THE
FAMILY ATL
OF THE
WORLD

THE
FAMILY ATLAS
OF THE
WORLD

PEERAGE BOOKS

First published in Great Britain in 1989 by
Peerage Books
Michelin House
81 Fulham Road
London SW3 6RB

ISBN 1 85052 129 8

Printed in Hong Kong by Mandarin Offset

CONTENTS

GENERAL REFERENCE

Abbreviations of measures used — ft Feet; mm {Millimetres / Millimeters}; cm {Centimetres / Centimeters}; m {Metres / Meters}; Km {Kilometres / Kilometers}; mb Millibars

City and Town symbols in order of size

∴ Sites of Archæological or Historical Importance

──── International Boundaries

─ ─ ─ International Boundaries (Undemarcated or Undefined)

··········· Internal Boundaries

∼─∼ Principal Roads

∼─∼ Tracks, Seasonal and other Roads

─┤ ├─ Road Tunnels

∼──∼ Principal Railways

∼──∼ Other Railways

─ ─ ─ Railways under construction

─┤─ ─ ┤─ Railway Tunnels

⊔⊔⊔⊔⊔⊔ Principal Canals

⋎ Passes

✿ Principal Airports

▲ 8848 Height above sea-level }
▼ 8050 Depth below sea-level } in metres
_1134_ Height of lake-level

─ ─ 3386 ─ Principal Shipping Routes (Distances in Nautical Miles)

∼∼∼ Perennial Streams

········ Seasonal Streams

⊂⊃ Seasonal Lakes, Salt Flats

Swamps, Marshes

⌣ Wells in Desert

▢ Permanent Ice

CONVERSION SCALE

ft	m
30 000	9000
	8000
24 000	7000
	6000
18 000	5000
	4000
12 000	3000
9000	2000
6000	1000
3000	500
Sea-Level 0	Sea-Level 0
	500
	1000
1000	
	2000
	3000
2000	4000
	5000
3000	6000
	7000
4000	8000
	9000
5000	10 000
	11 000
6000	12 000
7000	
fathoms	m

THE WORLD
Physical
1:150 000 000

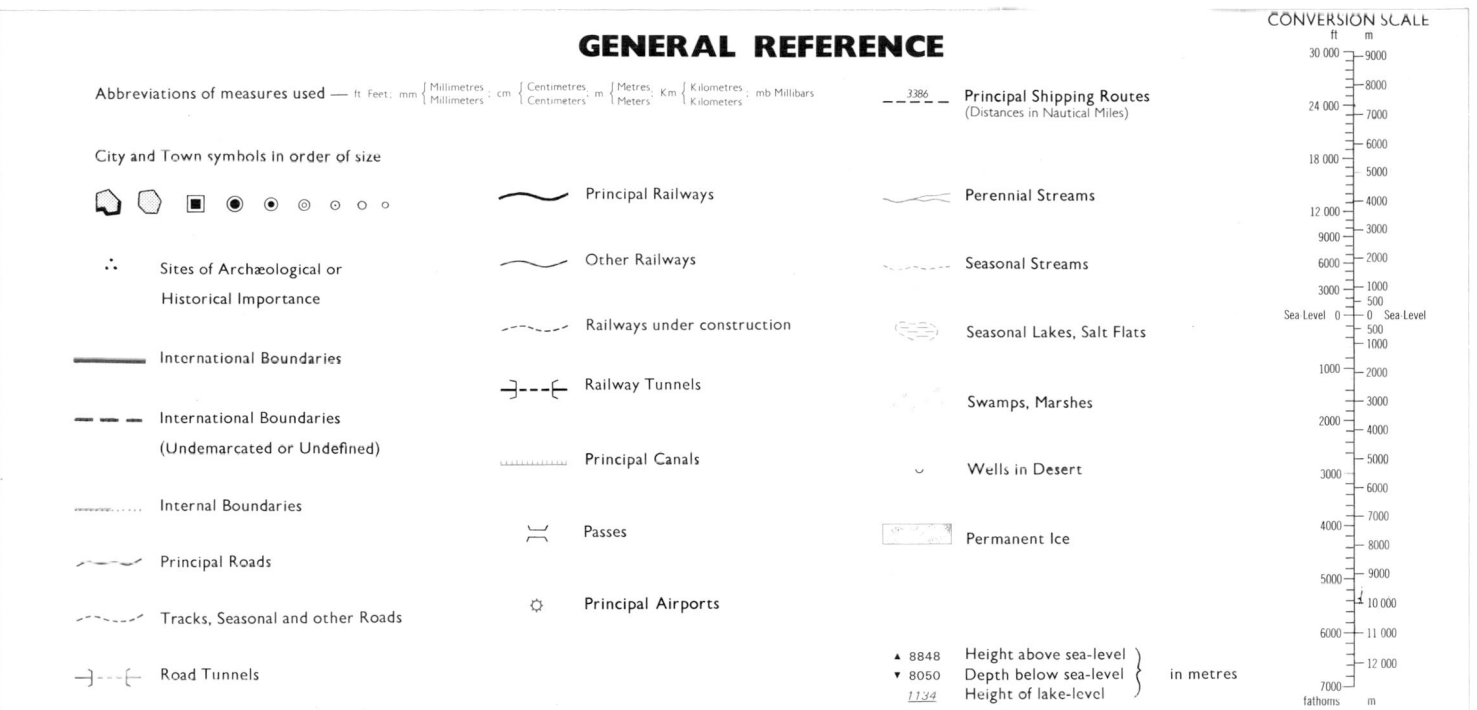

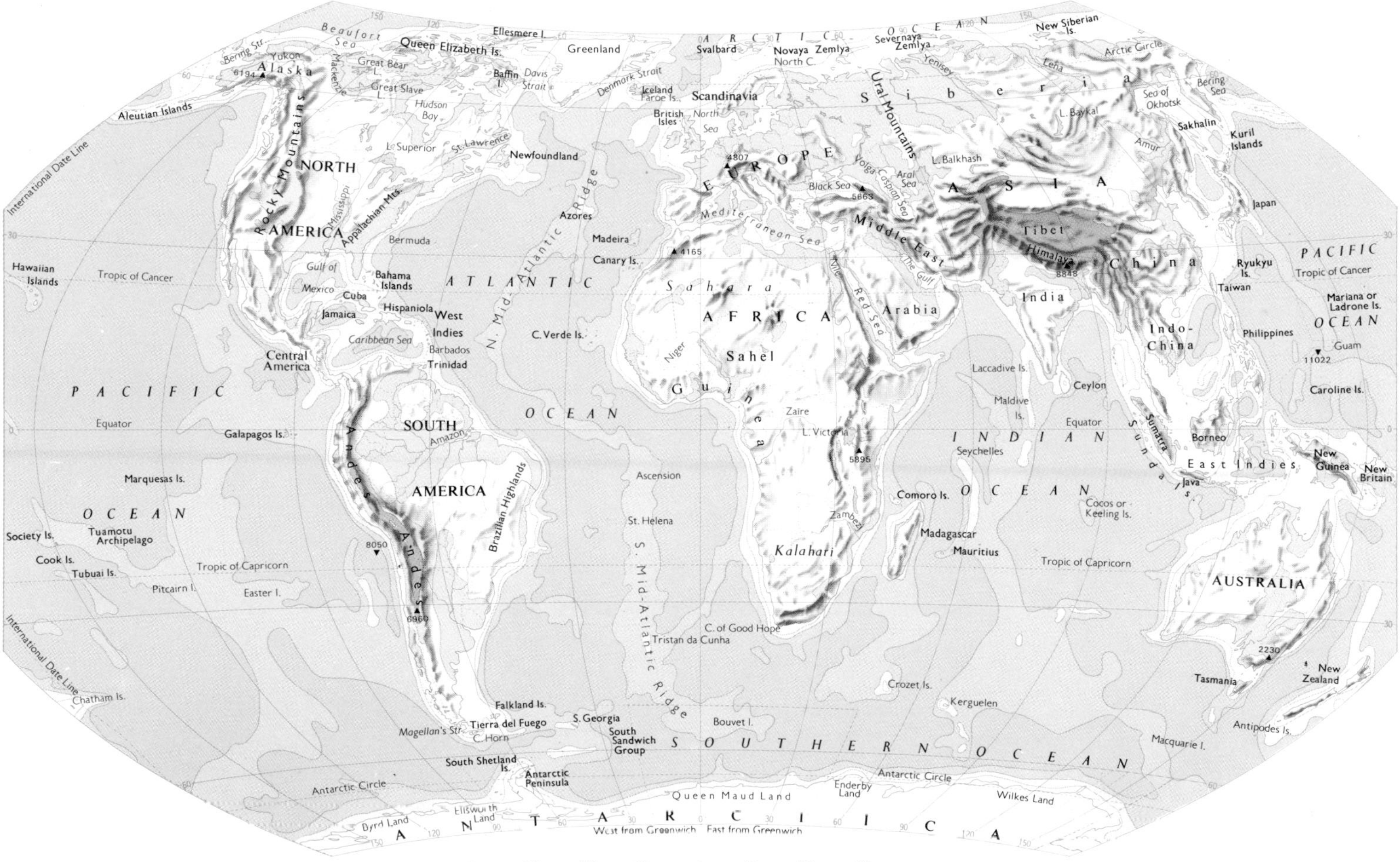

m	4000	2000	200	0	200	2000	4000	m
ft	12 000	6000	600	0	600	6000	12 000	ft

Projection: Hammer Equal Area

COPYRIGHT. GEORGE PHILIP & SON. LTD.

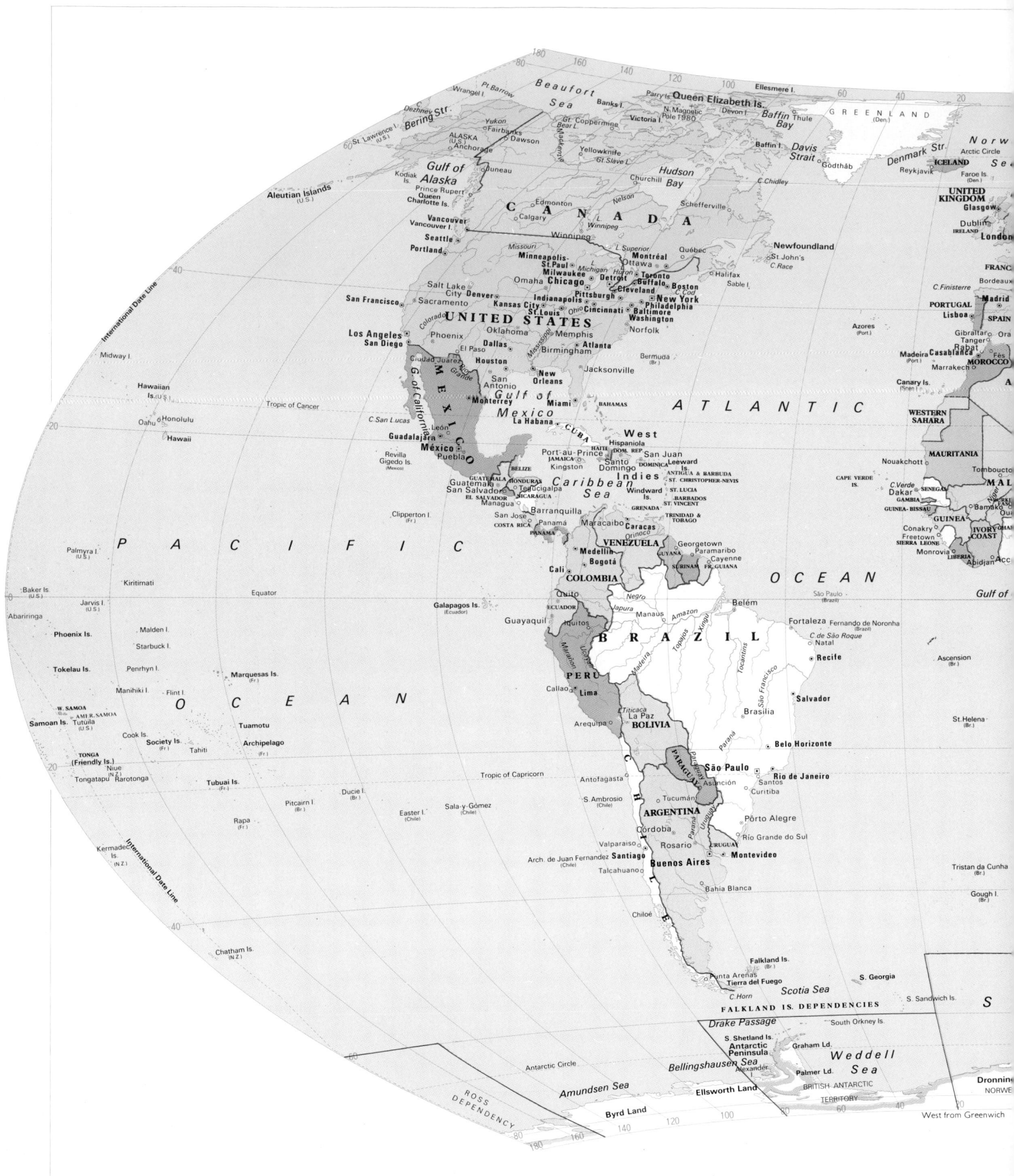

Projection: *Hammer Equal Area*

1:20 000 000

100   0   100   200   300   400   500 miles
100   0   200   400   600   800 km

ARCTIC OCEAN

Ural Mountains
Ob
Obshchiy
Volga Uplands
Pechora
Mezen
N. Dvina
Onega
L. Onega
White Sea
Kola Peninsula
Kanin Peninsula
Nordkinn
North Cape
Tundra

CASPIAN SEA
–28
Caucasus
5 65
5633
Elbruz
Terek
Rion
Kura
Van
Aras
Ararat 5165
Kizil Irmak
L. Tuz
Euphrates
Anatolia
3770
Cyprus 1951
Crete

BLACK SEA
2211
Crimea
Sea of Azov
Don
Manych
Tsimlyansk Res.
Volga
Oka
Rybinsk Res.
Moscow
Central Russian Uplands
Dnepr (Dnieper)
Bug
Danube
Ukraine
Pripyat
Pripyat Marshes
Dnestr (Dniester)
Prut
Carpathians
Transylvanian Alps
Wallachia
Moldavia
Danube
Balkans
Rhodope
Balkan Peninsula
Pindus
Morea
5121
C. Matapan

AEGEAN SEA
Ida 1786

Finland
Lapland
Kjølen Mts.
2123
L. Torne
Scandinavia
Sweden
Norway
Galdhøpiggen 2469
Ume
Indals
Mälaren
Vänern
Vättern
Gotland
Öland
L. Ladoga
L. Onega
Neva
L. Chudskoye
G. of Finland
G. of Bothnia
G. of Riga
Niemen
BALTIC SEA
North European Plain
Odra (Oder)
Wisła (Vistula)
Elbe
Weser
Harz 1142
Erz Geb.
Sudetes
Bohemian Heights
Moravian Heights
Plain of Hungary
Tisza
Bakony For.
Drava
Sava
Dinaric Alps
ADRIATIC SEA
Str. of Otranto
IONIAN SEA
Ionian Is.

3734
NORWEGIAN SEA
Arctic Circle
Iceland 1491
Hekla
Vatna Jökull 2119
SOUTH EAST ICELAND
Faroe Bank
FAEROES
Faroe Is.
Shetland Is.
Orkney Is.
Fair Isle
VIKING
FORTIES
FISHER
Dogger Bank
DOGGER
HUMBER
THAMES
HELIGOLAND
GERMAN BIGHT
Netherlands
Rhine
Ardennes
Meuse
Vosges
Black For.
Taunus
Jura
Alps
4807
Mt. Blanc
Apennines
Corsica
Sardinia
Ligurian Sea
Tyrrhenian Sea
Str. of Bonifacio
C. Blanco
Vesuvius 1277
Etna 3263
Sicily
Str. of Messina
Calabria
Malta

NORTH UTSIRE
SOUTH UTSIRE
Lindesnes
NORTH SEA
Jutland
Skagerrak
Kattegat
Denmark

ATLANTIC OCEAN
Rockall
ROCKALL
BAILEY
Fisher Bank
HEBRIDES
Hebrides
British Isles
Great Britain
Ben Nevis 1347
CROMARTY
FORTH
TYNE
DOVER
Snowdon 1085
Irish Sea
Ireland
IRISH SEA
Carnsore
LUNDY
FASTNET
Land's End
English Channel
PLYMOUTH
PORTLAND
WIGHT
Brittany
Finisterre
SOLE
SHANNON
Valentia I.
C. Clear
Seine
Loire
Garonne
Gironde
Bay of Biscay
BISCAY
4861
Cantabrian Mts.
Pic d'Aneto 3404
Pyrenees
Central Massif
Mt. Dore 1886
Rhône
G. of Lions
Old Castile
New Castile
Iberian Peninsula
Sa. de Guadarrama
Douro
Tagus
Sa. da Estrela
Guadiana
Sierra Morena
Guadalquivir
Sierra Nevada
Mulhacén 3478
Andalusia
Str. of Gibraltar
C. Trafalgar
C. St. Vincent
C. Spartel
Maritime Atlas
Plateau of the Shotts
MEDITERRANEAN SEA
Balearic Is.

ft   m
12 000 4000
6000   2000
3000   1000
1200   600
600   200
0   0
2000   600
4000   6000
12 000 m   ft

Projection Bonne   West from Greenwich 0 East from Greenwich

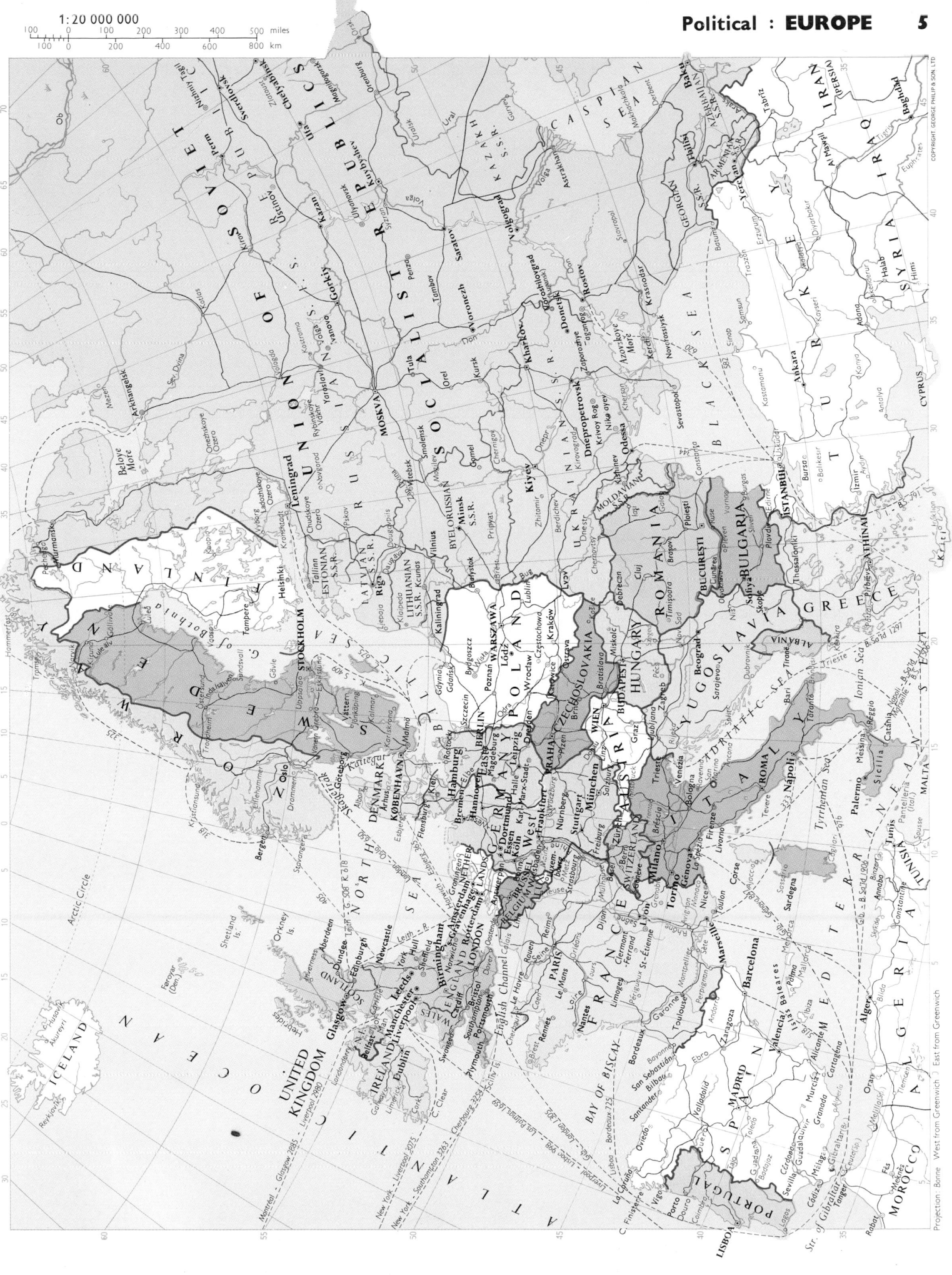

1:2 000 000

10 0 10 20 30 40 50 miles
10 0 10 20 30 40 50 60 70 80 km

East from Greenwich   COPYRIGHT GEORGE PHILIP & SON LTD.

West from Greenwich

Projection: Conical with two standard parallels.

ENGLISH CHANNEL

FRANCE

Rouen
Dieppe
Le Tréport
Le Havre
C. de la Hève
C. d'Antifer
Fécamp
Yvetot
St-Valery-en-Caux
Trouville
Honfleur
Lisieux
Bernay
Elbeuf
Pont-l'Évêque
Caudebec
Louviers
Seine
Bayeux
Caen
Arromanches
Vierville
Isigny
Carentan
Périers
St-Lô
Barfleur
Quineville
Valognes
Cherbourg
C. de la Hague
Alderney
Guernsey
St. Peter Port
Sark
Channel Islands
Jersey
St. Helier
Barneville

SCILLY ISLES
On same Scale
St. Ives
Penzance
Land's End
Isles of Scilly
St. Mary's

SUFFOLK
Lowestoft
Beccles
Bungay
Southwold
Aldeburgh
Orford Ness
Felixstowe
Harwich
The Naze
Walton on the Naze
Clacton
Ipswich
Woodbridge
Stowmarket
Needham Market
Sudbury
Saxmundham
Diss
Eye
Wymondham

CAMBRIDGE
Peterborough
Fletton
Ely
Newmarket
St. Edmunds
Bury St. Edmunds
Thetford
Mildenhall
Huntingdon
St. Ives
St. Neots
Royston
Saffron Walden
Haverhill

ESSEX
Colchester
Chelmsford
Braintree
Maldon
Witham
Mersea
Foulness
Southend
Shoeburyness
Basildon
Brentwood
Harlow
Epping
Enfield
Barnet

HERTFORD
Hertford
Welwyn
St. Albans
Hatfield
Hemel Hempstead
Watford
Stevenage
Letchworth
Hitchin

BEDFORD
Bedford
Luton
Dunstable
Leighton Buzzard
Biggleswade

NORTHAMPTON
Northampton
Wellingborough
Rushden
Kettering
Corby
Rockingham
Market Harborough

MILTON KEYNES
BUCKS
Buckingham
Bletchley
Aylesbury
High Wycombe
Marlow

OXFORD
Oxford
Banbury
Bicester
Woodstock
Witney
Abingdon
Wantage

WARWICK
Warwick
Leamington
Stratford-on-Avon
Rugby
Nuneaton
Hinckley
Coventry
Redditch

WEST MIDLAND
Birmingham
West Bromwich
Wolverhampton
Dudley
Tipton
Stourbridge
Walsall
Sutton Coldfield

WORCESTER
HEREFORD & WORCESTER
Worcester
Droitwich
Kidderminster
Bromsgrove
Malvern
Malvern Hills
Ledbury
Ross-on-Wye
Hereford
Leominster
Ludlow

SHROPSHIRE
Clee Hills
Bridgnorth

LONDON
Croydon
Bromley
Kingston
Hounslow
Hillingdon
Harrow
Ealing
Greenwich
Dartford
Gravesend
Tilbury
Rochester
Chatham
Gillingham
Maidstone
Sittingbourne
Sheppey
Sheerness
Herne Bay
Margate
Ramsgate
Deal
Dover
Folkestone
South Foreland
North Foreland
Canterbury
Faversham
Ashford
Thanet
New Romney
Hythe
Dungeness
Rye
Romney Marsh

KENT
Sevenoaks
Tonbridge
Tunbridge Wells
Crowborough

EAST SUSSEX
Hastings
Bexhill
Eastbourne
Beachy Hd.
Battle
Newhaven
Brighton
Hove

SURREY
Reigate
Crawley
Horsham
Dorking
Guildford
Leith Hill
Haslemere

WEST SUSSEX
Worthing
Littlehampton
Bognor Regis
Selsey Bill
Chichester

The Weald
The North Downs
The South Downs

HANTS
Winchester
Eastleigh
Basingstoke
Andover
Aldershot
Farnborough
Alton
Farnham
Fareham
Gosport
Havant
Hayling I.

Portsmouth
Southampton
ISLE OF WIGHT
Cowes
Newport
Ryde
Ventnor
Needles
St. Catherine's Point

BERKS
Reading
Newbury
Windsor
Maidenhead
Slough
Bracknell
Berkshire Downs
Wallingford

WILTS
Swindon
Marlborough
Devizes
Chippenham
Trowbridge
Melksham
Salisbury
Salisbury Plain
Stonehenge
Amesbury
Mere
Wilton

DORSET
Dorchester
Weymouth
Portland Bill
Poole
Bournemouth
Christchurch
Swanage
I. of Purbeck
St. Alban's Hd.
Blandford
Sherborne
Shaftesbury
Bridport
Lyme Regis
Beaminster

SOMERSET
Taunton
Bridgwater
Wellington
Yeovil
Chard
Glastonbury
Wells
Bruton
Frome
Mendip Hills
Quantock Hills
Polden Hills
Minehead
Exmoor
Dunkery Beacon 520
Lynton
Ilfracombe
Bree

AVON
Bristol
Bath
Clevedon
Weston-super-Mare
Avonmouth

GLOUCESTER
Gloucester
Cheltenham
Stroud
Cirencester
Cleeve Hill 330
Forest of Dean
Tewkesbury

DEVON
Exeter
Exmouth
Sidmouth
Honiton
Tiverton
Teignmouth
Torquay (Torbay)
Paignton
Dartmouth
Start Pt.
Kingsbridge
Salcombe
Newton Abbot
Dartmoor
Yes tor 618
Okehampton
Tavistock
Plymouth
Devonport
Barnstaple
Braunton
Bideford
Torridge
Taw
South Molton
Hartland Point
Holsworthy

CORNWALL
Launceston
Bodmin Moor
Brown Willy 419
Bodmin
Bude
Boscastle
Padstow
Newquay
St. Austell
Truro
Liskeard
Looe
Fowey
Mevagissey
St. Ives
Penzance
Camborne
Redruth
Helston
Falmouth
Lizard
St. Michael's Mount
Eddystone

WALES / CYMRU
POWYS
GWENT
Cardiff
Newport
Pontypool
Cwmbran
Ebbw Vale
Tredegar
Abergavenny
Monmouth
Chepstow
Merthyr Tydfil
Aberdare
Rhondda
Pontypridd
Maesteg
Bridgend
MID GLAMORGAN
SOUTH GLAMORGAN
WEST GLAMORGAN
Swansea
Neath
Port Talbot
Porthcawl
Gower
Llanelli
Burry Port
Brecon
Brecon Beacons 886
Black Mts.
Builth Wells
Llandrindod Wells
Rhayader
Newtown
Machynlleth
Welshpool
Montgomery
Radnor Forest
Hay-on-Wye

DYFED
Aberystwyth
Aberayron
Cardigan
Cardigan Bay
Fishguard
St. David's
St. David's Hd.
St. Bride's Bay
Milford Haven
Pembroke
Tenby
Carmarthen
Llandeilo
Llandovery
Newcastle Emlyn
Lampeter
Llanidloes
Tywi
Teifi
Towy

Bristol Channel
Lundy

ENGLISH CHANNEL

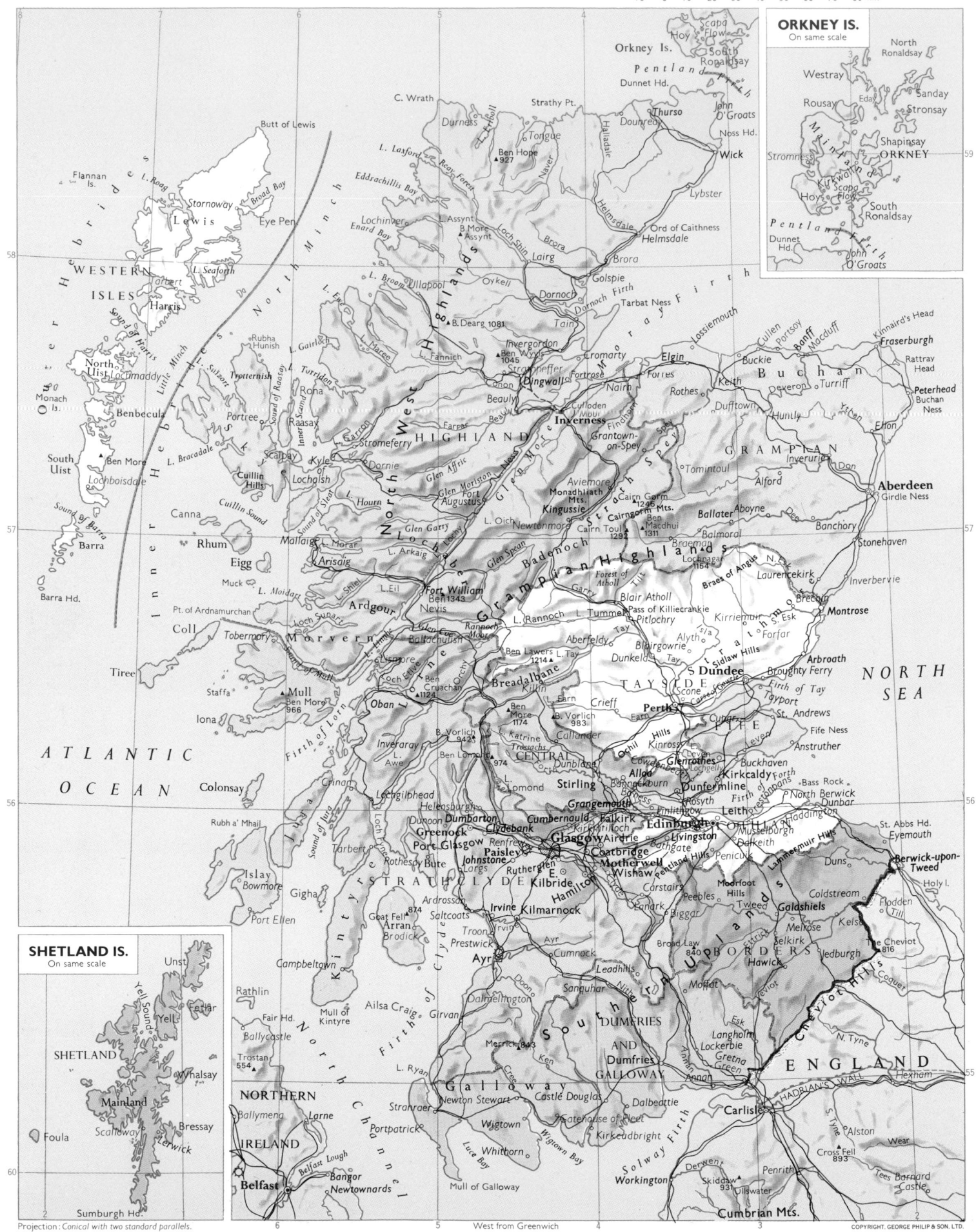

1:2 000 000

ORKNEY IS.
On same scale

SHETLAND IS.
On same scale

Projection: Conical with two standard parallels.

West from Greenwich

COPYRIGHT. GEORGE PHILIP & SON, LTD.

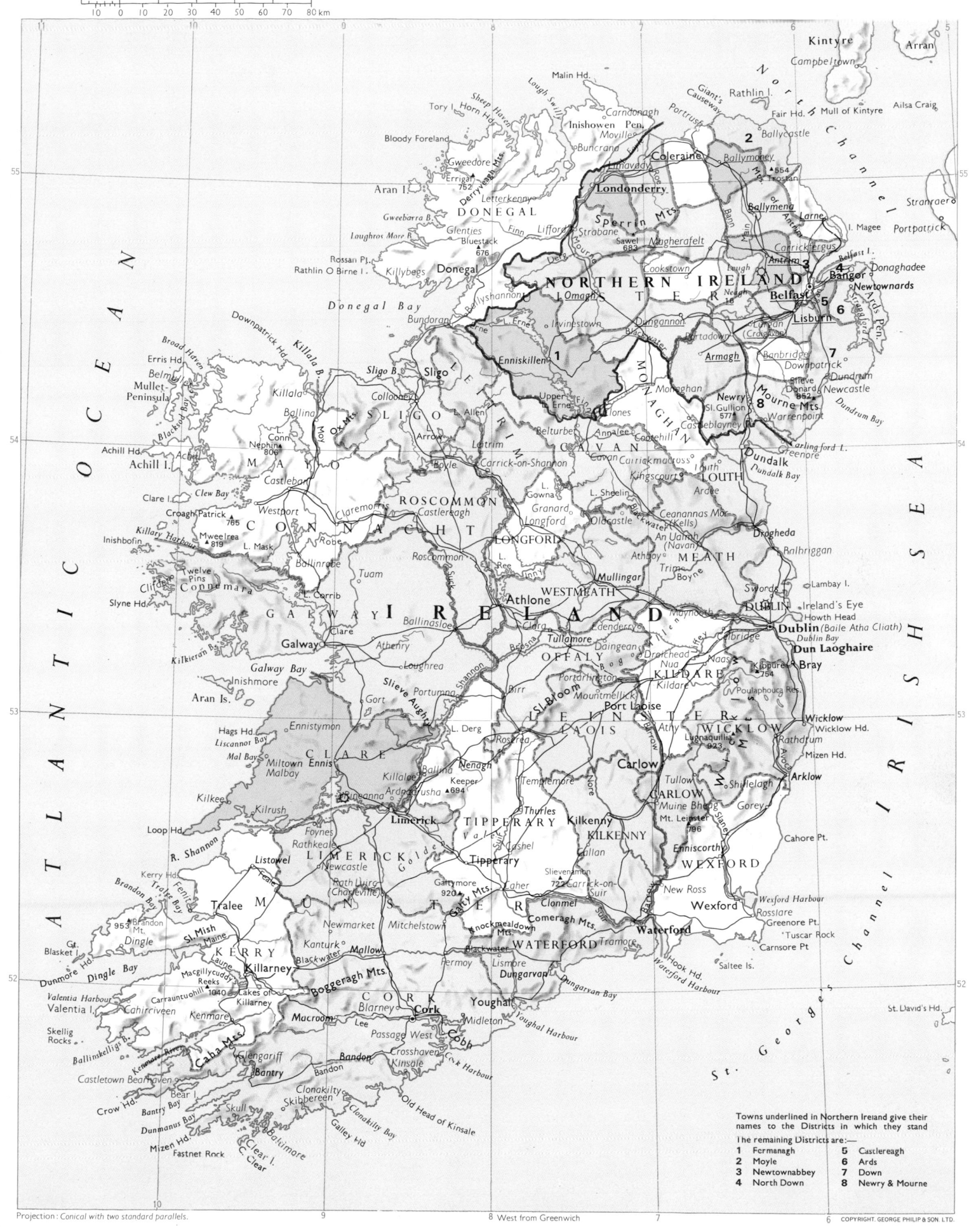

1:2 000 000

Projection: Conical with two standard parallels.

8 West from Greenwich

COPYRIGHT. GEORGE PHILIP & SON. LTD.

Towns underlined in Northern Ireland give their
names to the Districts in which they stand
The remaining Districts are:—

1 Fermanagh	5 Castlereagh
2 Moyle	6 Ards
3 Newtownabbey	7 Down
4 North Down	8 Newry & Mourne

1 : 4 000 000

20 0 40 60 miles
20 0 20 40 60 80 km

The DISTRICTS of Northern Ireland have been numbered and can be identified by reference to this table.

1 Londonderry 14 Craigavon
2 Limavady 15 Armagh
3 Coleraine 16 Newry & Mourne
4 Ballymoney 17 Banbridge
5 Moyle 18 Down
6 Larne 19 Lisburn
7 Ballymena 20 Antrim
8 Magherafelt 21 Newtownabbey
9 Cookstown 22 Carrickfergus
10 Strabane 23 North Down
11 Omagh 24 Ards
12 Fermanagh 25 Castlereagh
13 Dungannon 26 Belfast

ORKNEY
Kirkwall
59
HIGHLAND

SHETLAND
Lerwick
60

Metropolitan Counties :-
On 1st April 1986 the administrative functions of the six metropolitan counties such as planning, education, transportation, libraries and social services were transferred to the city and town boroughs and various non-elected residuary bodies.

WESTERN ISLES
Stornoway

58

HIGHLAND
Inverness
GRAMPIAN
Aberdeen

SCOTLAND

TAYSIDE
Dundee

FIFE
Glenrothes

CENTRAL
Stirling
Edinburgh
LOTHIAN
Glasgow

STRATHCLYDE

ATLANTIC

OCEAN

56

BORDERS
Newtown
St. Boswells

DUMFRIES AND GALLOWAY
Dumfries

NORTHUMBERLAND
Newcastle
TYNE AND WEAR
Durham

NORTH
SEA

Carlisle

DURHAM
CLEVELAND
Middlesbrough

CUMBRIA
Northallerton

ISLE OF MAN
Douglas

NORTH YORKSHIRE

54

LANCASHIRE
Preston
WEST YORKSHIRE
Wakefield
HUMBERSIDE
Hull

GREATER MANCHESTER
MERSEYSIDE Manchester
Liverpool
Barnsley
SOUTH YORKSHIRE

ENGLAND
Lincoln

Chester
CHESHIRE
DERBYSHIRE
Matlock
NOTTING-HAM-SHIRE
Nottingham
LINCOLNSHIRE

DONEGAL
Lifford

NORTHERN IRELAND
Tyrone
Fermanagh

Sligo
LEITRIM
Monaghan
Armagh
Belfast
Down
Dundalk

SLIGO
Carrick-on-Shannon
MONAGHAN
Cavan
LOUTH

MAYO
Castlebar

ROSCOMMON
LONGFORD
Longford
An Uaimh (Navan)
MEATH

CAVAN

GALWAY
Galway
Roscommon
Mullingar
WESTMEATH

IRELAND

OFFALY
Tullamore
KILDARE
Naas
DUBLIN
Dublin

CLARE
Ennis
LAOIS
Port Laoise
WICKLOW
Wicklow

LIMERICK
Limerick
TIPPERARY
Kilkenny
CARLOW
Carlow

KERRY
Tralee
KILKENNY
Clonmel
WEXFORD
Wexford

CORK
WATERFORD
Waterford

IRISH SEA

North Channel

ISLE OF MAN
Douglas

GWYNEDD
Caernarfon
Mold
CLWYD

WALES
Shrewsbury
SHROPSHIRE
STAFFORD-SHIRE
Stafford
LEICESTERSHIRE
Leicester
NORFOLK
Norwich

POWYS
HEREFORD AND WORCESTER
Worcester
WEST MIDLANDS
Birmingham
WARWICK-SHIRE
Warwick
NORTH-AMPTON-SHIRE
Northampton
CAMBRIDGE-SHIRE
Cambridge
SUFFOLK
Ipswich

Llandrindod Wells
Bedford
BEDFORD-SHIRE

DYFED
Carmarthen
Gloucester
GLOUCESTER-SHIRE
Oxford
OXFORDSHIRE
BUCK-INGHAM-SHIRE
Aylesbury
Hertford
HERTFORD-SHIRE
ESSEX
Chelmsford

WEST GLAMORGAN
Swansea
MID GLAMORGAN
GWENT
Cwmbran
Reading
BERKSHIRE
GREATER LONDON
Kingston
Maidstone

SOUTH GLAMORGAN
Cardiff
Bristol
AVON
WILTSHIRE
Trowbridge
SURREY
KENT

SOMERSET
Taunton
HAMPSHIRE
Winchester
WEST SUSSEX
Chichester
EAST SUSSEX
Lewes

DEVON
Exeter
DORSET
Dorchester
Newport
ISLE OF WIGHT

CORNWALL
Truro

CELTIC
SEA

ST. GEORGE'S CHANNEL

ENGLISH CHANNEL

FRANCE

50

o Norwich Administrative headquarters
MERSEYSIDE Metropolitan counties
Antrim Former Northern Ireland counties

Projection: Conical with two standard parallels

West from Greenwich 0 East from Greenwich
COPYRIGHT. GEORGE PHILIP & SON. LTD.

1:2 500 000

Projection: Conical with two standard parallels   East from Greenwich   COPYRIGHT. GEORGE PHILIP & SON. LTD.

1 : 5 000 000

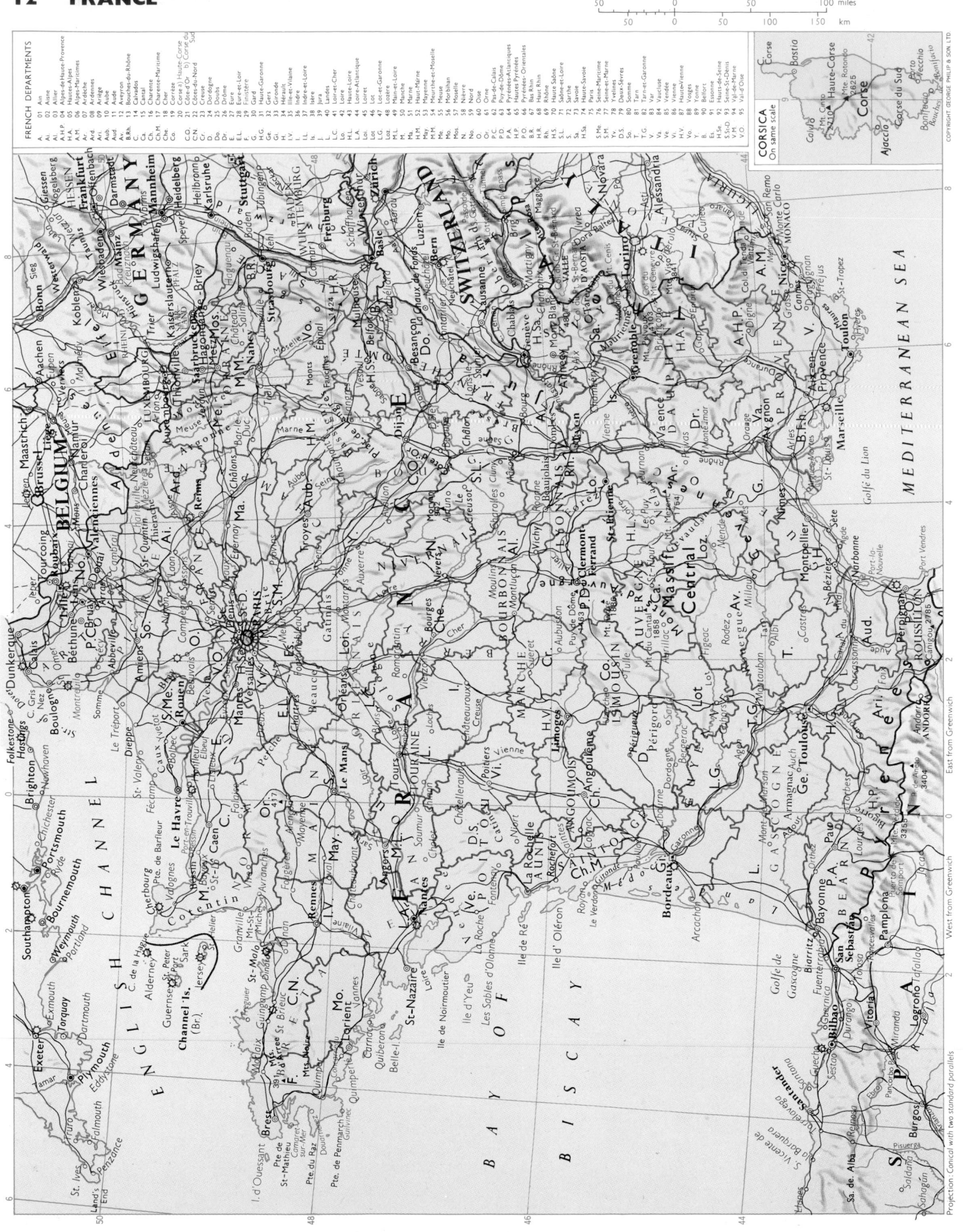

FRENCH DEPARTMENTS

A.	01 Ain
Ai.	02 Aisne
Al.	03 Allier
A.H.P.	04 Alpes-de-Haute-Provence
H.A.	05 Hautes-Alpes
A.M.	06 Alpes-Maritimes
Ard.	07 Ardèche
Ard.	08 Ardennes
Ari.	09 Ariège
Aub.	10 Aube
Aud.	11 Aude
Av.	12 Aveyron
B.Rh.	13 Bouches-du-Rhône
Cal.	14 Calvados
Ca.	15 Cantal
Ch.	16 Charente
Ch.M.	17 Charente-Maritime
Che.	18 Cher
Co.	19 Corrèze
C.O.	20 Corse a) Haute-Corse b) Corse du Sud
C.N.	21 Côte-d'Or
C.N.	22 Côtes-du-Nord
Cr.	23 Creuse
Do.	24 Dordogne
Do.	25 Doubs
Dr.	26 Drôme
E.L.	27 Eure
E.L.	28 Eure-et-Loir
F.	29 Finistère
Ga.	30 Gard
H.G.	31 Haute-Garonne
Ge.	32 Gers
Gi.	33 Gironde
H.	34 Hérault
I.V.	35 Ille-et-Vilaine
I.	36 Indre
I.L.	37 Indre-et-Loire
I.	38 Isère
J.	39 Jura
La.	40 Landes
L.C.	41 Loir-et-Cher
Lo.	42 Loire
H.L.	43 Haute-Loire
Lo.A.	44 Loire-Atlantique
Loi.	45 Loiret
Lot	46 Lot
L.G.	47 Lot-et-Garonne
Loz.	48 Lozère
M.L.	49 Maine-et-Loire
Ma.	50 Manche
Ma.	51 Marne
H.M.	52 Haute-Marne
May.	53 Mayenne
M.M.	54 Meurthe-et-Moselle
Me.	55 Meuse
Mo.	56 Morbihan
Mos.	57 Moselle
Ni.	58 Nièvre
No.	59 Nord
O.	60 Oise
Or.	61 Orne
P.C.	62 Pas-de-Calais
P.D.	63 Puy-de-Dôme
P.A.	64 Pyrénées-Atlantiques
H.P.	65 Hautes-Pyrénées
P.O.	66 Pyrénées-Orientales
B.R.	67 Bas-Rhin
H.R.	68 Haut-Rhin
Rh.	69 Rhône
H.S.	70 Haute-Saône
S.L.	71 Saône-et-Loire
Sa.	72 Sarthe
Sa.	73 Savoie
H.Sa.	74 Haute-Savoie
S.Me.	75 Paris
S.M.	76 Seine-Maritime
S.M.	77 Seine-et-Marne
Y.	78 Yvelines
D.S.	79 Deux-Sèvres
So.	80 Somme
T.	81 Tarn
T.G.	82 Tarn-et-Garonne
Va.	83 Var
Va.	84 Vaucluse
Ve.	85 Vendée
Vi.	86 Vienne
H.V.	87 Haute-Vienne
V.	88 Vosges
Y.	89 Yonne
B.	90 Belfort
Es.	91 Essonne
H.Se.	92 Hauts-de-Seine
S.S-D.	93 Seine-St-Denis
V.M.	94 Val-de-Marne
V.O.	95 Val-d'Oise

CORSICA
On same scale

Projection. Conical with two standard parallels

1:5 000 000

50   0   50   100 miles

50   0   50   100   150   km

East from Greenwich

West from Greenwich

Projection: Conical with two standard parallels

East from Greenwich

1:5 000 000

50 0 50 100 miles
50 0 50 100 150 km

SEA

Zatoka Gdańska

Wejherowo Sopot **Gdynia** Zelenogradsk (Königsberg) **Kaliningrad** (Königsberg) Chernyakhovsk **Vilnius** Molodechno Borisov Gorki

LITHUANIAN S.S.R.

Gdańsk (Danzig) Elbląg Braniewo Pregolya Gusev Suwałki Alitus Varena Lida **Minsk** Berezina **Mogilev** Krichev

Starogard Malbork Pojezierze Mazurskie ▲309 Gizycko Kętrzyn Augustów **R.S.F.S.R.**

Bydgoszcz Chojnice Chełmno Grudziądz Olsztyn Ostróda Mława Ciechanów Ostrołęka Grodno Mosty Skchara **Baranovichi** **Bobruysk** **Gomel**

Toruń Lipno Rypin 238 Sokółka **Białystok** Neman Volkovysk Slonim Bereza Ptich Drut Sozh

Gniezno Inowrocław Włocławek Płock Wkra Bug Ostrów Mazowiecka Brańsk Hajnówka **B Y E L O R U S S I A N   S.S.R.**

Września Koło Kutno Łowicz **Warszawa** (Warsaw) Mińsk Mazowiecki Siedlce Czeremcha Zhabinka **Brest** **Pinsk** Luninets Pripyat Kalinkovichi Chernigov

POLAND Konin Turek Łęczyca Pruszków Żyrardów Otwock Łuków Biała Podlaska Międzyrzec Podlaski Sarny ▲316 Uzh Desna

Kalisz **Łódź** Pilica Skierniewice Grójec Kozienice Puławy Włodawa Polesye Korosten

Krotoszyn Ostrów Wielkopolski Piotrków Trybunalski Radom Chełm Kovel Styr Goryn Sluch Novograd-Volynskiy Radomyshl **Kiyev** Borispol

Wrocław (Breslau) Oleśnica Brzeg Wieluń Radomsko Końskie **Lublin** Krasnik Zamość Vladimir Volynskiy **Lutsk** **Rovno** Korets Zhitomir Fastov Belaya Tserkov

Nysa Opole Częstochowa Jędrzejów Kielce Ostrowiec Świętokrzyski Sandomierz Sokal Dubno Ostrog Shepetovka **Zhitomir** **Berdichev** Kazatin

Zabrze Tarnowskie Góry Zawiercie Pinczów Tarnobrzeg 390▲ Radekhov Brody Kremenets Starokonstantinav **Vinnitsa**

Racibórz Gliwice Bytom Sosnowiec **Katowice** Dąbrowa Tarnowska Rzeszów Przeworsk Kamenka Bugskaya ▲384 **U K R A I N I A N   S.S.R.** Khmelnitskiy

Opava Ostrava Tychy **Kraków** Wisła (Vistula) **Tarnów** Jarosław Gorodok **Lvov** Zolochev Ternopol ▲471 Zhmerinka

Frýdek Místek Cieszyn Bielsko-Biała Wieliczka Jasło Przemyśl Sambor Dnestr Buchach Chortkov Kamenets-Podolskiy Pervomaisk

Bohumín Český Těšín 1725 Nowy Sącz Krosno Dukelský Pr. Sanok Drogobych Borislav Stryi Zaleshchiki Mogilev-Podolskiy Uman

Přerov 550 Jablunkovský Pr. Západné Beskydy Vychodné Beskydy 502 Turka Zhabye Chernovtsy Bug

SLOVAKIA Žilina 2655 Tatry 4780 Ivano-Frankovsk Kolomyya Snyatyn **Khotin** Yedintsy Soroki Kotovsk

Biele Karpaty Ružomberok Nízke Tatry Prešov **Košice** Nadvornaya ▲1881 Per Yablonitse **Chernovtsy** Starozhinets **Beltsy**

Kremnica Banská Bystrica Zvolen **Uzhgorod** Mukachevo 931 2061 Storozhinets Dorohoi **M O L D A V I A N**

Nitra Slovenské Rudohorie Banská Štiavnica Lučenec Sátoraljaújhely Beregovo Khust Sighetu Marmatiei Radauti Botoşani ▲429 **Kishinev** Bendery Tiraspol

Trnava Nitra Sajó Hernád Bodva **Miskolc** Tokaj **Nyíregyháza** **Satu Mare** Carei Suceava Dorohoi Iaşi **Odessa**

Bratislava N. Zámky Komárno Hron Eger Mezőkövesd Hajdúböszörmény **Baia Mare** Pietrosul 2305 Vatra-Dornei Roman

Győr Esztergom Vác Gyöngyös Hatvan Jászberény **Debrecen** Someş Dej 2102 Pietrosu Bistrita Piatra Neamţ Bacău Vaslui Belgorod-Dnestrovskiy

Budapest Újpest Hegyes Karcag Oradea **Cluj-Napoca** Turda **Tîrgu Mureş** Praid Odorheiu Secuiesc Piatra Neamţ Bîrlad Tecuci

Székesfehérvár Bakony Dunaújváros Szolnok Mezőtúr Salonta **Tîrgu Mureş** Aiud Miercurea Ciuc Bretcu Siret Kogul

HUNGARY Kecskemét Cegléd Nagykőrös Békéscsaba Gyula Criş Negru Mţii Bihor ▲1848 Medias Sighişoara Focşani Ozero Sasyk

Veszprém Dunaföldvár Kiskunfélegyháza Kiskőrös Csongrád Szentes **Transilvania** Abrud Crişul Alb **Sibiu** Făgăraş Gheorghe Galaţi Ismail

Balaton Kaposvár Szekszárd Baja Kiskunhalas Hódmezővásárhely Makó **Arad** Brad **Alba-Iulia** Deva Simeria Carpaţii Meridionali Olt Rîmnicu Sărat **Brăila** 467 Sulina

Pécs Mohács Senta Kikinda **Romania** Mureş Lugoj Hunedoara 2535 Turnu Roşu **Braşov** Cîmpina Buzău Tulcea

Timişoara Bečej Zrenjanin (Petrovgrad) Caransebeş Vf. Negoiu Vf. Omul 2507 Ialomiţa Câmpulung Ploieşti

Osijek Novi Sad Sremska Mitrovica Petrovaradin Vršac Reşiţa Porta Orientalis Peleaga 2509 350 2518 Paring Rîmnicu Vîlcea Tîrgovişte Dunărea (Danube)

Brod Vinkovci Odžak **Beograd** (Belgrade) Pančevo Bela Crkva Mehadia Târgu-Jiu Jiu Piteşti Argeş **Bucureşti** (Bucharest) Ialomiţa

Tešanj Bijeljina Zemun Smederevo Orşova Portile de Fier **Turnu-Severin** Valea Slatina Dîmboviţa Cernavodă **BLACK**

YUGOSLAVIA Tuzla Sava Požarevac 1346 Negotin **Craiova** Olt Caracal Vedea Olteniţa Călăraşi Silistra **Constanţa** **SEA**

Sarajevo Titova Užice Čačak Kragujevac Zaječar Timok Vidin Corabia Turnu Măgurele Zimnicea Giurgiu **Ruse** (Ruschuk) Mangalia Tolbukhin

BULGARIA Dunav (Danube)

COPYRIGHT. GEORGE PHILIP & SON. LTD.

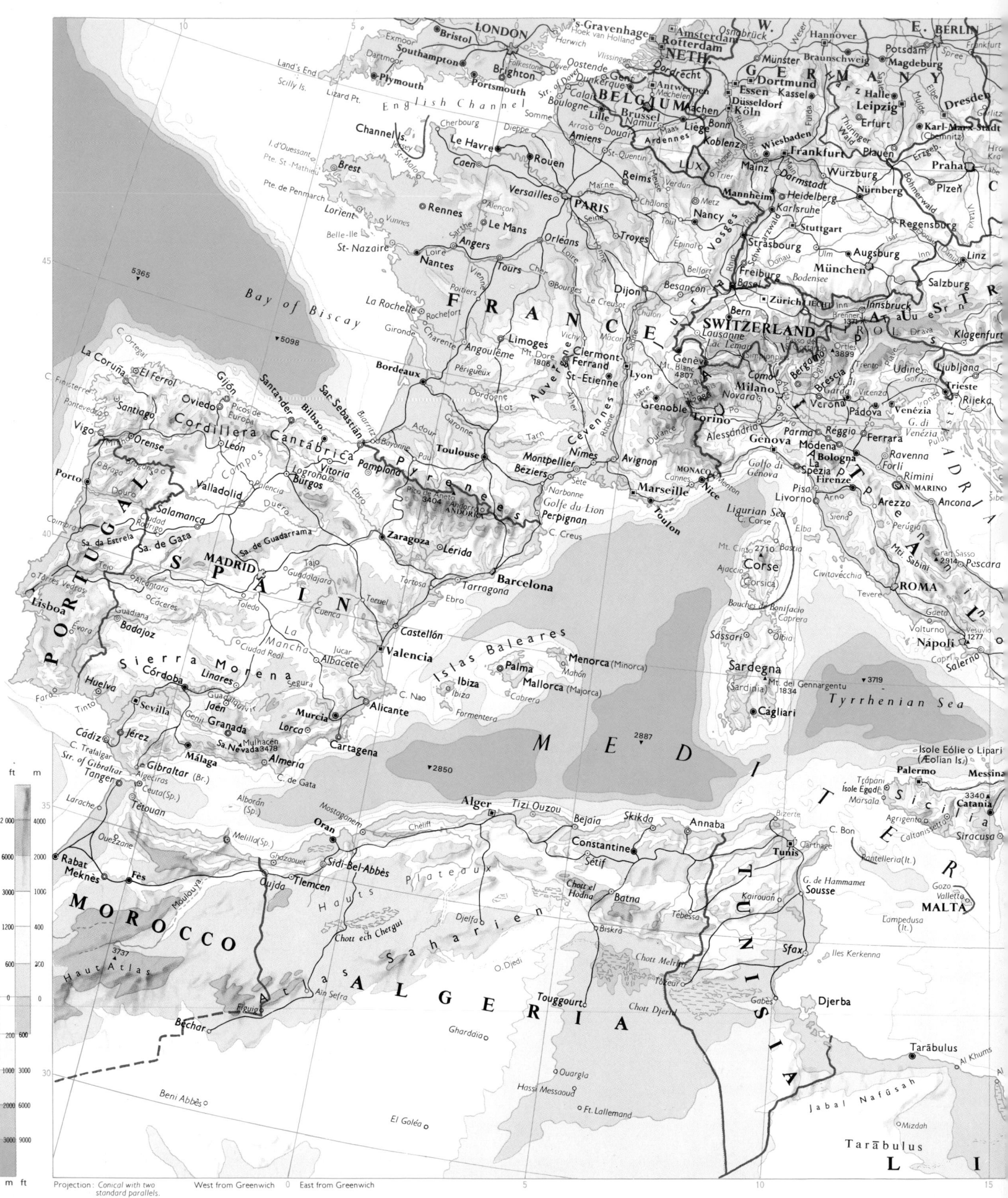

1:10 000 000

50   0   50   100   150   200 miles

50   0   100   200   300 km

------ Division between Greeks
and Turks in Cyprus;
Turks to the north.

COPYRIGHT. GEORGE PHILIP & SON. LTD.

NORWEGIAN SEA

ICELAND
on the same scale
as general map

1:5 000 000

20   0   20   40   60   80   100 miles
40 20 0   40   80   120   160 km

East from Greenwich

Projection. Conical with two standard parallels

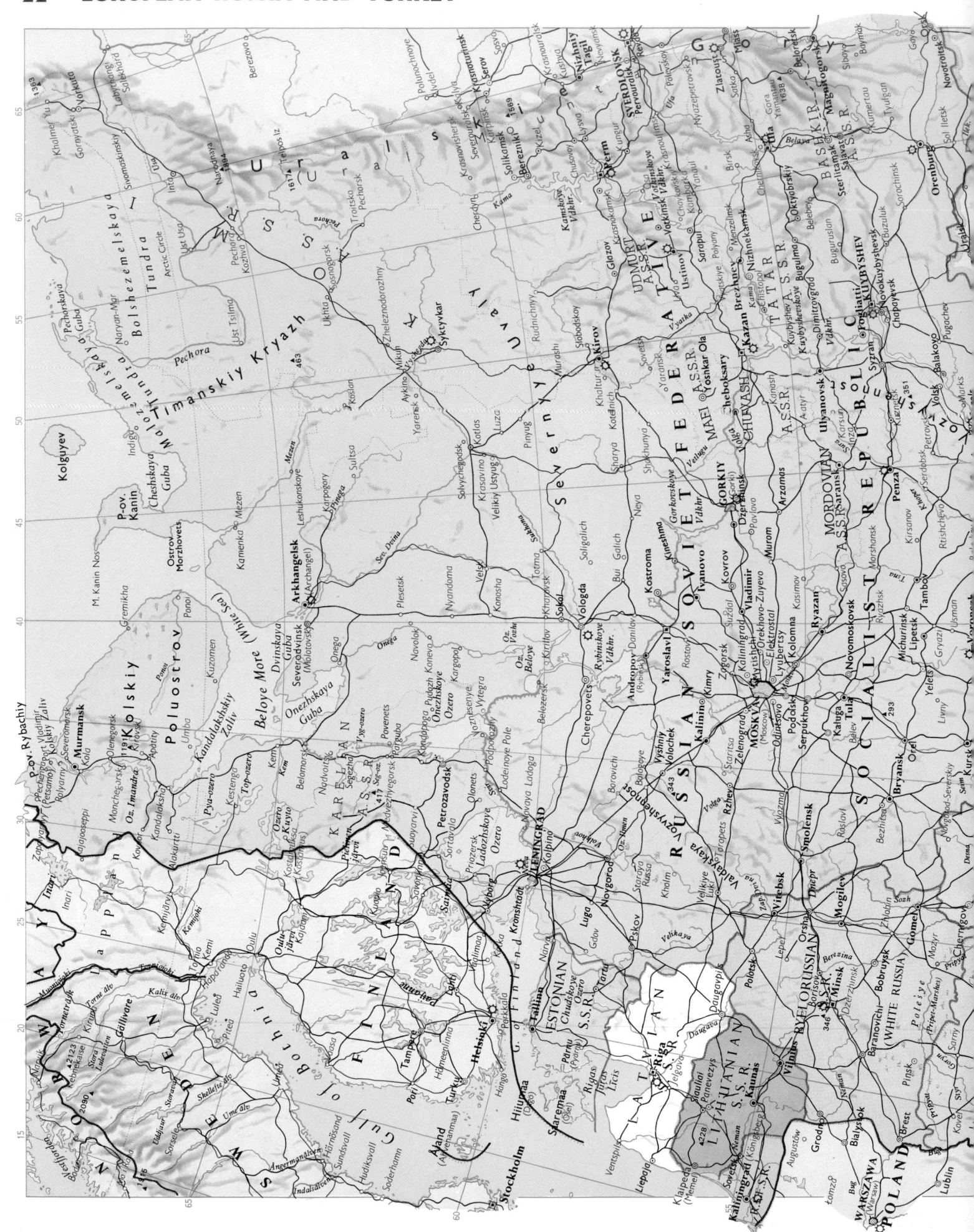

1:10 000 000

100   50   0   50   100   150   200 miles
100   0   100   200   300   km

1	Kabardino-Balkar A.S.S.R.
2	North Ossetian A.S.S.R. (Azer.)
3	Nakhichevan A.S.S.R.
4	Checheno-Ingush A.S.S.R.
5	Karagiye Depression

K I R G I Z   S T E P P E

K A Z A K H S k a y a   N i z m e n n o s t

P r i v o l z h s k a y a

K A L M Y K   A.S.S.R.

Ergeni Vozvyshennost

C A S P I A N   S E A

U K R A I N E

Zaliv Kara Bogaz Gol

D A G E S T A N   A.S.S.R.

B o l s h o i   K a v k a z   C a u c a s u s

GEORGIAN   S.S.R.

ADZHAR

A Z E R B A I J A N   S.S.R.

ARMENIAN   S.S.R.

A l b o r z

I R A N   (P E R S I A)

TEHRÁN

B L A C K   S E A

K u z e y   A n a d o l u   D a ğ l a r ı

T U R K E Y

A n a d o l u

T o r o s   D a ğ l a r ı

A r m e n i a

K ū h

I R A Q

S Y R I A

Bādiyat ash Sham

Baghdád

L E B A N O N

Dimashq (Damascus)

Bayrút (Beirut)

M E D I T E R R A N E A N   S E A

L e v a n t

CYPRUS

Dhodhekanisos

R O M A N I A

B U L G A R I A

MOLDAVIAN S.S.R.

KIEV (Kiyev)

Odessa

ISTANBUL

Ankara

Projection: Conical with two standard parallels

East from Greenwich

Division between Greeks and Turks
in Cyprus: Turks to the North.

R.S.F.S.R.
1. Daghestan A.S.S.R.
2. Kabardino–Balkar A.S.S.R.
3. Mari A.S.S.R.
4. Mordovian A.S.S.R.
5. North Ossetian A.S.S.R.
6. Tatar A.S.S.R.
7. Udmurt A.S.S.R.
8. Chuvash A.S.S.R.
9. Checheno–Ingush A.S.S.R.
AZERBAIJAN
10. Nakhichevan A.S.S.R.
GEORGIA
11. Abkhaz A.S.S.R.
12. Adzhar A.S.S.R.

Projection: Conical Orthomorphic with two standard parallels   East from Greenwich

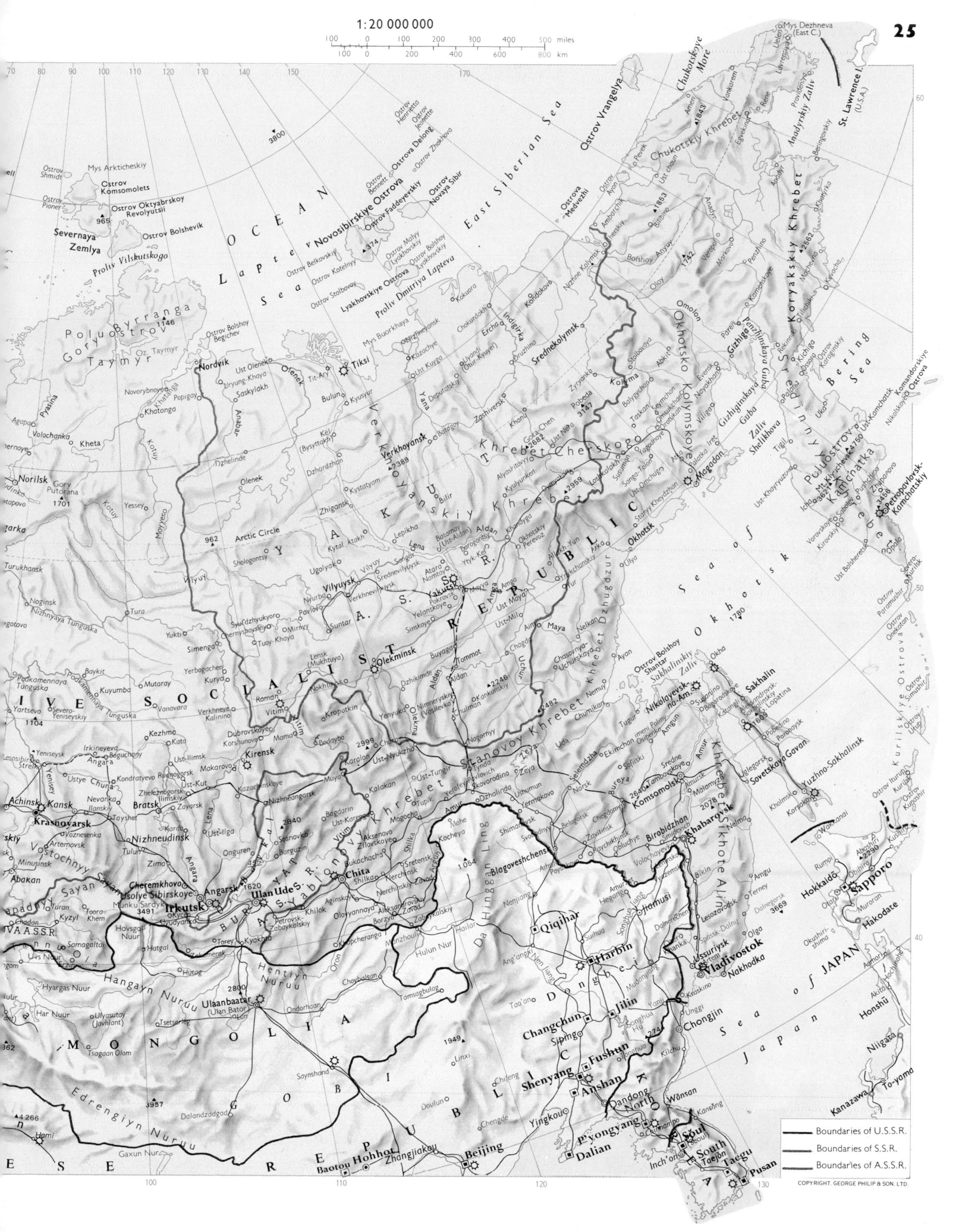

1:20 000 000

100   0   100   200   300   400   500 miles
100   0   200   400   600   800 km

OCEAN

Laptev Sea

East Siberian Sea

Chukotskoye More

Mys Dezhneva
(East C.)

St. Lawrence I.
(U.S.A.)

Ostrov Shmidt
Mys Arkticheskiy

Ostrov Komsomolets

Ostrov Pioner
Ostrov Oktyabrskoy Revolyutsii

Ostrov Bolshevik

Severnaya Zemlya

Proliv Vilkutskogo

Ostrov Vrangelya

Ostrova Medvezhi

Chukotskiy Khrebet

Anadyrskiy Zaliv

Koryakskiy Khrebet

Poluostrov Goryubyrranga
Taymyr

Oz. Taymyr

Ostrov Bolshoy Begichev

Novosibirskiye Ostrova

Ostrova Delong

Ostrov Novaya Sibir

Srednnyy Khrebet

Bering Sea

Gizhiga

Penzhinskaya Guba

Ostrov Karaginskiy

Norilsk
Gory Putorana

Nordvik

Tiksi

Verkhoyansk

Khrebet Cherskogo

Okhotsko Kolymskoye

Poluostrov Kamchatka

Petropavlovsk-Kamchatskiy

Arctic Circle

Y A K U T S K A Y A   A. S. S. R.

Yakutsk

SOCIALIST REPUBLIC

Okhotsk

Sea of Okhotsk

Olekminsk

Sakhalin

Nikolayevsk-na-Am.

Vilyuysk

E   S O C I A L I S T

Vitim

Stanovoy Khrebet

Komsomolsk

Yuzhno-Sakhalinsk

Kirensk

Achinsk   Kansk

Bratsk

Krasnoyarsk

Nizhneudinsk

Birobidzhan

Khabarovsk

Sovetskaya Gavan

Hokkaido

Sapporo

Cheremkhovo
Usolye Sibirskoye

Angarsk

Ulan Ude

Chita

Hakodate

Irkutsk

B U R Y A T   A. S. S. R.

Blagoveshchensk

Vladivostok

Nakhodka

JAPAN

Ulaanbaatar
(Ulan Bator)

Hentiyn Nuruu

Qiqihar

Harbin

Ussuriysk

Sea of Japan

Honshū

M O N G O L I A

Hangayn Nuruu

Changchun

Jilin

Chongjin

Hyargas Nuur

Har Nuur

G O B I

Shenyang   Fushun

Anshan

Dandong

North

Wŏnsan

Kanazawa
To-yama

Edrengiyn Nuruu

Yingkou

Chengde

P'yŏngyang

Dalian

Sŏul

South

Inch'ŏn   Taejŏn

Taegu

Pusan

Baotou   Hohhot

Zhangjiakou

Beijing

COPYRIGHT. GEORGE PHILIP & SON. LTD.

Boundaries of U.S.S.R.
Boundaries of S.S.R.
Boundaries of A.S.S.R.

1:50 000 000

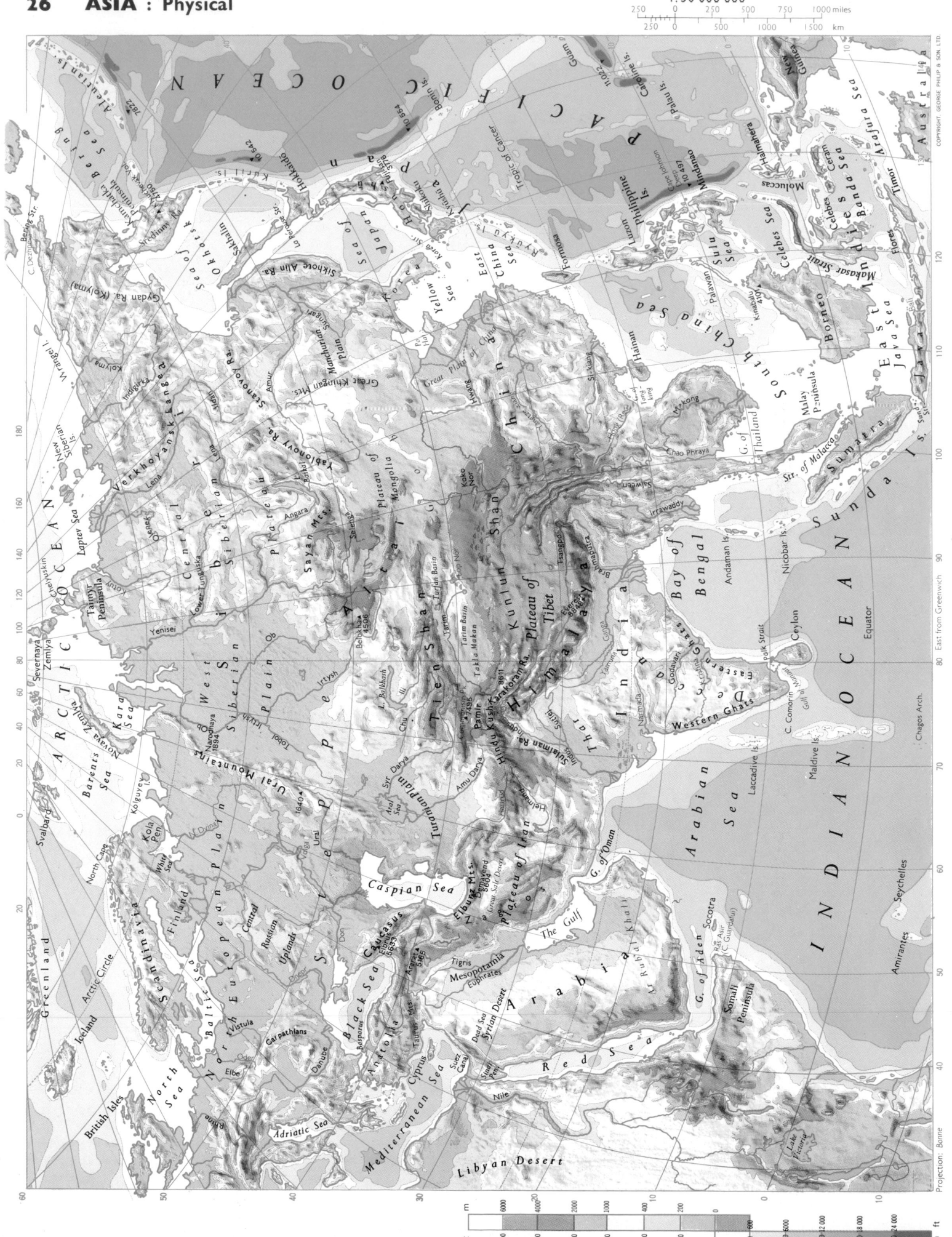

Projection: Bonne

1:50 000 000

250   0   250   500   750   1000 miles
250   0   500   1000   1500 km

COPYRIGHT. GEORGE PHILIP & SON, LTD.

East from Greenwich

Projection: Bonne

A R C T I C   O C E A N

P A C I F I C   O C E A N

I N D I A N   O C E A N

U. S. S. R.

C H I N A

MONGOLIA

INNER MONGOLIA

MANCHURIA

XINJIANG UYGUR

XIZANG (TIBET)

INDIA

PAKISTAN

AFGHANISTAN

IRAN (PERSIA)

SAUDI ARABIA

TURKEY

SYRIA

IRAQ

EUROPE

AFRICA

AUSTRALIA

INDONESIA

MALAYSIA

PHILIPPINES

THAILAND (SIAM)

BURMA

VIETNAM

LAOS

CAMBODIA

NEPAL

BHUTAN

BANGLADESH

SRI LANKA (CEYLON)

JAPAN

KOREA

OMAN

YEMEN

SOUTH YEMEN

KUWAIT

QATAR

BAHRAIN

UNITED ARAB EMIRATES

JORDAN

LEBANON

ISRAEL

CYPRUS

EGYPT

LIBYA

SUDAN

ETHIOPIA

SOMALI REP.

KENYA

TANZANIA

UGANDA

RWANDA

BURUNDI

ZAIRE

ZAMBIA

MALAWI

ICELAND

UNITED KINGDOM

Tokyo, Yokohama, Kyoto, Osaka, Nagoya, Nagasaki, Kobe, Sapporo, Hakodate, Hokkaido

Beijing, Shanghai, Tianjin, Qingdao, Dalian, Shenyang, Harbin, Changchun, Wuhan, Nanjing, Xi'an, Lanzhou, Chengdu, Chongqing, Kunming, Guangzhou, HONG KONG, Fuzhou, Changsha, Ürümqi, Kashi, Lhasa, Xining, Yining

Hanoi, Ho Chi Minh, Phnom Penh, Vientiane, Bangkok, Rangoon, Mandalay

Manila, Davao, Luzon, Mindanao, Borneo, Sumatera, Jakarta, Kuala Lumpur, Singapore, Brunei, Sabah, Sarawak

Delhi, Bombay, Calcutta, Madras, Hyderabad, Ahmadabad, Kanpur, Lucknow, Varanasi, Allahabad, Lahore, Amritsar, Karachi, Peshawar, Quetta, Colombo

Kabul, Herat, Qandahar, Mashhad, Tehrān, Esfahān, Shirāz, Zāhedān, Bandar 'Abbās

Baghdad, Al Başrah, Damascus (Dimashq), Halab, Bayrūt, Jerusalem, Ankara, Istanbul, Izmir, Erzurum, Al Madinah, Makkah (Mecca), Ar Riyād, Masqat, Aden, Sana

Moskva, Leningrad, Warszawa, Berlin, Wien, Paris, London, Roma, Beograd, Thessaloníki, Athínai, Odessa, Murmansk, Arkhangelsk, Sverdlovsk, Chelyabinsk, Magnitogorsk, Novosibirsk, Omsk, Tomsk, Krasnoyarsk, Irkutsk, Yakutsk, Khabarovsk, Vladivostok, Tashkent, Alma Ata, Samarkand, Baku, Tbilisi, Yerevan, Astrakhan, Rostov, Orenburg

Bering Sea, Sea of Okhotsk, Sea of Japan, Yellow Sea, East China Sea, South China Sea, Philippine Sea, Celebes Sea, Sulu Sea, Banda Sea, Java Sea, Bay of Bengal, Arabian Sea, Red Sea, Caspian Sea, Black Sea, Mediterranean Sea, Baltic Sea, North Sea, Barents Sea, Kara Sea, Laptev Sea

Kuril Is., Sakhalin, Kamchatka, Aleutian Is., Taiwan (Formosa), Hainan, Maldives, Seychelles, Socotra, Andaman Is., Nicobar Is., Lakshadweep, Ryukyu-retto

Tropic of Cancer, Equator, Arctic Circle

1:1 000 000

1949 Armistice line
1974 Cease-Fire line

10 5 0 10 20 miles
10 0 10 20 30 km

LEBANON

SYRIA

UNDER
ISRAELI
ADMINISTRATION

BIRKET RAM

M E D I T E R R A N E A N   S E A

Sūr (Tyre)

Qiryat Shemona

Nahariyya
'Akko (Acre)

Hagalil (Galilee)

KEFAR NAHUM (CAPERNAUM)

HEFA (Haifa)
Qiryat Yam
Qiryat Bialik
Qiryat Ata
Tirat Karmel

Yam Kinneret (Sea of Galilee)
Terverya 209

'ATLIT

Nazerat
Nazareth

Dar'ā

TEL MEGIDDO
Megiddo
'Afula

Irbid

CAESAREA
Or 'Aqiva
Hadera

Janin

J O R D A N

Netanya

Shomron (Samaria)

Ţūlkarm

SAMARIA

TEL ARSHAF
Herzliyya
Ramat HaSharon

Nabulus
SHECHEM
JACOB'S WELL

TEL AVIV
YAFO (Jaffa)
Ramat Gan
Bat Yam
Holon

UNDER

ISRAELI

ADMINISTRATION

SHILO

West

Rishon le Ziyyon
Nes Ziyyona
Ramla
Rehovot

Rām Allāh
Al Birah

'AMMAN

As Salt

Az Zarqā'

Bank

Lod (Lydda)

Ashdod

TEL GEZER

JERUSALEM
(Yerushalayim, Al Quds)

Ashqelon

Al 'Ayzariya (Bethany)

Qiryat Gat
BET GUVRIN
TEL LAKHISH

Bayt Lahm (Bethlehem)
BIRAK SULAYMĀN (SOLOMON'S POOLS)

QUMRĀN

Allenby Bridge

UNDER
ISRAELI
ADMINISTRATION

Gaza

Al Khalil (Hebron)

Gaza
Strip
Khān Yūnis

1949 Armistice Line

MESADA

Be'er Sheva

E G Y P T

Inset map (Continuation Southwards 1:2 500 000):

I S R A E L

Gaza
Strip
Khān Yūnis

Al Khalil (Hebron)

Be'er Sheva

Dimona

HORVOT SHIVTA

H a n e g e v

Mizpe Ramon

J O R D A N

E G Y P T

PETRA

1727

Elat
Al 'Aqaba

Continuation
Southwards
1:2 500 000
0 10 20 30 km

Projection: Conical with two standard parallels

East from Greenwich

COPYRIGHT. GEORGE PHILIP & SON. LTD.

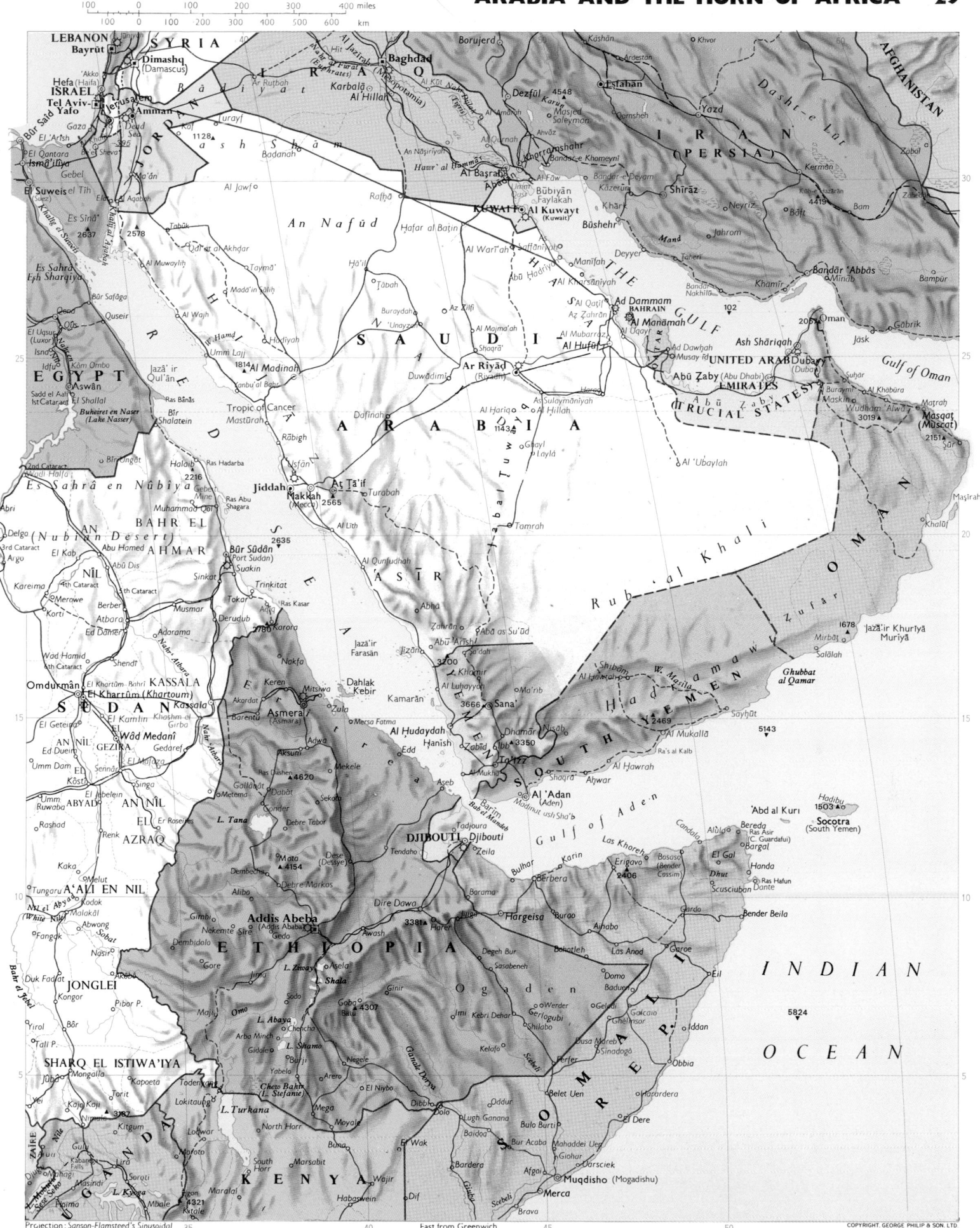

1:15 000 000

Projection: Sanson-Flamsteed's Sinusoidal   East from Greenwich   COPYRIGHT. GEORGE PHILIP & SON. LTD

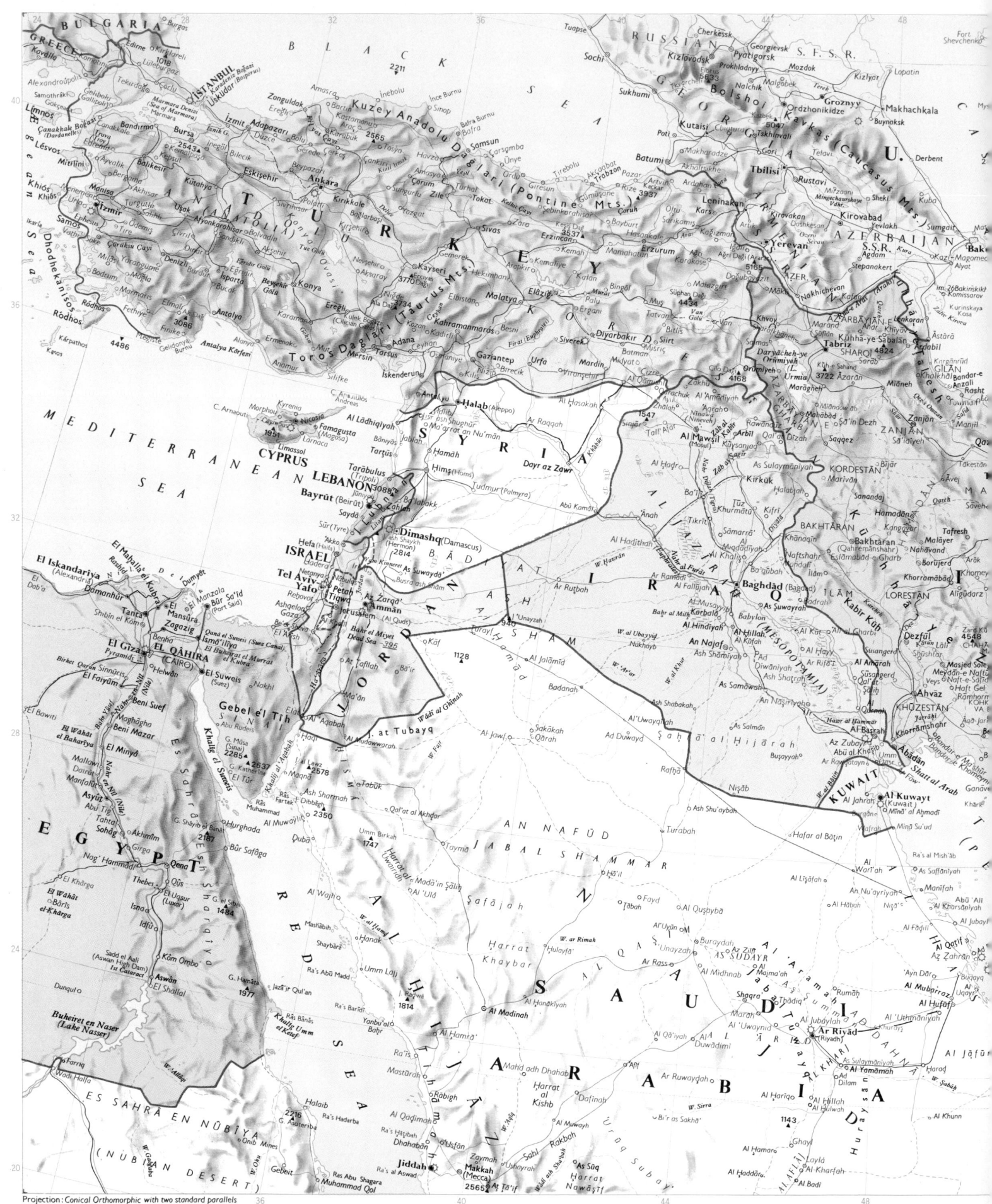

Division between Greeks and Turks
in Cyprus; Turks to the North.

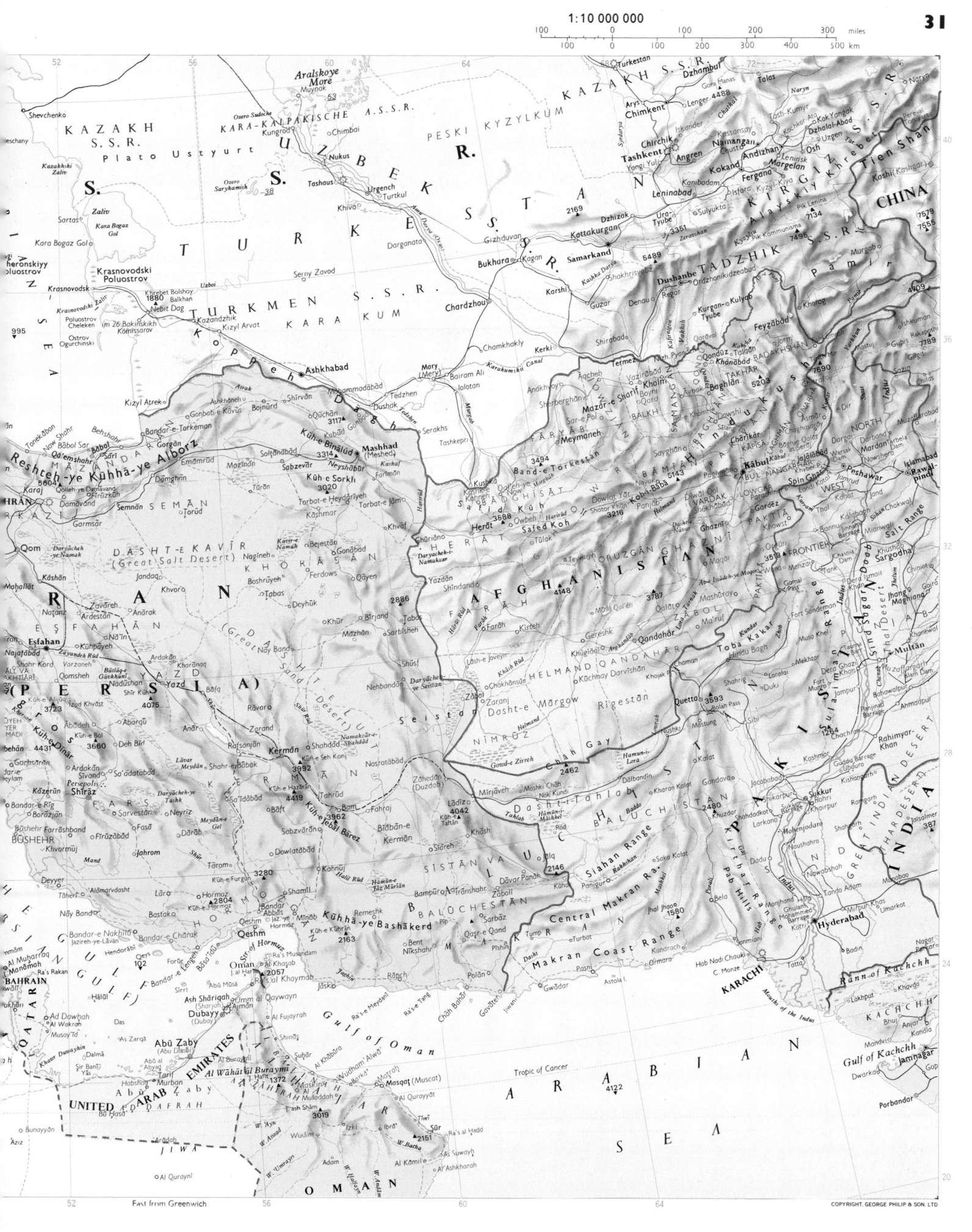

1:10 000 000

U.S.S.R.

SAMANGAN BADAKHSHAN
BALKH TAKHAR
FARYAB BAGHLAN
BADGHISAT
HERAT GHOWR BAMIAN VARDAK KAPISA NANGARHAR NORTH WEST FRONTIER
AFGHANISTAN
Herat Kabul KONARHA
Peshawar
Islamabad Srinagar
JAMMU AND KASHMIR
ORUZGAN GHAZNI PAKTIA Rawalpindi
PAKTIA PAKTIA
HELMAND ZABOL QANDAHAR PAKTIKA
NIMRUZ
Qandahar Quetta Sialkot HIMACHAL PRADESH
Lahore Amritsar
Faisalabad
PUNJAB Ludhiana Simla
BALUCHISTAN Chandigarh Ambala Dehra Dun
Multan Haridwar
Siahan Range PAKISTAN HARYANA Meerut
Central Makran Range Bikaner DELHI Moradabad
Sukkur Bareilly
Makran Coast Range Jaipur Agra
SIND RAJASTHAN Gwalior
Karachi Hyderabad
ARABIAN SEA Jodhpur Jhansi
Tropic of Cancer
Rann of Kachchh Udaipur Kota
GUJARAT INDIA BHARAT
Ahmadabad Indore MADHYA
Rajkot Vadodara Bhopal PRADESH
Jamnagar (Baroda)
Gulf of Kachchh Surat Nagpur
Diu
Gulf of Khambhat
DADRA & NAGAR HAVELI Nasik Aurangabad MAHARASHTRA Chandrapur
DAMAN Ajanta Range
BOMBAY Thane Satmala Hills
Pune (Poona) Sholapur Nanded
Mahabaleshwar ANDHRA PRADESH
Kolhapur Bijapur Hyderabad
Belgaum Secunderabad
GOA Panaji (Panjim) Gulbarga
Marmagao

Inset map (Continuation Southwards on same scale)

GOA Dharwad Kurnool
Gadag Bellary Adoni
KARNATAKA Erramala Hills
Mangalore Anantapur Nellore
Shimoga Pulicat Lake
Bangalore Kolar Madras
Mysore Vellore
Gold Fields
Salem Pondicherry
Coimbatore Cuddalore
TAMIL NADU Kumbakonam
Tiruchchirappalli Thanjavur
Madurai Nagappattinam
Palk Strait
KERALA Point Pedro
Cochin Jaffna
Ernakulam Palk Bay
Alleppey Gulf of Mannar (Manaar)
Quilon Trincomalee
Trivandrum
Nagercoil Anuradhapura
Cape Comorin SRI LANKA (CEYLON)
Kandy
Colombo Adam's Peak
Moratuwa
Galle Dondra Head

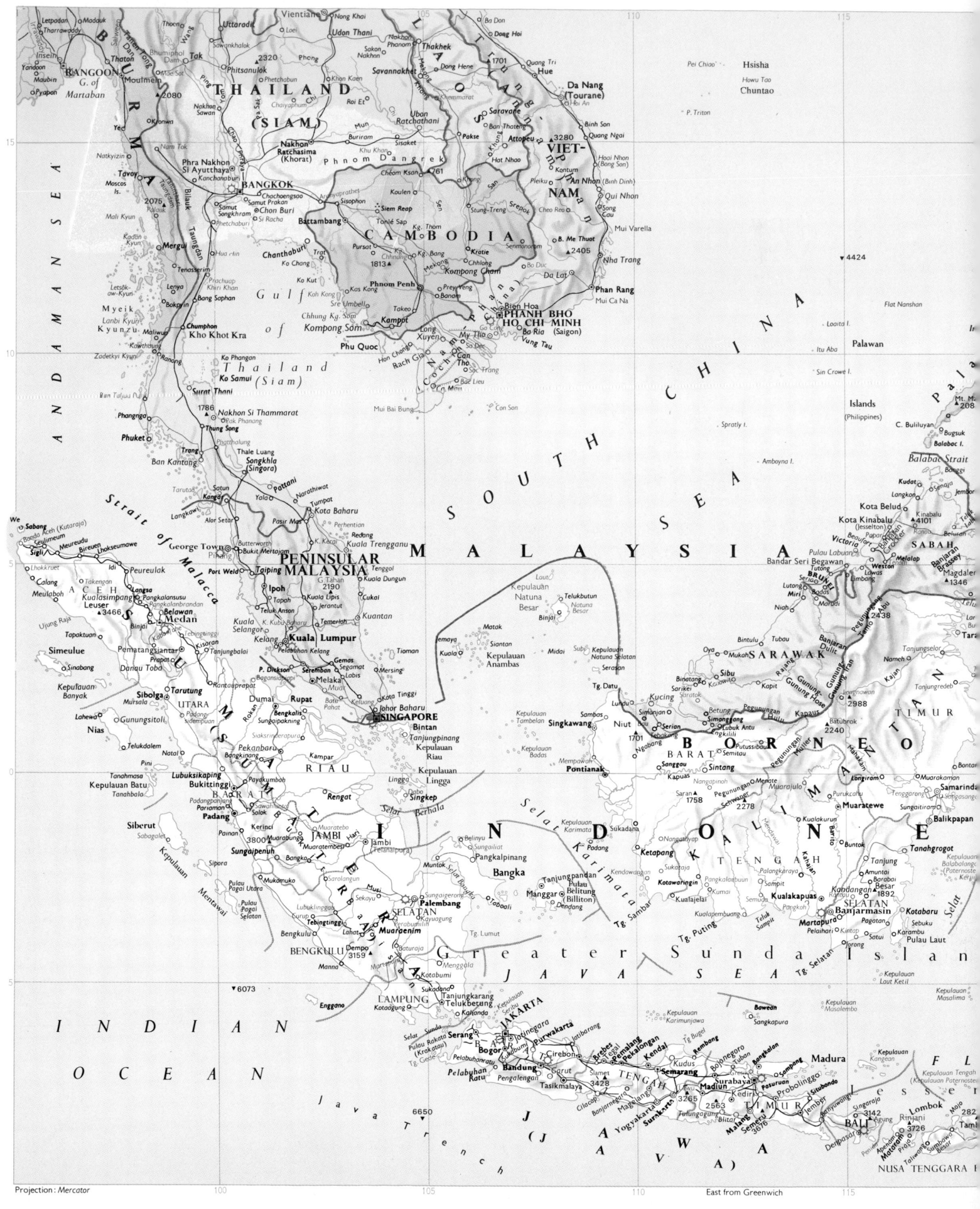

East from Greenwich

1:12 500 000

100 | 0 | 100 | 200 | 300 miles
100 | 0 | 100 | 200 | 300 | 400 | 500 km

JAVA AND MADURA

1:7 500 000

50 | 0 | 50 | 100 | 150 | 200 miles
50 | 0 | 50 | 100 | 150 | 200 | 250 | 300 km

PHILIPPINE

LUZON

MANILA

Polillo Islands

Mindoro

Panay
Iloilo
Bacolod
Cebu
Negros
Bohol

Mindanao
Zamboanga
Davao
General Santos
Sarangani Bay

SULU SEA

SULAWESI SEA

SULAWESI (CELEBES)

SULAWESI SEA

Kepulauan Sangihe

Kepulauan Talaud

Manado
Gorontalo

Halmahera
Ternate
Tidore

Morotai

PACIFIC OCEAN

Yap Islands

Caroline Islands
(U.S. Trust Territory of the Pacific Islands)

Belau
Babelthuap
Koror

MALUKU

Buru
Seram (Ceram)
Ambon
Buton

BANDA SEA

Misool
Fakfak

IRIAN JAYA

Jazirah Doberai
(Vogelkop)

Manokwari

Teluk Cenderawasih

Pegunungan Van Rees

Jayapura
(Hollandia)

Pegunungan Sudirman
Puncak Jaya 5029
Puncak Trikora 4750
Jayawijaya 4702

PAPUA NEW GUINEA

Kepulauan Aru
Trangan
Wokam

Kepulauan Kai
Kai Besar 7440

Kepulauan Tanimbar
Yamdena

Flores
NUSA TENGGARA TIMUR
Sumba
Kupang
Sumbawa
Alor
TIMOR TIMUR
Dili

ARAFURA SEA

Merauke

Sawu Sea

Equator

JAKARTA
Bogor
Bandung
BARAT
TENGAH
Semarang
Surakarta
Yogyakarta
TIMUR
Surabaya
Madura
Malang
Madiun
Kediri
Probolinggo
Bali

Kepulauan Karimunjawa

COPYRIGHT. GEORGE PHILIP & SON, LTD.

SEA OF JAPAN

PACIFIC OCEAN

CHŪGOKU

SHIKOKU

KYŪSHŪ

KINKI

TOKAIDO LINE

SOUTH KOREA

Pusan
Taegu
Kwangju
Mokpo
Chŏnju
Taejŏn
Chungju
Pohang
Masan
Chinju
Sunchon
Yŏsu

1:5 000 000

| 25 | 0 | 25 | 50 | 75 | 100 miles |

| 25 | 0 | 50 | 100 | 150 | km |

Projection: Conical with two standard parallels

East from Greenwich

Osumi-Shotō
Tane-ga-Shima 1935
Yaku-Shima
Tokara-Kaikyō
Tokara-Shima
Suwanose-Jima
Nansei-Shoto
Amami-Ō-Shima
Toku-no-Shima

Continuation Southwards on same scale

HOKKAIDŌ
SAPPORO
Sea of Okhotsk
Rebun-Tō
Rishiri-Tō
Wakkanai
Sōya-Misaki
Asahigawa
Abashiri
Abashiri-Wan
Shiretoko-Misaki
Nemuro-Kaikyō
Kushiro
Nemuro
Obihiro
Muroran
Hakodate
Okushiri-Tō
Otaru
Rumoi
Poroshiri-Dake 2052
Erimo-Misaki

TŌHOKU
Aomori
Hachinohe
Hirosaki
Morioka
Miyako
Akita
Kamaishi
Sakata
Sendai
Ishinomaki
Yamagata
Sado
Niigata
Fukushima
Kōriyama
Iwaki
Nagaoka
Toyama
Kanazawa
Noto-Hantō
CHŪBU
KANTŌ
TŌKYŌ
YOKOHAMA
Yokosuka
Utsunomiya
Maebashi
Mito
Chōshi
Bōsō-Hantō
Kasumi-ga-Ura
NAGOYA
Shizuoka
Hamamatsu
Toyohashi
Ōsaka
SAKAI
KŌBE
KYŌTO
Wakayama
Matsue
Tottori
Okayama
Hiroshima
Kure
Shimonoseki
KITAKYŪSHŪ
FUKUOKA
Saga
Sasebo
Nagasaki
Kumamoto
Ōmuta
Miyazaki
Kagoshima
Matsuyama
Takamatsu
Tokushima
KŌchi
Goto-Rettō
Shio-no-Misaki
Ashizuri-Misaki
Hachijō-Jima
Miyake-Jima
Nii-Jima

SEA OF JAPAN

PACIFIC OCEAN

1:10 000 000

| 100 | 50 | 0 | 50 | 100 | 150 | 200 miles |

| 100 | 0 | 100 | 200 | 300 | km |

Projection: Bonne

East from Greenwich

REFERENCE TO PREFECTURES

HOKKAIDŌ DISTRICT		KINKI DISTRICT	
1	Hokkaidō	24	Hyogo
TŌHOKU DISTRICT		25	Kyōto
2	Aomori	26	Shiga
3	Akita	27	Ōsaka
4	Iwate	28	Nara
5	Yamagata	29	Mie
6	Miyagi	30	Wakayama
7	Fukushima		
		CHŪGOKU DISTRICT	
CHŪBU DISTRICT		31	Tottori
8	Niigata	32	Okayama
9	Ishikawa	33	Shimane
10	Toyama	34	Hiroshima
11	Fukui	35	Yamaguchi
12	Gifu		
13	Nagano	SHIKOKU DISTRICT	
14	Yamanashi	36	Kagawa
15	Aichi	37	Tokushima
16	Shizuoka	38	Ehime
		39	Kōchi
KANTŌ DISTRICT			
17	Gumma	KYŪSHŪ DISTRICT	
18	Tochigi	40	Fukuoka
19	Saitama	41	Saga
20	Ibaraki	42	Nagasaki
21	Tōkyō	43	Kumamoto
22	Chiba	44	Ōita
23	Kanagawa	45	Miyazaki
		46	Kagoshima

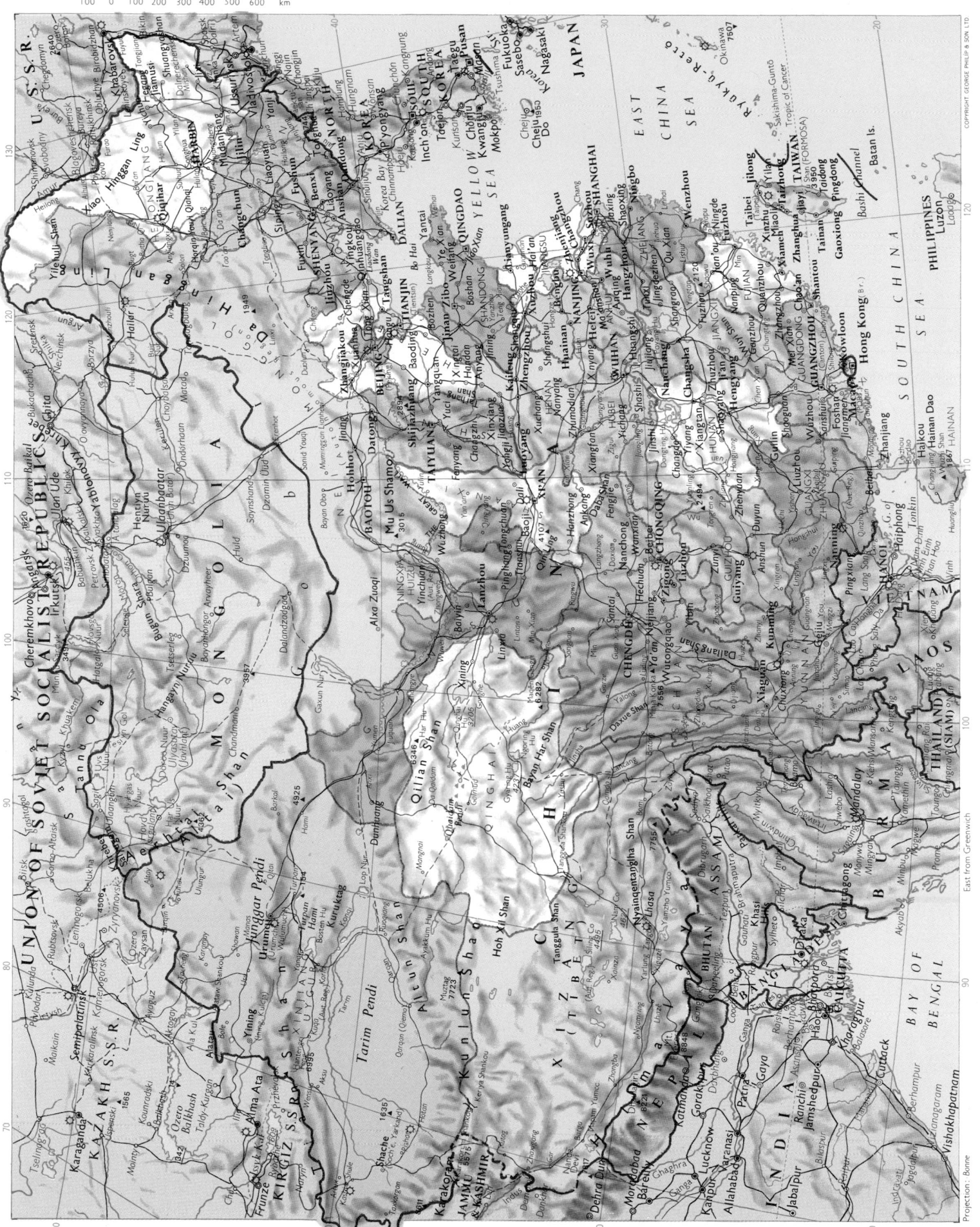

1:20 000 000

Projection: Bonne

East from Greenwich

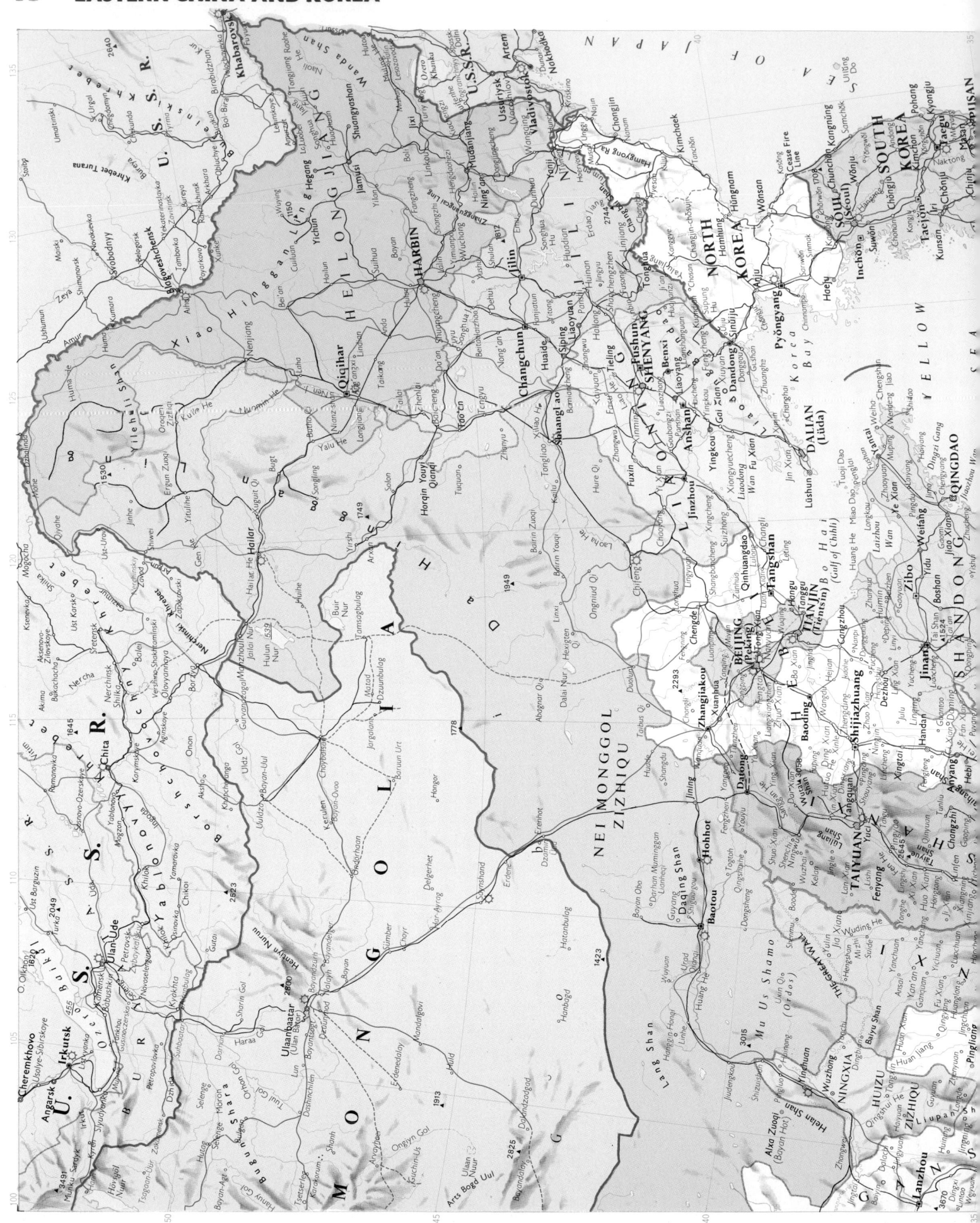

1:10 000 000

50   0   50   100   150   200   250 miles
50 0 50 100 150 200 250 300 350 400 km

P   A   C   I   F   I   C   O   C   E   A   N

E   A   S   T   C   H   I   N   A   S   E   A

S   O   U   T   H   C   H   I   N   A   S   E   A

JAPAN

KITAKYŪSHŪ
Fukuoka
Kurume
Sasebo   Sendai
Nagasaki   Minamata
Omuta   Makurazaki
Kagoshima

Tsushima
Goto-retto
Kōshiki-shima
Kusagaki-jima

Iki
Yōsu

Mokpo
Cheju
Cheju Do
(Quelpart)

Nansei-shotō

Tokara-guntō
Amami-ō-shima
Amami-guntō
Okino erabu-shima
Toku-no-shima
Naze
Ōku
Nogo
Okinawa
Naha
Kume
Okinawa-guntō

Tropic of Cancer

Miyako
Ryūkyū
Sekibi-shō
Yaeyama-rettō
Iriomote
Ishigaki
Yonaguni
Sakishima-guntō

Senkaku guntō

SHANGHAI
Chongming Dao
Nantong   Changshu
Songjiang
Suzhou   Jiaxing
Wuxi   Hangzhou
Zhenjiang
Changzhou
Wuhu
NANJING
Hefei
Huainan
Bengbu
Xuzhou

JIANGSU
ANHUI
ZHEJIANG
Ningbo
Shaoxing
Wenzhou

TAIWAN
(FORMOSA)
TAIBEI
(Taipei)
Jilong
Taoyuan
Yilan
Miaoli
Taizhong
Nantou
Hualian
Zhanghua
Jiayi
Yunlin
Taidong
Tainan
Gaoxiong
Pingdong
Fangliao

Penghu

PHILIPPINES
Luzon
Batan Is.
Babuyan Is.
Bashi Channel
Balintang Channel
Babuyan Channel
C. Engaño
Aparri
Vigan

NANCHANG
WUHAN
Hankou
Wuchang
Hanyang
Huangshi

HUBEI
JIANGXI
FUJIAN
Nanping
Fuzhou
Quanzhou
Xiamen
Zhangzhou
Shantou

Changsha
HUNAN
Hengyang
Shaoyang
Zhuzhou
Xiangtan

GUANGDONG
GUANGZHOU
(Canton)
Foshan
Jiangmen
Zhuhai
Macau
(Port.)
Shenzhen
HONGKONG
(Br.)
Kowloon

Guilin
GUANGXI-ZHUANGZU
ZIZHIQU
Nanning

HAINAN
Haikou
Zhanjiang

GUIZHOU
Guiyang

SICHUAN
CHONGQING
Zigong
Neijiang

Xi'an
Hanzhong

HENAN
Zhengzhou
Kaifeng
Luoyang

VIETNAM
HANOI
Haiphong

Xian

East from Greenwich

Projection: Lambert's Equivalent Azimuthal

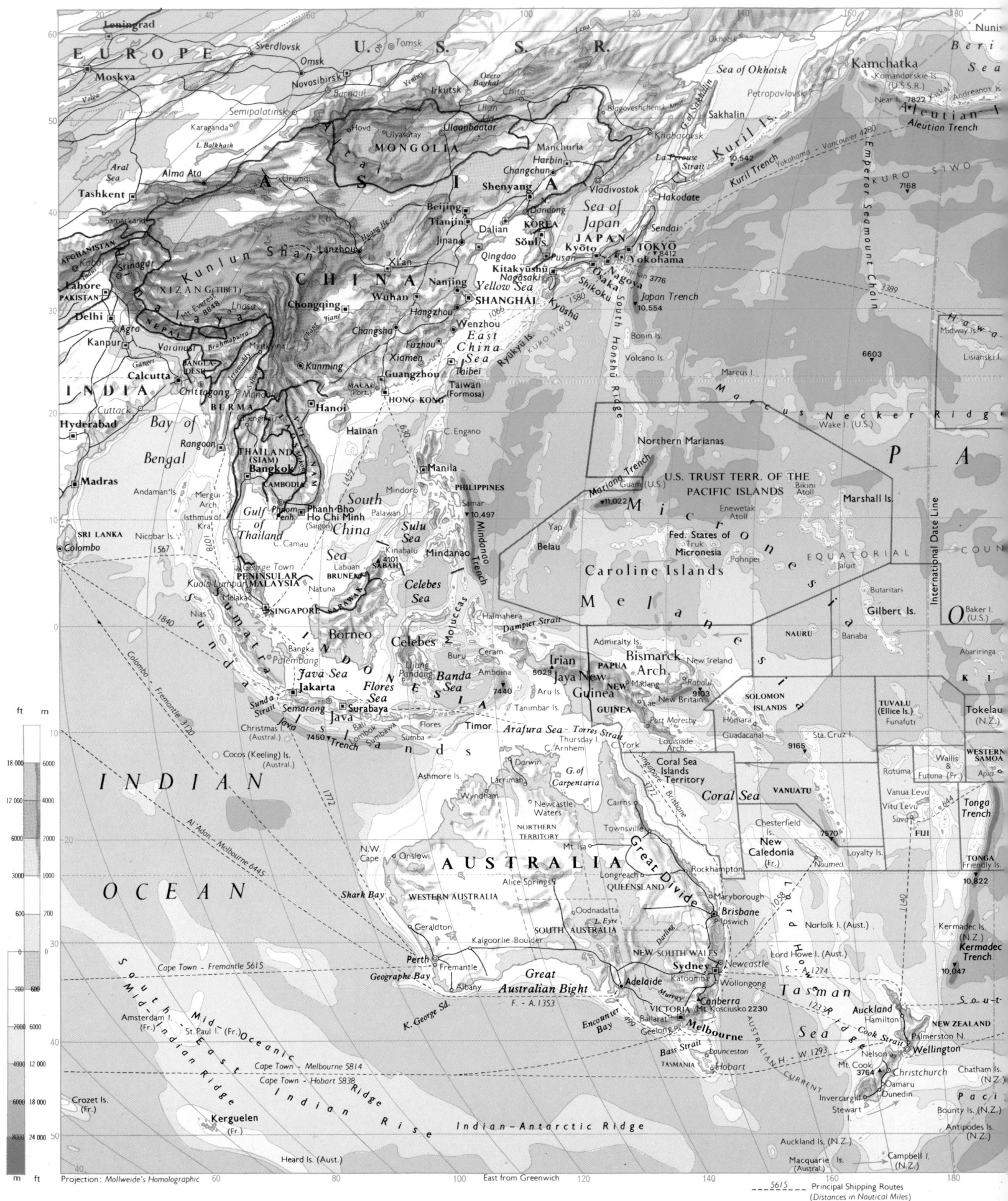

Principal Shipping Routes
(Distances in Nautical Miles)

ALASKA
C. 6050
Bristol Bay
Gulf of Alaska
imak
Prince of Wales I.
Juneau
Sitka
Prince Rupert
Queen Charlotte Is.
Kitimat

GREENLAND
C. Farewell

Churchill
Hudson Bay
Betcher Is.
Scheffervile
Hamilton Inlet

CANADA
Dawson Creek
Edmonton
Lynn Lake
Prince Albert
Saskatoon
L. Athabaska
L. Winnipeg
James Bay
Labrador
Strait of Belle Isle
NORTH

NORTH AMERICA
Vancouver
Vancouver I.
Victoria
Medicine Hat
Regina
Winnipeg
Duluth
L. Superior
Sault Ste. Marie
Montréal
Québec
Anticosti
Pr. Edward I.
Newfoundland
C. Race
Southampton 3091

Seattle
Tacoma
Portland
Spokane
Helena
Bismark
Butte
Boise
Cheyenne
Missouri
Minneapolis
St. Paul
Milwaukee
Michigan
Huron
Ottawa
Toronto
L. Ontario
Fredericton
Saint John
Sable I.
New York
C. Breton I.

Mendocino Seascarp
C. Mendocino
Sacramento
Oakland
San Francisco
4418
Salt Lake City
Denver
Kansas City
Des Moines
Erie
CHICAGO
Detroit
Buffalo
Pittsburgh
NEW YORK
Philadelphia
Baltimore
Washington
Richmond
Norfolk
ATLANTIC

6741
2419
UNITED STATES
Santa Fé
Oklahoma
St. Louis
Indianapolis
Cincinnati
Memphis
C. Hatteras
New York - Recife 3678
Bermuda (U.K.)
New York - Liverpool 4330

Los Angeles
San Diego
C. Blanco
2091
Murray Seascarp
El Paso
Dallas
Austin
Atlanta
Savannah
Jacksonville
OCEAN

Ciudad Juárez
Houston
San Antonio
Galveston
New Orleans
Mobile
Tampa
Miami

Hawaiian Is. (U.S.A.)
Tropic of Cancer
CALIFORNIAN CURRENT
Guadalupe
Pto. Eugenia
6225
Sierra Madre Or.
Gulf of California
Torreón
Monterrey
Gulf of Mexico
Florida Strait
BAHAMAS

Oahu
Honolulu
Hawaii
Clarion Fracture Zone
C. S. Lucas
Revilla Gigedo Is. (Mexico)
Aguascalientes
Tampico
San Luis Potosí
La Habana
Yucatan Channel
CUBA
West Indies
Hispaniola 9200
DOM. REP.
Santo Domingo
St. Thomas (U.S.)
Virgin Is.
Leeward Is.

ton I. (U.S.)
3277
Guadalajara
México
5700
Veracruz
Puebla
Mérida
7680
JAMAICA
HAITI
Kingston
PUERTO RICO
Guadeloupe (Fr.)
Martinique (Fr.)

4711
Acapulco
S.E. MONSOON DRIFT
BELIZE
GUATEMALA 3656
Guatemala
Tegucigalpa
HONDURAS
Caribbean Sea
Curaçao (Ne.)
Windward Is.
BARBADOS
TRINIDAD & TOBAGO

PACIFIC
Clipperton Fracture Zone
Clipperton I. (Fr.)
3666
SALVADOR
NICARAGUA
Managua
Barranquilla
Maracaibo
Caracas
Orinoco
VENEZUELA
CENTRAL AMERICA
San José
COSTA RICA
PANAMA
Panamá
Colón
Panama Canal
Medellín
Bogotá

Christmas Island Ridge
CURRENT
Palmyra Is. (U.S.)
Cocos I.
835
Cali
COLOMBIA

Teraina
Tabuaeran
Kiritimati
Equator
C. S. Francisco
Quito
ECUADOR
Chimborazo 6267
Iquitos
Manaus
Amazon

E N
Jarvis I. (U.S.)
Galápagos (Ecuador)
Guayaquil
Cuenca
BRAZIL

erbury I.
oenix Is.
Malden I.
Vostok I.
Flint I.
Starbuck I.
Tahiti - Panamá 4570
C. Pariñas
Chiclayo
Trujillo
Lobos Is.
SOUTH

IBATI
Tongareva
Penrhyn Is.
Manihiki
Suwarrow I. s
Caroline I.
Marquesas Is.
706
PERU
Lima
Callao
6369
AMERICA
10

ukapuka
ER.
MOA
Cook Islands (N.Z.)
Society Is.
1303
Leeward Is.
Tahiti
Tuamotu Archipelago
Auckland - Panamá 6510
Cuzco
Titicaca
Illampu & Ancohuma 6550
BOLIVIA

iue
Manuae
Windward Is.
FRENCH POLYNESIA
East Pacific Ridge
6866
La Paz
Peru-

Austral Is.
Seamount Chain
Rarotonga
Iquique
Chile
Antofagasta

estern
Tubuai Is. (Austral Is.)
Rapa Iti
Tuamotu Ridge
Pitcairn I. (U.K.)
Ducie I.
Tropic of Capricorn
Sala-y-Gomez (Chile)
Easter Is. (Chile)
San Félix (Chile)
San Ambrosio (Chile)
8050
Trench
79
Salta
Asunción
PARAGUAY

Southeast Pacific Basin
PERUVIAN CURRENT
Tucumán
Corrientes
Pto. Alegre
30

Arch. de Juan Fernández (Chile)
Aconcagua 6960
Córdoba
Rosario
Santa Fe
Paysandú
URUGUAY
Montevideo

Alejandro Selkirk
Robinson Crusoe
Valparaiso
Santiago
Buenos Aires
La Plata
Río de la Plata

Concepción
P.A. Valparaíso
1414
Neuquen
Paraná
ARGENTINA
Mar del Plata
SOUTH

Pacific - Antarctic Ridge
Chile Rise
P.A.
Buenos Aires - Montevideo 1355
1295
ATLANTIC
40

Pacific - Antarctic Basin
WEST WIND DRIFT
CAPE HORN CURRENT
Chonos Arch.
G. of Penas
Patagonian
Sta. Cruz
Argentine Basin 6212
OCEAN

s Basin
Wellington Is.
Punta Arenas
Str. of Magellan
Tierra del Fuego
C. Horn
Sta. Cruz
Punta Arenas
P. Deseado
Falkland Is. (U.K.)
Stanley
South Georgia
50

1:40 000 000

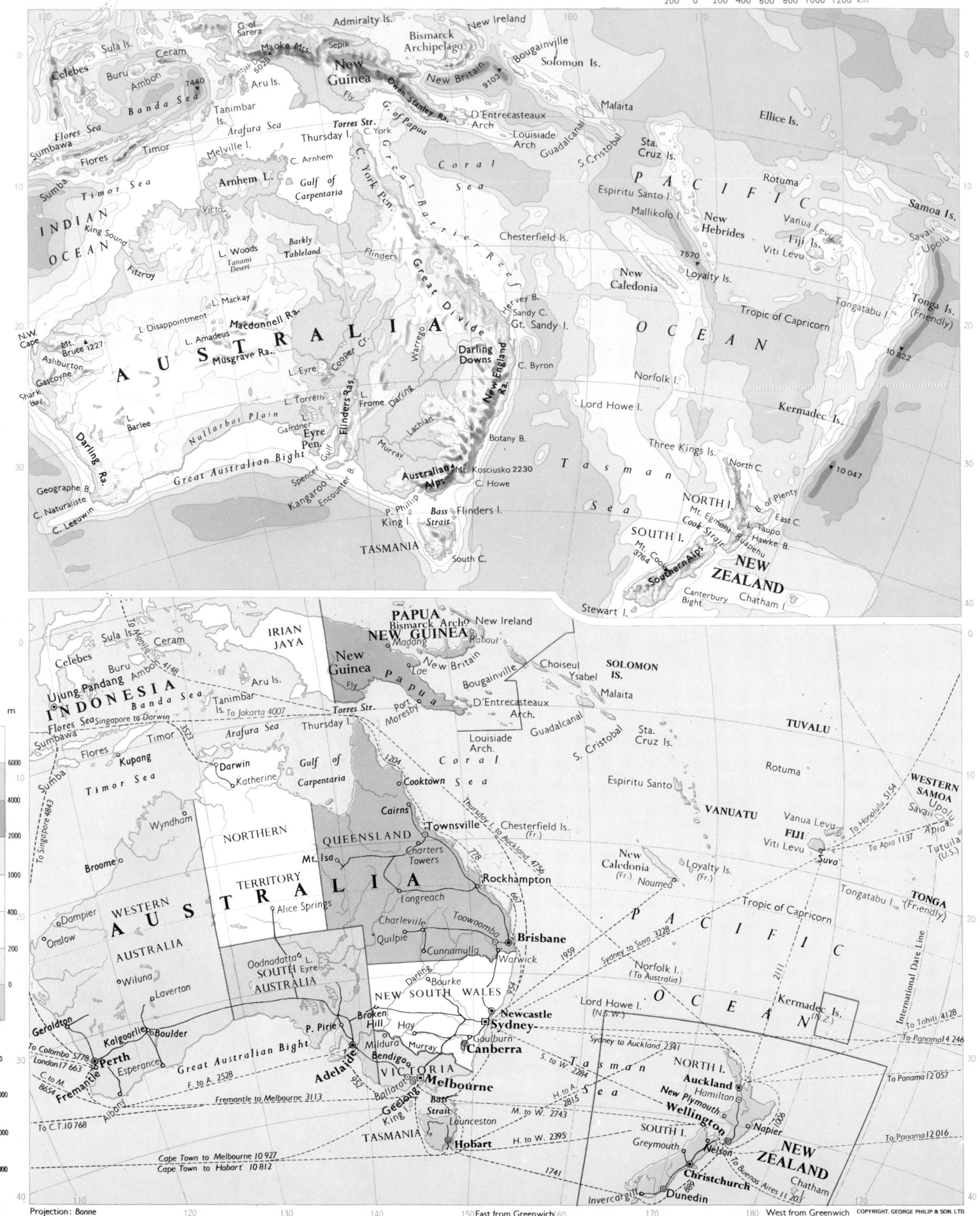

Projection: Bonne

150 East from Greenwich 160   West from Greenwich   COPYRIGHT. GEORGE PHILIP & SON. LTD.

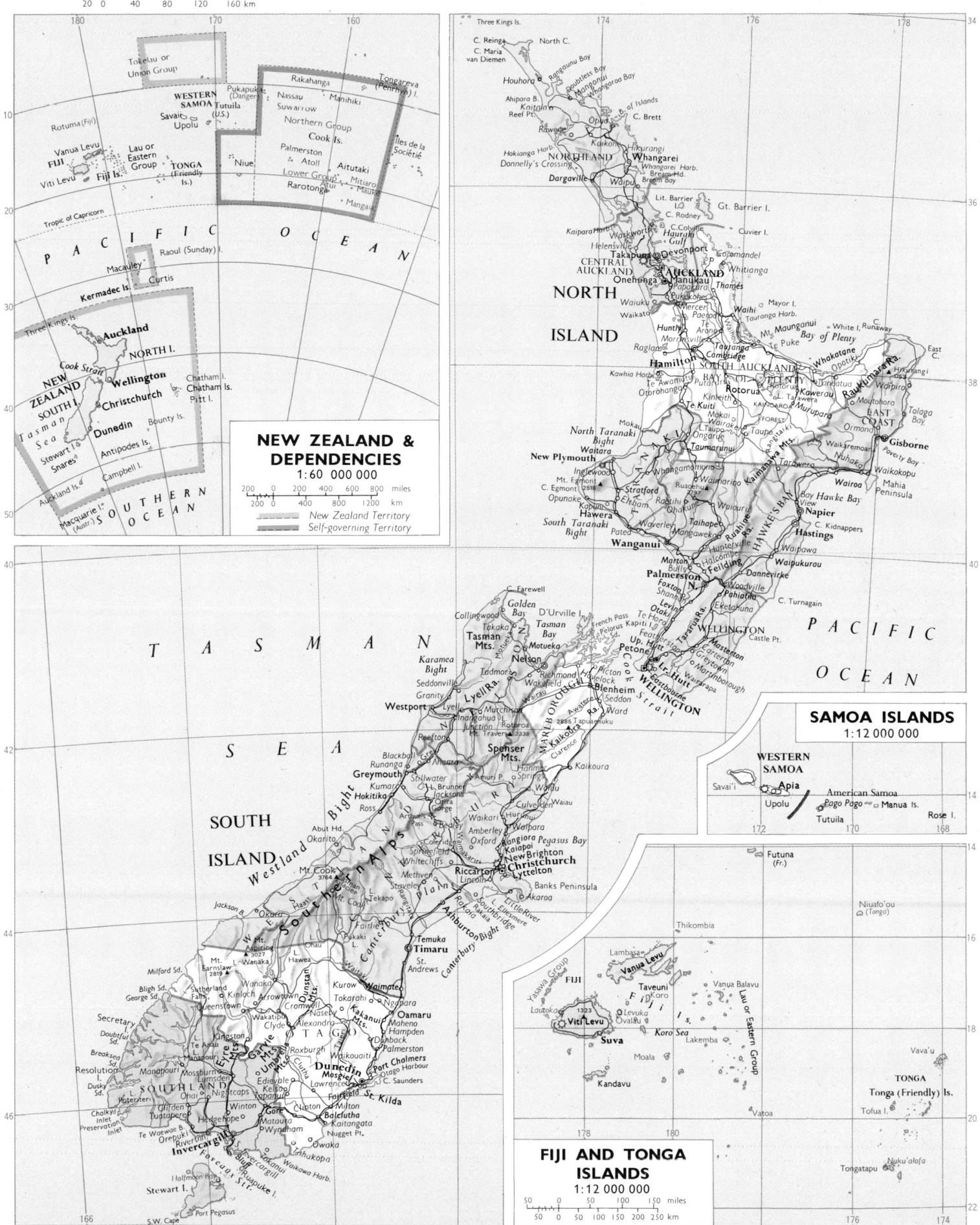

1:6 000 000

20 0 20 40 60 80 100 miles
20 0 40 80 120 160 km

NEW ZEALAND & DEPENDENCIES
1:60 000 000

200 0 200 400 600 800 miles
200 0 400 800 1200 km

New Zealand Territory
Self-governing Territory

SAMOA ISLANDS
1:12 000 000

WESTERN SAMOA

Savai'i Apia
Upolu Pago Pago Manua Is.
Tutuila Rose I.

American Samoa

FIJI AND TONGA ISLANDS
1:12 000 000

50 0 50 100 150 miles
50 0 50 100 150 200 250 km

FIJI

Vanua Levu
Taveuni
Koro
Viti Levu
Levuka
Ovalau
Suva Koro Sea
Kandavu

Lau or Eastern Group

TONGA
Tonga (Friendly) Is.

Projection: Conical with two standard parallels

COPYRIGHT. GEORGE PHILIP & SON, L.TD.

TASMANIA

Bass Strait

King Island

Flinders Island

CORAL SEA

Great Barrier Reef

Gulf of Carpentaria

Cape York Peninsula

Arnhem Land

NORTHERN TERRITORY

QUEENSLAND

GREAT ARTESIAN

Simpson Desert

Barkly Tableland

Great Dividing Range

Rockhampton
Gladstone
Yeppoon
Mackay
Bowen
Ayr
Townsville
Ingham
Cairns
Innisfail
Mareeba
Cooktown
Charters Towers
Hughenden
Winton
Cloncurry
Mount Isa
Normanton
Burketown
Croydon
Georgetown
Alice Springs
Tennant Creek

Macdonnell Ranges

Tropic of Capricorn

1:8 000 000

50   100   150   200 miles

50   0   50   100   150   200   250   300 km

T A S M A N   S E A

NEW SOUTH WALES

SOUTH AUSTRALIA

VICTORIA

Bass Strait

Great Dividing Range

Great Artesian Basin

Grey Range

Barrier Range

Flinders Range

BRISBANE

SYDNEY

CANBERRA

MELBOURNE

ADELAIDE

Newcastle

Broken Hill

Wollongong

Port Augusta

Whyalla

Geelong

Ballarat

Bendigo

King Island

Flinders Island

Furneaux Group

Cape Barren I.

Hogan Group

Kent Group

Spencer Gulf

Lake Eyre

Lake Torrens

Lake Gairdner

Lake Frome

Kangaroo I.

Murray Bridge

Mildura

Wagga Wagga

Albury

Dubbo

Tamworth

Coffs Harbour

Grafton

Lismore

Toowoomba

Ipswich

Gold Coast

Maryborough

Gympie

Fraser Island

Darling R.

Murray R.

Murrumbidgee R.

COMMONWEALTH TERR.

East from Greenwich

Projection: Bonne

COPYRIGHT GEORGE PHILIP & SON, LTD.

135   140   145   150

30   35   40

1:8 000 000

50 0 50 100 150 200 miles
50 0 50 100 150 200 250 300 km

East from Greenwich

Projection. Bonne

COPYRIGHT. GEORGE PHILIP & SON. LTD.

SOUTH AUSTRALIA

WESTERN AUSTRALIA

SOUTHERN OCEAN

Great Australian Bight

Great Victoria Desert

Nullarbor Plain

Hampton Tableland

Ayers Rock 868
Mt. Olga 1069
Mann Ra. Mt. Morris 1387
Musgrave Ranges
Everard Ranges
The Officer
Mt. Woodroffe 1549
L. Amadeus
Everard Park
L. Meramangye

Mt. Barée
Mt. Buttfield
Rawlinson Ra. 1126
Mt. Forrest
Cavenagh Ra.
Christopher L.
Rawlinson Ra.
Mt. Aloysius 1058
Blackstone Ra.
Mt. Squires 705
Warburton Ra.
Barrow Ra.
Macintosh Ra. Pt. Lillian 466
Saunders Pt. 466
Mt. Thirsoll
L. Yeo
Jubilee L.
Shell Lakes
Serpentine Lakes
Nurrari Lakes
Wyola L. L. Day-Day
L. Maurice
L. Wilson
Talbot Ra.

L. Breaden
Baker L.
L. Gillen
Ernest Giles Ra. 712
Rason L.
L. Throssell
L. Carnegie
Mt. Burnside
Brassey Ra.
Mt. Normanhurst
L. Buchanan
Cosmo Newberry
L. Wells
L. Carey
L. Raeside
L. Rebecca
Kirgella Rocks
Mt. Eureka 499
Granite Peak
Earaheedy
Wongawol

L. Minigwal
Great Victoria Desert

Barrow Ra.
Bates Ra.
Yandal
Mt. Keith
Wiluna
L. Way
Depot Springs
Barr Smith Ra.
Carnarvon Ra.
Mt. Essendon 906
Nabberu
L. Nabberu
Montague Ra.
Sandstone
Youanmi Downs
Cashmere Downs
Maynard Hills 543
Mt. Elvire
Mt. Alexander
Mt. Redcliffe 576
Melrose
Louisa
Ida Valley
Pinnacles
Mt. Keith
Yuinmery

Mt. Singleton 677
Paynes Find
Eaaroo
Ninghan
Bonnie Rock
Beacon
Bencubbin
Mukinbudin
Westonia
Southern Cross
Marvel Loch
Mt. Burges 554
Kalgoorlie-Boulder
Coolgardie
Kambalda
Bulla Bulling
Widgiemooltha

Kookynie
Leonora
Gwalia
Menzies
Malcolm
Niagara
Kanowna
Broad Arrow
Comet Vale
Goongarrie
Mt. Monger
Kurnalpi
Pinjin
Mulline

Norseman
L. Cowan
L. Dundas
L. Johnston
Peak Eleanora 503
L. Hope
L. Tay
Kumarl
Salmon Gums
Gilmore
Grass Patch
L. King
Newdegate
Ravensthorpe
Hopetoun
Mt. Ridley
Eastern Group
Mt. Malcolm
C. Arid
C. Pasley
Middle I.
Sandy Bight
South East Is.
Archipelago of the Recherche
Cape Le Grand
Esperance B.
Duke of Orleans B.
Esperance

Cocklebiddy Motel
Madura Motel
Mundrabilla
Eucla Motel
Wilson Bluff
Border
Nullarbor
Head of Bight
Yalata
Koonalda
Coorabie
Fowler's B.
C. Nuyts
Penong
Watson
Barton
Ooldea
Fisher
Moralinga
Cook
Hughes
Deakin
Reid
Forrest
Naretha
Haig
Nurina
Rawlinna
Loongana
Kitchener
Zanthus
Karonie
Kanandah
Naretha
L. Gidgi
L. Noseman

PERTH
Fremantle
Kwinana
Rockingham
Rottnest I.
Mandurah
Pinjarra
Waroona
Harvey
Bunbury
Busselton
C. Naturaliste
Dunsborough
Margaret River
Augusta
C. Leeuwin
Pt. D'Entrecasteaux
Northcliffe
Pemberton
Manjimup
Bridgetown
Nannup
Collie
Donnybrook
Boyup Brook
Kojonup
Wagin
Katanning
Broomehill
Gnowangerup
Jerramungup
Borden
Ongerup
Tambellup
Cranbrook
Mt. Barker
Denmark
Albany
King George Sound
Bald Hd.
West Cape Howe
Stirling Ra. 1073
Bluff Knoll
Pingrup
Nyabing
Lake Grace
Dumbleyung
Kukerin
Kulin
Hyden
Lake King
Wickepin
Narrogin
Williams
Boddington
Pingelly
Brookton
Beverley
York
Northam
Toodyay
Goomalling
Dowerin
Wyalkatchem
Trayning
Kellerberrin
Merredin
Kununoppin
Bruce Rock
Quairading
Corrigin
Narembeen
Bencubbin
Koorda
Bonnie Rock
Wongan Hills
Dalwallinu
Kalannie
Moora
Watheroo
Coorow
Carnamah
Three Springs
Mingenew
Dongara
Greenough
Geraldton
Northampton
Kalbarri
Horrocks
Yuna
Mullewa
Morawa
Perenjori
Latham
Wubin
Payne's Find

Murchison R.
Gascoyne R.
Carnarvon
Shark Bay
Denham
Dirk Hartog I.
Hamelin Pool
C. Cuvier
Bernier I.
Dorre I.
Peron Pen.
Geographe Channel
Houtman Abrolhos

Hamelin Pool
Gascoyne R.
Kennedy Ra.
Mt. Augustus 1105
Mt. Vernon
Mt. Fraser 799
Mt. Gould
Peak Hill
Cue
Mount Magnet
Yalgoo
Sandstone
Nicholson Ra.
Dividing Ra.
Tallering Peak 439
L. Moore
Ninghan

Three Rivers
New Springs
Waldburg Ra.
Robinson Ra.
Collier Ra.
Mileura
Meekatharra
Wiluna
Nannine
Murgoo
Byro
Woodleigh
Mullewa
L. Austin
Mt. Magnet
L. Annean

C. Farquhar
C. Ronsard
C. St. Cricq
Inscription
Steep Pt.
Peron
Useless Loop

1:40 000 000

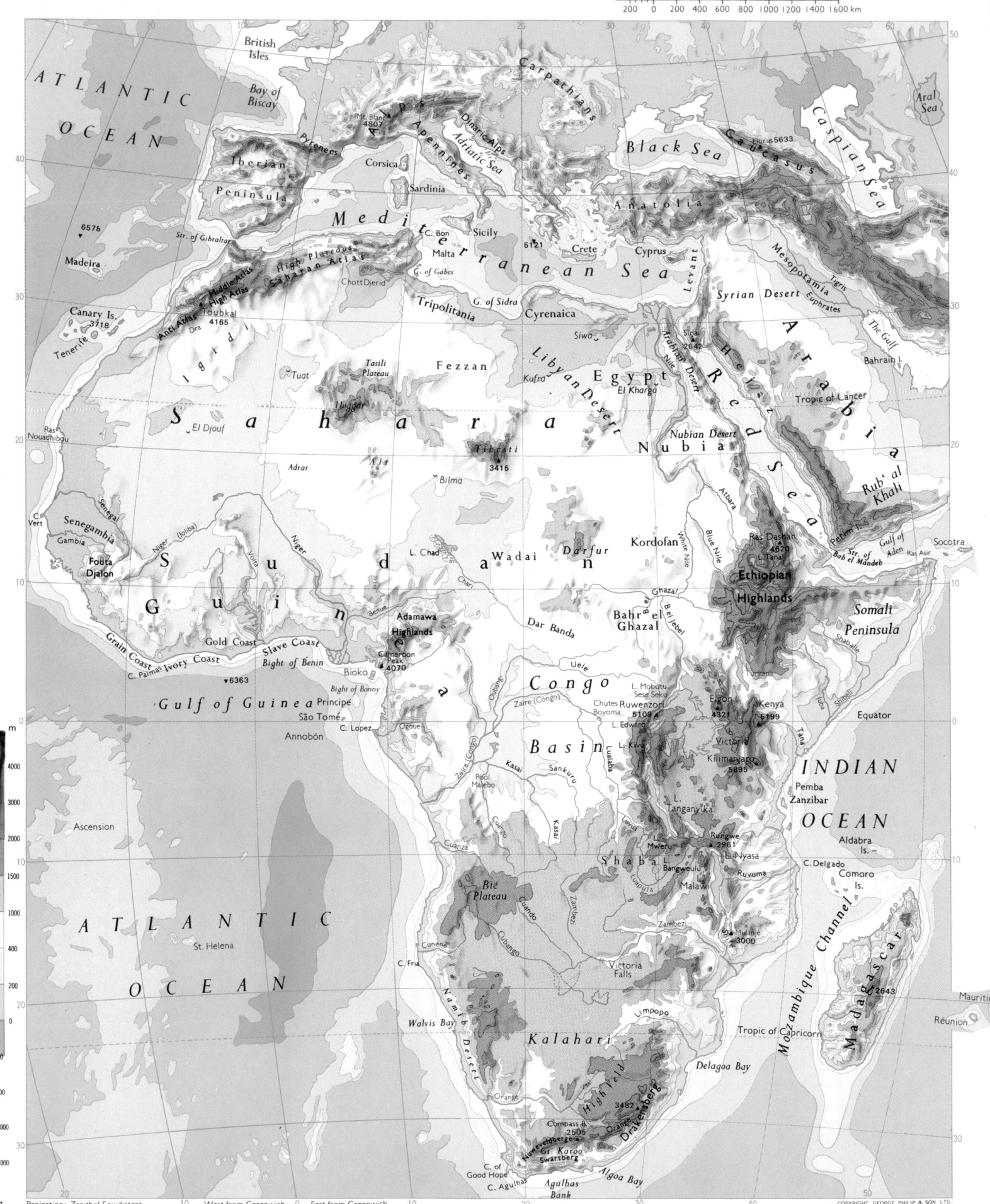

COPYRIGHT. GEORGE PHILIP & SON LTD

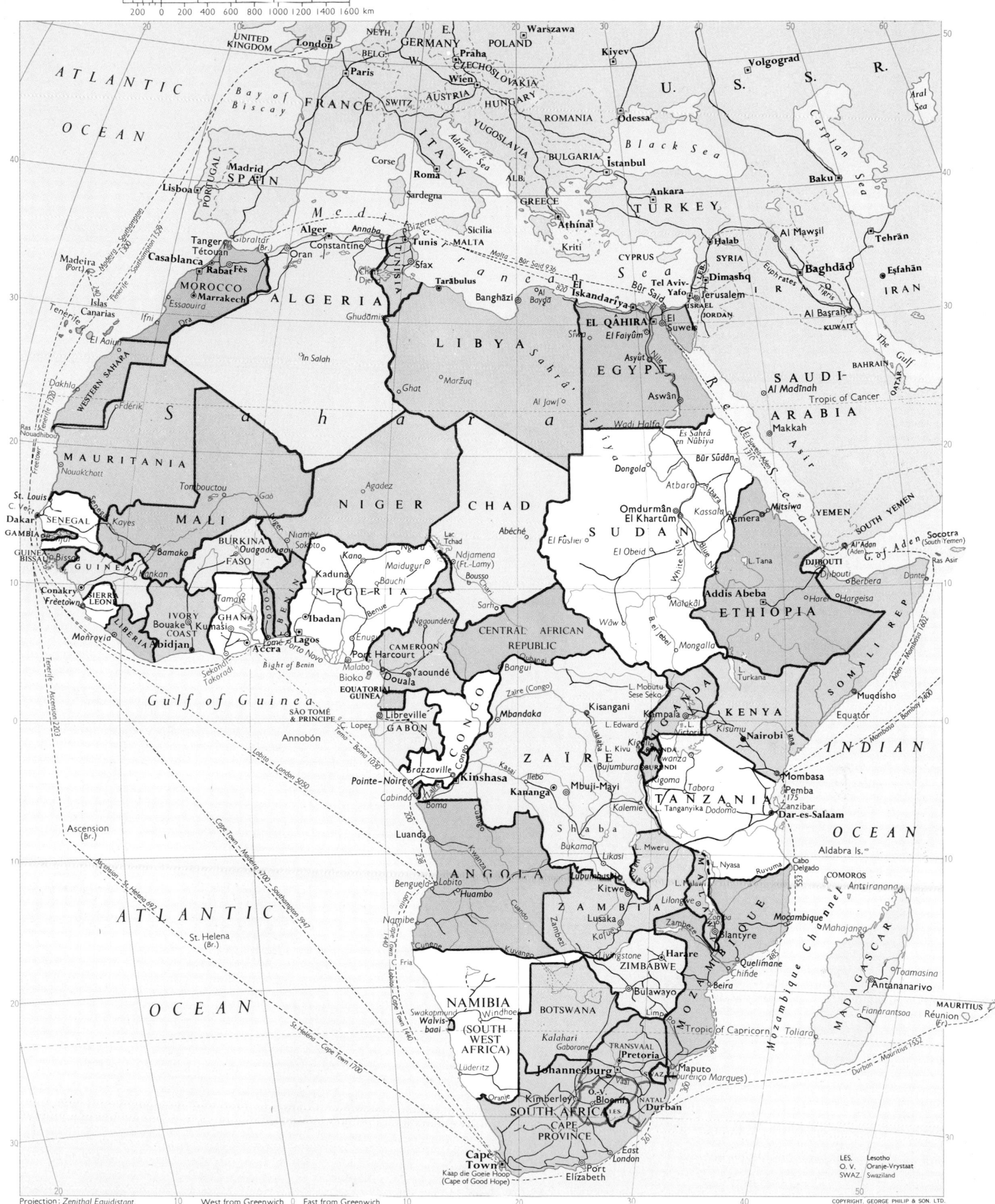

1:40 000 000

200   0   200   400   600   800   1000 miles
200   0   200 400 600 800 1000 1200 1400 1600 km

Projection: Zenithal Equidistant.   10   West from Greenwich   0   East from Greenwich   10   20   30   40

COPYRIGHT. GEORGE PHILIP & SON. LTD.

LES.   Lesotho
O.V.   Oranje-Vrystaat
SWAZ. Swaziland

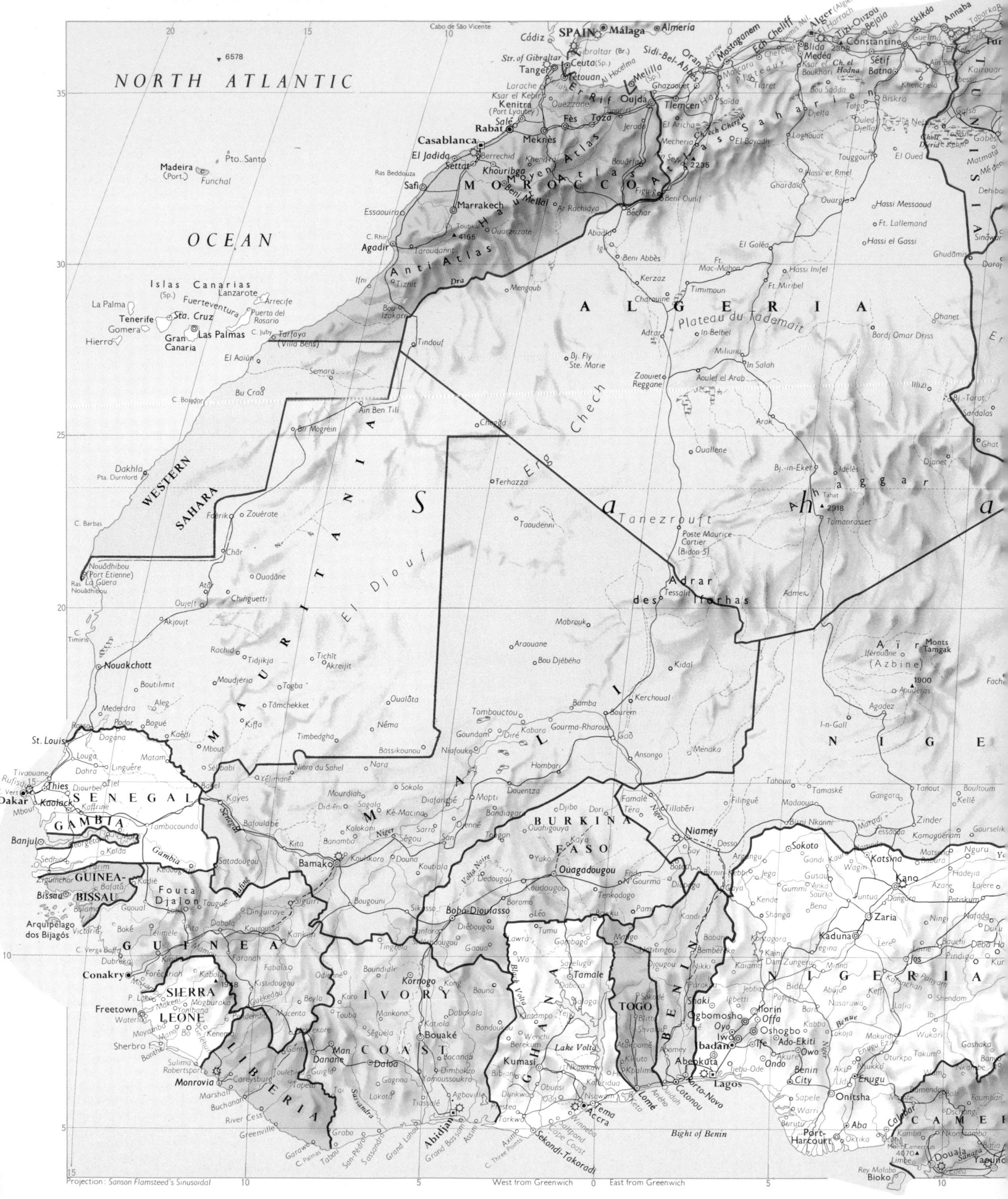

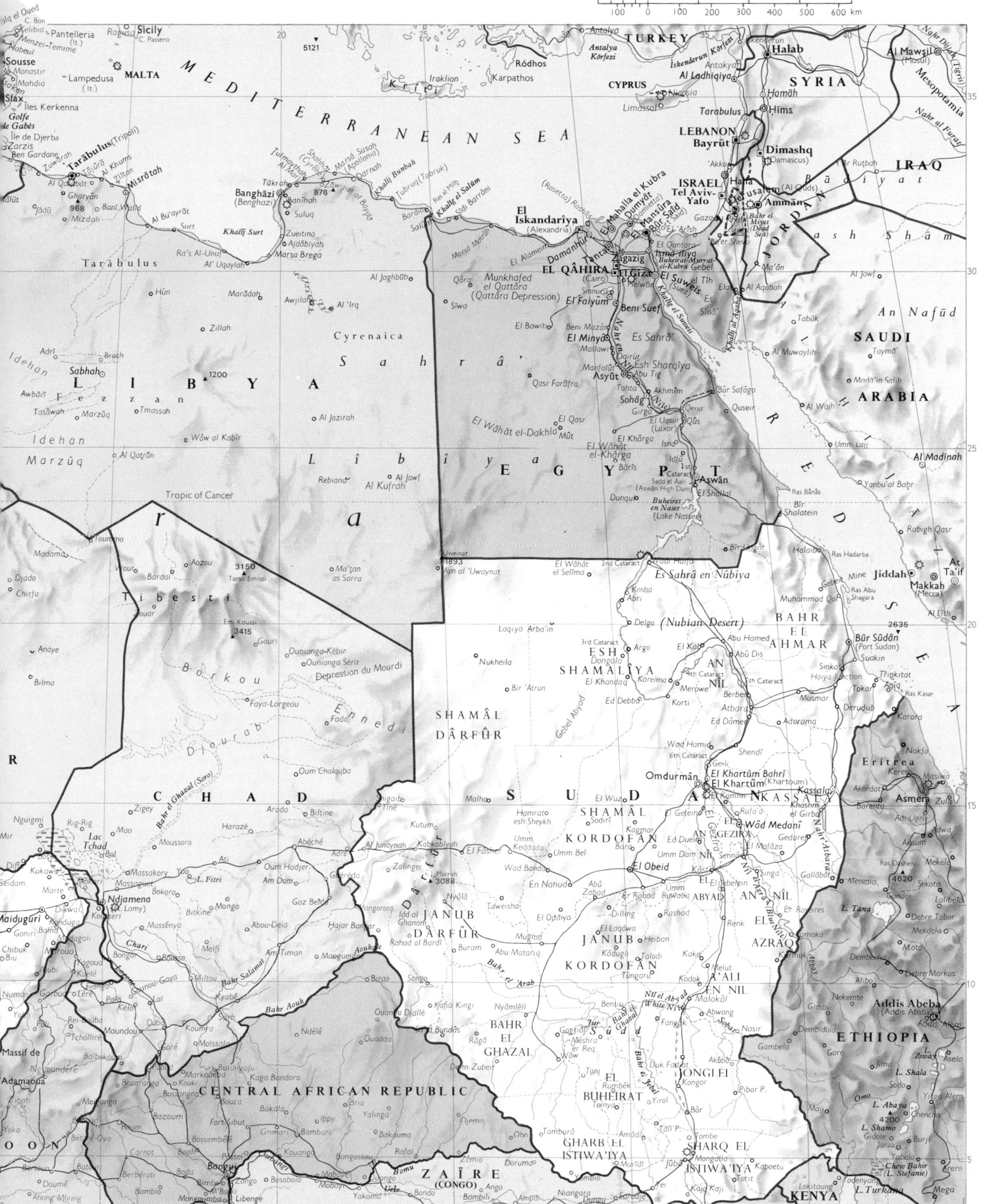

100   0   100   200   300   400 miles
100   0   100   200   300   400   500   600 km

MEDITERRANEAN SEA

TURKEY

CYPRUS

SYRIA

LEBANON
Bayrût

ISRAEL
Tel Aviv-
Yafo

IRAQ

JORDAN

SAUDI
ARABIA

LIBYA

Cyrenaica

Sahrâ'

Fezzan

Lîbîyegypt

Tropic of Cancer

Tibesti

Borkou

Ennedi

CHAD

SHAMÂL
DÂRFÛR

SUDAN

Eritrea

Asmera

CENTRAL AFRICAN REPUBLIC

ZAÏRE
(CONGO)

ETHIOPIA

Addis Abeba
(Addis Ababa)

KENYA

1 : 7 500 000

50 0 50 100 150 miles
50 0 50 100 150 200 250 km

SUDAN

ETHIOPIA

SOMALI REP.

KENYA

UGANDA

RWANDA

BURUNDI

TANZANIA

ZAMBIA

MALAWI

MOZAMBIQUE

LAKE VICTORIA 1134

LAKE TANGANYIKA

INDIAN OCEAN

Garamba National Park
Yakuluku National Park
Dungu
Faradje
Watsa
Aba
Kerripi
Kinyeti 3187
Opari
Nimule
Torit
Lotagipi Swamp
Lokichokio
Lokitaung
Todengang
Chew Bahir (L. Stefanie)
Mega
Moyale
Mandera
Dawa

Arua
Yura
Aru
Gulu
Kitgum
Loyoro
Kidepo Nat. Park 2749
1794
375
High Lava Plateau
Lake Turkana
Lake Rudolf
North Horr
Dukana
2007
El Wak
Buna
Beraha

Mahagi
Mahagi Port
Djugu
Bunia
Irumu
Masindi
Kachung
Moroto
Mt. Moroto 3084
Kulal 2293
South Horr
Nyiru 2752
Baragoi
Marsabit
Arba Jahan
Wajir
Habaswein
Lorian Swamp
Mado Gashi

Fort Portal
Margherita 5109
Kasese
Mubende
Mukono
Kampala
Entebbe
Jinja
Tororo
Mbale
Kitale
Eldoret
Kabarnet
Maralal
Archers Post
Laisamis
Isiolo
Garba Tula
Koreh Wells
Equator
Saka
Garissa

Masaka
Bukoba
Musoma
Serengeti National Park
Nairobi
Machakos
Kitui
Kathua
Bura
Kolbio
Galma-Galla

Kigali
Rwanda
Bujumbura (Usumbura)
Gitega
Biharamulo
Mwanza
Ngorongoro Crater 3188
Loolmalasin 3648
Kilimanjaro 5895
Moshi
Arusha
Tsavo National Park
Voi
Mombasa and Kilindini
Malindi

Kigoma-Ujiji
Tabora
Shinyanga
Kahama
Singida
Kondoa
Masai Steppe
Same
Lushoto
Tanga
Pemba I.
Chake Chake

Kalemie
Mpanda
Dodoma
Morogoro
Dar-es-Salaam
Zanzibar I.
Zanzibar
Bagamoyo

Sumbawanga
Mbeya
Tukuyu
Iringa
Njombe
Selous Game Reserve
Mafia I.
Utete
Kilwa Kivinje
Kilwa Kisiwani
Lindi
Mtwara
Mikindani

Kasama
Mpika
Livingstonia
Nkhata Bay
Songea
Tunduru
Masasi
C. Delgado

Projection: Modified Polyconic

East from Greenwich

COPYRIGHT. GEORGE PHILIP & SON. LTD.

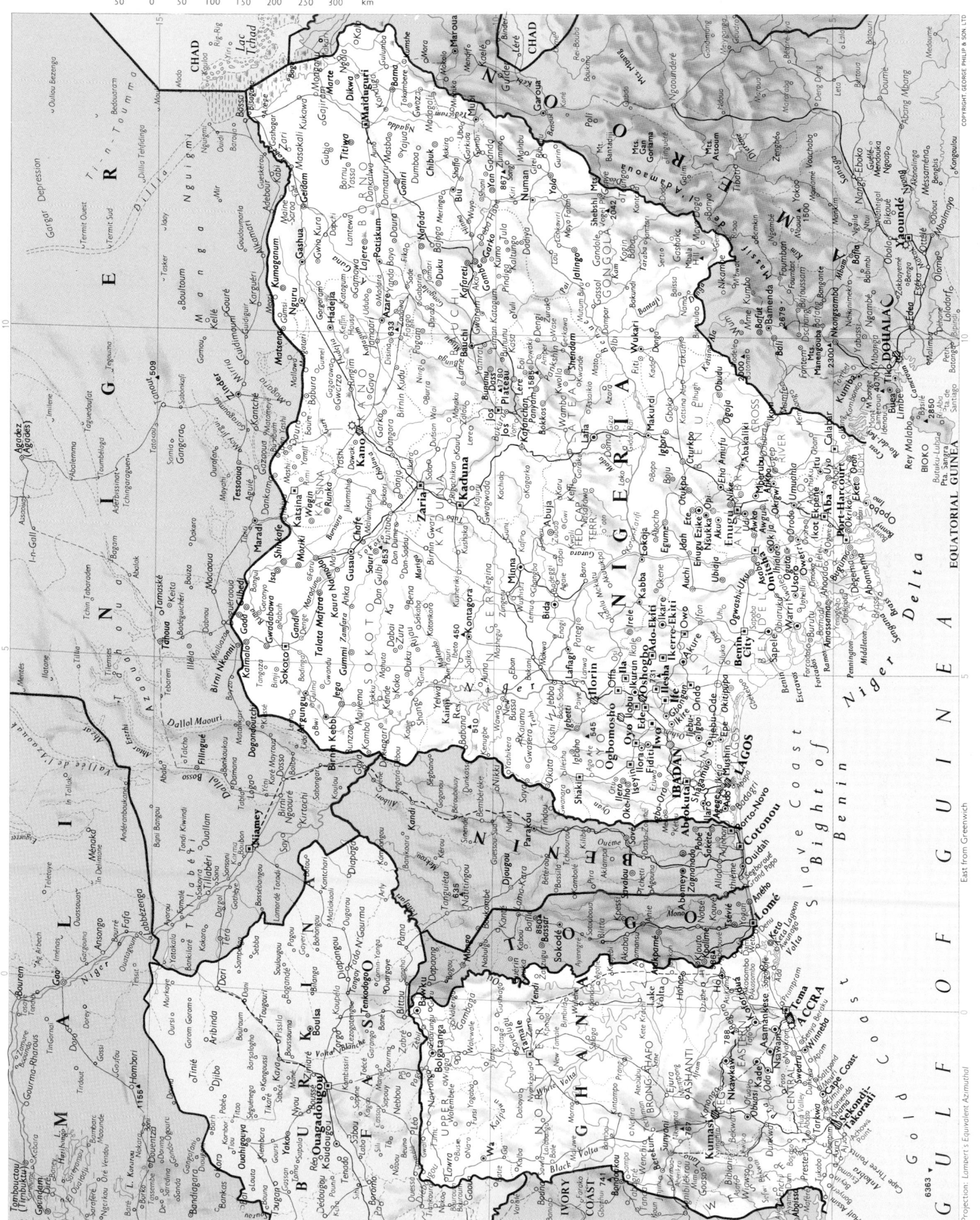

1:8 000 000

Projection: Lambert's Equivalent Azimuthal

East from Greenwich

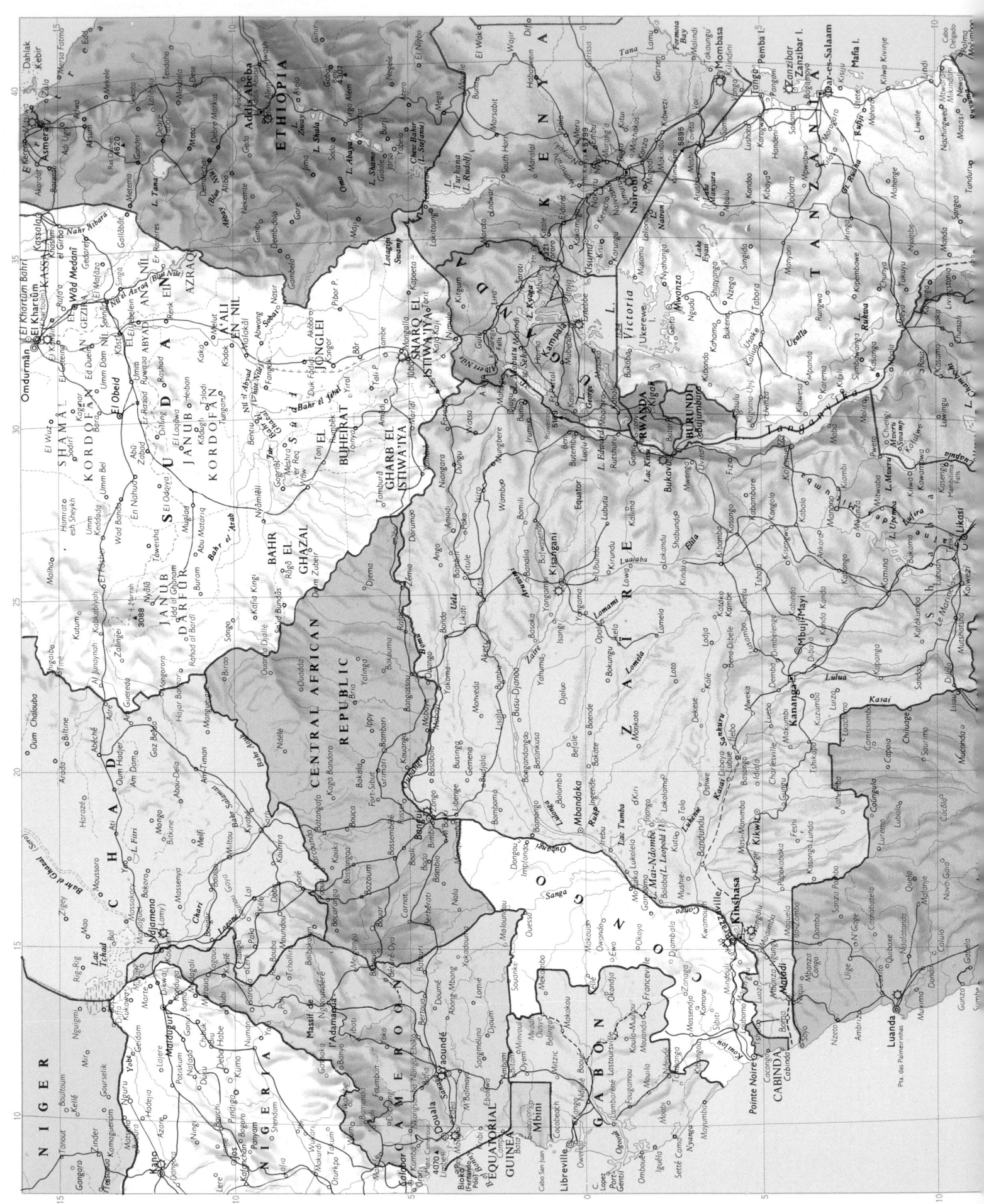

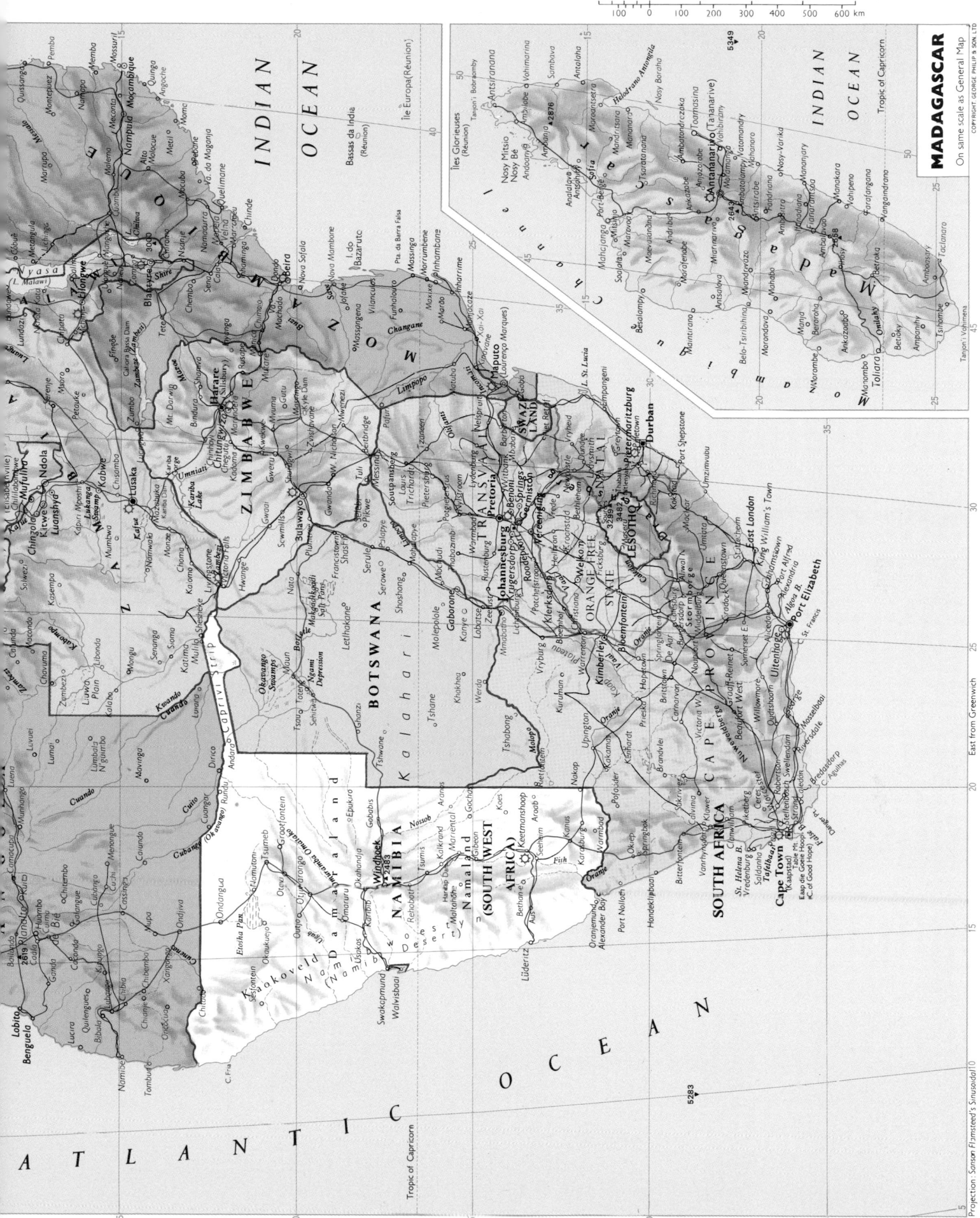

1:15 000 000

100   100   200   300   400 miles
100   0   100   200   300   400   500   600 km

MADAGASCAR
On same scale as General Map

COPYRIGHT GEORGE PHILIP & SON LTD

INDIAN

OCEAN

INDIAN   OCEAN

Tropic of Capricorn

ATLANTIC   OCEAN

Tropic of Capricorn

East from Greenwich

Projection Sanson Flamsteed's Sinusoidal

Projection: Lambert's Equivalent Azimuthal

1:8 000 000

50   0   50   100   150   200 miles
50   0   100   200   300 km

MALAWI

ZAMBEZIA

MOZAMBIQUE

M O Z A M B I Q U E   C H A N N E L

ZIMBABWE

HARARE
Chitungwiza

Bulawayo

Gwe ru

MASHONALAND
CENTRAL

MASHONALAND
WEST

MATABELELAND
SOUTH

Masvingo

MASVINGO

Iles Glorieuses (Réunion)

Antsiranana
Ambohitra
1475

Nosy Be

A N T S I R
A N A N A

2876

Mahajanga

Besalampy

M A D A G A S C A R

Maintirano

Morondava
Mahabo

ANTANANARIVO
ANTANANARIVO
(Tananarive)
2643

Antsirabe

Miandrivazo

Antsalova

Belo-
Tsiribihina

M A H A J A N G A

Fianarantsoa
FIANARANTSOA

2658

Manakara

Vohipeno

Farafangana

Manombo

Toliara

Tropic of Capricorn

1956

Taolanaro

V E N D A

Kruger
National
Park

T R A N S V A A L

PRETORIA
Temba

JOHANNESBURG
Benoni
Springs

Vereeniging

SWAZILAND

Maputo
(Lourenço Marques)

MAPUTO

N A T A L

LESOTHO
3096

DURBAN
KwaMashu
Umlazi
Mpumalanga

Pietermaritzburg

3482

Richards Bay

Lake St. Lucia

Empangeni

Port Shepstone

Margate

East London

I N D I A N

O C E A N

30   East from Greenwich   45

MADAGASCAR

On same scale as General Map

COPYRIGHT. GEORGE PHILIP & SON. LTD.

1 : 35 000 000

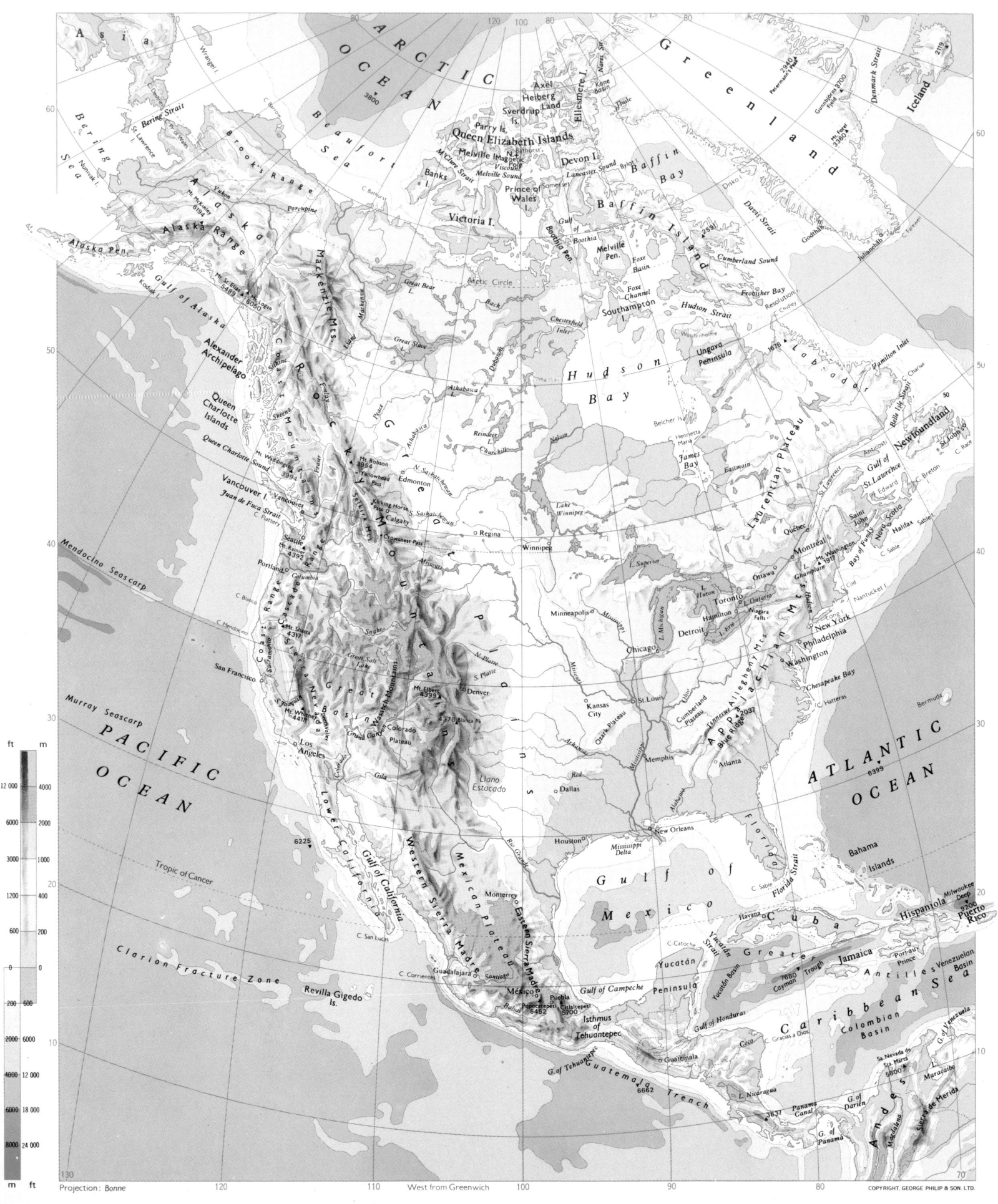

1 : 35 000 000

Scale bar: 200 0 200 400 600 800 miles / 400 0 400 800 1200 km

Projection: Bonne

West from Greenwich

COPYRIGHT. GEORGE. PHILIP & SON. LTD.

State capital ⊙

C.	CONNECTICUT	N.H.	NEW HAMPSHIRE
D.	DELAWARE	N.J.	NEW JERSEY
D.C.	DISTRICT OF COLUMBIA	R.I.	RHODE ISLAND
M.	MARYLAND	VER.	VERMONT
MASS	MASSACHUSETTS	SPM	ST. PIERRE ET MIQUELON

Projection: Bonne

ALASKA
1 : 30 000 000

100 0   100 200 300 miles
100 0   200   400 km

1:15 000 000

100 50 0 100 200 300 400 miles
100 0 100 200 300 400 500 600 km

G R E E N L A N D

A T L A N T I C

O C E A N

Baffin Bay

Devon Island
Lancaster Sound

Bylot I.
Pond Inlet
Brodeur
Peninsula
Milne Inlet

Davis Strait

Angmagssalik

Disko
Disko B.
Holsteinsborg
Sukkertoppen
Godthåb
Frederikshåb
Nanortalik
Kap Farvel

Cumberland Peninsula
C. Dyer
Cape Dyer
C. Mercy

Foxe Basin
Prince Charles I.
Nettilling L.
Cumberland Sd.
Frobisher Bay
Resolution I.

Gulf of Boothia

Committee B.
Melville Peninsula
Repulse B.
Rae Isthmus
Foxe Channel
Southampton I.
Coral Harbour
Bell Pen.
Coats I.
Mansel I.

Hudson Strait
Digges Is.
C. Chidley
Akpatok I.
Ungava Bay

H u d s o n   B a y

Ottawa Is.
Sleeper Is.
King George Is.
Belcher Is.

U n g a v a   P e n i n s u l a
Portland Promontory
Inoucdjouac (Port Harrison)
Payne L.
Kuujjuaq
Kaniapiskau

N E W F O U N D L A N D
Hopedale
Nain
C. Harrison
Indian Harbour
Rigolet
Cartwright
Battle Hbr.
Belle Isle

COAST OF LABRADOR
Schefferville
Churchill Falls
Churchill
Ashuanipi

Q U E B E C
L. Minto
L. Bienville
Great Whale River
La Grande
Fort George
Eastmain
Fort Rupert
Mistassini
Chibougamau

James Bay
Akimiski I.
Attawapiskat
Fort Albany
Charlton

O N T A R I O
Big Trout L.
Winisk
Severn
Ft. Severn
Albany
Moosonee
Armstrong
Nakina
Geraldton
L. Nipigon
Thunder Bay
Hearst
Cochrane
Timmins
Kirkland Lake
Rouyn
Noranda

L a k e   S u p e r i o r
Sault Ste. Marie
Sudbury
North Bay

St. Lawrence
Gulf of St. Lawrence
Sept-Îles
Port-Cartier
Baie-Comeau
I. d'Anticosti
Gaspé
Pén. de Gaspé

P.R. EDWARD I.
Charlottetown
Summerside
NEW BRUNSWICK
Moncton
Fredericton
Saint John
NOVA SCOTIA
Halifax
Dartmouth
Truro
Sydney
Glace Bay
Yarmouth
Liverpool
Shelburne
Sable I.

NEWFOUNDLAND
St. John's
Bonavista
Gander
Grand Falls
Corner Brook
Port aux Basques
C. Race

ST-PIERRE et MIQUELON (Fr.)
Cabot Str.
Cape Breton I.

Quebec
Lévis
Trois-Rivières
Shawinigan
Chicoutimi
Jonquière
Roberval
La Tuque
MONTRÉAL
Sherbrooke
Ottawa
Hull
Cornwall
L. Champlain

VERMONT
NEW HAMPSHIRE
Montpelier
Concord
Manchester
MAINE
Bangor
Portland
Augusta

TORONTO
Hamilton
London
Windsor
Niagara Falls
Kitchener
Guelph
Brantford
St. Catharines
Georgian Bay
Lake Huron
Owen Sound
Orillia
Peterboro
Belleville
Kingston
Oshawa

MASS.
Boston
Worcester
Springfield
Providence
New Haven
Bridgeport
CONN.

NEW YORK
Buffalo
Rochester
Syracuse
Utica
Albany
Binghamton
Elmira
PENNSYLVANIA

DETROIT
Toledo
Cleveland
Akron
Youngstown
OHIO

CHICAGO
Milwaukee
Racine
Kenosha
Madison
Rockford
Evanston
Gary
ILLINOIS
INDIANA
South Bend

WISCONSIN
Appleton
Green Bay
Sheboygan
Manitowoc

NEW JERSEY
NEW YORK
Newark
Jersey City
Trenton
Allentown
Reading

West from Greenwich

COPYRIGHT GEORGE PHILIP & SON, LTD.

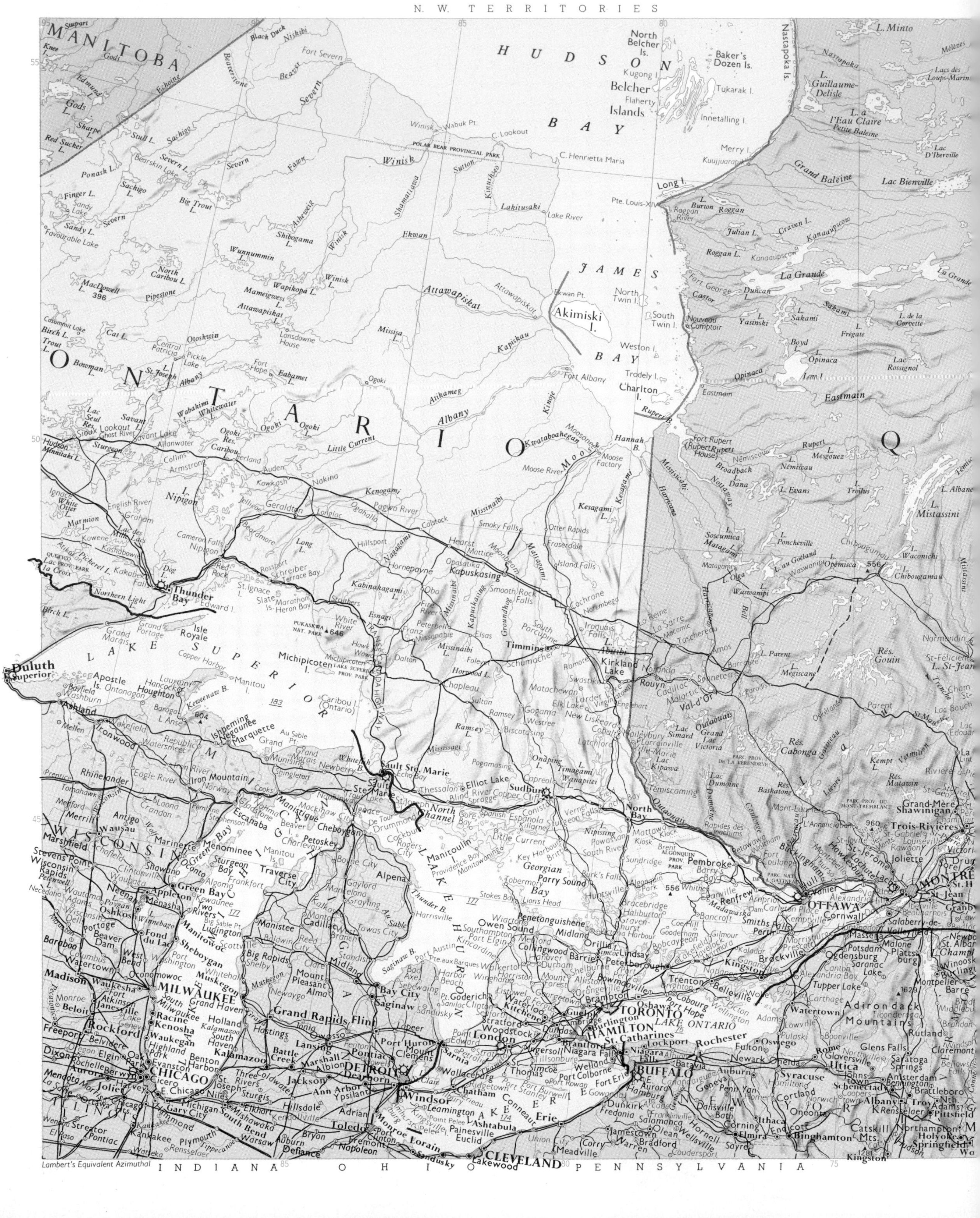
N. W. TERRITORIES
MANITOBA
ONTARIO
Q
HUDSON BAY
JAMES BAY
Belcher Islands
North Belcher Is.
Baker's Dozen Is.
Akimiski I.
Charlton I.
LAKE SUPERIOR
LAKE MICHIGAN
LAKE HURON
LAKE ERIE
LAKE ONTARIO
Georgian Bay
North Channel
Manitoulin I.
Isle Royale
WISCONSIN
ILLINOIS
NEW YORK
INDIANA
OHIO
PENNSYLVANIA
Thunder Bay
Sault Ste. Marie
Sudbury
North Bay
Timmins
Kapuskasing
Cochrane
Moosonee
Moose Factory
Fort Albany
Kirkland Lake
Rouyn
Val-d'Or
Chibougamau
Mistassini
Lac Bienville
La Grande
Eastmain
OTTAWA
MONTRÉAL
Trois-Rivières
Shawinigan
TORONTO
HAMILTON
St. Catharines
Niagara Falls
BUFFALO
Rochester
Syracuse
Kingston
London
Windsor
DETROIT
Flint
Saginaw
Bay City
Lansing
Grand Rapids
Kalamazoo
Toledo
CLEVELAND
Erie
CHICAGO
MILWAUKEE
Madison
Rockford
Green Bay
Duluth
Superior
Ashland
Marquette
Owen Sound
Barrie
Peterborough
Belleville
Pembroke
Algonquin Prov. Park
Adirondack Mountains
Lambert's Equivalent Azimuthal

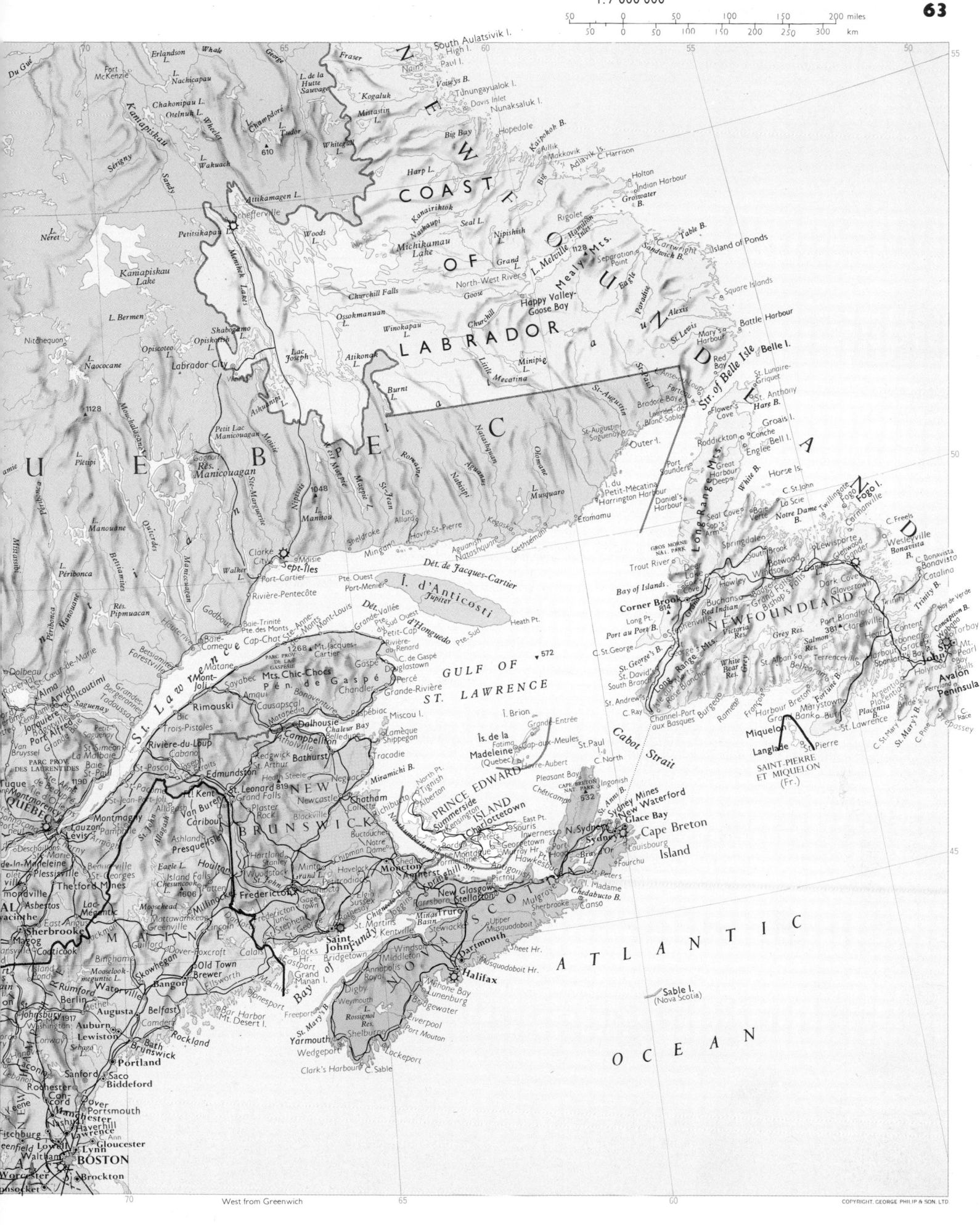

1:7 000 000

50   50   100   150   200 miles
50 50 100 150 200 250 300 km

West from Greenwich

COPYRIGHT. GEORGE PHILIP & SON. LTD

Projection: Lambert's Equivalent Azimuthal   West from Greenwich

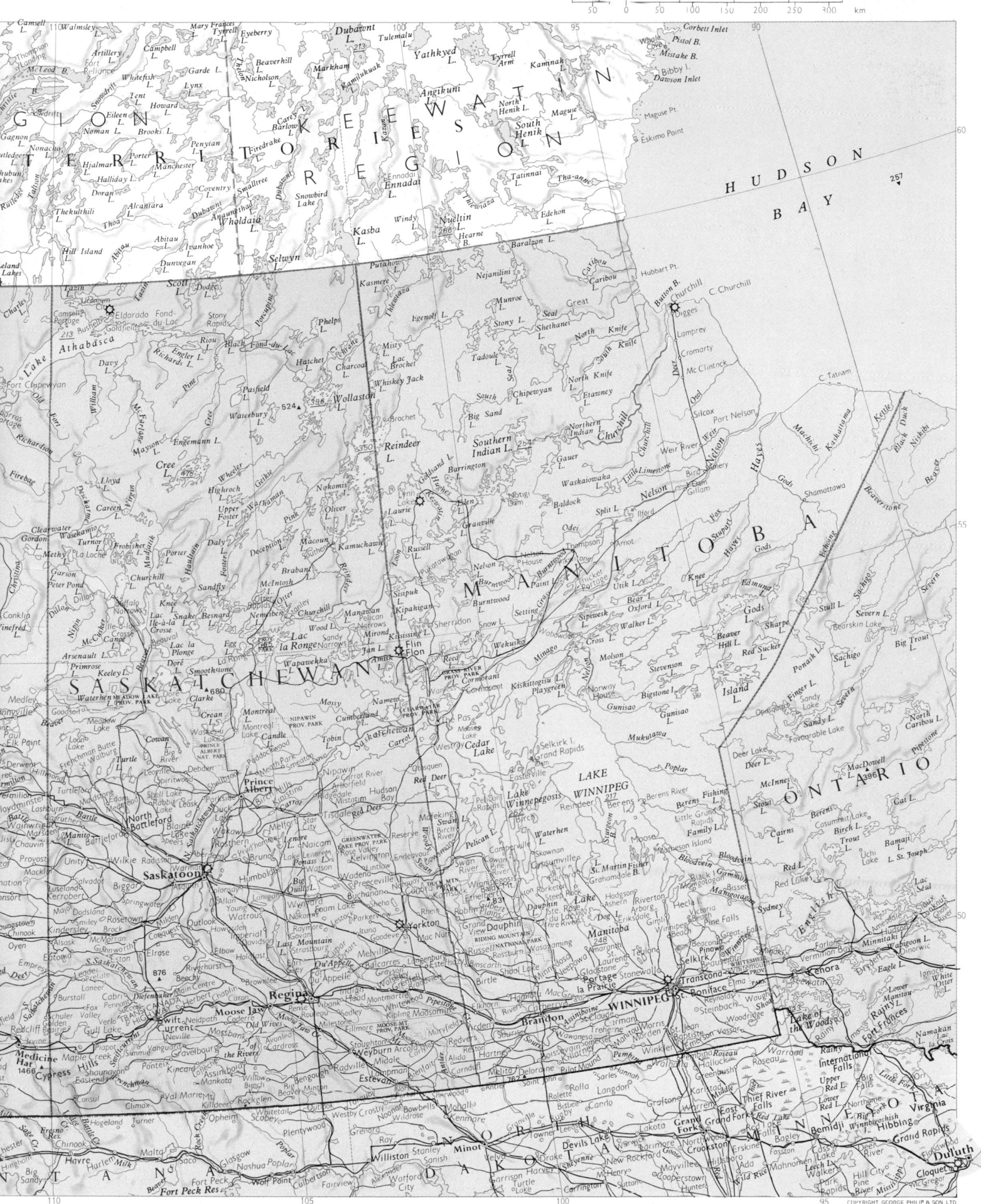

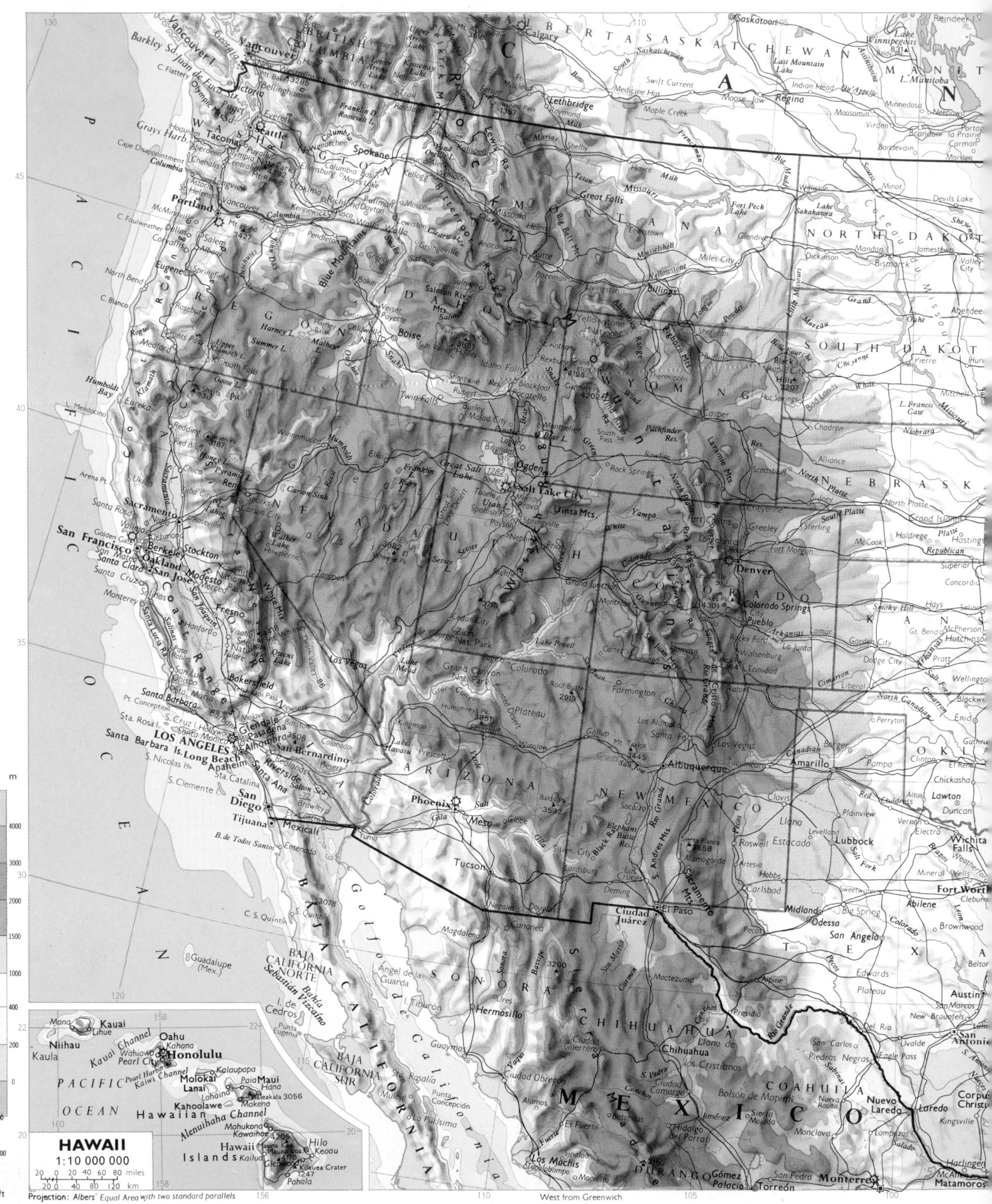

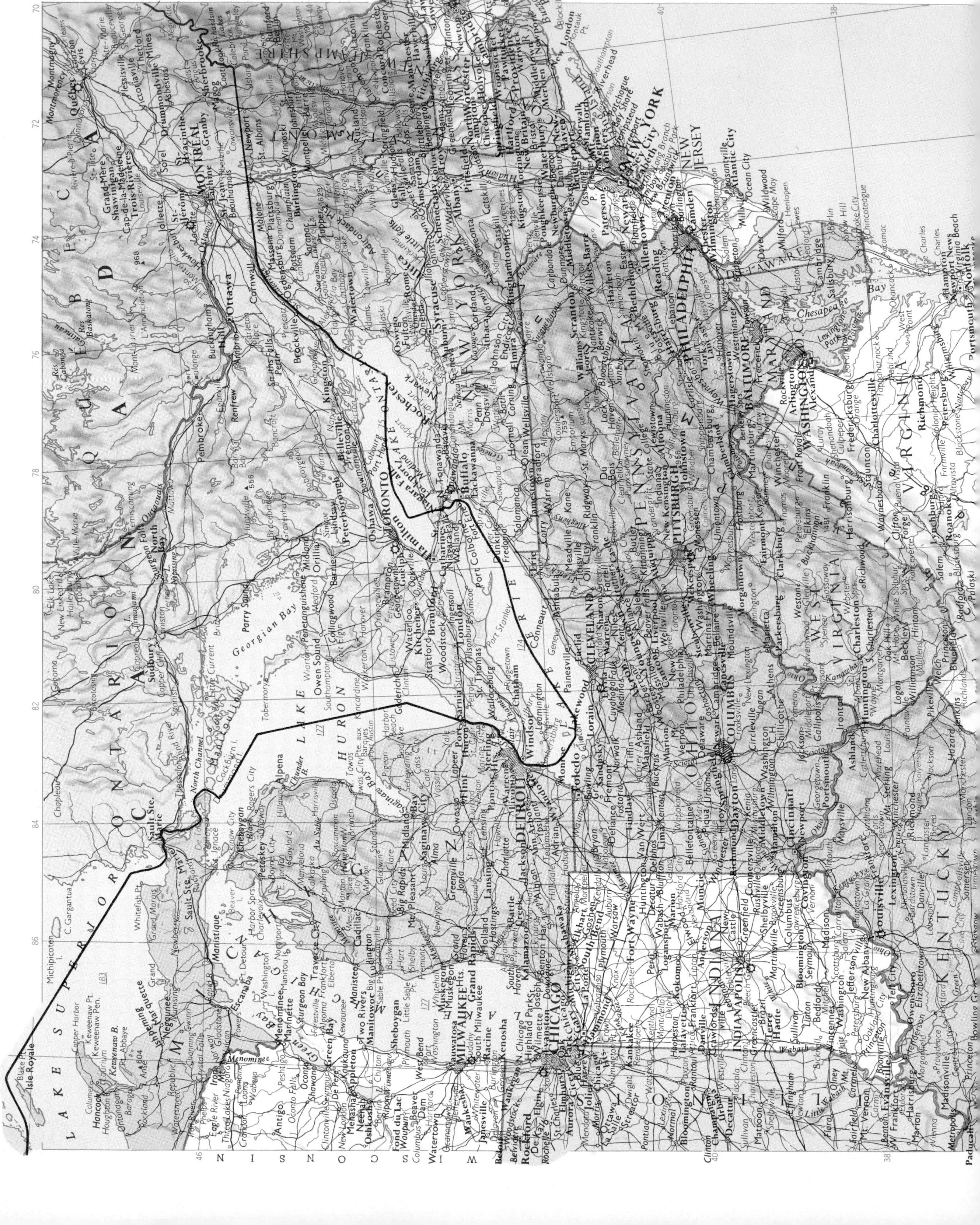
LAKE SUPERIOR
LAKE HURON
Georgian Bay
LAKE ONTARIO
LAKE ERIE
LAKE MICHIGAN
ONTARIO
QUEBEC
MICHIGAN
WISCONSIN
ILLINOIS
INDIANA
OHIO
KENTUCKY
WEST VIRGINIA
VIRGINIA
PENNSYLVANIA
NEW YORK
NEW JERSEY
MARYLAND
DELAWARE
MASS.
NEW HAMPSHIRE
VERMONT
CHICAGO
MILWAUKEE
DETROIT
TORONTO
BUFFALO
CLEVELAND
PITTSBURGH
COLUMBUS
INDIANAPOLIS
PHILADELPHIA
BALTIMORE
WASHINGTON
NEW YORK
BOSTON
MONTREAL
OTTAWA
Québec

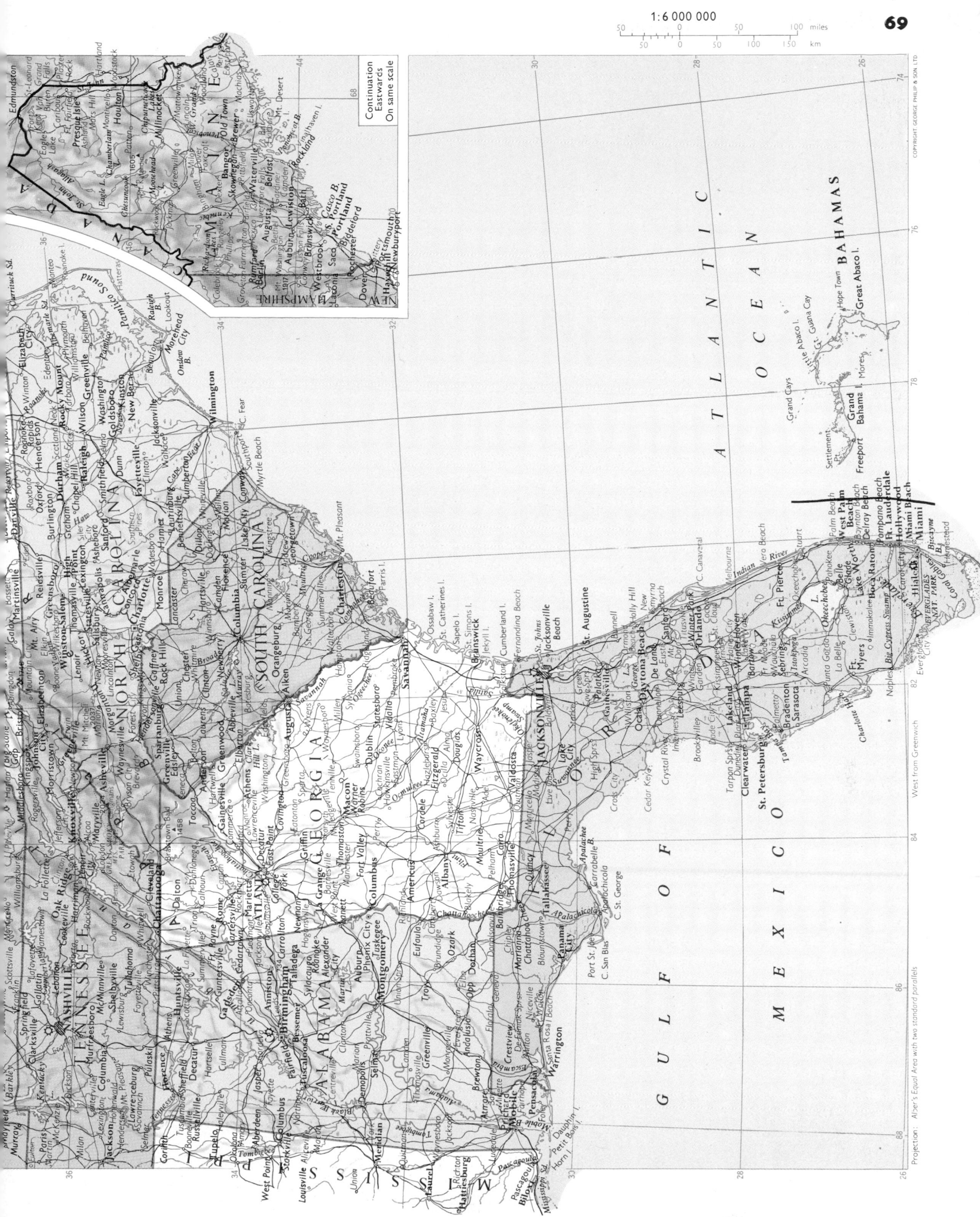

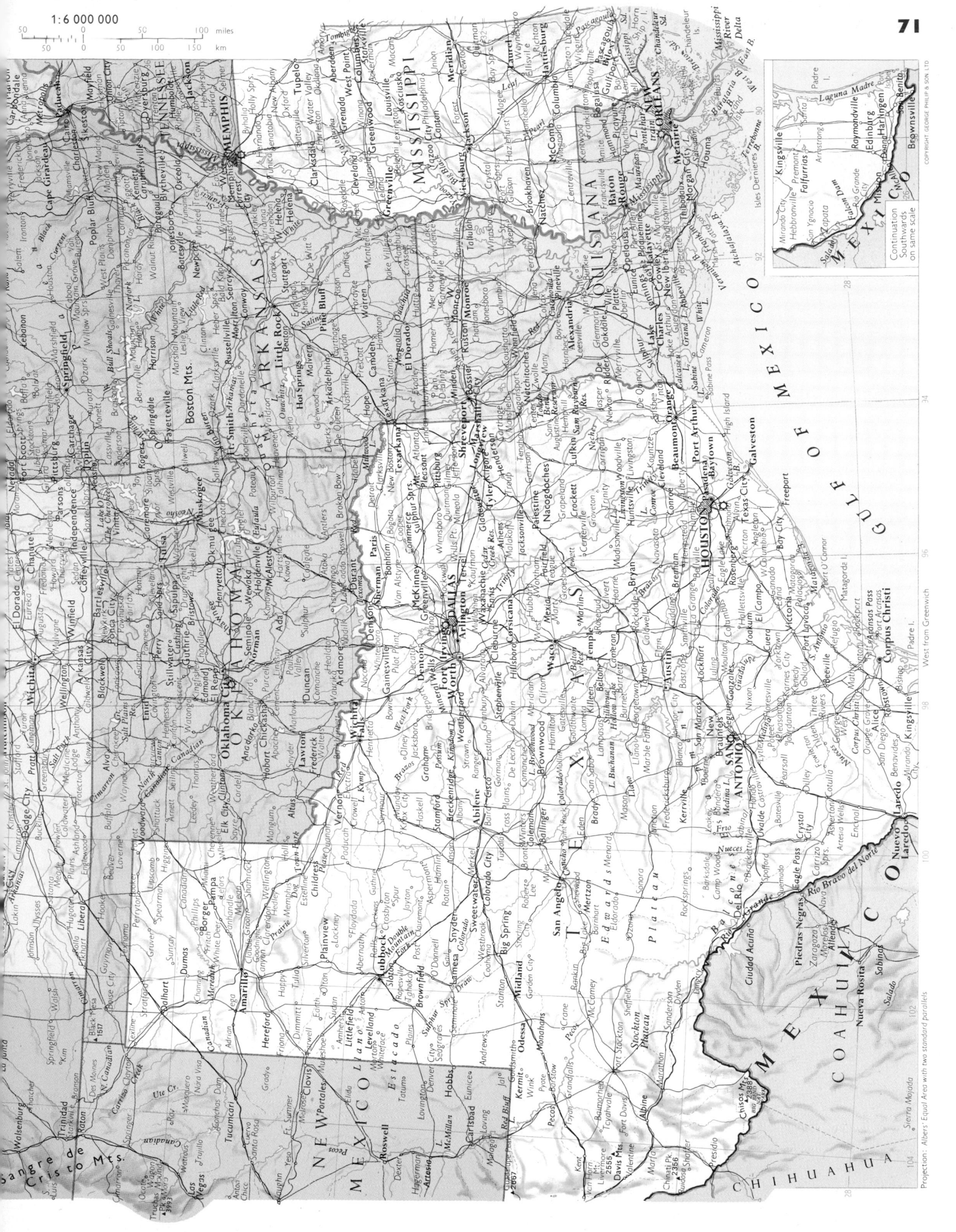

1:6 000 000

50　　　0　　　50　　　100 miles
50　0　50　100　150 km

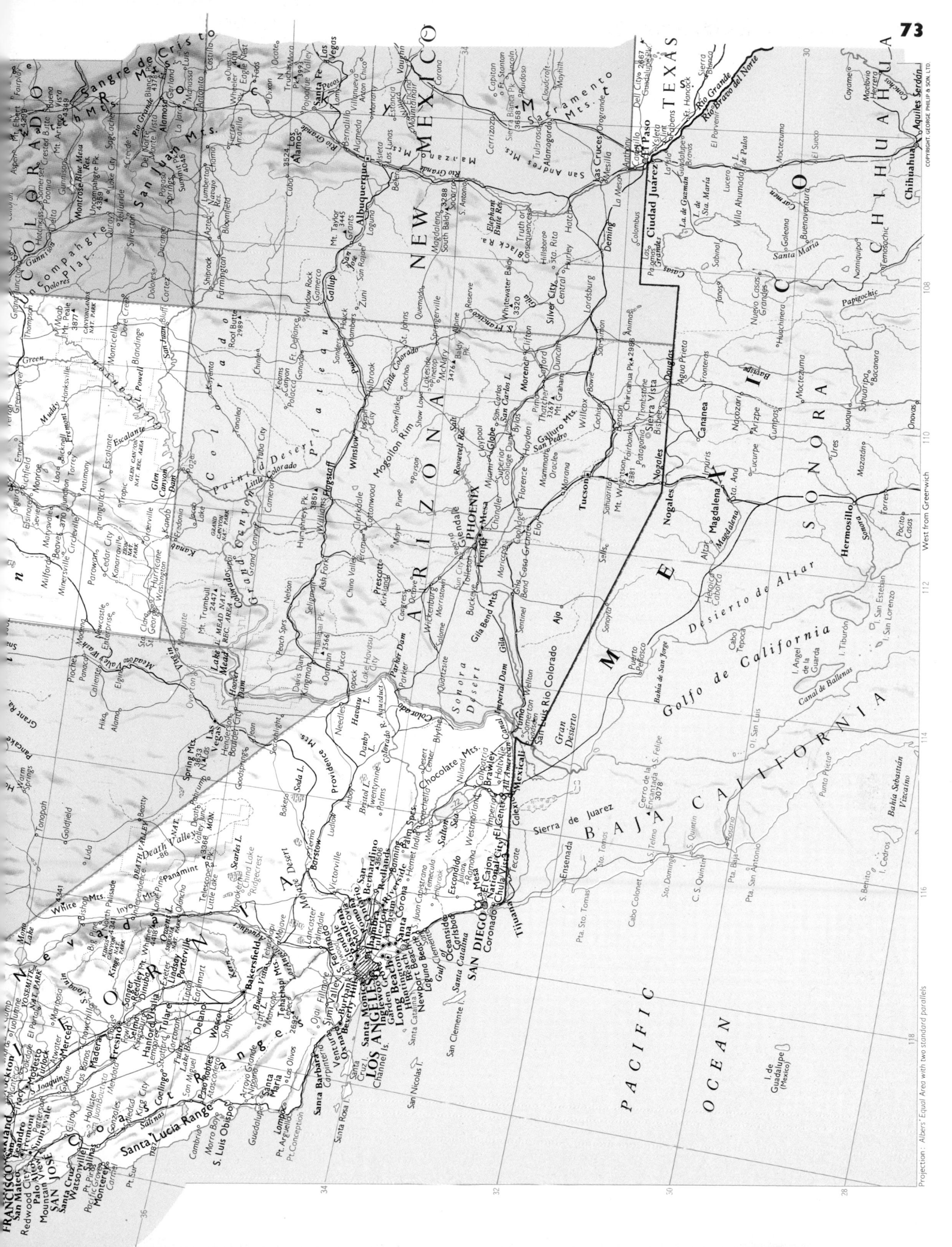

Projection: Albers' Equal Area with two standard parallels

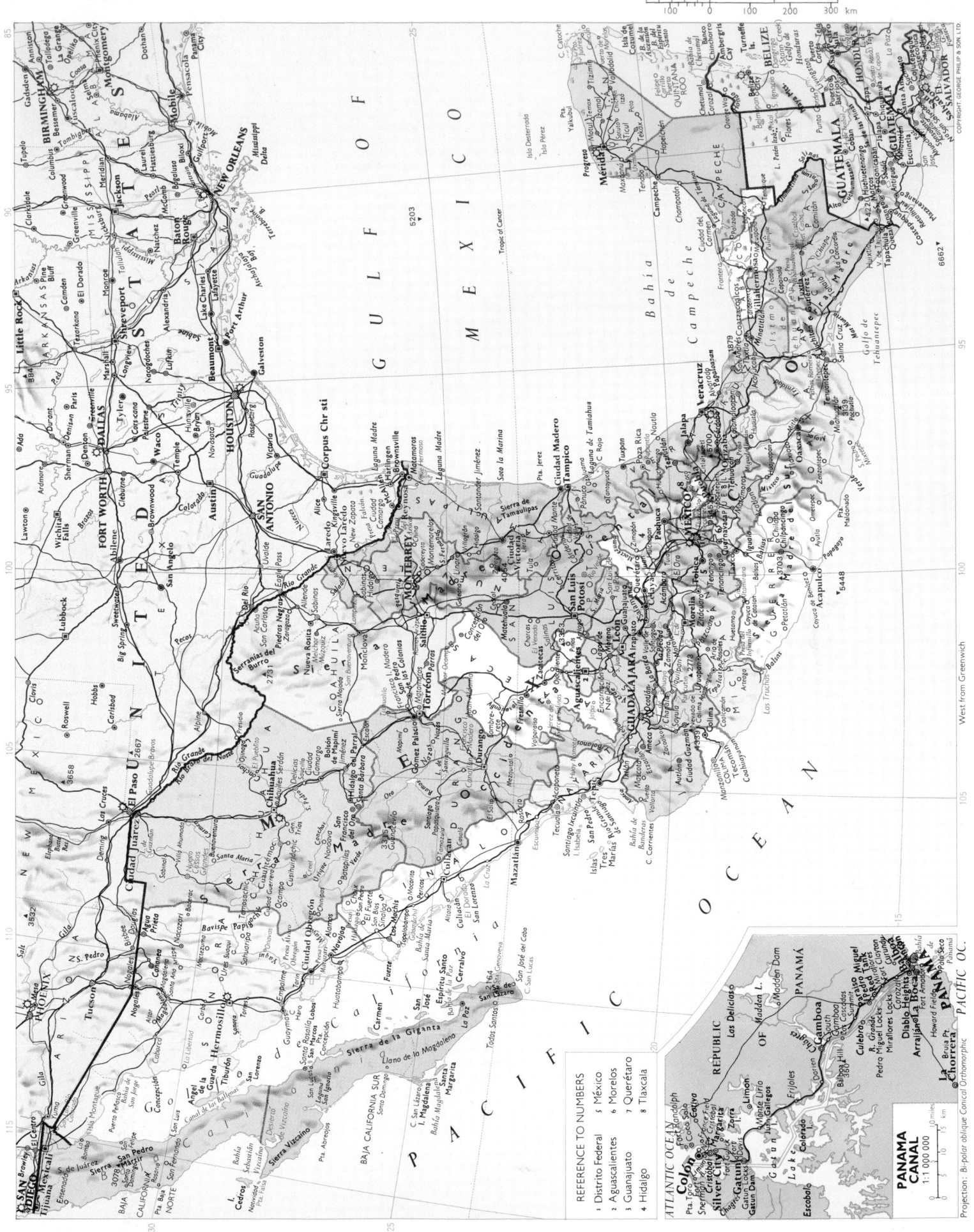

1:12 000 000

REFERENCE TO NUMBERS

1 Distrito Federal 5 México
2 Aguascalientes 6 Morelos
3 Guanajuato 7 Querétaro
4 Hidalgo 8 Tlaxcala

PANAMA CANAL
1:1 000 000

Projection: Bi-polar oblique Conical Orthomorphic

COPYRIGHT. GEORGE PHILIP & SON, LTD.

1:12 000 000

100   0   100   200 miles
100   0   100   200   300 km

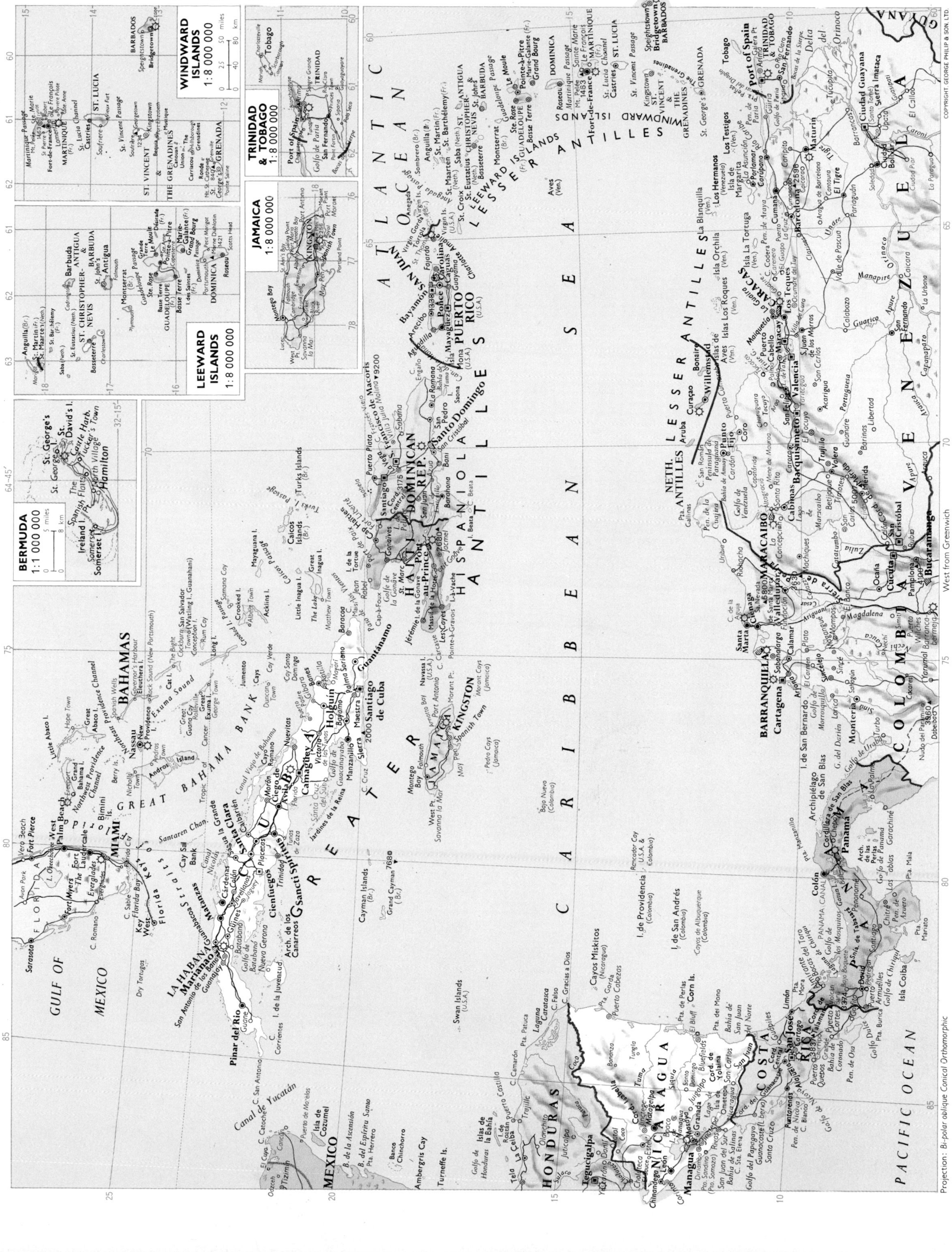

WINDWARD ISLANDS 1:8 000 000

TRINIDAD & TOBAGO 1:8 000 000

JAMAICA 1:8 000 000

LEEWARD ISLANDS 1:8 000 000

BERMUDA 1:1 000 000

COPYRIGHT GEORGE PHILIP & SON LTD.

ATLANTIC OCEAN

CARIBBEAN SEA

GULF OF MEXICO

PACIFIC OCEAN

GREATER ANTILLES

LESSER ANTILLES

WINDWARD ISLANDS

BAHAMAS

CUBA

JAMAICA

HISPANIOLA

HAITI

DOMINICAN REP.

PUERTO RICO

MEXICO

HONDURAS

NICARAGUA

COSTA RICA

PANAMA

COLOMBIA

VENEZUELA

GUIANA

West from Greenwich

Projection: Bi-polar oblique Conical Orthomorphic

1:30 000 000

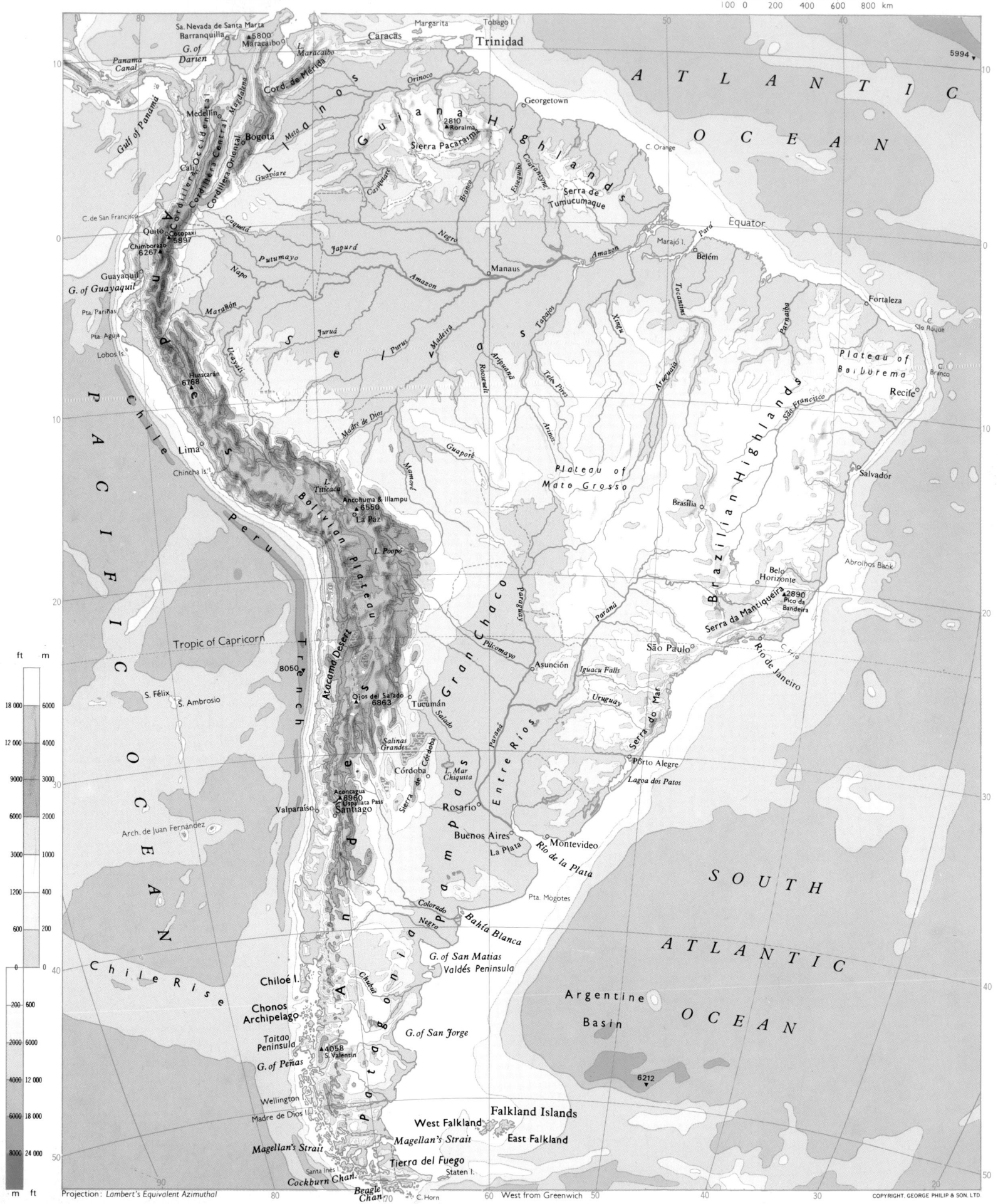

ATLANTIC OCEAN

Panama Canal
Sa. Nevada de Santa Marta
Barranquilla
5800
Maracaibo
G. of Darien
Caracas
Margarita
Tobago I.
Trinidad
5994

Medellín
Cordillera Occidental
Cordillera Central
Cordillera Oriental
Magdalena
Bogotá
Cali
Llanos
Orinoco
Meta
Guaviare
Guiana Highlands
Sierra Pacaraima
2810 Roraima
Georgetown
C. Orange
Cuyuni
Essequibo
Branco
Corentyne
Serra de Tumucumaque

C. de San Francisco
Quito
Cotopaxi 5897
Chimborazo 6267
Guayaquil
G. of Guayaquil
Pta. Pariñas
Pta. Aguja
Lobos Is.
Caquetá
Putumayo
Napo
Marañón
Japurá
Juruá
Purus
Negro
Amazon
Manaus
Amazon
Equator
Marajó I.
Pará
Belém
Fortaleza
C. São Roque

Huascarán 6768
Ucayali
Madeira
Tapajós
Xingu
Tocantins
Parnaíba
Plateau of Borborema
Recife

Lima
Chincha Is.
Chile
Peru
Trench
Madre de Dios
Guaporé
Mamoré
Roosevelt
Aripuanã
Teles Pires
Araguaia
Juruena
Arinos
São Francisco
Plateau of Mato Grosso
Brazilian Highlands
Salvador

L. Titicaca
Bolivian Plateau
Ancohuma & Illampu 6550
La Paz
L. Poopó
Gran Chaco
Paraguay
Brasília
Belo Horizonte
Abrolhos Bank
2890 Pico da Bandeira
Serra da Mantiqueira

Tropic of Capricorn
8050
Ojos del Salado 6863
Tucumán
Salado
Pilcomayo
Paraná
Asunción
São Paulo
Rio de Janeiro
C. Frio
Serra do Mar

S. Félix
S. Ambrosio
Atacama Desert
Salinas Grandes
Córdoba
Sierra de Córdoba
L. Mar Chiquita
Rosario
Uruguay
Iguaçu Falls
Paraná
Entre Ríos
Pôrto Alegre
Lagoa dos Patos

Arch. de Juan Fernández
Aconcagua 6960
Uspallata Pass
Valparaíso
Santiago
Pampas
Buenos Aires
La Plata
Montevideo
Río de la Plata
Pta. Mogotes

Chile Rise
Chiloé I.
Chonos Archipelago
Taitao Peninsula
4058 S. Valentin
G. of Peñas
Wellington
Madre de Dios I.
Colorado
Negro
Bahía Blanca
G. of San Matias
Valdés Peninsula
Chubut
Patagonia
G. of San Jorge

SOUTH
ATLANTIC
OCEAN

Argentine Basin
6212

PACIFIC OCEAN

Santa Inés
Cockburn Chan.
Magellan's Strait
Tierra del Fuego
Staten I.
West Falkland
Magellan's Strait
Falkland Islands
East Falkland

Beagle Chan.
C. Horn

West from Greenwich

ft m
18 000 6000
12 000 4000
9000 3000
6000 2000
3000 1000
1200 400
600 200
0 0
600 200
6000 2000
12 000 4000
18 000 6000
24 000 8000
m ft

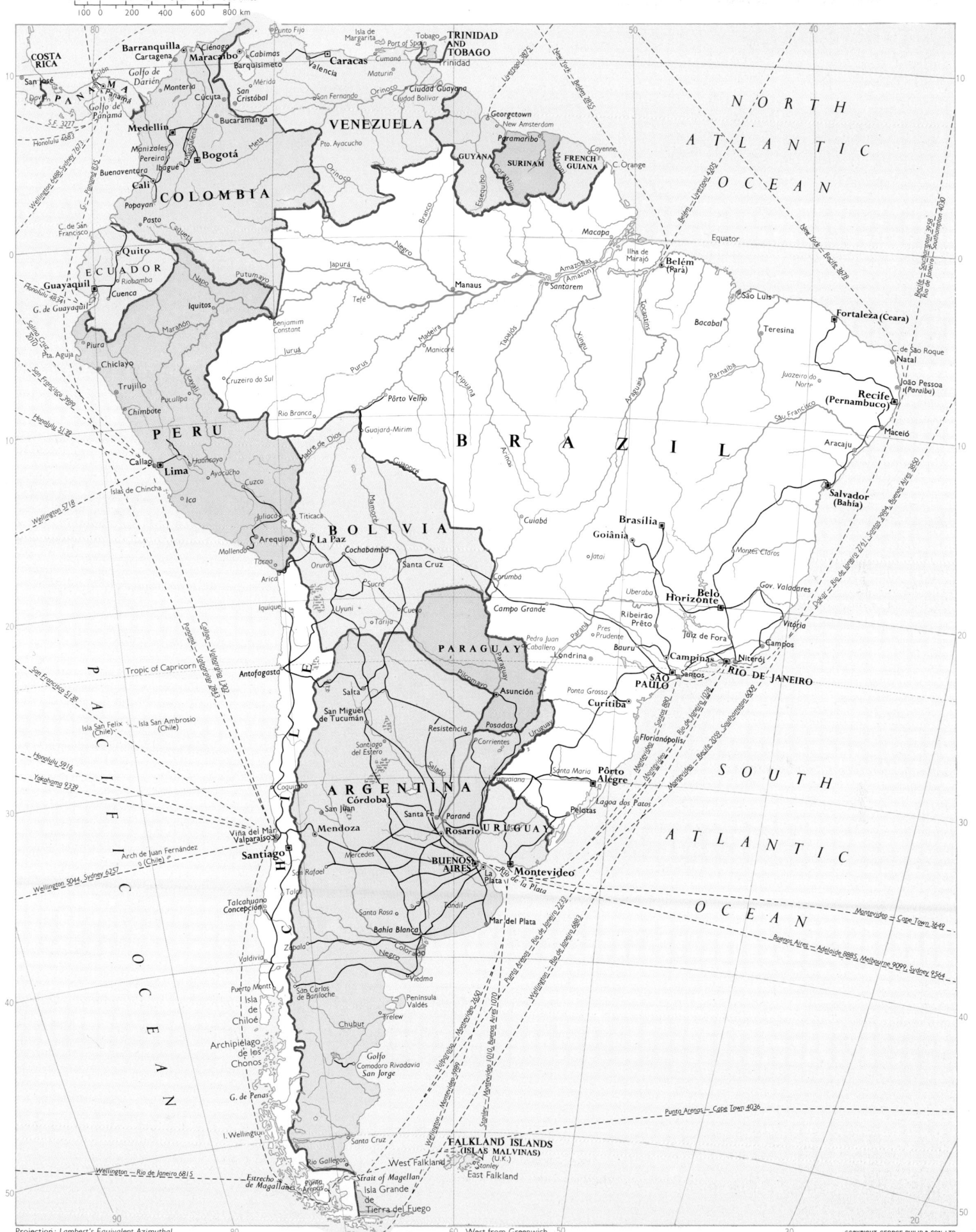

1:30 000 000

1:16 000 000

100 0 100 200 300 400 500 miles
100 0 100 200 300 400 500 600 700 800 km

A T L A N T I C   O C E A N

Paramaribo
Amsterdam
Nieuw Nickerie
Totness
Kwakoegron
Albina
Moengo
St. Laurent
Iracoubo
Sinnamary
Kourou
Cayenne
Approuague
C. Orange
SURINAM
FR. GUIANA
St. Georges
Oiapoque
Camopi

AMAPÁ
Amapá
C. do Norte
Macapá
Ilha de Maracá
Estuario do Rio Amazonas
Ilha Caviana
Ilha Mexiana

Equator

Serra do Navio
Mazagão
Afuá
Chaves
Ilha de Marajó
Gurupá
Breves
Muaná
Belém (Pará)
Vigia
Curuçá
Salinópolis
Bragança
Viseu
Guimarães
B. de São Marcos
São Luís (Maranhão)
Alcântara
Rosário
Barreirinhas
Tutóia
Luís Correia

Óbidos
Santarém
Amazonas (Amazon)
Altamira
Parintins
Aveiro
Brasilia Legal

PARÁ
Itaituba
Bacabal
Tucuruí
Paranaíba
Camocim
Granja
Itapipoca
Sobral
Maranguape
Fortaleza (Ceará)
Cascavel
Aracati
Baturité
Ipu
Rocas
Fernando de Noronha (Braz.)

MARANHÃO
Imperatriz
Grajaú
Carolina
Caxias
Teresina
Crateús
Senador Pompeu
Quixeramobim
Russas
Mossoró
RIO GRANDE DO NORTE
Ceará Mirim
C. de São Roque
Natal

CEARÁ

Amarante
Floriano
Uruçuí
PIAUÍ
Picos
Crato
Juàzeiro do Norte
Cajàzeiras
Patos
PARAÍBA
Campina Grande
João Pessoa (Paraíba)
Cabedelo

Conceição do Araguaia
Pedro Afonso
Petrolina
Juàzeiro
Paulo Afonso
Garanhuns
PERNAMBUCO
RECIFE (Pernambuco)
Olinda

B R A Z I L

Pôrto Nacional
Natividade
Barra
Xique-Xique
Jacobina
Propriá
SERGIPE
Aracaju
ALAGOAS
Maceió
Arapiraca

Parnaguá
Campo Formoso
Queimadas
Feira de Santana
BAHIA
Alagoinhas
Santo Amaro
Salvador (Bahia)
Todos os Santos
GOIÁS
Barreiras
Bom Jesus da Lapa
1850
Jequié
Valença
Ilhéus

Niquelândia
1678
Posse
Condeúba
Vitória da Conquista
Itabuna
Canavieiras

DIST. FED.
Brasília
Formosa
Montes Claros
Belmonte
Pôrto Seguro

Goiânia
Anápolis
MATO GROSSO
Planalto do Diamantino
Mato Grosso
Januária
Pedra Azul
Nanuque
Prado
Caravelas
Abrolhos

MATO GROSSO DO SUL
Araguari
Uberlândia
Patos de Minas
Diamantina
MINAS GERAIS
Ipatinga
Gov. Valadares
Teófilo Otoni
Mucuri
Conceição da Barra
São Mateus
Linhares

Campo Grande
Uberaba
Araxá
Belo Horizonte
ESPÍRITO SANTO
Vitória
Vila Velha
Trindade (Braz.)

Três Lagoas
Ribeirão Prêto
SÃO PAULO
Campinas
Juiz de Fora
Petrópolis
Niterói
RIO DE JANEIRO
Cabo Frio

Dourados
Marília
Bauru
Piracicaba
Botucatu

COPYRIGHT GEORGE PHILIP & SON, LTD.

1:16 000 000

100 50 0 100 200 300 miles
100 0 100 200 300 400 km

MATO GROSSO DO SUL

PARAGUAY

Asunción

BRASIL

PARANÁ

Curitiba

São Paulo

RIO DE JANEIRO

Santos

SANTA CATARINA

Florianópolis

RIO GRANDE DO SUL

Pôrto Alegre

Pelotas

Rio Grande

URUGUAY

MONTEVIDEO

Antofagasta

Tropic of Capricorn

San Miguel de Tucumán

Salta

Santiago del Estero

Córdoba

La Rioja

San Juan

Mendoza

Rosario

Santa Fe

Paraná

BUENOS AIRES

La Plata

Avellaneda

Viña del Mar
Valparaíso
SANTIAGO
Rancagua

Talca

Talcahuano
Concepción

Mar del Plata

Bahía Blanca

Neuquén

Valdivia

Osorno
Pto. Varas
Puerto Montt

I. de Chiloé

Trelew

Archipiélago de los Chonos

Comodoro Rivadavia

Golfo San Jorge

I. Wellington

Río Gallegos

Arch. Reina Adelaida

Estrecho de Magallanes
(Magellan's Str.)

Punta Arenas

Tierra del Fuego

FALKLAND ISLANDS
(ISLAS MALVINAS)
(Br.)

West Falkland

East Falkland

Stanley

South Georgia
(Br.)

SOUTH ATLANTIC OCEAN

Peru—Chile Trench

Cabo de Hornos (C. Horn)

Projection: Sanson-Flamsteed's Sinusoidal

60 West from Greenwich 55

INDEX

The number in dark type which follows each name in the index refers to the page number where that feature or place will be found.

The geographical co-ordinates which follow the place name are sometimes only approximate but are close enough for the place name to be located.

An open square □ signifies that the name refers to an administrative division of a country while a solid square ■ follows the name of a country.

Rivers have been indexed to their mouth or to where they join another river. All rivers are followed by the symbol →.

The alphabetic order of names composed of two or more words is governed primarily by the first word and then by the second. This is an example of the rule:

> East Tawas
> Eastbourne
> Easter Is.
> Eastern Ghats
> Eastleigh

Names composed of a proper name (*Mexico*) and a description (*Gulf of*) are positioned alphabetically by the proper name. If the same word occurs in the name of a town and a geographical feature, the town name is listed first followed by the name or names of the geographical features.

Names beginning with M', Mc are all indexed as if they were spelled Mac.

Names composed of the definite article (Le, La, Les, L') and a proper name are usually alphabetized by the proper name:

> Havre, Le
> Spezia, La

If the same place name occurs twice or more in the index and the places are in different countries, they will be followed by the country and be in the latter's alphabetical order:

> Boston, U.K.
> Boston, U.S.A.

If the same place name occurs two or more times in the index and all are in the same country, each is followed by the name of the administrative subdivision in which it is located. The names are placed in the alphabetical order of the subdivisions. For example:

> Columbus, Ga., U.S.A.
> Columbus, Miss., U.S.A.
> Columbus, Ohio, U.S.A.

If there is a mixture of these situations, the primary order is fixed by the alphabetical sequence of the countries and the secondary order by that of the country subdivisions:

> Rochester, U.K.
> Rochester, Minn., U.S.A.
> Rochester, N.Y., U.S.A.

Below is a list of abbreviations used in the index.

A.S.S.R. – Autonomous Soviet Socialist Republic	Fed. – Federal, Federation	Mont. – Montana	Pa. – Pennsylvania	Scot. – Scotland
Ala. – Alabama	Fla. – Florida	Mt.(s) – Mont, Monta, Monti, Muntii, Montaña, Mount, Mountain(s)	Pak. – Pakistan	Sd. – Sound
Arch. – Archipelago	Fr. – France, French		Pass. – Passage	Sp. – Spain, Spanish
Ariz. – Arizona	G. – Golfe, Golfo, Gulf, Guba		Pen. – Peninsula	St. – Saint
Ark. – Arkansas	Ga. – Georgia	N. – North, Northern	Pk. – Peak	Str. – Strait, Stretto
B. – Baie, Bahia, Bay, Boca, Bucht, Bugt	Gt. – Great	N.B. – New Brunswick	Plat. – Plateau	Tenn. – Tennessee
	Hts. – Heights	N.C. – North Carolina	Prov. – Province, Provincial	Terr. – Territory
B.C. – British Columbia	I.(s) – Ile, Ilha, Insel, Isla, Island(s)	N. Dak. – North Dakota	Pt. – Point	Tex. – Texas
Br. – British	III. – Illinois	N.H. – New Hampshire	Pta. – Ponta, Punta	U.K. – United Kingdom
C. – Cabo, Cap, Cape	Ind. – Indiana	N.J. – New Jersey	Pte. – Pointe	U.S.A. – United States of America
Calif. – California	K. – Kap, Kapp	N. Mex. – New Mexico	Qué. – Québec	
Chan. – Channel	Kans. – Kansas	N.S. – Nova Scotia	R. – Rio, River	U.S.S.R. – Union of Soviet Socialist Republics
Col. – Colombia	Ky. – Kentucky	N.S.W. – New South Wales	R.S.F.S.R. – Russian Soviet Federative Socialist Republic	
Colo. – Colorado	L. – Lac, Lacul, Lago, Lagoa, Lake, Limni, Loch, Lough	N.Y. – New York		Ut. P. – Uttar Pradesh
Conn. – Connecticut		N.Z. – New Zealand		Va. – Virginia
Cord. – Cordillera	La. – Louisiana	Nat. Park – National Park	Ra.(s) – Range(s)	Vic. – Victoria
D.C. – District of Columbia	Ld. – Land	Nebr. – Nebraska	Rep. – Republic	Vt. – Vermont
Del. – Delaware	Mad. P. – Madhya Pradesh	Neth. – Netherlands	Res. – Reserve, Reservoir	Wash. – Washington
Dep. – Dependency	Man. – Manitoba	Nev. – Nevada	S. – South	W. – West
Des. – Desert	Mass. – Massachusetts	Nfld. – Newfoundland	S. Africa – South Africa	W. Va. – West Virginia
Dist. – District	Md. – Maryland	Nic. – Nicaragua	S.C. – South Carolina	Wis. – Wisconsin
Dom. Rep. – Dominican Republic	Mich. – Michigan	Nig. – Nigeria	S. Dak. – South Dakota	Wyo. – Wyoming
	Minn. – Minnesota	Okla. – Oklahoma	S.S.R. – Soviet Socialist Republic	Yug. – Yugoslavia
E. – East	Miss. – Mississippi	Ont. – Ontario		
Fd. – Fjord	Mo. – Missouri	Oreg. – Oregon	Sa. – Serra, Sierra	
		P. – Pass, Paso, Pasul	Sask. – Saskatchewan	

Aachen

A

Aachen 14 50 47N 6 4 E
Aalborg = Ålborg 21 57 2N 9 54 E
A'âli en Nîl □ 51 9 30N 31 30 E
Aalsmeer 11 52 17N 4 43 E
Aalst 11 50 56N 4 2 E
Aalten 11 51 56N 6 35 E
Aarau 14 47 23N 8 4 E
Aare → 14 47 33N 8 14 E
Aarhus = Århus 21 56 8N 10 11 E
Aarschot 11 50 59N 4 49 E
Aba 53 5 10N 7 19 E
Ābādān 30 30 22N 48 20 E
Ābādeh 31 31 8N 52 40 E
Abadla 50 31 2N 2 45W
Abaetetuba 79 1 40S 48 50W
Abagnar Qi 38 43 52N 116 2 E
Abakan 25 53 40N 91 10 E
Abariringa 40 2 50S 171 40W
Abarqū 31 31 10N 53 20 E
'Abasān 28 31 19N 34 21 E
Abashiri 36 44 0N 144 15 E
Abashiri-Wan 36 44 0N 144 30 E
Abay 24 49 38N 72 53 E
Abaya, L. 51 6 30N 37 50 E
Abaza 24 52 39N 90 6 E
Abbay = Nîl el Azraq → 51 15 38N 32 31 E
Abbaye, Pt. 68 46 58N 88 4W
Abbeville, France 12 50 6N 1 49 E
Abbeville, La., U.S.A. 71 30 0N 92 7W
Abbeville, S.C., U.S.A. 69 34 12N 82 21W
Abbieglassie 45 27 15S 147 28 E
Abbotsford, Canada 64 49 5N 122 20W
Abbotsford, U.S.A. 70 44 55N 90 20W
Abbottabad 32 34 10N 73 15 E
Abd al Kūrī 29 12 5N 52 20 E
Abéché 51 13 50N 20 35 E
Åbenrå 21 55 3N 9 25 E
Abeokuta 53 7 3N 3 19 E
Aberaeron 7 52 15N 4 16W
Aberayron = Aberaeron 7 52 15N 4 16W
Abercorn = Mbala 54 8 46S 31 24 E
Abercorn 45 25 12S 151 5 E
Aberdare 7 51 43N 3 27W
Aberdeen, Australia 45 32 9S 150 56 E
Aberdeen, Canada 65 52 20N 106 8W
Aberdeen, S. Africa 56 32 28S 24 2 E
Aberdeen, U.K. 8 57 9N 2 6W
Aberdeen, Ala., U.S.A. 69 33 49N 88 33W
Aberdeen, Idaho, U.S.A. 72 42 57N 112 50W
Aberdeen, S. Dak., U.S.A. 70 45 30N 98 30W
Aberdeen, Wash., U.S.A. 72 47 0N 123 50W
Aberdovey 7 52 33N 4 3W
Aberfeldy 8 56 37N 3 50W
Abergavenny 7 51 49N 3 1W
Abernathy 71 33 49N 101 49W
Abert, L. 72 42 40N 120 8W
Aberystwyth 7 52 25N 4 6W
Abidjan 50 5 26N 3 58W
Abilene, Kans., U.S.A. 70 39 0N 97 16W
Abilene, Tex., U.S.A. 71 32 22N 99 40W
Abingdon, U.K. 7 51 40N 1 17W
Abingdon, Ill., U.S.A. 70 40 53N 90 23W
Abingdon, Va., U.S.A. 69 36 46N 81 56W
Abington Reef 44 18 0S 149 35 E
Abitau → 65 59 53N 109 3W
Abitau L. 65 60 27N 107 15W
Abitibi L. 62 48 40N 79 40W
Abkhaz A.S.S.R. □ 23 43 0N 41 0 E
Abkit 25 64 10N 157 10 E
Abminga 45 26 8S 134 51 E
Abohar 32 30 10N 74 10 E
Abomey 53 7 10N 2 5 E
Abong-Mbang 54 4 0N 13 8 E
Abonnema 53 4 41N 6 49 E
Abou-Deïa 51 11 20N 19 20 E
Aboyne 8 57 4N 2 48W
Abrantes 13 39 24N 8 7W
Abreojos, Pta. 74 26 50N 113 40W
Abri 51 20 50N 30 27 E
Abrolhos, Banka 79 18 0S 38 0W
Abrud 15 46 19N 23 5 E
Abruzzi □ 18 42 15N 14 0 E
Absaroka Ra. 72 44 40N 110 0W
Abū al Khaṣīb 30 30 25N 48 0 E
Abū 'Alī 30 27 20N 49 27 E
Abu 'Arīsh 29 16 53N 42 48 E
Abu Dhabi = Abū Ẓāby 31 24 28N 54 22 E
Abū Dīs, Jordan 28 31 47N 35 16 E
Abû Dis, Sudan 51 19 12N 33 38 E
Abū Ghaush 28 31 48N 35 6 E
Abu Hamed 51 19 32N 33 13 E
Abū Kamāl 30 34 30N 41 0 E
Abū Madd, Ra's 30 24 50N 37 7 E
Abu Matariq 51 10 59N 26 9 E
Abu Rudeis 30 28 54N 33 11 E
Abu Tig 51 27 4N 31 15 E
Abû Zabad 51 12 25N 29 10 E
Abū Ẓāby 31 24 28N 54 22 E
Abuja 53 9 16N 7 2 E
Abukuma-Gawa → 36 38 6N 140 52 E
Abunã 78 9 40S 65 20W
Abunã → 78 9 41S 65 20W
Abut Hd. 43 43 7S 170 15 E
Abwong 51 9 2N 32 14 E
Acámbaro 74 20 0N 100 40W
Acaponeta 74 22 30N 105 20W
Acapulco 74 16 51N 99 56W
Acarigua 78 9 33N 69 12W
Acatlán 74 18 10N 98 3W
Acayucan 74 17 59N 94 58W
Accomac 68 37 43N 75 40W
Accra 53 5 35N 0 6W
Accrington 6 53 46N 2 22W
Aceh □ 34 4 15N 97 30 E
Achalpur 32 21 22N 77 32 E
Achill 9 53 56N 9 55W
Achill Hd. 9 53 59N 10 15W
Achill I. 9 53 58N 10 5W
Achill Sound 9 53 53N 9 55W
Achinsk 25 56 20N 90 20 E
Ackerman 71 33 20N 89 8W
Acklins I. 75 22 30N 74 0W
Acme 64 51 33N 113 30W
Aconcagua, Cerro 80 32 39S 70 0W
Aconquija, Mt. 80 27 0S 66 0W
Açores, Is. dos = Azores 2 38 44N 29 0W
Acre = 'Akko 28 32 55N 35 4 E
Acre □ 78 9 1S 71 0W
Acre → 78 8 45S 67 22W
Ad Dahnā 30 24 30N 48 10 E
Ad Dammām 30 26 20N 50 5 E
Ad Dawhah 31 25 15N 51 35 E
Ad Dilam 30 23 55N 47 10 E
Ad Dīwānīyah 30 32 0N 45 0 E
Ada, Minn., U.S.A. 70 47 20N 96 30W
Ada, Okla., U.S.A. 71 34 50N 96 45W
Adaja → 13 41 32N 4 52W
Adam 31 22 15N 57 28 E
Adamaoua, Massif de l' 51 7 20N 12 20 E
Adamawa Highlands = Adamaoua, Massif de l' 51 7 20N 12 20 E
Adamello, Mt. 18 46 10N 10 34 E
Adaminaby 45 36 0S 148 45 E
Adams, N.Y., U.S.A. 68 43 50N 76 3W
Adams, Wis., U.S.A. 70 43 59N 89 50W
Adams, Mt. 72 46 10N 121 28W
Adam's Bridge 32 9 15N 79 40 E
Adams L. 64 51 10N 119 40W
Adam's Peak 32 6 48N 80 30 E
Adana 30 37 0N 35 16 E
Adapazarı 30 40 48N 30 25 E
Adarama 51 17 10N 34 52 E
Adaut 35 8 8S 131 7 E
Adavale 45 25 52S 144 32 E
Adda → 18 45 8N 9 53 E
Addis Ababa = Addis Abeba 51 9 2N 38 42 E
Addis Abeba 51 9 2N 38 42 E
Addis Alem 51 9 0N 38 17 E
Addo 56 33 32S 25 45 E
Adel 69 31 10N 83 28W
Adelaide, Australia 45 34 52S 138 30 E
Adelaide, S. Africa 57 32 42S 26 20 E
Adelaide Pen. 60 68 15N 97 30W
Adelaide River 46 13 15S 131 7 E
Adele, I. 46 15 32S 123 9 E
Aden = Al 'Adan 29 12 45N 45 0 E
Aden, G. of 29 12 30N 47 30 E
Adendorp 56 32 15S 24 30 E
Adi 35 4 15S 133 30 E
Adi Ugri 51 14 58N 38 48 E
Adieu, C. 47 32 0S 132 10 E
Adieu Pt. 46 15 14S 124 35 E
Adige → 18 45 9N 12 20 E
Adilabad 32 19 33N 78 20 E
Adin 72 41 10N 121 0W
Adin Khel 31 32 45N 68 5 E
Adirondack Mts. 68 44 0N 74 15W
Adlavik Is. 63 55 2N 57 45W
Admer 50 20 21N 5 27 E
Admiralty G. 46 14 20S 125 55 E
Admiralty I. 60 57 40N 134 35W
Admiralty Inlet 72 48 0N 122 40W
Admiralty Is. 40 2 0S 147 0 E
Ado 53 6 36N 2 56 E
Ado Ekiti 53 7 38N 5 12 E
Adonara 35 8 15S 123 5 E
Adoni 32 15 33N 77 18W
Adour → 12 43 32N 1 32W
Adra 13 36 43N 3 3W
Adrano 18 37 40N 14 49 E
Adrar 50 27 51N 0 11W
Adré 51 13 40N 22 20 E
Adrī 51 27 32N 13 2 E
Adrian, Mich., U.S.A. 68 41 55N 84 0W
Adrian, Tex., U.S.A. 71 35 19N 102 37W
Adriatic Sea 16 43 0N 16 0 E
Adua 35 1 45S 129 50 E
Adwa 51 14 15N 38 52 E
Adzhar A.S.S.R. □ 23 42 0N 42 0 E
Ægean Sea 17 37 0N 25 0 E
Æolian Is. = Eólie, Is. 18 38 30N 14 50 E
Aerht'ai Shan 37 46 40N 92 45 E
Afars & Issas, Terr. of = Djibouti ■ 29 12 0N 43 0 E
Afghanistan ■ 31 33 0N 65 0 E
Afgoi 29 2 7N 44 59 E
'Afif 30 23 53N 42 56 E
Afognak I. 60 58 10N 152 50W
Africa 48 10 0N 20 0 E
Afuá 79 0 15S 50 20W
Afula 28 32 37N 35 17 E
Afyonkarahisar 30 38 45N 30 33 E
Agadès = Agadez 53 16 58N 7 59 E
Agadez 53 16 58N 7 59 E
Agadir 50 30 28N 9 55W
Agano → 36 37 57N 139 8 E
Agapa 25 71 27N 89 15 E
Agartala 33 23 50N 91 23 E
Agassiz 64 49 14N 121 46W
Agats 35 5 33S 138 0 E
Agattu I. 60 52 25N 172 30 E
Agboville 50 5 55N 4 15W
Agde 12 43 19N 3 28 E
Agen 12 44 12N 0 38 E
Aghil Mts. 32 36 0N 77 0 E
Aginskoye 25 51 6N 114 32 E
Agra 32 27 17N 77 58 E
Agri → 18 40 13N 16 44 E
Ağri Daği 30 39 50N 44 15 E
Ağri Karakose 30 39 44N 43 3 E
Agrigento 18 37 19N 13 33 E
Agrinion 19 38 37N 21 27 E
Água Clara 79 20 25S 52 45W
Agua Prieta 74 31 20N 109 32W
Aguadas 78 5 40N 75 38W
Aguadilla 75 18 27N 67 10W
Aguanish 63 50 14N 62 2W
Aguanus → 63 50 13N 62 5W
Aguarico → 78 0 59S 75 11W
Aguas Blancas 80 24 15S 69 55W
Aguascalientes 74 21 53N 102 12W
Aguascalientes □ 74 22 0N 102 20W
Aguilas 13 37 23N 1 35W
Agulhas, C. 56 34 52S 20 0 E
Agung 34 8 20S 115 28 E
'Agur 28 31 42N 34 55 E
Agusan → 35 9 0N 125 30 E
Aha Mts. 56 19 45S 21 0 E
Ahaggar 50 23 0N 6 30 E
Ahar 30 38 35N 47 0 E
Ahipara B. 43 35 5S 173 5 E
Ahiri 32 19 30N 80 0 E
Ahmadabad 32 23 0N 72 40 E
Ahmadnagar 32 19 7N 74 46 E
Ahmadpur 32 29 12N 71 10 E
Ahmedabad = Ahmadabad 32 23 0N 72 40 E
Ahmednagar = Ahmadnagar 32 19 7N 74 46 E
Ahuachapán 75 13 54N 89 52W
Ahvāz 30 31 20N 48 40 E
Ahvenanmaa = Åland 21 60 15N 20 0 E
Aḥwar 29 13 30N 46 40 E
Aichi □ 36 35 0N 137 15 E
Aigues-Mortes 12 43 35N 4 12 E
Aihui 38 50 10N 127 30 E
Aija 78 9 50S 77 45W
Aiken 69 33 34N 81 50W
Aillik 63 55 11N 59 18W
Ailsa Craig 8 55 15N 5 7W
'Ailūn 28 32 18N 35 47 E
Aim 25 59 0N 133 55 E
Aimere 35 8 45S 121 3 E
Aimorés 79 19 30S 41 4W
Ain □ 12 46 5N 5 20 E
Aïn Banaiyan 31 23 0N 51 0 E
Aïn Beïda 50 35 50N 7 29 E
Aïn Ben Tili 50 25 59N 9 27W
Aïn-Sefra 50 32 47N 0 37W
Ainabo 29 9 0N 46 25 E
Ainsworth 70 42 33N 99 52W
Aïr 50 18 30N 8 0 E
Airdrie 8 55 53N 3 57W
Aire → 6 53 42N 0 55W
Airlie Beach 44 20 16S 148 43 E
Aisne □ 12 49 42N 3 40 E
Aisne → 12 49 26N 2 50 E
Aitkin 70 46 32N 93 43W
Aiud 15 46 19N 23 44 E
Aix-en-Provence 12 43 32N 5 27 E
Aix-la-Chapelle = Aachen 14 50 47N 6 4 E
Aiyansh 64 55 17N 129 2W
Áiyina 19 37 45N 23 26 E
Aiyion 19 38 15N 22 5 E
Aizawl 33 23 40N 92 44 E
Aizuwakamatsu 36 37 30N 139 56 E
Ajaccio 12 41 55N 8 40 E
Ajanta Ra. 32 20 28N 75 50 E
Ajdâbiyah 51 30 54N 20 4 E
'Ajmān 31 25 25N 55 30 E
Ajmer 32 26 28N 74 37 E
Ajo 73 32 18N 112 54W
Ak Dağ 30 36 30N 30 0 E
Akaroa 43 43 49S 172 59 E
Akashi 36 34 45N 135 0 E
Akelamo 35 1 35N 129 40 E
Akershus fylke □ 21 60 0N 11 10 E
Aketi 54 2 38N 23 47 E
Akhelóös → 19 38 36N 21 14 E
Akhisar 30 38 56N 27 48 E
Akhmîm 51 26 31N 31 47 E
Akimiski I. 62 52 50N 81 30W
Akita 36 39 45N 140 7 E
Akita □ 36 39 40N 140 30 E
Akjoujt 50 19 45N 14 15W
'Akko 28 32 55N 35 4 E
Akkol 24 45 0N 75 39 E
Aklavik 60 68 12N 135 0W
Akobo → 51 7 48N 33 3 E
Akola 32 20 42N 77 2 E
Akordat 51 15 30N 37 40 E
Akosombo Dam 53 6 20N 0 5 E
Akpatok I. 61 60 25N 68 8W
Akranes 20 64 19N 21 58W
Akreijit 50 18 19N 9 11W
Akron, Colo., U.S.A. 70 40 13N 103 15W
Akron, Ohio, U.S.A. 68 41 7N 81 31W
Aksai Chih 32 35 15N 79 55 E
Aksaray 30 38 25N 34 2 E
Aksarka 24 66 31N 67 50 E
Aksay 24 51 11N 53 0 E
Akşehir 30 38 18N 31 30 E
Aksenovo Zilovskoye 25 53 20N 117 40 E
Aksu 37 41 5N 80 10 E
Aksum 51 14 5N 38 40 E
Aktogay 24 46 57N 79 40 E
Aktyubinsk 23 50 17N 57 10 E
Aku 53 6 40N 7 18 E
Akure 53 7 15N 5 5 E
Akureyri 20 65 40N 18 6W
Akyab = Sittwe 33 20 18N 92 45 E
Al 'Adan 29 12 45N 45 0 E
Al Aḥsā 30 25 50N 49 0 E
Al Amādīyah 30 37 5N 43 30 E
Al Amārah 30 31 55N 47 15 E
Al 'Aqabah 28 29 31N 35 0 E
Al 'Aramah 30 25 30N 46 0 E
Al Ashkhara 31 21 50N 59 30 E
Al 'Ayzarīyah 28 31 47N 35 15 E
Al Badī' 30 22 0N 46 35 E
Al Baṣrah 30 30 30N 47 50 E
Al Bāzūrīyah 28 33 15N 35 16 E
Al Bīrah 28 31 55N 35 12 E
Al Bu'ayrāt 51 31 24N 15 44 E
Al Buqay'ah 28 32 15N 35 30 E
Al Fallūjah 30 33 20N 43 55 E
Al Fāw 30 30 0N 48 30 E
Al Fujayrah 31 25 7N 56 18 E
Al Hābah 30 27 10N 47 0 E
Al Haddār 30 21 58N 45 57 E
Al Ḥadīthah 30 34 0N 41 13 E
Al Ḥāmad 30 31 30N 39 30 E
Al Ḥamar 30 22 23N 46 6 E
Al Ḥamrā' 30 24 2N 38 55 E
Al Ḥarīq 30 23 29N 46 27 E
Al Ḥarīr, W. → 28 32 44N 35 59 E
Al Ḥasakah 30 36 35N 40 45 E
Al Ḥawrah 29 13 50N 47 35 E
Al Ḥayy 30 32 5N 46 5 E
Al Ḥijāz 29 26 0N 37 30 E
Al Ḥillah, Iraq 30 32 30N 44 25 E
Al Ḥillah, Si. Arabia 30 23 35N 46 50 E
Al Hindīyah 30 32 30N 44 10 E
Al Ḥiṣnn 28 32 29N 35 52 E
Al Hoceïma 50 35 8N 3 58W
Al Ḥudaydah 29 14 50N 43 0 E
Al Hufūf 30 25 25N 49 45 E
Al Ḥulwah 30 23 24N 46 48 E
Al Irq 51 29 5N 21 35 E
Al Ittihad = Madīnat ash Sha'b 29 12 50N 45 0 E
Al Jāfūrah 30 25 0N 50 15 E
Al Jaghbūb 51 29 42N 24 38 E
Al Jahrah 30 29 25N 47 40 E
Al Jalāmīd 30 31 20N 39 45 E
Al Jawf, Libya 51 24 10N 23 24 E
Al Jawf, Si. Arabia 30 29 55N 39 40 E
Al Jazirah, Asia 30 33 30N 44 0 E
Al Jazirah, Libya 51 26 10N 21 20 E
Al Jubayl 30 27 0N 49 50 E
Al Jubaylah 30 24 55N 46 25 E
Al Junaynah 51 13 27N 22 45 E
Al Khābūra 31 23 57N 57 5 E
Al Khalīl 28 31 32N 35 6 E
Al Khalūf 29 20 30N 58 13 E
Al Kharfah 30 22 0N 46 35 E
Al Kharj 30 24 0N 47 0 E
Al Kufrah 51 24 17N 23 15 E
Al Kūt 30 32 30N 46 0 E
Al Kuwayt 30 29 30N 48 0 E
Al Lādhiqīyah 30 35 30N 35 45 E
Al Lubban 28 32 9N 35 14 E
Al Luḥayyah 29 15 45N 42 40 E
Al Madīnah 29 24 35N 39 52 E
Al-Mafraq 28 32 17N 36 14 E
Al Majma'ah 30 25 57N 45 22 E
Al Manāmah 31 26 10N 50 30 E
Al Marj 51 32 25N 20 30 E
Al Mawṣil 30 36 15N 43 5 E
Al Mazra 28 31 16N 35 31 E
Al Midhnab 30 25 50N 44 18 E
Al Miqdādīyah 30 34 0N 45 0 E
Al Mish'āb 30 28 12N 48 36 E
Al Mubarraz 30 25 30N 49 40 E
Al Muḥarraq 31 26 15N 50 40 E
Al Mukallā 29 14 33N 49 2 E
Al Mukhā 29 13 18N 43 15 E
Al Musayyib 30 32 40N 44 25 E
Al Muwayliḥ 30 27 40N 35 30 E
Al Owuho = Otukpa 53 7 9N 7 41 E
Al Qaḍīmah 30 22 20N 39 13 E
Al Qā'iyah 30 24 33N 43 15 E
Al Qāmishli 30 37 10N 41 10 E
Al Qaṣabát 51 32 39N 14 1 E
Al Qaṣīm 30 26 0N 43 0 E
Al Qaṭīf 30 26 35N 50 0 E
Al Qaṭrūn 51 24 56N 15 3 E
Al Quaisūmah 30 28 10N 46 20 E
Al Quds = Jerusalem 28 31 47N 35 10 E
Al Qurayyāt 31 23 17N 58 53 E
Al Qurnah 30 31 1N 47 25 E
Al 'Ulā 30 26 35N 38 0 E
Al Uqaylah ash Sharqīgah 51 30 12N 19 10 E
Al Uqayr 30 25 40N 50 15 E
Al 'Uthmānīyah 30 25 5N 49 22 E
Al 'Uwaynid 30 24 50N 46 0 E
Al' 'Uwayqīlah 30 30 30N 42 10 E
Al 'Uyūn 30 26 30N 43 50 E
Al Wakrah 31 25 10N 51 40 E
Al Wari'āh 30 27 51N 47 25 E
Al Yamāmah 30 24 5N 47 30 E
Al Yāmūn 28 32 29N 35 14 E
Alabama □ 69 33 0N 87 0W
Alabama → 69 31 8N 87 57W
Alagoa Grande 79 7 3S 35 35W
Alagoas □ 79 9 0S 36 0W
Alagoinhas 79 12 7S 38 20W
Alajuela 75 10 2N 84 8W
Alakamisy 57 21 19S 47 14 E
Alakurtti 22 67 0N 30 30 E
Alameda 73 35 10N 106 43W
Alamo 73 36 21N 115 10W
Alamogordo 73 32 59N 106 0W
Alamos 74 27 0N 109 0W
Alamosa 73 37 30N 106 0W
Åland 21 60 15N 20 0 E
Ålands hav 21 60 0N 19 30 E
Alandur 32 13 0N 80 15 E
Alanya 30 36 38N 32 0 E
Alaotra, Farihin' 57 17 30S 48 30 E
Alapayevsk 24 57 52N 61 42 E
Alaşehir 23 38 23N 28 30 E
Alaska □ 60 65 0N 150 0W
Alaska, G. of 60 58 0N 145 0W
Alaska Highway 64 60 0N 130 0W
Alaska Pen. 60 56 0N 160 0W
Alaska Range 60 62 50N 151 0W
Alataw Shankou 37 45 5N 81 57 E
Alatyr 22 54 45N 46 35 E
Alausi 78 2 0S 78 50W
Alava, C. 72 48 10N 124 40W
Alawoona 45 34 45S 140 30 E
Alba 18 44 41N 8 1 E
Alba Iulia 15 46 8N 23 39 E
Albacete 13 39 0N 1 50W
Albacutya, L. 45 35 45S 141 58 E
Albania ■ 19 41 0N 20 0 E
Albany, Australia 47 35 1S 117 58 E
Albany, Ga., U.S.A. 69 31 40N 84 10W
Albany, Minn., U.S.A. 70 45 37N 94 38W
Albany, N.Y., U.S.A. 68 42 35N 73 47W
Albany, Oreg., U.S.A. 72 44 41N 123 0W
Albany, Tex., U.S.A. 71 32 45N 99 20W
Albany → 62 52 17N 81 31W
Albardón 80 31 20S 68 30W
Albarracín, Sierra de 13 40 30N 1 30W
Albatross B. 44 12 45S 141 30 E
Albemarle 69 35 27N 80 15W
Albemarle Sd. 69 36 0N 76 30W
Alberche → 13 39 58N 4 46W

Angellala

Albert, L. = Mobutu Sese Seko, L. 54 1 30N 31 0 E
Albert, L. 45 35 30S 139 10 E
Albert Canyon 64 51 8N 117 41W
Albert Edward Ra. 46 18 17S 127 57 E
Albert Lea 70 43 32N 93 20W
Albert Nile → 54 3 36N 32 2 E
Alberta □ 64 54 40N 115 0W
Albertinia 56 34 11S 21 34 E
Alberton 63 46 50N 64 0W
Albertville = Kalemie 54 5 55S 29 9 E
Albi 12 43 56N 2 9 E
Albia 70 41 0N 92 50W
Albina 79 5 37N 54 15W
Albina, Ponta 56 15 52S 11 44 E
Albion, Idaho, U.S.A. 72 42 21N 113 37W
Albion, Mich., U.S.A. 68 42 15N 84 45W
Albion, Nebr., U.S.A. 70 41 47N 98 0W
Ålborg 21 57 2N 9 54 E
Alborz, Reshteh-ye Kūhhā-ye 31 36 0N 52 0 E
Albreda 64 52 35N 119 10W
Albuquerque 73 35 5N 106 47W
Albuquerque, Cayos de 75 12 10N 81 50W
Alburquerque 13 39 15N 6 59W
Albury 45 36 3S 146 56 E
Alcalá de Henares 13 40 28N 3 22W
Alcalá la Real 13 37 27N 3 57W
Alcamo 18 37 59N 12 55 E
Alcaníz 13 41 2N 0 8W
Alcântara, Brazil 79 2 20S 44 30W
Alcántara, Spain 13 39 41N 6 57W
Alcantara L. 65 60 57N 108 9W
Alcaraz, Sierra de 13 38 40N 2 20W
Alcaudete 13 37 35N 4 5W
Alcázar de San Juan 13 39 24N 3 12W
Alcira 13 39 9N 0 30W
Alcoa 69 35 50N 84 0W
Alcobaça 13 39 32N 9 0W
Alcova 72 42 37N 106 52W
Alcoy 13 38 43N 0 30W
Aldabra Is. 3 9 22S 46 28 E
Aldan 25 58 40N 125 30 E
Aldan → 25 63 28N 129 35 E
Aldeburgh 7 52 9N 1 35 E
Alder 72 45 27N 112 3W
Alderney 7 49 42N 2 12W
Aldershot 7 51 15N 0 43W
Aledo 70 41 10N 90 50W
Aleg 50 17 3N 13 55W
Alegrete 80 29 40S 56 0W
Aleisk 24 52 40N 83 0 E
Alejandro Selkirk, I. 41 33 50S 80 15W
Aleksandrovsk-Sakhalinskiy 25 50 50N 142 20 E
Aleksandrovskiy Zavod 25 50 40N 117 50 E
Aleksandrovskoye 24 60 35N 77 50 E
Alemania 80 25 40S 65 30W
Alençon 12 48 27N 0 4 E
Alenuihaha Chan. 66 20 25N 156 0W
Aleppo = Ḥalab 30 36 10N 37 15 E
Aléria 18 42 5N 9 26 E
Alert Bay 64 50 30N 126 55W
Alès 12 44 9N 4 5 E
Alessándria 18 44 54N 8 37 E
Ålesund 20 62 28N 6 12 E
Aleutian Is. 60 52 0N 175 0W
Aleutian Trench 40 48 0N 180 0 E
Alexander 70 47 51N 103 40W
Alexander, Mt. 47 28 58S 120 16 E
Alexander Arch. 60 57 0N 135 0W
Alexander B. 56 28 36S 16 33 E
Alexander Bay 56 28 40S 16 30 E
Alexander City 69 32 58N 85 57W
Alexandra, Australia 45 37 8S 145 40 E
Alexandra, N.Z. 43 45 14S 169 25 E
Alexandra Falls 64 60 29N 116 18W
Alexandretta = İskenderun 30 36 32N 36 10 E
Alexandria = El Iskandarîya 51 31 0N 30 0 E
Alexandria, Australia 44 19 5S 136 40 E
Alexandria, B.C., Canada 64 52 35N 122 27W
Alexandria, Ont., Canada 62 45 19N 74 38W
Alexandria, S. Africa 56 33 38S 26 28 E
Alexandria, Ind., U.S.A. 68 40 18N 85 40W
Alexandria, La., U.S.A. 71 31 20N 92 30W
Alexandria, Minn., U.S.A. 70 45 50N 95 20W
Alexandria, S. Dak., U.S.A. 70 43 40N 97 45W
Alexandria, Va., U.S.A. 68 38 47N 77 1W
Alexandria Bay 68 44 20N 75 52W
Alexandrina, L. 45 35 25S 139 10 E
Alexandroúpolis 19 40 50N 25 54 E
Alexis → 63 52 33N 56 8W
Alexis Creek 64 52 10N 123 20W
Alford 8 57 13N 2 42W
Alfreton 6 53 6N 1 22W
Alga 23 49 53N 57 20 E
Algarve 13 36 58N 8 20W
Algeciras 13 36 9N 5 28W
Algemesí 13 39 11N 0 27W
Alger 50 36 42N 3 8 E
Algeria ■ 50 28 30N 2 0 E
Alghero 18 40 34N 8 20 E
Algiers = Alger 50 36 42N 3 8 E
Algoa B. 56 33 50S 25 45 E
Algoma 68 44 35N 87 27W
Algona 70 43 4N 94 14W
Alhama de Murcia 13 37 51N 1 25W
Alhambra 73 34 2N 118 10W
Alhucemas = Al Hoceïma 50 35 8N 3 58W
'Alī al Gharbī 30 32 30N 46 45 E
'Alī Khēl 32 33 57N 69 43 E
Aliákmon → 19 40 30N 22 36 E
Alibo 51 9 52N 37 5 E
Alicante 13 38 23N 0 30W
Alice, S. Africa 56 32 48S 26 55 E
Alice, U.S.A. 71 27 47N 98 1W
Alice →, Queens., Australia 44 24 2S 144 50 E
Alice →, Queens., Australia 44 15 35S 142 20 E
Alice Arm 64 55 29N 129 31W
Alice Downs 46 17 45S 127 56 E
Alice Springs 44 23 40S 133 50 E
Alicedale 56 33 15S 26 4 E
Aliceville 69 33 9N 88 10W
Alick Cr. → 44 20 55S 142 20 E
Alida 65 49 25N 101 55W
Aligarh, Ut. P., India 32 27 55N 78 10 E
Aligarh, India 32 27 55N 78 10 E
Alīgūdarz 30 33 25N 49 45 E
Alingsås 21 57 56N 12 31 E
Alipur 32 29 25N 70 55 E
Alipur Duar 33 26 30N 89 35 E
Aliquippa 68 40 38N 80 18W
Aliwal North 56 30 45S 26 45 E
Alix 64 52 24N 113 11W
Aljustrel 13 37 55N 8 10W
Alkmaar 11 52 37N 4 45 E
All American Canal 73 32 45N 115 0W
Allahabad 33 25 25N 81 58 E
Allakh-Yun 25 60 50N 137 5 E
Allan 65 51 53N 106 4W
Allanmyo 33 19 30N 95 17 E
Allanridge 56 27 45S 26 40 E
Allanwater 62 50 14N 90 10W
Allegan 68 42 32N 85 52W
Allegheny → 68 40 27N 80 0W
Allegheny Mts. 68 38 0N 80 0W
Allen, Bog of 9 53 15N 7 0W
Allen, L. 9 54 12N 8 5W
Allenby Br. = Jisr al Ḥusayn 28 31 53N 35 33 E
Allende 74 28 20N 100 50W
Allentown 68 40 36N 75 30W
Alleppey 32 9 30N 76 28 E
Alliance, Nebr., U.S.A. 70 42 10N 102 50W
Alliance, Ohio, U.S.A. 68 40 53N 81 7W
Allier □ 12 46 25N 3 0 E
Allier → 12 46 57N 3 4 E
Alliston 62 44 9N 79 52W
Alloa 8 56 7N 3 49W
Allora 45 28 2S 152 0 E
Alma, Canada 63 48 35N 71 40W
Alma, Ga., U.S.A. 69 31 33N 82 28W
Alma, Kans., U.S.A. 70 39 1N 96 22W
Alma, Mich., U.S.A. 68 43 25N 84 40W
Alma, Nebr., U.S.A. 70 40 10N 99 25W
Alma, Wis., U.S.A. 70 44 19N 91 54W
'Almā ash Sha'b 28 33 7N 35 9 E
Alma Ata 24 43 15N 76 57 E
Almada 13 38 40N 9 9W
Almaden, Australia 44 17 22S 144 40 E
Almadén, Spain 13 38 49N 4 52W
Almanor, L. 72 40 15N 121 11W
Almansa 13 38 51N 1 5W
Almanzor, Pico de 13 40 15N 5 18W
Almanzora → 13 37 14N 1 46W
Almazán 13 41 30N 2 30W
Almeirim 79 1 30S 52 34W
Almelo 11 52 22N 6 42 E
Almendralejo 13 38 41N 6 26W
Almería 13 36 52N 2 27W
Almirante 75 9 10N 82 30W
Almora 32 29 38N 79 40 E
Alnwick 6 55 25N 1 42W
Alon 33 22 12N 95 5 E
Alor 35 8 15S 124 30 E
Alor Setar 34 6 7N 100 22 E
Aloysius Mt. 47 26 0S 128 38 E
Alpena 68 45 6N 83 24W
Alpes-de-Haute-Provence □ 12 44 8N 6 10 E
Alpes-Maritimes □ 12 43 55N 7 10 E
Alpha 44 23 39S 146 37 E
Alphonse 3 7 0S 52 45 E
Alpine, Ariz., U.S.A. 73 33 57N 109 4W
Alpine, Tex., U.S.A. 71 30 25N 103 35W
Alps 14 47 0N 8 0 E
Alroy Downs 44 19 20S 136 5 E
Alsace 12 48 15N 7 25 E
Alsask 65 51 21N 109 59W
Alsásua 13 42 54N 2 10W
Alsten 20 65 58N 12 40 E
Alta 20 69 57N 23 10 E
Alta Gracia 80 31 40S 64 30W
Alta Lake 64 50 10N 123 0W
Altaelva → 20 69 46N 23 45 E
Altafjorden 20 70 5N 23 5 E
Altagracia 78 10 45N 71 30W
Altai = Aerht'ai Shan 37 46 40N 92 45 E
Altai Mts. 26 46 40N 92 45 E
Altamaha → 69 31 19N 81 17W
Altamira 79 3 12S 52 10W
Altanbulag 37 50 16N 106 30 E
Altar 74 30 40N 111 50W
Altata 74 24 30N 108 0W
Altavista 68 37 9N 79 22W
Altay 37 47 48N 88 10 E
Alto Adige = Trentino Alto Adige □ 18 46 30N 11 0 E
Alto-Alentejo 13 39 0N 7 40W
Alto Araguaia 79 17 15S 53 20W
Alto Cuchumatanes = Cuchumatanes, Sierra de los 75 15 35N 91 25W
Alto Molocue 55 15 50S 37 35 E
Alton 70 38 55N 90 5W
Alton Downs 45 26 7S 138 57 E
Altona 14 53 32N 9 56 E
Altoona 68 40 32N 78 24W
Altun Shan 37 38 30N 88 0 E
Alturas 72 41 36N 120 37W
Altus 71 34 30N 99 25W
Alùla 29 11 50N 50 45 E
Alusi 35 7 35S 131 40 E
Alva 71 36 50N 98 50W
Alvarado, Mexico 74 18 40N 95 50W
Alvarado, U.S.A. 71 32 25N 97 15W
Alvaro Obregón, Presa 74 27 55N 109 52W
Alvear 80 29 5S 56 30W
Alvesta 21 56 54N 14 35 E
Alvie 45 38 14S 143 30 E
Alvin 71 29 23N 95 12W
Älvkarleby 21 60 34N 17 26 E
Älvsborgs län □ 21 58 30N 12 30 E
Älvsbyn 20 65 40N 21 0 E
Alwar 32 27 38N 76 34 E
Alxa Zuoqi 38 38 50N 105 40 E
Alyaskitovyy 25 64 45N 141 30 E
Alyata 23 39 58N 49 25 E
Alyth 8 56 38N 3 15W
Alzada 70 45 3N 104 22W
Am Dam 51 12 40N 20 35 E
Am-Timan 51 11 0N 20 10 E
Amadeus, L. 47 24 54S 131 0 E
Amâdi, Sudan 51 5 29N 30 25 E
Amadi, Zaïre 54 3 40N 26 40 E
Amadjuak 61 64 0N 72 39W
Amadjuak L. 61 65 0N 71 8W
Amagasaki 36 34 42N 135 20 E
Amakusa-Shotō 36 32 15N 130 10 E
Amalner 32 21 5N 75 5 E
Amambay, Cordillera de 80 23 0S 55 45W
Amangeldy 24 50 10N 65 10 E
Amapá 79 2 5N 50 50W
Amapá □ 79 1 40N 52 0W
Amarante 79 6 14S 42 50W
Amaranth 65 50 36N 98 43W
Amargosa 79 13 2S 39 36W
Amarillo 71 35 14N 101 46W
Amaro, Mt. 18 42 5N 14 6 E
Amasra 30 41 45N 32 30 E
Amassama 53 5 1N 6 2 E
Amasya 30 40 40N 35 50 E
Amatikulu 57 29 3S 31 33 E
Amatitlán 75 14 29N 90 38W
Amazon = Amazonas → 79 0 5S 50 0W
Amazonas □ 78 4 0S 62 0W
Amazonas → 79 0 5S 50 0W
Ambahakily 57 21 36S 43 41 E
Ambala 32 30 23N 76 56 E
Ambalavao 57 21 50S 46 56 E
Ambalindum 44 23 23S 135 0 E
Ambam 54 2 20N 11 15 E
Ambanja 57 13 40S 48 27 E
Ambarchik 25 69 40N 162 20 E
Ambarijeby 57 14 56S 47 41 E
Ambaro, Helodranon' 57 13 23S 48 38 E
Ambartsevo 24 57 30N 83 52 E
Ambato 78 1 5S 78 42W
Ambato Boeny 57 16 28S 46 43 E
Ambatofinandrahana 57 20 33S 46 48 E
Ambatolampy 57 19 20S 47 35 E
Ambatondrazaka 57 17 55S 48 28 E
Ambatosoratra 57 17 37S 48 31 E
Ambenja 57 15 17S 46 58 E
Amberg 14 49 25N 11 52 E
Ambergris Cay 74 18 0N 88 0W
Amberley 43 43 9S 172 44 E
Ambikapur 33 23 15N 83 15 E
Ambilobé 57 13 10S 49 3 E
Ambinanindrano 57 20 5S 48 23 E
Ambleside 6 54 26N 2 58W
Ambo 78 10 5S 76 10W
Ambodifototra 57 16 59S 49 52 E
Ambodilazana 57 18 6S 49 10 E
Ambohimahasoa 57 21 7S 47 13 E
Ambohimanga 57 20 52S 47 36 E
Ambohitra 57 12 30S 49 10 E
Ambon 35 3 35S 128 20 E
Ambositra 57 20 31S 47 25 E
Ambovombé 57 25 11S 46 5 E
Amboy 73 34 33N 115 51W
Amboyna I. 34 7 50N 112 50 E
Ambriz 54 7 48S 13 8 E
Amby 45 26 30S 148 11 E
Amchitka I. 60 51 30N 179 0W
Amderma 24 69 45N 61 30 E
Ameca 74 20 30N 104 0W
Ameca → 74 20 40N 105 15W
Amecameca 74 19 7N 98 46W
Ameland 11 53 27N 5 45 E
Amen 25 68 45N 180 0 E
American Falls 72 42 46N 112 56W
American Falls Res. 72 43 0N 112 50W
American Samoa ■ 43 14 20S 170 40W
Americus 69 32 0N 84 10W
Amersfoort, Neth. 11 52 9N 5 23 E
Amersfoort, S. Africa 57 26 59S 29 53 E
Amery, Australia 47 31 9S 117 5 E
Amery, Canada 65 56 34N 94 3W
Ames 70 42 0N 93 40W
Amga 25 60 50N 132 0 E
Amga → 25 62 38N 134 32 E
Amgu 25 45 45N 137 15 E
Amgun → 25 52 56N 139 38 E
Amherst, Burma 33 16 2N 97 20 E
Amherst, Canada 63 45 48N 64 8W
Amherst, U.S.A. 71 34 0N 102 24W
Amherstburg 62 42 6N 83 6W
Amiata, Mte. 18 42 54N 11 40 E
Amiens 12 49 54N 2 16 E
Amirante Is. 3 6 0S 53 0 E
Amisk L. 65 54 35N 102 15W
Amite 71 30 47N 90 31W
Amlwch 6 53 24N 4 21W
'Ammān 28 31 57N 35 52 E
Ammanford 7 51 48N 4 0W
Ammi'ad 28 32 55N 35 32 E
Amorgós 19 36 50N 25 57 E
Amory 69 33 59N 88 29W
Amos 62 48 35N 78 5W
Amoy = Xiamen 38 24 25N 118 4 E
Ampanihy 57 24 40S 44 45 E
Ampasindava, Helodranon' 57 13 40S 48 15 E
Ampasindava, Saikanosy 57 13 42S 47 55 E
Ampenan 34 8 35S 116 13 E
Ampotaka 57 25 3S 44 41 E
Ampoza 57 22 20S 44 44 E
Amqa 28 32 59N 35 10 E
Amqui 63 48 28N 67 27W
Amravati 32 20 55N 77 45 E
Amreli 32 21 35N 71 17 E
Amritsar 32 31 35N 74 57 E
Amroha 32 28 53N 78 30 E
Amsterdam, Neth. 11 52 23N 4 54 E
Amsterdam, U.S.A. 68 42 58N 74 10W
Amsterdam, I. 3 38 30S 77 30 E
Amudarya → 24 43 40N 59 0 E
Amundsen Gulf 60 71 0N 124 0W
Amuntai 34 2 28S 115 25 E
Amur → 25 52 56N 141 10 E
Amurang 35 1 5N 124 40 E
Amuri Pass 43 42 31S 172 11 E
Amursk 25 50 14N 136 54 E
Amurzet 25 47 50N 131 5 E
An Nafūd 30 28 15N 41 0 E
An Najaf 30 32 3N 44 15 E
An Nāqūrah 28 33 7N 35 8 E
An Nāşirīyah 30 31 0N 46 15 E
An Nhon 34 13 55N 109 7 E
An Nîl □ 51 19 30N 33 0 E
An Nîl el Abyad □ 51 14 0N 32 15 E
An Nîl el Azraq □ 51 12 30N 34 30 E
An Nu'ayrīyah 30 27 30N 48 30 E
An Uaimh 9 53 39N 6 40W
Anabar → 25 73 8N 113 36 E
'Anabtā 28 32 19N 35 7 E
Anaconda 72 46 7N 113 0W
Anacortes 72 48 30N 122 40W
Anadarko 71 35 4N 98 15W
Anadolu 30 38 0N 30 0 E
Anadyr 25 64 35N 177 20 E
Anadyr → 25 64 55N 176 5 E
Anadyrskiy Zaliv 25 64 0N 180 0 E
'Ānah 30 34 25N 42 0 E
Anaheim 73 33 50N 118 0W
Anahim Lake 64 52 28N 125 18W
Anáhuac 74 27 14N 100 9W
Anakapalle 33 17 42N 83 6 E
Anakie 44 23 32S 147 45 E
Analalava 57 14 35S 48 0 E
Anambas, Kepulauan 34 3 20N 106 30 E
Anamoose 70 47 55N 100 20W
Anamosa 70 42 7N 91 30W
Anamur 30 36 8N 32 58 E
Anan 36 33 54N 134 40 E
Anantnag 32 33 45N 75 10 E
Anápolis 79 16 15S 48 50W
Anār 31 30 55N 55 13 E
Anārak 31 33 25N 53 40 E
Anatolia = Anadolu 30 38 0N 30 0 E
Anatone 72 46 9N 117 4W
Anatsogno 57 23 33S 43 46 E
Añatuya 80 28 20S 62 50W
Anaunethad L. 65 60 55N 104 25W
Anaye 51 19 15N 12 50 E
Anchorage 60 61 10N 149 50W
Ancohuma, Nevada 78 16 0S 68 50W
Ancón 78 11 50S 77 10W
Ancona 18 43 37N 13 30 E
Ancud 80 42 0S 73 50W
Ancud, G. de 80 42 0S 73 0W
Anda 38 46 24N 125 19 E
Andado 44 25 25S 135 15 E
Andalgalá 80 27 40S 66 30W
Åndalsnes 20 62 35N 7 43 E
Andalucía □ 13 37 35N 5 0W
Andalusia 69 31 19N 86 30W
Andalusia □ = Andalucía □ 13 37 35N 5 0W
Andaman Is. 3 12 30N 92 30 E
Andaman Sea 34 13 0N 96 0 E
Andara 56 18 2S 21 9 E
Andenne 11 50 30N 5 5 E
Anderson, Calif., U.S.A. 72 40 30N 122 19W
Anderson, Ind., U.S.A. 68 40 5N 85 40W
Anderson, Mo., U.S.A. 71 36 43N 94 29W
Anderson, S.C., U.S.A. 69 34 32N 82 40W
Anderson → 60 69 42N 129 0W
Anderson, Mt. 57 25 5S 30 42 E
Andes 78 5 40N 75 53W
Andes, Cord. de los 78 20 0S 68 0W
Andfjorden 20 69 10N 16 20 E
Andhra Pradesh □ 32 16 0N 79 0 E
Andikíthira 19 35 52N 23 15 E
Andizhan 24 41 10N 72 0 E
Andkhvoy 31 36 52N 65 8 E
Andoany 57 13 25S 48 16 E
Andong 38 36 40N 128 43 E
Andorra ■ 13 42 30N 1 30 E
Andorra La Vella 13 42 31N 1 32 E
Andover 7 51 13N 1 29W
Andrahary, Mt. 57 13 37S 49 17 E
Andramasina 57 19 11S 47 35 E
Andranopasy 57 21 17S 43 44 E
Andreanof Is. 60 52 0N 178 0W
Andrewilla 45 26 31S 139 17 E
Andrews, S.C., U.S.A. 69 33 29N 79 30W
Andrews, Tex., U.S.A. 71 32 18N 102 33W
Ándria 18 41 13N 16 17 E
Andriba 57 17 30S 46 58 E
Androka 57 24 58S 44 2 E
Andropov 22 58 5N 38 50 E
Ándros 19 37 50N 24 57 E
Andros I. 75 24 30N 78 0W
Andros Town 75 24 43N 77 47W
Andújar 13 38 3N 4 5W
Andulo 54 11 25S 16 45 E
Anegada I. 75 18 45N 64 20W
Anegada Passage 75 18 15N 63 45W
Anécho 53 6 12N 1 34 E
Aneto, Pico de 13 42 37N 0 40 E
Angamos, Punta 80 23 1S 70 32W
Ang'angxi 38 47 10N 123 48 E
Angara → 25 58 30N 97 0 E
Angarsk 25 52 30N 104 0 E
Angas Downs 47 25 2S 132 14 E
Angas Hills 46 23 0S 127 50 E
Angaston 45 34 30S 139 8 E
Ånge 20 62 31N 15 35 E
Ángel de la Guarda, I. 74 29 30N 113 30W
Angeles 35 15 9N 120 33 E
Ängelholm 21 56 15N 12 58 E
Angellala 45 26 24S 146 54 E

Balashov

Ashdot Yaaqov 28 32 39N 35 35 E
Asheboro 69 35 43N 79 46W
Asherton 71 28 25N 99 43W
Asheville 69 35 39N 82 30W
Asheweig → 62 54 17N 87 12W
Ashford, Australia 45 29 15S 151 3 E
Ashford, U.K. 7 51 8N 0 53 E
Ashford, U.S.A. 72 46 45N 122 2W
Ashikaga 36 36 28N 139 29 E
Ashizuri-Zaki 36 32 44N 133 0 E
Ashkhabad 24 38 0N 57 50 E
Ashland, Kans., U.S.A. 71 37 13N 99 43W
Ashland, Ky., U.S.A. 68 38 25N 82 40W
Ashland, Maine, U.S.A. 63 46 34N 68 26W
Ashland, Mont., U.S.A. 72 45 41N 106 12W
Ashland, Nebr., U.S.A. 70 41 5N 96 27W
Ashland, Ohio, U.S.A. 68 40 52N 82 20W
Ashland, Oreg., U.S.A. 72 42 10N 122 38W
Ashland, Va., U.S.A. 68 37 46N 77 30W
Ashland, Wis., U.S.A. 70 46 40N 90 52W
Ashley 70 46 3N 99 23W
Ashmont 64 54 7N 111 35W
Ashmore Reef 46 12 14S 123 5 E
Ashq'elon 28 31 42N 34 35 E
Ashtabula 68 41 52N 80 50W
Ashton, S. Africa 56 33 50S 20 5 E
Ashton, U.S.A. 72 44 6N 111 30W
Ashton-under-Lyne 6 53 30N 2 8W
Ashuanipi, L. 63 52 45N 66 15W
Asia 26 45 0N 75 0 E
Asia, Kepulauan 35 1 0N 131 13 E
Asifabad 32 19 20N 79 24 E
Asike 35 6 39S 140 24 E
Asilah 50 35 29N 6 0W
Asinara 18 41 5N 8 15 E
Asinara, G. dell' 18 41 0N 8 30 E
Asino 24 57 0N 86 0 E
'Asir □ 29 18 40N 42 30 E
Asir, Ras 29 11 55N 51 10 E
Askersund 21 58 53N 14 55 E
Askham 56 26 59S 20 47 E
Askja 20 65 3N 16 48W
Āsmār 31 35 10N 71 27 E
Asmara = Asmera 51 15 19N 38 55 E
Asmera 51 15 19N 38 55 E
Aso 36 33 0N 131 5 E
Asotin 72 46 20N 117 3W
Aspen 73 39 12N 106 56W
Aspermont 71 33 11N 100 15W
Aspiring, Mt. 43 44 23S 168 46 E
Asquith 65 52 8N 107 13W
Assam □ 33 26 0N 93 0 E
Asse 11 50 24N 4 10 E
Assen 11 53 0N 6 35 E
Assini 50 5 9N 3 17W
Assiniboia 65 49 40N 105 59W
Assiniboine → 65 49 53N 97 8W
Assis 80 22 40S 50 20W
Assisi 18 43 4N 12 36 E
Assynt, L. 8 58 25N 5 15W
Astara 23 38 30N 48 50 E
Asti 18 44 54N 8 11 E
Astipálaia 19 36 32N 26 22 E
Astorga 13 42 29N 6 8W
Astoria 72 46 16N 123 50W
Astrakhan 23 46 25N 48 5 E
Astrakhan-Bazàr 23 39 14N 48 30 E
Asturias 13 43 15N 6 0W
Asunción 80 25 10S 57 30W
Asunción, La 78 11 2N 63 53W
Aswân 51 24 4N 32 57 E
Aswân High Dam = Sadd el Aali 51 23 54N 32 54 E
Asyût 51 27 11N 31 4 E
At Ţafilah 30 30 45N 35 30 E
At Tā'if 29 21 5N 40 27 E
Aţ Ţur 28 31 47N 35 14 E
Aţ Ţurrah 28 32 39N 35 59 E
Atacama, Desierto de 80 24 0S 69 20W
Atacama, Salar de 80 23 30S 68 20W
Atakpamé 53 7 31N 1 13 E
Atalaya 78 10 45S 73 50W
Atami 36 35 5N 139 4 E
Atapupu 35 9 0S 124 51 E
Atâr 50 20 30N 13 5W
Atara 25 63 10N 129 10 E
Atascadero 73 35 32N 120 44W
Atasu 24 48 30N 71 0 E
Atauro 35 8 10S 125 30 E
Atbara 51 17 42N 33 59 E
'Atbara → 51 17 40N 33 56 E
Atbasar 24 51 48N 68 20 E
Atchafalaya B. 71 29 30N 91 20W
Atchison 70 39 40N 95 10W
Ath 11 50 38N 3 47 E
Athabasca 64 54 45N 113 20W
Athabasca → 65 58 40N 110 50W
Athabasca, L. 65 59 15N 109 15W
Athboy 9 53 37N 6 55W
Athenry 9 53 18N 8 45W
Athens = Athínai 19 37 58N 23 46 E
Athens, Ala., U.S.A. 69 34 49N 86 58W
Athens, Ga., U.S.A. 69 33 56N 83 24W
Athens, Ohio, U.S.A. 68 39 25N 82 6W
Athens, Tenn., U.S.A. 69 35 45N 84 38W
Athens, Tex., U.S.A. 71 32 11N 95 48W
Atherton 44 17 17S 145 30 E
Athínai 19 37 58N 23 46 E
Athlone 9 53 26N 7 57W
Atholl, Forest of 8 56 51N 3 50W
Atholville 63 47 59N 66 43W
Áthos 19 40 9N 24 22 E
Athy 9 53 0N 7 0W
Ati 51 13 13N 18 20 E
Atico 78 16 14S 73 40W
Atikokan 62 48 45N 91 37W
Atikonak L. 63 52 40N 64 32W
Atka 25 60 50N 151 48 E
Atkinson 70 42 35N 98 59W
Atlanta, Ga., U.S.A. 69 33 50N 84 24W
Atlanta, Tex., U.S.A. 71 33 7N 94 8W
Atlantic 70 41 25N 95 0W
Atlantic City 68 39 25N 74 25W
Atlantic Ocean 2 0 0 20 0W
Atlas Mts. = Haut Atlas 50 32 30N 5 0W
Atlin 60 59 31N 133 41W
Atlin, L. 64 59 26N 133 45W
'Atlit 28 32 42N 34 56 E
Atmore 69 31 2N 87 30W
Atoka 71 34 22N 96 10W
Atoyac → 74 16 30N 97 31W
Atrak → 31 37 50N 57 0 E
Atsuta 36 43 24N 141 26 E
Attalla 69 34 2N 86 5W
Attawapiskat 62 52 56N 82 24W
Attawapiskat → 62 52 57N 82 18W
Attawapiskat, L. 62 52 18N 87 54W
Attica 68 40 20N 87 15W
Attikamagen L. 63 55 0N 66 30W
'Attīl 28 32 23N 35 4 E
Attleboro 68 41 56N 71 18W
Attock 32 33 52N 72 20 E
Attopeu 34 14 48N 106 50 E
Attur 32 11 35N 78 30 E
Atuel → 80 36 17S 66 50W
Åtvidaberg 21 58 12N 16 0 E
Atwater 73 37 21N 120 37W
Atwood 70 39 52N 101 3W
Au Sable → 68 44 25N 83 20W
Au Sable Pt. 62 46 40N 86 10W
Aube □ 12 48 15N 4 10 E
Aube → 12 48 34N 3 43 E
Auburn, Ala., U.S.A. 69 32 37N 85 30W
Auburn, Calif., U.S.A. 72 38 53N 121 4W
Auburn, Ind., U.S.A. 68 41 20N 85 0W
Auburn, N.Y., U.S.A. 68 42 57N 76 39W
Auburn, Nebr., U.S.A. 70 40 25N 95 50W
Auburn Range 45 25 15S 150 30 E
Auburndale 69 28 5N 81 45W
Aubusson 12 45 57N 2 11 E
Auch 12 43 39N 0 36 E
Auckland 43 36 52S 174 46 E
Auckland Is. 40 50 40S 166 5 E
Aude □ 12 43 8N 2 28 E
Aude → 12 43 13N 3 14 E
Auden 62 50 14N 87 53W
Audubon 70 41 43N 94 56W
Augathella 45 25 48S 146 35 E
Augrabies Falls 56 28 35S 20 20 E
Augsburg 14 48 22N 10 54 E
Augusta, Italy 18 37 14N 15 12 E
Augusta, Ark., U.S.A. 71 35 17N 91 25W
Augusta, Ga., U.S.A. 69 33 29N 81 59W
Augusta, Kans., U.S.A. 71 37 40N 97 0W
Augusta, Maine, U.S.A. 63 44 20N 69 46W
Augusta, Mont., U.S.A. 72 47 30N 112 29W
Augusta, Wis., U.S.A. 70 44 41N 91 8W
Augustów 15 53 51N 23 0 E
Augustus, Mt. 47 24 20S 116 50 E
Augustus Downs 44 18 35S 139 55 E
Augustus I. 46 15 20S 124 30 E
Ault 70 40 40N 104 42W
Aunis 12 46 5N 0 50W
Auponhia 35 1 58S 125 27 E
Aurangabad, Bihar, India 33 24 45N 84 18 E
Aurangabad, Maharashtra, India 32 19 50N 75 23 E
Aurillac 12 44 55N 2 26 E
Aurora, S. Africa 56 32 40S 18 29 E
Aurora, Colo., U.S.A. 70 39 44N 104 55W
Aurora, Ill., U.S.A. 68 41 42N 88 12W
Aurora, Mo., U.S.A. 71 36 58N 93 42W
Aurora, Nebr., U.S.A. 70 40 55N 98 0W
Aurukun Mission 44 13 20S 141 45 E
Aus 56 26 35S 16 12 E
Aust-Agder fylke □ 21 58 55N 7 40 E
Austerlitz = Slavkov 14 49 10N 16 52 E
Austin, Minn., U.S.A. 70 43 37N 92 59W
Austin, Nev., U.S.A. 72 39 30N 117 1W
Austin, Tex., U.S.A. 71 30 20N 97 45W
Austin, L. 47 27 40S 118 0 E
Austral Downs 44 20 30S 137 45 E
Austral Is. = Tubuai Is. 41 25 0S 150 0W
Austral Seamount Chain 41 24 0S 150 0W
Australia ■ 3 23 0S 135 0 E
Australian Alps 45 36 30S 148 30 E
Australian Cap. Terr. □ 45 35 30S 149 0 E
Austria ■ 14 47 0N 14 0 E
Austvågøy 20 68 20N 14 40 E
Autlán 74 19 40N 104 30W
Autun 12 46 58N 4 17 E
Auvergne, Australia 46 15 39S 130 1 E
Auvergne, France 12 45 20N 3 15 E
Auxerre 12 47 48N 3 32 E
Avallon 12 47 30N 3 53 E
Avalon Pen. 63 47 30N 53 20W
Aveiro, Brazil 79 3 10S 55 5W
Aveiro, Portugal 13 40 37N 8 38W
Āvej 30 35 40N 49 15 E
Avellaneda 80 34 50S 58 10W
Avellino 18 40 54N 14 46 E
Aversa 18 40 58N 14 11 E
Avery 72 47 22N 115 56W
Aves, I. de 75 15 45N 63 55W
Aves, Is. de 75 12 0N 67 30W
Avesta 21 60 9N 16 10 E
Aveyron □ 12 44 22N 2 45 E
Aviá Terai 80 26 45S 60 50W
Avignon 12 43 57N 4 50 E
Ávila 13 40 39N 4 43W
Avilés 13 43 35N 5 57W
Avoca, Australia 45 37 5S 143 26 E
Avoca, Ireland 9 52 52N 6 13W
Avoca → 45 35 40S 143 43 E
Avola 64 51 45N 119 19W
Avon 70 43 0N 98 3W
Avon □ 7 51 30N 2 40W
Avon →, Australia 47 31 40S 116 7 E
Avon →, Avon, U.K. 7 51 30N 2 43W
Avon →, Hants., U.K. 7 50 44N 1 45W
Avon →, Warwick, U.K. 7 52 0N 2 9W
Avonlea 65 50 0N 105 0W
Avonmouth 7 51 30N 2 42W
Avranches 12 48 40N 1 20W
'Awālī 31 26 0N 50 30 E
'Awartā 28 32 10N 35 17 E
Awash 29 9 1N 40 10 E
Awatere → 43 41 37S 174 10 E
Awbārī 51 26 46N 12 57 E
Awe, L. 8 56 15N 5 15W
Awgu 53 6 4N 7 24 E
Awjilah 51 29 8N 21 7 E
Axarfjörður 20 66 15N 16 45W
Axel Heiberg I. 58 80 0N 90 0W
Axim 50 4 51N 2 15W
Axminster 7 50 47N 3 1W
Ayabaca 78 4 40S 79 53W
Ayabe 36 35 20N 135 20 E
Ayacucho, Argentina 80 37 5S 58 20W
Ayacucho, Peru 78 13 0S 74 0W
Ayaguz 24 48 10N 80 0 E
Ayamonte 13 37 12N 7 24W
Ayan 25 56 30N 138 16 E
Ayaviri 78 14 50S 70 35W
Āybak 31 36 15N 68 5 E
Ayers Rock 47 25 23S 131 5 E
Ayios Evstrátios 19 39 34N 24 58 E
Aykin 22 62 15N 49 56 E
Aylesbury 7 51 48N 0 49W
Aylmer L. 60 64 0N 110 8W
'Ayn 'Arīk 28 31 54N 35 8 E
Ayn Dār 30 25 55N 49 10 E
Ayn Zālah 30 36 45N 42 35 E
Ayon, Ostrov 25 69 50N 169 0 E
Ayr, Australia 44 19 35S 147 25 E
Ayr, U.K. 8 55 28N 4 37W
Ayr → 8 55 29N 4 40W
Ayre, Pt. of 6 54 27N 4 21W
Aytos 19 42 42N 27 16 E
Ayu, Kepulauan 35 0 35N 131 5 E
Ayutla 74 16 58N 99 17W
Ayvalık 30 39 20N 26 46 E
Az Zahrān 30 26 10N 50 7 E
Az Zarqā 28 32 5N 36 4 E
Az-Zilfī 30 26 12N 44 52 E
Az Zubayr 30 30 20N 47 50 E
Azamgarh 33 26 5N 83 13 E
Āzarbāyjān-e Gharbī □ 30 37 0N 44 30 E
Āzarbāyjān-e Sharqī □ 30 37 20N 47 0 E
Azare 53 11 55N 10 10 E
Azbine = Aïr 50 18 30N 8 0 E
Azerbaijan S.S.R. □ 23 40 20N 48 0 E
Azogues 78 2 35S 78 0W
Azor 28 32 2N 34 48 E
Azores 2 38 44N 29 0W
Azov 23 47 3N 39 25 E
Azov Sea = Azovskoye More 24 46 0N 36 30 E
Azovskoye More 24 46 0N 36 30 E
Azovy 24 64 55N 64 35 E
Aztec 73 36 54N 108 0W
Azúa de Compostela 75 18 25N 70 44W
Azuaga 13 38 16N 5 39W
Azuero, Pen. de 75 7 30N 80 30W
Azul 80 36 42S 59 43W

B

Ba Don 34 17 45N 106 26 E
Ba Ria 34 10 30N 107 10 E
Ba Xian 38 39 8N 116 22 E
Baa 35 10 50S 123 0 E
Baarle Nassau 11 51 27N 4 56 E
Baarn 11 52 12N 5 17 E
Bab el Mandeb 29 12 35N 43 25 E
Babahoyo 78 1 40S 79 30W
Babakin 47 32 7S 118 1 E
Babana 53 10 31N 3 46 E
Babar 35 8 0S 129 30 E
Babb 72 48 56N 113 27W
Babinda 44 17 20S 145 56 E
Babine 64 55 22N 126 37W
Babine → 64 55 45N 127 44W
Babine L. 64 54 48N 126 0W
Babo 35 2 30S 133 30 E
Bābol 31 36 40N 52 50 E
Bābol Sar 31 36 45N 52 45 E
Baboua 54 5 49N 14 58 E
Babura 53 12 51N 8 59 E
Babuyan Chan. 35 18 40N 121 30 E
Babylon 30 32 40N 44 30 E
Bacabal 79 4 15S 44 45W
Bacan 35 8 27S 126 27 E
Bacan, Kepulauan 35 0 35S 127 30 E
Bacan, Pulau 35 0 50S 127 30 E
Bacarra 35 18 15N 120 37 E
Bacău 15 46 35N 26 55 E
Bacerac 74 30 18N 108 50W
Bachelina 24 57 45N 67 20 E
Back → 60 65 10N 104 0W
Backstairs Passage 45 35 40S 138 5 E
Bacolod 35 10 40N 122 57 E
Bad → 70 44 22N 100 22W
Bad Axe 68 43 48N 82 59W
Bad Ischl 14 47 44N 13 38 E
Bad Lands 70 43 40N 102 10W
Badagara 32 11 35N 75 40 E
Badajoz 13 38 50N 6 59W
Badakhshān □ 31 36 30N 71 0 E
Badalona 13 41 26N 2 15 E
Badalzai 32 29 50N 65 35 E
Badampahar 33 22 10N 86 10 E
Badanah 30 30 58N 41 30 E
Badarinath 32 30 45N 79 30 E
Badas 34 4 33N 114 25 E
Badas, Kepulauan 34 0 45N 107 5 E
Baddo → 31 28 0N 64 20 E
Bade 35 7 10S 139 35 E
Baden 14 48 1N 16 13 E
Baden-Baden 14 48 45N 8 15 E
Baden-Württemberg □ 14 48 40N 9 0 E
Badgastein 14 47 7N 13 9 E
Badger 63 49 0N 56 4W
Bādghīsāt □ 31 35 0N 63 0 E
Badin 32 24 38N 68 54 E
Badong 39 31 1N 110 23 E
Baduen 29 7 15N 47 40 E
Badulla 32 7 1N 81 7 E
Baeza 13 37 57N 3 25W
Bafatá 50 12 8N 14 40W
Baffin B. 58 72 0N 64 0W
Baffin I. 61 68 0N 75 0W
Bafia 54 4 40N 11 10 E
Bafing → 50 13 49N 10 50W
Bafoulabé 50 13 50N 10 55W
Bāfq 31 31 40N 55 25 E
Bafra 30 41 34N 35 54 E
Bāft 31 29 15N 56 38 E
Bafut 53 6 6N 10 2 E
Bafwasende 54 1 3N 27 5 E
Bagamoyo 54 6 28S 38 55 E
Baganga 35 7 34N 126 33 E
Bagani 56 18 7S 21 41 E
Bagansiapiapi 34 2 12N 100 50 E
Bagdarin 25 54 26N 113 36 E
Bagé 80 31 20S 54 15W
Bagenalstown = Muine Bheag 9 52 42N 6 57W
Baggs 72 41 8N 107 46W
Baghdād 30 33 20N 44 30 E
Baghlān 31 36 12N 69 0 E
Baghlān □ 31 36 0N 68 30 E
Bagley 70 47 30N 95 22W
Bagotville 63 48 22N 70 54W
Baguio 35 16 26N 120 34 E
Bahama, Canal Viejo de 75 22 10N 77 30W
Bahamas ■ 75 24 0N 75 0W
Baharampur 33 24 2N 88 27 E
Bahawalpur 32 29 24N 71 40 E
Bahía = Salvador 79 13 0S 38 30W
Bahía □ 79 12 0S 42 0W
Bahía, Is. de la 75 16 45N 86 15W
Bahía Blanca 80 38 35S 62 13W
Bahía de Caráquez 78 0 40S 80 27W
Bahía Laura 80 48 10S 66 30W
Bahía Negra 78 20 5S 58 5W
Bahr Aouk → 54 8 40N 19 0 E
Bahr el Ahmar □ 51 20 0N 35 0 E
Bahr el Ghazâl □ 51 7 0N 28 0 E
Bahr Salamat → 51 9 20N 18 0 E
Bahraich 33 27 38N 81 37 E
Bahrain ■ 31 26 0N 50 35 E
Baia Mare 15 47 40N 23 35 E
Baïbokoum 51 7 46N 15 43 E
Baicheng 38 45 38N 122 42 E
Baidoa 29 3 8N 43 30 E
Baie Comeau 63 49 12N 68 10W
Baie-St-Paul 63 47 28N 70 32W
Baie Trinité 63 49 25N 67 20W
Baie Verte 63 49 55N 56 12W
Ba'ījī 30 35 0N 43 30 E
Baikal, L. = Baykal, Oz. 25 53 0N 108 0 E
Baile Atha Cliath = Dublin 9 53 20N 6 18W
Bailundo 55 12 10S 15 50 E
Bainbridge 69 30 53N 84 34W
Baing 35 10 14S 120 34 E
Bainville 70 48 8N 104 10W
Bā'ir 30 30 45N 36 55 E
Baird 71 32 25N 99 25W
Baird Mts. 60 67 10N 160 15W
Bairin Youqi 38 43 30N 118 35 E
Bairin Zuoqi 38 43 58N 119 15 E
Bairnsdale 45 37 48S 147 36 E
Baitadi 33 29 35N 80 25 E
Baixo-Alentejo 13 38 0N 8 30W
Baiyin 38 36 45N 104 14 E
Baiyu Shan 38 37 15N 107 30 E
Baja 15 46 12N 18 59 E
Baja, Pta. 74 29 50N 116 0W
Baja California 74 31 10N 115 12W
Bajimba, Mt. 45 29 17S 152 6 E
Bajo Nuevo 75 15 40N 78 50W
Bajool 44 23 40S 150 35 E
Bakala 51 6 15N 20 20 E
Bakchar 24 57 1N 82 5 E
Bakel 50 14 56N 12 20W
Baker, Calif., U.S.A. 73 35 16N 116 8W
Baker, Mont., U.S.A. 70 46 22N 104 12W
Baker, Oreg., U.S.A. 72 44 50N 117 55W
Baker, L., Australia 47 26 54S 126 5 E
Baker, L., Canada 60 64 0N 96 0W
Baker I. 40 0 10N 176 35W
Baker Lake 60 64 20N 96 3W
Baker Mt. 72 48 50N 121 49W
Bakers Creek 44 21 13S 149 7 E
Baker's Dozen Is. 62 56 45N 78 45W
Bakersfield 73 35 25N 119 0W
Bākhtarān 30 34 23N 47 0 E
Bākhtarān □ 30 34 0N 46 30 E
Bakinskikh Komissarov, im. 26 30 39 20N 49 15 E
Bakkafjörður 20 66 2N 14 48W
Bakkagerði 20 65 31N 13 49W
Bakony Forest = Bakony Hegyseg 15 47 10N 17 30 E
Bakony Hegyseg 15 47 10N 17 30 E
Bakouma 51 5 40N 22 56 E
Baku 23 40 25N 49 45 E
Bal'ā 28 32 20N 35 6 E
Bala, L. = Tegid, L. 6 52 53N 3 38W
Balabac, Str. 34 7 53N 117 5 E
Balabac I. 34 8 0N 117 0 E
Balabakk 30 34 0N 36 10 E
Balabalangan, Kepulauan 34 2 20S 117 30 E
Balaghat 32 21 49N 80 12 E
Balaghat Ra. 32 18 50N 76 30 E
Balaguer 13 41 50N 0 50 E
Balaklava, Australia 45 34 7S 138 22 E
Balaklava, U.S.S.R. 23 44 30N 33 30 E
Balakovo 22 52 4N 47 55 E
Balashov 22 51 30N 43 10 E

Balasore

Balasore = Baleshwar 33 21 35N 87 3 E
Balaton 15 46 50N 17 40 E
Balboa 75 9 0N 79 30W
Balboa Hill 74 9 6N 79 44W
Balbriggan 9 53 35N 6 10W
Balcarce 80 38 0S 58 10W
Balcarres 65 50 50N 103 35W
Balchik 19 43 28N 28 11 E
Balclutha 43 46 15S 169 45 E
Bald Hd. 47 35 6S 118 1 E
Bald I. 47 34 57S 118 27 E
Bald Knob 71 35 20N 91 35W
Baldock L. 65 56 33N 97 57W
Baldwin, Fla., U.S.A. 69 30 15N 82 10W
Baldwin, Mich., U.S.A. 68 43 54N 85 53W
Baldwinsville 68 43 10N 76 19W
Baleares, Is. 13 39 30N 3 0 E
Balearic Is. = Baleares, Is. 13 39 30N 3 0 E
Baler 35 15 46N 121 34 E
Baleshwar 33 21 35N 87 3 E
Balfe's Creek 44 20 12S 145 55 E
Balfour 57 26 38S 28 35 E
Balfouriyya 28 32 38N 35 18 E
Bali, Cameroon 53 5 54N 10 0 E
Bali, Indonesia 34 8 20S 115 0 E
Bali □ 34 8 20S 115 0 E
Bali, Selat 35 8 18S 114 25 E
Balikesir 30 39 35N 27 58 E
Balikpapan 34 1 10S 116 55 E
Balimbing 35 5 5N 119 58 E
Balipara 33 26 50N 92 45 E
Baliza 79 16 0S 52 20W
Balkan Mts. = Stara Planina 19 43 15N 23 0 E
Balkan Pen. 4 42 0N 22 0 E
Balkh 31 36 44N 66 47 E
Balkh □ 31 36 30N 67 0 E
Balkhash 24 46 50N 74 50 E
Balkhash, Ozero 24 46 0N 74 50 E
Balla 33 24 10N 91 35 E
Ballachulish 8 56 40N 5 10W
Balladonia 47 32 27S 123 51 E
Ballarat 45 37 33S 143 50 E
Ballard, L. 47 29 20S 120 10 E
Ballater 8 57 2N 3 2W
Ballenas, Canal de 74 29 10N 113 45W
Ballenas, Canal de 74 29 10N 113 45W
Ballidu 47 30 35S 116 45 E
Ballina, Australia 45 28 50S 153 31 E
Ballina, Mayo, Ireland 9 54 7N 9 10W
Ballina, Tipp., Ireland 9 52 49N 8 27W
Ballinasloe 9 53 20N 8 12W
Ballinger 71 31 45N 99 58W
Ballinrobe 9 53 36N 9 13W
Ballinskelligs B. 9 51 46N 10 11W
Ballycastle 9 55 12N 6 15W
Ballymena 9 54 53N 6 18W
Ballymena □ 9 54 53N 6 18W
Ballymoney 9 55 5N 6 30W
Ballymoney □ 9 55 5N 6 23W
Ballyshannon 9 54 30N 8 10W
Balmaceda 80 46 0S 71 50W
Balmoral, Australia 45 37 15S 141 48 E
Balmoral, U.K. 8 57 3N 3 13W
Balmorhea 71 31 2N 103 41W
Balonne → 45 28 47S 147 56 E
Balrampur 33 27 30N 82 20 E
Balranald 45 34 38S 143 33 E
Balsas → 74 17 55N 102 10W
Balta, U.S.A. 70 48 12N 100 7W
Balta, U.S.S.R. 23 48 2N 29 45 E
Baltic Sea 21 56 0N 20 0 E
Baltimore, Ireland 9 51 29N 9 22W
Baltimore, U.S.A. 68 39 18N 76 37W
Baluchistan □ 31 27 30N 65 0 E
Balygychan 25 63 56N 154 12 E
Bam 31 29 7N 58 14 E
Bama 53 11 33N 13 41 E
Bamako 50 12 34N 7 55W
Bamba 50 17 5N 1 24W
Bambari 51 5 40N 20 35 E
Bambaroo 44 18 50S 146 10 E
Bamberg, Germany 14 49 54N 10 53 E
Bamberg, U.S.A. 69 33 19N 81 1W
Bambili 54 3 40N 26 0 E
Bamenda 53 5 57N 10 11 E
Bamfield 64 48 45N 125 10W
Bāmīān □ 31 35 0N 67 0 E
Bamiancheng 38 43 15N 124 2 E
Bampūr 31 27 15N 60 21 E
Ban Don = Surat Thani 34 9 6N 99 20 E
Banaba 40 0 45S 169 50 E
Banalia 54 1 32N 25 5 E
Banam 34 11 20N 105 17 E
Banamba 50 13 29N 7 22W
Banana 44 24 28S 150 8 E
Bananal, I. do 79 11 30S 50 30W
Banaras = Varanasi 33 25 22N 83 0 E
Banbridge 9 54 21N 6 17W
Banbridge □ 9 54 21N 6 16W
Banbury 7 52 4N 1 21W
Banchory 8 57 3N 2 30W
Bancroft 62 45 3N 77 51W
Band-e Torkestān 31 35 30N 64 0 E
Banda 32 25 30N 80 26 E
Banda, Kepulauan 35 4 37S 129 50 E
Banda, La 80 27 45S 64 10W
Banda Aceh 34 5 35N 95 20 E
Banda Banda, Mt. 45 31 10S 152 28 E
Banda Elat 35 5 40S 133 5 E
Banda Sea 35 6 0S 130 0 E
Bandai-San 36 37 36N 140 4 E
Bandanaira 35 4 32S 129 54 E
Bandar = Machilipatnam 33 16 12N 81 8 E
Bandār 'Abbās 31 27 15N 56 15 E
Bandar-e Anzalī 30 37 30N 49 30 E
Bandar-e Chārak 31 26 45N 54 20 E
Bandar-e Deylam 30 30 5N 50 10 E
Bandar-e Khomeyni 30 30 30N 49 5 E
Bandar-e Lengeh 31 26 35N 54 58 E
Bandar-e Ma'shur 30 30 35N 49 10 E
Bandar-e Nakhīlū 31 26 58N 53 30 E
Bandar-e Rīg 31 29 29N 50 38 E
Bandar-e Torkeman 31 37 0N 54 10 E
Bandar Maharani = Muar 34 2 3N 102 34 E
Bandar Penggaram = Batu Pahat 34 1 50N 102 56 E
Bandar Seri Begawan 34 4 52N 115 0 E
Bandawe 55 11 58S 34 5 E
Bandeira, Pico da 79 20 26S 41 47W
Bandera, Argentina 80 28 55S 62 20W
Bandera, U.S.A. 71 29 45N 99 3W
Banderas, B. de 74 20 40N 105 30W
Bandiagara 50 14 12N 3 29W
Bandırma 30 40 20N 28 0 E
Bandon 9 51 44N 8 45W
Bandon → 9 51 40N 8 41W
Bandundu 54 3 15S 17 22 E
Bandung 35 6 54S 107 36 E
Bandya 47 27 40S 122 5 E
Banes 75 21 0N 75 42W
Banff, Canada 64 51 10N 115 34W
Banff, U.K. 8 57 40N 2 32W
Banff Nat. Park 64 51 30N 116 15W
Banfora 50 10 40N 4 40W
Bang Saphan 34 11 14N 99 28 E
Bangalore 32 12 59N 77 40 E
Bangassou 54 4 55N 23 7 E
Banggai 35 1 40S 123 30 E
Banggi, P. 34 7 17N 117 12 E
Banghāzī 51 32 11N 20 3 E
Bangil 35 7 36S 112 50 E
Bangka, Pulau, Sulawesi, Indonesia 35 1 50N 125 5 E
Bangka, Pulau, Sumatera, Indonesia 34 2 0S 105 50 E
Bangka, Selat 34 2 30S 105 30 E
Bangkalan 35 7 2S 112 46 E
Bangkinang 34 0 18N 101 5 E
Bangko 34 2 5S 102 9 E
Bangkok 34 13 45N 100 35 E
Bangladesh ■ 33 24 0N 90 0 E
Bangong Tso 32 34 0N 78 20 E
Bangor, N. Ireland, U.K. 9 54 40N 5 40W
Bangor, Wales, U.K. 6 53 13N 4 9W
Bangor, U.S.A. 63 44 48N 68 42W
Bangued 35 17 40N 120 37 E
Bangui 54 4 23N 18 35 E
Bangweulu, L. 54 11 0S 30 0 E
Bani 75 18 16N 70 22W
Banī Na'īm 28 31 31N 35 10 E
Banī Suhaylah 28 31 21N 34 19 E
Banī Walīd 51 31 36N 13 53 E
Banīnah 51 32 0N 20 12 E
Bāniyās 30 35 10N 36 0 E
Banja Luka 18 44 49N 17 11 E
Banjar 35 7 24S 108 30 E
Banjarmasin 34 3 20S 114 35 E
Banjarnegara 35 7 24S 109 42 E
Banjul 50 13 28N 16 40W
Banka Banka 44 18 50S 134 0 E
Bankipore 33 25 35N 85 10 E
Banks I., B.C., Canada 64 53 20N 130 0W
Banks I., N.W.T., Canada 60 73 15N 121 30W
Banks Pen. 43 43 45S 173 15 E
Banks Str. 44 40 40S 148 10 E
Bankura 33 23 11N 87 18 E
Bann →, Down, U.K. 9 54 30N 6 31W
Bann →, Londonderry, U.K. 9 55 10N 6 34W
Banning 73 33 58N 116 52W
Banningville = Bandundu 54 3 15S 17 22 E
Bannockburn 8 56 5N 3 55W
Bannu 32 33 0N 70 18 E
Banská Bystrica 15 48 46N 19 14 E
Banská Štiavnica 15 48 25N 18 55 E
Banswara 32 23 32N 74 24 E
Banten 35 6 5S 106 8 E
Bantry 9 51 40N 9 28W
Bantry, B. 9 51 35N 9 50W
Bantul 35 7 55S 110 19 E
Banu 32 35 35N 69 5 E
Banyak, Kepulauan 34 2 10N 97 10 E
Banyo 53 6 52N 11 45 E
Banyumas 35 7 32S 109 18 E
Banyuwangi 35 8 13S 114 21 E
Banzyville = Mobayi 54 4 15N 21 8 E
Baocheng 39 33 12N 106 56 E
Baode 38 39 1N 111 5 E
Baoding 38 38 50N 115 28 E
Baoji 39 34 20N 107 5 E
Baojing 39 28 45N 109 41 E
Baokang 39 31 54N 111 12 E
Baoshan 37 25 10N 99 5 E
Baotou 38 40 32N 110 2 E
Baoying 39 33 17N 119 20 E
Bapatla 33 15 55N 80 30 E
Bāqa el Gharbīyya 28 32 25N 35 2 E
Ba'qūbah 30 33 45N 44 50 E
Bar 19 42 8N 19 8 E
Bar Harbor 63 44 15N 68 20W
Bar-le-Duc 12 48 47N 5 10 E
Barabai 34 2 32S 115 34 E
Barabinsk 24 55 20N 78 20 E
Baraboo 70 43 28N 89 46W
Baracaldo 13 43 18N 2 59W
Baracoa 75 20 20N 74 30W
Baraga 70 46 49N 88 29W
Barahona 75 18 13N 71 7W
Barail Range 33 25 15N 93 20 E
Barakhola 33 25 0N 92 45 E
Barakpur 33 22 44N 88 30 E
Barakula 45 26 30S 150 33 E
Baralaba 44 24 13S 149 50 E
Baralzon L. 65 60 0N 98 3W
Baramula 32 34 15N 74 20 E
Baran 32 25 9N 76 40 E
Baranof I. 60 57 0N 135 10W
Baranovichi 22 53 10N 26 0 E
Barão de Melgaço 78 11 50S 60 45W
Barapasi 35 2 15S 137 5 E
Barat Daya, Kepulauan 35 7 30S 128 0 E
Barataria B. 71 29 15N 89 45W
Barbacena 79 21 15S 43 56W
Barbacoas 78 1 45N 78 0W
Barbados ■ 75 13 0N 59 30W
Barberton, S. Africa 57 25 42S 31 2 E
Barberton, U.S.A. 68 41 0N 81 40W
Barbourville 69 36 57N 83 52W
Barbuda I. 75 17 30N 61 40W
Barca, La 74 20 20N 102 40W
Barcaldine 44 23 43S 145 6 E
Barcelona, Spain 13 41 21N 2 10 E
Barcelona, Venezuela 78 10 10N 64 40W
Barcelos 78 1 0S 63 0W
Barcoo → 44 25 30S 142 50 E
Barddhaman 33 23 14N 87 39 E
Bardera 29 2 20N 42 27 E
Bardi, Ra's 30 24 17N 37 31 E
Bardia 51 31 45N 25 0 E
Bardsey I. 6 52 46N 4 47W
Bardstown 68 37 50N 85 29W
Bareilly 32 28 22N 79 27 E
Barentu 51 15 2N 37 35 E
Barga 37 30 40N 81 20 E
Bargal 29 11 25N 51 0 E
Bargara 44 24 50S 152 25 E
Barge, La 72 42 12N 110 4W
Barguzin 25 53 37N 109 37 E
Barhi 33 24 15N 85 25 E
Bari 18 41 6N 16 52 E
Bari Doab 32 30 20N 73 0 E
Barīm 29 12 39N 43 25 E
Barinas 78 8 36N 70 15W
Baring, C. 60 70 0N 117 30W
Bârîs 51 24 42N 30 31 E
Barisal 33 22 45N 90 20 E
Barisan, Bukit 34 3 30S 102 15 E
Barito → 34 4 0S 114 50 E
Barkā' 31 23 40N 58 0 E
Barkley Sound 64 48 50N 125 10W
Barkly Downs 44 20 30S 138 30 E
Barkly East 56 30 58S 27 33 E
Barkly Tableland 44 17 50S 136 40 E
Barkly West 56 28 5S 24 31 E
Barksdale 71 29 47N 100 2W
Barlee, L. 47 29 15S 119 30 E
Barletta 18 41 20N 16 17 E
Barlow L. 65 62 0N 103 0W
Barmedman 45 34 9S 147 21 E
Barmer 32 25 45N 71 20 E
Barmera 45 34 15S 140 28 E
Barmouth 6 52 44N 4 3W
Barnard Castle 6 54 33N 1 55W
Barnato 45 31 38S 145 0 E
Barnaul 24 53 20N 83 40 E
Barnesville 69 33 6N 84 9W
Barnet 7 51 37N 0 15W
Barneveld 11 52 7N 5 36 E
Barngo 44 25 3S 147 20 E
Barnhart 71 31 10N 101 8W
Barnsley 6 53 33N 1 29W
Barnstaple 7 51 5N 4 3W
Barnsville 70 46 43N 96 28W
Baro 53 8 35N 6 18 E
Baroda = Vadodara 32 22 20N 73 10 E
Baroe 56 33 13S 24 33 E
Baron Ra. 46 23 30S 127 45 E
Barpeta 33 26 20N 91 10 E
Barques, Pte. aux 68 44 5N 82 55W
Barquísimeto 78 10 4N 69 19W
Barra, Brazil 79 11 5S 43 10W
Barra, U.K. 8 57 0N 7 30W
Barra, Sd. of 8 57 4N 7 25W
Barra do Corda 79 5 30S 45 10W
Barra do Piraí 79 22 30S 43 50W
Barra Falsa, Pta. da 57 22 58S 35 37 E
Barra Hd. 8 56 47N 7 40W
Barraba 45 30 21S 150 35 E
Barrackpur = Barakpur 33 22 44N 88 30 E
Barranca, Lima, Peru 78 10 45S 77 50W
Barranca, Loreto, Peru 78 4 50S 76 50W
Barrancabermeja 78 7 0N 73 50W
Barrancas 78 8 55N 62 5W
Barrancos 13 38 10N 6 58W
Barranqueras 80 27 30S 59 0W
Barranquilla 78 11 0N 74 50W
Barras 79 4 15S 42 18W
Barraute 62 48 26N 77 38W
Barre 68 44 15N 72 30W
Barreiras 79 12 8S 45 0W
Barreirinhas 79 2 30S 42 50W
Barreiro 13 38 40N 9 6W
Barreiros 79 8 49S 35 12W
Barren, Nosy 57 18 25S 43 40 E
Barretos 79 20 30S 48 35W
Barrhead 64 54 10N 114 24W
Barrie 62 44 24N 79 40W
Barrier Ra. 45 31 0S 141 30 E
Barrière 64 51 12N 120 7W
Barrington L. 65 56 55N 100 15W
Barrington Tops 45 32 6S 151 28 E
Barringun 45 29 1S 145 41 E
Barrow 60 71 16N 156 50W
Barrow → 9 52 10N 6 57W
Barrow Creek 44 21 30S 133 55 E
Barrow I. 46 20 45S 115 20 E
Barrow-in-Furness 6 54 8N 3 15W
Barrow Pt. 44 14 20S 144 40 E
Barrow Ra. 47 26 0S 127 40 E
Barry 7 51 23N 3 19W
Barry's Bay 62 45 29N 77 41W
Barsi 32 18 10N 75 50 E
Barsoi 33 25 48N 87 57 E
Barstow, Calif., U.S.A. 73 34 58N 117 2W
Barstow, Tex., U.S.A. 71 31 28N 103 24W
Bartica 78 6 25N 58 40W
Bartin 30 41 38N 32 21 E
Bartlesville 71 36 50N 95 58W
Bartlett 71 30 46N 97 30W
Bartlett, L. 64 63 5N 118 20W
Barton 47 30 31S 132 39 E
Barton-upon-Humber 6 53 41N 0 27W
Bartow 69 27 53N 81 49W
Barú, Volcan 75 8 55N 82 35W
Bas-Rhin □ 12 48 40N 7 30 E
Bāsa'idū 31 26 35N 55 20 E
Basankusa 54 1 5N 19 50 E
Basel 14 47 35N 7 35 E
Bashkir A.S.S.R. □ 22 54 0N 57 0 E
Basilan 35 6 35N 122 0 E
Basilan Str. 35 6 50N 122 0 E
Basildon 7 51 34N 0 29 E
Basilicata □ 18 40 30N 16 0 E
Basim = Washim 32 20 3N 77 0 E
Basin 72 44 22N 108 2W
Basingstoke 7 51 15N 1 5W
Baskatong, Rés. 62 46 46N 75 50W
Basle = Basel 14 47 35N 7 35 E
Basoka 54 1 16N 23 40 E
Basongo 54 4 15S 20 20 E
Basque Provinces = Vascongadas □ 13 42 50N 2 45W
Basra = Al Başrah 30 30 30N 47 50 E
Bass Rock 8 56 5N 2 40W
Bass Str. 44 39 15S 146 30 E
Bassano 64 50 48N 112 20W
Bassano del Grappa 18 45 45N 11 45 E
Bassar 53 9 19N 0 57 E
Bassas da India 55 22 0S 39 0 E
Basse-Terre 75 16 0N 61 40W
Bassein 33 16 45N 94 30 E
Basseterre 75 17 17N 62 43W
Bassett, Nebr., U.S.A. 70 42 37N 99 30W
Bassett, Va., U.S.A. 69 36 48N 79 59W
Bassigny 12 48 0N 5 30 E
Bassikounou 50 15 55N 6 1W
Bastak 31 27 15N 54 25 E
Bastar 33 19 15N 81 40 E
Basti 33 26 52N 82 55 E
Bastia 12 42 40N 9 30 E
Bastogne 11 50 1N 5 43 E
Bastrop 71 30 5N 97 22W
Bat Yam 28 32 2N 34 44 E
Bata 54 1 57N 9 50 E
Bataan 35 14 40N 120 25 E
Batabanó 75 22 40N 82 20W
Batabanó, G. de 75 22 30N 82 30W
Batac 35 18 3N 120 34 E
Batagoy 25 67 38N 134 38 E
Batalha 13 39 40N 8 50W
Batamay 25 63 30N 129 15 E
Batang, China 37 30 1N 99 0 E
Batang, Indonesia 35 6 55S 109 45 E
Batangafo 51 7 25N 18 20 E
Batangas 35 13 35N 121 10 E
Batanta 35 0 55S 130 40 E
Batavia 68 43 0N 78 10W
Batchelor 46 13 4S 131 1 E
Bateman's B. 45 35 40S 150 12 E
Batemans Bay 45 35 44S 150 11 E
Batesburg 69 33 54N 81 32W
Batesville, Ark., U.S.A. 71 35 48N 91 40W
Batesville, Miss., U.S.A. 71 34 17N 89 58W
Batesville, Tex., U.S.A. 71 28 59N 99 38W
Bath, U.K. 7 51 22N 2 22W
Bath, Maine, U.S.A. 63 43 50N 69 49W
Bath, N.Y., U.S.A. 68 42 20N 77 17W
Bathgate 8 55 54N 3 38W
Bathurst = Banjul 50 13 28N 16 40W
Bathurst, Australia 45 33 25S 149 31 E
Bathurst, Canada 63 47 37N 65 43W
Bathurst, S. Africa 56 33 30S 26 50 E
Bathurst, C. 60 70 34N 128 0W
Bathurst B. 44 14 16S 144 25 E
Bathurst Harb. 44 43 15S 146 10 E
Bathurst I. 46 11 30S 130 10 E
Bathurst Inlet 60 66 50N 108 1W
Batinah 31 24 0N 56 0 E
Batlow 45 35 31S 148 9 E
Batman 30 37 55N 41 5 E
Batna 50 35 34N 6 15 E
Baton Rouge 71 30 30N 91 5W
Batopilas 74 27 0N 107 45W
Batouri 54 4 30N 14 25 E
Battambang 34 13 7N 103 12 E
Batticaloa 32 7 43N 81 45 E
Battir 28 31 44N 35 8 E
Battle 7 50 55N 0 30 E
Battle → 65 52 43N 108 15W
Battle Camp 44 15 20S 144 40 E
Battle Creek 68 42 20N 85 6W
Battle Harbour 63 52 16N 55 35W
Battle Lake 70 46 20N 95 43W
Battle Mountain 72 40 45N 117 0W
Battleford 65 52 45N 108 15W
Batu 29 6 55N 39 45 E
Batu, Kepulauan 34 0 30S 98 25 E
Batu Pahat 34 1 50N 102 56 E
Batuata 35 6 12S 122 42 E
Batumi 23 41 30N 41 30 E
Baturaja 34 4 11S 104 15 E
Baturité 79 4 28S 38 45W
Bau 34 1 25N 110 9 E
Baubau 35 5 25S 122 38 E
Bauchi 53 10 22N 9 48 E
Bauchi □ 53 10 30N 10 0 E
Baudette 70 48 46N 94 35W
Bauer, C. 45 32 44S 134 4 E
Bauhinia Downs 44 24 35S 149 18 E
Bauru 79 22 10S 49 0W
Baús 79 18 22S 52 47W
Bautzen 14 51 11N 14 25 E
Bavaria = Bayern □ 14 49 7N 11 30 E
Bavispe → 74 29 30N 109 11W
Bawdwin 33 23 5N 97 20 E
Bawean 34 5 46S 112 35 E
Bawku 53 11 3N 0 19W
Bawlake 33 19 11N 97 21 E
Baxley 69 31 43N 82 23W
Baxter Springs 71 37 3N 94 45W
Bay, L. de 35 14 20N 121 11 E
Bay Bulls 63 47 19N 52 50W
Bay City, Mich., U.S.A. 68 43 35N 83 51W

Bay City, Oreg., U.S.A.	**72** 45 45N 123 58W	Beaver →, B.C., Canada	**64** 59 52N 124 20W	Belfast, L.	**9** 54 40N 5 50W	Ben Cruachan	**8** 56 26N 5 8W	Berezovo	**22** 64 0N 65 0 E

Bay City, Oreg., U.S.A. **72** 45 45N 123 58W
Bay City, Tex., U.S.A. **71** 28 59N 95 55W
Bay de Verde **63** 48 5N 52 54W
Bay Minette **69** 30 54N 87 43W
Bay St. Louis **71** 30 18N 89 22W
Bay Springs **71** 31 58N 89 18W
Bay View **43** 39 25S 176 50 E
Bayamo **75** 20 20N 76 40W
Bayamón **75** 18 24N 66 10W
Bayan **38** 46 5N 127 24 E
Bayan Har Shan **37** 34 0N 98 0 E
Bayan Hot = Alxa Zuoqi **38** 38 50N 105 40 E
Bayan Obo **38** 41 52N 109 59 E
Bayanaul **24** 50 45N 75 45 E
Bayanhongor **37** 46 8N 102 43 E
Bayard **70** 41 48N 103 17W
Bayázeh **31** 33 30N 54 40 E
Baybay **35** 10 40N 124 55 E
Bayburt **30** 40 15N 40 20 E
Bayern □ **14** 49 7N 11 30 E
Bayeux **12** 49 17N 0 42W
Bayfield **70** 46 50N 90 48W
Baykal, Oz. **25** 53 0N 108 0 E
Baykit **25** 61 50N 95 50 E
Baykonur **24** 47 48N 65 50 E
Baymak **22** 52 36N 58 19 E
Baynes Mts. **56** 17 15S 13 0 E
Bayombong **35** 16 30N 121 10 E
Bayonne **12** 43 30N 1 28W
Bayovar **78** 5 50S 81 0W
Bayram-Ali **24** 37 37N 62 10 E
Bayreuth **14** 49 56N 11 35 E
Bayrūt **30** 33 53N 35 31 E
Bayt Awlá **28** 31 37N 35 2 E
Bayt Fajjár **28** 31 38N 35 9 E
Bayt Fūrīk **28** 32 11N 35 20 E
Bayt Hānūn **28** 31 32N 34 32 E
Bayt Jālā **28** 31 43N 35 11 E
Bayt Lahm **28** 31 43N 35 12 E
Bayt Rīma **28** 32 2N 35 6 F
Bayt Sāhūr **28** 31 42N 35 13 E
Bayt Ummar **28** 31 38N 35 7 E
Bayt 'ūr al Tahtā **28** 31 54N 35 5 E
Baytin **28** 31 56N 35 14 E
Baytown **71** 29 42N 94 57W
Baytūniyā **28** 31 54N 35 10 E
Baza **13** 37 30N 2 47W
Bazaruto, I. do **57** 21 40S 35 28 E
Bazhong **39** 31 52N 106 46 E
Beach **70** 46 57N 103 58W
Beachport **45** 37 29S 140 0 E
Beachy Head **7** 50 44N 0 16 E
Beacon, Australia **47** 30 26S 117 52 E
Beacon, U.S.A. **68** 41 32N 73 58W
Beaconia **65** 50 25N 96 31W
Beagle, Canal **80** 55 0S 68 30W
Beagle Bay **46** 16 58S 122 40 E
Bealanana **57** 14 33N 48 44 E
Bear I. **9** 51 38N 9 50W
Bear L., B.C., Canada **64** 56 10N 126 52W
Bear L., Man., Canada **65** 55 8N 96 0W
Bear L., U.S.A. **72** 42 0N 111 20W
Bearcreek **72** 45 11N 109 6W
Beardmore **62** 49 36N 87 57W
Beardstown **70** 40 0N 90 25W
Béarn **12** 43 20N 0 30W
Bearpaw Mts. **72** 48 15N 109 30W
Bearskin Lake **62** 53 58N 91 2W
Beata, C. **75** 17 40N 71 30W
Beatrice **70** 40 20N 96 40W
Beatrice, C. **44** 14 20S 136 55 E
Beatton → **64** 56 15N 120 45W
Beatton River **64** 57 26N 121 20W
Beatty **73** 36 58N 116 46W
Beauce, Plaine de la **12** 48 10N 1 45 E
Beauceville **63** 46 13N 70 46W
Beaudesert **45** 27 59S 153 0 E
Beaufort, Malaysia **34** 5 30N 115 40 E
Beaufort, N.C., U.S.A. **69** 34 45N 76 40W
Beaufort, S.C., U.S.A. **69** 32 25N 80 40W
Beaufort Sea **58** 72 0N 140 0W
Beaufort West **56** 32 18S 22 36 E
Beauharnois **62** 45 20N 73 52W
Beaulieu → **64** 62 3N 113 11W
Beauly **8** 57 29N 4 27W
Beauly → **8** 57 26N 4 28W
Beaumaris **6** 53 16N 4 7W
Beaumont **71** 30 5N 94 8W
Beaune **12** 47 2N 4 50 E
Beauséjour **65** 50 5N 96 35W
Beauvais **12** 49 25N 2 8 E
Beauval **65** 55 9N 107 37W
Beaver, Alaska, U.S.A. **60** 66 20N 147 30W
Beaver, Okla., U.S.A. **71** 36 52N 100 31W
Beaver, Utah, U.S.A. **73** 38 20N 112 45W

Beaver →, B.C., Canada **64** 59 52N 124 20W
Beaver →, Ont., Canada **62** 55 55N 87 48W
Beaver →, Sask., Canada **65** 55 26N 107 45W
Beaver City **70** 40 13N 99 50W
Beaver Dam **70** 43 28N 88 50W
Beaver Falls **68** 40 44N 80 20W
Beaver Hill L. **65** 54 5N 94 50W
Beaver I. **68** 45 40N 85 31W
Beaverhill L., Alta., Canada **64** 53 27N 112 32W
Beaverhill L., N.W.T., Canada **65** 63 2N 104 22W
Beaverlodge **64** 55 11N 119 29W
Beavermouth **64** 51 32N 117 23W
Beaverstone → **62** 54 59N 89 25W
Beawar **32** 26 3N 74 18 E
Beboa **57** 17 22S 44 33 E
Beccles **7** 52 27N 1 33 E
Bečej **19** 45 36N 20 3 E
Béchar **50** 31 38N 2 18W
Beckley **68** 37 50N 81 8W
Bedford, Canada **62** 45 7N 72 59W
Bedford, S. Africa **56** 32 40S 26 10 E
Bedford, U.K. **7** 52 8N 0 29W
Bedford, Ind., U.S.A. **68** 38 50N 86 30W
Bedford, Iowa, U.S.A. **70** 40 40N 94 41W
Bedford, Ohio, U.S.A. **68** 41 23N 81 32W
Bedford, Va., U.S.A. **68** 37 25N 79 30W
Bedford □ **7** 52 4N 0 28W
Bedford, C. **44** 15 14S 145 21 E
Bedford Downs **46** 17 19S 127 20 E
Bedourie **44** 24 30S 139 30 E
Beech Grove **68** 39 40N 86 2W
Beechworth **45** 36 22S 146 43 E
Beechy **65** 50 53N 107 24W
Beenleigh **45** 27 43S 153 10 E
Be'er Sheva' **28** 31 15N 34 48 E
Be'er Sheva' → **28** 31 12N 34 40 E
Be'eri **28** 31 25N 34 30 E
Be'erotayim **28** 32 19N 34 59 E
Beersheba = Be'er Sheva' **28** 31 15N 34 48 E
Beeston **6** 52 55N 1 11W
Beetaloo **44** 17 15S 133 50 E
Beeville **71** 28 27N 97 44W
Befale **54** 0 25N 20 45 E
Befandriana **57** 21 55S 44 0 E
Befotaka **57** 23 49S 47 0 E
Bega **45** 36 41S 149 51 E
Behara **57** 24 55S 46 20 E
Behbehán **30** 30 30N 50 15 E
Behshahr **31** 36 45N 53 35 E
Bei Jiang → **39** 23 2N 112 58 E
Bei'an **38** 48 10N 126 20 E
Beibei **39** 29 47N 106 22 E
Beihai **39** 21 28N 109 6 E
Beijing **38** 39 55N 116 20 E
Beijing □ **38** 39 55N 116 20 E
Beilen **11** 52 52N 6 27 E
Beilpajah **44** 32 54S 143 52 E
Beira **55** 19 50S 34 52 E
Beira-Alta **13** 40 35N 7 35W
Beira-Baixa **13** 40 2N 7 30W
Beira-Litoral **13** 40 5N 8 30W
Beirut = Bayrūt **30** 33 53N 35 31 E
Beit Lähiyah **28** 31 32N 34 30 E
Beitaolaizhao **38** 44 58N 125 58 E
Beitbridge **57** 22 12S 30 0 E
Beizhen **38** 37 20N 118 2 E
Beja, Portugal **13** 38 2N 7 53W
Béja, Tunisia **50** 36 43N 9 12 E
Bejaia **50** 36 42N 5 2 E
Bejestán **31** 34 30N 58 5 E
Bekasi **35** 6 14S 106 59 E
Békéscsaba **15** 46 40N 21 5 E
Bekily **57** 24 13S 45 19 E
Bela, India **33** 25 50N 82 0 E
Bela, Pakistan **32** 26 12N 66 20 E
Bela Crkva **19** 44 55N 21 27 E
Bela Vista, Brazil **80** 22 12S 56 20W
Bela Vista, Mozam. **57** 26 10S 32 44 E
Belau Is. **40** 7 30N 134 30 E
Belavenona **57** 24 50S 47 4 E
Belawan **34** 3 33N 98 32 E
Belaya **22** 56 0N 54 32 E
Belaya Tserkov **23** 49 45N 30 10 E
Belcher Is. **62** 56 15N 78 45W
Belebey **22** 54 7N 54 7 E
Belém **79** 1 20S 48 30W
Belén, Paraguay **80** 23 30S 57 6W
Belen, U.S.A. **73** 34 40N 106 50W
Belet Uen **29** 4 30N 45 5 E
Belev **22** 53 50N 36 5 E
Belfast, S. Africa **57** 25 42S 30 2 E
Belfast, U.K. **9** 54 35N 5 56W
Belfast, U.S.A. **63** 44 30N 69 0W
Belfast □ **9** 54 35N 5 56W

Belfast, L. **9** 54 40N 5 50W
Belfield **70** 46 54N 103 11W
Belfort **12** 47 38N 6 50 E
Belfry **72** 45 10N 109 2W
Belgaum **32** 15 55N 74 35 E
Belgium ■ **11** 50 30N 5 0 E
Bolgorod **23** 50 35N 36 35 E
Belgorod-Dnestrovskiy **23** 46 11N 30 23 E
Belgrade = Beograd **19** 44 50N 20 37 E
Belgrade **72** 45 50N 111 10W
Belhaven **69** 35 34N 76 35W
Beli Drim → **19** 42 6N 20 25 E
Belinga **54** 1 10N 13 2 E
Belinyu **34** 1 35S 105 50 E
Belitung **34** 3 10S 107 50 E
Belize ■ **74** 17 0N 88 30W
Belize City **74** 17 25N 88 0W
Belkovskiy, Ostrov **25** 75 32N 135 44 E
Bell → **62** 49 48N 77 38W
Bell Bay **44** 41 6S 146 53 E
Bell I. **63** 50 46N 55 35W
Bell-Irving → **64** 56 12N 129 5W
Bell Peninsula **61** 63 50N 82 0W
Bell Ville **80** 32 40S 62 40W
Bella Bella **64** 52 10N 128 10W
Bella Coola **64** 52 25N 126 40W
Bella Unión **80** 30 15S 57 40W
Bella Vista **80** 28 33S 59 0W
Bellaire **68** 40 1N 80 46W
Bellary **32** 15 10N 76 56 E
Bellata **45** 29 53S 149 46 E
Belle, La **69** 26 45N 81 22W
Belle Fourche **70** 44 43N 103 52W
Belle Fourche → **70** 44 25N 102 19W
Belle Glade **69** 26 43N 80 38W
Belle-Ile **12** 47 20N 3 10W
Belle Isle **63** 51 57N 55 25W
Belle Isle, Str. of **63** 51 30N 56 30W
Belle Plaine, Iowa, U.S.A. **70** 41 51N 92 18W
Belle Plaine, Minn., U.S.A. **70** 44 35N 93 48W
Belledune **63** 47 55N 65 50W
Bellefontaine **68** 40 20N 83 45W
Bellefonte **68** 40 56N 77 45W
Belleoram **63** 47 31N 55 25W
Belleville, Canada **62** 44 10N 77 23W
Belleville, Ill., U.S.A. **70** 38 30N 90 0W
Belleville, Kans., U.S.A. **70** 39 51N 97 38W
Bellevue, Canada **64** 49 35N 114 22W
Bellevue, U.S.A. **72** 43 25N 114 23W
Bellin **61** 60 0N 70 0W
Bellingen **45** 30 25S 152 50 E
Bellingham **72** 48 45N 122 27W
Bellinzona **14** 46 11N 9 1 E
Bello **78** 6 20N 75 33W
Bellows Falls **68** 43 10N 72 30W
Belluno **18** 46 8N 12 13 E
Bellville **71** 29 58N 96 18W
Bélmez **13** 38 17N 5 17W
Belmont, Australia **45** 33 4S 151 42 E
Belmont, S. Africa **56** 29 28S 24 22 E
Belmonte **79** 16 0S 39 0W
Belmopan **74** 17 18N 88 30W
Belmullet **9** 54 13N 9 58W
Belo Horizonte **79** 19 55S 43 56W
Belo-sur-Mer **57** 20 42S 44 0 E
Belo-Tsiribihina **57** 19 40S 44 30 E
Belogorsk **25** 51 0N 128 20 E
Beloha **57** 25 10S 45 3 E
Beloit, Kans., U.S.A. **70** 39 32N 98 9W
Beloit, Wis., U.S.A. **70** 42 35N 89 0W
Belomorsk **22** 64 35N 34 30 E
Belonia **33** 23 15N 91 30 E
Beloretsk **22** 53 58N 58 24 E
Belovo **24** 54 30N 86 0 E
Beloye, Oz. **22** 60 10N 37 35 E
Beloye More **22** 66 30N 38 0 E
Belozersk **22** 60 0N 37 30 E
Beltana **45** 30 48S 138 25 E
Belterra **79** 2 45S 55 0W
Belton, S.C., U.S.A. **69** 34 31N 82 39W
Belton, Tex., U.S.A. **71** 31 4N 97 30W
Belton Res. **71** 31 8N 97 32W
Beltsy **23** 47 48N 28 0 E
Belturbet **9** 54 6N 7 28W
Belukha **24** 49 50N 86 50 E
Beluran **34** 5 48N 117 35 E
Belvidere **70** 42 15N 88 55W
Belyando → **44** 21 38S 146 50 E
Belyy, Ostrov **24** 73 30N 71 0 E
Belyy Yar **24** 58 26N 84 39 E
Belzoni **71** 33 12N 90 30W
Bemaraha, Lembalemban' i **57** 18 40S 44 45 E
Bemarivo **57** 21 45S 44 45 E
Bemarivo → **57** 15 27S 47 40 E
Bemavo **57** 21 33S 45 25 E
Bembéréke **53** 10 11N 2 43 E
Bemidji **70** 47 30N 94 50W
Ben 'Ammi **28** 33 0N 35 7 E

Ben Cruachan **8** 56 26N 5 8W
Ben Dearg **8** 57 47N 4 58W
Ben Gardane **51** 33 11N 11 11 E
Ben Hope **8** 58 24N 4 36W
Ben Lawers **8** 56 33N 4 13W
Ben Lomond, N.S.W., Australia **45** 30 1S 151 43 E
Ben Lomond, Tas., Australia **44** 41 38S 147 42 E
Ben Lomond, U.K. **8** 56 12N 4 39W
Ben Macdhui **8** 57 4N 3 40W
Ben Mhor **8** 57 16N 7 21W
Ben More, Central, U.K. **8** 56 23N 4 31W
Ben More, Strathclyde, U.K. **8** 56 26N 6 2W
Ben More Assynt **8** 58 7N 4 51W
Ben Nevis **8** 56 48N 5 0W
Ben Vorlich **8** 56 22N 4 15W
Ben Wyvis **8** 57 40N 4 35W
Bena **53** 11 20N 5 50 E
Bena Dibele **54** 4 4S 22 50 E
Benagerie **45** 31 25S 140 22 E
Benalla **45** 36 30S 146 0 E
Benares = Varanasi **33** 25 22N 83 0 E
Benavides **71** 27 35N 98 28W
Benbecula **8** 57 26N 7 21W
Benbonyathe, Mt. **45** 30 25S 139 11 E
Bencubbin **47** 30 48S 117 52 E
Bend **72** 44 2N 121 15W
Bendel □ **53** 6 0N 6 0 E
Bender Beila **29** 9 30N 50 48 E
Bendering **47** 32 23S 118 18 E
Bendery **23** 46 50N 29 30 E
Bendigo **45** 36 40S 144 15 E
Bene Beraq **28** 32 6N 34 51 E
Benenitra **57** 23 27S 45 5 E
Benevento **18** 41 7N 14 45 E
Bengal, Bay of **33** 15 0N 90 0 E
Bengbu **39** 32 58N 117 20 E
Benghazi = Banghāzī **51** 32 11N 20 3 E
Bengkalis **34** 1 30N 102 10 E
Bengkulu **34** 3 50S 102 12 E
Bengkulu □ **34** 3 48S 102 16 E
Bengough **65** 49 25N 105 10W
Benguela **55** 12 37S 13 25 E
Benguérua, I. **57** 21 58S 35 28 E
Beni **54** 0 30N 29 27 E
Beni → **78** 10 23S 65 24W
Beni Abbès **50** 30 5N 2 5W
Beni Mazâr **51** 28 32N 30 44 E
Beni Mellal **50** 32 21N 6 21W
Beni Ounif **50** 32 0N 1 10W
Beni Suef **51** 29 5N 31 6 E
Beniah L. **64** 63 23N 112 17W
Benidorm **13** 38 33N 0 9W
Benin ■ **53** 10 0N 2 0 E
Benin, Bight of **53** 5 0N 3 0 E
Benin City **53** 6 20N 5 31 E
Benjamin Constant **78** 4 40S 70 15W
Benkelman **70** 40 7N 101 32W
Benlidi **44** 24 35S 144 50 E
Bennett **64** 59 56N 134 53W
Bennett, Ostrov **25** 76 21N 148 56 E
Bennettsville **69** 34 38N 79 39W
Bennington **68** 42 52N 73 12W
Benoni **57** 26 11S 28 18 E
Benson **73** 31 59N 110 19W
Bent **31** 26 20N 59 31 E
Benteng **35** 6 10S 120 30 E
Bentinck I. **44** 17 3S 139 35 E
Benton, Ark., U.S.A. **71** 34 30N 92 35W
Benton, Ill., U.S.A. **70** 38 0N 88 55W
Benton Harbor **68** 42 10N 86 28W
Benue □ **53** 7 30N 7 30 E
Benue → **53** 7 48N 6 46 E
Benxi **38** 41 20N 123 48 E
Beo **35** 4 25N 126 50 E
Beograd **19** 44 50N 20 37 E
Beowawe **72** 40 35N 116 30W
Beppu **36** 33 15N 131 30 E
Berau, Teluk **35** 2 30S 132 30 E
Berber **51** 18 0N 34 0 E
Berbera **29** 10 30N 45 2 E
Berbérati **54** 4 15N 15 40 E
Berbice → **78** 6 20N 57 32W
Berdichev **23** 49 57N 28 30 E
Berdsk **24** 54 47N 83 2 E
Berdyansk **23** 46 45N 36 50 E
Berea **68** 37 35N 84 18W
Berebere **35** 2 25N 128 45 E
Bereda **29** 11 45N 51 0 E
Berekum **50** 7 29N 2 34W
Berens → **65** 52 25N 97 2W
Berens I. **65** 52 18N 97 18W
Berens River **65** 52 25N 97 0W
Berevo, Mahajanga, Madag. **57** 17 14S 44 17 E
Berevo, Toliara, Madag. **57** 19 44S 44 58 F
Berezina → **22** 52 33N 30 14 E
Berezniki **22** 59 24N 56 46 E

Berezovo **22** 64 0N 65 0 E
Bergama **30** 39 8N 27 15 E
Bérgamo **18** 45 42N 9 40 E
Bergen, Neth. **11** 52 40N 4 43 E
Bergen, Norway **21** 60 23N 5 20 E
Bergen-op-Zoom **11** 51 30N 4 18 E
Bergerac **12** 44 51N 0 30 E
Bergum **11** 53 13N 5 59 E
Bergville **57** 28 52S 29 18 E
Berhala, Selat **34** 1 0S 104 15 E
Berhampore = Baharampur **33** 24 2N 88 27 E
Berhampur **33** 19 15N 84 54 E
Bering Sea **60** 58 0N 167 0 E
Bering Str. **60** 66 0N 170 0W
Beringen **11** 51 3N 5 14 E
Beringovskiy **25** 63 3N 179 19 E
Berja **13** 36 50N 2 56W
Berkeley, U.K. **7** 51 41N 2 28W
Berkeley, U.S.A. **72** 37 52N 122 20W
Berkeley Springs **68** 39 38N 78 12W
Berkshire □ **7** 51 30N 1 20W
Berland → **64** 54 0N 116 50W
Berlin, Germany **14** 52 32N 13 24 E
Berlin, Md., U.S.A. **68** 38 19N 75 12W
Berlin, N.H., U.S.A. **68** 44 29N 71 10W
Berlin, Wis., U.S.A. **68** 43 58N 88 55W
Bermejo →, Formosa, Argentina **80** 26 51S 58 23W
Bermejo →, San Juan, Argentina **80** 32 30S 67 30W
Bermuda ■ **2** 32 45N 65 0W
Bern **14** 46 57N 7 28 E
Bernado **73** 34 30N 106 53W
Bernalillo **73** 35 17N 106 37W
Bernardo de Irigoyen **80** 26 15S 53 40W
Bernburg **14** 51 40N 11 42 E
Berne = Bern **14** 46 57N 7 28 E
Bernier I. **47** 24 50S 113 12 E
Beror Hayil **28** 31 34N 34 38 E
Beroroha **57** 21 40S 45 10 E
Beroun **14** 49 57N 14 5 E
Berrechid **50** 33 18N 7 36W
Berri **45** 34 14S 140 35 E
Berry, Australia **45** 34 46S 150 43 E
Berry, France **12** 46 50N 2 0 E
Berry Is. **75** 25 40N 77 50W
Berryville **71** 36 23N 93 35W
Berthold **70** 48 19N 101 45W
Berthoud **70** 40 21N 105 5W
Bertoua **54** 4 30N 13 45 E
Bertrand **70** 40 35N 99 38W
Berufjörður **20** 64 48N 14 29W
Berwick **68** 41 4N 76 17W
Berwick-upon-Tweed **6** 55 47N 2 0W
Berwyn Mts. **6** 52 54N 3 26W
Besalampy **57** 16 43S 44 29 E
Besançon **12** 47 15N 6 0 E
Besar **34** 2 40S 116 0 E
Besnard L. **65** 55 25N 106 0W
Besni **30** 37 41N 37 52 E
Besor, N. → **28** 31 28N 34 22 E
Bessemer, Ala., U.S.A. **69** 33 25N 86 57W
Bessemer, Mich., U.S.A. **70** 46 27N 90 0W
Bet Alfa **28** 32 31N 35 25 E
Bet Dagan **28** 32 1N 34 49 E
Bet Guvrin **28** 31 37N 34 54 E
Bet Ha'Emeq **28** 32 58N 35 8 E
Bet Hashitta **28** 32 31N 35 27 E
Bet Qeshet **28** 32 41N 35 21 E
Bet She'an **28** 32 30N 35 30 E
Bet Shemesh **28** 31 44N 35 0 E
Bet Yosef **28** 32 34N 35 33 E
Betafo **57** 19 50S 46 51 E
Bétaré Oya **54** 5 40N 14 5 E
Bethal **57** 26 27S 29 28 E
Bethanien **56** 26 31S 17 8 E
Bethany = Al 'Ayzarîyah **28** 31 47N 35 15 E
Bethany, S. Africa **56** 29 34S 25 59 E
Bethany, U.S.A. **70** 40 18N 94 0W
Bethel **60** 60 50N 161 50W
Bethlehem = Bayt Lahm **28** 31 43N 35 12 E
Bethlehem, S. Africa **57** 28 14S 28 18 E
Bethlehem, U.S.A. **68** 40 39N 75 24W
Bethulie **56** 30 30S 25 59 E
Béthune **12** 50 30N 2 38 E
Bethungra **45** 34 45S 147 51 E
Betioky **57** 23 48S 44 20 E
Betoota **44** 25 45S 140 42 E
Betroka **57** 23 16S 46 0 E
Betsiamites **63** 48 56N 68 40W
Betsiamites → **63** 48 56N 68 38W
Betsiboka → **57** 16 3S 46 36 E
Bettiah **33** 26 48N 84 33 E

8

Bronte Park

Bol 51 13 30N 15 0 E
Bolama 50 11 30N 15 30W
Bolan Pass 31 29 50N 67 20 E
Bolaños ► 74 21 14N 104 8W
Bolbec 12 49 30N 0 30 E
Bole 37 45 11N 81 37 E
Bolesławiec 14 51 17N 15 37 E
Bolgatanga 53 10 44N 0 53W
Boli 38 45 46N 130 31 E
Bolinao C. 35 16 23N 119 55 E
Bolívar, Argentina 80 36 15S 60 53W
Bolívar, Colombia 78 2 0N 77 0W
Bolivar, Mo., U.S.A. 71 37 38N 93 22W
Bolivar, Tenn., U.S.A. 71 35 14N 89 0W
Bolivia ■ 78 17 6S 64 0W
Bolivian Plateau 76 20 0S 67 30W
Bollnäs 21 61 21N 16 24 E
Bollon 45 28 2S 147 29 E
Bolobo 54 2 6S 16 20 E
Bologna 18 44 30N 11 20 E
Bologoye 22 57 55N 34 0 E
Bolomba 54 0 35N 19 0 E
Bolong 35 7 6N 122 14 E
Bolsena, L. di 18 42 35N 11 55 E
Bolshereche 24 56 4N 74 45 E
Bolshevik, Ostrov 25 78 30N 102 0 E
Bolshezemelskaya Tundra 22 67 0N 56 0 E
Bolshoi Kavkas 23 42 50N 44 0 E
Bolshoy Anyuy ► 25 68 30N 160 49 E
Bolshoy Atlym 24 62 25N 66 50 E
Bolshoy Begichev, Ostrov 25 74 20N 112 30 E
Bolshoy Lyakhovskiy, Ostrov 25 73 35N 142 0 E
Bolsward 11 53 3N 5 32 E
Bolton 6 53 35N 2 26W
Bolu 30 40 45N 31 35 E
Bolvadin 30 38 45N 31 4 E
Bolzano 18 46 30N 11 20 E
Bom Despacho 79 19 43S 45 15W
Bom Jesus da Lapa 79 13 15S 43 25W
Boma 54 5 50S 13 4 E
Bomaderry 45 34 52S 150 37 E
Bombala 45 36 56S 149 15 E
Bombay 32 18 55N 72 50 E
Bomboma 54 2 25N 18 55 E
Bomili 54 1 45N 27 5 E
Bomongo 54 1 27N 18 21 E
Bomu ► 54 4 40N 22 30 E
Bon, C. 51 37 1N 11 2 E
Bonaire 75 12 10N 68 15W
Bonang 45 37 11S 148 41 E
Bonanza 75 13 54N 84 35W
Bonaparte Archipelago 46 14 0S 124 30 E
Bonaventure 63 48 5N 65 32W
Bonavista 63 48 40N 53 5W
Bonavista, C. 63 48 42N 53 5W
Bondo 54 3 55N 23 53 E
Bondoukou 50 8 2N 2 47W
Bondowoso 35 7 55S 113 49 E
Bone, Teluk 35 4 10S 120 50 E
Bone Rate 35 7 25S 121 5 E
Bone Rate, Kepulauan 35 6 30S 121 10 E
Bo'ness 8 56 0N 3 38W
Bong Son = Hoai Nhon 34 14 28N 109 1 E
Bongandanga 54 1 24N 21 3 E
Bongor 51 10 35N 15 20 E
Bonham 71 33 30N 96 10W
Bonifacio 12 41 24N 9 10 E
Bonifacio, Bouches de 18 41 12N 9 15 E
Bonin Is. 40 27 0N 142 0 E
Bonn 14 50 43N 7 6 E
Bonne Terre 71 37 57N 90 33W
Bonners Ferry 72 48 38N 116 21W
Bonney, L. 45 37 50S 140 20 E
Bonnie Downs 44 22 7S 143 50 E
Bonnie Rock 47 30 29S 118 22 E
Bonny, Bight of 54 3 30N 9 20 E
Bonnyville 65 54 20N 110 45W
Bonoi 35 1 45S 137 41 E
Bontang 34 0 10N 117 30 E
Bonthain 35 5 34S 119 56 E
Bonthe 50 7 30N 12 33W
Bontoc 35 17 7N 120 58 E
Bonython Ra. 46 23 40S 128 45 E
Boogardie 47 28 2S 117 45 E
Bookabie 47 31 50S 132 41 E
Booker 71 36 29N 100 30W
Boolaboolka, L. 45 32 38S 143 10 E
Booligal 45 33 58S 144 53 E
Boom 11 51 6N 4 20 E
Boonah 45 27 58S 152 41 E
Boone, Iowa, U.S.A. 70 42 5N 93 53W
Boone, N.C., U.S.A. 69 36 14N 81 43W
Booneville, Ark., U.S.A. 71 35 10N 93 54W
Booneville, Miss., U.S.A. 69 34 39N 88 34W
Boonville, Ind., U.S.A. 68 38 3N 87 13W
Boonville, Mo., U.S.A. 70 38 57N 92 45W
Boonville, N.Y., U.S.A. 68 43 31N 75 20W
Boorindal 45 30 22S 146 11 E
Boorowa 45 34 28S 148 44 E
Boothia, Gulf of 61 71 0N 90 0W
Boothia Pen. 60 71 0N 94 0W
Bootle, Cumbria, U.K. 6 54 17N 3 24W
Bootle, Merseyside, U.K. 6 53 28N 3 1W
Booué 54 0 5S 11 55 E
Bophuthatswana □ 56 25 49S 25 30 E
Boquilla, Presa de la 74 27 40N 105 30W
Bôr, Sudan 51 6 10N 31 40 E
Bor, Yugoslavia 19 44 8N 22 7 E
Borah, Pk. 72 44 19N 113 46W
Borama 29 9 55N 43 7 E
Borås 21 57 43N 12 56 E
Borāzjān 31 29 22N 51 10 E
Borba 78 4 12S 59 34W
Borda, C. 45 35 45S 136 34 E
Bordeaux 12 44 50N 0 36W
Borden, Australia 47 34 3S 118 12 E
Borden, Canada 63 46 18N 63 47W
Borders □ 8 55 35N 2 50W
Bordertown 45 36 19S 140 45 E
Borðeyri 20 65 12N 21 6W
Bordj Fly Ste. Marie 50 27 19N 2 32W
Bordj-in-Eker 50 24 9N 5 3 E
Bordj Omar Driss 50 28 10N 6 40 E
Bordj-Tarat 50 25 55N 9 3 E
Borgarnes 20 64 32N 21 55W
Børgefjellet 20 65 20N 13 45 E
Borger, Neth. 11 52 54N 6 44 E
Borger, U.S.A. 71 35 40N 101 20W
Borgholm 21 56 52N 16 39 E
Borisoglebsk 23 51 27N 42 5 E
Borisov 22 54 17N 28 28 E
Borja 78 4 20S 77 40W
Borkou 51 18 15N 18 50 E
Borkum 14 53 36N 6 42 E
Borlänge 21 60 29N 15 26 E
Borneo 34 1 0N 115 0 E
Bornholm 21 55 10N 15 0 E
Borno □ 53 12 30N 12 30 E
Borobudur 35 7 36S 110 13 E
Borogontsy 25 62 42N 131 8 E
Boromo 50 11 45N 2 58W
Borongan 35 11 37N 125 26 E
Bororen 44 24 13S 151 33 E
Borovichi 22 58 25N 33 55 E
Borroloola 44 16 4S 136 17 E
Borth 7 52 29N 4 3W
Borujerd 30 33 55N 48 50 E
Borzya 25 50 24N 116 31 E
Bosa 18 40 17N 8 32 E
Bosanska Gradiška 18 45 10N 17 15 E
Bosaso 29 11 12N 49 18 E
Boscastle 7 50 42N 4 42W
Bose 39 23 53N 106 35 E
Boshan 38 36 28N 117 49 E
Boshoek 56 25 30S 27 9 E
Boshof 56 28 31S 25 13 E
Boshrūyeh 31 33 50N 57 30 E
Bosna ► 19 45 4N 18 29 E
Bosna i Hercegovina □ 18 44 0N 18 0 E
Bosnia = Bosna i Hercegovina □ 18 44 0N 18 0 E
Bosnik 35 1 5S 136 10 E
Bōsō-Hantō 36 35 20N 140 20 E
Bosobolo 54 4 15N 19 50 E
Bosporus = Karadeniz Boğazı 30 41 10N 29 10 E
Bossangoa 51 6 35N 17 30 E
Bossekop 20 69 57N 23 15 E
Bossembélé 51 5 25N 17 40 E
Bossier City 71 32 28N 93 48W
Bosso 51 13 43N 13 19 E
Bosten Hu 37 41 55N 87 40 E
Boston, U.K. 6 52 59N 0 2W
Boston, U.S.A. 68 42 20N 71 0W
Boston Bar 64 49 52N 121 30W
Boswell, Canada 64 49 28N 116 45W
Boswell, U.S.A. 71 34 1N 95 50W
Botany Bay 45 34 0S 151 14 E
Bothaville 56 27 23S 26 34 E
Bothnia, G. of 20 63 0N 20 0 E
Bothwell 44 42 20S 147 1 E
Botletle ► 56 20 10S 23 15 E
Botoşani 15 47 42N 26 41 E
Botswana ■ 56 22 0S 24 0 E
Bottineau 70 48 49N 100 25W
Bottrop 11 51 34N 6 59 E
Botucatu 80 22 55S 48 30W
Botwood 63 49 6N 55 23W
Bou Djébéha 50 18 25N 2 45W
Bou Izakarn 50 29 12N 9 46W
Bouaké 50 7 40N 5 2W
Bouar 54 6 0N 15 40 E
Bouârfa 50 32 32N 1 58 E
Bouca 51 6 45N 18 25 E
Boucaut B. 44 12 0S 134 25 E
Bouches-du-Rhône □ 12 43 37N 5 2 E
Bougainville C. 46 13 57S 126 4 E
Bougainville Reef 44 15 30S 147 5 E
Bougie = Bejaia 50 36 42N 5 2 E
Bougouni 50 11 30N 7 20W
Bouillon 11 49 44N 5 3 E
Boulder, Colo., U.S.A. 70 40 3N 105 10W
Boulder, Mont., U.S.A. 72 46 14N 112 4W
Boulder City 73 35 58N 114 50W
Boulder Dam = Hoover Dam 73 36 0N 114 45W
Boulia 44 22 52S 139 51 E
Boulogne-sur-Mer 12 50 42N 1 36 E
Boultoum 53 14 45N 10 25 E
Bouna 50 9 10N 3 0W
Boundiali 50 9 30N 6 20W
Bountiful 72 40 57N 111 58W
Bounty I. 40 48 0S 178 30 E
Bourbonnais 12 46 28N 3 0 E
Bourem 53 17 0N 0 24W
Bourg-en-Bresse 12 46 13N 5 12 E
Bourges 12 47 9N 2 25 E
Bourgogne 12 47 0N 4 50 E
Bourke 45 30 8S 145 55 E
Bournemouth 7 50 43N 1 53W
Bousso 51 10 34N 16 52 E
Boutilimit 50 17 45N 14 40W
Bouvet I. = Bouvetøya 3 54 26S 3 24 E
Bouvetøya 3 54 26S 3 24 E
Bovigny 11 50 12N 5 55 E
Bovill 72 46 58N 116 27W
Bow Island 64 49 50N 111 23W
Bowbells 70 48 47N 102 19W
Bowdle 70 45 30N 99 40W
Bowelling 47 33 25S 116 30 E
Bowen 44 20 0S 148 16 E
Bowen Mts. 45 37 0S 148 0 E
Bowie, Ariz., U.S.A. 73 32 15N 109 30W
Bowie, Tex., U.S.A. 71 33 33N 97 50W
Bowland, Forest of 6 54 0N 2 30W
Bowling Green, Ky., U.S.A. 68 37 0N 86 25W
Bowling Green, Ohio, U.S.A. 68 41 22N 83 40W
Bowling Green, C. 44 19 19S 147 25 E
Bowman 70 46 12N 103 21W
Bowmans 45 34 10S 138 17 E
Bowmanville 62 43 55N 78 41W
Bowmore 8 55 45N 6 18W
Bowral 45 34 26S 150 27 E
Bowraville 45 30 37S 152 52 E
Bowron ► 64 54 3N 121 50W
Bowser L. 64 56 30N 129 30W
Bowsman 65 52 14N 101 12W
Boxtel 11 51 36N 5 20 E
Boyce 71 31 25N 92 39W
Boyer ► 64 58 27N 115 57W
Boyle 9 53 58N 8 19W
Boyne ► 9 53 43N 6 15W
Boyne City 68 45 13N 85 1W
Boyni Qara 31 36 20N 67 0 E
Boynton Beach 69 26 31N 80 3W
Boyoma, Chutes 48 0 35N 25 23 E
Boyup Brook 47 33 50S 116 23 E
Bozeman 72 45 40N 111 0W
Bozen = Bolzano 18 46 30N 11 20 E
Bozoum 51 6 25N 16 35 E
Brabant □ 11 50 46N 4 30 E
Brabant L. 65 55 58N 103 43W
Brač 18 43 20N 16 40 E
Bracadale, L. 8 57 20N 6 30W
Bracciano, L. di 18 42 8N 12 11 E
Bracebridge 62 45 2N 79 19W
Brach 51 27 31N 14 20 E
Bräcke 20 62 45N 15 26 E
Brackettville 71 29 21N 100 20W
Brad 15 46 10N 22 50 E
Bradenton 69 27 25N 82 35W
Bradford, U.K. 6 53 47N 1 45W
Bradford, U.S.A. 68 41 58N 78 41W
Bradley, Ark., U.S.A. 71 33 7N 93 39W
Bradley, S. Dak., U.S.A. 70 45 10N 97 40W
Bradore Bay 63 51 27N 57 18W
Bradshaw 46 15 21S 130 16 E
Brady 71 31 8N 99 25W
Braemar 45 33 12S 139 35 E
Braga 13 41 35N 8 25W
Bragança, Brazil 79 1 0S 47 2W
Bragança, Portugal 13 41 48N 6 50W
Brahmanbaria 33 23 58N 91 15 E
Brahmani ► 33 20 39N 86 46 E
Brahmaputra ► 33 24 2N 90 59 E
Braich-y-pwll 6 52 47N 4 46W
Braidwood 45 35 27S 149 49 E
Brăila 15 45 19N 27 59 E
Brainerd 70 46 20N 94 10W
Braintree 7 51 53N 0 34 E
Brak ► 56 29 35S 22 55 E
Brakwater 56 22 28S 17 3 E
Bralorne 64 50 50N 122 50W
Brampton 62 43 45N 79 45W
Bramwell 44 12 8S 142 37 E
Branco ► 78 1 20S 61 50W
Brandenburg 14 52 24N 12 33 E
Brandfort 56 28 40S 26 30 E
Brandon 65 49 50N 99 57W
Brandon, Mt. 9 52 15N 10 15W
Brandon B. 9 52 17N 10 8W
Brandvlei 56 30 25S 20 30 E
Braniewo 15 54 25N 19 50 E
Brańsk 15 52 45N 22 50 E
Branson, Colo., U.S.A. 71 37 4N 103 53W
Branson, Mo., U.S.A. 71 36 40N 93 18W
Brantford 62 43 10N 80 15W
Branxholme 45 37 52S 141 49 E
Bras d'Or, L. 63 45 50N 60 50W
Brasil, Planalto 78 18 0S 46 30W
Brasiléia 78 11 0S 68 45W
Brasília 79 15 47S 47 55W
Braşov 15 45 38N 25 35 E
Brasschaat 11 51 19N 4 27 E
Brassey, Banjaran 34 5 0N 117 15 E
Brassey Ra. 47 25 8S 122 15 E
Brasstown Bald, Mt. 69 34 54N 83 45W
Bratislava 14 48 10N 17 7 E
Bratsk 25 56 10N 101 30 E
Brattleboro 68 42 53N 72 37W
Braunschweig 14 52 17N 10 28 E
Braunton 7 51 6N 4 9W
Brava 29 1 20N 44 8 E
Bravo del Norte ► 74 25 57N 97 9W
Brawley 73 32 58N 115 30W
Bray 9 53 12N 6 6W
Bray, Mt. 44 14 0S 134 30 E
Bray-sur-Seine 12 48 25N 3 14 E
Brazeau ► 64 52 55N 115 14W
Brazil 68 39 32N 87 8W
Brazil ■ 79 12 0S 50 0W
Brazilian Highlands = Brasil, Planalto 76 18 0S 46 30W
Brazos ► 71 28 53N 95 23W
Brazzaville 54 4 9S 15 12 E
Brčko 19 44 54N 18 46 E
Breadalbane, Australia 44 23 50S 139 35 E
Breadalbane, U.K. 8 56 30N 4 15W
Breaden, L. 47 25 51S 125 28 E
Breaksea Sd. 43 45 35S 166 35 E
Bream Bay 43 35 56S 174 28 E
Bream Head 43 35 51S 174 36 E
Brebes 35 6 52S 109 3 E
Brechin 8 56 44N 2 40W
Breckenridge, Colo., U.S.A. 72 39 30N 106 2W
Breckenridge, Minn., U.S.A. 70 46 20N 96 36W
Breckenridge, Tex., U.S.A. 71 32 48N 98 55W
Brecon 7 51 57N 3 23W
Brecon Beacons 7 51 53N 3 27W
Breda 11 51 35N 4 45 E
Bredasdorp 56 34 33S 20 2 E
Bredbo 45 35 58S 149 10 E
Bregenz 14 47 30N 9 45 E
Breiðafjörður 20 65 15N 23 15W
Brejo 79 3 41S 42 47W
Bremen 14 53 4N 8 47 E
Bremer I. 44 12 5S 136 45 E
Bremerhaven 14 53 34N 8 35 E
Bremerton 72 47 30N 122 38W
Brenham 71 30 5N 96 27W
Brenner Pass 14 47 0N 11 30 E
Brent, Canada 62 46 2N 78 29W
Brent, U.K. 7 51 33N 0 18W
Brentwood 7 51 37N 0 19 E
Bréscia 18 45 33N 10 13 E
Breskens 11 51 23N 3 33 E
Breslau = Wrocław 14 51 5N 17 5 E
Bressanone 18 46 43N 11 40 E
Bressay I. 8 60 10N 1 5W
Bresse 12 46 50N 5 10 E
Brest, France 12 48 24N 4 31W
Brest, U.S.S.R. 22 52 10N 23 40 E
Bretagne 12 48 0N 3 0W
Bretçu 15 46 7N 26 18 E
Breton 64 53 7N 114 28W
Breton Sd. 71 29 40N 89 12W
Brett, C. 43 35 10S 174 20 E
Brevard 69 35 19N 82 42W
Brewarrina 45 30 0S 146 51 E
Brewer 63 44 43N 68 50W
Brewster 72 48 10N 119 51W
Brewton 69 31 9N 87 2W
Breyten 57 26 16S 30 0 E
Brezhnev 24 55 42N 52 19 E
Bria 51 6 30N 21 58 E
Briançon 12 44 54N 6 39 E
Bribie I. 45 27 0S 152 58 E
Bridgend 7 51 30N 3 35W
Bridgeport, Calif., U.S.A. 73 38 14N 119 15W
Bridgeport, Conn., U.S.A. 68 41 12N 73 12W
Bridgeport, Nebr., U.S.A. 70 41 42N 103 10W
Bridgeport, Tex., U.S.A. 71 33 15N 97 45W
Bridger 72 45 20N 108 58W
Bridgeton 68 39 29N 75 10W
Bridgetown, Australia 47 33 58S 116 7 E
Bridgetown, Barbados 75 13 0N 59 30W
Bridgetown, Canada 63 44 55N 65 18W
Bridgewater, Canada 63 44 25N 64 31W
Bridgewater, U.S.A. 70 43 34N 97 29W
Bridgewater, C. 45 38 23S 141 23 E
Bridgnorth 7 52 33N 2 25W
Bridgwater 7 51 7N 3 0W
Bridlington 6 54 6N 0 11W
Bridport, Australia 44 40 59S 147 23 E
Bridport, U.K. 7 50 43N 2 45W
Brie, Plaine de la 12 48 35N 3 10 E
Brig 14 46 18N 7 59 E
Brigg 6 53 33N 0 30W
Briggsdale 70 40 40N 104 20W
Brigham City 72 41 30N 112 1W
Bright 45 36 42S 146 56 E
Brighton, Australia 45 35 5S 138 30 E
Brighton, Canada 62 44 2N 77 44W
Brighton, U.K. 7 50 50N 0 9W
Brighton, U.S.A. 70 39 59N 104 50W
Brilliant 64 49 19N 117 38W
Brindisi 19 40 39N 17 55 E
Brinkley 71 34 55N 91 15W
Brinkworth 45 33 42S 138 26 E
Brion, I. 63 47 46N 61 26W
Brisbane 45 27 25S 153 2 E
Brisbane ► 45 27 24S 153 9 E
Bristol, U.K. 7 51 26N 2 35W
Bristol, Conn., U.S.A. 68 41 44N 72 57W
Bristol, S. Dak., U.S.A. 70 45 25N 97 43W
Bristol, Tenn., U.S.A. 69 36 36N 82 11W
Bristol B. 60 58 0N 160 0W
Bristol Channel 7 51 18N 4 30W
Bristol L. 73 34 23N 116 50W
Bristow 71 35 55N 96 28W
British Columbia □ 64 55 0N 125 15W
British Guiana = Guyana ■ 78 5 0N 59 0W
British Honduras = Belize ■ 74 17 0N 88 30W
British Isles 4 55 0N 4 0W
Brits 57 25 37S 27 48 E
Britstown 56 30 37S 23 30 E
Britt 62 45 46N 80 34W
Brittany = Bretagne 12 48 0N 3 0W
Britton 70 45 50N 97 47W
Brixton 44 23 32S 144 57 E
Brlik 24 43 40N 73 49 E
Brno 14 49 10N 16 35 E
Broad ► 69 33 59N 82 39W
Broad Arrow 47 30 23S 121 15 E
Broad B. 8 58 14N 6 16W
Broad Haven 9 54 20N 9 55W
Broad Law 8 55 30N 3 22W
Broad Sd. 44 22 0S 149 45 E
Broadhurst Ra. 46 22 30S 122 30 E
Broads, The 6 52 45N 1 30 E
Broadus 70 45 28N 105 27W
Broadview 65 50 22N 102 35W
Brochet 65 57 53N 101 40W
Brochet, L. 65 58 36N 101 35W
Brock 65 51 26N 108 43W
Brocken 14 51 48N 10 40 E
Brockport 68 43 12N 77 56W
Brockville 62 44 35N 75 41W
Brockway 70 47 18N 105 46W
Brodeur Pen. 61 72 30N 88 10W
Brodick 8 55 34N 5 9W
Brogan 72 44 14N 117 32W
Broken Bow, Nebr., U.S.A. 70 41 25N 99 35W
Broken Bow, Okla., U.S.A. 71 34 2N 94 43W
Broken Hill = Kabwe 55 14 30S 28 29 E
Broken Hill 45 31 58S 141 29 E
Bromfield 7 52 25N 2 45W
Bromley 7 51 20N 0 5 E
Brønderslev 21 57 16N 9 57 E
Bronkhorstspruit 57 25 46S 28 45 E
Bronte 71 31 54N 100 18W
Bronte Park 44 42 8S 146 30 E

Brookfield

Brookfield 70 39 50N 93 4W
Brookhaven 71 31 40N 90 25W
Brookings, Oreg., U.S.A. 72 42 4N 124 10W
Brookings, S. Dak., U.S.A. 70 44 20N 96 45W
Brookmere 64 49 52N 120 53W
Brooks 64 50 35N 111 55W
Brooks B. 64 50 15N 127 55W
Brooks L. 65 61 55N 106 35W
Brooks Ra. 60 68 40N 147 0W
Brooksville 69 28 32N 82 21W
Brookville 68 39 25N 85 0W
Brooloo 45 26 30S 152 43 E
Broom, L. 8 57 55N 5 15W
Broome 46 18 0S 122 15 E
Broomehill 47 33 51S 117 39 E
Brora 8 58 0N 3 50W
Brora → 8 58 4N 3 52W
Brosna → 9 53 8N 8 0W
Brothers 72 43 56N 120 39W
Broughton Island 61 67 33N 63 0W
Broughty Ferry 8 56 29N 2 50W
Brouwershaven 11 51 45N 3 55 E
Browerville 70 46 3N 94 50W
Brown, Pt. 45 32 32S 133 50 E
Brown Willy 7 50 35N 4 34W
Brownfield 71 33 10N 102 15W
Browning 72 48 35N 113 0W
Brownlee 65 50 43N 106 1W
Brownsville, Oreg., U.S.A. 72 44 29N 123 0W
Brownsville, Tenn., U.S.A. 71 35 35N 89 15W
Brownsville, Tex., U.S.A. 71 25 56N 97 25W
Brownwood 71 31 45N 99 0W
Brownwood, L. 71 31 51N 98 35W
Browse I. 46 14 7S 123 33 E
Bruay-en-Artois 12 50 29N 2 33 E
Bruce, Mt. 46 22 37S 118 8 E
Bruce Rock 47 31 52S 118 8 E
Bruck an der Leitha 14 48 1N 16 47 E
Brue → 7 51 10N 2 59W
Bruges = Brugge 11 51 13N 3 13 E
Brugge 11 51 13N 3 13 E
Brûlé 64 53 15N 117 58W
Brumado 79 14 14S 41 40W
Brunchilly 44 18 50S 134 30 E
Brundidge 69 31 43N 85 45W
Bruneau 72 42 57N 115 55W
Bruneau → 72 42 57N 115 58W
Brunei = Bandar Seri Begawan 34 4 52N 115 0 E
Brunei ■ 34 4 50N 115 0 E
Brunette Downs 44 18 40S 135 55 E
Brunner, L. 43 42 37S 171 27 E
Bruno 65 52 20N 105 30W
Brunsbüttelkoog 14 53 52N 9 13 E
Brunswick = Braunschweig 14 52 17N 10 28 E
Brunswick, Ga., U.S.A. 69 31 10N 81 30W
Brunswick, Maine, U.S.A. 63 43 53N 69 50W
Brunswick, Md., U.S.A. 68 39 20N 77 38W
Brunswick, Mo., U.S.A. 70 39 26N 93 10W
Brunswick, Pen. de 80 53 30S 71 30W
Brunswick B. 46 15 15S 124 50 E
Brunswick Junction 47 33 15S 115 50 E
Bruny I. 44 43 20S 147 15 E
Brush 70 40 17N 103 33W
Brusque 80 27 5S 49 0W
Brussel 11 50 51N 4 21 E
Brussels = Brussel 11 50 51N 4 21 E
Bruthen 45 37 42S 147 50 E
Bruxelles = Brussel 11 50 51N 4 21 E
Bryan, Ohio, U.S.A. 68 41 30N 84 30W
Bryan, Tex., U.S.A. 71 30 40N 96 27W
Bryan, Mt. 45 33 30S 139 0 E
Bryansk 22 53 13N 34 25 E
Bryant 70 44 35N 97 28W
Bryne 21 58 44N 5 38 E
Bryson City 69 35 28N 83 25W
Bu Craa 50 26 45N 12 50W
Buapinang 35 4 40S 121 30 E
Buayan 35 6 3N 125 6 E
Bucak 30 37 28N 30 36 E
Bucaramanga 78 7 0N 73 0W
Buccaneer Arch. 46 16 7S 123 20 E
Buchan 8 57 32N 2 8W
Buchan Ness 8 57 29N 1 48W
Buchanan, Canada 65 51 40N 102 45W
Buchanan, Liberia 50 5 57N 10 2W
Buchanan, L., Queens., Australia 44 21 35S 145 52 E
Buchanan, L., W. Austral., Australia 47 25 33S 123 2 E
Buchanan, L., U.S.A. 71 30 50N 98 25W
Buchans 63 48 50N 56 52W
Bucharest = Bucureşti 15 44 27N 26 10 E
Buckeye 73 33 28N 112 40W
Buckhannon 68 39 2N 80 10W
Buckhaven 8 56 10N 3 2W
Buckie 8 57 40N 2 58W
Buckingham, Canada 62 45 37N 75 24W
Buckingham, U.K. 7 52 0N 0 59W
Buckingham □ 7 51 50N 0 55W
Buckingham B. 44 12 10S 135 40 E
Buckland Newton 7 50 45N 2 25W
Buckle Hd. 46 14 26S 127 52 E
Buckleboo 45 32 54S 136 12 E
Buckley 72 47 10N 122 2W
Bucklin 71 37 37N 99 40W
Buctouche 63 46 30N 64 45W
Bucureşti 15 44 27N 26 10 E
Bucyrus 68 40 48N 83 0W
Budalin 33 22 20N 95 10 E
Budapest 15 47 29N 19 5 E
Bude 7 50 49N 4 33W
Budennovsk 23 44 50N 44 10 E
Budgewoi Lake 45 33 13S 151 34 E
Búðareyri 20 65 2N 14 13W
Búðir 20 64 49N 23 23W
Budjala 54 2 50N 19 40 E
Buea 53 4 10N 9 9 E
Buena Vista, Colo., U.S.A. 73 38 56N 106 6W
Buena Vista, Va., U.S.A. 68 37 47N 79 23W
Buena Vista L. 73 35 15N 119 21W
Buenaventura, Colombia 78 3 53N 77 4W
Buenaventura, Mexico 74 29 50N 107 30W
Buenos Aires 80 34 30S 58 20W
Buenos Aires, L. 80 46 35S 72 30W
Buffalo, Mo., U.S.A. 71 37 40N 93 5W
Buffalo, N.Y., U.S.A. 68 42 55N 78 50W
Buffalo, Okla., U.S.A. 71 36 55N 99 42W
Buffalo, S. Dak., U.S.A. 70 45 39N 103 31W
Buffalo, Wyo., U.S.A. 72 44 25N 106 50W
Buffalo → 64 60 5N 115 5W
Buffalo Head Hills 64 57 25N 115 55W
Buffalo L. 64 52 27N 112 54W
Buffalo Narrows 65 55 51N 108 29W
Buffels → 56 29 36S 17 3 E
Buford 69 34 5N 84 0W
Bug →, Poland 15 52 31N 21 5 E
Bug →, U.S.S.R. 23 46 59N 31 58 E
Buga 78 4 0N 76 15W
Bugel, Tanjung 34 6 26S 111 3 E
Bugsuk 34 8 15N 117 15 E
Bugt 38 48 47N 121 56 E
Bugulma 22 54 33N 52 48 E
Buguma 53 4 42N 6 55 E
Buguruslan 22 53 39N 52 26 E
Buheirat-Murrat-el-Kubra 51 30 15N 32 40 E
Buhl, Idaho, U.S.A. 72 42 35N 114 54W
Buhl, Minn., U.S.A. 70 47 30N 92 46W
Buick 71 37 38N 91 2W
Builth Wells 7 52 10N 3 26W
Buir Nur 37 47 50N 117 42 E
Bujumbura 54 3 16S 29 18 E
Bukachacha 25 52 55N 116 50 E
Bukama 54 9 10S 25 50 E
Bukavu 54 2 20S 28 52 E
Bukene 54 4 15S 32 48 E
Bukhara 24 39 48N 64 25 E
Bukittinggi 34 0 20S 100 20 E
Bukoba 54 1 20S 31 49 E
Bukombe 52 3 31S 32 4 E
Bula 35 3 6S 130 30 E
Bulahdelah 45 32 23S 152 13 E
Bulan 35 12 40N 123 52 E
Bulandshahr 32 28 28N 77 51 E
Bulawayo 55 20 7S 28 32 E
Bulgan 37 48 45N 103 34 E
Bulgaria ■ 19 42 35N 25 30 E
Bulgroo 45 25 47S 143 58 E
Bulgunnia 45 30 10S 134 53 E
Bulhar 29 10 25N 44 30 E
Buli, Teluk 35 1 5N 128 25 E
Buliluyan, C. 34 8 20N 117 15 E
Bulkley → 64 55 15N 127 40W
Bull Shoals L. 71 36 40N 93 5W
Bullara 46 22 40S 114 3 E
Bullaring 47 32 30S 117 45 E
Buller → 43 41 44S 171 36 E
Bulli 45 34 15S 150 57 E
Bullock Creek 44 17 43S 144 31 E
Bulloo → 45 28 43S 142 30 E
Bulloo Downs, Queens., Australia 45 28 31S 142 57 E
Bulloo Downs, W. Austral., Australia 47 24 0S 119 32 E
Bulloo L. 45 28 43S 142 25 E
Bulls 43 40 10S 175 24 E
Bulo Burti 29 3 50N 45 33 E
Bulsar = Valsad 32 20 40N 72 58 E
Bultfontein 56 28 18S 26 10 E
Bulu Karakelong 35 4 35N 126 50 E
Bulukumba 35 5 33S 120 11 E
Bulun 25 70 37N 127 30 E
Bumba 54 2 13N 22 30 E
Bumhpa Bum 33 26 51N 97 14 E
Buna 54 2 58N 39 30 E
Bunbah, Khalīj 51 32 20N 23 15 E
Bunbury 47 33 20S 115 35 E
Buncrana 9 55 8N 7 28W
Bundaberg 45 24 54S 152 22 E
Bundey → 44 21 46S 135 37 E
Bundi 32 25 30N 75 35 E
Bundooma 44 24 54S 134 16 E
Bundoran 9 54 24N 8 17W
Bungil Cr. → 44 27 5S 149 5 E
Bungo-Suidō 36 33 0N 132 15 E
Bungun Shara 37 49 0N 104 0 E
Bunia 54 1 35N 30 20 E
Bunji 32 35 45N 74 40 E
Bunkie 71 31 1N 92 12W
Bunnell 69 29 28N 81 12W
Buntok 34 1 40S 114 58 E
Bununu Dass 53 10 0N 9 31 E
Bunyu 34 3 35N 117 50 E
Buol 35 1 15N 121 32 E
Buon Me Thuot 34 12 40N 108 3 E
Buorkhaya, Mys 25 71 50N 132 40 E
Buqayq 30 26 0N 49 45 E
Buqei'a 28 32 58N 35 20 E
Bur Acaba 29 3 12N 44 20 E
Bûr Safâga 51 26 43N 33 57 E
Bûr Sa'îd 51 31 16N 32 18 E
Bûr Sûdân 51 19 32N 37 9 E
Bura 52 1 4S 39 58 E
Burao 29 9 32N 45 32 E
Buras 71 29 20N 89 33W
Buraydah 30 26 20N 44 8 E
Buraymī, Al Wāhāt al 31 24 10N 55 43 E
Burbank 73 34 9N 118 23W
Burcher 45 33 30S 147 16 E
Burdekin → 44 19 38S 147 25 E
Burdett 64 49 50N 111 32W
Burdur 30 37 45N 30 22 E
Burdwan = Barddhaman 33 23 14N 87 39 E
Bure → 6 52 38N 1 45 E
Bureya → 25 49 27N 129 30 E
Burgas 19 42 33N 27 29 E
Burgenland □ 14 47 20N 16 20 E
Burgeo 63 47 37N 57 38W
Burgersdorp 56 31 0S 26 20 E
Burges, Mt. 47 30 50S 121 5 E
Burgos 13 42 21N 3 41W
Burgsvik 21 57 3N 18 19 E
Burgundy = Bourgogne 12 47 0N 4 50 E
Burias 35 12 55N 123 5 E
Burica, Pta. 75 8 3N 82 51W
Burin, Canada 63 47 1N 55 14W
Būrīn, Jordan 28 32 11N 35 15 E
Buriram 34 15 0N 103 0 E
Burji 51 5 29N 37 51 E
Burkburnett 71 34 7N 98 35W
Burke 72 47 31N 115 56W
Burke → 44 23 12S 139 33 E
Burketown 44 17 45S 139 33 E
Burkina Faso ■ 50 12 0N 1 0W
Burk's Falls 62 45 37N 79 24W
Burley 72 42 37N 113 55W
Burlington, Colo., U.S.A. 70 39 21N 102 18W
Burlington, Iowa, U.S.A. 70 40 50N 91 5W
Burlington, Kans., U.S.A. 70 38 15N 95 47W
Burlington, N.C., U.S.A. 69 36 7N 79 27W
Burlington, N.J., U.S.A. 68 40 5N 74 50W
Burlington, Vt., U.S.A. 68 44 27N 73 14W
Burlington, Wash., U.S.A. 72 48 29N 122 19W
Burlington, Wis., U.S.A. 68 42 41N 88 18W
Burlyu-Tyube 24 46 30N 79 10 E
Burma ■ 33 21 0N 96 30 E
Burnaby I. 64 52 25N 131 19W
Burnet 71 30 45N 98 11W
Burney 72 40 56N 121 41W
Burngup 47 33 2S 118 42 E
Burnie 44 41 4S 145 56 E
Burnley 6 53 47N 2 15W
Burns, Oreg., U.S.A. 72 43 40N 119 4W
Burns, Wyo., U.S.A. 70 41 13N 104 18W
Burns Lake 64 54 20N 125 45W
Burnside → 60 66 51N 108 4W
Burnside, L. 47 25 22S 123 0 E
Burntwood → 65 56 8N 96 34W
Burntwood L. 65 55 22N 100 26W
Burqā 28 32 18N 35 11 E
Burqân 30 29 0N 47 57 E
Burqin 37 47 43N 87 0 E
Burra 45 33 40S 138 55 E
Burramurra 44 20 25S 137 15 E
Burren Junction 45 30 7S 148 59 E
Burrendong Dam 45 32 39S 149 6 E
Burrinjuck Res. 45 35 0S 148 36 E
Burro, Serranías del 74 29 0N 102 0W
Burrundie 46 13 32S 131 42 E
Burruyacú 80 26 30S 64 40W
Burry Port 7 51 41N 4 17W
Bursa 30 40 15N 29 5 E
Burstall 65 50 39N 109 54W
Burton L. 62 54 45N 78 20W
Burton-upon-Trent 6 52 48N 1 39W
Burtundy 45 33 45S 142 15 E
Buru 35 3 30S 126 30 E
Burundi ■ 54 3 15S 30 0 E
Burutu 53 5 20N 5 29 E
Burwell 70 41 49N 99 8W
Bury 6 53 36N 2 19W
Bury St. Edmunds 7 52 15N 0 42 E
Buryat A.S.S.R. □ 25 53 0N 110 0 E
Buşayyah 30 30 0N 46 10 E
Būshehr 31 28 55N 50 55 E
Būshehr □ 31 28 20N 51 45 E
Bushell 65 59 31N 108 45W
Bushire = Būshehr 31 28 55N 50 55 E
Bushnell, Ill., U.S.A. 70 40 32N 90 30W
Bushnell, Nebr., U.S.A. 70 41 18N 103 50W
Businga 54 3 16N 20 59 E
Buskerud fylke □ 21 60 13N 9 0 E
Busra ash Shām 30 32 30N 36 25 E
Busselton 47 33 42S 115 15 E
Bussum 11 52 16N 5 10 E
Busto Arsizio 18 45 40N 8 50 E
Busu-Djanoa 54 1 43N 21 23 E
Busuanga 35 12 10N 120 0 E
Buta 54 2 50N 24 53 E
Butare 54 2 31S 29 52 E
Butaritari 40 3 30N 174 0 E
Bute 8 55 48N 5 2W
Bute Inlet 64 50 40N 124 53W
Butembo 54 0 9N 29 18 E
Butha Qi 38 48 0N 122 32 E
Butler, Mo., U.S.A. 70 38 17N 94 18W
Butler, Pa., U.S.A. 68 40 52N 79 52W
Butte, Mont., U.S.A. 72 46 0N 112 31W
Butte, Nebr., U.S.A. 70 42 56N 98 54W
Butterworth = Gcuwa 57 32 20S 28 11 E
Butterworth 34 5 24N 100 23 E
Buttfield, Mt. 47 24 45S 128 9 E
Button B. 65 58 45N 94 23W
Butty Hd. 47 33 54S 121 39 E
Butuan 35 8 57N 125 33 E
Butung 35 5 0S 122 45 E
Buturlinovka 23 50 50N 40 35 E
Buxton, S. Africa 56 27 38S 24 42 E
Buxton, U.K. 6 53 16N 1 54W
Buy 22 58 28N 41 28 E
Buyaga 25 59 50N 127 0 E
Buzău 15 45 10N 26 50 E
Buzău → 15 45 26N 27 44 E
Buzen 36 33 35N 131 5 E
Buzi → 55 19 50S 34 43 E
Buzuluk 22 52 48N 52 12 E
Buzzards Bay 68 41 45N 70 38W
Bydgoszcz 15 53 10N 18 0 E
Byelorussian S.S.R. □ 22 53 30N 27 0 E
Byers 70 39 46N 104 13W
Byhalia 71 34 53N 89 41W
Bylas 73 33 11N 110 9W
Bylot I. 61 73 13N 78 34W
Byro 47 26 5S 116 11 E
Byrock 45 30 40S 146 27 E
Byron Bay 45 28 43S 153 37 E
Byrranga, Gory 25 75 0N 100 0 E
Byske 20 64 57N 21 11 E
Byske älv → 20 64 57N 21 13 E
Bytom 15 50 25N 18 54 E

C

Ca Mau = Quan Long 34 9 7N 105 8 E
Caála 55 12 46S 15 30 E
Caamano Sd. 64 52 55N 129 25W
Cabanatuan 35 15 30N 120 58 E
Cabano 63 47 40N 68 56W
Cabedelo 79 7 0S 34 50W
Cabimas 78 10 23N 71 25W
Cabinda 54 5 33S 12 11 E
Cabinda □ 54 5 0S 12 30 E
Cabinet Mts. 72 48 0N 115 30W
Cabo Blanco 80 47 15S 65 47W
Cabo Frio 79 22 51S 42 3W
Cabo Pantoja 78 1 0S 75 10W
Cabonga, Réservoir 62 47 20N 76 40W
Cabool 71 37 10N 92 8W
Caboolture 45 27 5S 152 58 E
Cabora Bassa Dam 55 15 20S 32 50 E
Caborca 74 30 40N 112 10W
Cabot Strait 63 47 15N 59 40W
Cabrera, I. 13 39 8N 2 57 E
Cabri 65 50 35N 108 25W
Cabriel → 13 39 14N 1 3W
Čačak 19 43 54N 20 20 E
Cáceres, Brazil 78 16 5S 57 40W
Cáceres, Spain 13 39 26N 6 23W
Cache Bay 62 46 22N 80 0W
Cachimbo, Serra do 79 9 30S 55 0W
Cachoeira 79 12 30S 39 0W
Cachoeira de Itapemirim 79 20 51S 41 7W
Cachoeira do Sul 80 30 3S 52 53W
Cacólo 54 10 9S 19 21 E
Caconda 55 13 48S 15 8 E
Cacongo 54 5 11S 12 5 E
Caddo 71 34 8N 96 18W
Cadell Cr. → 44 22 35S 141 51 E
Cader Idris 6 52 43N 3 56W
Cadibarrawirracanna, L. 45 28 52S 135 27 E
Cadillac, Canada 62 48 14N 78 23W
Cadillac, U.S.A. 68 44 16N 85 25W
Cadiz, Phil. 35 10 57N 123 15 E
Cádiz, Spain 13 36 30N 6 20W
Cádiz, G. de 13 36 40N 7 0W
Cadney Park 45 27 55S 134 3 E
Cadomin 64 53 2N 117 20W
Cadotte → 64 56 43N 117 10W
Cadoux 47 30 46S 117 7 E
Caen 12 49 10N 0 22W
Caernarfon 6 53 8N 4 17W
Caernarfon B. 6 53 4N 4 40W
Caernarvon = Caernarfon 6 53 8N 4 17W
Caerphilly 7 51 34N 3 13W
Caesarea 28 32 30N 34 53 E
Caeté 79 19 55S 43 40W
Caetité 79 13 50S 42 32W
Cafu 56 16 30S 15 8 E
Cagayan → 35 18 25N 121 42 E
Cagayan de Oro 35 8 30N 124 40 E
Cágliari 18 39 15N 9 6 E
Cágliari, G. di 18 39 8N 9 10 E
Caguas 75 18 14N 66 4W
Caha Mts. 9 51 45N 9 40W
Cahama 56 16 17S 14 19 E
Caher 9 52 23N 7 56W
Cahersiveen 9 51 57N 10 13W
Cahore Pt. 9 52 34N 6 11W
Cahors 12 44 27N 1 27 E
Cahuapanas 78 5 15S 77 0W
Caia 55 17 51S 35 24 E
Caibarién 75 22 30N 79 30W
Caicara 78 7 38N 66 10W
Caicó 79 6 20S 37 0W
Caicos Is. 75 21 40N 71 40W
Caicos Passage 75 22 45N 72 45W
Cairn Gorm 8 57 7N 3 40W
Cairn Toul 8 57 3N 3 44W
Cairngorm Mts. 8 57 6N 3 42W
Cairns 44 16 57S 145 45 E
Cairo = El Qâhira 51 30 1N 31 14 E
Cairo, Ga., U.S.A. 69 30 52N 84 12W
Cairo, Ill., U.S.A. 71 37 0N 89 10W
Caithness, Ord of 8 58 9N 3 37W
Caiundo 55 15 50S 17 28 E
Caiza 78 20 2S 65 40W
Cajamarca 78 7 5S 78 28W
Cajàzeiras 79 6 52S 38 30W
Calabar 53 4 57N 8 20 E
Calábria □ 18 39 24N 16 30 E
Calafate 80 50 19S 72 15W
Calahorra 13 42 18N 1 59W
Calais, France 12 50 57N 1 56 E
Calais, U.S.A. 63 45 11N 67 20W
Calama, Brazil 78 8 0S 62 50W
Calama, Chile 80 22 30S 68 55W
Calamar, Bolívar, Colombia 78 10 15N 74 55W
Calamar, Vaupés, Colombia 78 1 58N 72 32W
Calamian Group 35 11 50N 119 55 E
Calamocha 13 40 50N 1 17W
Calang 34 4 37N 95 37 E
Calapan 35 13 25N 121 7 E
Calatayud 13 41 20N 1 40W
Calauag 35 13 55N 122 15 E
Calavite, Cape 35 13 26N 120 20 E
Calbayog 35 12 4N 124 38 E
Calca 78 13 22S 72 0W
Calcasieu L. 71 30 0N 93 17W
Calcutta 33 22 36N 88 24 E
Calder → 6 53 44N 1 21W
Caldera 80 27 5S 70 55W
Caldwell, Idaho, U.S.A. 72 43 45N 116 42W

Casper

Caldwell, Kans., U.S.A. 71 37 5N 97 37W
Caldwell, Tex., U.S.A. 71 30 30N 96 42W
Caledon 56 34 14S 19 26 E
Caledon → 56 30 31S 26 5 E
Caledon B. 44 12 45S 137 0 E
Calella 13 41 37N 2 40 E
Calemba 56 16 0S 15 44 E
Calera, La 80 32 50S 71 10W
Calexico 73 32 40N 115 33W
Calf of Man 6 54 4N 4 48W
Calgary 64 51 0N 114 10W
Calhoun 69 34 30N 84 55W
Cali 78 3 25N 76 35W
Calicut 32 11 15N 75 43 E
Caliente 73 37 36N 114 34W
California 70 38 37N 92 30W
California □ 73 37 25N 120 0W
California, Baja 74 32 10N 115 12W
California, Baja, T.N. □ 74 30 0N 115 0W
California, Baja, T.S. □ 74 25 50N 111 50W
California, G. de 74 27 0N 111 0W
California, Lr. = California, Baja 74 32 10N 115 12W
Calingasta 80 31 15S 69 30W
Calipatria 73 33 8N 115 30W
Calistoga 72 38 36N 122 32W
Calitzdorp 56 33 33S 21 42 E
Callabonna, L. 45 29 40S 140 5 E
Callan 9 52 33N 7 25W
Callander 8 56 15N 4 14W
Callao 78 12 0S 77 0W
Callaway 70 41 20N 99 56W
Callide 44 24 18S 150 28 E
Calling Lake 64 55 15N 113 12W
Calliope 44 24 0S 151 16 E
Calne 6 51 26N 2 0W
Calola 56 16 25S 17 48 E
Caloundra 45 26 45S 153 10 E
Calstock 62 49 47N 84 9W
Caltagirone 18 37 13N 14 30 E
Caltanissetta 18 37 30N 14 3 E
Calulo 54 10 1S 14 56 E
Calumet 68 47 14N 88 27W
Calunda 55 12 7S 23 36 E
Calvados □ 12 49 5N 0 15W
Calvert 71 30 59N 96 40W
Calvert → 44 16 17S 137 44 E
Calvert Hills 44 17 15S 137 20 E
Calvert I. 64 51 30N 128 0W
Calvert Ra. 46 24 0S 122 30 E
Calvi 12 42 34N 8 45 E
Calvinia 56 31 28S 19 45 E
Cam → 7 52 21N 0 16 E
Camabatela 54 8 20S 15 26 E
Camacupa 55 11 58S 17 22 E
Camagüey 75 21 20N 78 0W
Camaná 78 16 30S 72 50W
Camaret 12 48 16N 4 37W
Camargo 78 20 38S 65 15 E
Camarón, C. 75 16 0N 85 0W
Camarones 80 44 50S 65 40W
Camas 72 45 35N 122 24W
Camas Valley 72 43 0N 123 46W
Cambay = Khambhat 32 22 23N 72 33 E
Cambodia ■ 34 12 15N 105 0 E
Camborne 7 50 13N 5 18W
Cambrai 12 50 11N 3 14 E
Cambria 73 35 39N 121 6W
Cambrian Mts. 7 52 25N 3 52W
Cambridge, Canada 62 43 23N 80 15W
Cambridge, N.Z. 43 37 54S 175 29 E
Cambridge, U.K. 7 52 13N 0 8 E
Cambridge, Idaho, U.S.A. 72 44 36N 116 40W
Cambridge, Mass., U.S.A. 68 42 20N 71 8W
Cambridge, Md., U.S.A. 68 38 33N 76 2W
Cambridge, Minn., U.S.A. 70 45 34N 93 15W
Cambridge, Nebr., U.S.A. 70 40 20N 100 12W
Cambridge, Ohio, U.S.A. 68 40 1N 81 35W
Cambridge Bay 60 69 10N 105 0W
Cambridge Gulf 46 14 55S 128 15 E
Cambridgeshire □ 7 52 12N 0 7 E
Camden, Ala., U.S.A. 69 31 59N 87 15W
Camden, Ark., U.S.A. 71 33 40N 92 50W
Camden, Maine, U.S.A. 63 44 14N 69 6W
Camden, N.J., U.S.A. 68 39 57N 75 7W
Camden, S.C., U.S.A. 69 34 17N 80 34W
Camden Sound 46 15 27S 124 25 E
Camdenton 71 38 1N 92 45W
Cameron, Ariz., U.S.A. 73 35 55N 111 31W
Cameron, La., U.S.A. 71 29 50N 93 18W
Cameron, Mo., U.S.A. 70 39 42N 94 14W
Cameron, Tex., U.S.A. 71 30 53N 97 0W
Cameron Falls 62 49 8N 88 19W
Cameron Hills 64 59 48N 118 0W
Cameroon ■ 54 6 0N 12 30 E
Cameroun, Mt. 54 4 13N 9 10 E
Cametá 79 2 12S 49 30W
Caminha 13 41 50N 8 50W
Camino 72 38 47N 120 40W
Camira Creek 45 29 15S 152 58 E
Camissombo 54 8 7S 20 38 E
Camocim 79 2 55S 40 50W
Camooweal 44 19 56S 138 7 E
Camopi → 79 3 10N 52 20W
Camp Crook 70 45 36N 103 59W
Camp Wood 71 29 41N 100 0W
Campana, I. 80 48 20S 75 20W
Campania □ 18 40 50N 14 45 E
Campbell 56 28 48S 23 44 E
Campbell I. 40 52 30S 169 0 E
Campbell L. 65 63 14N 106 55W
Campbell River 64 50 5N 125 20W
Campbell Town 44 41 52S 147 30 E
Campbellsville 68 37 23N 85 21W
Campbellton 63 47 57N 66 43W
Campbelltown 45 34 4S 150 49 E
Campbeltown 8 55 25N 5 36W
Campeche 74 19 50N 90 32W
Campeche □ 74 19 50N 90 32W
Campeche, B. de 74 19 30N 93 0W
Camperdown 45 38 14S 143 9 E
Camperville 65 51 59N 100 9W
Campina Grande 79 7 20S 35 47W
Campinas 80 22 50S 47 0W
Campo 54 2 22N 9 50 E
Campo Belo 79 20 52S 45 16W
Campo Formoso 79 10 30S 40 20W
Campo Grande 79 20 25S 54 40W
Campo Maíor 79 4 50S 42 12W
Campo Mourão 79 24 3S 52 22W
Campoalegre 78 2 41N 75 20W
Campobasso 18 41 34N 14 40 E
Campos 79 21 50S 41 20W
Campos Belos 79 13 10S 47 3W
Campuya → 78 1 40S 73 30W
Camrose 64 53 0N 112 50W
Camsell Portage 65 59 37N 109 15W
Can Tho 34 10 2N 105 46 E
Canada ■ 60 60 0N 100 0W
Cañada de Gómez 80 32 40S 61 30W
Canadian 71 35 56N 100 25W
Canadian → 71 35 27N 95 3W
Çanakkale 30 40 8N 26 30 E
Çanakkale Boğazı 30 40 3N 26 12 E
Canal Flats 64 50 10N 115 48W
Canandaigua 68 42 55N 77 18W
Cananea 74 31 0N 110 20W
Canarias, Is. 50 28 30N 16 0W
Canarreos, Arch. de los 75 21 35N 81 40W
Canary Is. = Canarias, Is. 50 28 30N 16 0W
Canaveral, C. 69 28 28N 80 31W
Canavieiras 79 15 39S 39 0W
Canbelego 45 31 32S 146 18 E
Canberra 45 35 15S 149 8 E
Canby, Calif., U.S.A. 72 41 26N 120 58W
Canby, Minn., U.S.A. 70 44 44N 96 15W
Canby, Oreg., U.S.A. 72 45 16N 122 42W
Cancún 74 21 8N 86 44W
Candala 29 11 30N 49 58 E
Candelo 45 36 47S 149 43 E
Candia = Iráklion 19 35 20N 25 12 E
Candle L. 65 53 50N 105 18W
Cando 70 48 30N 99 14W
Canea = Khaniá 19 35 30N 24 4 E
Canelones 80 34 32S 56 17W
Cañete, Chile 80 37 50S 73 30W
Cañete, Peru 78 13 8S 76 30W
Cangas 13 42 16N 8 47W
Canguaretama 79 6 20S 35 5W
Canguçu 80 31 22S 52 43W
Cangxi 39 31 47N 105 59 E
Cangzhou 38 38 19N 116 52 E
Canim Lake 64 51 47N 120 54W
Canipaan 34 8 33N 117 15 E
Çankırı 30 40 40N 33 37 E
Canmore 64 51 7N 115 18W
Cann River 45 37 35S 149 7 E
Canna 8 57 3N 6 33W
Cannanore 32 11 53N 75 27 E
Cannes 12 43 32N 7 0 E
Cannock 6 52 42N 2 2W
Cannon Ball → 70 46 20N 100 38W
Cannondale, Mt. 44 25 13S 148 57 E
Canoas 80 29 56S 51 11W
Canoe L. 65 55 10N 108 15W
Canon City 70 38 27N 105 14W
Canora 65 51 40N 102 30W
Canowindra 45 33 35S 148 38 E
Canso 63 45 20N 61 0W
Cantabria □ 13 43 10N 4 0W
Cantabrian Mts. = Cantábrica, Cordillera 13 43 0N 5 10W
Cantábrica, Cordillera 13 43 0N 5 10W
Cantal □ 12 45 5N 2 45 E
Canterbury, Australia 44 25 23S 141 53 E
Canterbury, U.K. 7 51 17N 1 5 E
Canterbury □ 43 43 45S 171 19 E
Canterbury Bight 43 44 16S 171 55 E
Canterbury Plains 43 43 55S 171 22 E
Canton = Guangzhou 39 23 5N 113 10 E
Canton, Ga., U.S.A. 69 34 13N 84 29W
Canton, Ill., U.S.A. 70 40 32N 90 0W
Canton, Miss., U.S.A. 71 32 40N 90 1W
Canton, Mo., U.S.A. 70 40 10N 91 33W
Canton, N.Y., U.S.A. 68 44 32N 75 3W
Canton, Ohio, U.S.A. 68 40 47N 81 22W
Canton, Okla., U.S.A. 71 36 5N 98 36W
Canton, S. Dak., U.S.A. 70 43 20N 96 35W
Canton L. 71 36 12N 98 40W
Canudos 78 7 13S 58 5W
Canutama 78 6 30S 64 20W
Canutillo 73 31 58N 106 36W
Canyon, Tex., U.S.A. 71 35 0N 101 57W
Canyon, Wyo., U.S.A. 72 44 43N 110 36W
Canyonlands Nat. Park 73 38 25N 109 30W
Canyonville 72 42 55N 123 14W
Cao Xian 39 34 50N 115 35 E
Cap-aux-Meules 63 47 23N 61 52W
Cap-Chat 63 49 6N 66 40W
Cap-de-la-Madeleine 62 46 22N 72 31W
Cap-Haïtien 75 19 40N 72 20W
Cap St.-Jacques = Vung Tau 34 10 21N 107 4 E
Capaia 54 8 27S 20 13 E
Capanaparo → 78 7 1N 67 7W
Cape → 44 20 49S 146 51 E
Cape Barren I. 44 40 25S 148 15 E
Cape Breton Highlands Nat. Park 63 46 50N 60 40W
Cape Breton I. 63 46 0N 60 30W
Cape Charles 68 37 15N 75 59W
Cape Coast 53 5 5N 1 15W
Cape Dorset 61 64 14N 76 32W
Cape Dyer 61 66 30N 61 22W
Cape Fear → 69 34 30N 78 25W
Cape Girardeau 71 37 20N 89 30W
Cape Jervis 45 35 40S 138 5 E
Cape May 68 39 1N 74 53W
Cape Preston 46 20 51S 116 12 E
Cape Province □ 56 32 0S 23 0 E
Cape Tormentine 63 46 8N 63 47W
Cape Town 56 33 55S 18 22 E
Cape Verde Is. ■ 2 17 10N 25 20W
Cape York Peninsula 44 12 0S 142 30 E
Capela 79 10 30S 37 0W
Capella 44 23 2S 148 1 E
Capernaum = Kefar Nahum 28 32 54N 35 34 E
Capim → 79 1 40S 47 47W
Capitan 73 33 33N 105 41W
Capraia 18 43 2N 9 50 E
Capreol 62 46 43N 80 56W
Caprera 18 41 12N 9 28 E
Capri 18 40 34N 14 15 E
Capricorn Group 44 23 30S 151 55 E
Capricorn Ra. 46 23 20S 116 50 E
Caprivi Strip 56 18 0S 23 0 E
Captain's Flat 45 35 35S 149 27 E
Caquetá → 78 1 15S 69 15W
Caracal 15 44 8N 24 22 E
Caracas 78 10 30N 66 55W
Caracol 79 9 15S 43 22W
Caradoc 45 30 35S 143 5 E
Carajás, Serra dos 79 6 0S 51 30W
Carangola 79 20 44S 42 5W
Carani 47 30 57S 116 28 E
Caransebeş 15 45 28N 22 18 E
Caratasca, L. 75 15 20N 83 40W
Caratinga 79 19 50S 42 10W
Caraúbas 79 5 43S 37 33W
Caravaca 13 38 8N 1 52W
Caravelas 79 17 45S 39 15W
Caraveli 78 15 45S 73 25W
Carballo 13 43 13N 8 41W
Carberry 65 49 50N 99 25W
Carbó 74 29 42N 110 58W
Carbon 64 51 30N 113 9W
Carbonara, C. 18 39 8N 9 30 E
Carbondale, Colo., U.S.A. 72 39 30N 107 10W
Carbondale, Ill., U.S.A. 71 37 45N 89 10W
Carbondale, Pa., U.S.A. 68 41 37N 75 30W
Carbonear 63 47 42N 53 13W
Carbonia 18 39 10N 8 30 E
Carcajou 64 57 47N 117 6W
Carcasse, C. 75 18 30N 74 28W
Carcassonne 12 43 13N 2 20 E
Carcross 60 60 13N 134 45W
Cardabia 46 23 2S 113 48 E
Cardamon Hills 32 9 30N 77 15 E
Cárdenas, Cuba 75 23 0N 81 30W
Cárdenas, San Luis Potosí, Mexico 74 22 0N 99 41W
Cárdenas, Tabasco, Mexico 74 17 59N 93 21W
Cardiff 7 51 28N 3 11W
Cardigan 7 52 6N 4 41W
Cardigan B. 7 52 30N 4 30W
Cardona 13 41 56N 1 40 E
Cardross 65 49 50N 105 40W
Cardston 64 49 15N 113 20W
Cardwell 44 18 14S 146 2 E
Careen L. 65 57 0N 108 11W
Carei 15 47 40N 22 29 E
Careme 35 6 55S 108 27 E
Carey, Idaho, U.S.A. 72 43 19N 113 58W
Carey, Ohio, U.S.A. 68 40 58N 83 22W
Carey, L. 47 29 0S 122 15 E
Carey L. 65 62 12N 102 55W
Careysburg 50 6 34N 10 30W
Cargados Garajos 3 17 0S 59 0 E
Carhué 80 37 10S 62 50W
Cariacica 79 20 16S 40 25W
Caribbean Sea 75 15 0N 75 0W
Cariboo Mts. 64 53 0N 121 0W
Caribou 63 46 55N 68 0W
Caribou →, Man., Canada 65 59 20N 94 44W
Caribou →, N.W.T., Canada 64 61 27N 125 45W
Caribou I. 62 47 22N 85 49W
Caribou Is. 64 61 55N 113 15W
Caribou L., Man., Canada 65 59 21N 96 10W
Caribou L., Ont., Canada 62 50 25N 89 5W
Caribou Mts. 64 59 12N 115 40W
Carinda 45 30 28S 147 41 E
Carinhanha 79 14 15S 44 46W
Carinthia □ = Kärnten □ 14 46 52N 13 30 E
Caripito 78 10 8N 63 6W
Caritianas 78 9 20S 63 6W
Carleton Place 62 45 8N 76 9W
Carletonville 56 26 23S 27 22 E
Carlin 72 40 44N 116 5W
Carlingford, L. 9 54 0N 6 5W
Carlinville 70 39 20N 89 55W
Carlisle, U.K. 6 54 54N 2 55W
Carlisle, U.S.A. 68 40 12N 77 10W
Carlota, La 80 33 30S 63 20W
Carlow 9 52 50N 6 58W
Carlow □ 9 52 43N 6 50W
Carlsbad, Calif., U.S.A. 73 33 11N 117 25W
Carlsbad, N. Mex., U.S.A. 71 32 20N 104 14W
Carlyle, Canada 65 49 40N 102 20W
Carlyle, U.S.A. 70 38 38N 89 23W
Carmacks 60 62 5N 136 16W
Carman 65 49 30N 98 0W
Carmangay 64 50 10N 113 10W
Carmanville 63 49 23N 54 19W
Carmarthen 7 51 52N 4 20W
Carmarthen B. 7 51 40N 4 30W
Carmel-by-the-Sea 73 36 38N 121 55W
Carmel Mt. 28 32 45N 35 3 E
Carmelo 80 34 0S 58 20W
Carmen 78 9 43N 75 8W
Carmen, I. 74 26 0N 111 20W
Carmen de Patagones 80 40 50S 63 0W
Carmi 68 38 6N 88 10W
Carmila 44 21 55S 149 24 E
Carmona 13 37 28N 5 42W
Carnarvon, Queens., Australia 44 24 48S 147 45 E
Carnarvon, W. Austral., Australia 47 24 51S 113 42 E
Carnarvon, S. Africa 56 30 56S 22 8 E
Carnarvon Ra., Queens., Australia 44 25 15S 148 30 E
Carnarvon Ra., W. Austral., Australia 47 25 20S 120 45 E
Carndonagh 9 55 15N 7 16W
Carnduff 65 49 10N 101 50W
Carnegie, L. 47 26 5S 122 30 E
Carnic Alps = Karnische Alpen 14 46 36N 13 0 E
Carniche, Alpi 18 46 36N 13 0 E
Carnot 54 4 59N 15 56 E
Carnot B. 46 17 20S 122 15 E
Carnsore Pt. 9 52 10N 6 20W
Caro 68 43 29N 83 27W
Carol City 69 25 5N 80 16W
Carolina, Brazil 75 7 10S 47 30W
Carolina, S. Africa 57 26 5S 30 6 E
Carolina, La 13 38 17N 3 38W
Caroline I. 41 9 15S 150 3W
Caroline Is. 3 8 0N 150 0 E
Caron 65 50 30N 105 50W
Caroni → 78 8 21N 62 43W
Caroona 45 31 24S 150 26 E
Carpathians, Mts. 15 49 30N 21 0 E
Carpaţii Meridionali 15 45 30N 25 0 E
Carpentaria, G. of 44 14 0S 139 0 E
Carpentaria Downs 44 18 44S 144 20 E
Carpinteria 73 34 25N 119 31W
Carpolac = Morea 45 36 45S 141 18 E
Carr Boyd Ra. 46 16 15S 128 35 E
Carrabelle 69 29 52N 84 40W
Carranya 46 19 14S 127 46 E
Carrara 18 44 5N 10 7 E
Carrauntoohill, Mt. 9 52 0N 9 49W
Carrick-on-Shannon 9 53 57N 8 7W
Carrick-on-Suir 9 52 22N 7 30W
Carrickfergus 9 54 43N 5 50W
Carrickfergus □ 9 54 43N 5 49W
Carrickmacross 9 54 0N 6 43W
Carrieton 45 32 25S 138 31 E
Carrington 70 47 30N 99 7W
Carrizal Bajo 80 28 5S 71 20W
Carrizo Cr. → 71 36 30N 103 40W
Carrizo Springs 71 28 28N 99 50W
Carrizozo 73 33 40N 105 57W
Carroll 70 42 2N 94 55W
Carrollton, Ga., U.S.A. 69 33 36N 85 5W
Carrollton, Ill., U.S.A. 70 39 20N 90 25W
Carrollton, Ky., U.S.A. 68 38 40N 85 10W
Carrollton, Mo., U.S.A. 70 39 19N 93 24W
Carron → 8 57 30N 5 30W
Carron, L. 8 57 22N 5 35W
Carrot → 65 53 50N 101 17W
Carrot River 65 53 17N 103 35W
Carruthers 65 52 52N 109 16W
Çarşamba 30 41 15N 36 45 E
Carse of Gowrie 8 56 30N 3 10W
Carson 70 46 27N 101 29W
Carson City 72 39 12N 119 46W
Carson Sink 72 39 50N 118 40W
Carstairs 8 55 42N 3 41W
Cartagena, Colombia 78 10 25N 75 33W
Cartagena, Spain 13 37 38N 0 59W
Cartago, Colombia 78 4 45N 75 55W
Cartago, C. Rica 75 9 50N 85 52W
Cartersville 69 34 11N 84 48W
Carterton 43 41 2S 175 31 E
Carthage, Ark., U.S.A. 71 34 4N 92 32W
Carthage, Ill., U.S.A. 70 40 25N 91 10W
Carthage, Mo., U.S.A. 71 37 10N 94 20W
Carthage, S. Dak., U.S.A. 70 44 14N 97 38W
Carthage, Tex., U.S.A. 71 32 8N 94 20W
Cartier I. 46 12 31S 123 29 E
Cartwright 63 53 41N 56 58W
Caruaru 79 8 15S 35 55W
Carúpano 78 10 39N 63 15W
Caruthersville 71 36 10N 89 40W
Carvoeiro 78 1 30S 61 59W
Casa Grande 73 32 53N 111 51W
Casablanca 50 33 36N 7 36W
Casale Monferrato 18 45 8N 8 28 E
Casas Grandes 74 30 22N 108 0W
Cascade, Idaho, U.S.A. 72 44 30N 116 2W
Cascade, Mont., U.S.A. 72 47 16N 111 46W
Cascade Locks 72 45 44N 121 54W
Cascade Ra. 72 47 0N 121 30W
Cascavel 80 24 57S 53 28W
Caserta 18 41 5N 14 20 E
Cashel 9 52 31N 7 53W
Cashmere 72 47 31N 120 30W
Cashmere Downs 47 28 57S 119 35 E
Casiguran 35 16 22N 122 7 E
Casilda 80 33 10S 61 10W
Casino 45 28 52S 153 3 E
Casiquiare → 78 2 1N 67 7W
Caslan 64 54 38N 112 31W
Casma 78 9 30S 78 20W
Caspe 13 41 14N 0 1W
Casper 72 42 52N 106 20W

Clipperton, I.

Cherryvale 71 37 20N 95 33W
Cherskiy .... 25 68 45N 161 18 E
Cherskogo Khrebet 25 65 0N 143 0 E
Cherwell → 7 51 46N 1 18W
Chesapeake 68 36 43N 76 15W
Chesapeake Bay .. 68 38 0N 76 12W
Cheshire □ 6 53 14N 2 30W
Cheshskaya Guba . 22 67 20N 47 0 E
Cheslatta L. 64 53 49N 125 20W
Chester, U.K. 6 53 12N 2 53W
Chester, Calif.,
U.S.A. 72 40 22N 121 14W
Chester, Ill., U.S.A. 71 37 58N 89 50W
Chester, Mont.,
U.S.A. 72 48 31N 111 0W
Chester, Pa., U.S.A. 68 39 54N 75 20W
Chester, S.C., U.S.A. 69 34 44N 81 13W
Chesterfield 6 53 14N 1 26W
Chesterfield, Îles .. 40 19 52S 158 15 E
Chesterfield Inlet .. 60 63 30N 90 45W
Chesterton Range . 45 25 30S 147 27 E
Chesuncook L. 63 46 0N 69 10W
Chéticamp 63 46 37N 60 59W
Chetumal 74 18 30N 88 20W
Chetumal, B. de ... 74 18 40N 88 10W
Chetwynd 64 55 45N 121 36W
Cheviot, The 6 55 29N 2 8W
Cheviot Hills 6 55 20N 2 30W
Cheviot Ra. ...... 44 25 20S 143 45 E
Chew Bahir ...... 51 4 40N 36 50 E
Chewelah 72 48 17N 117 43W
Cheyenne, Okla.,
U.S.A. 71 35 35N 99 40W
Cheyenne, Wyo.,
U.S.A. 70 41 9N 104 49W
Cheyenne → 70 44 40N 101 15W
Cheyenne Wells ... 70 38 51N 102 10W
Cheyne B. .... 47 34 35S 118 50 E
Chhapra .... 33 25 48N 84 44 E
Chhatarpur .... 32 24 55N 79 35 E
Chhindwara ...... 32 22 2N 78 59 E
Chhlong .... 34 12 15N 105 58 E
Chi → .... 34 15 11N 104 43 E
Chiamis .... 35 7 20S 108 21 E
Chiamussu =
Jiamusi .... 38 46 40N 130 26 E
Chiange .... 55 15 35S 13 40 E
Chiapa → 74 16 42N 93 0W
Chiapas □ 74 17 0N 92 45W
Chiba .... 36 35 30N 140 7 E
Chiba □ .... 36 35 30N 140 20 E
Chibabava .... 57 20 17S 33 35 E
Chibatu .... 35 7 6S 107 59 E
Chibemba, Cunene,
Angola .... 55 15 48S 14 8 E
Chibemba, Huila,
Angola .... 56 16 20S 15 20 E
Chibia .... 55 15 10S 13 42 E
Chibougamau 62 49 56N 74 24W
Chibougamau L. .. 62 49 50N 74 20W
Chibuk .... 53 10 52N 12 50 E
Chic-Chocs, Mts. .. 63 48 55N 66 0W
Chicacole =
Srikakulam ..... 33 18 14N 83 58 E
Chicago 68 41 53N 87 40W
Chicago Heights .. 68 41 29N 87 37W
Chichagof I. 64 58 0N 136 0W
Chichester 7 50 50N 0 47W
Chichibu .... 36 36 5N 139 10 E
Ch'ich'ihaerh =
Qiqihar .... 38 47 26N 124 0 E
Chickasha 71 35 0N 98 0W
Chiclana de la
Frontera 13 36 26N 6 9W
Chiclayo 78 6 42S 79 50W
Chico 72 39 45N 121 54W
Chico →, Chubut,
Argentina 80 44 0S 67 0W
Chico →,
Santa Cruz,
Argentina 80 50 0S 68 30W
Chicomo .... 57 24 31S 34 6 E
Chicopee 68 42 6N 72 37W
Chicoutimi 63 48 28N 71 5W
Chicualacuala .... 57 22 6S 31 42 E
Chidambaram .... 32 11 20N 79 45 E
Chidenguele ...... 57 24 55S 34 11 E
Chidley, C. 61 60 23N 64 26W
Chiede .... 56 17 15S 16 22 E
Chiengi .... 54 8 45S 29 10 E
Chiese → .... 18 45 8N 10 25 E
Chieti .... 18 42 22N 14 10 E
Chifeng .... 38 42 18N 118 58 E
Chignecto B. 63 45 30N 64 40W
Chiguana 78 21 0S 67 58W
Chihli, G. of = Bo
Hai .... 38 39 0N 120 0 E
Chihuahua 74 28 40N 106 3W
Chihuahua □ 74 28 40N 106 3W
Chiili .... 24 44 20N 66 15 E
Chik Bollapur ..... 32 13 25N 77 45 E
Chikmagalur ...... 32 13 15N 75 45 E
Chilako → 64 53 53N 122 57W
Chilapa 74 17 40N 99 11W
Chilas .... 32 35 25N 74 5 E
Chilaw .... 32 7 30N 79 50 E
Chilcotin → 64 51 44N 122 23W
Childers .... 45 25 15S 152 17 E
Childress 71 34 30N 100 15W
Chile ■ 80 35 0S 72 0W
Chile Rise 41 38 0S 92 0W
Chilete 78 7 10S 78 50W
Chililabombwe .... 55 12 18S 27 43 E
Chilin = Jilin ..... 38 43 44N 126 30 E
Chilka L. .... 33 19 40N 85 25 E
Chilko → 64 52 0N 123 40W
Chilko, L. 64 51 20N 124 10W
Chillagoe .... 44 17 7S 144 33 E
Chillán 80 36 40S 72 10W
Chillicothe, Ill.,
U.S.A. 70 40 55N 89 32W
Chillicothe, Mo.,
U.S.A. 70 39 45N 93 30W
Chillicothe, Ohio,
U.S.A. 68 39 20N 82 58W
Chilliwack 64 49 10N 121 54W
Chiloane, I. .... 57 20 40S 34 55 E
Chiloé, I. de 80 42 30S 73 50W
Chilpancingo 74 17 30N 99 30W
Chiltern Hills 7 51 44N 0 42W
Chilton 68 44 1N 88 12W
Chiluage .... 54 9 30S 21 50 E
Chilumba .... 52 10 28S 34 12 E
Chilwa, L. .... 55 15 15S 35 40 E
Chimay .... 11 50 3N 4 20 E
Chimbay .... 24 42 57N 59 47 E
Chimborazo 78 1 29S 78 55W
Chimbote 78 9 0S 78 35W
Chimkent .... 24 42 18N 69 36 E
Chimoio .... 55 19 4S 33 30 E
Chin □ .... 33 22 0N 93 0 E
Chin Ling Shan =
Qinling Shandi .. 39 33 50N 108 10 E
China 74 25 40N 99 20W
China ■ .... 37 30 0N 110 0 E
Chinan = Jinan ... 38 36 38N 117 1 E
Chinandega 75 12 35N 87 12W
Chinati Pk. 71 30 0N 104 25W
Chincha Alta 78 13 25S 76 7W
Chinchilla .... 45 26 45S 150 38 E
Chinchón 13 40 9N 3 26W
Chinchorro, Banco 74 18 35N 87 20W
Chinchou = Jinzhou 38 41 5N 121 3 E
Chincoteague 68 37 58N 75 21W
Chinde .... 55 18 35S 36 30 E
Chindwin → ..... 33 21 26N 95 15 E
Chingola .... 55 12 31S 27 53 E
Ch'ingtao =
Qingdao .... 38 36 5N 120 20 E
Chinguetti 50 20 25N 12 24W
Chingune .... 57 20 33S 35 0 E
Chinhae .... 38 35 9N 128 47 E
Chinhanguanine ... 57 25 21S 32 30 E
Chinhoyi .... 55 17 20S 30 8 E
Chiniot .... 32 31 45N 73 0 E
Chinju .... 38 35 12N 128 2 E
Chinle 73 36 14N 109 38W
Chinnampo .... 38 38 52N 125 10 E
Chino Valley 73 34 54N 112 28W
Chinon .... 12 47 10N 0 15 E
Chinook, Canada .. 65 51 28N 110 59W
Chinook, U.S.A. ... 72 48 35N 109 19W
Chinsali .... 54 10 30S 32 2 E
Chinteche .... 52 11 50S 34 5 E
Chióggia .... 18 45 13N 12 15 E
Chios = Khíos .... 19 38 27N 26 9 E
Chipata .... 55 13 38S 32 28 E
Chipatujah .... 35 7 45S 108 0 E
Chipewyan L. 65 58 0N 98 27W
Chipley 69 30 45N 85 32W
Chipman 63 46 6N 65 53W
Chippenham 7 51 27N 2 7W
Chippewa → 70 44 25N 92 10W
Chippewa Falls ... 70 44 55N 91 22W
Chiquián 78 10 10S 77 0W
Chiquimula 75 14 51N 89 37W
Chiquinquira 78 5 37N 73 50W
Chirala .... 32 15 50N 80 26 E
Chirchik .... 24 41 29N 69 35 E
Chiricahua Pk. 73 31 53N 109 14W
Chirikof I. 60 55 50N 155 40W
Chiriquí, G. de 75 8 0N 82 10W
Chiriquí, L. de 75 9 10N 82 0W
Chirmiri .... 33 23 15N 82 20 E
Chiromo .... 55 16 30S 35 7 E
Chirripó Grande,
Cerro 75 9 29N 83 29W
Chisamba .... 55 14 55S 28 20 E
Chisapani Garhi ... 33 27 30N 84 2 E
Chisholm 64 54 55N 114 10W
Chisos Mts. 71 29 20N 103 15W
Chistopol .... 22 55 25N 50 38 E
Chita .... 25 52 0N 113 35 E
Chitado .... 55 17 10S 14 8 E
Chitembo .... 55 13 30S 16 50 E
Chitral .... 31 35 50N 71 56 E
Chitré 75 7 59N 80 27W
Chittagong .... 33 22 19N 91 48 E
Chittagong □ ..... 33 24 5N 91 0 E
Chittaurgarh ...... 32 24 52N 74 38 E
Chittoor .... 32 13 15N 79 5 E
Chiusi .... 18 43 1N 11 58 E
Chivasso .... 18 45 10N 7 52 E
Chivilcoy 80 34 55S 60 0W
Chkalov = Orenburg 22 51 45N 55 6 E
Chobe National Park 56 18 0S 25 0 E
Choele Choel 80 39 11S 65 40W
Choix 74 26 40N 108 23W
Chojnice .... 15 53 42N 17 32 E
Chokurdakh ...... 25 70 38N 147 55 E
Cholet 12 47 4N 0 52W
Choluteca 75 13 20N 87 14W
Choma .... 55 16 48S 26 59 E
Chomutov .... 14 50 28N 13 23 E
Chon Buri .... 34 13 21N 101 1 E
Chonan .... 38 36 48N 127 9 E
Chone 78 0 40S 80 0W
Chong'an .... 39 27 45N 118 0 E
Chongde .... 39 30 32N 120 26 E
Chongjin .... 38 41 47N 129 50 E
Chŏngju, N. Korea . 38 39 40N 125 5 E
Chŏngju, S. Korea . 38 36 39N 127 27 E
Chongli .... 38 40 58N 115 15 E
Chongming Dao ... 39 31 40N 121 30 E
Chongqing .... 39 29 35N 106 25 E
Chongzuo .... 39 22 23N 107 20 E
Chŏnju .... 38 35 50N 127 4 E
Chonos, Arch. de
los 80 45 0S 75 0W
Chorley 6 53 39N 2 39W
Chorregon .... 44 22 40S 143 32 E
Chorrera, La 74 8 50N 79 50W
Chŏrwŏn .... 38 38 15N 127 10 E
Chorzów .... 15 50 18N 18 57 E
Chos-Malal 80 37 20S 70 15W
Chosan .... 38 40 50N 125 47 E
Chōshi .... 36 35 45N 140 51 E
Choszczno .... 14 53 7N 15 25 E
Choteau 72 47 50N 112 10W
Chotila .... 32 22 23N 71 15 E
Chowchilla 73 37 11N 120 12W
Choybalsan ...... 37 48 4N 114 30 E
Christchurch, N.Z. . 43 43 33S 172 47 E
Christchurch, U.K. . 7 50 44N 1 33W
Christiana .... 56 27 52S 25 8 E
Christie B. 65 62 32N 111 10W
Christina → 65 56 40N 111 3W
Christmas Cr. → . 46 18 29S 125 23 E
Christmas Creek .. 46 18 29S 125 23 E
Christmas I. =
Kiritimati 2 1 58N 157 27W
Christmas I. ...... 3 10 30S 105 40 E
Christopher L. .... 47 24 49S 127 42 E
Chu .... 24 43 36N 73 42 E
Chu Chua 64 51 22N 120 10W
Ch'uanchou =
Quanzhou ..... 39 24 55N 118 34 E
Chūbu □ .... 36 36 45N 137 30 E
Chubut → 80 43 20S 65 5W
Chuchi L. 64 55 12N 124 30W
Chudskoye, Oz. ... 22 58 13N 27 30 E
Chūgoku □ ...... 36 35 0N 133 0 E
Chūgoku-Sanchi .. 36 35 0N 133 0 E
Chugwater 70 41 48N 104 47W
Chuka .... 52 0 23S 37 38 E
Chukotskiy Khrebet 25 68 0N 175 0 E
Chukotskoye More 25 68 0N 175 0W
Chula Vista 73 32 39N 117 8W
Chulman .... 25 56 52N 124 52 E
Chulucanas 78 5 8S 80 10W
Chulym → ...... 24 57 43N 83 51 E
Chumbicha 80 29 0S 66 10W
Chumikan .... 25 54 40N 135 10 E
Chumphon .... 34 10 35N 99 14 E
Chuna → .... 25 57 47N 94 37 E
Chun'an .... 39 29 35N 119 3 E
Chunchŏn .... 38 37 58N 127 44 E
Chungking =
Chongqing ..... 39 29 35N 106 25 E
Chunya .... 54 8 30S 33 27 E
Chuquibamba 78 15 47S 72 44W
Chuquicamata 80 22 15S 69 0W
Chuquisaca □ 78 23 30S 63 30W
Chur .... 14 46 52N 9 32 E
Churachandpur ... 33 24 20N 93 40 E
Churchill 65 58 47N 94 11W
Churchill →, Man.,
Canada 65 58 47N 94 12W
Churchill →, Nfld.,
Canada 63 53 19N 60 10W
Churchill, C. 65 58 46N 93 12W
Churchill Falls 63 53 36N 64 19W
Churchill L. 65 55 55N 108 20W
Churchill Pk. 64 58 10N 125 10W
Churu .... 32 28 20N 74 50 E
Chushal .... 32 33 40N 78 40 E
Chusovoy .... 22 58 15N 57 40 E
Chuvash A.S.S.R.□ 22 55 30N 47 0 E
Ci Xian .... 38 36 20N 114 25 E
Cianjur .... 35 6 49S 107 8 E
Cibadok .... 35 6 53S 106 47 E
Cibatu .... 35 7 8S 107 59 E
Cicero 68 41 48N 87 48W
Ciechanów .... 15 52 52N 20 38 E
Ciego de Avila 75 21 50N 78 50W
Ciénaga 78 11 1N 74 15W
Cienfuegos 75 22 10N 80 30W
Cieszyn .... 15 49 45N 18 35 E
Cieza 13 38 17N 1 23W
Cijulang .... 35 7 42S 108 27 E
Cikajang .... 35 7 25S 107 48 E
Cikampek .... 35 6 23S 107 28 E
Cilacap .... 35 7 43S 109 0 E
Cilician Gates P. .. 30 37 20N 34 52 E
Cimahi .... 35 6 53S 107 33 E
Cimarron, Kans.,
U.S.A. 71 37 50N 100 20W
Cimarron, N. Mex.,
U.S.A. 71 36 30N 104 52W
Cimarron → 71 36 10N 96 17W
Cimone, Mte. ..... 18 44 10N 10 40 E
Cîmpina .... 15 45 10N 25 45 E
Cîmpulung .... 15 45 17N 25 3 E
Cinca → .... 13 41 26N 0 21 E
Cincinnati 68 39 10N 84 26W
Ciney .... 11 50 18N 5 5 E
Cinto, Mte. .... 12 42 24N 8 54 E
Circle, Alaska,
U.S.A. 60 65 50N 144 10W
Circle, Mont., U.S.A. 70 47 26N 105 35W
Circleville, Ohio,
U.S.A. 68 39 35N 82 57W
Circleville, Utah,
U.S.A. 73 38 12N 112 24W
Cirebon .... 35 6 45S 108 32 E
Cirencester 7 51 43N 1 59W
Cisco 71 32 25N 99 0W
Ciskei □ .... 57 33 0S 27 0 E
Citlaltépetl 74 19 0N 97 20W
Citrusdal .... 56 32 35S 19 0 E
Ciudad Altamirano . 74 18 20N 100 40W
Ciudad Bolívar 78 8 5N 63 36W
Ciudad Camargo .. 74 27 41N 105 10W
Ciudad de Valles .. 74 22 0N 99 0W
Ciudad del Carmen 74 18 38N 91 50W
Ciudad Delicias =
Delicias 74 28 10N 105 30W
Ciudad Guayana .. 78 8 0N 62 30W
Ciudad Guerrero .. 74 28 33N 107 28W
Ciudad Guzmán ... 74 19 40N 103 30W
Ciudad Juárez 74 31 40N 106 28W
Ciudad Madero ... 74 22 19N 97 50W
Ciudad Mante 74 22 50N 99 0W
Ciudad Obregón .. 74 27 28N 109 59W
Ciudad Real 13 38 59N 3 55W
Ciudad Rodrigo ... 13 40 35N 6 32W
Ciudad Trujillo =
Santo Domingo . 75 18 30N 69 59W
Ciudad Victoria ... 74 23 41N 99 9W
Civitanova Marche 18 43 18N 13 41 E
Civitavécchia ..... 18 42 6N 11 46 E
Çivril .... 30 38 20N 29 43 E
Cizre .... 30 37 19N 42 10 E
Clackline .... 47 31 40S 116 32 E
Clacton-on-Sea ... 7 51 47N 1 10 E
Claire, L. 64 58 35N 112 5W
Clairemont 71 33 9N 100 44W
Clanton 69 32 48N 86 36W
Clanwilliam ...... 56 32 11S 18 52 E
Clara 9 53 20N 7 38W
Clara → .... 44 19 8S 142 30 E
Clare, Australia ... 45 33 50S 138 37 E
Clare, U.S.A. 68 43 47N 84 45W
Clare □ 9 52 20N 9 0W
Clare → 9 53 22N 9 5W
Clare I. 9 53 48N 10 0W
Claremont 68 43 23N 72 20W
Claremont Pt. .... 44 14 1S 143 41 E
Claremore 71 36 40N 95 37W
Claremorris 9 53 45N 9 0W
Clarence →,
Australia .... 45 29 25S 153 22 E
Clarence →, N.Z. 43 42 10S 173 56 E
Clarence, I. 80 54 0S 72 0W
Clarence Str.,
Australia .... 46 12 0S 131 0 E
Clarence Str., U.S.A. 64 55 40N 132 10W
Clarendon, Ark.,
U.S.A. 71 34 41N 91 20W
Clarendon, Tex.,
U.S.A. 71 34 58N 100 54W
Clarenville 63 48 10N 54 1W
Claresholm 64 50 0N 113 33W
Clarinda 70 40 45N 95 0W
Clarion 70 42 41N 93 46W
Clarion Fracture
Zone 41 20 0N 120 0W
Clark 70 44 55N 97 45W
Clark Fork 72 48 9N 116 9W
Clark Fork → 72 48 9N 116 15W
Clark Hill Res. 69 33 45N 82 20W
Clarkdale 73 34 53N 112 3W
Clarke City 63 50 12N 66 38W
Clarke I. .... 44 40 32S 148 10 E
Clarke L. 65 54 24N 106 54W
Clarke Ra. .... 44 20 45S 148 20 E
Clark's Fork → .. 72 45 39N 108 43W
Clark's Harbour ... 63 43 25N 65 38W
Clarksburg 68 39 18N 80 21W
Clarksdale 71 34 12N 90 33W
Clarkston 72 46 28N 117 2W
Clarksville, Ark.,
U.S.A. 71 35 29N 93 27W
Clarksville, Tenn.,
U.S.A. 69 36 32N 87 20W
Clarksville, Tex.,
U.S.A. 71 33 37N 94 59W
Clatskanie 72 46 9N 123 12W
Claude 71 35 8N 101 22W
Claveria .... 35 18 37N 121 4 E
Clay Center 70 39 27N 97 9W
Claypool 73 33 27N 110 55W
Clayton, Idaho,
U.S.A. 72 44 12N 114 31W
Clayton, N. Mex.,
U.S.A. 71 36 30N 103 10W
Cle Elum 72 47 15N 120 57W
Clear, C. 9 51 26N 9 30W
Clear I. 9 51 26N 9 30W
Clear L. 72 39 5N 122 47W
Clear Lake, S. Dak.,
U.S.A. 70 44 48N 96 41W
Clear Lake, Wash.,
U.S.A. 72 48 27N 122 15W
Clear Lake Res. ... 72 41 55N 121 10W
Clearfield, Pa.,
U.S.A. 68 41 0N 78 27W
Clearfield, Utah,
U.S.A. 72 41 10N 112 0W
Clearmont 72 44 43N 106 29W
Clearwater, Canada 64 51 38N 120 2W
Clearwater, U.S.A. . 69 27 58N 82 45W
Clearwater →,
Alta., Canada ... 64 52 22N 114 57W
Clearwater →,
Alta., Canada ... 65 56 44N 111 23W
Clearwater Cr. → 64 61 36N 125 30W
Clearwater Mts. ... 72 46 20N 115 30W
Clearwater Prov.
Park 65 54 0N 101 0W
Cleburne 71 32 18N 97 25W
Cleethorpes 6 53 33N 0 2W
Cleeve Cloud 7 51 56N 2 0W
Clerke Reef ...... 46 17 22S 119 20 E
Clermont .... 44 22 49S 147 39 E
Clermont-Ferrand . 12 45 46N 3 4 E
Clervaux .... 11 50 4N 6 2 E
Cleveland, Australia 45 27 30S 153 15 E
Cleveland, Miss.,
U.S.A. 71 33 43N 90 43W
Cleveland, Ohio,
U.S.A. 68 41 28N 81 43W
Cleveland, Okla.,
U.S.A. 71 36 21N 96 33W
Cleveland, Tenn.,
U.S.A. 69 35 9N 84 52W
Cleveland, Tex.,
U.S.A. 71 30 18N 95 0W
Cleveland □ ...... 6 54 35N 1 8 E
Cleveland, C. ..... 44 19 11S 147 1 E
Clew B. 9 53 54N 9 50W
Clewiston 69 26 44N 80 50W
Clifden, Ireland ... 9 53 30N 10 2W
Clifden, N.Z. ..... 43 46 1S 167 42 E
Clifton, Australia .. 45 27 59S 151 53 E
Clifton, Ariz., U.S.A. 73 33 8N 109 23W
Clifton, Tex., U.S.A. 71 31 46N 97 35W
Clifton Beach ..... 44 16 46S 145 39 E
Clifton Forge 68 37 49N 79 51W
Clifton Hills ...... 45 27 1S 138 54 E
Climax 65 49 10N 108 20W
Clinch → 69 36 0N 84 29W
Clingmans Dome .. 69 35 35N 83 30W
Clint 73 31 37N 106 11W
Clinton, B.C.,
Canada 64 51 6N 121 35W
Clinton, Ont.,
Canada 62 43 37N 81 32W
Clinton, N.Z. ..... 43 46 12S 169 23 E
Clinton, Ark., U.S.A. 71 35 37N 92 30W
Clinton, Ill., U.S.A. 70 40 8N 89 0W
Clinton, Ind., U.S.A. 68 39 40N 87 22W
Clinton, Iowa, U.S.A. 70 41 50N 90 12W
Clinton, Mass.,
U.S.A. 68 42 26N 71 40W
Clinton, Mo., U.S.A. 70 38 20N 93 46W
Clinton, N.C., U.S.A. 69 35 5N 78 15W
Clinton, Okla., U.S.A. 71 35 30N 99 0W
Clinton, S.C., U.S.A. 69 34 30N 81 54W
Clinton, Tenn.,
U.S.A. 69 36 6N 84 10W
Clinton C. .... 44 22 30S 150 45 E
Clinton Colden L. .. 60 63 58N 107 27W
Clintonville 70 44 35N 88 46W
Clipperton, I. 41 10 18N 109 13W

Danlí

Danlí **75** 14 4N 86 35W
Dannemora, Sweden **21** 60 12N 17 51 E
Dannemora, U.S.A. **68** 44 41N 73 44W
Dannevirke **43** 40 12S 176 8 E
Dannhauser **57** 28 0S 30 3 E
Danshui **39** 25 12N 121 25 E
Dansville **68** 42 32N 77 41W
Dante **29** 10 25N 51 16 E
Danube → **15** 45 20N 29 40 E
Danville, Ill., U.S.A. **68** 40 10N 87 40W
Danville, Ky., U.S.A. **68** 37 40N 84 45W
Danville, Va., U.S.A. **69** 36 40N 79 20W
Danzhai **39** 26 11N 107 48 E
Danzig = Gdańsk **15** 54 22N 18 40 E
Dao **35** 10 30N 121 57 E
Dao Xian **39** 25 36N 111 31 E
Daoud = Aïn Beïda **50** 35 50N 7 29 E
Daqing Shan **38** 40 40N 111 0 E
Daqu Shan **39** 30 25N 122 20 E
Dar-es-Salaam, Tanzania **52** 6 50S 39 12 E
Dar es Salaam, Tanzania **54** 6 50S 39 12 E
Dar'ā **28** 32 36N 36 7 E
Dārāb **31** 28 50N 54 30 E
Daraj **50** 30 10N 10 28 E
Darband **32** 34 20N 72 50 E
Darbhanga **33** 26 15N 85 55 E
Darby **72** 46 2N 114 7W
Dardanelle **71** 35 12N 93 9W
Dardanelles = Çanakkale Boğazı **30** 40 0N 20 10 E
Dârfûr **51** 13 40N 24 0 E
Dargai **32** 34 25N 71 55 E
Dargan Ata **24** 40 29N 62 10 E
Dargaville **43** 35 57S 173 52 E
Darhan Muminggan Lianheqi **38** 41 40N 110 28 E
Darien **74** 9 7N 79 46W
Darién, G. del **78** 9 0N 77 0W
Darjeeling = Darjiling **33** 27 3N 88 18 E
Darjiling **33** 27 3N 88 18 E
Dark Cove **63** 48 47N 54 13W
Darkan **47** 33 20S 116 43 E
Darling → **45** 34 4S 141 54 E
Darling Downs **45** 27 30S 150 30 E
Darling Ra. **47** 32 30S 116 0 E
Darlington, U.K. **6** 54 33N 1 33W
Darlington, S.C., U.S.A. **69** 34 18N 79 50W
Darlington, Wis., U.S.A. **70** 42 43N 90 7W
Darlot, L. **47** 27 48S 121 35 E
Darłowo **14** 54 25N 16 25 E
Darmstadt **14** 49 51N 8 40 E
Darnah **51** 32 40N 22 35 E
Darnall **57** 29 23S 31 18 E
Darnley B. **60** 69 30N 123 30W
Darr **44** 23 13S 144 7 E
Darr → **44** 23 39S 143 50 E
Darrington **72** 48 14N 121 37W
Darror → **29** 10 30N 50 0 E
Dart → **7** 50 24N 3 36W
Dartmoor **7** 50 36N 4 0W
Dartmouth, Australia **44** 23 31S 144 44 E
Dartmouth, Canada **63** 44 40N 63 30W
Dartmouth, U.K. **7** 50 21N 3 35W
Dartmouth, L. **45** 26 4S 145 18 E
Darvaza **24** 40 11N 58 24 E
Darvel, Teluk **35** 4 50N 118 20 E
Darwha **32** 20 15N 77 45 E
Darwin **46** 12 25S 130 51 E
Darwin River **46** 12 50S 130 58 E
Dās **31** 25 20N 53 30 E
Dasht → **31** 25 10N 61 40 E
Dasht-e Kavīr **31** 34 30N 55 0 E
Dasht-e Lūt **31** 31 30N 58 0 E
Dasht-e Mārgow **31** 30 40N 62 30 E
Dasseneiland **56** 33 25S 18 3 E
Datia **32** 25 39N 78 27 E
Datian **39** 25 40N 117 50 E
Datong, Anhui, China **39** 30 48N 117 44 E
Datong, Shanxi, China **38** 40 6N 113 18 E
Datu, Tanjung **34** 2 5N 109 39 E
Datu Piang **35** 7 2N 124 30 E
Daugava → **22** 57 4N 24 3 E
Daugavpils **22** 55 53N 26 32 E
Daulpur **32** 26 45N 77 59 E
Dauphin **65** 51 9N 100 5W
Dauphin I. **69** 30 16N 88 10W
Dauphin L. **65** 51 20N 99 45W
Dauphiné **12** 45 15N 5 25 E
Daura **53** 11 31N 11 24 E
Davangere **32** 14 25N 75 55 E
Davao **35** 7 0N 125 40 E
Davao, G. of **35** 6 30N 125 48 E
Dāvar Panāh **31** 27 25N 62 15 E
Davenport, Iowa, U.S.A. **70** 41 30N 90 40W
Davenport, Wash., U.S.A. **72** 47 40N 118 5W
Davenport Downs **44** 24 8S 141 7 E
Davenport Ra. **44** 20 28S 134 0 E
David **75** 8 30N 82 30W
David City **70** 41 18N 97 10W
Davidson **65** 51 16N 105 59W
Davis **72** 38 33N 121 44W
Davis Dam **73** 35 11N 114 35W
Davis Inlet **63** 55 50N 60 59W
Davis Mts. **71** 30 42N 104 15W
Davis Str. **61** 65 0N 58 0W
Davos **14** 46 48N 9 49 E
Davy L. **65** 58 53N 108 18W
Dawes Ra. **44** 24 40S 150 40 E
Dawson, Canada **60** 64 10N 139 30W
Dawson, Ga., U.S.A. **69** 31 45N 84 28W
Dawson, N. Dak., U.S.A. **70** 46 56N 99 45W
Dawson, I. **80** 53 50S 70 50W
Dawson Creek **64** 55 45N 120 15W
Dawson Inlet **65** 61 50N 93 25W
Dawson Range **44** 24 30S 149 48 E
Daxian **39** 31 15N 107 23 E
Daxin **39** 22 50N 107 11 E
Daxue Shan **37** 30 30N 101 30 E
Daye **39** 30 6N 114 58 E
Dayong **39** 29 11N 110 30 E
Dayr Abū Sa'īd **28** 32 30N 35 42 E
Dayr al-Ghuṣūn **28** 32 21N 35 4 E
Dayr az Zawr **30** 35 20N 40 5 E
Dayr Dirwān **28** 31 55N 35 15 E
Daysland **64** 52 50N 112 20W
Dayton, Ohio, U.S.A. **68** 39 45N 84 10W
Dayton, Tenn., U.S.A. **69** 35 30N 85 1W
Dayton, Wash., U.S.A. **72** 46 20N 118 10W
Daytona Beach **69** 29 14N 81 0W
Dayu **39** 25 24N 114 22 E
Dayville **72** 44 33N 119 37W
Dazhu **39** 30 41N 107 15 E
Dazu **39** 29 40N 105 42 E
De Aar **56** 30 39S 24 0 E
De Funiak Springs **69** 30 42N 86 10W
De Grey **46** 20 12S 119 12 E
De Grey → **46** 20 12S 119 13 E
De Kalb **70** 41 55N 88 45W
De Land **69** 29 1N 81 19W
De Leon **71** 32 9N 98 35W
De Pere **68** 44 28N 88 1W
De Queen **71** 34 3N 94 24W
De Quincy **71** 30 30N 93 27W
De Ridder **71** 30 48N 93 15W
De Smet **70** 44 25N 97 35W
De Soto **70** 38 7N 90 33W
De Tour **68** 45 59N 83 56W
De Witt **71** 34 19N 91 20W
Dead Sea **28** 31 30N 35 30 E
Deadwood **70** 44 23N 103 44W
Deadwood L. **64** 59 10N 128 30W
Deakin **47** 30 46S 128 58 E
Deal **7** 51 13N 1 25 E
Deal I. **44** 39 30S 147 20 E
Dealesville **56** 28 41S 25 44 E
Dean, Forest of **7** 51 50N 2 35W
Deán Funes **80** 30 20S 64 20W
Dearborn **62** 42 18N 83 15W
Dease → **64** 59 56N 128 32W
Dease L. **64** 58 40N 130 5W
Dease Lake **64** 58 25N 130 6W
Death Valley **73** 36 19N 116 52W
Death Valley Junc. **73** 36 21N 116 30W
Death Valley Nat. Monument **73** 36 30N 117 0W
Deba Habe **53** 10 14N 11 20 E
Debao **39** 23 21N 106 46 E
Debar **19** 41 31N 20 30 E
Debden **65** 53 30N 106 50W
Debolt **64** 55 12N 118 1W
Deborah East, L. **47** 30 45S 119 0 E
Deborah West, L. **47** 30 45S 118 50 E
Debre Markos **51** 10 20N 37 40 E
Debre Tabor **51** 11 50N 38 26 E
Debrecen **15** 47 33N 21 42 E
Decatur, Ala., U.S.A. **69** 34 35N 87 0W
Decatur, Ga., U.S.A. **69** 33 47N 84 17W
Decatur, Ill., U.S.A. **70** 39 50N 89 0W
Decatur, Ind., U.S.A. **68** 40 50N 84 56W
Decatur, Tex., U.S.A. **71** 33 15N 97 35W
Deccan **32** 18 0N 79 0 E
Deception L. **65** 56 33N 104 13W
Decorah **70** 43 20N 91 50W
Dedéagach = Alexandroúpolis **19** 40 50N 25 54 E
Dédougou **50** 12 30N 3 25W
Dee →, Scotland, U.K. **8** 57 4N 2 7W
Dee →, Wales, U.K. **6** 53 15N 3 7W
Deep B. **64** 61 15N 116 35W
Deep Well **44** 24 20S 134 0 E
Deepwater **45** 29 25S 151 51 E
Deer → **65** 58 23N 94 13W
Deer Lake, Nfld., Canada **63** 49 11N 57 27W
Deer Lake, Ont., Canada **65** 52 36N 94 20W
Deer Lodge **72** 46 25N 112 40W
Deer Park **72** 47 55N 117 21W
Deer River **70** 47 21N 93 44W
Deeral **44** 17 14S 145 55 E
Deerdepoort **56** 24 37S 26 27 E
Defiance **68** 41 20N 84 20W
Deganya **28** 32 43N 35 34 E
Degeh Bur **29** 8 11N 43 31 E
Degema **53** 4 50N 6 48 E
Deggendorf **14** 48 49N 12 59 E
Deh Bīd **31** 30 39N 53 11 E
Dehi Titan **32** 33 45N 63 50 E
Dehibat **50** 32 0N 10 47 E
Dehkareqan **30** 37 43N 45 55 E
Dehra Dun **32** 30 20N 78 4 E
Dehui **38** 44 30N 125 40 E
Deinze **11** 50 59N 3 32 E
Dej **15** 47 10N 23 52 E
Dekese **54** 3 24S 21 24 E
Del Norte **73** 37 40N 106 27W
Del Rio **71** 29 23N 100 50W
Delano **73** 35 48N 119 13W
Delareyville **56** 26 41S 25 26 E
Delavan **70** 42 40N 88 39W
Delaware **68** 40 20N 83 0W
Delaware □ **68** 39 0N 75 40W
Delaware → **68** 39 20N 75 25W
Delegate **45** 37 4S 148 56 E
Delft **11** 52 1N 4 22 E
Delfzijl **11** 53 20N 6 55 E
Delgado, C. **54** 10 45S 40 40 E
Delgo **51** 20 6N 30 40 E
Delhi **32** 28 38N 77 17 E
Delia **64** 51 38N 112 23W
Delice → **30** 39 45N 34 15 E
Delicias **74** 28 10N 105 30W
Dell City **73** 31 58N 105 19W
Dell Rapids **70** 43 53N 96 44W
Delmiro Gouveia **79** 9 24S 38 6W
Delong, Ostrova **25** 76 40N 149 20 E
Deloraine, Australia **44** 41 30S 146 40 E
Deloraine, Canada **65** 49 15N 100 29W
Delphi **68** 40 37N 86 40W
Delphos **68** 40 51N 84 17W
Delportshoop **56** 28 22S 24 20 E
Delray Beach **69** 26 27N 80 4W
Delta, Colo., U.S.A. **73** 38 44N 108 5W
Delta, Utah, U.S.A. **72** 39 21N 112 29W
Delungra **45** 29 39S 150 51 E
Demanda, Sierra de la **13** 42 15N 3 0W
Demba **54** 5 28S 22 15 E
Dembecha **51** 10 32N 37 30 E
Dembidolo **51** 8 34N 34 50 E
Demer → **11** 50 57N 4 42 E
Deming **73** 32 10N 107 50W
Demini → **78** 0 46S 62 56W
Demopolis **69** 32 30N 87 48W
Dempo, Mt. **34** 4 2S 103 15 E
Den Burg **11** 53 3N 4 47 E
Den Haag = 's-Gravenhage **11** 52 7N 4 17 E
Den Helder **11** 52 57N 4 45 E
Den Oever **11** 52 56N 5 2 E
Denain **11** 50 20N 3 22 E
Denau **24** 38 16N 67 54 E
Denbigh **6** 53 12N 3 26W
Dendang **34** 3 7S 107 56 E
Dendermonde **11** 51 2N 4 5 E
Deng Xian **39** 32 34N 112 4 E
Dengi **53** 9 25N 9 55 E
Denham **47** 25 56S 113 31 E
Denham Ra. **44** 21 55S 147 46 E
Denham Sd. **47** 25 45S 113 15 E
Denia **13** 38 49N 0 8 E
Denial B. **45** 32 14S 133 32 E
Deniliquin **45** 35 30S 144 58 E
Denison, Iowa, U.S.A. **70** 42 0N 95 18W
Denison, Tex., U.S.A. **71** 33 50N 96 40W
Denison Plains **46** 18 35S 128 0 E
Denizli **30** 37 42N 29 2 E
Denmark **47** 34 59S 117 25 E
Denmark ■ **21** 55 30N 9 0 E
Denmark Str. **2** 66 0N 30 0W
Denpasar **34** 8 45S 115 14 E
Denton, Mont., U.S.A. **72** 47 25N 109 56W
Denton, Tex., U.S.A. **71** 33 12N 97 10W
D'Entrecasteaux Pt. **47** 34 50S 115 57 E
Denver **70** 39 45N 105 0W
Denver City **71** 32 58N 102 48W
Deoghar **33** 24 30N 86 42 E
Deolali **32** 19 58N 73 50 E
Deoria **33** 26 31N 83 48 E
Deosai Mts. **32** 35 40N 75 0 E
Deping **38** 37 25N 116 58 E
Depot Springs **47** 27 55S 120 3 E
Deputatskiy **25** 69 18N 139 54 E
Dêqên **37** 28 34N 98 51 E
Deqing **39** 23 8N 111 42 E
Dera Ghazi Khan **32** 30 5N 70 43 E
Dera Ismail Khan **32** 31 50N 70 50 E
Derbent **23** 42 5N 48 15 E
Derby, Australia **46** 17 18S 123 38 E
Derby, U.K. **6** 52 55N 1 28W
Derby □ **6** 52 55N 1 28W
Derg → **9** 54 42N 7 26W
Derg, L. **9** 53 0N 8 20W
Dergaon **33** 26 45N 94 0 E
Dernieres Isles **71** 29 0N 90 45W
Derry = Londonderry **9** 55 0N 7 20W
Derryveagh Mts. **9** 55 0N 8 40W
Derudub **51** 17 31N 36 7 E
Derwent **65** 53 41N 110 58W
Derwent →, Derby, U.K. **6** 52 53N 1 17W
Derwent →, N. Yorks., U.K. **6** 53 45N 0 57W
Derwent Water, L. **6** 54 35N 3 9W
Des Moines, Iowa, U.S.A. **70** 41 35N 93 37W
Des Moines, N. Mex., U.S.A. **71** 36 50N 103 51W
Des Moines → **70** 40 23N 91 25W
Desaguadero → **78** 18 24S 67 5W
Deschaillons **63** 46 32N 72 7W
Descharme → **65** 56 51N 109 13W
Deschutes → **72** 45 30N 121 0W
Dese **29** 11 5N 39 40 E
Desert Center **73** 33 45N 115 27W
Deskenatlata L. **64** 60 55N 112 3W
Desna → **22** 50 33N 30 32 E
Desolación, I. **80** 53 0S 74 0W
Despeñaperros, Paso **13** 38 24N 3 30W
Dessau **14** 51 49N 12 15 E
Dessye = Dese **29** 11 5N 39 40 E
D'Estrees B. **45** 35 55S 137 45 E
Detmold **14** 51 55N 8 50 E
Detour Pt. **68** 45 37N 86 35W
Detroit, Mich., U.S.A. **62** 42 23N 83 5W
Detroit, Tex., U.S.A. **71** 33 40N 95 10W
Detroit Lakes **70** 46 50N 95 50W
Deurne, Belgium **11** 51 12N 4 24 E
Deurne, Neth. **11** 51 27N 5 49 E
Deutsche Bucht **14** 54 0N 8 0 E
Deux-Sèvres □ **12** 46 35N 0 20W
Deva **15** 45 53N 22 55 E
Devakottai **32** 9 55N 78 45 E
Deventer **11** 52 15N 6 10 E
Deveron → **8** 57 40N 2 31W
Devils Lake **70** 48 5N 98 50W
Devils Paw **64** 58 47N 134 0W
Devizes **7** 51 21N 2 0W
Devon **64** 53 24N 113 44W
Devon I. **58** 75 10N 85 0W
Devonport, Australia **44** 41 10S 146 22 E
Devonport, N.Z. **43** 36 49S 174 49 E
Devonport, U.K. **7** 50 23N 4 11W
Devonshire □ **7** 50 50N 3 40W
Dewas **32** 22 59N 76 3 E
Dewetsdorp **56** 29 33S 26 39 E
Dewsbury **6** 53 42N 1 38W
Dexter, Mo., U.S.A. **71** 36 50N 90 0W
Dexter, N. Mex., U.S.A. **71** 33 15N 104 25W
Dey-Dey, L. **47** 29 12S 131 4 E
Deyhūk **31** 33 15N 57 30 E
Deyyer **31** 27 55N 51 55 E
Dezadeash L. **64** 60 28N 136 58W
Dezfūl **30** 32 20N 48 30 E
Dezhneva, Mys **25** 66 5N 169 40W
Dezhou **38** 37 26N 116 18 E
Dhafra **31** 23 20N 54 0 E
Dhahira **31** 23 40N 57 0 E
Dhahran = Aẓ Ẓahrān **30** 26 10N 50 7 E
Dhaka **33** 23 43N 90 26 E
Dhaka □ **33** 24 25N 90 25 E
Dhamar **29** 14 30N 44 20 E
Dhamtari **33** 20 42N 81 35 E
Dhanbad **33** 23 50N 86 30 E
Dhangarhi **33** 28 55N 80 40 E
Dhankuta **33** 26 55N 87 40 E
Dhar **32** 22 35N 75 26 E
Dharmapuri **32** 12 10N 78 10 E
Dharwad **32** 15 22N 75 15 E
Dharwar **32** 15 43N 75 1 E
Dhaulagiri **33** 28 39N 83 28 E
Dhenkanal **33** 20 45N 85 35 E
Dhidhimótikhon **19** 41 22N 26 29 E
Dhíkti **19** 35 8N 25 22 E
Dhírfis **19** 38 40N 23 54 E
Dhodhekánisos **19** 36 35N 27 0 E
Dhrol **32** 22 33N 70 25 E
Dhubaibah **31** 23 25N 54 35 E
Dhuburi **33** 26 2N 89 59 E
Dhule **32** 20 58N 74 50 E
Diablo Heights **74** 8 58N 79 34W
Diafarabé **50** 14 9N 4 57W
Diamantina **79** 18 17S 43 40W
Diamantina → **45** 26 45S 139 10 E
Diamantino **79** 14 30S 56 30W
Diamond Harbour **33** 22 11N 88 14 E
Diamond Is. **44** 17 25S 151 5 E
Diamond Mts. **72** 40 0N 115 58W
Diamondville **72** 41 51N 110 30W
Diancheng **39** 21 30N 111 4 E
Diapaga **53** 12 5N 1 46 E
Dībā **31** 25 45N 56 16 E
Dibaya **54** 6 30S 22 57 E
Dibaya-Lubue **54** 4 12S 19 54 E
Dibbi **29** 4 10N 41 52 E
Dibete **56** 23 45S 26 32 E
Dibrugarh **33** 27 29N 94 55 E
Dickinson **70** 46 50N 102 48W
Dickson, U.S.A. **69** 36 5N 87 22W
Dickson, U.S.S.R. **24** 73 40N 80 5 E
Didiéni **50** 13 53N 8 6W
Didsbury **64** 51 35N 114 10W
Diébougou **50** 11 0N 3 15W
Diefenbaker L. **65** 51 0N 106 55W
Diego Garcia **3** 7 50S 72 50 E
Diekirch **11** 49 52N 6 10 E
Dieppe **12** 49 54N 1 4 E
Dieren **11** 52 3N 6 6 E
Dierks **71** 34 9N 94 0W
Diest **11** 50 58N 5 4 E
Differdange **11** 49 31N 5 54 E
Digby **63** 44 38N 65 50W
Digges **65** 58 40N 94 0W
Digges Is. **61** 62 40N 77 50W
Dighinala **33** 23 15N 92 5 E
Dighton **70** 38 30N 100 26W
Digne **12** 44 5N 6 12 E
Digos **35** 6 45N 125 20 E
Digranes **20** 66 4N 14 44 E
Digul → **35** 7 7S 138 42 E
Dihang → **33** 27 48N 95 30 E
Dijlah, Nahr → **30** 31 0N 47 25 E
Dijon **12** 47 20N 5 0 E
Dikomu di Kai **56** 24 58S 24 36 E
Diksmuide **11** 51 2N 2 52 E
Dikson = Dickson **24** 73 40N 80 5 E
Dikwa **53** 12 4N 13 30 E
Dili **35** 8 39S 125 34 E
Dilley **71** 28 40N 99 12W
Dilling **51** 12 3N 29 35 E
Dillon, Canada **65** 55 56N 108 35W
Dillon, Mont., U.S.A. **72** 45 9N 112 36W
Dillon, S.C., U.S.A. **69** 34 26N 79 20W
Dillon → **65** 55 56N 108 56W
Dilolo **54** 10 28S 22 18 E
Dilston **44** 41 22S 147 10 E
Dimashq **30** 33 30N 36 18 E
Dimbaza **57** 32 50S 27 14 E
Dimbokro **50** 6 45N 4 46W
Dimboola **45** 36 28S 142 7 E
Dîmboviţa → **15** 44 5N 26 35 E
Dimbulah **44** 17 8S 145 4 E
Dimitrovgrad, Bulgaria **19** 42 5N 25 35 E
Dimitrovgrad, U.S.S.R. **22** 54 14N 49 39 E
Dimmitt **71** 34 36N 102 16W
Dimona **28** 31 2N 35 1 E
Dinagat **35** 10 10N 125 40 E
Dinajpur **33** 25 33N 88 43 E
Dinan **12** 48 28N 2 2W
Dinant **11** 50 16N 4 55 E
Dinar **30** 38 5N 30 15 E
Dinara Planina **18** 44 0N 16 30 E
Dinard **12** 48 38N 2 6W
Dinaric Alps = Dinara Planina **18** 44 0N 16 30 E
Dindigul **32** 10 25N 78 0 E
Ding Xian **38** 38 30N 114 59 E
Dingbian **38** 37 35N 107 32 E
Dinghai **39** 30 1N 122 6 E
Dingle **9** 52 9N 10 17W
Dingle B. **9** 52 3N 10 20W
Dingnan **39** 24 45N 115 0 E
Dingo **44** 23 38S 149 19 E
Dingtao **39** 35 5N 115 35 E
Dinguiraye **50** 11 18N 10 49W
Dingwall **8** 57 36N 4 26W
Dingxi **38** 35 30N 104 33 E
Dingxiang **38** 38 30N 112 58 E
Dinokwe **56** 23 29S 26 37 E
Dinosaur National Monument **72** 40 30N 108 58W
Dinuba **73** 36 31N 119 22W
Diourbel **50** 14 39N 16 12W
Dipolog **35** 8 36N 123 20 E
Dir **31** 35 8N 71 59 E
Diré **50** 16 20N 3 25W
Dire Dawa **29** 9 35N 41 45 E
Diriamba **75** 11 51N 86 19W
Dirico **55** 17 50S 20 42 E
Dirk Hartog I. **47** 25 50S 113 5 E
Dirranbandi **45** 28 33S 148 17 E

Gerede

Fresno 73 36 47N 119 50W
Fresno Res. 72 48 40N 110 0W
Frew ➤ 44 20 0S 135 38 E
Frewena 44 19 25S 135 25 E
Freycinet Pen. 44 42 10S 148 25 E
Fria, C. 56 18 0S 12 0 E
Frías 80 28 40S 65 5W
Friedrichshafen 14 47 39N 9 29 E
Friendly, Is. =
Tonga ■ 43 19 50S 174 30W
Friesland □ 11 53 5N 5 50 E
Frijoles 74 9 11N 79 48W
Frio ➤ 71 28 30N 98 10W
Friona 71 34 40N 102 42W
Frisian Is. 4 53 30N 6 0 E
Fritch 71 35 40N 101 35W
Friuli-Venezia
Giulia □ 18 46 0N 13 0 E
Frobisher B. 61 62 30N 66 0W
Frobisher Bay 61 63 44N 68 31W
Frobisher L. 65 56 20N 108 15W
Frohavet 20 63 50N 9 35 E
Froid 70 48 20N 104 29W
Fromberg 72 42 25N 108 58W
Frome 7 51 16N 2 17W
Frome, L. 45 30 45S 139 45 E
Frome Downs 45 31 13S 139 45 E
Front Range 72 40 0N 105 40W
Front Royal 68 38 55N 78 10W
Frontera 74 18 30N 92 40W
Frosinone 18 41 38N 13 20 E
Frostburg 68 39 43N 78 57W
Frostisen 20 68 14N 17 10 E
Frøya 20 63 43N 8 40 E
Frunze 24 42 54N 74 46 E
Frutal 79 20 0S 49 0W
Frýdek-Místek 15 49 40N 18 20 E
Fu Xian, Liaoning,
China 38 39 38N 121 58 E
Fu Xian, Shaanxi,
China 38 36 0N 109 20 E
Fucheng 38 37 50N 116 10 E
Fuchou = Fuzhou 39 26 5N 119 16 E
Fuchū 36 34 34N 133 14 E
Fuchuan 39 24 50N 111 5 E
Fuchun Jiang ➤ 39 30 5N 120 5 E
Fuding 39 27 20N 120 12 E
Fuente Ovejuna 13 38 15N 5 25W
Fuentes de Oñoro 13 40 33N 6 52W
Fuerte ➤ 74 25 50N 109 25W
Fuerte Olimpo 78 21 0S 57 51W
Fuerteventura 50 28 30N 14 0W
Fugløysund 20 70 15N 20 20 E
Fugou 39 34 3N 114 25 E
Fuhai 37 47 2N 87 25 E
Fuji 36 35 9N 138 39 E
Fuji-no-miya 36 35 10N 138 40 E
Fuji-San 36 35 22N 138 44 E
Fujian □ 39 26 0N 118 0 E
Fujin 38 47 16N 132 1 E
Fujisawa 36 35 22N 139 29 E
Fukien = Fujian □ 39 26 0N 118 0 E
Fukuchiyama 36 35 19N 135 9 E
Fukue-Shima 36 32 40N 128 45 E
Fukui 36 36 0N 136 10 E
Fukui □ 36 36 0N 136 12 E
Fukuoka 36 33 39N 130 21 E
Fukuoka □ 36 33 30N 131 0 E
Fukushima 36 37 44N 140 28 E
Fukushima □ 36 37 30N 140 15 E
Fukuyama 36 34 35N 133 20 E
Fulda 14 50 32N 9 41 E
Fulda ➤ 14 51 27N 9 40 E
Fuling 39 29 40N 107 20 E
Fullerton, Calif.,
U.S.A. 73 33 52N 117 58W
Fullerton, Nebr.,
U.S.A. 70 41 25N 98 0W
Fulton, Mo., U.S.A. 70 38 50N 91 55W
Fulton, N.Y., U.S.A. 68 43 20N 76 22W
Fulton, Tenn., U.S.A. 69 36 31N 88 53W
Funabashi 36 35 45N 140 0 E
Funafuti 40 8 30S 179 0 E
Funchal 50 32 38N 16 54W
Fundación 78 10 31N 74 11W
Fundão 13 40 8N 7 30W
Fundy, B. of 63 45 0N 66 0W
Funing, Jiangsu,
China 39 33 45N 119 50 E
Funing, Yunnan,
China 39 23 35N 105 45 E
Funiu Shan 39 33 30N 112 20 E
Funtua 53 11 30N 7 18 E
Fuping 38 38 48N 114 12 E
Fuqing 39 25 41N 119 21 E
Furāt, Nahr al ➤ 30 31 0N 47 25 E
Furneaux Group 44 40 10S 147 50 E
Furness 6 54 12N 3 10W
Fürth 14 49 29N 11 0 E
Fury and Hecla Str. 61 69 56N 84 0W
Fusagasuga 78 4 21N 74 22W
Fushan 38 37 30N 121 15 E
Fushun 38 41 50N 123 56 E
Fusong 38 42 20N 127 15 E
Fusui 39 22 40N 107 56 E
Futuna 43 14 25S 178 20 E
Fuxin 38 42 5N 121 48 E
Fuyang, Anhui,
China 39 33 0N 115 48 E
Fuyang, Zhejiang,
China 39 30 5N 119 57 E
Fuyu 38 45 12N 124 43 E
Fuyuan 38 48 20N 134 5 E
Fuzhou 39 26 5N 119 16 E
Fylde 6 53 50N 2 58W
Fyn 21 55 20N 10 30 E
Fyne, L. 8 56 0N 5 20W

G

Gaanda 53 10 10N 12 27 E
Gabela 54 11 0S 14 24 E
Gabès 50 33 53N 10 2 E
Gabès, G. de 51 34 0N 10 30 E
Gabon ■ 54 0 10S 10 0 E
Gaborone 56 24 45S 25 57 E
Gabrovo 19 42 52N 25 19 E
Gachsārān 31 30 15N 50 45 E
Gadag 32 15 30N 75 45 E
Gadarwara 32 22 50N 78 50 E
Gadhada 32 22 0N 71 35 E
Gadsden, Ala.,
U.S.A. 69 34 1N 86 0W
Gadsden, Ariz.,
U.S.A. 73 32 35N 114 47W
Gadwal 32 16 10N 77 50 E
Gaffney 69 35 3N 81 40W
Gafsa 50 34 24N 8 43 E
Gagetown 63 45 46N 66 10W
Gagnoa 50 6 56N 5 16W
Gagnon 63 51 50N 68 5W
Gagnon, L. 65 62 3N 110 27W
Gai Xian 38 40 22N 122 20 E
Gail 71 32 48N 101 25W
Gainesville, Fla.,
U.S.A. 69 29 38N 82 20W
Gainesville, Ga.,
U.S.A. 69 34 17N 83 47W
Gainesville, Mo.,
U.S.A. 71 36 35N 92 26W
Gainesville, Tex.,
U.S.A. 71 33 40N 97 10W
Gainsborough 6 53 23N 0 46W
Gairdner L. 45 31 30S 136 0 E
Gairloch, L. 8 57 43N 5 45W
Galangue 55 13 42S 16 9 E
Galápagos 41 0 0 89 0W
Galashiels 8 55 37N 2 50W
Galaţi 15 45 27N 28 2 E
Galatina 19 40 10N 18 10 E
Galax 69 36 42N 80 57W
Galbraith 44 16 25S 141 30 E
Galcaio 29 6 30N 47 30 E
Galdhøpiggen 21 61 38N 8 18 E
Galela 35 1 50N 127 49 E
Galesburg 70 40 57N 90 23W
Galich 22 58 23N 42 12 E
Galicia □ 13 42 43N 7 45W
Galilee = Hagalil 28 32 53N 35 18 E
Galilee, L. 44 22 20S 145 50 E
Galilee, Sea of =
Yam Kinneret 28 32 45N 35 35 E
Galiuro Mts. 73 32 40N 110 30W
Gallabat 51 12 58N 36 11 E
Gallatin 69 36 24N 86 27W
Galle 32 6 5N 80 10 E
Gállego ➤ 13 41 39N 0 51W
Gallegos ➤ 80 51 35S 69 0W
Galley Hd. 9 51 32N 8 56W
Gallinas, Pta. 78 12 28N 71 40W
Gallipoli = Gelibolu 30 40 28N 26 43 E
Gallipoli 19 40 8N 18 0 E
Gallipolis 68 38 50N 82 10W
Gällivare 20 67 9N 20 40 E
Galloway 8 55 0N 4 25W
Galloway, Mull of 8 54 38N 4 50W
Gallup 73 35 30N 108 45W
Gal'on 28 31 38N 34 51 E
Galong 45 34 37S 148 34 E
Galoya 32 8 10N 80 55 E
Galty Mts. 9 52 22N 8 10W
Galtymore 9 52 22N 8 12W
Galula 52 8 40S 33 0 E
Galva 70 41 10N 90 0W
Galveston 71 29 15N 94 48W
Galveston B. 71 29 30N 94 50W
Gálvez 80 32 0S 61 14W
Galway 9 53 16N 9 4W
Galway □ 9 53 16N 9 3W
Galway B. 9 53 10N 9 20W
Gambaga 53 10 30N 0 28W
Gambela 51 8 14N 34 38 E
Gambia ■ 50 13 25N 16 0W
Gambia ➤ 50 13 28N 16 34W
Gambier, C. 46 11 56S 130 57 E
Gambier Is. 45 35 3S 136 30 E
Gamboa 74 9 8N 79 42W
Gamboma 54 1 55S 15 52 E
Gamerco 73 35 33N 108 56W
Gamlakarleby =
Kokkola 20 63 50N 23 8 E
Gammon ➤ 65 51 24N 95 44W
Gan Jiang ➤ 37 29 15N 116 0 E
Gan Shemu'el 28 32 28N 34 56 E
Gan Yavne 28 31 48N 34 42 E
Ganado, Ariz.,
U.S.A. 73 35 46N 109 41W
Ganado, Tex., U.S.A. 71 29 4N 96 31W
Gananoque 62 44 20N 76 10W
Ganaveh 31 29 35N 50 35 E
Gancheng 39 18 51N 108 37 E
Gand = Gent 11 51 2N 3 42 E
Ganda 55 13 3S 14 35 E
Gandak ➤ 33 25 39N 85 13 E
Gandava 32 28 32N 67 32 E
Gander 63 48 58N 54 35W
Gander L. 63 48 58N 54 35W
Gandhi Sagar 32 24 40N 75 40 E
Gandi 53 12 55N 5 49 E
Ganedidalem = Gani 35 0 48S 128 14 E
Ganga ➤ 33 23 20N 90 30 E
Ganganagar 32 29 56N 73 56 E
Gangara 53 14 35N 8 29 E
Gangaw 33 22 5N 94 5 E
Gangdisê Shan 33 31 20N 81 0 E
Ganges =
Ganga ➤ 33 23 20N 90 30 E
Gangtok 33 27 20N 88 37 E
Gani 35 0 48S 128 14 E
Gannett Pk. 72 43 15N 109 38W
Gannvalley 70 44 3N 98 57W
Ganquan 38 36 20N 109 20 E
Gansu □ 38 36 0N 104 0 E
Ganta 50 7 15N 8 59W
Gantheaume, C. 45 36 4S 137 32 E
Gantheaume B. 47 27 40S 114 10 E
Ganyem 35 2 46S 140 12 E
Ganyu 39 34 50N 119 8 E
Ganzhou 39 25 51N 114 56 E
Gao'an 39 28 26N 115 17 E
Gaomi 38 36 20N 119 42 E
Gaoping 38 35 45N 112 55 E
Gaoua 50 10 20N 3 8W
Gaoual 50 11 45N 13 25W
Gaoxiong 39 22 38N 120 18 E
Gaoyou 39 32 47N 119 26 E
Gaoyou Hu 39 32 45N 119 20 E
Gaoyuan 38 37 8N 117 58 E
Gap 12 44 33N 6 5 E
Gar 37 32 10N 79 58 E
Garachiné 75 8 0N 78 12W
Garanhuns 79 8 50S 36 30W
Garawe 50 4 35N 8 0W
Garber 71 36 30N 97 36W
Garberville 72 40 11N 123 50W
Gard 29 9 30N 49 6 E
Gard □ 12 44 2N 4 10 E
Garda, L. di 18 45 40N 10 40 E
Garde L. 65 62 50N 106 13W
Garden City, Kans.,
U.S.A. 71 38 0N 100 45W
Garden City, Tex.,
U.S.A. 71 31 52N 101 28W
Garden Grove 73 33 47N 117 55W
Gardēz 31 33 37N 69 9 E
Gardiner 72 45 3N 110 42W
Gardner 68 42 35N 72 0W
Gardner Canal 64 53 27N 128 8W
Gardnerville 72 38 59N 119 47W
Garfield 72 47 3N 117 8W
Gargano, Mte. 18 41 43N 15 43 E
Garibaldi Prov. Park 64 49 50N 122 40W
Garies 56 30 32S 17 59 E
Garigliano ➤ 18 41 13N 13 44 E
Garissa 52 0 25S 39 40 E
Garland 72 41 47N 112 10W
Garm 24 39 0N 70 20 E
Garmsār 31 35 20N 52 25 E
Garner 70 43 4N 93 37W
Garnett 70 38 18N 95 12W
Garoe 29 8 25N 48 33 E
Garonne ➤ 12 45 2N 0 36W
Garoua 53 9 19N 13 21 E
Garrison, Mont.,
U.S.A. 72 46 30N 112 56W
Garrison, N. Dak.,
U.S.A. 70 47 39N 101 27W
Garrison, Tex.,
U.S.A. 71 31 50N 94 28W
Garrison Res. =
Sakakawea, L. 70 47 30N 102 0W
Garry ➤ 8 56 47N 3 47W
Garry L. 60 65 58N 100 18W
Garsen 54 2 20S 40 5 E
Garson L. 65 56 19N 110 2W
Garub 56 26 37S 16 0 E
Garut 35 7 14S 107 53 E
Garvie Mts. 43 45 30S 168 50 E
Garwa = Garoua 53 9 19N 13 21 E
Gary 68 41 35N 87 20W
Garzê 37 31 39N 99 58 E
Garzón 78 2 10N 75 40W
Gasan Kuli 24 37 40N 54 20 E
Gascogne 12 43 45N 0 20 E
Gascogne, G. de 12 44 0N 2 0W
Gascony =
Gascogne 12 43 45N 0 20 E
Gascoyne ➤ 47 24 52S 113 37 E
Gascoyne Junc. T.O. 47 25 2S 115 17 E
Gashaka 53 7 20N 11 29 E
Gashua 53 12 54N 11 0 E
Gaspé 63 48 52N 64 30W
Gaspé, C. de 63 48 48N 64 7W
Gaspé, Pén. de 63 48 45N 65 40W
Gaspésie, Parc
Prov. de la 63 48 55N 65 50W
Gassaway 68 38 42N 80 43W
Gastonia 69 35 17N 81 10W
Gastre 80 42 20S 69 15W
Gata, C. de 13 36 41N 2 13W
Gata, Sierra de 13 40 20N 6 45W
Gataga ➤ 64 58 35N 126 59W
Gateshead 6 54 57N 1 37W
Gatesville 71 31 29N 97 45W
Gâtinais 12 48 5N 2 40 E
Gatineau ➤ 62 45 27N 75 42W
Gatineau, Parc de la 62 45 40N 76 0W
Gatun 74 9 16N 79 55W
Gatun, L. 75 9 7N 79 56W
Gatun Dam 74 9 16N 79 55W
Gatun Locks 74 9 16N 79 55W
Gatyana 57 32 16S 28 31 E
Gau 43 18 2S 179 18 E
Gauer L. 65 57 0N 97 50W
Gauhati 33 26 10N 91 45 E
Gaula ➤ 20 63 21N 10 14 E
Gausta, Mt. 21 59 48N 8 40 E
Gaväter 31 25 10N 61 31 E
Gävleborgs län □ 21 61 30N 16 15 E
Gawachab 56 27 4S 17 55 E
Gawilgarh Hills 32 21 15N 76 45 E
Gawler 45 34 30S 138 42 E
Gaxun Nur 37 42 22N 100 30 E
Gay 22 51 27N 58 27 E
Gaya, India 33 24 47N 85 4 E
Gaya, Niger 53 11 52N 3 28 E
Gaylord 68 45 1N 84 41W
Gayndah 45 25 35S 151 32 E
Gaza 28 31 30N 34 28 E
Gaza □ 57 23 10S 32 45 E
Gaza Strip 28 31 29N 34 25 E
Gazaoua 53 13 32N 7 55 E
Gaziantep 30 37 6N 37 23 E
Gazli 24 40 14N 63 24 E
Gboko 53 7 17N 9 4 E
Gbongan 53 7 28N 4 20 E
Gcuwa 57 32 20S 28 11 E
Gdańsk 15 54 22N 18 40 E
Gdańska, Zatoka 15 54 30N 19 20 E
Gdov 22 58 48N 27 55 E
Gdynia 15 54 35N 18 33 E
Ge'a 28 31 38N 34 37 E
Gebe 35 0 5N 129 25 E
Gebeit Mine 51 21 3N 36 29 E
Gebel Mûsa 30 28 32N 33 59 E
Gedaref 51 14 2N 35 28 E
Gede, Tanjung 34 6 46S 105 12 E
Gedera 28 31 49N 34 46 E
Gedser 21 54 35N 11 55 E
Geelong 45 38 10S 144 22 E
Geelvink Chan. 47 28 30S 114 0 E
Geidam 51 12 57N 11 57 E
Geikie ➤ 65 57 45N 103 52W
Geili 51 16 1N 32 37 E
Geita 54 2 48S 32 12 E
Gejiu 37 23 20N 103 10 E
Gela 18 37 6N 14 18 E
Geladi 29 6 59N 46 30 E
Gelderland □ 11 52 5N 6 10 E
Geldermalsen 11 51 53N 5 17 E
Geldrop 11 51 25N 5 32 E
Geleen 11 50 57N 5 49 E
Gelehun 50 8 20N 11 40W
Gelibolu 30 40 28N 26 43 E
Gelsenkirchen 14 51 30N 7 5 E
Gemas 34 2 37N 102 36 E
Gembloux 11 50 34N 4 43 E
Gemena 54 3 13N 19 48 E
Gemerek 30 39 15N 36 10 E
Gen He ➤ 38 50 16N 119 32 E
Gendringen 11 51 52N 6 21 E
General Acha 80 37 20S 64 38W
General Alvear,
Buenos Aires,
Argentina 80 36 0S 60 0W
General Alvear,
Mendoza,
Argentina 80 35 0S 67 40W
General Artigas 80 26 52S 56 16W
General Belgrano 80 36 35S 58 47W
General Guido 80 36 40S 57 50W
General Juan
Madariaga 80 37 0S 57 0W
General La Madrid 80 37 17S 61 20W
General MacArthur 35 11 18N 125 28 E
General Martin
Miguel de Güemes 80 24 50S 65 0W
General Paz 80 27 45S 57 36W
General Pico 80 35 45S 63 50W
General Pinedo 80 27 15S 61 20W
General Santos 35 6 5N 125 14 E
General Trías 74 28 21N 106 22W
General Villegas 80 35 0S 63 0W
Genesee 72 46 31N 116 59W
Genesee ➤ 68 43 16N 77 36W
Geneseo, Ill., U.S.A. 70 41 25N 90 10W
Geneseo, Kans.,
U.S.A. 70 38 32N 98 8W
Geneva = Genève 14 46 12N 6 9 E
Geneva, Ala., U.S.A. 69 31 2N 85 52W
Geneva, N.Y., U.S.A. 68 42 53N 77 0W
Geneva, Nebr.,
U.S.A. 70 40 35N 97 35W
Geneva, Ohio,
U.S.A. 68 41 49N 80 58W
Geneva, L. =
Léman, Lac 14 46 26N 6 30 E
Geneva, L. 68 42 38N 88 30W
Genève 14 46 12N 6 9 E
Genil ➤ 13 37 42N 5 19W
Genk 11 50 58N 5 32 E
Gennargentu, Mti.
del 18 40 0N 9 10 E
Gennep 11 51 41N 5 59 E
Genoa = Génova 18 44 24N 8 56 E
Genoa, Australia 45 37 29S 149 35 E
Genoa, U.S.A. 70 41 31N 97 44W
Génova 18 44 24N 8 56 E
Génova, G. di 18 44 0N 9 0 E
Gent 11 51 2N 3 42 E
Geographe B. 47 33 30S 115 15 E
Geographe Chan. 47 24 30S 113 0 E
Georga, Zemlya 24 80 30N 49 0 E
George 56 33 58S 22 29 E
George ➤ 63 58 49N 66 10W
George, L., N.S.W.,
Australia 45 35 10S 149 25 E
George, L.,
S. Austral.,
Australia 45 37 25S 140 0 E
George, L.,
W. Austral.,
Australia 46 22 45S 123 40 E
George, L., Uganda 54 0 5N 30 10 E
George, L., U.S.A. 69 29 15N 81 35W
George River = Port
Nouveau-Québec 61 58 30N 65 59W
George Sound 43 44 52S 167 25 E
George Town,
Australia 44 41 5S 146 49 E
George Town,
Bahamas 75 23 33N 75 47W
George Town,
Malaysia 34 5 25N 100 15 E
George West 71 28 18N 98 5W
Georgetown,
Australia 44 18 17S 143 33 E
Georgetown, Ont.,
Canada 62 43 40N 79 56W
Georgetown, P.E.I.,
Canada 63 46 13N 62 24W
Georgetown,
Gambia 50 13 30N 14 47W
Georgetown,
Guyana 78 6 50N 58 12W
Georgetown, Colo.,
U.S.A. 72 39 46N 105 49W
Georgetown, Ky.,
U.S.A. 68 38 13N 84 33W
Georgetown, Ohio,
U.S.A. 68 38 50N 83 50W
Georgetown, S.C.,
U.S.A. 69 33 22N 79 15W
Georgetown, Tex.,
U.S.A. 71 30 40N 97 45W
Georgia □ 69 32 0N 82 0W
Georgia, Str. of 64 49 25N 124 0W
Georgian B. 62 45 15N 81 0W
Georgian S.S.R. □ 23 42 0N 43 0 E
Georgievsk 23 44 12N 43 28 E
Georgina ➤ 44 23 30S 139 47 E
Georgina Downs 44 21 10S 137 40 E
Georgiu-Dezh 23 51 3N 39 30 E
Gera 14 50 53N 12 11 E
Geraardsbergen 11 50 45N 3 53 E
Geral, Serra 80 26 25S 50 0W
Geral de Goiás,
Serra 79 12 0S 46 0W
Geraldine 72 47 36N 110 18W
Geraldton, Australia 47 28 48S 114 32 E
Geraldton, Canada 62 49 44N 86 59W
Gerede 30 40 45N 32 10 E

Gypsumville

Grande, B. 80 50 30S 68 20W
Grande, La 72 45 15N 118 0W
Grande Baie 63 48 19N 70 52W
Grande Baleine, R. de la → 62 55 16N 77 47W
Grande Cache 64 53 53N 119 8W
Grande de Santiago → ... 74 21 20N 105 50W
Grande-Entrée 63 47 30N 61 40W
Grande Prairie 64 55 10N 118 50W
Grande-Rivière 63 48 26N 64 30W
Grande-Vallée 63 49 14N 65 8W
Grandes-Bergeronnes 63 48 16N 69 35W
Grandfalls 71 31 21N 102 51W
Grandoe Mines ... 64 56 29N 129 54W
Grandview 72 46 13N 119 58W
Grange, La, Ga., U.S.A. 69 33 4N 85 0W
Grange, La, Ky., U.S.A. 68 38 20N 85 20W
Grange, La, Tex., U.S.A. 71 29 54N 96 52W
Grangemouth 8 56 1N 3 43W
Granger, Wash., U.S.A. 72 46 25N 120 5W
Granger, Wyo., U.S.A. 72 41 35N 109 58W
Grangeville 72 45 57N 116 4W
Granite City 70 38 45N 90 3W
Granite Falls 70 44 45N 95 35W
Granite Peak ..... 47 25 40S 121 20 E
Granite Pk. 72 45 8N 109 52W
Granity .... 43 41 39S 171 51 E
Granja 79 3 7S 40 50W
Granja de Torrehermosa ... 13 38 19N 5 35W
Granollers .... 13 41 39N 2 18 E
Grant 70 40 53N 101 42W
Grant, I. .... 46 11 10S 132 52 E
Grant, Mt. 72 38 34N 118 48W
Grant City 70 40 30N 94 25W
Grant Range Mts. . 73 38 30N 115 30W
Grantham 6 52 55N 0 39W
Grantown-on-Spey 8 57 19N 3 36W
Grants 73 35 14N 107 51W
Grants Pass 72 42 30N 123 22W
Grantsburg 70 45 46N 92 44W
Grantsville 72 40 35N 112 32W
Granville, France .. 12 48 50N 1 35W
Granville, N. Dak., U.S.A. 70 48 18N 100 48W
Granville, N.Y., U.S.A. 68 43 24N 73 16W
Granville L. 65 56 18N 100 30W
Grapeland 71 31 30N 95 31W
Gras, L. de 60 64 30N 110 30W
Graskop .... 57 24 56S 30 49 E
Grass → 65 56 3N 96 33W
Grass Range 72 47 0N 109 0W
Grass River Prov. Park 65 54 40N 100 50W
Grass Valley, Calif., U.S.A. 72 39 18N 121 0W
Grass Valley, Oreg., U.S.A. 72 45 22N 120 48W
Grasse .... 12 43 38N 6 56 E
Grassmere .... 45 31 24S 142 38 E
Gravelbourg 65 49 50N 106 35W
's-Gravenhage ..... 11 52 7N 4 17 E
Gravesend, Australia 45 29 35S 150 20 E
Gravesend, U.K. .. 7 51 25N 0 22 E
Gravois, Pointe-à- . 75 16 15N 73 56W
Grayling 68 44 40N 84 42W
Grayling → 64 59 21N 125 0W
Grays Harbor 72 46 55N 124 8W
Grays L. 72 43 8N 111 30W
Grayson 65 50 45N 102 40W
Graz .... 14 47 4N 15 27 E
Greasy L. 64 62 55N 122 12W
Great Abaco I. 75 26 25N 77 10W
Great Australia Basin .... 44 26 0S 140 0 E
Great Australian Bight .... 47 33 30S 130 0 E
Great Bahama Bank 75 23 15N 78 0W
Great Barrier I. .... 43 36 11S 175 25 E
Great Barrier Reef . 44 18 0S 146 50 E
Great Basin 72 40 0N 116 30W
Great Bear → ... 60 65 0N 124 0W
Great Bear L. 60 65 30N 120 0W
Great Bend 70 38 25N 98 55W
Great Blasket I. ... 9 52 5N 10 30W
Great Britain 4 54 0N 2 15W
Great Central 64 49 20N 125 10W
Great Dividing Ra. . 44 23 0S 146 0 E
Great Exuma I. 75 23 30N 75 50W
Great Falls, Canada 65 50 27N 96 1W
Great Falls, U.S.A. . 72 47 27N 111 12W
Great Fish → = Groot Vis → ... 56 33 28S 27 5 E
Great Guana Cay .. 75 24 0N 76 20W
Great Harbour Deep 63 50 25N 56 32W
Great Inagua I. 75 21 0N 73 20W
Great Indian Desert = Thar Desert .. 32 28 0N 72 0 E
Great I. 65 58 53N 96 35W
Great Karoo ...... 56 31 55S 21 0 E
Great Lake .... 44 41 50S 146 40 E
Great Orme's Head 6 53 20N 3 52W
Great Ouse → ... 6 52 47N 0 22 E
Great Palm I. ..... 44 18 45S 146 40 E
Great Plains 58 47 0N 105 0W
Great Ruaha → .. 54 7 56S 37 52 E
Great Saint Bernard P. = Grand St-Bernard, Col du . 14 45 50N 7 10 E
Great Salt Lake ... 72 41 0N 112 30W
Great Salt Lake Desert 72 40 20N 113 50W
Great Salt Plains Res. 71 36 40N 98 15W
Great Sandy Desert 46 21 0S 124 0 E
Great Slave L. 64 61 23N 115 38W
Great Smoky Mts. Nat. Park 69 35 39N 83 30W
Great Stour = Stour → ...... 7 51 15N 1 20 E
Great Victoria Desert 47 29 30S 126 30 E
Great Wall .... 38 38 30N 109 30 E
Great Whernside .. 6 54 9N 1 59W
Great Yarmouth ... 6 52 40N 1 45 E
Greater Antilles ... 75 17 40N 74 0W
Greater London □ . 7 51 30N 0 5W
Greater Manchester □ .. 6 53 30N 2 15W
Greater Sunda Is. . 34 7 0S 112 0 E
Gredos, Sierra de . 13 40 20N 5 0W
Greece ■ .... 19 40 0N 23 0 E
Greeley, Colo., U.S.A. 70 40 30N 104 40W
Greeley, Nebr., U.S.A. 70 41 36N 98 32W
Green →, Ky., U.S.A. 68 37 54N 87 30W
Green →, Utah, U.S.A. 73 38 11N 109 53W
Green B. 68 45 0N 87 30W
Green Bay 68 44 30N 88 0W
Green C. .... 45 37 13S 150 1 E
Green Cove Springs 69 29 59N 81 40W
Green Hd. .... 47 30 5S 114 56 E
Green Island ..... 43 45 55S 170 26 E
Green River 73 38 59N 110 10W
Greenbush 70 48 46N 96 10W
Greencastle 68 39 40N 86 48W
Greenfield, Ind., U.S.A. 68 39 47N 85 51W
Greenfield, Iowa, U.S.A. 70 41 18N 94 28W
Greenfield, Mass., U.S.A. 68 42 38N 72 38W
Greenfield, Miss., U.S.A. 71 37 28N 93 50W
Greenland ■ 2 66 0N 45 0W
Greenock 8 55 57N 4 46W
Greenore 9 54 2N 6 8W
Greenore Pt. 9 52 15N 6 20W
Greenough → ... 47 28 51S 114 38 E
Greensboro, Ga., U.S.A. 69 33 34N 83 12W
Greensboro, N.C., U.S.A. 69 36 7N 79 46W
Greensburg, Ind., U.S.A. 68 39 20N 85 30W
Greensburg, Kans., U.S.A. 71 37 38N 99 20W
Greensburg, Pa., U.S.A. 68 40 18N 79 31W
Greenville, Liberia . 50 5 1N 9 6W
Greenville, Ala., U.S.A. 69 31 50N 86 37W
Greenville, Calif., U.S.A. 72 40 8N 120 57W
Greenville, Ill., U.S.A. 70 38 53N 89 22W
Greenville, Maine, U.S.A. 63 45 30N 69 32W
Greenville, Mich., U.S.A. 68 43 12N 85 14W
Greenville, Miss., U.S.A. 71 33 25N 91 0W
Greenville, N.C., U.S.A. 69 35 37N 77 26W
Greenville, Ohio, U.S.A. 68 40 5N 84 38W
Greenville, Pa., U.S.A. 68 41 23N 80 22W
Greenville, S.C., U.S.A. 69 34 54N 82 24W
Greenville, Tenn., U.S.A. 69 36 13N 82 51W
Greenville, Tex., U.S.A. 71 33 5N 96 5W
Greenwater Lake Prov. Park 65 52 32N 103 30W
Greenwich .... 7 51 28N 0 0 E
Greenwood, Canada 64 49 10N 118 40W
Greenwood, Miss., U.S.A. 71 33 30N 90 4W
Greenwood, S.C., U.S.A. 69 34 13N 82 13W
Greenwood, Mt. ... 46 13 48S 130 4 E
Gregory 70 43 14N 99 20W
Gregory → ...... 44 17 53S 139 17 E
Gregory, L., S. Austral., Australia .... 45 28 55S 139 0 E
Gregory, L., W. Austral., Australia .... 47 25 38S 119 58 E
Gregory Downs ... 44 18 35S 138 45 E
Gregory Ra., Queens., Australia 44 19 30S 143 40 E
Gregory Ra., W. Austral., Australia .... 46 21 20S 121 12 E
Greifswald .... 14 54 6N 13 23 E
Gremikha .... 22 67 50N 39 40 E
Grenada 71 33 45N 89 50W
Grenada ■ 75 12 10N 61 40W
Grenadines 75 12 40N 61 20W
Grenen .... 21 57 44N 10 40 E
Grenfell, Australia . 45 33 52S 148 8 E
Grenfell, Canada .. 65 50 30N 102 56W
Grenoble .... 12 45 12N 5 42 E
Grenora 70 48 38N 103 54W
Grenville, C. ...... 44 12 0S 143 13 E
Grenville Chan. ... 64 53 40N 129 46W
Gresham 72 45 30N 122 25W
Gresik .... 35 7 13S 112 38 E
Gretna Green 8 55 0N 3 3W
Grevenmacher .... 11 49 41N 6 26 E
Grey → .... 43 42 27S 171 12 E
Grey, C. .... 44 13 0S 136 35 E
Grey Range ...... 45 27 0S 143 30 E
Grey Res. 63 48 20N 56 30W
Greybull 72 44 30N 108 3W
Greymouth .... 43 42 29S 171 13 E
Greytown, N.Z. .... 43 41 5S 175 29 E
Greytown, S. Africa 57 29 1S 30 36 E
Gribbell I. 64 53 23N 129 0W
Gridley 72 39 27N 121 47W
Griekwastad ...... 56 28 49S 23 15 E
Griffin 69 33 17N 84 14W
Griffith .... 45 34 18S 146 2 E
Grimari .... 51 5 43N 20 6 E
Grimsby 6 53 35N 0 5W
Grímsey 20 66 33N 18 0W
Grimshaw 64 56 10N 117 40W
Grimstad .... 21 58 22N 8 35 E
Grinnell 70 41 45N 92 43W
Gris-Nez, C. ...... 12 50 52N 1 35 E
Groais I. 63 50 55N 55 35W
Groblersdal ...... 57 25 15S 29 25 E
Grodno .... 22 53 42N 23 52 E
Grodzisk Wielkopolski .... 14 52 15N 16 22 E
Groesbeck 71 31 32N 96 34W
Grójec .... 15 51 50N 20 58 E
Grong .... 20 64 25N 12 8 E
Groningen .... 11 53 15N 6 35 E
Groningen □ ..... 11 53 16N 6 40 E
Groom 71 35 12N 100 59W
Groot → .... 56 33 45S 24 36 E
Groot Berg → .... 56 32 47S 18 8 E
Groot-Brakrivier ... 56 34 2S 22 18 E
Groot-Kei → ..... 57 32 41S 28 22 E
Groot Vis → ..... 56 33 28S 27 5 E
Groote Eylandt .... 44 14 0S 136 40 E
Grootfontein ...... 56 19 31S 18 6 E
Grootlaagte → .. 56 20 55S 21 27 E
Grootvloer .... 56 30 0S 20 40 E
Gros C. 64 61 59N 113 32W
Gross Glockner ... 14 47 5N 12 40 E
Grossenhain ...... 14 51 17N 13 32 E
Grosseto .... 18 42 45N 11 7 E
Groswater B. 63 54 20N 57 40W
Groton 70 45 27N 98 6W
Grouard Mission .. 64 55 33N 116 9W
Groundhog → ... 62 48 45N 82 58W
Grouse Creek 72 41 44N 113 57W
Groveton, N.H., U.S.A. 68 44 34N 71 30W
Groveton, Tex., U.S.A. 71 31 5N 95 4W
Groznyy .... 23 43 20N 45 45 E
Grudziądz .... 15 53 30N 18 47 E
Grundy Center 70 42 22N 92 45W
Gruver 71 36 19N 101 20W
Gryazi .... 22 52 30N 39 58 E
Gua .... 33 22 18N 85 20 E
Guacanayabo, G. de 75 20 40N 77 20W
Guadalajara, Mexico 74 20 40N 103 20W
Guadalajara, Spain 13 40 37N 3 12W
Guadalcanal ...... 40 9 32S 160 12 E
Guadalete → 13 36 35N 6 13W
Guadalhorce → .. 13 36 41N 4 27W
Guadalquivir → .. 13 36 47N 6 22W
Guadalupe = Guadeloupe ■ .. 75 16 20N 61 40W
Guadalupe 73 34 59N 120 33W
Guadalupe → ... 71 28 30N 96 53W
Guadalupe, Sierra de 13 39 28N 5 30W
Guadalupe Bravos . 74 31 20N 106 10W
Guadalupe I. 41 29 0N 118 50W
Guadalupe Pk. 73 31 50N 105 30W
Guadarrama, Sierra de 13 41 0N 4 0W
Guadeloupe ■ 75 16 20N 61 40W
Guadeloupe Passage 75 16 50N 62 15W
Guadiana → 13 37 14N 7 22W
Guadix 13 37 18N 3 11W
Guafo, Boca del .. 80 43 35S 74 0W
Guaira 80 24 5S 54 10W
Guaira, La 78 10 36N 66 56W
Guaitecas, Is. 80 44 0S 74 30W
Guajará-Mirim 78 10 50S 65 20W
Guajira, Pen. de la . 78 12 0N 72 0W
Gualeguay 80 33 10S 59 14W
Gualeguaychú 80 33 3S 59 31W
Guam .... 3 13 27N 144 45 E
Guamúchil 74 25 25N 108 3W
Guan Xian .... 37 31 2N 103 38 E
Guanabacoa 75 23 8N 82 18W
Guanacaste, Cordillera del ... 75 10 40N 85 4W
Guanaceví 74 25 40N 106 0W
Guanahani = San Salvador 75 24 0N 74 40W
Guanajay 75 22 56N 82 42W
Guanajuato 74 21 0N 101 20W
Guanajuato □ 74 20 40N 101 20W
Guandacol 80 29 30S 68 40W
Guane 75 22 10N 84 7W
Guang'an .... 39 30 28N 106 35 E
Guangde .... 39 30 54N 119 25 E
Guangdong □ .... 39 23 0N 113 0 E
Guanghua .... 39 32 22N 111 38 E
Guangshun .... 39 26 8N 106 21 E
Guangxi Zhuangzu Zizhiqu □ ...... 39 24 0N 109 0 E
Guangyuan .... 39 32 26N 105 51 E
Guangze .... 39 27 30N 117 12 E
Guangzhou .... 39 23 5N 113 10 E
Guanipa → 78 9 56N 62 26W
Guantánamo 75 20 10N 75 14W
Guantao .... 38 36 42N 115 25 E
Guanyun .... 39 34 20N 119 18 E
Guápiles 75 10 10N 83 46W
Guaporé → 78 11 55S 65 4W
Guaqui 78 16 41S 68 54W
Guarapuava 80 25 20S 51 30W
Guarda 13 40 32N 7 20W
Guardafui, C. = Asir, Ras .... 29 11 55N 51 10 E
Guasdualito 78 7 15N 70 44W
Guasipati 78 7 28N 61 54W
Guatemala 75 14 40N 90 22W
Guatemala ■ 75 15 40N 90 30W
Guatire 78 10 28N 66 32W
Guaviare → 78 4 3N 67 44W
Guaxupé 79 21 10S 47 5W
Guayama 75 17 59N 66 7W
Guayaquil 78 2 15S 79 52W
Guayaquil, G. de .. 78 3 10S 81 0W
Guaymas 74 27 59N 110 54W
Guazhou .... 39 32 17N 119 21 E
Gudbrandsdalen .. 21 61 33N 10 0 E
Guddu Barrage ... 32 28 30N 69 50 E
Gudivada .... 33 16 30N 81 3 E
Gudur .... 32 14 12N 79 55 E
Guecho 13 43 21N 2 59W
Guékédou 50 8 40N 10 5W
Guelma .... 50 36 25N 7 29 E
Guelph 62 43 35N 80 20W
Güera, La 50 20 51N 17 0W
Guéréda .... 51 14 31N 22 5 E
Guéret .... 12 46 11N 1 51 E
Guernica 13 43 19N 2 40W
Guernsey, U.K. 7 49 30N 2 35W
Guernsey, U.S.A. .. 70 42 19N 104 45W
Guerrero □ 74 17 30N 100 0W
Gueydan 71 30 3N 92 30W
Gui Jiang → .... 39 23 30N 111 15 E
Gui Xian .... 39 23 8N 109 35 E
Guichi .... 39 30 39N 117 27 E
Guidong .... 39 26 7N 113 57 E
Guiglo 50 6 45N 7 30W
Guijá .... 57 24 27S 33 0 E
Guildford 7 51 14N 0 34W
Guilford 63 45 12N 69 25W
Guilin .... 39 25 18N 110 15 E
Guilvinec 12 47 48N 4 17W
Guimarães 79 2 9S 44 42W
Guimaras .... 35 10 35N 122 37 E
Guinea ■ 50 10 20N 11 30W
Guinea, Gulf of ... 3 3 0N 2 30 E
Guinea-Bissau ■ .. 50 12 0N 15 0W
Güines 75 22 50N 82 0W
Guingamp 12 48 34N 3 10W
Guiping .... 39 23 21N 110 2 E
Güiria 78 10 32N 62 18W
Guiuan .... 35 11 5N 125 55 E
Guixi .... 39 28 16N 117 15 E
Guiyang, Guizhou, China .... 39 26 32N 106 40 E
Guiyang, Hunan, China .... 39 25 46N 112 42 E
Guizhou □ .... 39 27 0N 107 0 E
Gujarat □ .... 32 23 20N 71 0 E
Gujranwala .... 32 32 10N 74 12 E
Gujrat .... 32 32 40N 74 2 E
Gulbarga .... 32 17 20N 76 50 E
Gulf, The .... 31 27 0N 50 0 E
Gulfport 71 30 21N 89 3W
Gulgong .... 45 32 20S 149 49 E
Gull Lake 65 50 10N 108 29W
Gulshad .... 24 46 45N 74 25 E
Gulu .... 54 2 48N 32 17 E
Gum Lake .... 45 32 42S 143 9 E
Gumlu .... 44 19 53S 147 41 E
Gumma □ .... 36 36 30N 138 20 E
Gummi .... 53 12 4N 5 9 E
Gümüsane .... 30 40 30N 39 30 E
Gumzai .... 35 5 28S 134 42 E
Guna .... 32 24 40N 77 19 E
Gundagai .... 45 35 3S 148 6 E
Gundih .... 35 7 10S 110 56 E
Gungu .... 54 5 43S 19 20 E
Gunisao → 65 53 56N 97 53W
Gunisao L. 65 53 33N 96 15W
Gunnbjørn Fjeld ... 58 68 45N 31 0W
Gunnedah .... 45 30 59S 150 15 E
Gunningbar Cr. → 45 31 14S 147 6 E
Gunnison, Colo., U.S.A. 73 38 32N 106 56W
Gunnison, Utah, U.S.A. 72 39 11N 111 48W
Gunnison → 73 39 3N 108 30W
Guntakal .... 32 15 11N 77 27 E
Guntersville 69 34 18N 86 16W
Guntur .... 33 16 23N 80 30 E
Gunungapi .... 35 6 45S 126 30 E
Gunungsitoli ...... 34 1 15N 97 30 E
Gunza .... 54 10 50S 13 50 E
Guo He → ...... 39 32 59N 117 10 E
Guoyang .... 39 33 32N 116 12 E
Gupis .... 32 36 15N 73 20 E
Gürchañ .... 30 34 55N 49 25 E
Gurdaspur .... 32 32 5N 75 31 E
Gurdon 71 33 55N 93 10W
Gurgaon .... 32 28 27N 77 1 E
Gurkha .... 33 28 5N 84 40 E
Gurley .... 45 29 45S 149 48 E
Gurupá 79 1 25S 51 35W
Gurupá, I. Grande de 79 1 25S 51 45W
Gurupi → 79 1 13S 46 6W
Guryev .... 23 47 5N 52 0 E
Gusau .... 53 12 12N 6 40 E
Gushan .... 38 39 50N 123 35 E
Gushi .... 39 32 11N 115 41 E
Gustine 73 37 14N 121 0W
Güstrow .... 14 53 47N 12 12 E
Gutha .... 47 28 58S 115 55 E
Guthalongra ...... 44 19 52S 147 50 E
Guthrie 71 35 55N 97 30W
Guttenberg 70 42 46N 91 10W
Guyana ■ 78 5 0N 59 0W
Guyang .... 38 41 0N 110 5 E
Guyenne .... 12 44 30N 0 40 E
Guymon 71 36 45N 101 30W
Guyra .... 45 30 15S 151 40 E
Guyuan .... 38 36 0N 106 20 E
Guzhen .... 39 33 22N 117 18 E
Guzinozersk ...... 25 51 20N 106 35 E
Guzmán, L. de 74 31 25N 107 25W
Gwa .... 33 17 36N 94 34 E
Gwaai .... 55 19 15S 27 45 E
Gwabegar .... 45 30 31S 149 0 E
Gwadabawa ...... 53 13 28N 5 15 E
Gwādar .... 31 25 10N 62 18 E
Gwalia .... 47 28 54S 121 20 E
Gwalior .... 32 26 12N 78 10 E
Gwanda .... 55 20 55S 29 0 E
Gwaram .... 53 10 15N 10 25 E
Gwarzo .... 53 12 20N 8 55 E
Gweebarra B. 9 54 52N 8 21W
Gweedore 9 55 4N 8 15W
Gwent □ 7 51 45N 2 55W
Gweru .... 55 19 28S 29 45 E
Gwinn 68 46 15N 87 29W
Gwoza .... 53 11 5N 13 40 E
Gwydir → .... 45 29 27S 149 48 E
Gwynedd □ 6 53 0N 4 0W
Gyaring Hu .... 37 34 50N 97 40 E
Gydanskiy P-ov. .. 24 70 0N 78 0 E
Gympie .... 45 26 11S 152 38 E
Gyoda .... 36 36 10N 139 30 E
Gyöngyös .... 15 47 48N 19 56 E
Györ .... 15 47 41N 17 40 E
Gypsum Pt. 64 61 53N 114 35W
Gypsumville 65 51 45N 98 40W

H

Hospet

Heber Springs 71 35 29N 91 59W
Hebert 65 50 30N 107 10W
Hebgen, L. 72 44 50N 111 15W
Hebi 38 35 57N 114 7 E
Hebrides 8 57 30N 7 0W
Hebrides, Inner Is. 8 57 20N 6 40W
Hebrides, Outer Is. 8 57 30N 7 40W
Hebron = Al Khalīl 28 31 32N 35 6 E
Hebron, Canada 61 58 5N 62 30W
Hebron, N. Dak., U.S.A. 70 46 56N 102 2W
Hebron, Nebr., U.S.A. 70 40 15N 97 33W
Hecate Str. 64 53 10N 130 30W
Hechi 39 24 40N 108 2 E
Hechuan 39 30 2N 106 12 E
Hecla 70 45 56N 98 8W
Hecla I. 65 51 10N 96 43W
Hede 20 62 23N 13 30 E
Hedemora 21 60 18N 15 58 E
Hedley 71 34 53N 100 39W
Heemstede 11 52 22N 4 37 E
Heerde 11 52 24N 6 2 E
Heerenveen 11 52 57N 5 55 E
Heerlen 11 50 55N 6 0 E
Ḥefa 28 32 46N 35 0 E
Hefei 39 31 52N 117 18 E
Hegang 38 47 20N 130 19 E
Heidelberg, Germany 14 49 23N 8 41 E
Heidelberg, C. Prov., S. Africa 56 34 6S 20 59 E
Heidelberg, Trans., S. Africa 57 26 30S 28 23 E
Heilbron 57 27 16S 27 59 E
Heilbronn 14 49 8N 9 13 E
Heilongjiang □ 38 48 0N 126 0 E
Heilunkiang = Heilongjiang □ 38 48 0N 126 0 E
Heinola 21 61 13N 26 2 E
Heinze Is. 33 14 25N 97 45 E
Hejaz = Al Ḥijāz 29 26 0N 37 30 E
Hejian 38 38 25N 116 5 E
Hejiang 39 28 43N 105 46 E
Hekimhan 30 38 50N 38 0 E
Hekla 20 63 56N 19 35W
Hekou 37 22 30N 103 59 E
Helan Shan 38 39 0N 105 55 E
Helena, Ark., U.S.A. 71 34 30N 90 35W
Helena, Mont., U.S.A. 72 46 40N 112 0W
Helensburgh 8 56 0N 4 44W
Helensville 43 36 41S 174 29 E
Ḥelez 28 31 36N 34 39 E
Helgoland 14 54 10N 7 51 E
Heligoland = Helgoland 14 54 10N 7 51 E
Hellendoorn 11 52 24N 6 27 E
Hellevoetsluis 11 51 50N 4 8 E
Hellín 13 38 31N 1 40W
Helmand □ 31 31 20N 64 0 E
Helmand → 31 31 12N 61 34 E
Helmand, Hamun 31 31 15N 61 15 E
Helmond 11 51 29N 5 41 E
Helmsdale 8 58 7N 3 40W
Helper 72 39 44N 110 56W
Helsingborg 21 56 3N 12 42 E
Helsingfors 21 60 15N 25 3 E
Helsingør 21 56 2N 12 35 E
Helsinki 21 60 15N 25 3 E
Helston 7 50 7N 5 17W
Helvellyn 6 54 31N 3 1W
Helwân 51 29 50N 31 20 E
Hemet 73 33 45N 116 59W
Hemingford 70 42 21N 103 4W
Hemphill 71 31 21N 93 49W
Hempstead 71 30 5N 96 5W
Hemse 21 57 15N 18 22 E
Henan □ 39 34 0N 114 0 E
Henares → 13 40 24N 3 30W
Henderson, Ky., U.S.A. 68 37 50N 87 38W
Henderson, N.C., U.S.A. 69 36 20N 78 25W
Henderson, Nev., U.S.A. 73 36 2N 115 0W
Henderson, Pa., U.S.A. 69 35 25N 88 40W
Henderson, Tex., U.S.A. 71 32 5N 94 49W
Hendersonville 69 35 21N 82 28W
Hendon 45 28 5S 151 50 E
Heng Xian 39 22 40N 109 17 E
Hengdaohezi 38 44 52N 129 0 E
Hengelo 11 52 3N 6 19 E
Hengshan, Hunan, China 39 27 16N 112 45 E
Hengshan, Shaanxi, China 38 37 58N 109 5 E
Hengshui 38 37 41N 115 40 E
Hengyang 39 26 52N 112 33 E
Henlopen, C. 68 38 48N 75 5W
Hennenman 56 27 59S 27 1 E
Hennessey 71 36 8N 97 53W
Henrietta 71 33 50N 98 15W
Henrietta, Ostrov 25 77 6N 156 30 E
Henrietta Maria C. 62 55 9N 82 20W
Henry 70 41 5N 89 20W
Henryetta 71 35 30N 96 0W
Hentiyn Nuruu 37 48 30N 108 30 E
Henty 45 35 30S 147 0 E
Henzada 33 17 38N 95 26 E
Heping 39 24 29N 115 0 E
Heppner 72 45 21N 119 34W
Hepu 39 21 40N 109 12 E
Héraðsflói 20 65 42N 14 12W
Héraðsvötn → 20 65 45N 19 25W
Herald Cays 44 16 58S 149 9 E
Herāt 31 34 20N 62 7 E
Herāt □ 31 35 0N 62 0 E
Hérault □ 12 43 34N 3 15 E
Herbert → 44 18 31S 146 17 E
Herbert Downs 44 23 7S 139 9 E
Herberton 44 17 20S 145 25 E
Hercegnovi 19 42 30N 18 33 E
Hercegovina = Bosna i Hercegovina □ 18 44 0N 18 0 E
Herðubreið 20 65 11N 16 21W
Hereford, U.K. 7 52 4N 2 42W
Hereford, U.S.A. 71 34 50N 102 28W
Hereford and Worcester □ 7 52 10N 2 30W
Herentals 11 51 12N 4 51 E
Herford 14 52 7N 8 40 E
Herington 70 38 43N 97 0W
Herjehogna 21 61 43N 12 7 E
Herkimer 68 43 0N 74 59W
Herman 70 45 51N 96 8W
Hermann 70 38 40N 91 25W
Hermannsburg Mission 46 23 57S 132 45 E
Hermanus 56 34 27S 19 12 E
Hermidale 45 31 30S 146 42 E
Hermiston 72 45 50N 119 16W
Hermitage 43 43 44S 170 5 E
Hermite, I. 80 55 50S 68 0W
Hermon, Mt. = Ash Shaykh, J. 30 33 25N 35 50 E
Hermosillo 74 29 10N 111 0W
Hernád → 15 47 56N 21 8 E
Hernandarias 80 25 20S 54 40W
Hernando 71 34 50N 89 59W
Herne 11 51 33N 7 12 E
Herne Bay 7 51 22N 1 8 E
Herning 21 56 8N 8 58 E
Heroica = Caborca 74 30 40N 112 10W
Heroica Nogales = Nogales 74 31 20N 110 56W
Heron Bay 62 48 40N 86 25W
Herreid 70 45 53N 100 5W
Herrera 13 37 26N 4 55W
Herrick 44 41 5S 147 55 E
Herrin 71 37 50N 89 0W
Herstal 11 50 40N 5 38 E
Hertford 7 51 47N 0 4W
Hertford □ 7 51 51N 0 5W
's-Hertogenbosch 11 51 42N 5 17 E
Hertzogville 56 28 9S 25 30 E
Hervey Bay 44 25 0S 153 5 E
Herzliyya 28 32 10N 34 50 E
Hesse = Hessen □ 14 50 40N 9 20 E
Hessen □ 14 50 40N 9 20 E
Hettinger 70 46 0N 102 38W
Hevron → 28 31 12N 34 42 E
Hewett, C. 61 70 16N 67 45W
Hexham 6 54 58N 2 7W
Hexigten Qi 38 43 18N 117 30 E
Hexrivier 56 33 30S 19 35 E
Heysham 6 54 5N 2 53W
Heywood 45 38 8S 141 37 E
Hi-no-Misaki 36 35 26N 132 38 E
Hialeach 69 25 49N 80 17W
Hiawatha, Kans., U.S.A. 70 39 55N 95 33W
Hiawatha, Utah, U.S.A. 72 39 29N 111 1W
Hibbing 70 47 30N 93 0W
Hibbs B. 44 42 35S 145 15 E
Hibernia Reef 46 12 0S 123 23 E
Hickory 69 35 46N 81 17W
Hicks Pt. 45 37 49S 149 17 E
Hida-Sammyaku 36 36 30N 137 40 E
Hidalgo 74 24 15N 99 26W
Hidalgo, Presa M. 74 26 30N 108 35W
Hidalgo del Parral 74 26 58N 105 40W
Hierro 50 27 44N 18 0 E
Higashiōsaka 36 34 40N 135 37 E
Higgins 71 36 9N 100 1W
Higginsville 47 31 42S 121 38 E
High Atlas = Haut Atlas 50 32 30N 5 0W
High I. 63 56 40N 61 10W
High Island 71 29 32N 94 22W
High Level 64 58 31N 117 8W
High Point 69 35 57N 79 58W
High Prairie 64 55 30N 116 30W
High River 64 50 30N 113 50W
High Springs 69 29 50N 82 40W
High Wycombe 7 51 37N 0 45W
Highbury 44 16 25S 143 9 E
Highland □ 8 57 30N 5 0W
Highland Park 68 42 10N 87 50W
Highmore 70 44 35N 99 26W
Highrock L. 65 57 5N 105 32W
Hiiumaa 22 58 50N 22 45 E
Ḥijārah, Ṣaḥrā' al 30 30 25N 44 30 E
Ḥijāz □ 29 24 0N 40 0 E
Hijo = Tagum 35 7 33N 125 53 E
Hiko 73 37 30N 115 13W
Hikone 36 35 15N 136 10 E
Hildesheim 14 52 9N 9 55 E
Hill → 47 30 23S 115 3 E
Hill City, Idaho, U.S.A. 72 43 20N 115 2W
Hill City, Kans., U.S.A. 70 39 25N 99 51W
Hill City, Minn., U.S.A. 70 46 57N 93 35W
Hill City, S. Dak., U.S.A. 70 43 58N 103 35W
Hill Island L. 65 60 30N 109 50W
Hillegom 11 52 18N 4 35 E
Hillingdon 7 51 33N 0 29W
Hillman 68 45 5N 83 52W
Hillmond 65 53 26N 109 41W
Hillsboro, Kans., U.S.A. 70 38 22N 97 10W
Hillsboro, N. Dak., U.S.A. 70 47 23N 97 9W
Hillsboro, N.H., U.S.A. 68 43 8N 71 56W
Hillsboro, N. Mex., U.S.A. 73 33 0N 107 35W
Hillsboro, Oreg., U.S.A. 72 45 31N 123 0W
Hillsboro, Tex., U.S.A. 71 32 0N 97 10W
Hillsdale 68 41 55N 84 40W
Hillside 46 21 45S 119 23 E
Hillsport 62 49 27N 85 34W
Hillston 45 33 30S 145 31 E
Hilo 66 19 44N 155 5W
Hilversum 11 52 14N 5 10 E
Himachal Pradesh □ 32 31 30N 77 0 E
Himalaya, Mts. 33 29 0N 84 0 E
Himatnagar 32 23 37N 72 57 E
Himeji 36 34 50N 134 40 E
Himi 36 36 50N 137 0 E
Ḥimş 30 34 40N 36 45 E
Hinchinbrook I. 44 18 20S 146 15 E
Hinckley, U.K. 7 52 33N 1 21W
Hinckley, U.S.A. 72 39 18N 112 41W
Hindmarsh L. 45 36 5S 141 55 E
Hindu Kush 31 36 0N 71 0 E
Hindubagh 32 30 56N 67 57 E
Hindupur 32 13 49N 77 32 E
Hines Creek 64 56 20N 118 40W
Hinganghat 32 20 30N 78 52 E
Hingham 72 48 34N 110 29W
Hingoli 32 19 41N 77 15 E
Hinna = Imi 29 6 28N 42 10 E
Hinsdale 72 48 26N 107 2W
Hinton, Canada 64 53 26N 117 34W
Hinton, U.S.A. 68 37 40N 80 51W
Hippolytushoef 11 52 54N 4 58 E
Hirakud Dam 33 21 32N 83 45 E
Hiratsuka 36 35 19N 139 21 E
Hirosaki 36 40 34N 140 28 E
Hiroshima 36 34 24N 132 30 E
Hiroshima □ 36 34 50N 133 0 E
Hisar 32 29 12N 75 45 E
Hispaniola 75 19 0N 71 0W
Hita 36 33 20N 130 58 E
Hitachi 36 36 36N 140 39 E
Hitchin 7 51 57N 0 16W
Hitoyoshi 36 32 13N 130 45 E
Hitra 20 63 30N 8 45 E
Ḥiyyon, N. → 28 30 25N 35 10 E
Hjalmar L. 65 61 33N 109 25W
Hjälmaren 21 59 18N 15 40 E
Hjørring 21 57 29N 9 59 E
Hluhluwe 57 28 1S 32 15 E
Ho 53 6 37N 0 27 E
Ho Chi Minh City = Phanh Bho Ho Chi Minh 34 10 58N 106 40 E
Hoai Nhon 34 14 28N 109 1 E
Hoare B. 61 65 17N 62 30W
Hobart, Australia 44 42 50S 147 21 E
Hobart, U.S.A. 71 35 0N 99 5W
Hobbs 71 32 40N 103 3W
Hoboken 11 51 11N 4 21 E
Hobro 21 56 39N 9 46 E
Hoburgen 21 56 55N 18 7 E
Hodgson 65 51 13N 97 36W
Hódmezővásárhely 15 46 28N 20 22 E
Hodna, Chott el 50 35 30N 5 10 E
Hodonín 14 48 50N 17 10 E
Hoek van Holland 11 52 0N 4 7 E
Hoëveld 57 26 30S 30 0 E
Hof, Germany 14 50 18N 11 55 E
Hof, Iceland 20 64 33N 14 40W
Höfðakaupstaður 20 65 50N 20 19W
Hofmeyr 56 31 39S 25 50 E
Hofsjökull 20 64 49N 18 48W
Hofsós 20 65 53N 19 26W
Hōfu 36 34 3N 131 34 E
Hogan Group 44 39 13S 147 1 E
Hogansville 69 33 14N 84 50W
Hogeland 72 48 51N 108 40W
Hoh Xil Shan 37 35 0N 89 0 E
Hohe Rhön 14 50 24N 9 58 E
Hohe Venn 11 50 30N 6 5 E
Hohenwald 69 35 35N 87 30W
Hohhot 38 40 52N 111 40 E
Hoi An 34 15 30N 108 19 E
Hoisington 70 38 33N 98 50W
Hokianga Harbour 43 35 31S 173 22 E
Hokitika 43 42 42S 171 0 E
Hokkaidō □ 36 43 30N 143 0 E
Holbrook, Australia 45 35 42S 147 18 E
Holbrook, U.S.A. 73 35 54N 110 10W
Holden, Canada 64 53 13N 112 11W
Holden, U.S.A. 72 39 0N 112 26W
Holdenville 71 35 5N 96 25W
Holderness 6 53 45N 0 5W
Holdfast 65 50 58N 105 25W
Holdrege 70 40 26N 99 22W
Holguín 75 20 50N 76 20W
Hollams Bird I. 56 24 40S 14 30 E
Holland 68 42 47N 86 7W
Hollandia = Jayapura 35 2 28S 140 38 E
Holleton 47 31 55S 119 0 E
Hollidaysburg 68 40 26N 78 25W
Hollis 71 34 45N 99 55W
Hollister, Calif., U.S.A. 73 36 51N 121 24W
Hollister, Idaho, U.S.A. 72 42 21N 114 40W
Holly 70 38 7N 102 7W
Holly Hill 69 29 15N 81 3W
Holly Springs 71 34 45N 89 25W
Hollywood, Calif., U.S.A. 66 34 7N 118 25W
Hollywood, Fla., U.S.A. 69 26 0N 80 9W
Holman Island 60 70 42N 117 41W
Hólmavík 20 65 42N 21 40W
Holmes Reefs 44 16 27S 148 0 E
Holmsund 20 63 41N 20 20 E
Holon 28 32 2N 34 47 E
Holroyd → 44 14 10S 141 36 E
Holstebro 21 56 22N 8 37 E
Holsworthy 7 50 48N 4 21W
Holt 20 63 33N 19 48W
Holton, Canada 63 54 31N 57 12W
Holton, U.S.A. 70 39 28N 95 44W
Holtville 73 32 50N 115 27W
Holwerd 11 53 22N 5 54 E
Holy Cross 60 62 10N 159 52W
Holy I., England, U.K. 6 55 42N 1 48W
Holy I., Wales, U.K. 6 53 17N 4 37W
Holyhead 6 53 18N 4 38W
Holyoke, Colo., U.S.A. 70 40 39N 102 18W
Holyoke, Mass., U.S.A. 68 42 14N 72 37W
Holyrood 63 47 27N 53 8W
Homalin 33 24 55N 95 0 E
Hombori 53 15 20N 1 38W
Home B. 61 68 40N 67 10W
Home Hill 44 19 43S 147 25 E
Homedale 72 43 42N 116 59W
Homer, Alaska, U.S.A. 60 59 40N 151 35W
Homer, La., U.S.A. 71 32 50N 93 4W
Homestead, Australia 44 20 20S 145 40 E
Homestead, Fla., U.S.A. 69 25 29N 80 27W
Homestead, Oreg., U.S.A. 72 45 5N 116 57W
Hominy 71 36 26N 96 24W
Homoine 57 23 55S 35 8 E
Homs = Ḥimş 30 34 40N 36 45 E
Hon Chong 34 10 25N 104 30 E
Honan = Henan □ 39 34 0N 114 0 E
Honbetsu 36 43 7N 143 37 E
Honda 78 5 12N 74 45W
Hondeklipbaai 56 30 19S 17 17 E
Hondo 71 29 22N 99 6W
Hondo → 74 18 25N 88 21W
Honduras ■ 75 14 40N 86 30W
Honduras, G. de 75 16 50N 87 0W
Hønefoss 21 60 10N 10 18 E
Honey L. 72 40 13N 120 14W
Honfleur 12 49 25N 0 13 E
Hong → 26 20 17N 106 34 E
Hong Kong ■ 39 22 11N 114 14 E
Hong'an 39 31 20N 114 40 E
Honghai Wan 39 22 40N 115 0 E
Honghu 39 29 50N 113 30 E
Hongjiang 39 27 7N 109 59 E
Hongshui He → 39 23 48N 109 30 E
Hongtong 38 36 16N 111 40 E
Honguedo, Détroit d' 63 49 15N 64 0W
Hongze Hu 39 33 15N 118 35 E
Honiara 40 9 27S 159 57 E
Honiton 7 50 48N 3 11W
Honjō 36 39 23N 140 3 E
Honolulu 66 21 19N 157 52W
Honshū 36 36 0N 138 0 E
Hood, Pt. 47 34 23S 119 34 E
Hood Mt. 72 45 24N 121 41W
Hood River 72 45 45N 121 31W
Hoodsport 72 47 24N 123 7W
Hoogeveen 11 52 44N 6 30 E
Hoogezand 11 53 11N 6 45 E
Hooghly → = Hughli → 33 21 56N 88 4 E
Hook Hd. 9 52 8N 6 57W
Hook I. 44 20 4S 149 0 E
Hook of Holland = Hoek van Holland 11 52 0N 4 7 E
Hooker 71 36 55N 101 10W
Hooker Creek 46 18 23S 130 38 E
Hoopeston 68 40 30N 87 40W
Hoopstad 56 27 50S 25 55 E
Hoorn 11 52 38N 5 4 E
Hoover Dam 73 36 0N 114 45W
Hope, Canada 64 49 25N 121 25 E
Hope, Ark., U.S.A. 71 33 40N 93 36W
Hope, N. Dak., U.S.A. 70 47 21N 97 42W
Hope, L. 45 28 24S 139 18 E
Hope Pt. 60 68 20N 166 50W
Hope Town 75 26 35N 76 57W
Hopedale 63 55 28N 60 13W
Hopefield 56 33 3S 18 22 E
Hopei = Hebei □ 38 39 0N 116 0 E
Hopelchén 74 19 46N 89 50W
Hopetoun, Vic., Australia 45 35 42S 142 22 E
Hopetoun, W. Austral., Australia 47 33 57S 120 7 E
Hopetown 56 29 34S 24 3 E
Hopkins 70 40 31N 94 45W
Hopkins, L. 46 24 15S 128 35 E
Hopkinsville 69 36 52N 87 26W
Hopland 72 39 0N 123 7W
Hoquiam 72 46 50N 123 55W
Hordaland fylke □ 21 60 25N 6 15 E
Horden Hills 46 20 15S 130 0 E
Hormoz 31 27 35N 55 0 E
Hormoz, Jaz. ye 31 27 8N 56 28 E
Hormozgān □ 31 27 30N 56 0 E
Hormuz Str. 31 26 30N 56 30 E
Horn, Austria 14 48 39N 15 40 E
Horn, Ísafjarðarsýsla, Iceland 20 66 28N 22 28W
Horn, Suður-Múlasýsla, Iceland 20 65 10N 13 31W
Horn → 64 61 30N 118 1W
Horn, Cape = Hornos, C. de 80 55 50S 67 30W
Horn Head 9 55 13N 8 0W
Horn I., Australia 44 10 37S 142 17 E
Horn I., U.S.A. 69 30 17N 88 40W
Horn Mts. 64 62 15N 119 15W
Hornavan 20 66 15N 17 30 E
Hornbeck 71 31 22N 93 20W
Hornbrook 72 41 58N 122 37W
Horncastle 6 53 13N 0 8W
Hornell 68 42 23N 77 41W
Hornell L. 64 62 20N 119 25W
Hornepayne 62 49 14N 84 48W
Hornos, C. de 80 55 50S 67 30W
Hornsby 45 33 42S 151 2 E
Hornsea 6 53 55N 0 10W
Horqin Youyi Qianqi 38 46 5N 122 3 E
Horqueta 80 23 15S 56 55W
Horse Cr. → 70 41 57N 103 58W
Horse Is. 63 50 15N 55 50W
Horsefly L. 64 52 25N 121 0W
Horsens 21 55 52N 9 51 E
Horsham, Australia 45 36 44S 142 13 E
Horsham, U.K. 7 51 4N 0 20W
Horten 21 59 25N 10 32 E
Horton 70 39 42N 95 30W
Horton → 60 69 56N 126 52W
Horwood, L. 62 48 5N 82 20W
Hose, Gunung-Gunung 34 2 5N 114 6 E
Hoshangabad 32 22 45N 77 45 E
Hoshiarpur 32 31 30N 75 58 E
Hosmer 70 45 36N 99 29W
Hospet 32 15 15N 76 20 E

Hospitalet de Llobregat

Hospitalet de
  Llobregat ...... 13 41 21N 2 6 E
Hoste, I. 80 55 0S 69 0W
Hot Creek Ra. 72 39 0N 116 0W
Hot Springs, Ark.,
  U.S.A. 71 34 30N 93 0W
Hot Springs, S. Dak.,
  U.S.A. 70 43 25N 103 30W
Hotagen .... 20 63 50N 14 30 E
Hotan .... 37 37 25N 79 55 E
Hotazel .... 56 27 17S 22 58 E
Hotchkiss 73 38 47N 107 47W
Hotham, C. .... 46 12 2S 131 18 E
Hoting .... 20 64 8N 16 15 E
Hottentotsbaai .... 56 26 8S 14 59 E
Houck 73 35 15N 109 15W
Houffalize .... 11 50 8N 5 48 E
Houghton 70 47 9N 88 39W
Houghton L. 68 44 20N 84 40W
Houghton-le-Spring 6 54 51N 1 28W
Houhora .... 43 34 49S 173 9 E
Houlton 63 46 5N 67 50W
Houma 71 29 35N 90 44W
Houston, Canada .. 64 54 25N 126 39W
Houston, Mo., U.S.A. 71 37 20N 92 0W
Houston, Tex.,
  U.S.A. 71 29 50N 95 20W
Houtman Abrolhos 47 28 43S 113 48 E
Hovd .... 37 48 2N 91 37 E
Hove 7 50 50N 0 10W
Hövsgöl Nuur ..... 37 51 0N 100 30 E
Howard, Australia 45 25 16S 152 32 E
Howard, Kans.,
  U.S.A. 71 37 30N 96 16W
Howard, S. Dak.,
  U.S.A. 70 44 2N 97 30W
Howard I. .... 44 12 10S 135 24 E
Howard L. 65 62 15N 105 57W
Howatharra ...... 47 28 29S 114 33 E
Howe 72 43 48N 113 0W
Howe, C. .... 45 37 30S 150 0 E
Howell 68 42 38N 83 56W
Howick .... 57 29 28S 30 14 E
Howick Group .... 44 14 20S 145 30 E
Howitt, L. .... 45 27 40S 138 40 E
Howley 63 49 12N 57 2W
Howrah = Haora .. 33 22 37N 88 20 E
Howth Hd. 9 53 21N 6 0W
Hoy I. 8 58 50N 3 15W
Høyanger .... 21 61 13N 6 4 E
Hpungan Pass .... 33 27 30N 96 55 E
Hradec Králové ... 14 50 15N 15 50 E
Hron → .... 15 47 49N 18 45 E
Hrvatska .... 18 45 20N 16 0 E
Hsenwi .... 33 23 22N 97 55 E
Hsiamen = Xiamen 38 24 25N 118 4 E
Hsian = Xi'an ..... 39 34 15N 109 0 E
Hsinhailien =
  Lianyungang .... 39 34 40N 119 11 E
Hsüchou = Xuzhou 39 34 18N 117 10 E
Hua Hin .... 34 12 34N 99 58 E
Hua Xian, Henan,
  China .... 39 35 30N 114 30 E
Hua Xian, Shaanxi,
  China .... 39 34 30N 109 48 E
Huacheng .... 39 24 4N 115 37 E
Huacho 78 11 10S 77 35W
Huachón 78 10 35S 76 0W
Huachuan .... 38 46 50N 130 21 E
Huade .... 38 41 55N 113 59 E
Huadian .... 38 43 0N 126 40 E
Huai He → ...... 39 33 0N 118 30 E
Huai'an .... 39 33 30N 119 10 E
Huaide .... 38 43 30N 124 40 E
Huainan .... 39 32 38N 116 58 E
Huaiyang .... 39 33 40N 114 52 E
Huaiyuan .... 39 24 31N 108 22 E
Huajianzi .... 38 41 23N 125 20 E
Huajuapan de Leon 74 17 50N 97 48W
Hualapai Pk. 73 35 8N 113 58W
Hualian .... 39 23 59N 121 37 E
Huallaga → 78 5 0S 75 30W
Huambo .... 55 12 42S 15 54 E
Huan Jiang → ... 38 34 28N 109 0 E
Huan Xian .... 38 36 33N 107 7 E
Huancabamba 78 5 10S 79 15W
Huancane 78 15 10S 69 44W
Huancapi 78 13 40S 74 0W
Huancavelica 78 12 50S 75 5W
Huancayo 78 12 5S 75 12W
Huang Hai = Yellow
  Sea .... 38 35 0N 123 0 E
Huang He → .... 38 37 55N 118 50 E
Huangchuan ...... 39 32 15N 115 10 E
Huangliu .... 39 18 20N 108 50 E
Huanglong .... 38 35 30N 109 59 E
Huangshi .... 39 30 10N 115 3 E
Huangyan .... 39 28 38N 121 19 E
Huánuco 78 9 55S 76 15W
Huaraz 78 9 30S 77 32W
Huarmey 78 10 5S 78 5W
Huascarán 78 9 8S 77 36W
Huascarán, Nevado 76 9 7S 77 37W
Huasco 80 28 30S 71 15W
Huatabampo 74 26 50N 109 50W
Huay Namota 74 21 56N 104 30W
Huayllay 78 11 3S 76 21W
Hubbard 71 31 50N 96 50W
Hubbart Pt. 65 59 21N 94 41W
Hubei □ .... 39 31 0N 112 0 E
Hubli-Dharwad =
  Dharwad ...... 32 15 22N 75 15 E
Huddersfield 6 53 38N 1 49W
Hudiksvall .... 21 61 43N 17 10 E
Hudson, Canada .. 65 50 6N 92 9W
Hudson, Mich.,
  U.S.A. 68 41 50N 84 20W
Hudson, N.Y., U.S.A. 68 42 15N 73 46W
Hudson, Wis., U.S.A. 70 44 57N 92 45W
Hudson, Wyo.,
  U.S.A. 72 42 54N 108 37W
Hudson → 68 40 42N 74 2W
Hudson Bay 61 52 51N 102 23W
Hudson Falls 68 43 18N 73 34W
Hudson Str. 61 62 0N 70 0W
Hudson's Hope ... 64 56 0N 121 54W
Hue .... 34 16 30N 107 35 E
Huelva 13 37 18N 6 57W
Huesca 13 42 8N 0 25W
Huetamo 74 18 36N 100 54W
Hugh → .... 44 25 1S 134 1 E
Hughenden ...... 44 20 52S 144 10 E
Hughes, Australia . 47 30 42S 129 31 E
Hughes, U.S.A. ... 60 66 0N 154 20W
Hughli → .... [illegible] 21 50N [illegible] 4 E
Hugo 70 39 12N 103 27W
Hugoton 71 37 11N 101 22W
Hui Xian .... 38 35 27N 113 12 E
Hui'an .... 39 25 1N 118 43 E
Huichang .... 39 25 32N 115 45 E
Huichapán 74 20 24N 99 40W
Huihe .... 38 48 12N 119 17 E
Huila, Nevado del . 78 3 0N 76 0W
Huilai .... 39 23 0N 116 18 E
Huimin .... 38 37 27N 117 28 E
Huinan .... 38 42 40N 126 2 E
Huinca Renancó .. 80 34 51S 64 22W
Huining .... 38 35 38N 105 0 E
Huinong .... 38 39 5N 106 35 E
Huize .... 37 26 24N 103 15 E
Huizhou .... 39 23 0N 114 23 E
Hukawng Valley ... 33 26 30N 96 30 E
Hukou .... 39 29 45N 116 21 E
Hukuntsi .... 56 23 58S 21 45 E
Hulan .... 38 46 1N 126 37 E
Ḥulayfā' .... 30 25 58N 40 45 E
Huld .... 37 45 5N 105 30 E
Hulda .... 28 31 50N 34 51 E
Hulin .... 38 45 48N 132 59 E
Hull, Canada 62 45 25N 75 44W
Hull, U.K. 6 53 45N 0 20W
Hull → 6 53 43N 0 25W
Hulst .... 11 51 17N 4 2 E
Hulun Nur .... 38 49 0N 117 30 E
Huma .... 38 51 43N 126 38 E
Huma He → ..... 38 51 42N 126 42 E
Humahuaca 80 23 10S 65 25W
Humaitá, Brazil ... 78 7 35S 63 1W
Humaitá, Paraguay 80 27 2S 58 31W
Humansdorp ..... 56 34 2S 24 46 E
Humbe .... 56 16 40S 14 55 E
Humber → 6 53 40N 0 10W
Humberside □ 6 53 50N 0 30W
Humbert River .... 46 16 30S 130 45 E
Humble 71 29 59N 93 18W
Humboldt, Canada 65 52 15N 105 9W
Humboldt, Iowa,
  U.S.A. 70 42 42N 94 15W
Humboldt, Tenn.,
  U.S.A. 71 35 50N 88 55W
Humboldt → 72 40 2N 118 31W
Hume, L. .... 45 36 0S 147 0 E
Humphreys Pk. ... 73 35 24N 111 38W
Hün .... 51 29 2N 16 0 E
Húnaflói 20 65 50N 20 50W
Hunan □ .... 39 27 30N 112 0 E
Hunchun .... 38 42 52N 130 28 E
Hundred Mile House 64 51 38N 121 18W
Hunedoara .... 15 45 40N 22 50 E
Hungary ■ .... 15 47 20N 19 20 E
Hungary, Plain of .. 4 47 0N 20 0 E
Hungerford .... 45 28 58S 144 24 E
Hŭngnam .... 38 39 49N 127 45 E
Hunsberge .... 56 27 45S 17 12 E
Hunsrück .... 14 49 30N 7 0 E
Hunstanton ...... 6 52 57N 0 30 E
Hunter 70 47 12N 97 17W
Hunter I., Australia . 44 40 30S 144 45 E
Hunter I., Canada . 64 51 55N 128 0W
Hunter Ra. .... 45 32 45S 150 15 E
Hunterville .... 43 39 56S 175 35 E
Huntingburg 68 38 20N 86 58W
Huntingdon, Canada 62 45 6N 74 10W
Huntingdon, U.K. .. 7 52 20N 0 11W
Huntingdon, U.S.A. 68 40 28N 78 1W
Huntington, Ind.,
  U.S.A. 68 40 52N 85 30W
Huntington, Oreg.,
  U.S.A. 72 44 22N 117 21W
Huntington, Utah,
  U.S.A. 72 39 24N 111 1W
Huntington, W. Va.,
  U.S.A. 68 38 20N 82 30W
Huntington Beach . 73 33 40N 118 0W
Huntington Park .. 73 33 58N 118 15W
Huntly, N.Z. ...... 43 37 34S 175 11 E
Huntly, U.K. 8 57 27N 2 48W
Huntsville, Canada 62 45 20N 79 14W
Huntsville, Ala.,
  U.S.A. 69 34 45N 86 35W
Huntsville, Tex.,
  U.S.A. 71 30 45N 95 35W
Huo Xian .... 38 36 36N 111 42 E
Huonville .... 44 43 0S 147 5 E
Huoqiu .... 39 32 20N 116 12 E
Huoshao Dao ..... 39 22 40N 121 30 E
Hupeh □ = Hubei □ 39 31 0N 112 0 E
Hure Qi .... 38 42 45N 121 45 E
Hurley, N. Mex.,
  U.S.A. 73 32 45N 108 7W
Hurley, Wis., U.S.A. 70 46 26N 90 10W
Huron 70 44 22N 98 12W
Huron, L. 68 45 0N 83 0W
Hurricane 73 37 10N 113 12W
Hurunui → ...... 43 42 54S 173 18 E
Húsavík 20 66 3N 17 21W
Huskvarna .... 21 57 47N 14 15 E
Hussar 64 51 3N 112 41W
Hutchinson, Kans.,
  U.S.A. 71 38 3N 97 59W
Hutchinson, Minn.,
  U.S.A. 70 44 50N 94 22W
Hutou .... 38 45 58N 133 38 E
Huttig 71 33 5N 92 10W
Hutton, Mt. .... 45 25 51S 148 20 E
Ḥuwwārah .... 28 32 9N 35 15 E
Huy .... 11 50 31N 5 15 E
Hvammur 20 65 13N 21 49W
Hvar .... 18 43 11N 16 28 E
Hvítá 20 64 40N 21 5W
Hvítá → 20 64 0N 20 58W
Hvítárvatn 20 64 37N 19 50W
Hwang Ho = Huang
  He → .... 38 37 55N 118 50 E
Hwange .... 55 18 18S 26 30 E
Hwange Nat. Park . 56 19 0S 26 30 E
Hyannis 70 42 0N 101 45W
Hyargas Nuur ..... 37 49 0N 93 0 E
Hyden .... 47 32 24S 118 53 E
Hyderabad, India .. 32 17 22N 78 29 E
Hyderabad, Pakistan 32 25 23N 68 24 E
Hyères .... 12 43 8N 6 9 E
Hyesan .... 38 41 20N 128 10 E
Hyland → 64 59 52N 128 12W
Hyndman Pk. 72 43 50N 114 10W
Hyōgo □ .... 36 35 15N 135 0 E
Hyrum 72 41 35N 111 56W
Hysham 72 46 21N 107 11W
Hythe .... 7 51 4N 1 5 E
Hyvinge = Hyvinkää 21 60 38N 24 50 E
Hyvinkää .... 21 60 38N 24 50 E

I

I-n-Gall .... 53 16 51N 7 1 E
Iaco → 78 9 3S 68 34W
Iakora .... 57 23 6S 46 40 E
Ialomiţa → ...... 15 44 42N 27 51 E
Iaşi .... 17 47 10N 27 40 E
Iba .... 35 15 22N 120 0 E
Ibadan .... 53 7 22N 3 58 E
Ibagué 78 4 20N 75 20W
Ibar → .... 19 43 43N 20 45 E
Ibaraki □ .... 36 36 10N 140 10 E
Ibarra 78 0 21N 78 7W
Iberian Peninsula .. 4 40 0N 5 0W
Iberville 62 45 19N 73 17W
Iberville, Lac D' ... 62 55 55N 73 15W
Ibi .... 53 8 15N 9 44 E
Ibiá 79 19 30S 46 30W
Ibicuy 80 33 55S 59 10W
Ibioapaba, Sa. da . 79 4 0S 41 30W
Ibiza .... 13 38 54N 1 26 E
Ibonma .... 35 3 29S 133 31 E
Ibotirama 79 12 13S 43 12W
Ibu .... 35 1 35N 127 33 E
Icá 78 14 0S 75 48W
Iça → 78 2 55S 67 58W
Içana 78 0 21N 67 19W
Iceland ■ 20 65 0N 19 0W
Icha .... 25 55 30N 156 0 E
Ich'ang = Yichang . 39 30 40N 111 20 E
Ichchapuram ..... 33 19 10N 84 40 E
Ichihara .... 36 35 28N 140 5 E
Ichikawa .... 36 35 44N 139 55 E
Ichilo → 78 15 57S 64 50W
Ichinomiya .... 36 35 18N 136 48 E
Ichinoseki .... 36 38 55N 141 8 E
Icy Str. 64 58 20N 135 30W
Ida Grove 70 42 20N 95 25W
Ida Valley .... 47 28 42S 120 29 E
Idabel 71 33 53N 94 50W
Idaho □ 72 44 10N 114 0W
Idaho City 72 43 50N 115 52W
Idaho Falls 72 43 30N 112 1W
Idaho Springs 72 39 49N 105 30W
Idd el Ghanam .... 51 11 30N 24 19 E
Iddan .... 29 6 10N 48 55 E
Idehan .... 51 27 10N 11 30 E
Idehan Marzūq .... 51 24 50N 13 51 E
Idelès .... 50 23 50N 5 53 E
Idfû .... 51 25 0N 32 49 E
Ídhi Óros .... 19 35 15N 24 45 E
Ídhra .... 19 37 20N 23 28 E
Idi .... 34 5 2N 97 37 E
Idiofa .... 54 4 55S 19 42 E
Idlip .... 30 35 55N 36 38 E
Idna .... 28 31 34N 34 58 E
Idutywa .... 57 32 8S 28 18 E
Ieper .... 11 50 51N 2 53 E
Ierápetra .... 19 35 0N 25 44 E
Ierzu .... 18 39 48N 9 32 E
Ifanadiana .... 57 21 19S 47 39 E
Ife .... 53 7 30N 4 31 E
Iffley .... 44 18 53S 141 12 E
Ifni 50 29 29N 10 12W
Iforas, Adrar des .. 50 19 40N 1 40 E
Igarapava 79 20 3S 47 47W
Igarapé Açu 79 1 4S 47 33W
Igarka .... 25 67 30N 86 33 E
Igbetti .... 53 8 44N 4 8 E
Igbo-Ora .... 53 7 29N 3 15 E
Iggesund .... 21 61 39N 17 10 E
Iglésias .... 18 39 19N 8 27 E
Igli 50 30 25N 2 19W
Igloolik 61 69 20N 81 49W
Ignace 62 49 30N 91 40W
Iguaçu → 80 25 36S 54 36W
Iguaçu, Cat. del ... 80 25 41S 54 26W
Iguaçu Falls =
  Iguaçu, Cat. del . 80 25 41S 54 26W
Iguala 74 18 20N 99 40W
Igualada .... 13 41 37N 1 37 E
Iguassu =
  Iguaçu → 80 25 36S 54 36W
Iguatu 79 6 20S 39 18W
Iguéla .... 54 2 0S 9 16 E
Ihiala .... 53 5 51N 6 55 E
Ihosy .... 57 22 24S 46 8 E
Ihotry, L. .... 57 21 56S 43 41 E
Ii .... 20 65 19N 25 22 E
Iida .... 36 35 35N 137 50 E
Iijoki → .... 20 65 20N 25 20 E
Iisalmi .... 20 63 32N 27 10 E
Iizuka .... 36 33 38N 130 42 E
Ijebu-Igbo .... 53 6 56N 4 1 E
Ijebu-Ode .... 53 6 47N 3 58 E
IJmuiden .... 11 52 28N 4 35 E
IJssel → .... 11 52 35N 5 50 E
IJsselmeer .... 11 52 45N 5 20 E
Ikare .... 53 7 32N 5 40 E
Ikaría .... 19 37 35N 26 10 E
Ikeja .... 53 6 36N 3 23 E
Ikela .... 54 1 6S 23 6 E
Ikerre-Ekiti ...... 53 7 25N 5 19 E
Iki .... 36 33 45N 129 42 E
Ikire .... 53 7 23N 4 15 E
Ikopa → .... 57 16 45S 46 40 E
Ikot Ekpene ...... 53 5 12N 7 40 E
Ikurun .... 53 7 54N 4 40 E
Ila .... 53 8 0N 4 39 E
Ilagan .... 35 17 7N 121 53 E
Īlām .... 30 33 0N 46 0 E
Ilanskiy .... 25 56 14N 96 3 E
Ilbilbie .... 44 21 45S 149 20 E
Île-à-la Crosse 65 55 27N 107 53W
Île-à-la-Crosse, Lac 65 55 40N 107 45W
Île-de-France ..... 12 49 0N 2 20 E
Ilebo .... 54 4 17S 20 55 E
Ilek .... 24 51 32N 53 21 E
Ilek → .... 22 51 30N 53 22 E
Ilero .... 53 8 0N 3 20 E
Ilesha .... 53 7 37N 4 40 E
Ilford 65 56 4N 95 35W
Ilfracombe, Australia 44 23 30S 144 30 E
Ilfracombe, U.K. 7 51 13N 4 8W
Ilhéus 79 14 49S 39 2W
Ili → .... 24 45 53N 77 10 E
Ilich .... 24 40 50N 68 27 E
Iliff 70 40 50N 103 3W
Iligan .... 35 8 12N 124 13 E
Iliodhrómia ...... 19 39 12N 23 50 E
Ilion 68 43 0N 75 3W
Ilkeston 6 52 59N 1 19W
Illampu =
  Ancohuma,
  Nevada 78 16 0S 68 50W
Illana B. .... 35 7 35N 123 45 E
Illapel 80 32 0S 71 10W
'Illār .... 28 32 23N 35 7 E
Ille-et-Vilaine □ ... 12 48 10N 1 30W
Iller → .... 14 48 23N 9 58 E
Illimani 78 16 30S 67 50W
Illinois □ 67 40 15N 89 30W
Illinois → 67 38 55N 90 28W
Illium = Troy ..... 30 39 57N 26 12 E
Ilmen, Oz. .... 22 58 15N 31 10 E
Ilo 78 17 40S 71 20W
Ilobu .... 53 7 45N 4 25 E
Iloilo .... 35 10 45N 122 33 E
Ilora .... 53 7 45N 3 50 E
Ilorin .... 53 8 30N 4 35 E
Ilwaki .... 35 7 55S 126 30 E
Imabari .... 36 34 4N 133 0 E
Imaloto → ...... 57 23 27S 45 13 E
Imandra, Oz. ..... 22 67 30N 33 0 E
Imari .... 36 33 15N 129 52 E
Imbler 72 45 31N 118 0W
imeni 26 Bakinskikh
  Komissarov,
  Azerbaijan,
  U.S.S.R. .... 23 39 19N 49 12 E
imeni 26 Bakinskikh
  Komissarov,
  Turkmen S.S.R.,
  U.S.S.R. .... 23 39 22N 54 10 E
Imeni Poliny
  Osipenko ...... 25 52 30N 136 29 E
Imeri, Serra 78 0 50N 65 25W
Imerimandroso .... 57 17 26S 48 35 E
Imi .... 29 6 28N 42 10 E
Imlay 72 40 45N 118 9W
Immingham 6 53 37N 0 12W
Immokalee 69 26 25N 81 26W
Imo □ .... 53 5 15N 7 20 E
Imola .... 18 44 20N 11 42 E
Imperatriz 79 5 30S 47 29W
Impéria .... 18 43 52N 8 0 E
Imperial, Canada .. 65 51 21N 105 28W
Imperial, Calif.,
  U.S.A. 73 32 52N 115 34W
Imperial, Nebr.,
  U.S.A. 70 40 38N 101 39W
Imperial Dam 73 32 50N 114 30W
Imperieuse Reef .. 46 17 36S 118 50 E
Impfondo .... 54 1 40N 18 0 E
Imphal .... 33 24 48N 93 56 E
Imuruan B. .... 35 10 40N 119 10 E
In Belbel .... 50 27 55N 1 12 E
In Salah .... 50 27 10N 2 32 E
Ina .... 36 35 50N 138 0 E
Ina-Bonchi .... 36 35 45N 137 58 E
Inangahua Junc. .. 43 41 52S 171 59 E
Inanwatan .... 35 2 10S 132 14 E
Iñapari 78 11 0S 69 40W
Inari .... 20 68 54N 27 5 E
Inarijärvi .... 20 69 0N 28 0 E
Inawashiro-Ko .... 36 37 29N 140 6 E
Inca .... 13 39 43N 2 54 E
İnce-Burnu .... 30 42 7N 34 56 E
Inchon .... 38 37 27N 126 40 E
Incomáti → ..... 57 25 46S 32 43 E
Indalsälven → ... 20 62 36N 17 30 E
Indaw .... 33 24 15N 96 5 E
Independence,
  Calif., U.S.A. 73 36 51N 118 14W
Independence, Iowa,
  U.S.A. 70 42 27N 91 52W
Independence,
  Kans., U.S.A. ... 71 37 10N 95 43W
Independence, Mo.,
  U.S.A. 70 39 3N 94 25W
Independence,
  Oreg., U.S.A. ... 72 44 53N 123 12W
Independence Mts. 72 41 30N 116 2W
India ■ .... 32 20 0N 78 0 E
Indian → 69 27 59N 80 34W
Indian-Antarctic
  Ridge .... 40 49 0S 120 0 E
Indian Cabins 64 59 52N 117 40W
Indian Harbour 63 54 27N 57 13W
Indian Head 65 50 30N 103 41W
Indian Ocean ..... 3 5 0S 75 0 E
Indiana 68 40 38N 79 9W
Indiana □ 68 40 0N 86 0W
Indianapolis 68 39 42N 86 10W
Indianola, Iowa,
  U.S.A. 70 41 20N 93 32W
Indianola, Miss.,
  U.S.A. 71 33 27N 90 40W
Indiga .... 22 67 50N 48 50 E
Indigirka → ..... 25 70 48N 148 54 E
Indio 73 33 46N 116 15W
Indonesia ■ ...... 34 5 0S 115 0 E
Indore .... 32 22 42N 75 53 E
Indramayu .... 35 6 20S 108 19 E
Indravati → ..... 33 19 20N 80 20 E
Indre □ .... 12 46 50N 1 39 E
Indre-et-Loire □ ... 12 47 20N 0 40 E
Indus → .... 32 24 20N 67 47 E
İnebolu .... 30 41 55N 33 40 E

Khalmer Yu

Kampot . . . . 34 10 36N 104 10 E
Kampuchea =
Cambodia ■ . . . . 34 12 15N 105 0 E
Kampung → . . . . 35 5 44S 138 24 E
Kampungbaru =
Tolitoli . . . . 35 1 5N 120 50 E
Kamrau, Teluk . . . . 35 3 30S 133 36 E
Kamsack 65 51 34N 101 54W
Kamskoye Vdkhr. . . 22 58 0N 56 0 E
Kamuchawie L. . . . 65 56 18N 101 59W
Kamui-Misaki . . . . . 36 43 20N 140 21 E
Kamyshin . . . . 23 50 10N 45 24 E
Kanaaupscow 62 54 2N 76 30W
Kanab 73 37 3N 112 29W
Kanab Creek 73 37 0N 112 40W
Kanagawa □ . . . . . 36 35 20N 139 20 E
Kanairiktok → . . . 63 55 2N 60 18W
Kananga . . . . 54 5 55S 22 18 E
Kanarraville 73 37 34N 113 12W
Kanash . . . . 22 55 30N 47 32 E
Kanawha → 68 38 50N 82 8W
Kanazawa . . . . 36 36 30N 136 38 E
Kanchanaburi . . . . . 34 14 2N 99 31 E
Kanchenjunga . . . . 33 27 50N 88 10 E
Kanchipuram . . . . . 32 12 52N 79 45 E
Kanda Kanda . . . . . 54 6 52S 23 48 E
Kandahar =
Qandahār . . . . . . 31 31 32N 65 30 E
Kandalaksha . . . . . 22 67 9N 32 30 E
Kandalakshkiy Zaliv 22 66 0N 35 0 E
Kandalu . . . . 32 29 55N 63 20 E
Kandangan . . . . 34 2 50S 115 20 E
Kandi . . . . 53 11 7N 2 55 E
Kandla . . . . 32 23 0N 70 10 E
Kandos . . . . 45 32 45S 149 58 E
Kandy . . . . 32 7 18N 80 43 E
Kane 68 41 39N 78 53W
Kane Basin 58 79 1N 73 0W
Kangaroo I. . . . . . . 45 35 45S 137 0 E
Kangaroo Mts. . . . . 44 23 25S 142 0 E
Kangavar . . . . 30 34 40N 48 0 E
Kangean, Kepulauan 34 6 55S 115 23 E
Kanggye . . . . 38 41 0N 126 35 E
Kangnŭng . . . . 38 37 45N 128 54 E
Kango . . . . 54 0 11N 10 5 E
Kangto . . . . 33 27 50N 92 35 E
Kaniapiskau → . . 63 56 40N 69 30W
Kaniapiskau L. 63 54 10N 69 55W
Kanin, P-ov. . . . . . . 22 68 0N 45 0 E
Kanin Nos, Mys . . . 22 68 45N 43 20 E
Kaniva . . . . 45 36 22S 141 18 E
Kankakee 68 41 6N 87 50W
Kankakee → 68 41 23N 88 16W
Kankan 50 10 23N 9 15W
Kanker . . . . 33 20 10N 81 40 E
Kankunskiy . . . . 25 57 37N 126 8 E
Kannapolis 69 35 32N 80 37W
Kannauj . . . . 32 27 3N 79 56 E
Kannod . . . . 32 22 45N 76 40 E
Kano . . . . 53 12 2N 8 30 E
Kano □ . . . . 53 11 45N 9 0 E
Kanowit . . . . 34 2 14N 112 20 E
Kanowna . . . . 47 30 32S 121 31 E
Kanoya . . . . 36 31 25N 130 50 E
Kanpetlet . . . . 33 21 10N 93 59 E
Kanpur . . . . 32 26 28N 80 20 E
Kansas □ 70 38 40N 98 0W
Kansas → 70 39 7N 94 36W
Kansas City, Kans.,
U.S.A. 70 39 0N 94 40W
Kansas City, Mo.,
U.S.A. 70 39 3N 94 30W
Kansk . . . . 25 56 20N 95 37 E
Kansu = Gansu □ . . 38 36 0N 104 0 E
Kantang . . . . 34 7 25N 99 31 E
Kantché . . . . 53 13 31N 8 30 E
Kanturk 9 52 10N 8 55W
Kanuma . . . . 36 36 34N 139 42 E
Kanus . . . . 56 27 50S 18 39 E
Kanye . . . . 56 25 0S 25 28 E
Kaohsiung =
Gaoxiong . . . . . . 39 22 38N 120 18 E
Kaokoveld . . . . 56 19 15S 14 30 E
Kaolack 50 14 5N 16 8W
Kapanga . . . . 54 8 30S 22 40 E
Kapchagai . . . . 24 43 51N 77 14 E
Kapela . . . . 18 44 40N 15 40 E
Kapfenberg . . . . 14 47 26N 15 18 E
Kapiri Mposhi . . . . 55 13 59S 28 43 E
Kāpīsā □ . . . . 31 35 0N 69 20 E
Kapiskau → 62 52 47N 81 55W
Kapit . . . . 34 2 0N 112 55 E
Kapiti I. . . . . 43 40 50S 174 56 E
Kapoeta . . . . 51 4 50N 33 35 E
Kaposvár . . . . 15 46 25N 17 47 E
Kapps . . . . 56 22 32S 17 18 E
Kapuas → . . . . . . 34 0 25S 109 20 E
Kapuas Hulu,
Pegunungan . . . . 34 1 30N 113 30 E
Kapunda . . . . 45 34 20S 138 56 E
Kapuskasing 62 49 25N 82 30W
Kapuskasing → . . 62 49 49N 82 0W
Kaputar, Mt. . . . . . 45 30 15S 150 10 E
Kara . . . . 24 69 10N 65 0 E
Kara Bogaz Gol,
Zaliv . . . . 23 41 0N 53 30 E
Kara Kalpak
A.S.S.R. □ . . . . . 24 43 0N 60 0 E
Kara Kum =
Karakum, Peski . 24 39 30N 60 0 E
Kara Sea . . . . 24 75 0N 70 0 E
Karabük . . . . 30 41 12N 32 37 E
Karabutak . . . . 24 49 59N 60 14 E
Karachi . . . . 32 24 53N 67 0 E
Karad . . . . 32 17 15N 74 10 E
Karadeniz Boğazı . . 30 41 10N 29 10 E
Karaganda . . . . 24 49 50N 73 10 E
Karagayly . . . . 24 49 26N 76 0 E
Karaginskiy, Ostrov 25 58 45N 164 0 E
Karagiye Depression 23 43 27N 51 45 E
Karaikal . . . . 32 10 59N 79 50 E
Karaikkudi . . . . 32 10 0N 78 45 E
Karaj . . . . 31 35 48N 51 0 E
Karakas . . . . 24 48 20N 83 30 E
Karakitang . . . . 35 3 14N 125 28 E
Karakoram Pass . . 32 35 33N 77 50 E
Karakoram Ra. . . . . 32 35 30N 77 0 E
Karakum, Peski . . . 24 39 30N 60 0 E
Karalon . . . . 25 57 5N 115 50 E
Karaman . . . . 30 37 14N 33 13 E
Karamay . . . . 37 45 30N 84 58 E
Karambu . . . . 34 3 53S 116 6 E
Karamea Bight . . . . 43 41 22S 171 40 E
Karanganyar . . . . . . 35 7 38S 109 37 E
Karasburg . . . . 56 28 0S 18 44 E
Karasino . . . . 24 66 50N 86 50 E
Karasjok . . . . 20 69 27N 25 30 E
Karasuk . . . . 24 53 44N 78 2 E
Karatau . . . . 24 43 10N 70 28 E
Karatau, Khrebet . . 24 43 30N 69 30 E
Karawanken . . . . . . 18 46 30N 14 40 E
Karazhal . . . . 24 48 2N 70 49 E
Karbalā . . . . 30 32 36N 44 3 E
Karcag . . . . 15 47 19N 20 57 E
Karda . . . . 25 55 0N 103 16 E
Kardhítsa . . . . 19 39 23N 21 54 E
Kareeberge . . . . 56 30 59S 21 50 E
Karelian A.S.S.R. □ 22 65 30N 32 30 E
Kargānrūd . . . . 30 37 55N 49 0 E
Kargasok . . . . 24 59 3N 80 53 E
Kargat . . . . 24 55 10N 80 15 E
Kargil . . . . 32 34 32N 76 12 E
Kargopol . . . . 22 61 30N 38 58 E
Kariba Dam . . . . . . 55 16 30S 28 35 E
Kariba Gorge . . . . . 55 16 30S 28 50 E
Kariba L. . . . . 55 16 40S 28 25 E
Karibib . . . . 56 22 0S 15 56 E
Karimata, Kepulauan 34 1 25S 109 0 E
Karimata, Selat . . . 34 2 0S 108 40 E
Karimnagar . . . . 32 18 26N 79 10 E
Karimunjawa,
Kepulauan . . . . . 34 5 50S 110 30 E
Karin . . . . 29 10 50N 45 52 E
Kariya . . . . 36 34 58N 137 1 E
Karkaralinsk . . . . . . 24 49 26N 75 30 E
Karkinitskiy Zaliv . . 23 45 56N 33 0 E
Karkur . . . . 28 32 29N 34 57 E
Karl-Marx-Stadt . . . 14 50 50N 12 55 E
Karlovac . . . . 18 45 31N 15 36 E
Karlovy Vary . . . . . . 14 50 13N 12 51 E
Karlsborg . . . . 21 58 33N 14 33 E
Karlshamn . . . . 21 56 10N 14 51 E
Karlskoga . . . . 21 59 22N 14 33 E
Karlskrona . . . . 21 56 10N 15 35 E
Karlsruhe . . . . 14 49 3N 8 23 E
Karlstad, Sweden . . 21 59 23N 13 30 E
Karlstad, U.S.A. . . . 70 48 38N 96 30W
Karnal . . . . 32 29 42N 77 2 E
Karnali → . . . . 33 29 0N 83 20 E
Karnaphuli Res. . . . 33 22 40N 92 20 E
Karnataka □ . . . . . . 32 13 15N 77 0 E
Karnes City 71 28 53N 97 53W
Karnische Alpen . . 14 46 36N 13 0 E
Kärnten □ . . . . 14 46 52N 13 30 E
Karonga . . . . 54 9 57S 33 55 E
Karoonda . . . . 45 35 1S 139 59 E
Karora . . . . 51 17 44N 38 15 E
Karpathos . . . . 19 35 37N 27 10 E
Karpinsk . . . . 22 59 45N 60 1 E
Karpogory . . . . 22 63 59N 44 27 E
Kars . . . . 30 40 40N 43 5 E
Karsakpay . . . . 24 47 55N 66 40 E
Karshi . . . . 24 38 53N 65 48 E
Karsun . . . . 22 54 14N 46 57 E
Kartaly . . . . 24 53 3N 60 40 E
Karufa . . . . 35 3 50S 133 20 E
Karumba . . . . 44 17 31S 140 50 E
Karungu . . . . 54 0 50S 34 10 E
Karwar . . . . 32 14 55N 74 13 E
Kasai → . . . . 54 3 30S 16 10 E
Kasama . . . . 54 10 16S 31 9 E
Kasane . . . . 56 17 34S 24 50 E
Kasanga . . . . 54 8 30S 31 10 E
Kasangulu . . . . 54 4 33S 15 15 E
Kasaragod . . . . 32 12 30N 74 58 E
Kasba L. 65 60 20N 102 10W
Kasempa . . . . 55 13 30S 25 44 E
Kasenga . . . . 54 10 20S 28 45 E
Kashabowie 62 48 40N 90 26W
Kāshān . . . . 31 34 5N 51 30 E
Kashi . . . . 37 39 30N 76 2 E
Kashiwazaki . . . . . . 36 37 22N 138 33 E
Kashk-e Kohneh . . 31 34 55N 62 30 E
Kāshmar . . . . 31 35 16N 58 26 E
Kashmir . . . . 32 34 0N 76 0 E
Kashun Noerh =
Gaxun Nur . . . . . 37 42 22N 100 30 E
Kasimov . . . . 22 54 55N 41 20 E
Kasiruta . . . . 35 0 25S 127 12 E
Kaskaskia → 70 37 58N 89 57W
Kaskattama → . . . 65 57 3N 90 4W
Kaskinen . . . . 20 62 22N 21 15 E
Kaskö . . . . 20 62 22N 21 15 E
Kaslo 64 49 55N 116 55W
Kasmere L. 65 59 34N 101 10W
Kasongo . . . . 54 4 30S 26 33 E
Kasongo Lunda . . . 54 6 35S 16 49 E
Kásos . . . . 19 35 20N 26 55 E
Kassala . . . . 51 15 30N 36 0 E
Kassalâ □ . . . . 51 15 20N 36 26 E
Kassel . . . . 14 51 19N 9 32 E
Kassue . . . . 35 6 58S 139 21 E
Kastamonu . . . . 30 41 25N 33 43 E
Kastellorizon =
Megiste . . . . 17 36 8N 29 34 E
Kastoría . . . . 19 40 30N 21 19 E
Kasulu . . . . 54 4 37S 30 5 E
Kasur . . . . 32 31 5N 74 25 E
Kata . . . . 25 58 46N 102 40 E
Katako Kombe . . . . 54 3 25S 24 20 E
Katamatite . . . . 45 36 6S 145 41 E
Katangi . . . . 32 21 56N 79 50 E
Katangli . . . . 25 51 42N 143 14 E
Katha . . . . 33 24 10N 96 30 E
Katherine . . . . 46 14 27S 132 20 E
Kathiawar . . . . 32 22 20N 71 0 E
Katihar . . . . 33 25 34N 87 36 E
Katima Mulilo . . . . . 56 17 28S 24 13 E
Katingan =
Mendawai → . . 34 3 30S 113 0 E
Katiola 50 8 10N 5 10W
Katkopberg . . . . . . 56 30 0S 20 0 E
Katmandu . . . . 33 27 45N 85 20 E
Katoomba . . . . 45 33 41S 150 19 E
Katowice . . . . 15 50 17N 19 5 E
Katrine, L. 8 56 15N 4 30W
Katrineholm . . . . . . 21 59 9N 16 12 E
Katsepe . . . . 57 15 45S 46 15 E
Katsina . . . . 53 13 0N 7 32 E
Katsuura . . . . 36 35 10N 140 20 E
Kattegatt . . . . 21 57 0N 11 20 E
Katwe . . . . 52 0 8S 29 52 E
Katwijk-aan-Zee . . 11 52 12N 4 24 E
Kauai 66 22 0N 159 30W
Kauai Chan. 66 21 45N 158 50W
Kaufman 71 32 35N 96 20W
Kaukauna 68 44 20N 88 13W
Kaukauveld . . . . 56 20 0S 20 15 E
Kaukonen . . . . 20 67 31N 24 53 E
Kauliranta . . . . 20 66 27N 23 41 E
Kaunas . . . . 22 54 54N 23 54 E
Kaura Namoda . . . . 53 12 37N 6 33 E
Kautokeino . . . . 20 69 0N 23 4 E
Kavacha . . . . 25 60 16N 169 51 E
Kavali . . . . 32 14 55N 80 1 E
Kaválla . . . . 19 40 57N 24 28 E
Kavkaz, Bolshoi . . . 23 42 50N 44 0 E
Kaw 79 4 30N 52 15W
Kawagoe . . . . 36 35 55N 139 29 E
Kawaguchi . . . . 36 35 52N 139 45 E
Kawaihae 66 20 3N 155 50W
Kawambwa . . . . 54 9 48S 29 3 E
Kawardha . . . . 33 22 0N 81 17 E
Kawasaki . . . . 36 35 35N 139 42 E
Kawene 62 48 45N 91 15W
Kawerau . . . . 43 38 7S 176 42 E
Kawhia Harbour . . . 43 38 5S 174 51 E
Kawio, Kepulauan . 35 4 30N 125 30 E
Kawnro . . . . 33 22 48N 99 8 E
Kawthoolei □ =
Kawthule □ . . . . 33 18 0N 97 30 E
Kawthule □ . . . . . . 33 18 0N 97 30 E
Kaya 53 13 4N 1 10W
Kayah □ . . . . 33 19 15N 97 15 E
Kayan → . . . . 34 2 55N 117 35 E
Kaycee 72 43 45N 106 46W
Kayeli . . . . 35 3 20S 127 10 E
Kayenta 73 36 46N 110 15W
Kayes 50 14 25N 11 30W
Kayoa . . . . 35 0 1N 127 28 E
Kayrunnera . . . . 45 30 40S 142 30 E
Kayseri . . . . 30 38 45N 35 30 E
Kaysville 72 41 2N 111 58W
Kayuagung . . . . 34 3 24S 104 50 E
Kazachinskoye . . . . 25 56 16N 107 36 E
Kazachye . . . . 25 70 52N 135 58 E
Kazakh S.S.R. □ . . 23 50 0N 70 0 E
Kazan . . . . 22 55 48N 49 3 E
Kazanlŭk . . . . 19 42 38N 25 20 E
Kāzerūn . . . . 31 29 38N 51 40 E
Kazumba . . . . 54 6 25S 22 5 E
Kazym → . . . . 24 63 54N 65 50 E
Ké-Macina 50 13 58N 5 22W
Kéa . . . . 19 37 35N 24 22 E
Keams Canyon 73 35 53N 110 9W
Kearney 70 40 45N 99 3W
Keban . . . . 23 38 50N 38 50 E
Kebnekaise . . . . . . 20 67 53N 18 33 E
Kebri Dehar . . . . . . 29 6 45N 44 17 E
Kebumen . . . . 35 7 42S 109 40 E
Kechika → 64 59 41N 127 12W
Kecskemét . . . . 15 46 57N 19 42 E
Kedgwick 63 47 40N 67 20W
Kedia Hill . . . . 56 21 28S 24 37 E
Kediri . . . . 35 7 51S 112 1 E
Kédougou 50 12 35N 12 10W
Keeley L. 65 54 54N 108 8W
Keeling Is. = Cocos
Is. . . . . 3 12 10S 96 55 E
Keene 68 42 57N 72 17W
Keeper Hill 9 52 46N 8 17W
Keer-Weer, C. . . . . 44 14 0S 141 32 E
Keetmanshoop . . . . 56 26 35S 18 8 E
Keewatin 70 47 23N 93 0W
Keewatin □ 65 63 20N 95 0W
Keewatin → 65 56 29N 100 46W
Kefallinía . . . . 19 38 20N 20 30 E
Kefamenanu . . . . . . 35 9 28S 124 29 E
Kefar 'Eqron . . . . . 28 31 52N 34 49 E
Kefar Hasīdim . . . . 28 32 47N 35 5 E
Kefar Nahum . . . . . 28 32 54N 35 34 E
Kefar Sava . . . . 28 32 11N 34 54 E
Kefar Szold . . . . . . 28 33 11N 35 39 E
Kefar Vitkin . . . . . . 28 32 22N 34 53 E
Kefar Yehezqel . . . 28 32 34N 35 22 E
Kefar Yona . . . . 28 32 20N 34 54 E
Kefar Zekharya . . . 28 31 43N 34 57 E
Kefar Zetim . . . . . . 28 32 48N 35 27 E
Keffi . . . . 53 8 55N 7 43 E
Keflavík 20 64 2N 22 35W
Keg River 64 57 54N 117 55W
Kegaska 63 50 9N 61 18W
Keighley 6 53 52N 1 54W
Keimoes . . . . 56 28 41S 20 59 E
Keith, Australia . . . 45 36 6S 140 20 E
Keith, U.K. 8 57 33N 2 58W
Keith Arm 60 64 20N 122 15W
Kekri . . . . 32 26 0N 75 10 E
Kël . . . . 25 69 30N 124 10 E
Kelan . . . . 38 38 43N 111 31 E
Kelang . . . . 34 3 2N 101 26 E
Kelibia . . . . 51 36 50N 11 3 E
Kellé . . . . 54 0 8S 14 38 E
Keller 72 48 2N 118 44W
Kellerberrin . . . . . . 47 31 36S 117 38 E
Kellogg 72 47 30N 116 5W
Kelloselkä . . . . 20 66 56N 28 53 E
Kells = Ceanannus
Mor 9 53 42N 6 53W
Kélo . . . . 51 9 10N 15 45 E
Kelowna 64 49 50N 119 25W
Kelsey Bay 64 50 25N 126 0W
Kelso, N.Z. . . . . . . 43 45 54S 169 15 E
Kelso, U.K. 8 55 36N 2 27W
Kelso, U.S.A. 72 46 10N 122 57W
Keluang . . . . 34 2 3N 103 18 E
Kelvington 65 52 10N 103 30W
Kem . . . . 22 65 0N 34 38 E
Kem → . . . . 22 64 57N 34 41 E
Kema . . . . 35 1 22N 125 8 E
Kemah . . . . 30 39 32N 39 5 E
Kemano 64 53 35N 128 0W
Kemerovo . . . . 24 55 20N 86 5 E
Kemi . . . . 20 65 44N 24 34 E
Kemi älv =
Kemijoki → . . . 20 65 47N 24 32 E
Kemijärvi . . . . 20 66 43N 27 22 E
Kemijoki → . . . . . 20 65 47N 24 32 E
Kemmerer 72 41 52N 110 30W
Kemmuna =
Comino . . . . 18 36 0N 14 20 E
Kemp L. 71 33 45N 99 15W
Kempsey . . . . 45 31 1S 152 50 E
Kempt, L. 62 47 25N 74 22W
Kempten . . . . 14 47 42N 10 18 E
Kemptville 62 45 0N 75 38W
Kendal, Indonesia . 34 6 56S 110 14 E
Kendal, U.K. 6 54 19N 2 44W
Kendall . . . . 45 31 35S 152 44 E
Kendall → . . . . . . 44 14 4S 141 35 E
Kendallville 68 41 25N 85 15W
Kendari . . . . 35 3 50S 122 30 E
Kendawangan . . . . 34 2 32S 110 17 E
Kende . . . . 53 11 30N 4 12 E
Kendenup . . . . 47 34 30S 117 38 E
Kendrapara . . . . 33 20 35N 86 30 E
Kendrew . . . . 56 32 32S 24 30 E
Kendrick 72 46 43N 116 41W
Kenedy 71 28 49N 97 51W
Kenema 50 7 50N 11 14W
Keng Tawng . . . . . 33 20 45N 98 18 E
Keng Tung . . . . 33 21 0N 99 30 E
Kenge . . . . 54 4 50S 17 4 E
Kenhardt . . . . 56 29 19S 21 12 E
Kenitra 50 34 15N 6 40W
Kenmare, Ireland . . 9 51 52N 9 35W
Kenmare, U.S.A. . . 70 48 40N 102 4W
Kenmare → 9 51 40N 10 0W
Kennebec 70 43 56N 99 54W
Kennedy Ra. . . . . . 47 24 45S 115 10 E
Kennedy Taungdeik 33 23 15N 93 45 E
Kennet → 7 51 24N 0 58W
Kenneth Ra. . . . . . . 47 23 50S 117 8 E
Kennett 71 36 7N 90 0W
Kennewick 72 46 11N 119 2W
Kénogami 63 48 25N 71 15W
Kenogami → 62 51 6N 84 28W
Kenora 65 49 47N 94 29W
Kenosha 68 42 33N 87 48W
Kensington, Canada 63 46 28N 63 34W
Kensington, U.S.A. 70 39 48N 99 2W
Kensington Downs 44 22 31S 144 19 E
Kent, Ohio, U.S.A. . 68 41 8N 81 20W
Kent, Oreg., U.S.A. 72 45 11N 120 45W
Kent, Tex., U.S.A. . 71 31 5N 104 12W
Kent □ . . . . 7 51 12N 0 40 E
Kent Group . . . . . . 44 39 30S 147 20 E
Kent Pen. 60 68 30N 107 0W
Kentau . . . . 24 43 32N 68 36 E
Kentland 68 40 45N 87 25W
Kenton 68 40 40N 83 35W
Kentucky □ 68 37 20N 85 0W
Kentucky → 68 38 41N 85 11W
Kentucky L. 69 36 25N 88 0W
Kentville 63 45 6N 64 29W
Kentwood 71 31 0N 90 30W
Kenya ■ . . . . 54 1 0N 38 0 E
Kenya, Mt. . . . . 54 0 10S 37 18 E
Keokuk 70 40 25N 91 24W
Kepi . . . . 35 6 32S 139 19 E
Kepsut . . . . 30 39 40N 28 9 E
Kerala □ . . . . 32 11 0N 76 15 E
Kerang . . . . 45 35 40S 143 55 E
Keraudren, C. . . . . 46 19 58S 119 45 E
Kerch . . . . 23 45 20N 36 20 E
Kerchoual . . . . 50 17 12N 0 20 E
Kerem Maharal . . . 28 32 39N 34 59 E
Keren . . . . 51 15 45N 38 28 E
Kerguelen . . . . 3 49 15S 69 10 E
Kericho . . . . 54 0 22S 35 15 E
Kerinci . . . . 34 1 40S 101 15 E
Kerki . . . . 24 37 50N 65 12 E
Kérkira . . . . 19 39 38N 19 50 E
Kerkrade . . . . 11 50 53N 6 4 E
Kermadec Is. 40 30 0S 178 15W
Kermadec Trench . 40 30 30S 176 0W
Kermān . . . . 31 30 15N 57 1 E
Kermān □ . . . . 31 30 0N 57 0 E
Kermānshāh =
Bākhtarān . . . . . . 30 34 23N 47 0 E
Kermit 71 31 56N 103 3W
Kern → 73 35 16N 119 18W
Kerrobert 65 51 56N 109 8W
Kerrville 71 30 1N 99 8W
Kerry □ 9 52 7N 9 35W
Kerry Hd. 9 52 26N 9 56W
Kertosono . . . . 35 7 38S 112 9 E
Kerulen → . . . . . . 37 48 48N 117 0 E
Kerzaz 50 29 29N 1 37W
Kesagami → 62 51 40N 79 45W
Kesagami L. 62 50 23N 80 15W
Keski-Suomen
lääni □ . . . . 20 62 0N 25 30 E
Kestell . . . . 57 28 17S 28 42 E
Kestenga . . . . 22 66 0N 31 50 E
Keswick 6 54 35N 3 9W
Ket → . . . . 24 58 55N 81 32 E
Keta . . . . 53 5 49N 1 0 E
Ketapang . . . . 34 1 55S 110 0 E
Ketchikan 60 55 25N 131 40W
Ketchum 72 43 41N 114 27W
Kettering 7 52 24N 0 44W
Kettle → 65 56 40N 89 34W
Kettle Falls 72 48 41N 118 2W
Kevin 72 48 45N 111 58W
Kewanee 70 41 18N 89 55W
Kewaunee 68 44 27N 87 30W
Keweenaw B. 68 46 56N 88 23W
Keweenaw Pen. . . . 68 47 30N 88 0W
Keweenaw Pt. 68 47 26N 87 40W
Key Harbour 62 45 50N 80 45W
Key West 75 24 33N 82 0W
Keyser 68 39 26N 79 0W
Keystone 70 43 54N 103 27W
Kezhma . . . . 25 58 59N 101 9 E
Khabarovo . . . . 24 69 30N 60 30 E
Khabarovsk . . . . . . 25 48 30N 135 5 E
Khābūr → . . . . 30 35 0N 40 30 E
Khairpur . . . . 32 27 32N 68 49 E
Khakhea . . . . 56 24 48S 23 22 E
Khalkhāl . . . . 30 37 37N 48 32 E
Khalkís . . . . 19 38 27N 23 42 E
Khalmer-Sede =
Tazovskiy . . . . . . 24 67 30N 78 44 E
Khalmer Yu . . . . . . 22 67 58N 65 1 E

Lafia

Kong 50 8 54N 4 36W
Kong, Koh 34 11 20N 103 0 E
Kongju 38 36 30N 127 0 E
Konglu 33 27 13N 97 57 E
Kongolo 54 5 22S 27 0 E
Kongor 51 7 1N 31 27 E
Kongsberg 21 59 39N 9 39 E
Kongsvinger 21 60 12N 12 2 E
Königsberg =
Kaliningrad 22 54 42N 20 32 E
Konin 15 52 12N 18 15 E
Konjic 19 43 42N 17 58 E
Konkiep 56 26 49S 17 15 E
Konosha 22 61 0N 40 5 E
Konotop 23 51 12N 33 7 E
Konqi He → 37 40 45N 90 10 E
Końskie 15 51 15N 20 23 E
Konstanz 14 47 39N 9 10 E
Kontagora 53 10 23N 5 27 E
Kontum 34 14 24N 108 0 E
Konya 30 37 52N 32 35 E
Konya Ovasi 30 38 30N 33 0 E
Konza 54 1 45S 37 7 E
Kookynie 47 29 17S 121 22 E
Kooline 46 22 57S 116 20 E
Kooloonong 45 34 48S 143 10 E
Koolyanobbing 47 30 48S 119 36 E
Koondrook 45 35 33S 144 8 E
Koorawatha 45 34 2S 148 33 E
Koorda 47 30 48S 117 35 E
Kooskia 72 46 9N 115 59W
Kootenai → 72 49 15N 117 39W
Kootenay L. 64 49 45N 116 50W
Kootenay Nat. Park 64 51 0N 116 0W
Kootjieskolk 56 31 15S 20 21 E
Kopaonik Planina 19 43 10N 21 50 E
Kópavogur 20 64 6N 21 55W
Koper 18 45 31N 13 44 E
Kopervik 21 59 17N 5 17 E
Kopeysk 24 55 7N 61 37 E
Kopi 45 33 24S 135 40 E
Köping 21 59 31N 16 3 E
Kopparberg 21 59 52N 15 0 E
Kopparbergs län □ 21 61 20N 14 15 E
Koppeh Dāgh 31 38 0N 58 0 E
Koppies 57 27 20S 27 30 E
Korab 19 41 44N 20 40 E
Korça 19 40 37N 20 50 E
Korce = Korça 19 40 37N 20 50 E
Korčula 18 42 57N 17 8 E
Kordestan 30 35 30N 42 0 E
Kordestān □ 30 36 0N 47 0 E
Korea, North ■ 38 40 0N 127 0 E
Korea, South ■ 38 36 0N 128 0 E
Korea Bay 38 39 0N 124 0 E
Korea Strait 39 34 0N 129 30 E
Koreh Wells 51 0 3N 38 45 E
Korhogo 50 9 29N 5 28W
Korim 35 0 58S 136 10 E
Korinthiakós Kólpos 19 38 16N 22 30 E
Kórinthos 19 37 56N 22 55 E
Kōriyama 36 37 24N 140 23 E
Koro, Fiji 43 17 19S 179 23 E
Koro, Ivory C. 50 8 32N 7 30W
Koro, Mali 50 14 1N 2 58W
Koro Sea 43 17 30S 179 45W
Korogwe 54 5 5S 38 25 E
Koroit 45 38 18S 142 24 E
Körös → 15 46 43N 20 12 E
Korraraika,
Helodranon' i 57 17 45S 43 57 E
Korsakov 25 46 36N 142 42 E
Korshunovo 25 58 37N 110 10 E
Korsör 21 55 20N 11 9 E
Korti 51 18 6N 31 33 E
Kortrijk 11 50 50N 3 17 E
Koryakskiy Khrebet 25 61 0N 171 0 E
Kos 19 36 50N 27 15 E
Koschagyl 23 46 40N 54 0 E
Kościan 14 52 5N 16 40 E
Kosciusko 71 33 3N 89 34W
Kosciusko, Mt. 45 36 27S 148 16 E
Kosciusko I. 64 56 0N 133 40W
Kosha 51 20 50N 30 30 E
K'oshih = Kashi 37 39 30N 76 2 E
Kosi-meer 57 27 0S 32 50 E
Košice 15 48 42N 21 15 E
Koslan 22 63 28N 48 52 E
Kosŏng 38 38 40N 128 22 E
Kosovska-Mitrovica 19 42 54N 20 52 E
Kostamuksa 22 62 34N 32 44 E
Koster 56 25 52S 26 54 E
Kôstî 51 13 8N 32 43 E
Kostroma 22 57 50N 40 58 E
Koszalin 14 54 11N 16 8 E
Kota 32 25 14N 75 49 E
Kota Baharu 34 6 7N 102 14 E
Kota Belud 34 6 21N 116 26 E
Kota Kinabalu 34 6 0N 116 4 E
Kota Tinggi 34 1 44N 103 53 E
Kotaagung 34 5 38S 104 29 E
Kotabaru 34 3 20S 116 20 E
Kotabumi 34 4 49S 104 54 E
Kotagede 35 7 54S 110 26 E
Kotamobagu 35 0 57N 124 31 E
Kotaneelee → 64 60 11N 123 42W
Kotawaringin 34 2 28S 111 27 E
Kotcho L. 64 59 7N 121 12W
Kotelnich 22 58 20N 48 10 E
Kotelnyy, Ostrov 25 75 10N 139 0 E
Kotka 21 60 28N 26 58 E
Kotlas 22 61 15N 47 0 E
Kotli 32 33 30N 73 55 E
Kotor 19 42 25N 18 47 E
Kotri 32 25 22N 68 22 E
Kottayam 32 9 35N 76 33 E
Kotturu 32 14 45N 76 10 E
Kotuy → 25 71 54N 102 6 E
Kotzebue 60 66 50N 162 40W
Kouango 54 5 0N 20 10 E
Koudougou 50 12 10N 2 20W
Kougaberge 56 33 48S 23 50 E
Kouilou → 54 4 10S 12 5 E
Kouki 54 7 22N 17 3 E
Koula Moutou 54 1 15S 12 25 E
Koulen 34 13 50N 104 40 E
Koulikoro 50 12 40N 7 50W
Koumala 44 21 38S 149 15 E
Koumra 51 8 50N 17 35 E
Kounradskiy 24 46 59N 75 0 E
Kountze 71 30 20N 94 22W
Kouroussa 50 10 45N 9 45W
Kousseri 51 12 0N 14 55 E
Koutiala 50 12 25N 5 23W
Kovdor 22 67 34N 30 24 E
Kovel 22 51 10N 24 20 E
Kovrov 22 56 25N 41 25 E
Kowkash 62 50 20N 87 12W
Kowloon 39 22 20N 114 15 E
Koyabuti 35 2 36S 140 37 E
Koyuk 60 64 55N 161 20W
Koyukuk → 60 64 56N 157 30W
Kozan 30 37 35N 35 50 E
Kozáni 19 40 19N 21 47 E
Kozhikode = Calicut 32 11 15N 75 43 E
Kozhva 22 65 10N 57 0 E
Kpalimé 53 6 57N 0 44 E
Kra, Isthmus of =
Kra, Kho Khot 34 10 15N 99 30 E
Kra, Kho Khot 34 10 15N 99 30 E
Kragan 35 6 43S 111 38 E
Kragerø 21 58 52N 9 25 E
Kragujevac 19 44 2N 20 56 E
Krakatau = Rakata,
Pulau 34 6 10S 105 20 E
Kraków 15 50 4N 19 57 E
Kraksaan 35 7 43S 113 23 E
Kraljevo 19 43 44N 20 41 E
Kramatorsk 23 48 50N 37 30 E
Kramfors 20 62 55N 17 48 E
Krankskop 57 28 0S 30 47 E
Krasavino 22 60 58N 46 29 E
Kraskino 25 42 44N 130 48 E
Kraśnik 15 50 55N 22 5 E
Krasnodar 23 45 5N 39 0 E
Krasnokamsk 22 58 4N 55 48 E
Krasnoselkupsk 24 65 20N 82 10 E
Krasnoturinsk 22 59 46N 60 12 E
Krasnoufimsk 22 56 57N 57 46 E
Krasnouralsk 22 58 21N 60 3 E
Krasnovishersk 22 60 23N 57 3 E
Krasnovodsk 23 40 0N 52 52 E
Krasnoyarsk 25 56 8N 93 0 E
Krasnyy Luch 23 48 13N 39 0 E
Krasnyy Yar 23 46 43N 48 23 E
Kratie 34 12 32N 106 10 E
Krau 35 3 19S 140 5 E
Krawang 35 6 19N 107 18 E
Krefeld 14 51 20N 6 32 E
Kremenchug 23 49 5N 33 25 E
Kremenchugskoye
Vdkhr. 23 49 20N 32 30 E
Kremmling 72 40 10N 106 30W
Kremnica 15 48 45N 18 50 E
Kribi 54 2 57N 9 56 E
Krishna → 33 15 57N 80 59 E
Krishnanagar 33 23 24N 88 33 E
Kristiansand 21 58 9N 8 1 E
Kristianstad 21 56 2N 14 9 E
Kristianstads län □ 21 56 15N 14 0 E
Kristiansund 20 63 7N 7 45 E
Kristiinankaupunki 20 62 16N 21 21 E
Kristinehamn 21 59 18N 14 13 E
Kristinestad 20 62 16N 21 21 E
Kriti 19 35 15N 25 0 E
Krivoy Rog 23 47 51N 33 20 E
Krk 18 45 8N 14 40 E
Krokodil → 57 25 14S 32 18 E
Kronobergs län □ 21 56 45N 14 30 E
Kronshtadt 22 60 5N 29 45 E
Kroonstad 56 27 43S 27 19 E
Kropotkin,
R.S.F.S.R.,
U.S.S.R. 23 45 28N 40 28 E
Kropotkin,
R.S.F.S.R.,
U.S.S.R. 25 59 0N 115 30 E
Krosno 15 49 42N 21 46 E
Krotoszyn 15 51 42N 17 23 E
Kruger Nat. Park 57 23 30S 31 40 E
Krugersdorp 57 26 5S 27 46 E
Kruisfontein 56 33 59S 24 43 E
Krung Thep =
Bangkok 34 13 45N 100 35 E
Kruševac 19 43 35N 21 28 E
Kruzof I. 64 57 10N 135 40W
Krymskiy Poluostrov 23 45 0N 34 0 E
Ksar el Boukhari 50 35 51N 2 52 E
Ksar el Kebir 50 35 0N 6 0W
Ksar es Souk = Ar
Rachidiya 50 31 58N 4 20W
Kuala 34 2 55N 105 47 E
Kuala Kubu Baharu 34 3 34N 101 39 E
Kuala Lipis 34 4 10N 102 3 E
Kuala Lumpur 34 3 9N 101 41 E
Kuala Trengganu 34 5 20N 103 8 E
Kualajelai 34 2 58S 110 46 E
Kualakapuas 34 2 55S 114 20 E
Kualakurun 34 1 10S 113 50 E
Kualapembuang 34 3 14S 112 38 E
Kualasimpang 34 4 17N 98 3 E
Kuandang 35 0 56N 123 1 E
Kuandian 38 40 45N 124 45 E
Kuangchou =
Guangzhou 39 23 5N 113 10 E
Kuantan 34 3 49N 103 20 E
Kuba 23 41 21N 48 32 E
Kubak 31 27 10N 63 10 E
Kuban → 23 45 20N 37 30 E
Kucing 34 1 33N 110 25 E
Kuda 32 23 10N 71 15 E
Kudat 34 6 55N 116 55 E
Kudus 35 6 48S 110 51 E
Kudymkar 24 59 1N 54 39 E
Kueiyang = Guiyang 39 26 32N 106 40 E
Kufrinjah 28 32 20N 35 41 E
Kufstein 14 47 35N 12 11 E
Kugong I. 62 56 18N 79 50W
Kūh-e 'Alijūq 31 31 30N 51 41 E
Kūh-e Dīnār 31 30 40N 51 0 E
Kūh-e-Hazārām 31 29 35N 57 20 E
Kūh-e-Jebāl Bārez 31 29 0N 58 0 E
Kūh-e Sorkh 31 35 30N 58 45 E
Kūh-e Taftān 31 28 40N 61 0 E
Kūhak 31 27 12N 63 10 E
Kūhhā-ye-
Bashākerd 31 26 45N 59 0 E
Kūhhā-ye Sabalān 30 38 15N 47 45 E
Kūhpāyeh 31 32 44N 52 20 E
Kuile He → 38 49 32N 124 42 E
Kuito 55 12 22S 16 55 E
Kuji 36 40 11N 141 46 E
Kukawa 51 12 58N 13 27 E
Kukerin 47 33 13S 118 0 E
Kulasekarappattinam
32 8 20N 78 0 E
Kuldja = Yining 37 43 58N 81 10 E
Kulin 47 32 40S 118 2 E
Kulja 47 30 28S 117 18 E
Kulm 70 46 22N 98 58W
Kulsary 23 46 59N 54 1 E
Kulumbura 46 13 55S 126 35 E
Kulunda 24 52 35N 78 57 E
Kulwin 45 35 0S 142 42 E
Kulyab 24 37 55N 69 50 E
Kum Tekei 24 43 10N 79 30 E
Kuma → 23 44 55N 47 0 E
Kumaganum 53 13 8N 10 38 E
Kumagaya 36 36 9N 139 22 E
Kumai 34 2 44S 111 43 E
Kumamba,
Kepulauan 35 1 36S 138 45 E
Kumamoto 36 32 45N 130 45 E
Kumamoto □ 36 32 55N 130 55 E
Kumanovo 19 42 9N 21 42 E
Kumara 43 42 37S 171 12 E
Kumarl 47 32 47S 121 33 E
Kumasi 50 6 41N 1 38W
Kumba 54 4 36N 9 24 E
Kumbarilla 45 27 15S 150 55 E
Kumertau 22 52 46N 55 47 E
Kumla 21 59 8N 15 10 E
Kumo 53 10 1N 11 12 E
Kumon Bum 33 26 30N 97 15 E
Kunama 45 35 35S 148 4 E
Kunashir, Ostrov 25 44 0N 146 0 E
Kundip 47 33 42S 120 10 E
Kungala 45 29 58S 153 7 E
Kunghit I. 64 52 6N 131 3W
Kungrad 24 43 6N 58 54 E
Kungsbacka 21 57 30N 12 5 E
Kungur 22 57 25N 56 57 E
Kungurri 44 21 3S 148 46 E
Kuningan 35 6 59S 108 29 E
Kunlong 33 23 20N 98 50 E
Kunlun Shan 33 36 0N 86 30 E
Kunming 37 25 1N 102 41 E
Kunsan 38 35 59N 126 45 E
Kunshan 39 31 22N 120 58 E
Kununurra 46 15 40S 128 50 E
Kunwarara 44 22 55S 150 9 E
Kunya-Urgench 24 42 19N 59 10 E
Kuopio 20 62 53N 27 35 E
Kuopion lääni □ 20 63 25N 27 10 E
Kupa → 18 45 28N 16 24 E
Kupang 35 10 19S 123 39 E
Kuqa 37 41 35N 82 30 E
Kura → 23 39 50N 49 20 E
Kuranda 44 16 48S 145 35 E
Kurashiki 36 34 40N 133 50 E
Kurayoshi 36 35 26N 133 50 E
Kure 36 34 14N 132 32 E
Kurgaldzhino 24 50 35N 70 20 E
Kurgan 24 55 26N 65 18 E
Kuria Maria Is. =
Khūrīyā Mūrīyā,
Jazā 'ir 29 17 30N 55 58 E
Kuridala 44 21 16S 140 29 E
Kurigram 33 25 49N 89 39 E
Kuril Is. = Kurilskiye
Ostrova 25 45 0N 150 0 E
Kuril Trench 40 44 0N 153 0 E
Kurilsk 25 45 14N 147 53 E
Kurilskiye Ostrova 25 45 0N 150 0 E
Kurmuk 51 10 33N 34 21 E
Kurnool 32 15 45N 78 0 E
Kurow 43 44 44S 170 29 E
Kurrajong 45 33 33S 150 42 E
Kurri Kurri 45 32 50S 151 28 E
Kursk 22 51 42N 36 11 E
Kuršumlija 19 43 9N 21 19 E
Kuruktag 37 41 0N 89 0 E
Kuruman 56 27 28S 23 28 E
Kuruman → 56 26 56S 20 39 E
Kurume 36 33 15N 130 30 E
Kurunegala 32 7 30N 80 23 E
Kurya 25 61 15N 108 10 E
Kusawa L. 64 60 20N 136 13W
Kushiro 36 43 0N 144 25 E
Kushiro → 36 42 59N 144 23 E
Kushka 24 35 20N 62 18 E
Kushtia 33 23 55N 89 5 E
Kushva 22 58 18N 59 45 E
Kuskokwim → 60 60 17N 162 27W
Kuskokwim Bay 60 59 50N 162 56W
Kussharo-Ko 36 43 38N 144 21 E
Kustanay 24 53 10N 63 35 E
Kütahya 30 39 30N 30 2 E
Kutaisi 23 42 19N 42 40 E
Kutaraja = Banda
Aceh 34 5 35N 95 20 E
Kutch, Gulf of =
Kachchh, Gulf of 32 22 50N 69 15 E
Kutch, Rann of =
Kachchh, Rann of 32 24 0N 70 0 E
Kutno 15 52 15N 19 23 E
Kuttabul 44 21 5S 148 48 E
Kutu 54 2 40S 18 11 E
Kutum 51 14 10N 24 40 E
Kuujjuaq 61 58 6N 68 15W
Kuwait = Al Kuwayt 30 29 30N 48 0 E
Kuwait ■ 30 29 30N 47 30 E
Kuwana 36 35 0N 136 43 E
Kuybyshev,
R.S.F.S.R.,
U.S.S.R. 22 53 8N 50 6 E
Kuybyshev,
R.S.F.S.R.,
U.S.S.R. 24 55 27N 78 19 E
Kuybyshevskoye
Vdkhr. 22 55 2N 49 30 E
Kūysanjaq 30 36 5N 44 38 E
Kuyto, Oz. 22 64 40N 31 0 E
Kuyumba 25 60 58N 96 59 E
Kuzey Anadolu
Dağlari 30 41 30N 35 0 E
Kuznetsk 22 53 12N 46 40 E
Kuzomen 22 66 22N 36 50 E
Kvænangen 20 70 5N 21 15 E
Kvarner 18 44 50N 14 10 E
Kvarnerič 18 44 43N 14 37 E
Kwabhaca 57 30 51S 29 0 E
Kwadacha → 64 57 28N 125 38W
Kwakhanai 56 21 39S 21 16 E
Kwakoegron 79 5 12N 55 25W
KwaMashu 57 29 45S 30 58 E
Kwamouth 54 3 9S 16 12 E
Kwando → 56 18 27S 23 32 E
Kwangju 38 35 9N 126 54 E
Kwangsi-Chuang =
Guangxi Zhuangzu
Zizhiqu □ 39 24 0N 109 0 E
Kwangtung =
Guangdong □ 39 23 0N 113 0 E
Kwara □ 53 8 0N 5 0 E
Kwataboahegan → 62 51 9N 80 50W
Kwatisore 35 3 18S 134 50 E
Kweichow =
Guizhou □ 39 27 0N 107 0 E
Kwekwe 55 18 58S 29 48 E
Kwiguk 60 63 45N 164 35W
Kwinana New Town 47 32 15S 115 47 E
Kwoka 35 0 31S 132 27 E
Kyabé 51 9 30N 19 0 E
Kyabra Cr. → 45 25 36S 142 55 E
Kyabram 45 36 19S 145 4 E
Kyakhta 25 50 30N 106 25 E
Kyangin 33 18 20N 95 20 E
Kyaukpadaung 33 20 52N 95 8 E
Kyaukpyu 33 19 28N 93 30 E
Kyaukse 33 21 36N 96 10 E
Kyle Dam 55 20 15S 31 0 E
Kyle of Lochalsh 8 57 17N 5 43W
Kyneton 45 37 10S 144 29 E
Kynuna 44 21 37S 141 55 E
Kyō-ga-Saki 36 35 45N 135 15 E
Kyoga, L. 54 1 35N 33 0 E
Kyogle 45 28 40S 153 0 E
Kyongju 38 35 51N 129 14 E
Kyongpyaw 33 17 12N 95 10 E
Kyōto 36 35 0N 135 45 E
Kyōto □ 36 35 15N 135 45 E
Kyren 25 51 45N 101 45 E
Kyrenia 30 35 20N 33 20 E
Kystatyam 25 67 20N 123 10 E
Kytal Ktakh 25 65 30N 123 40 E
Kyulyunken 25 64 10N 137 5 E
Kyunhla 33 23 25N 95 15 E
Kyuquot 64 50 3N 127 25W
Kyūshū 36 33 0N 131 0 E
Kyūshū-Sanchi 36 32 35N 131 17 E
Kyustendil 19 42 16N 22 41 E
Kyusyur 25 70 39N 127 15 E
Kywong 45 34 58S 146 44 E
Kyzyl 25 51 50N 94 30 E
Kyzyl-Kiya 24 40 16N 72 8 E
Kyzylkum, Peski 24 42 30N 65 0 E
Kzyl-Orda 24 44 48N 65 28 E

L

Labak 35 6 32N 124 5 E
Labe = Elbe → 14 53 50N 9 0 E
Labé 50 11 24N 12 16W
Laberge, L. 64 61 11N 135 12W
Labis 34 2 22N 103 2 E
Laboulaye 80 34 10S 63 30W
Labrador, Coast
of □ 63 53 20N 61 0W
Labrador City 63 52 57N 66 55W
Lábrea 78 7 15S 64 51W
Labuan, Pulau 34 5 21N 115 13 E
Labuha 35 0 30S 127 30 E
Labuhan 35 6 22S 105 50 E
Labuhanbajo 35 8 28S 120 1 E
Labuk, Telok 34 6 10N 117 50 E
Labytnangi 22 66 39N 66 21 E
Lac Allard 63 50 33N 63 24W
Lac Bouchette 63 48 16N 72 11W
Lac du Flambeau 70 46 1N 89 51W
Lac Édouard 62 47 40N 72 16W
Lac La Biche 64 54 45N 111 58W
Lac la Martre 60 63 8N 117 16W
Lac-Mégantic 63 45 35N 70 53W
Lac Seul, Res. 62 50 25N 92 30W
Lacantúm → 74 16 36N 90 40W
Laccadive Is. =
Lakshadweep Is. 3 10 0N 72 30 E
Lacepede B. 45 36 40S 139 40 E
Lacepede Is. 46 16 55S 122 0 E
Lachine 62 45 30N 73 40W
Lachlan → 45 34 22S 143 55 E
Lachute 62 45 39N 74 21W
Lackawanna 68 42 49N 78 50W
Lacombe 64 52 30N 113 44W
Laconia 68 43 32N 71 30W
Lacrosse 72 46 51N 117 58W
Ladakh Ra. 32 34 0N 78 0 E
Ladismith 56 33 28S 21 15 E
Lādīz 31 28 55N 61 15 E
Ladoga, L. =
Ladozhskoye
Ozero 22 61 15N 30 30 E
Ladozhskoye Ozero 22 61 15N 30 30 E
Lady Grey 56 30 43S 27 13 E
Ladybrand 56 29 9S 27 29 E
Ladysmith, Canada 64 49 0N 123 49W
Ladysmith, S. Africa 57 28 32S 29 46 E
Ladysmith, U.S.A. 70 45 27N 91 4W
Lae 40 6 40S 147 2 E
Læsø 21 57 15N 10 53 E
Lafayette, Colo.,
U.S.A. 70 40 0N 105 2W
Lafayette, Ga.,
U.S.A. 69 34 44N 85 15W
Lafayette, Ind.,
U.S.A. 68 40 22N 86 52W
Lafayette, La.,
U.S.A. 71 30 18N 92 0W
Lafayette, Tenn.,
U.S.A. 69 36 35N 86 0W
Laferte → 64 61 53N 117 44W
Lafia 53 8 30N 8 34 E

Maracay

Madre, Sierra, Phil. 35 17 0N 122 0 E
Madre de Dios → 78 10 59S 66 8W
Madre de Dios, I. .. 80 50 20S 75 10W
Madre del Sur, Sierra 74 17 30N 100 0W
Madre Occidental, Sierra 74 27 0N 107 0W
Madre Oriental, Sierra 74 25 0N 100 0W
Madrid 13 40 25N 3 45W
Madura, Selat .... 35 7 30S 113 20 E
Madura Motel .... 47 31 55S 127 0 E
Madurai .... 32 9 55N 78 10 E
Madurantakam .... 32 12 30N 79 50 E
Mae Sot .... 34 16 43N 98 34 E
Maebashi .... 36 36 24N 139 4 E
Maesteg 7 51 36N 3 40W
Maestra, Sierra ... 75 20 15N 77 0W
Maestrazgo, Mts. del 13 40 30N 0 25W
Maevatanana ..... 57 16 56S 46 49 E
Mafeking 65 52 40N 101 10W
Mafeteng .... 56 29 51S 27 15 E
Maffra .... 45 37 53S 146 58 E
Mafia I. .... 54 7 45S 39 50 E
Mafikeng .... 56 25 50S 25 38 E
Mafra, Brazil 80 26 10S 50 0W
Mafra, Portugal ... 13 38 55N 9 20W
Magadan .... 25 59 38N 150 50 E
Magadi .... 54 1 54S 36 19 E
Magaliesburg ..... 57 26 0S 27 32 E
Magallanes, Estrecho de 80 52 30S 75 0W
Magangué 78 9 14N 74 45W
Magburaka 50 8 47N 12 0W
Magdalena, Argentina 80 35 5S 57 30W
Magdalena, Bolivia 78 13 13S 63 57W
Magdalena, Malaysia .... 34 4 25N 117 55 E
Magdalena, Mexico 74 30 50N 112 0W
Magdalena, U.S.A. . 73 34 10N 107 20W
Magdalena →, Colombia 78 11 6N 74 51W
Magdalena →, Mexico 74 30 40N 112 25W
Magdalena, B. 74 24 30N 112 10W
Magdalena, Llano de la 74 25 0N 111 30W
Magdeburg ...... 14 52 8N 11 36 E
Magdelaine Cays .. 44 16 33S 150 18 E
Magdi'el .... 28 32 10N 34 54 E
Magee 71 31 53N 89 45W
Magee, I. 9 54 48N 5 44W
Magelang .... 35 7 29S 110 13 E
Magellan's Str. = Magallanes, Estrecho de 80 52 30S 75 0W
Magenta, L. ...... 47 33 30S 119 2 E
Maggiore, L. ...... 18 46 0N 8 35 E
Maghār .... 28 32 54N 35 24 E
Magherafelt 9 54 44N 6 37W
Magnitogorsk ..... 22 53 27N 59 4 E
Magnolia, Ark., U.S.A. 71 33 18N 93 12W
Magnolia, Miss., U.S.A. 71 31 8N 90 28W
Magog 63 45 18N 72 9W
Magosa = Famagusta ..... 30 35 8N 33 55 E
Magpie L. 63 51 0N 64 41W
Magrath 64 49 25N 112 50W
Maguarinho, C. ... 79 0 15S 48 30W
Maguse L. 65 61 40N 95 10W
Maguse Pt. 65 61 20N 93 50W
Magwe .... 33 20 10N 95 0 E
Mahābād .... 30 36 50N 45 45 E
Mahabo .... 57 20 23S 44 40 E
Mahagi .... 54 2 20N 31 0 E
Mahajamba → ... 57 15 33S 47 8 E
Mahajamba, Helodranon' i ... 57 15 24S 47 5 E
Mahajanga .... 57 15 40S 46 25 E
Mahajanga □ ..... 57 17 0S 47 0 E
Mahajilo → ...... 57 19 42S 45 22 E
Mahakam → .... 34 0 35S 117 17 E
Mahalapye .... 56 23 1S 26 51 E
Mahallāt .... 31 33 55N 50 30 E
Mahanadi → .... 33 20 20N 86 25 E
Mahanoro .... 57 19 54S 48 48 E
Maharashtra □ .... 32 20 30N 75 30 E
Mahari Mts. ...... 52 6 20S 30 0 E
Mahasolo .... 57 19 7S 46 22 E
Mahbubnagar .... 32 16 45N 77 59 E
Mahdia .... 51 35 28N 11 0 E
Mahé .... 3 5 0S 55 30 E
Mahenge .... 54 8 45S 36 41 E
Maheno .... 43 45 10S 170 50 E
Mahesana .... 32 23 39N 72 26 E
Mahia Pen. .... 43 39 9S 177 55 E
Mahnomen 70 47 22N 95 57W
Mahón .... 13 39 53N 4 16 E
Mahone Bay 63 44 30N 64 20W
Mai-Ndombe, L. ... 54 2 0S 18 20 E
Maicurú → 79 2 14S 54 17W
Maidenhead 7 51 31N 0 42W
Maidstone, Canada 65 53 5N 109 20W
Maidstone, U.K. ... 7 51 16N 0 31 E
Maiduguri .... 53 12 0N 13 20 E
Maijdi .... 33 22 48N 91 10 E
Maikala Ra. ...... 33 22 0N 81 0 E
Main →, Germany 14 50 0N 8 18 E
Main →, U.K. 9 54 49N 6 20W
Main Centre 65 50 35N 107 21W
Maine .... 12 48 0N 0 0 E
Maine □ 63 45 20N 69 0W
Maine → 9 52 10N 9 40W
Maine-et-Loire □ .. 12 47 31N 0 30W
Maingkwan .... 33 26 15N 96 37 E
Mainit, L. .... 35 9 31N 125 30 E
Mainland, Orkney, U.K. 8 59 0N 3 10W
Mainland, Shetland, U.K. 8 60 15N 1 22W
Maintirano .... 57 18 3S 44 1 E
Mainz .... 14 50 0N 8 17 E
Maipú 80 36 52S 57 50W
Maiquetía 78 10 36N 66 57W
Mairabari .... 33 26 30N 92 22 E
Maisi, Pta. de 75 20 10N 74 10W
Maitland, N.S.W., Australia .... 45 32 33S 151 36 E
Maitland, S. Austral., Australia .... 45 34 23S 137 40 E
Maiz, Is. del 75 12 15N 83 4W
Maizuru .... 36 35 25N 135 22 E
Majalengka .... 35 6 50S 108 13 E
Majd el Kurūm .... 28 32 56N 35 15 E
Majene .... 35 3 38S 118 57 E
Maji .... 51 6 12N 35 30 E
Major 65 51 52N 109 37W
Majorca, I. = Mallorca .... 13 39 30N 3 0 E
Maka 50 13 40N 14 10W
Makale .... 35 3 6S 119 51 E
Makari .... 54 12 35N 14 28 E
Makarikari = Makgadikgadi Salt Pans .... 56 20 40S 25 45 E
Makarovo .... 25 57 40N 107 45 E
Makasar = Ujung Pandang .... 35 5 10S 119 20 E
Makasar, Selat .... 35 1 0S 118 20 E
Makat .... 23 47 39N 53 19 E
Makedhonía □ .... 19 40 39N 22 0 E
Makedonija □ .... 19 41 53N 21 40 E
Makena 66 20 39N 156 27W
Makeni 50 8 55N 12 5W
Makeyevka .... 23 48 0N 38 0 E
Makgadikgadi Salt Pans .... 56 20 40S 25 45 E
Makhachkala ..... 23 43 0N 47 30 E
Makian .... 35 0 20N 127 20 E
Makindu .... 54 2 18S 37 50 E
Makinsk .... 24 52 37N 70 26 E
Makkah .... 29 21 30N 39 54 E
Makkovik 63 55 10N 59 10W
Maklakovo .... 25 58 16N 92 29 E
Makó .... 15 46 14N 20 33 E
Makokou .... 54 0 40N 12 50 E
Makoua .... 54 0 5S 15 50 E
Makrai .... 32 22 2N 77 0 E
Makran .... 31 26 13N 61 30 E
Makran Coast Range .... 31 25 40N 64 0 E
Maksimkin Yar ..... 24 58 42N 86 50 E
Mākū .... 30 39 15N 44 31 E
Makumbi .... 54 5 50S 20 43 E
Makunda .... 56 22 30S 20 7 E
Makurazaki .... 36 31 15N 130 20 E
Makurdi .... 53 7 43N 8 35 E
Makwassie .... 56 27 17S 26 0 E
Mal B. 9 52 50N 9 30W
Mala, Pta. 75 7 28N 80 2W
Malabang .... 35 7 36N 124 3 E
Malabar Coast ..... 32 11 0N 75 0 E
Malacca, Str. of ... 34 3 0N 101 0 E
Malad City .... 72 42 10N 112 20 E
Málaga, Spain 13 36 43N 4 23W
Malaga, U.S.A. 71 32 12N 104 2W
Málaga □ 13 36 38N 4 58W
Malaimbandy ..... 57 20 20S 45 36 E
Malakâl .... 51 9 33N 31 40 E
Malakand .... 32 34 40N 71 55 E
Malakoff 71 32 10N 95 55W
Malamyzh .... 25 50 0N 136 50 E
Malang .... 35 7 59S 112 45 E
Malange .... 54 9 36S 16 17 E
Mälaren .... 21 59 30N 17 10 E
Malargüe 80 35 32S 69 30W
Malartic 62 48 9N 78 9W
Malatya .... 30 38 25N 38 20 E
Malawi ■ .... 55 11 55S 34 0 E
Malawi, L. .... 55 12 30S 34 30 E
Malay Pen. .... 34 7 25N 100 0 E
Malaybalay .... 35 8 5N 125 7 E
Malāyer .... 30 34 19N 48 51 E
Malaysia ■ .... 34 5 0N 110 0 E
Malazgirt .... 30 39 10N 42 33 E
Malbaie, La 63 47 40N 70 10W
Malbon .... 44 21 5S 140 17 E
Malbooma .... 45 30 41S 134 11 E
Malbork .... 15 54 3N 19 1 E
Malcolm .... 47 28 51S 121 25 E
Malcolm, Pt. ...... 47 33 48S 123 45 E
Maldegem .... 11 51 14N 3 26 E
Malden 71 36 35N 90 0W
Malden I. 41 4 3S 155 1W
Maldives ■ .... 3 5 0N 73 0 E
Maldonado 80 35 0S 55 0W
Maldonado, Punta . 74 16 19N 98 35W
Malé Karpaty ..... 14 48 30N 17 20 E
Maléa, Ákra ...... 19 36 28N 23 7 E
Malegaon .... 32 20 30N 74 38 E
Malema .... 55 14 57S 37 20 E
Malgomaj .... 20 64 40N 16 30 E
Malha .... 51 15 8N 25 10 E
Malhão, Sa. do ... 13 37 25N 8 0W
Malheur → 72 44 3N 116 59W
Malheur L. 72 43 19N 118 42W
Mali ■ 50 17 0N 3 0W
Mali → .... 33 25 40N 97 40 E
Malih → .... 28 32 20N 35 34 E
Malik .... 35 0 39S 123 16 E
Malili .... 35 2 42S 121 6 E
Malindi .... 54 3 12S 40 5 E
Malines = Mechelen 11 51 2N 4 29 E
Maling .... 35 1 0N 121 0 E
Malita .... 35 6 19N 125 39 E
Mallacoota Inlet ... 45 37 34S 149 40 E
Mallaig 8 57 0N 5 50W
Mallawi .... 51 27 44N 30 44 E
Mallorca .... 13 39 30N 3 0 E
Mallow 9 52 8N 8 40W
Malmberget ...... 20 67 11N 20 40 E
Malmédy .... 11 50 25N 6 2 E
Malmesbury ...... 56 33 28S 18 41 E
Malmö .... 21 55 36N 12 59 E
Malmöhus län □ .. 21 55 45N 13 30 E
Malolos .... 35 14 50N 120 49 E
Malone 68 44 50N 74 19W
Malozemelskaya Tundra .... 22 67 0N 50 0 E
Malpelo 78 4 3N 81 35W
Malta, Idaho, U.S.A. 72 42 15N 113 30W
Malta, Mont., U.S.A. 72 48 20N 107 55W
Malta ■ .... 18 35 50N 14 30 E
Maltahöhe .... 56 24 55S 17 0 E
Malton 6 54 9N 0 48W
Maluku .... 35 1 0S 127 0 E
Maluku □ .... 35 3 0S 128 0 E
Malvan .... 32 16 2N 73 30 E
Malvern, U.K. 7 52 7N 2 19W
Malvern, U.S.A. ... 71 34 22N 92 50W
Malvern Hills 7 52 0N 2 19W
Malvinas, Is. = Falkland Is. 80 51 30S 59 0W
Malyy Lyakhovskiy, Ostrov .... 25 74 7N 140 36 E
Mama .... 25 58 18N 112 54 E
Mamahatun ...... 30 39 50N 40 23 E
Mamaia .... 15 44 18N 28 37 E
Mamanguape 79 6 50S 35 4W
Mamasa .... 35 2 55S 119 20 E
Mambasa .... 52 1 22N 29 3 E
Mamberamo → .. 35 2 0S 137 50 E
Mambilima Falls .. 54 10 31S 28 45 E
Mamburao .... 35 13 13N 120 39 E
Mameigwess L. ... 62 52 35N 87 50W
Mamfe .... 53 5 50N 9 15 E
Mammoth 73 32 46N 110 43W
Mamoré → 78 10 23S 65 53W
Mamou 50 10 15N 12 0W
Mamuju .... 35 2 41S 118 50 E
Man 50 7 30N 7 40W
Man, I. of 6 54 15N 4 30W
Man Na .... 33 23 27N 97 19 E
Mana 79 5 45N 53 55W
Manaar, Gulf of = Mannar, G. of ... 32 8 30N 79 0 E
Manacapuru 78 3 16S 60 37W
Manacor .... 13 39 34N 3 13 E
Manado .... 35 1 29N 124 51 E
Managua 75 12 6N 86 20W
Managua, L. 75 12 20N 86 30W
Manakara .... 57 22 8S 48 1 E
Manambao → ... 57 17 35S 44 0 E
Manambato ...... 57 13 43S 49 7 E
Manambolo → .. 57 19 18S 44 22 E
Manambolosy .... 57 16 2S 49 40 E
Mananara .... 57 16 10S 49 46 E
Mananara → .... 57 23 21S 47 42 E
Mananjary .... 57 21 13S 48 20 E
Manantenina ..... 57 24 17S 47 19 E
Manaos = Manaus 78 3 0S 60 0W
Manapouri .... 43 45 34S 167 39 E
Manapouri, L. .... 43 45 32S 167 32 E
Manas .... 37 44 17N 85 56 E
Manas → .... 33 26 12N 90 40 E
Manasir .... 31 24 30N 51 10 E
Manassa 73 37 12N 105 58W
Manaung .... 33 18 45N 93 40 E
Manaus 78 3 0S 60 0W
Manawan L. 65 55 24N 103 14W
Manay .... 35 7 17N 126 33 E
Mancelona 68 44 54N 85 5W
Mancha, La 13 39 10N 2 54W
Manche □ 12 49 10N 1 20W
Manchegorsk ..... 22 67 40N 32 40 E
Manchester, U.K. .. 6 53 30N 2 15W
Manchester, Conn., U.S.A. 68 41 47N 72 30W
Manchester, Ga., U.S.A. 69 32 53N 84 32W
Manchester, Iowa, U.S.A. 70 42 28N 91 27W
Manchester, Ky., U.S.A. 68 37 9N 83 45W
Manchester, N.H., U.S.A. 68 42 58N 71 29W
Manchester L. 65 61 28N 107 29W
Mand → .... 31 28 20N 52 30 E
Manda .... 54 10 30S 34 40 E
Mandabé .... 57 21 0S 44 55 E
Mandal .... 21 58 2N 7 25 E
Mandalay .... 33 22 0N 96 4 E
Mandale = Mandalay ...... 33 22 0N 96 4 E
Mandalī .... 30 33 43N 45 28 E
Mandan 70 46 50N 101 0W
Mandar, Teluk .... 35 3 35S 119 15 E
Mandasor = Mandsaur ...... 32 24 3N 75 8 E
Mandaue .... 35 10 20N 123 56 E
Mandi .... 32 31 39N 76 58 E
Mandimba .... 55 14 20S 35 40 E
Mandioli .... 35 0 40S 127 20 E
Mandla .... 33 22 39N 80 30 E
Mandoto .... 57 19 34S 46 17 E
Mandrare → .... 57 25 10S 46 30 E
Mandritsara ...... 57 15 50S 48 49 E
Mandsaur .... 32 24 3N 75 8 E
Mandurah .... 47 32 36S 115 48 E
Mandvi .... 32 22 51N 69 22 E
Mandya .... 32 12 30N 77 0 E
Maneroo .... 44 23 22S 143 53 E
Maneroo Cr. → .. 44 23 21S 143 53 E
Manfalût .... 51 27 20N 30 52 E
Manfred .... 45 33 19S 143 45 E
Mangaia 43 21 55S 157 55W
Mangalia .... 15 43 50N 28 35 E
Mangalore .... 32 12 55N 74 47 E
Manggar .... 34 2 50S 108 10 E
Manggawitu ...... 35 4 8S 133 32 E
Mangkalihat, Tanjung .... 35 1 2N 118 59 E
Mangla Dam ..... 32 33 9N 73 44 E
Mangnai .... 37 37 52N 91 43 E
Mango .... 53 10 20N 0 30 E
Mangoche .... 55 14 25S 35 16 E
Mangoky → .... 57 21 29S 43 41 E
Mangole .... 35 1 50S 125 55 E
Mangonui .... 43 35 1S 173 32 E
Mangueigne ...... 51 10 30N 21 15 E
Mangueira, L. da .. 80 33 0S 52 50W
Mangum 71 34 50N 99 30W
Manhattan 70 39 10N 96 40W
Manhiça .... 57 25 23S 32 49 E
Manhuaçu 79 20 15S 42 2W
Mania → .... 57 19 42S 45 22 E
Manica .... 57 18 58S 32 59 E
Manica e Sofala □ 57 19 10S 33 45 E
Manicoré 78 5 48S 61 16W
Manicouagan → . 63 49 30N 68 30W
Manīfah .... 30 27 44N 49 0 E
Manifold .... 44 22 41S 150 40 E
Manifold, C. ...... 44 22 41S 150 50 E
Manigotagan 65 51 6N 96 18W
Manihiki 41 10 24S 161 1W
Manila, Phil. ...... 35 14 40N 121 3 E
Manila, U.S.A. 72 41 0N 109 44W
Manila Bay .... 35 14 0N 120 0 E
Manilla .... 45 30 45S 150 43 E
Manipur □ .... 33 25 0N 94 0 E
Manipur → ..... 33 23 45N 94 20 E
Manisa .... 30 38 38N 27 30 E
Manistee 68 44 15N 86 20W
Manistee → 68 44 15N 86 21W
Manistique 68 45 59N 86 18W
Manito L. 65 52 43N 109 43W
Manitoba □ 65 55 30N 97 0W
Manitoba, L. 65 51 0N 98 45W
Manitou 65 49 15N 98 32W
Manitou I. 62 47 22N 87 30W
Manitou Is. 68 45 8N 86 0W
Manitou L. 63 50 55N 65 17W
Manitou Springs .. 70 38 52N 104 55W
Manitoulin I. 62 45 40N 82 30W
Manitowaning 62 45 46N 81 49W
Manitowoc 68 44 8N 87 40W
Manizales 78 5 5N 75 32W
Manja .... 57 21 26S 44 20 E
Manjacaze .... 57 24 45S 34 0 E
Manjakandriana ... 57 18 55S 47 47 E
Manjhand .... 32 25 50N 68 10 E
Manjil .... 30 36 46N 49 30 E
Manjimup .... 47 34 15S 116 6 E
Manjra → ...... 32 18 49N 77 52 E
Mankato, Kans., U.S.A. 70 39 49N 98 11W
Mankato, Minn., U.S.A. 70 44 8N 93 59W
Mankayane .... 57 26 40S 31 4 E
Mankono 50 8 1N 6 10W
Mankota 65 49 25N 107 5W
Manly .... 45 33 48S 151 17 E
Manmad .... 32 20 18N 74 28 E
Mann Ranges, Mts. 47 26 6S 130 5 E
Manna .... 34 4 25S 102 55 E
Mannahill .... 45 32 25S 140 0 E
Mannar .... 32 9 1N 79 54 E
Mannar, G. of ..... 32 8 30N 79 0 E
Mannar I. .... 32 9 5N 79 45 E
Mannheim .... 14 49 28N 8 29 E
Manning, Canada . 64 56 53N 117 39W
Manning, U.S.A. ... 69 33 40N 80 9W
Manning Prov. Park 64 49 5N 120 45W
Mannington 68 39 35N 80 25W
Mannum .... 45 34 50S 139 20 E
Mano 50 8 3N 12 2W
Manokwari .... 35 0 54S 134 0 E
Manombo .... 57 22 57S 43 28 E
Manono .... 54 7 15S 27 25 E
Manouane, L. 63 50 45N 70 45W
Manresa .... 13 41 48N 1 50 E
Mans, Le .... 12 48 0N 0 10 E
Mansa .... 54 11 13S 28 55 E
Mansel I. 61 62 0N 80 0W
Mansfield, Australia 45 37 4S 146 6 E
Mansfield, U.K. ... 6 53 8N 1 12W
Mansfield, La., U.S.A. 71 32 2N 93 40W
Mansfield, Ohio, U.S.A. 68 40 45N 82 30W
Mansfield, Wash., U.S.A. 72 47 51N 119 44W
Manson Creek 64 55 37N 124 32W
Manta 78 1 0S 80 40W
Mantalingajan, Mt. . 34 8 55N 117 45 E
Manteca 73 37 50N 121 12W
Manteo 69 35 55N 75 41W
Mantes-la-Jolie ... 12 49 0N 1 41 E
Manthani .... 32 18 40N 79 35 E
Manti 72 39 23N 111 32W
Mantiqueira, Serra da 79 22 0S 44 0W
Manton 68 44 23N 85 25W
Mántova .... 18 45 20N 10 42 E
Mänttä .... 20 62 0N 24 40 E
Mantua = Mántova 18 45 20N 10 42 E
Manu 78 12 10S 70 51W
Manua Is. 43 14 13S 169 35W
Manuae 41 19 30S 159 0W
Manuel Alves → . 79 11 19S 48 28W
Manui .... 35 3 35S 123 5 E
Manville 70 42 48N 104 36W
Many 71 31 36N 93 28W
Manyara, L. ...... 54 3 40S 35 50 E
Manych-Gudilo, Oz. 23 46 24N 42 38 E
Manyoni .... 54 5 45S 34 55 E
Manzai .... 32 32 12N 70 15 E
Manzanares 13 39 0N 3 22W
Manzanillo, Cuba .. 75 20 20N 77 31W
Manzanillo, Mexico 74 19 0N 104 20W
Manzanillo, Pta. ... 75 9 30N 79 40W
Manzano Mts. 73 34 30N 106 45W
Manzhouli .... 38 49 35N 117 25 E
Manzini .... 57 26 30S 31 25 E
Mao .... 51 14 4N 15 19 E
Maoke, Pegunungan 35 3 40S 137 30 E
Maoming .... 39 21 50N 110 54 E
Mapam Yumco ... 33 30 45N 81 28 E
Mapia, Kepulauan . 35 0 50N 134 20 E
Mapimí 74 25 50N 103 50W
Mapimí, Bolsón de 74 27 30N 104 15W
Mapinhane .... 57 22 20S 35 0 E
Maple Creek 65 49 55N 109 29W
Mapleton 72 44 4N 123 58W
Mapuera → 78 1 5S 57 2W
Maputo .... 57 25 58S 32 32 E
Maputo, B. de .... 57 25 50S 32 45 E
Maqnā .... 30 28 25N 34 50 E
Maquela do Zombo 54 6 0S 15 15 E
Maquinchao 80 41 15S 68 50W
Maquoketa 70 42 4N 90 40W
Mar, Serra do 80 25 30S 49 0W
Mar Chiquita, L. ... 80 30 40S 62 50W
Mar del Plata 80 38 0S 57 30W
Mara .... 52 1 30S 34 32 E
Maraā 78 1 52S 65 25W
Marabá 79 5 20S 49 5W
Maracá, I. de 79 2 10N 50 30W
Maracaibo 78 10 40N 71 37W
Maracaibo, L. de .. 78 9 40N 71 30W
Maracay 78 10 15N 67 28W

Marādah

Marādah .... 51 29 15N 19 15 E
Maradi .... 53 13 29N 7 20 E
Marāgheh .... 30 37 30N 46 12 E
Marāh .... 30 25 0N 45 35 E
Marajó, I. de 79 1 0S 49 30W
Maralal .... 54 1 0N 36 38 E
Maralinga .... 47 30 13S 131 32 E
Marama .... 45 35 10S 140 10 E
Marampa 50 8 45N 12 28W
Marana 73 32 30N 111 9W
Maranboy .... 46 14 40S 132 39 E
Marand .... 30 38 30N 45 45 E
Maranguape 79 3 55S 38 50W
Maranhão = São Luís 79 2 39S 44 15W
Maranhão □ 79 5 0S 46 0W
Maranoa → .... 45 27 50S 148 37 E
Marañón → 78 4 30S 73 35W
Marão .... 57 24 18S 34 2 E
Marathon, Australia 44 20 51S 143 32 E
Marathon, Canada . 62 48 44N 86 23W
Marathón, Greece . 19 38 11N 23 58 E
Marathon, U.S.A. .. 71 30 15N 103 15W
Maratua .... 35 2 10N 118 35 E
Marbella 13 36 30N 4 57W
Marble Bar .... 46 21 9S 119 44 E
Marble Falls 71 30 30N 98 15W
Marburg .... 14 50 49N 8 36 E
March .... 7 52 33N 0 5 E
Marche .... 12 46 5N 1 20 E
Marche □ .... 18 43 22N 13 10 E
Marche-en-Famenne 11 50 14N 5 19 E
Marches = Marche □ .... 18 43 22N 13 10 E
Marcus .... 40 24 0N 153 45 E
Marcus Necker Ridge .... 40 20 0N 175 0 E
Mardan .... 32 34 20N 72 0 E
Mardie .... 46 21 12S 115 59 E
Mardin .... 30 37 20N 40 43 E
Maree L. 8 57 40N 5 30W
Mareeba .... 44 16 59S 145 28 E
Marek = Stanke Dimitrov .... 19 42 17N 23 9 E
Marek .... 35 4 41S 120 24 E
Maremma .... 18 42 45N 11 15 E
Marengo 70 41 42N 92 5W
Marerano .... 57 21 23S 44 52 E
Marfa 71 30 15N 104 0W
Margaret Bay 64 51 20N 127 35W
Margaret L. 64 58 56N 115 25W
Margarita 74 9 20N 79 55W
Margarita, I. de ... 78 11 0N 64 0W
Margate, S. Africa . 57 30 50S 30 20 E
Margate, U.K. .... 7 51 23N 1 24 E
Margelan .... 24 40 27N 71 42 E
Marguerite 64 52 30N 122 25W
Mari A.S.S.R. □ ... 22 56 30N 48 0 E
Maria I., N. Terr., Australia .... 44 14 52S 135 45 E
Maria I., Tas., Australia .... 44 42 35S 148 0 E
Maria van Diemen, C. .... 43 34 29S 172 40 E
Marian L. 64 63 0N 116 15W
Mariana Trench ... 40 13 0N 145 0 E
Marianao 75 23 8N 82 24W
Marianna, Ark., U.S.A. 71 34 48N 90 48W
Marianna, Fla., U.S.A. 69 30 45N 85 15W
Marias → 72 47 56N 110 30W
Mariato, Punta 75 7 12N 80 52W
Ma'rib .... 29 15 25N 45 21 E
Maribor .... 18 46 36N 15 40 E
Marico → .... 56 23 35S 26 57 E
Maricopa, Ariz., U.S.A. 73 33 5N 112 2W
Maricopa, Calif., U.S.A. 73 35 7N 119 27W
Marîdî .... 51 4 55N 29 25 E
Marie-Galante 75 15 56N 61 16W
Mariecourt 61 61 30N 72 0W
Mariehamn .... 21 60 5N 19 55 E
Marienberg .... 11 52 30N 6 35 E
Marienbourg .... 11 50 6N 4 31 E
Mariental .... 56 24 36S 18 0 E
Mariestad .... 21 58 43N 13 50 E
Marietta, Ga., U.S.A. 69 34 0N 84 30W
Marietta, Ohio, U.S.A. 68 39 27N 81 27W
Mariinsk .... 24 56 10N 87 20 E
Marília 79 22 13S 50 0W
Marillana .... 46 22 37S 119 16 E
Marín 13 42 23N 8 42W
Marina Plains .... 44 14 37S 143 57 E
Marinduque .... 35 13 25N 122 0 E
Marine City 68 42 45N 82 29W
Marinel, Le .... 54 10 25S 25 17 E
Marinette 68 45 4N 87 40W
Maringá 80 23 26S 52 2W
Marion, Ala., U.S.A. 69 32 33N 87 20W
Marion, Ill., U.S.A. . 71 37 45N 88 55W
Marion, Ind., U.S.A. 68 40 35N 85 40W
Marion, Iowa, U.S.A. 70 42 2N 91 36W
Marion, Kans., U.S.A. 70 38 25N 97 2W
Marion, Mich., U.S.A. 68 44 7N 85 8W
Marion, N.C., U.S.A. 69 35 42N 82 0W
Marion, Ohio, U.S.A. 68 40 38N 83 8W
Marion, S.C., U.S.A. 69 34 11N 79 22W
Marion, Va., U.S.A. 69 36 51N 81 29W
Marion, L. 69 33 30N 80 15W
Marion I. .... 3 47 0S 38 0 E
Mariposa 73 37 31N 119 59W
Mariscal Estigarribia 78 22 3S 60 40W
Maritsa → .... 19 41 40N 26 34 E
Marīvān .... 30 35 30N 46 25 E
Markazī □ .... 31 35 0N 49 30 E
Marked Tree 71 35 35N 90 24W
Marken .... 11 52 26N 5 12 E
Market Drayton ... 6 52 55N 2 30W
Market Harborough 7 52 29N 0 55W
Markham L. 65 62 30N 102 35W
Markovo .... 25 64 40N 169 40 E
Marks .... 22 51 45N 46 50 E
Marksville 71 31 10N 92 2W
Marla .... 45 27 19S 133 33 E
Marlborough .... 44 22 46S 149 52 E
Marlborough □ ... 43 41 45S 173 33 E
Marlborough Downs 7 51 25N 1 55W
Marlin 71 31 25N 96 50W
Marlow 71 34 40N 97 58W
Marmagao .... 32 15 25N 73 56 E
Marmara .... 30 40 05N 27 00 E
Marmara, Sea of = Marmara Denizi . 30 40 45N 28 15 E
Marmara Denizi ... 30 40 45N 28 15 E
Marmaris .... 30 36 50N 28 14 E
Marmarth 70 46 21N 103 52W
Marmion L. 62 48 55N 91 20W
Marmion Mt. .... 47 29 16S 119 50 E
Marmolada, Mte. .. 18 46 25N 11 55 E
Marmora 62 44 28N 77 41W
Marne □ .... 12 48 50N 4 10 E
Marne → .... 12 48 48N 2 24 E
Maroala .... 57 15 23S 47 59 E
Maroantsetra .... 57 15 26S 49 44 E
Maromandia .... 57 14 13S 48 5 E
Marondera .... 55 18 5S 31 42 E
Maroni → 79 5 30N 54 0W
Maroochydore .... 45 26 29S 153 5 E
Maroona .... 45 37 27S 142 54 E
Marosakoa .... 57 15 26S 46 38 E
Maroua .... 53 10 40N 14 20 E
Marovoay .... 57 16 6S 46 39 E
Marquard .... 56 28 40S 27 28 E
Marquesas Is. 41 9 30S 140 0W
Marquette 68 46 30N 87 21W
Marracuene .... 57 25 45S 32 35 E
Marrakech 50 31 9N 8 0W
Marrawah .... 44 40 55S 144 42 E
Marree .... 45 29 39S 138 1 E
Marrilla .... 46 22 31S 114 25 E
Marrimane .... 57 22 58S 33 34 E
Marromeu .... 57 18 15S 36 25 E
Marrowie Creek ... 45 33 23S 145 40 E
Marrupa .... 55 13 8S 37 30 E
Mars, Le 70 43 0N 96 0W
Marsá Matrûh .... 51 31 19N 27 9 E
Marsá Susah .... 51 32 52N 21 59 E
Marsabit .... 54 2 18N 38 0 E
Marsala .... 18 37 48N 12 25 E
Marsaxlokk .... 18 35 47N 14 32 E
Marsden .... 45 33 47S 147 32 E
Marseille .... 12 43 18N 5 23 E
Marseilles = Marseille .... 12 43 18N 5 23 E
Marsh I. 71 29 35N 91 50W
Marsh L. 70 45 5N 96 0W
Marshall, Liberia .. 50 6 8N 10 22W
Marshall, Ark., U.S.A. 71 35 58N 92 40W
Marshall, Mich., U.S.A. 68 42 17N 84 59W
Marshall, Minn., U.S.A. 70 44 25N 95 45W
Marshall, Mo., U.S.A. 70 39 8N 93 15W
Marshall, Tex., U.S.A. 71 32 29N 94 20W
Marshall → .... 44 22 59S 136 59 E
Marshall Is. .... 40 9 0N 171 0 E
Marshalltown 70 42 5N 92 56W
Marshfield, Mo., U.S.A. 71 37 20N 92 58W
Marshfield, Wis., U.S.A. 70 44 42N 90 10W
Marstrand .... 21 57 53N 11 35 E
Mart 71 31 34N 96 51W
Martaban .... 33 16 30N 97 35 E
Martaban, G. of ... 33 16 5N 96 30 E
Martapura, Kalimantan, Indonesia .... 34 3 22S 114 47 E
Martapura, Sumatera, Indonesia .... 34 4 19S 104 22 E
Marte .... 53 12 23N 13 46 E
Martelange .... 11 49 49N 5 43 E
Martha's Vineyard . 68 41 25N 70 35W
Martin, S. Dak., U.S.A. 70 43 11N 101 45W
Martin, Tenn., U.S.A. 71 36 23N 88 51W
Martin, L. 69 32 45N 85 50W
Martinborough ... 43 41 14S 175 29 E
Martinique 75 14 40N 61 0W
Martinique Passage 75 15 15N 61 0W
Martinsburg 68 39 30N 77 57W
Martinsville, Ind., U.S.A. 68 39 29N 86 23W
Martinsville, Va., U.S.A. 69 36 41N 79 52W
Marton .... 43 40 4S 175 23 E
Martos 13 37 44N 3 58W
Marudi .... 34 4 11N 114 19 E
Ma'ruf .... 31 31 30N 67 6 E
Marugame .... 36 34 15N 133 40 E
Marulan .... 45 34 43S 150 3 E
Marunga .... 56 17 28S 20 2 E
Marwar .... 32 25 43N 73 45 E
Mary .... 24 37 40N 61 50 E
Mary Frances L. ... 65 63 19N 106 13W
Mary Kathleen ... 44 20 44S 139 48 E
Maryborough = Port Laoise 9 53 2N 7 20W
Maryborough, Queens., Australia 45 25 31S 152 37 E
Maryborough, Vic., Australia .... 45 37 0S 143 44 E
Maryfield 65 49 50N 101 35W
Maryland □ 68 39 10N 76 40W
Maryport 6 54 43N 3 30W
Mary's Harbour ... 63 52 18N 55 51W
Marystown 63 47 10N 55 10W
Marysvale 73 38 25N 112 17W
Marysville, Canada 64 49 35N 116 0W
Marysville, Calif., U.S.A. 72 39 14N 121 40W
Marysville, Kans., U.S.A. 70 39 50N 96 49W
Marysville, Ohio, U.S.A. 68 40 15N 83 20W
Maryvale .... 45 28 4S 152 12 E
Maryville 69 35 50N 84 0W
Marzūq .... 51 25 53N 13 57 E
Masada = Mesada 28 31 20N 35 19 E
Masai Steppe .... 52 4 30S 36 30 E
Masaka .... 54 0 21S 31 45 E
Masalembo, Kepulauan .... 34 5 35S 114 30 E
Masalima, Kepulauan .... 34 5 4S 117 5 E
Masamba .... 35 2 30S 120 15 E
Masan .... 38 35 11N 128 32 E
Masandam, Ras ... 31 26 30N 56 30 E
Masasi .... 54 10 45S 38 52 E
Masaya 75 12 0N 86 7W
Masbate .... 35 12 21N 123 36 E
Mascara .... 50 35 26N 0 6 E
Mascarene Is. .... 3 22 0S 55 0 E
Mascota 74 20 30N 104 50W
Masela .... 35 8 9S 129 51 E
Maseru .... 56 29 18S 27 30 E
Mashābih .... 30 25 35N 36 30 E
Mashan .... 39 23 40N 108 11 E
Mashhad .... 31 36 20N 59 35 E
Mashike .... 36 43 31N 141 30 E
Mashkel, Hamun-i- 31 28 30N 63 0 E
Mashki Chāh .... 31 29 5N 62 30 E
Mashonaland Central □ .... 57 17 30S 31 0 E
Mashonaland East □ .... 57 18 0S 32 0 E
Mashonaland West □ .... 57 17 30S 29 30 E
Masi .... 20 69 26N 23 40 E
Masi Manimba .... 54 4 40S 17 54 E
Masindi .... 54 1 40N 31 43 E
Masisea 78 8 35S 74 22W
Masisi .... 52 1 23S 28 49 E
Masjed Soleyman . 30 31 55N 49 18 E
Mask, L. 9 53 36N 9 24W
Masoala, Tanjon' i . 57 15 59S 50 13 E
Masoarivo .... 57 19 3S 44 19 E
Masohi .... 35 3 20S 128 55 E
Masomeloka .... 57 20 17S 48 37 E
Mason 71 30 45N 99 15W
Mason City 70 43 9N 93 12W
Masqat .... 31 23 37N 58 36 E
Massa .... 18 44 2N 10 7 E
Massachusetts □ . 68 42 25N 72 0W
Massada .... 28 33 41N 35 36 E
Massaguet .... 51 12 28N 15 26 E
Massakory .... 51 13 0N 15 49 E
Massangena .... 57 21 34S 33 0 E
Massawa = Mitsiwa 51 15 35N 39 25 E
Massena 68 44 52N 74 55W
Massénya .... 51 11 21N 16 9 E
Masset 64 54 2N 132 10W
Massif Central ... 12 45 30N 3 0 E
Massillon 68 40 47N 81 30W
Massinga .... 57 23 15S 35 22 E
Masterton .... 43 40 56S 175 39 E
Mastuj .... 32 36 20N 72 36 E
Mastung .... 31 29 50N 66 56 E
Masuda .... 36 34 40N 131 51 E
Masvingo .... 55 20 8S 30 49 E
Mataboor .... 35 1 41S 138 3 E
Matachewan 62 47 56N 80 39W
Matad .... 37 47 11N 115 27 E
Matadi .... 54 5 52S 13 31 E
Matagalpa 75 13 0N 85 58W
Matagami 62 49 45N 77 34W
Matagami, L. 62 49 50N 77 40W
Matagorda 71 28 43N 96 0W
Matagorda B. 71 28 30N 96 15W
Matagorda I. 71 28 10N 96 40W
Matak, P. .... 34 3 18N 106 16 E
Matakana .... 45 32 59S 145 54 E
Matam 50 15 34N 13 17W
Matamoros, Coahuila, Mexico 74 25 33N 103 15W
Matamoros, Puebla, Mexico 74 18 2N 98 17W
Matamoros, Tamaulipas, Mexico 74 25 50N 97 30W
Ma'ţan as Sarra ... 51 21 45N 22 0 E
Matane 63 48 50N 67 33W
Matanuska 60 61 39N 149 19W
Matanzas 75 23 0N 81 40W
Matapan, C. = Taínaron, Ákra .. 19 36 22N 22 27 E
Matapédia 63 48 0N 66 59W
Matara .... 32 5 58N 80 30 E
Mataram .... 34 8 41S 116 10 E
Matarani 78 77 0S 72 10W
Mataranka .... 46 14 55S 133 4 E
Matatiele .... 57 30 20S 28 49 E
Mataura .... 43 46 11S 168 51 E
Matehuala 74 23 40N 100 40W
Matera .... 18 40 40N 16 37 E
Matheson Island ... 65 51 45N 96 56W
Mathis 71 28 4N 97 48W
Mathura .... 32 27 30N 77 40 E
Mati .... 35 6 55N 126 15 E
Matías Romero ... 74 16 53N 95 2W
Matima .... 56 20 15S 24 26 E
Matlock 6 53 8N 1 32W
Matmata .... 50 33 37N 9 59 E
Mato Grosso □ ... 79 14 0S 55 0W
Mato Grosso, Planalto do 79 15 0S 55 0W
Matochkin Shar ... 24 73 10N 56 40 E
Matosinhos 13 41 11N 8 42W
Matrah .... 31 23 37N 58 30 E
Matsena .... 53 13 5N 10 5 E
Matsue .... 36 35 25N 133 10 E
Matsumae .... 36 41 26N 140 7 E
Matsumoto .... 36 36 15N 138 0 E
Matsusaka .... 36 34 34N 136 32 E
Matsutō .... 36 36 31N 136 34 E
Matsuyama .... 36 33 45N 132 45 E
Mattagami → 62 50 43N 81 29W
Mattancheri .... 32 9 50N 76 15 E
Mattawa 62 46 20N 78 45W
Mattawamkeag ... 63 45 30N 68 21W
Matterhorn .... 14 45 58N 7 39 E
Matthew Town 75 20 57N 73 40W
Matthew's Ridge .. 78 7 37N 60 10W
Mattice 62 49 40N 83 20W
Matuba .... 57 24 28S 32 49 E
Matucana 78 11 55S 76 25W
Matun .... 32 33 22N 69 58 E
Maturín 78 9 45N 63 11W
Mau Ranipur .... 32 25 16N 79 8 E
Maud, Pt. .... 46 23 6S 113 45 E
Maude .... 45 34 29S 144 18 E
Maudin Sun .... 33 16 0N 94 30 E
Maués 78 3 20S 57 45W
Mauganj .... 33 24 50N 81 55 E
Maui .... 66 20 45N 156 20 E
Mauke 43 20 9S 157 20W
Maulamyaing .... 33 16 30N 97 40 E
Maumee 68 41 35N 83 40W
Maumee → 68 41 42N 83 28W
Maumere .... 35 8 38S 122 13 E
Maun .... 56 20 0S 23 26 E
Mauna Kea 66 19 50N 155 28W
Mauna Loa 66 21 8N 157 10W
Maungmagan Kyunzu .... 33 14 0N 97 48 E
Maupin 72 45 12N 121 9W
Maurepas L. 71 30 18N 90 35W
Maures .... 12 43 15N 6 15 E
Maurice L. .... 47 29 30S 131 0 E
Mauritania ■ 50 20 50N 10 0W
Mauritius ■ .... 3 20 0S 57 0 E
Mauston 70 43 48N 90 5W
Mavinga .... 55 15 50S 20 21 E
Mavqi'im .... 28 31 38N 34 32 E
Mawk Mai .... 33 20 14N 97 37 E
Mawlaik .... 33 23 40N 94 26 E
Max 70 47 50N 101 20W
Maxcanú 74 20 40N 92 0W
Maxesibeni .... 57 30 49S 29 23 E
Maxhamish L. 64 59 50N 123 17W
Maxixe .... 57 23 54S 35 17 E
Maxwelton .... 44 20 43S 142 41 E
May Downs .... 44 22 38S 148 55 E
May Pen 75 17 58N 77 15W
Maya → .... 25 54 31N 134 41 E
Maya Mts. 74 16 30N 89 0W
Mayaguana 75 22 30N 72 44W
Mayagüez 75 18 12N 67 9W
Mayarí 75 20 40N 75 41W
Maybell 72 40 30N 108 4W
Maydena .... 44 42 45S 146 30 E
Mayenne 12 48 20N 0 38W
Mayenne □ 12 48 10N 0 40W
Mayer 73 34 28N 112 17W
Mayerthorpe 64 53 57N 115 8W
Mayfield 69 36 45N 88 40W
Mayhill 73 32 58N 105 30W
Maykop .... 23 44 35N 40 25 E
Maynard Hills .... 47 28 28S 119 49 E
Mayne → .... 44 23 40S 141 55 E
Maynooth 9 53 22N 6 38W
Mayo 60 63 38N 135 57W
Mayo □ 9 53 47N 9 7W
Mayo L. 60 63 45N 135 0W
Mayon Volcano ... 35 13 15N 123 41 E
Mayor I. .... 43 37 16S 176 17 E
Mayson L. 65 57 55N 107 10W
Maysville 68 38 39N 83 46W
Maythalūn .... 28 32 21N 35 16 E
Mayu .... 35 1 30N 126 30 E
Mayville 70 47 30N 97 23W
Mayya .... 25 61 44N 130 18 E
Mazabuka .... 55 15 52S 27 44 E
Mazagán = El Jadida 50 33 11N 8 17W
Mazagão 79 0 7S 51 16W
Mazán 78 3 30S 73 0W
Māzandarān □ ... 31 36 30N 52 0 E
Mazar-e Sharīf ... 31 36 41N 67 0 E
Mazarredo 80 47 10S 66 50W
Mazarrón 13 37 38N 1 19W
Mazaruni → 78 6 25N 58 35W
Mazatenango 75 14 35N 91 30W
Mazatlán 74 23 10N 106 30W
Māzhān .... 31 32 30N 59 0 E
Mazīnān .... 31 36 19N 56 56 E
Mazoe → .... 55 16 20S 33 30 E
Mazu Dao .... 39 26 10N 119 55 E
Mazurian Lakes = Mazurski, Pojezierze .... 15 53 50N 21 0 E
Mazurski, Pojezierze 15 53 50N 21 0 E
Mbabane .... 57 26 18S 31 6 E
Mbaïki .... 54 3 53N 18 1 E
Mbala .... 54 8 46S 31 24 E
Mbale .... 54 1 8N 34 12 E
Mbalmayo .... 54 3 33N 11 33 E
Mbamba Bay .... 54 11 13S 34 49 E
Mbandaka .... 54 0 1N 18 18 E
Mbanza Congo ... 54 6 18S 14 16 E
Mbanza Ngungu .. 54 5 12S 14 53 E
Mbarara .... 54 0 35S 30 40 E
Mbashe → .... 57 32 15S 28 54 E
Mbeya .... 54 8 54S 33 29 E
Mbini □ .... 54 1 30N 10 0 E
Mbour 50 14 22N 16 54W
Mbout 50 16 1N 12 38W
Mbuji-Mayi .... 54 6 9S 23 40 E
Mbulu .... 54 3 45S 35 30 E
Mchinji .... 55 13 47S 32 58 E
Mdina .... 18 35 51N 14 25 E
Mead, L. 73 36 1N 114 44W
Meade 71 37 18N 100 25W
Meadow .... 47 26 35S 114 40 E
Meadow Lake 65 54 10N 108 26W
Meadow Lake Prov. Park 65 54 27N 109 0W
Meadow Valley Wash → 73 36 39N 114 35W
Meadville 68 41 39N 80 9W
Meaford 62 44 36N 80 35W
Mealy Mts. 63 53 10N 58 0W
Meander River ... 64 59 2N 117 42W
Meares, C. 72 45 37N 124 0W
Mearim → 79 3 4S 44 35W
Meath □ 9 53 32N 6 40W
Meath Park 65 53 27N 105 22W
Meaux .... 12 48 58N 2 50 E
Mecca = Makkah . 29 21 30N 39 54 E
Mecca 73 33 37N 116 3W
Mechelen .... 11 51 2N 4 29 E
Mecheria 50 33 35N 0 18W
Mecklenburger Bucht .... 14 54 20N 11 40 E
Meconta .... 55 14 59S 39 50 E
Meda .... 46 17 22S 123 59 E

Miranda

Medan 34 3 40N 98 38 E
Medanosa, Pta. 80 48 8S 66 0W
Medéa 50 36 12N 2 50 E
Medellín 78 6 15N 75 35W
Medemblik 11 52 46N 5 8 E
Mederdra 50 17 0N 15 38W
Medford, Oreg., U.S.A. 72 42 20N 122 52W
Medford, Wis., U.S.A. 70 45 9N 90 21W
Mediaş 15 46 9N 24 22 E
Medical Lake 72 47 35N 117 42W
Medicine Bow 72 41 56N 106 11W
Medicine Bow Pk. 72 41 21N 106 19W
Medicine Bow Ra. 72 41 10N 106 25W
Medicine Hat 65 50 0N 110 45W
Medicine Lake 70 48 30N 104 30W
Medicine Lodge 71 37 20N 98 37W
Medina = Al Madīnah 29 24 35N 39 52 E
Medina, N. Dak., U.S.A. 70 46 57N 99 20W
Medina, N.Y., U.S.A. 68 43 15N 78 27W
Medina, Ohio, U.S.A. 68 41 9N 81 50W
Medina → 71 29 10N 98 20W
Medina del Campo 13 41 18N 4 55W
Medina L. 71 29 35N 98 58W
Medina-Sidonia 13 36 28N 5 57W
Medinipur 33 22 25N 87 21 E
Mediterranean Sea 16 35 0N 15 0 E
Medley 65 54 25N 110 16W
Médoc 12 45 10N 0 50W
Medport = Marsaxlokk 18 35 47N 14 32 E
Medstead 65 53 19N 108 5W
Medveditsa → 23 49 35N 42 41 E
Medvezhi, Ostrava 25 71 0N 161 0 E
Medvezhyegorsk 22 63 0N 34 25 E
Medway → 7 51 28N 0 45 E
Meeberrie 47 26 57S 115 51 E
Meekatharra 47 26 32S 118 29 E
Meeker 72 40 1N 107 58W
Meerut 32 29 1N 77 42 E
Meeteetse 72 44 10N 108 56W
Mega 51 3 57N 38 19 E
Mégara 19 37 58N 23 22 E
Meghalaya □ 33 25 50N 91 0 E
Megiddo 28 32 36N 35 11 E
Mégiscane, L. 62 48 35N 75 55W
Megiste 17 36 8N 29 34 E
Mehadia 15 44 56N 22 23 E
Mei Jiang → 39 24 25N 116 35 E
Mei Xian 39 24 16N 116 6 E
Meiganga 54 6 30N 14 25 E
Meiktila 33 20 53N 95 54 E
Me'ir Shefeya 28 32 35N 34 58 E
Meissen 14 51 10N 13 29 E
Meitan 39 27 45N 107 29 E
Mejillones 80 23 10S 70 30W
Meka 47 27 25S 116 48 E
Mékambo 54 1 2N 13 50 E
Mekdela 51 11 24N 39 10 E
Mekhtar 32 30 30N 69 15 E
Meknès 50 33 57N 5 33W
Mekong → 34 9 30N 106 15 E
Mekongga 35 3 39S 121 15 E
Melagiri Hills 32 12 20N 77 30 E
Melaka 34 2 15N 102 15 E
Melalap 34 5 10N 116 5 E
Melanesia 40 4 0S 155 0 E
Melbourne, Australia 45 37 50S 145 0 E
Melbourne, U.S.A. 69 28 4N 80 35W
Melchor Múzquiz 74 27 50N 101 30W
Melchor Ocampo 74 24 52N 101 40W
Mélèzes → 61 57 30N 71 0W
Melfi 51 11 0N 17 59 E
Melfort 65 52 50N 104 37W
Melilla 50 35 21N 2 57W
Melilot 28 31 22N 34 37 E
Melita 65 49 15N 101 0W
Melitopol 23 46 50N 35 22 E
Melk 14 48 13N 15 20 E
Mellansel 20 63 25N 18 17 E
Mellen 70 46 19N 90 36W
Mellerud 21 58 41N 12 28 E
Mellette 70 45 11N 98 29W
Melo 80 32 20S 54 10W
Melolo 35 9 53S 120 40 E
Melrose, N.S.W., Australia 45 32 42S 146 57 E
Melrose, W. Austral., Australia 47 27 50S 121 15 E
Melrose, U.K. 8 53 35N 2 44W
Melrose, U.S.A. 71 34 27N 103 33W
Melstone 72 46 36N 107 50W
Melton Mowbray 6 52 46N 0 52W
Melun 12 48 32N 2 39 E
Melut 51 10 30N 32 13 E
Melville 65 50 55N 102 50W
Melville, C. 44 14 11S 144 30 E
Melville, L. 63 53 30N 60 0W
Melville B. 44 12 0S 136 45 E
Melville I., Australia 46 11 30S 131 0 E
Melville I., Canada 58 75 30N 112 0W
Melville Pen. 61 68 0N 84 0W
Melvin → 64 59 11N 117 31W
Memba 55 14 11S 40 30 E
Memboro 35 9 30S 119 30 E
Memel = Klaipeda 22 55 43N 21 10 E
Memel 57 27 38S 29 36 E
Memmingen 14 47 59N 10 12 E
Mempawah 34 0 30N 109 5 E
Memphis, Tenn., U.S.A. 71 35 7N 90 0W
Memphis, Tex., U.S.A. 71 34 45N 100 30W
Mena 71 34 40N 94 15W
Menai Strait 6 53 14N 4 10W
Ménaka 53 15 59N 2 18 E
Menan = Chao Phraya → 34 13 32N 100 36 E
Menarandra → 57 25 17S 44 30 E
Menard 71 30 57N 99 48W
Menasha 68 44 13N 88 27W
Menate 34 0 12S 113 3 E
Mendawai → 34 3 30S 113 0 E
Mende 12 44 31N 3 30 E
Menderes → 30 37 25N 28 45 E
Mendip Hills 7 51 17N 2 40W
Mendocino 72 39 26N 123 50W
Mendocino, C. 72 40 26N 124 25W
Mendocino Seascarp 41 41 0N 140 0W
Mendota, Calif., U.S.A. 73 36 46N 120 24W
Mendota, Ill., U.S.A. 70 41 35N 89 5W
Mendoza 80 32 50S 68 52W
Mene Grande 78 9 49N 70 56W
Menemen 30 38 34N 27 3 E
Menen 11 50 47N 3 7 E
Menfi 18 37 36N 12 57 E
Mengcheng 39 33 18N 116 31 E
Menggala 34 4 30S 105 15 E
Mengshan 39 24 14N 110 55 E
Mengzi 37 23 20N 103 22 E
Menihek L. 63 54 0N 67 0W
Menin = Menen 11 50 47N 3 7 E
Menindee 45 32 20S 142 25 E
Menindee, L. 45 32 20S 142 25 E
Meningie 45 35 35S 139 0 E
Menominee 68 45 9N 87 39W
Menominee → 68 45 5N 87 36W
Menomonie 70 44 50N 91 54W
Menongue 55 14 48S 17 52 E
Menorca 13 40 0N 4 0 E
Mentawai, Kepulauan 34 2 0S 99 0 E
Menton 12 43 50N 7 29 E
Mentz Dam 56 33 10S 25 9 E
Menzelinsk 22 55 53N 53 1 E
Menzies 47 29 40S 120 58 E
Me'ona 28 33 1N 35 15 E
Meppel 68 52 42N 6 12 E
Mer Rouge 71 32 47N 91 48W
Merabéllou, Kólpos 19 35 10N 25 50 E
Meramangye, L. 47 28 25S 132 13 E
Meran = Merano 18 46 40N 11 10 E
Merano 18 46 40N 11 10 E
Merauke 35 8 29S 140 24 E
Merbabu 35 7 30S 110 40 E
Merbein 45 34 10S 142 2 E
Merca 29 1 48N 44 50 E
Merced 73 37 18N 120 30W
Mercedes, Buenos Aires, Argentina 80 34 40S 59 30W
Mercedes, Corrientes, Argentina 80 29 10S 58 5W
Mercedes, San Luis, Argentina 80 33 40S 65 21W
Mercedes, Uruguay 80 33 12S 58 0W
Merceditas 80 28 20S 70 35W
Mercer 43 37 16S 175 5 E
Mercy C. 61 65 0N 63 30W
Meredith, C. 80 52 15S 60 40W
Meredith, L. 71 35 30N 101 35W
Merga = Nukheila 51 19 1N 26 21 E
Mergui Arch. = Myeik Kyunzu 34 11 30N 97 30 E
Mérida, Mexico 74 20 9N 89 40W
Mérida, Spain 13 38 55N 6 25W
Mérida, Venezuela 78 8 24N 71 8W
Mérida, Cord. de 76 9 0N 71 0W
Meriden 68 41 33N 72 47W
Meridian, Idaho, U.S.A. 72 43 41N 116 25W
Meridian, Miss., U.S.A. 69 32 20N 88 42W
Meridian, Tex., U.S.A. 71 31 55N 97 37W
Meriruma 79 1 15N 54 50W
Merkel 71 32 30N 100 0W
Merksem 11 51 16N 4 25 E
Mermaid Reef 46 17 6S 119 36 E
Merowe 51 18 29N 31 46 E
Merredin 47 31 28S 118 18 E
Merrick 8 55 8N 4 30W
Merrill, Oreg., U.S.A. 72 42 2N 121 37W
Merrill, Wis., U.S.A. 70 45 11N 89 41W
Merriman 70 42 55N 101 42W
Merritt 64 50 10N 120 45W
Merriwa 45 32 6S 150 22 E
Merriwagga 45 33 47S 145 43 E
Merry I. 62 55 29N 77 31W
Merrygoen 45 31 51S 149 12 E
Merryville 71 30 47N 93 31W
Mersa Fatma 29 14 57N 40 17 E
Mersch 11 49 44N 6 7 E
Merseburg 14 51 20N 12 0 E
Mersey → 6 53 20N 2 56W
Merseyside □ 6 53 25N 2 55W
Mersin 30 36 51N 34 36 E
Mersing 34 2 25N 103 50 E
Merthyr Tydfil 7 51 45N 3 23W
Mértola 13 37 40N 7 40 E
Mertzon 71 31 17N 100 48W
Meru 54 0 3N 37 40 E
Mesa 73 33 20N 111 56W
Mesa, La, Calif., U.S.A. 73 32 48N 117 5W
Mesa, La, N. Mex., U.S.A. 73 32 6N 106 48W
Mesada 28 31 20N 35 19 E
Mesgouez, L. 62 51 20N 75 0W
Meshed = Mashhad 31 36 20N 59 35 E
Meshra er Req 51 8 25N 29 18 E
Mesick 68 44 24N 85 42W
Mesilinka → 64 56 6N 124 30W
Mesilla 73 32 20N 106 50W
Mesolóngion 19 38 21N 21 28 E
Mesopotamia = Al Jazirah 30 33 30N 44 0 E
Mesquite 73 36 47N 114 6W
Mess Cr. → 64 57 55N 131 14W
Messina, Italy 18 38 10N 15 32 E
Messina, S. Africa 57 22 20S 30 0 E
Messina, Str. di 18 38 5N 15 35 E
Messíni 19 37 4N 22 1 E
Messiniakós, Kólpos 19 36 45N 22 5 E
Mesta → 19 41 30N 24 0 E
Meta → 78 6 12N 67 28W
Metairie 71 29 59N 90 9W
Metaline Falls 72 48 52N 117 22W
Metán 80 25 30S 65 0W
Metangula 55 12 40S 34 50 E
Metema 51 12 56N 36 13 E
Methven 43 43 38S 171 40 E
Methy L. 65 56 28N 109 30W
Metil 55 16 24S 39 0 E
Metlakatla 64 55 10N 131 33W
Metropolis 71 37 10N 88 47W
Mettur Dam 32 11 45N 77 45 E
Metulla 28 33 17N 35 34 E
Metz 12 49 8N 6 10 E
Meulaboh 34 4 11N 96 3 E
Meureudu 34 5 19N 96 10 E
Meurthe-et-Moselle □ 12 48 52N 6 0 E
Meuse □ 12 49 8N 5 25 E
Meuse → 11 50 45N 5 41 E
Mexborough 6 53 29N 1 18W
Mexia 71 31 38N 96 32W
Mexiana, I. 79 0 0 49 30W
Mexicali 74 32 40N 115 30W
México, Mexico 74 19 20N 99 10W
Mexico, U.S.A. 70 39 10N 91 55W
México □ 74 19 20N 99 10W
Mexico ■ 74 25 0N 105 0W
Mexico, G. of 74 25 0N 90 0W
Meymaneh 31 35 53N 64 38 E
Mezen 22 65 50N 44 20 E
Mezen → 22 66 11N 43 59 E
Mezőkövesd 15 47 49N 20 35 E
Mezőtúr 15 47 0N 20 41 E
Mezquital 74 23 29N 104 23W
Mhow 32 22 33N 75 50 E
Miahuatlán 74 16 21N 96 36W
Miallo 44 16 28S 145 22 E
Miami, Ariz., U.S.A. 73 33 25N 110 54W
Miami, Fla., U.S.A. 69 25 45N 80 15W
Miami, Tex., U.S.A. 71 35 44N 100 38W
Miami → 68 39 20N 84 40W
Miami Beach 69 25 49N 80 6W
Miamisburg 68 39 40N 84 11W
Mian Xian 39 33 10N 106 32 E
Mianchi 39 34 48N 111 48 E
Mīāndowāb 30 37 0N 46 5 E
Miandrivazo 57 19 31S 45 29 E
Mīāneh 30 37 30N 47 40 E
Mianwali 32 32 38N 71 28 E
Mianyang, Hubei, China 39 30 25N 113 25 E
Mianyang, Sichuan, China 39 31 22N 104 47 E
Miaoli 39 24 37N 120 49 E
Miarinarivo 57 18 57S 46 55 E
Miass 22 54 59N 60 6 E
Michigan □ 67 44 40N 85 40W
Michigan, L. 68 44 0N 87 0W
Michigan City 68 41 42N 86 56W
Michikamau L. 63 54 20N 63 10W
Michipicoten 62 47 55N 84 55W
Michipicoten I. 62 47 40N 85 40W
Michoacan □ 74 19 0N 102 0W
Michurinsk 22 52 58N 40 27 E
Miclere 44 22 34S 147 32 E
Mico, Pta. 75 12 0N 83 30W
Micronesia 40 11 0N 160 0 E
Mid Glamorgan □ 7 51 40N 3 25W
Mid-Indian Ridge 40 40 0S 75 0 E
Mid-Oceanic Ridge 40 42 0S 90 0 E
Midai, P. 34 3 0N 107 47 E
Midale 65 49 25N 103 20W
Middelburg, Neth. 11 51 30N 3 36 E
Middelburg, C. Prov., S. Africa 56 31 30S 25 0 E
Middelburg, Trans., S. Africa 57 25 49S 29 28 E
Middelwit 56 24 51S 27 3 E
Middle Alkali L. 72 41 30N 120 3W
Middle Loup → 70 41 17N 98 23W
Middleport 68 39 0N 82 5W
Middlesboro 69 36 36N 83 43W
Middlesbrough 6 54 35N 1 14W
Middleton, Australia 44 22 22S 141 32 E
Middleton, Canada 63 44 57N 65 4W
Middletown, Conn., U.S.A. 68 41 37N 72 40W
Middletown, N.Y., U.S.A. 68 41 28N 74 28W
Middletown, Ohio, U.S.A. 68 39 29N 84 25W
Midi, Canal du → 12 43 45N 1 21 E
Midland, Australia 45 31 54S 115 59 E
Midland, Canada 62 44 45N 79 50W
Midland, Mich., U.S.A. 68 43 37N 84 17W
Midland, Tex., U.S.A. 71 32 0N 102 3W
Midleton 9 51 52N 8 12W
Midlothian 71 32 30N 97 0W
Midongy, Tangorombohitr' i 57 23 30S 47 0 E
Midongy Atsimo 57 23 35S 47 1 E
Midway Is. 2 28 13N 177 22W
Midwest 72 43 27N 106 19W
Midyat 30 37 25N 41 23 E
Mie □ 36 34 30N 136 10 E
Międzychód 14 52 35N 15 53 E
Międzyrzec Podlaski 15 51 58N 22 45 E
Mienga 56 17 12S 19 48 E
Miercurea Ciuc 15 46 21N 25 48 E
Mieres 13 43 18N 5 48W
Migdāl 28 32 51N 35 30 E
Migdal Afeq 28 32 5N 34 58 E
Miguel Alemán, Presa 74 18 15N 96 40W
Miguel Alves 79 4 11S 42 55W
Mihara 36 34 24N 133 5 E
Mikínai 19 37 43N 22 46 E
Mikkeli 21 61 43N 27 15 E
Mikkeli □ 20 62 0N 28 0 E
Mikkwa → 64 58 25N 114 46W
Míkonos 19 37 30N 25 25 E
Mikun 22 62 20N 50 0 E
Mikura-Jima 36 33 52N 139 36 E
Milaca 70 45 45N 93 40W
Milagro 78 2 11S 79 36W
Milan = Milano 18 45 28N 9 10 E
Milan, Mo., U.S.A. 70 40 10N 93 5W
Milan, Tenn., U.S.A. 69 35 55N 88 45W
Milang 45 32 2S 139 10 E
Milano 18 45 28N 9 10 E
Milâs 30 37 20N 27 50 E
Milazzo 18 38 13N 15 13 E
Milbank 70 45 17N 96 38W
Milden 65 51 29N 107 32W
Mildura 45 34 13S 142 9 E
Miles, Australia 45 26 40S 150 9 E
Miles, U.S.A. 71 31 39N 100 11W
Miles City 70 46 24N 105 50W
Milestone 65 49 59N 104 31W
Mileura 47 26 22S 117 20 E
Milford, Del., U.S.A. 68 38 52N 75 27W
Milford, Utah, U.S.A. 73 38 20N 113 0W
Milford Haven 7 51 43N 5 2W
Milford Sd. 43 44 41S 167 47 E
Milgun 47 25 6S 118 18 E
Milh, Bahr al 30 32 40N 43 35 E
Milh, Ras al 51 31 54N 25 6 E
Miliana 50 27 20N 2 32 E
Miling 47 30 30S 116 17 E
Milk → 72 48 5N 106 15W
Milk River 64 49 10N 112 5W
Mill City 72 44 45N 122 28W
Mille 69 33 7N 83 15W
Mille Lacs, L. 70 46 10N 93 30W
Mille Lacs, L. des 62 48 45N 90 35W
Millen 69 32 50N 81 57W
Miller 70 44 35N 98 59W
Millicent 45 37 34S 140 21 E
Millinocket 63 45 45N 68 45W
Millmerran 45 27 53S 151 16 E
Mills L. 64 61 30N 118 20W
Milltown Malbay 9 52 51N 9 25W
Millville 68 39 22N 75 0W
Millwood Res. 71 33 45N 94 0W
Milne → 44 21 10S 137 33 E
Milne Inlet 61 72 30N 80 0W
Milnor 70 46 19N 97 29W
Milo 64 50 34N 112 53W
Mílos 19 36 44N 24 25 E
Milparinka 45 29 46S 141 57 E
Milton, N.Z. 43 46 7S 169 59 E
Milton, U.K. 8 57 18N 4 32W
Milton, Fla., U.S.A. 69 30 38N 87 0W
Milton, Pa., U.S.A. 68 41 0N 76 53W
Milton-Freewater 72 45 57N 118 24W
Milton Keynes 7 52 3N 0 42W
Miltou 51 10 14N 17 26 E
Milwaukee 68 43 9N 87 58W
Milwaukie 72 45 27N 122 39W
Min Jiang →, Fujian, China 39 26 0N 119 35 E
Min Jiang →, Sichuan, China 37 28 45N 104 40 E
Min Xian 39 34 25N 104 0 E
Mina 73 38 21N 118 9W
Mina Pirquitas 80 22 40S 66 30W
Mīnā Su'ud 30 28 45N 48 28 E
Mīnā'al Aḥmadī 30 29 5N 48 10 E
Mīnāb 31 27 10N 57 1 E
Minago → 65 54 33N 98 59W
Minaki 65 49 59N 94 40W
Minamata 36 32 10N 130 30 E
Minas 80 34 20S 55 10W
Minas, Sierra de las 75 15 9N 89 31W
Minas Basin 63 45 20N 64 12W
Minas de Rio Tinto 13 37 42N 6 35W
Minas Gerais □ 79 18 50S 46 0W
Minatitlán 74 17 58N 94 35W
Minbu 33 20 10N 94 52 E
Mindanao 35 8 0N 125 0 E
Mindanao Sea = Bohol Sea 35 9 0N 124 0 E
Mindanao Trench 35 8 0N 128 0 E
Minden, Germany 14 52 18N 8 45 E
Minden, U.S.A. 71 32 40N 93 20W
Mindiptana 35 5 55S 140 22 E
Mindoro 35 13 0N 121 0 E
Mindoro Strait 35 12 30N 120 30 E
Mindouli 54 4 12S 14 28 E
Minehead 7 51 12N 3 29W
Mineola 71 32 40N 95 30W
Mineral Wells 71 32 50N 98 5W
Minersville 73 38 14N 112 58W
Mingan 63 50 20N 64 0W
Mingechaurskoye Vdkhr. 23 40 56N 47 20 E
Mingela 44 19 52S 146 38 E
Mingenew 47 29 12S 115 21 E
Mingera Cr. → 44 20 38S 137 45 E
Minggang 39 32 24N 114 3 E
Mingin 33 22 50N 94 30 E
Mingxi 39 26 18N 117 12 E
Minho □ 13 41 25N 8 20W
Minho → 13 41 58N 8 40W
Minidoka 72 42 47N 113 34W
Minigwal L. 47 29 31S 123 14 E
Minilya 47 23 55S 114 0 E
Minilya → 47 23 45S 114 0 E
Minipi, L. 63 52 25N 60 45W
Mink L. 64 61 54N 117 40W
Minna 53 9 37N 6 30 E
Minneapolis, Kans., U.S.A. 70 39 11N 97 40W
Minneapolis, Minn., U.S.A. 70 44 58N 93 20W
Minnedosa 65 50 14N 99 50W
Minnesota □ 70 46 40N 94 0W
Minnie Creek 47 24 3S 115 42 E
Minnitaki L. 62 49 57N 92 10W
Miño → 13 41 52N 8 40W
Minorca = Menorca 13 40 0N 4 0 E
Minore 45 32 14S 148 27 E
Minot 70 48 10N 101 15W
Minqing 39 26 15N 118 50 E
Minsk 22 53 52N 27 30 E
Mińsk Mazowiecki 15 52 10N 21 33 E
Mintaka Pass 32 37 0N 74 58 E
Minto 60 64 55N 149 20W
Minton 65 49 10N 104 35W
Minturn 72 39 35N 106 25W
Minusinsk 25 53 50N 91 20 E
Minutang 33 28 15N 96 30 E
Minvoul 54 2 9N 12 8 E
Mir 51 14 5N 11 59 E
Miraflores Locks 74 8 59N 79 36W
Miraj 32 16 50N 74 45 E
Miram 44 21 15S 148 55 E
Miram Shah 32 33 0N 70 2 E
Miramar 57 23 50S 35 35 E
Miramichi B. 63 47 15N 65 0W
Miranda 79 20 10S 56 15W

Nairn

Morton, Wash.,
U.S.A. 72 46 33N 122 17W
Morundah 45 34 57S 146 19 E
Moruya 45 35 58S 150 3 E
Morvan 12 47 5N 4 0 E
Morven 45 26 22S 147 5 E
Morvern 8 56 38N 5 44W
Morwell 45 38 10S 146 22 E
Morzhovets, Ostrov 22 66 44N 42 35 E
Moscos Is. 34 14 0N 97 30 E
Moscow = Moskva 22 55 45N 37 35 E
Moscow 72 46 45N 116 59W
Mosel → 11 50 22N 7 36 E
Moselle =
Mosel → 11 50 22N 7 36 E
Moselle □ 12 48 59N 6 33 E
Moses Lake 72 47 9N 119 17W
Mosgiel 43 45 53S 170 21 E
Moshi 54 3 22S 37 18 E
Moshupa 56 24 46S 25 29 E
Mosjøen 20 65 51N 13 12 E
Moskenesøya 20 67 58N 13 0 E
Moskenstraumen 20 67 47N 12 45 E
Moskva 22 55 45N 37 35 E
Moskva → 22 55 5N 38 51 E
Mosomane 56 24 2S 26 19 E
Mosquera 78 2 35N 78 24W
Mosquero 71 35 48N 103 57W
Mosquitos, G. de los 75 9 15N 81 10W
Moss 21 59 27N 10 40 E
Moss Vale 45 34 32S 150 25 E
Mossaka 54 1 15S 16 45 E
Mossbank 65 49 56N 105 56W
Mossburn 43 45 41S 168 15 E
Mosselbaai 56 34 11S 22 8 E
Mossendjo 54 2 55S 12 42 E
Mossgiel 45 33 15S 144 5 E
Mossman 44 16 21S 145 15 E
Mossoró 79 5 10S 37 15W
Mossuril 55 14 58S 40 42 E
Mossy → 65 54 5N 102 58W
Most 14 50 31N 13 38 E
Mosta 18 35 54N 14 24 E
Mostaganem 50 35 54N 0 5 E
Mostar 19 43 22N 17 50 E
Mostardas 80 31 2S 50 51W
Mosul = Al Mawşil 30 36 15N 43 5 E
Motagua → 75 15 44N 88 14W
Motala 21 58 32N 15 1 E
Motherwell 8 55 48N 4 0W
Motihari 33 26 30N 84 55 E
Motozintla de
Mendoza 74 15 21N 92 14W
Mott 70 46 25N 102 29W
Motueka 43 41 7S 173 1 E
Motul 74 21 0N 89 20W
Mouanda 54 1 28S 13 7 E
Mouchalagane → 63 50 56N 68 41W
Moúdhros 19 39 50N 25 18 E
Moudjeria 50 17 50N 12 28W
Mouila 54 1 50S 11 0 E
Moulamein 45 35 3S 144 1 E
Moule 75 16 20N 61 22W
Moulins 12 46 35N 3 19 E
Moulmein 33 16 30N 97 40 E
Moulton 71 29 35N 97 8W
Moultrie 69 31 11N 83 47W
Moultrie, L. 69 33 25N 80 10W
Mound City, Mo.,
U.S.A. 70 40 2N 95 25W
Mound City, S. Dak.,
U.S.A. 70 45 46N 100 3W
Moundou 51 8 40N 16 10 E
Moundsville 68 39 53N 80 43W
Mount Airy 69 36 31N 80 37W
Mount Amherst 46 18 24S 126 58 E
Mount Angel 72 45 4N 122 46W
Mount Augustus 47 24 20S 116 56 E
Mount Barker,
S. Austral.,
Australia 45 35 5S 138 52 E
Mount Barker,
W. Austral.,
Australia 47 34 38S 117 40 E
Mount Carmel 68 38 20N 87 48W
Mount Clemens 62 42 35N 82 50W
Mount Coolon 44 21 25S 147 25 E
Mount Darwin 55 16 47S 31 38 E
Mount Desert I. 63 44 15N 68 25W
Mount Dora 69 28 49N 81 32W
Mount Douglas 44 21 35S 146 50 E
Mount Edgecumbe 64 57 8N 135 22W
Mount Elizabeth 46 16 0S 125 50 E
Mount Fletcher 57 30 40S 28 30 E
Mount Forest 62 43 59N 80 43W
Mount Gambier 45 37 50S 140 46 E
Mount Garnet 44 17 37S 145 6 E
Mount Hope,
N.S.W., Australia 45 32 51S 145 51 E
Mount Hope,
S. Austral.,
Australia 45 34 7S 135 23 E
Mount Hope, U.S.A. 68 37 52N 81 9W
Mount Horeb 70 43 0N 89 42W
Mount Howitt 45 26 31S 142 16 E
Mount Isa 44 20 42S 139 26 E
Mount Keith 47 27 15S 120 30 E
Mount Larcom 44 23 48S 150 59 E
Mount Lofty Ra. 45 34 35S 139 5 E
Mount McKinley
Nat. Park 60 64 0N 150 0W
Mount Magnet 47 28 2S 117 47 E
Mount Margaret 45 26 54S 143 21 E
Mount Maunganui 43 37 40S 176 14 E
Mount Molloy 44 16 42S 145 20 E
Mount Monger 47 31 0S 122 0 E
Mount Morgan 44 23 40S 150 25 E
Mount Morris 68 42 43N 77 50W
Mount Mulligan 44 16 45S 144 47 E
Mount Narryer 47 26 30S 115 55 E
Mount Oxide Mine 44 19 30S 139 29 E
Mount Pearl 63 47 31N 52 47W
Mount Perry 45 25 13S 151 42 E
Mount Phillips 47 24 25S 116 15 E
Mount Pleasant,
Iowa, U.S.A. 70 40 58N 91 35W
Mount Pleasant,
Mich., U.S.A. 68 43 35N 84 47W
Mount Pleasant,
S.C., U.S.A. 69 32 45N 79 48W
Mount Pleasant,
Tenn., U.S.A. 69 35 31N 87 11W
Mount Pleasant,
Tex., U.S.A. 71 33 5N 95 0W
Mount Pleasant,
Utah, U.S.A. 72 39 40N 111 29W
Mount Rainier Nat.
Park. 72 46 50N 121 43W
Mount Revelstoke
Nat. Park 64 51 5N 118 30W
Mount Robson Prov.
Park 64 53 0N 119 0W
Mount Sandiman 47 24 25S 115 30 E
Mount Shasta 72 41 20N 122 18W
Mount Sterling, Ill.,
U.S.A. 70 39 59N 90 40W
Mount Sterling, Ky.,
U.S.A. 68 38 3N 83 57W
Mount Surprise 44 18 10S 144 17 E
Mount Vernon,
Australia 47 24 9S 118 2 E
Mount Vernon, Ind.,
U.S.A. 70 38 17N 88 57W
Mount Vernon, N.Y.,
U.S.A. 68 40 57N 73 49W
Mount Vernon, Ohio,
U.S.A. 68 40 20N 82 30W
Mount Vernon,
Wash., U.S.A. 72 48 25N 122 20W
Mountain City, Nev.,
U.S.A. 72 41 54N 116 0W
Mountain City,
Tenn., U.S.A. 69 36 30N 81 50W
Mountain Grove 71 37 5N 92 20W
Mountain Home,
Ark., U.S.A. 71 36 20N 92 25W
Mountain Home,
Idaho, U.S.A. 72 43 11N 115 45W
Mountain Iron 70 47 30N 92 37W
Mountain Park 64 52 50N 117 15W
Mountain View, Ark.,
U.S.A. 71 35 52N 92 10W
Mountain View,
Calif., U.S.A. 73 37 26N 122 5W
Mountainair 73 34 35N 106 15W
Mountmellick 9 53 7N 7 20W
Moura, Australia 44 24 35S 149 58 E
Moura, Brazil 78 1 32S 61 38W
Mourdi, Dépression
du 51 18 10N 23 0 E
Mourdiah 50 14 35N 7 25W
Moure, La 70 46 27N 98 17W
Mourilyan 44 17 35S 146 3 E
Mourne → 9 54 45N 7 39W
Mourne Mts. 9 54 10N 6 0W
Mouscron 11 50 45N 3 12 E
Moussoro 51 13 41N 16 35 E
Moutong 35 0 28N 121 13 E
Moville 9 55 11N 7 3W
Moy → 9 54 5N 8 50W
Moyale, Ethiopia 29 3 34N 39 4 E
Moyale, Kenya 54 3 30N 39 0 E
Moyamba 50 8 4N 12 30W
Moyen Atlas 50 33 0N 5 0W
Moyle □ 9 55 10N 6 15W
Moyo 34 8 10S 117 40 E
Moyobamba 78 6 0S 77 0W
Moyyero → 25 68 44N 103 42 E
Mozambique =
Moçambique 55 15 3S 40 42 E
Mozambique ■ 55 19 0S 35 0 E
Mozambique Chan. 57 17 30S 42 30 E
Mozdok 23 43 45N 44 48 E
Mozyr 22 52 0N 29 15 E
Mpanda 54 6 23S 31 1 E
Mpika 55 11 51S 31 25 E
Mporokoso 52 9 25S 30 5 E
Mpumalanga 57 29 50S 30 33 E
Mpwapwa 54 6 23S 36 30 E
Msaken 51 35 49N 10 33 E
Msoro 55 13 35S 31 50 E
Mtubatuba 57 28 30S 32 8 E
Mtwara-Mikindani 52 10 20S 40 20 E
Mu Us Shamo 38 39 0N 109 0 E
Muaná 79 1 25S 49 15W
Muar 34 2 3N 102 34 E
Muarabungo 34 1 28S 102 52 E
Muaraenim 34 3 40S 103 50 E
Muarajuloi 34 0 12S 114 3 E
Muarakaman 34 0 2S 116 45 E
Muaratebo 34 1 30S 102 26 E
Muaratembesi 34 1 42S 103 8 E
Muaratewe 34 0 58S 114 52 E
Mubende 54 0 33N 31 22 E
Mubi 53 10 18N 13 16 E
Muck 8 56 50N 6 15W
Muckadilla 45 26 35S 148 23 E
Muconda 54 10 31S 21 15 E
Mucuri 79 18 0S 39 36W
Mucusso 56 18 1S 21 25 E
Mudanjiang 38 44 38N 129 30 E
Muddy → 73 38 0N 110 22W
Mudgee 45 32 32S 149 31 E
Mudjatik → 65 56 1N 107 36W
Muêda 52 11 36S 39 28 E
Mueller Ra. 46 18 18S 126 46 E
Muerto, Mar 74 16 10N 94 10W
Mufulira 55 12 32S 28 15 E
Muğla 30 37 15N 28 22 E
Mugu 33 29 45N 82 30 E
Muhammad Qol 51 20 53N 37 9 E
Muharraqa = Sa'ad 28 31 28N 34 33 E
Muikamachi 36 37 15N 138 50 E
Muine Bheag 9 52 42N 6 57W
Muir, L. 47 34 30S 116 40 E
Mukah 34 2 55N 112 5 E
Mukden =
Shenyang 38 41 48N 123 27 E
Mukhtuya = Lensk 25 60 48N 114 55 E
Mukinbudin 47 30 55S 118 5 E
Mukomuko 34 2 30S 101 10 E
Muktsar 32 30 30N 74 30 E
Mukur 32 32 50N 67 42 E
Mukutawa → 65 53 10N 97 24W
Mulchén 80 37 45S 72 20W
Mulde → 14 51 50N 12 15 E
Mule Creek 70 43 19N 104 8W
Muleba 52 1 50S 31 37 E
Muleshoe 71 34 17N 102 42W
Mulgathing 45 30 15S 134 8 E
Mulgrave 63 45 38N 61 31W
Mulhacén 13 37 4N 3 20W
Mülheim 14 51 26N 6 53 E
Mulhouse 14 47 40N 7 20 E
Muling He → 38 45 53N 133 30 E
Mull 8 56 27N 6 0W
Mullaittvu 32 9 15N 80 49 E
Mullen 70 42 5N 101 0W
Mullengudgery 45 31 43S 147 23 E
Mullens 68 37 34N 81 22W
Muller, Pegunungan 34 0 30N 113 30 E
Mullet Pen. 9 54 10N 10 2W
Mullewa 47 28 29S 115 30 E
Mulligan → 45 26 40S 139 0 E
Mullin 71 31 33N 98 38W
Mullingar 9 53 31N 7 20W
Mullins 69 34 12N 79 15W
Mullumbimby 45 28 30S 153 30 E
Multan 32 30 15N 71 36 E
Mulvane 71 37 30N 97 15W
Mumbwa 55 15 0S 27 0 E
Muna 35 5 0S 122 30 E
München 14 48 8N 11 33 E
Munchen-Gladbach
=
Mönchengladbach 14 51 12N 6 23 E
Muncho Lake 64 59 0N 125 50W
Muncie 68 40 10N 85 20W
Mundala 35 4 30S 141 0 E
Mundare 64 53 35N 112 20W
Munday 71 33 26N 99 39W
Münden 14 51 25N 9 42 E
Mundiwindi 46 23 47S 120 9 E
Mundo Novo 79 11 50S 40 29W
Mundrabilla 47 31 52S 127 51 E
Mungallala 45 26 28S 147 34 E
Mungallala Cr. → 45 28 53S 147 5 E
Mungana 44 17 8S 144 27 E
Mungbere 54 2 36N 28 28 E
Munger 33 25 23N 86 30 E
Mungindi 45 28 58S 149 1 E
Munhango 55 12 10S 18 38 E
Munich = München 14 48 8N 11 33 E
Munising 68 46 25N 86 39W
Munku-Sardyk 25 51 45N 100 20 E
Muñoz Gamero,
Pen. 80 52 30S 73 5 E
Munroe L. 65 59 13N 98 35W
Münster 14 51 58N 7 37 E
Munster □ 9 52 20N 8 40W
Muntadgin 47 31 45S 118 33 E
Muntok 34 2 5S 105 10 E
Munyak 24 43 30N 59 15 E
Muonio 20 67 57N 23 40 E
Mupa 55 16 5S 15 50 E
Muping 38 37 22N 121 36 E
Muqdisho 29 2 2N 45 25 E
Mur → 14 46 35N 16 3 E
Murallón, Cuerro 80 49 48S 73 30W
Murang'a 54 0 45S 37 9 E
Murashi 22 59 30N 49 0 E
Murchison → 47 27 45S 114 0 E
Murchison Falls =
Kabarega Falls 54 2 15N 31 30 E
Murchison House 47 27 39S 114 14 E
Murchison Ra. 44 20 0S 134 10 E
Murcia 13 38 20N 1 10W
Murcia □ 13 37 50N 1 30W
Murdo 70 43 56N 100 43W
Murdoch Pt. 44 14 37S 144 55 E
Mureş → 15 46 15N 20 13 E
Mureşul =
Mureş → 15 46 15N 20 13 E
Murfreesboro 69 35 50N 86 21W
Murgab 24 38 10N 74 2 E
Murgon 45 26 15S 151 54 E
Murgoo 47 27 24S 116 28 E
Muria 35 6 36S 110 53 E
Müritz See 14 53 25N 12 40 E
Murmansk 22 68 57N 33 10 E
Murom 22 55 35N 42 3 E
Muroran 36 42 25N 141 0 E
Muroto-Misaki 36 33 15N 134 10 E
Murphy 72 43 11N 116 33W
Murphysboro 71 37 50N 89 20W
Murray, Ky., U.S.A. 69 36 40N 88 20W
Murray, Utah, U.S.A. 72 40 41N 111 58W
Murray →,
Australia 45 35 20S 139 22 E
Murray →, Canada 64 56 11N 120 45W
Murray, L. 69 34 8N 81 30W
Murray Bridge 45 35 6S 139 14 E
Murray Downs 44 21 4S 134 40 E
Murray Harbour 63 46 0N 62 28W
Murray Seascarp 41 30 0N 135 0W
Murraysburg 56 31 58S 23 47 E
Murree 32 33 56N 73 28 E
Murrin Murrin 47 28 58S 121 33 E
Murrumbidgee → 45 34 43S 143 12 E
Murrumburrah 45 34 32S 148 22 E
Murrurundi 45 31 42S 150 51 E
Mursala 34 1 41N 98 28 E
Murtle L. 64 52 8N 119 38W
Murtoa 45 36 35S 142 28 E
Murwara 33 23 46N 80 28 E
Murwillumbah 45 28 18S 153 27 E
Mürzzuschlag 14 47 36N 15 41 E
Muş 30 38 45N 41 30 E
Mûsa, G. 30 28 33N 33 59 E
Musa Khel 32 30 59N 69 52 E
Mūsā Qal'eh 31 32 20N 64 50 E
Musaffargarh 32 30 10N 71 10 E
Musala 19 42 13N 23 37 E
Musan 38 42 12N 129 12 E
Musay'id 31 25 0N 51 33 E
Muscat = Masqat 31 23 37N 58 36 E
Muscat & Oman =
Oman ■ 29 23 0N 58 0 E
Muscatine 70 41 25N 91 5W
Musgrave Ras. 47 26 0S 132 0 E
Mushie 54 2 56S 16 55 E
Mushin 53 6 32N 3 21 E
Musi → 34 2 20S 104 56 E
Muskeg → 64 60 20N 123 20W
Muskegon 68 43 15N 86 17W
Muskegon → 68 43 25N 86 0W
Muskegon Hts. 68 43 12N 86 17W
Muskogee 71 35 50N 95 25W
Muskwa → 64 58 47N 122 48W
Musmar 51 18 13N 35 40 E
Musoma 54 1 30S 33 48 E
Musquaro, L. 63 50 38N 61 5W
Musquodoboit
Harbour 63 44 50N 63 9W
Musselburgh 8 55 57N 3 3W
Musselshell → 72 47 21N 107 58W
Mussoorie 32 30 27N 78 6 E
Mussuco 56 17 2S 19 3 E
Mustang 33 29 10N 83 55 E
Musters, L. 80 45 20S 69 25W
Muswellbrook 45 32 16S 150 56 E
Mût, Egypt 51 25 28N 28 58 E
Mut, Turkey 30 36 40N 33 28 E
Mutanda 57 21 0S 33 34 E
Mutaray 25 60 56N 101 0 E
Mutare 55 18 58S 32 38 E
Muting 35 7 23S 140 20 E
Mutsu-Wan 36 41 5N 140 55 E
Muttaburra 44 22 38S 144 29 E
Muxima 54 9 33S 13 58 E
Muya 25 56 27N 115 50 E
Muzaffarabad 32 34 25N 73 30 E
Muzaffarnagar 32 29 26N 77 40 E
Muzaffarpur 33 26 7N 85 23 E
Muzhi 24 65 25N 64 40 E
Muzon C. 64 54 40N 132 40W
Muztag 37 36 20N 87 28 E
Mvuma 55 19 16S 30 30 E
Mwanza, Tanzania 54 2 30S 32 58 E
Mwanza, Zaïre 54 7 55S 26 43 E
Mweelrea 9 53 37N 9 48W
Mweka 54 4 50S 21 34 E
Mwenezi 55 21 15S 30 48 E
Mwenga 54 3 1S 28 28 E
Mweru, L. 54 9 0S 28 40 E
Mwinilunga 55 11 43S 24 25 E
Mwirasandu 52 0 56S 30 22 E
My Tho 34 10 29N 106 23 E
Myanaung 33 18 18N 95 22 E
Myaungmya 33 16 30N 94 40 E
Mycenae = Mikinai 19 37 43N 22 46 E
Myeik Kyunzu 34 11 30N 97 30 E
Myingyan 33 21 30N 95 20 E
Myitkyina 33 25 24N 97 26 E
Mymensingh 33 24 45N 90 24 E
Mynydd Du 7 51 45N 3 45W
Mýrdalsjökull 20 63 40N 19 6W
Myrtle Beach 69 33 43N 78 50W
Myrtle Creek 72 43 0N 123 9W
Myrtle Point 72 43 0N 124 4W
Mysore 32 12 17N 76 41 E
Mysore □ =
Karnataka □ 32 13 15N 77 0 E
Myton 72 40 10N 110 2W
Mývatn 20 65 36N 17 0W
Mzimkulu → 57 30 44S 30 28 E
Mzimvubu → 57 31 38S 29 33 E

N

Naab → 14 49 1N 12 2 E
Na'an 28 31 53N 34 52 E
Naantali 21 60 29N 22 2 E
Naas 9 53 12N 6 40W
Nababiep 56 29 36S 17 46 E
Nabawa 47 28 30S 114 48 E
Nabberu, L. 47 25 50S 120 30 E
Nabeul 51 36 30N 10 44 E
Nabire 35 3 15S 135 26 E
Nabisipi → 63 50 14N 62 13W
Nablus = Nābulus 28 32 14N 35 15 E
Naboomspruit 57 24 32S 28 40 E
Nābulus 28 32 14N 35 15 E
Naches 72 46 48N 120 42W
Nachingwea 54 10 23S 38 49 E
Nackara 45 32 48S 139 12 E
Naco 73 31 24N 109 58W
Nacogdoches 71 31 33N 94 39W
Nacozari 74 30 24N 109 39W
Nadiad 32 22 41N 72 56 E
Nadūshan 31 32 2N 53 35 E
Nadvoitsy 22 63 52N 34 14 E
Nadym 24 65 35N 72 42 E
Nadym → 24 66 12N 72 0 E
Nafada 53 11 8N 11 20 E
Naftshahr 30 34 0N 45 30 E
Nafūd ad Dahy 30 22 0N 45 0 E
Naga 35 13 38N 123 15 E
Naga Hills 33 26 0N 94 30 E
Nagagami → 62 49 40N 84 40W
Nagaland □ 33 26 0N 94 30 E
Nagano 36 36 40N 138 10 E
Nagano □ 36 36 15N 138 0 E
Nagaoka 36 37 27N 138 51 E
Nagappattinam 32 10 46N 79 51 E
Nagar Parkar 32 24 30N 70 35 E
Nagasaki 36 32 47N 129 50 E
Nagasaki □ 36 32 50N 129 40 E
Nagaur 32 27 15N 73 45 E
Nagercoil 32 8 12N 77 26 E
Nagīneh 31 34 20N 57 15 E
Nagoorin 44 24 17S 151 15 E
Nagornyy 25 55 58N 124 57 E
Nagoya 36 35 10N 136 50 E
Nagpur 32 21 8N 79 10 E
Nagykanizsa 14 46 28N 17 0 E
Nagykörös 15 47 5N 19 48 E
Naha 39 26 13N 127 42 E
Nahalal 28 32 41N 35 12 E
Nahanni Butte 64 61 2N 123 31W
Nahanni Nat. Park 64 61 15N 125 0W
Nahariyya 28 33 1N 35 5 E
Nahāvand 30 34 10N 48 22 E
Nahf 28 32 56N 35 18 E
Nahlin 64 58 55N 131 38W
Naicam 65 52 30N 104 30W
Nā'ifah 29 19 59N 50 46 E
Nain, Canada 63 56 34N 61 40W
Nā'īn, Iran 31 32 54N 53 0 E
Nainpur 32 22 30N 80 10 E
Naira 35 4 28S 130 0 E
Nairn 8 57 35N 3 54W

Nairobi

Nairobi **54** 1 17S 36 48 E
Naivasha **54** 0 40S 36 30 E
Najafābād **31** 32 40N 51 15 E
Najd **30** 26 30N 42 0 E
Najibabad **32** 29 40N 78 20 E
Najin **38** 42 12N 130 15 E
Nakadōri-Shima **36** 32 57N 129 4 E
Nakamura **36** 33 0N 133 0 E
Nakfa **51** 16 40N 38 32 E
Nakhichevan A.S.S.R. □ **23** 39 14N 45 30 E
Nakhodka **25** 42 53N 132 54 E
Nakhon Phanom **34** 17 23N 104 43 E
Nakhon Ratchasima **34** 14 59N 102 12 E
Nakhon Sawan **34** 15 35N 100 10 E
Nakhon Si Thammarat **34** 8 29N 100 0 E
Nakina, B.C., Canada **64** 59 12N 132 52W
Nakina, Ont., Canada **62** 50 10N 86 40W
Nakskov **21** 54 50N 11 8 E
Naktong → **38** 35 7N 128 57 E
Nakuru **54** 0 15S 36 4 E
Nakusp **64** 50 20N 117 45W
Nal → **32** 25 20N 65 30 E
Nalchik **23** 43 30N 43 33 E
Nalgonda **32** 17 6N 79 15 E
Nallamalai Hills **32** 15 30N 78 50 E
Nalón → **13** 43 32N 6 4W
Nālūt **51** 31 54N 11 0 E
Nam Co **37** 30 30N 90 45 E
Nam-Phan **34** 10 30N 106 0 E
Namacunde **56** 17 18S 15 50 E
Namacurra **57** 17 30S 36 50 E
Namak, Daryācheh-ye **31** 34 30N 52 0 E
Namak, Kavir-e **31** 34 30N 57 30 E
Namaland **56** 24 30S 17 0 E
Namangan **24** 41 0N 71 40 E
Namapa **55** 13 43S 39 50 E
Namaqualand **56** 30 0S 17 25 E
Namasagali **52** 1 2N 33 0 E
Namber **35** 1 2S 134 49 E
Nambour **45** 26 32S 152 58 E
Nambucca Heads **45** 30 37S 153 0 E
Nameh **34** 2 34N 116 21 E
Namew L. **65** 54 14N 101 56W
Namib Desert = Namibwoestyn **56** 22 30S 15 0 E
Namibe **55** 15 7S 12 11 E
Namibe □ **56** 16 35S 12 30 E
Namibia ■ **56** 22 0S 18 9 E
Namibwoestyn **56** 22 30S 15 0 E
Namlea **35** 3 18S 127 5 E
Namoi → **45** 30 12S 149 30 E
Nampa **72** 43 34N 116 34W
Nampula **55** 15 6S 39 15 E
Namrole **35** 3 46S 126 46 E
Namse Shankou **33** 30 0N 82 25 E
Namsen → **20** 64 27N 11 42 E
Namsos **20** 64 29N 11 30 E
Namtay **25** 62 43N 129 37 E
Namtu **33** 23 5N 97 28 E
Namu **64** 51 52N 127 50W
Namur **11** 50 27N 4 52 E
Namur □ **11** 50 17N 5 0 E
Namutoni **56** 18 49S 16 55 E
Namwala **55** 15 44S 26 30 E
Nanaimo **64** 49 10N 124 0W
Nanam **38** 41 44N 129 40 E
Nanan **39** 24 59N 118 21 E
Nanango **45** 26 40S 152 0 E
Nan'ao, China **39** 23 28N 117 5 E
Nanao, Japan **36** 37 0N 137 0 E
Nanbu **39** 31 18N 106 3 E
Nanchang **39** 28 42N 115 55 E
Nancheng **39** 27 33N 116 35 E
Nanching = Nanjing **39** 32 2N 118 47 E
Nanchong **39** 30 43N 106 2 E
Nanchuan **39** 29 9N 107 6 E
Nancy **12** 48 42N 6 12 E
Nanda Devi **32** 30 23N 79 59 E
Nandan **39** 24 58N 107 29 E
Nanded **32** 19 10N 77 20 E
Nandewar Ra. **45** 30 15S 150 35 E
Nandi **43** 17 42S 177 20 E
Nandurbar **32** 21 20N 74 15 E
Nandyal **32** 15 30N 78 30 E
Nanga **47** 26 7S 113 45 E
Nanga-Eboko **54** 4 41N 12 22 E
Nanga Parbat **32** 35 10N 74 35 E
Nangapinoh **34** 0 20S 111 44 E
Nangarhár □ **31** 34 20N 70 0 E
Nangatayap **34** 1 32S 110 34 E
Nanjiang **39** 32 28N 106 51 E
Nanjing **39** 32 2N 118 47 E
Nankang **39** 25 40N 114 45 E
Nanking = Nanjing **39** 32 2N 118 47 E
Nanning **39** 22 48N 108 20 E
Nannup **47** 33 59S 115 48 E
Nanpi **38** 38 2N 116 45 E
Nanping **39** 26 38N 118 10 E
Nansei-Shotō **37** 26 0N 128 0 E
Nantes **12** 47 12N 1 33W
Nanticoke **68** 41 12N 76 1W
Nanton **64** 50 21N 113 46W
Nantong **39** 32 1N 120 52 E
Nantucket I. **58** 41 16N 70 3W
Nanuque **79** 17 50S 40 21W
Nanutarra **46** 22 32S 115 30 E
Nanxiong **39** 25 6N 114 15 E
Nanyang **39** 33 11N 112 30 E
Nanyuan **38** 39 44N 116 22 E
Nanyuki **54** 0 2N 37 4 E
Nanzhang **39** 31 45N 111 50 E
Náo, C. de la **13** 38 44N 0 14 E
Naococane L. **63** 52 50N 70 45W
Naoetsu **36** 37 12N 138 10 E
Naoli He → **38** 47 18N 134 9 E
Napa **72** 38 18N 122 17W
Napanee **62** 44 15N 77 0W
Napier **43** 39 30S 176 56 E
Napier Broome B. **46** 14 2S 126 37 E
Napier Downs **46** 17 11S 124 36 E
Napier Pen. **44** 12 4S 135 43 E
Naples = Nápoli **18** 40 50N 14 17 E
Naples **69** 26 10N 81 45W
Napo → **78** 3 20S 72 40W
Napoleon, N. Dak., U.S.A. **70** 46 32N 99 49W
Napoleon, Ohio, U.S.A. **68** 41 24N 84 7W
Nápoli **18** 40 50N 14 17 E
Nappa Merrie **45** 27 36S 141 7 E
Nara, Japan **36** 34 40N 135 49 E
Nara, Mali **50** 15 10N 7 20W
Nara □ **36** 34 30N 136 0 E
Nara Visa **71** 35 39N 103 10W
Naracoorte **45** 36 58S 140 45 E
Naradhan **45** 33 34S 146 17 E
Narasapur **33** 16 26N 81 40 E
Narathiwat **34** 6 30N 101 48 E
Narayanganj **33** 23 40N 90 33 E
Narayanpet **32** 16 45N 77 30 E
Narbonne **12** 43 11N 3 0 E
Nardò **19** 40 10N 18 0 E
Narembeen **47** 32 7S 118 24 E
Nares Stræde **58** 80 0N 70 0W
Naretha **47** 31 0S 124 45 E
Narin **32** 36 5N 69 0 E
Narindra, Helodranon' i **57** 14 55S 47 30 E
Narmada → **32** 21 38N 72 36 E
Narodnaya **22** 65 5N 60 0 E
Narok **52** 1 55S 35 52 E
Narooma **45** 36 14S 150 4 E
Narrabri **45** 30 19S 149 46 E
Narran → **45** 28 37S 148 12 E
Narrandera **45** 34 42S 146 31 E
Narraway → **64** 55 44N 119 55W
Narrogin **47** 32 58S 117 14 E
Narromine **45** 32 12S 148 12 E
Narsimhapur **32** 22 54N 79 14 E
Narva **22** 59 23N 28 12 E
Narvik **20** 68 28N 17 26 E
Naryan-Mar **22** 68 0N 53 0 E
Naryilco **45** 28 37S 141 53 E
Narym **24** 59 0N 81 30 E
Narymskoye **24** 49 10N 84 15 E
Naryn **24** 41 26N 75 58 E
Nasa **20** 66 29N 15 23 E
Nasarawa **53** 8 32N 7 41 E
Naseby **43** 45 1S 170 10 E
Naser, Buheirat en **51** 23 0N 32 30 E
Nashua, Iowa, U.S.A. **70** 42 55N 92 34W
Nashua, Mont., U.S.A. **72** 48 10N 106 25W
Nashua, N.H., U.S.A. **68** 42 50N 71 25W
Nashville, Ark., U.S.A. **71** 33 56N 93 50W
Nashville, Ga., U.S.A. **69** 31 3N 83 15W
Nashville, Tenn., U.S.A. **69** 36 12N 86 46W
Nasik **32** 19 58N 73 50 E
Nasirabad **32** 26 15N 74 45 E
Naskaupi → **63** 53 47N 60 51W
Nass → **64** 55 0N 129 40W
Nassau **75** 25 0N 77 20W
Nassau, B. **80** 55 20S 68 0W
Nasser, L. = Naser, Buheirat en **51** 23 0N 32 30 E
Nässjö **21** 57 39N 14 42 E
Nat Kyizin **33** 14 57N 97 59 E
Nata **56** 20 12S 26 12 E
Natagaima **78** 3 37N 75 6W
Natal, Brazil **79** 5 47S 35 13W
Natal, Canada **64** 49 43N 114 51W
Natal, Indonesia **34** 0 35N 99 7 E
Natal □ **57** 28 30S 30 30 E
Naṭanz **31** 33 30N 51 55 E
Natashquan **63** 50 14N 61 46W
Natashquan → **63** 50 7N 61 50W
Natchez **71** 31 35N 91 25W
Natchitoches **71** 31 47N 93 4W
Nathalia **45** 36 1S 145 13 E
Nathdwara **32** 24 55N 73 50 E
Natimuk **45** 36 42S 142 0 E
Nation → **64** 55 30N 123 32W
National City **73** 32 39N 117 7W
Natitingou **53** 10 20N 1 26 E
Natividad, I. **74** 27 50N 115 10W
Natoma **70** 39 14N 99 0W
Natron, L. **54** 2 20S 36 0 E
Natuna Besar, Kepulauan **34** 4 0N 108 15 E
Natuna Selatan, Kepulauan **34** 2 45N 109 0 E
Naturaliste C. **44** 40 50S 148 15 E
Naubinway **62** 46 7N 85 27W
Naumburg **14** 51 10N 11 48 E
Nauru ■ **3** 1 0S 166 0 E
Naushahra = Nowshera **32** 34 0N 72 0 E
Nauta **78** 4 31S 73 35W
Nautanwa **33** 27 20N 83 25 E
Nautla **74** 20 20N 96 50W
Navajo Res. **73** 36 55N 107 30W
Navalcarnero **13** 40 17N 4 5W
Navan = An Uaimh **9** 53 39N 6 40W
Navarino, I. **80** 55 0S 67 40W
Navarra □ **13** 42 40N 1 40W
Navasota **71** 30 20N 96 5W
Navassa **75** 18 30N 75 0W
Naver → **8** 58 34N 4 15W
Navoi **24** 40 9N 65 22 E
Navojoa **74** 27 0N 109 30W
Navolok **22** 62 33N 39 57 E
Návpaktos **19** 38 23N 21 50 E
Návplion **19** 37 33N 22 50 E
Navsari **32** 20 57N 72 59 E
Nawabshah **32** 26 15N 68 25 E
Nawakot **33** 27 55N 85 10 E
Nawalgarh **32** 27 50N 75 15 E
Nawāsīf, Harrat **30** 21 20N 42 10 E
Náxos **19** 37 8N 25 25 E
Nāy Band **31** 27 20N 52 40 E
Nayakhan **25** 61 56N 159 0 E
Nayarit □ **74** 22 0N 105 0W
Nazareth = Nazerat **28** 32 42N 35 17 E
Nazas **74** 25 10N 104 6W
Nazas → **74** 25 35N 103 25W
Naze, The **7** 51 53N 1 19 E
Nazerat **28** 32 42N 35 17 E
Nazir Hat **33** 22 35N 91 49 E
Nazko **64** 53 1N 123 37W
Nazko → **64** 53 7N 123 34W
Ncheu **55** 14 50S 34 47 E
Ndala **52** 4 45S 33 15 E
Ndalatando **54** 9 12S 14 48 E
Ndélé **51** 8 25N 20 36 E
Ndendé **54** 2 22S 11 23 E
Ndjamena **51** 12 10N 14 59 E
Ndjolé **54** 0 10S 10 45 E
Ndola **55** 13 0S 28 34 E
Neagh, Lough **9** 54 35N 6 25W
Neah Bay **72** 48 25N 124 40W
Neale L. **46** 24 15S 130 0 E
Near Is. **60** 53 0N 172 0 E
Neath **7** 51 39N 3 49W
Nebine Cr. → **45** 29 27S 146 56 E
Nebit Dag **23** 39 30N 54 22 E
Nebo **44** 59 12N 32 25 E
Nebraska □ **70** 41 30N 100 0W
Nebraska City **70** 40 40N 95 52W
Nébrodi, Monti **18** 37 55N 14 50 E
Necedah **70** 44 2N 90 7W
Nechako → **64** 53 30N 122 44W
Neches → **71** 29 55N 93 52W
Neckar → **14** 49 31N 8 26 E
Necochea **80** 38 30S 58 50W
Needles **73** 34 50N 114 35W
Needles, The **7** 50 39N 1 35W
Neemuch = Nimach **32** 24 30N 74 56 E
Neenah **68** 44 10N 88 30W
Neepawa **65** 50 15N 99 30W
Neft-chala = imeni 26 Bakinskikh Komissarov **23** 39 19N 49 12 E
Nefta **50** 33 53N 7 50 E
Neftyannyye Kamni **23** 40 20N 50 55 E
Negapatam = Nagappattinam **32** 10 46N 79 51 E
Negaunee **68** 46 30N 87 36W
Negba **28** 31 40N 34 41 E
Negele **29** 5 20N 39 36 E
Negev Desert = Hanegev **28** 30 50N 35 0 E
Negoiul, Vf. **15** 45 38N 24 35 E
Negombo **32** 7 12N 79 50 E
Negotin **19** 44 16N 22 37 E
Negra Pt. **35** 18 40N 120 50 E
Negro →, Argentina **80** 41 2S 62 47W
Negro →, Brazil **78** 3 0S 60 0W
Negro →, Uruguay **80** 33 24S 58 22W
Negros **35** 9 30N 122 40 E
Nehbandān **31** 31 35N 60 5 E
Nei Monggol Zizhiqu □ **38** 42 0N 112 0 E
Neidpath **65** 50 12N 107 20W
Neihart **72** 47 0N 110 44W
Neijiang **39** 29 35N 104 55 E
Neilton **72** 17 24N 123 52W
Neisse → **14** 52 4N 14 46 E
Neiva **78** 2 56N 75 18W
Neixiang **39** 33 10N 111 52 E
Nejanilini L. **65** 59 33N 97 48W
Nekemte **51** 9 4N 36 30 E
Neksø **21** 55 4N 15 8 E
Nelia **44** 20 39S 142 12 E
Neligh **70** 42 11N 98 2W
Nelkan **25** 57 40N 136 4 E
Nellore **32** 14 27N 79 59 E
Nelma **25** 47 39N 139 0 E
Nelson, Canada **64** 49 30N 117 20W
Nelson, N.Z. **43** 41 18S 173 16 E
Nelson, U.K. **6** 53 50N 2 14W
Nelson, U.S.A. **73** 35 35N 113 16W
Nelson □ **43** 42 11S 172 15 E
Nelson → **65** 54 33N 98 2W
Nelson, C. **45** 38 26S 141 32 E
Nelson, Estrecho **80** 51 30S 75 0W
Nelson Forks **64** 59 30N 124 0W
Nelson House **65** 55 47N 98 51W
Nelson L. **65** 55 48N 100 7W
Nelspoort **56** 32 7S 23 0 E
Nelspruit **57** 25 29S 30 59 E
Néma **50** 16 40N 7 15W
Neman → **22** 55 25N 21 10 E
Nemeiben L. **65** 55 20N 105 20W
Nemunas = Neman → **22** 55 25N 21 10 E
Nemuro **36** 43 20N 145 35 E
Nemuro-Kaikyō **36** 43 30N 145 30 E
Nemuy **25** 55 40N 136 9 E
Nen Jiang → **38** 45 28N 124 30 E
Nenagh **9** 52 52N 8 11W
Nenana **60** 64 30N 149 20W
Nene → **6** 52 38N 0 13 E
Nenjiang **38** 49 10N 125 10 E
Nenusa, Kepulauan **35** 4 45N 127 1 E
Neodesha **71** 37 30N 95 37W
Neosho **71** 36 56N 94 28W
Neosho → **71** 35 59N 95 10W
Nepal ■ **33** 28 0N 84 30 E
Nepalganj **33** 28 5N 81 40 E
Nephi **72** 39 43N 111 52W
Nephin **9** 54 1N 9 21W
Nerchinsk **25** 52 0N 116 39 E
Nerchinskiy Zavod **25** 51 20N 119 40 E
Néret L. **63** 54 45N 70 44W
Neretva → **19** 43 1N 17 27 E
Nerva **13** 37 42N 6 30W
Nes **20** 65 53N 17 24W
Nes Ziyyona **28** 31 56N 34 48W
Neskaupstaður **20** 65 9N 13 42W
Ness, Loch **8** 57 15N 4 30W
Nesttun **21** 60 19N 5 21 E
Netanya **28** 32 20N 34 51 E
Nète → **11** 51 7N 4 14 E
Nether Stowey **7** 51 0N 3 10W
Netherbury **7** 50 46N 2 45W
Netherdale **44** 21 10S 148 33 E
Netherlands ■ **11** 52 0N 5 30 E
Netherlands Antilles ■ **78** 12 15N 69 0W
Netherlands Guiana = Surinam ■ **79** 4 0N 56 0W
Nettilling L. **61** 66 30N 71 0W
Netzahualcoyotl, Presa **74** 17 10N 93 30W
Neubrandenburg **14** 53 33N 13 17 E
Neuchâtel **14** 47 0N 6 55 E
Neuchâtel, Lac de **14** 46 53N 6 50 E
Neufchâteau **11** 49 50N 5 25 E
Neumünster **14** 54 4N 9 58 E
Neunkirchen **14** 49 23N 7 12 E
Neuquén **80** 38 55S 68 0W
Neuruppin **14** 52 56N 12 48 E
Neuse → **69** 35 5N 76 30W
Neusiedler See **14** 47 50N 16 47 E
Neuss **11** 51 12N 6 39 E
Neustrelitz **14** 53 22N 13 4 E
Neva → **22** 59 50N 30 30 E
Nevada **71** 37 51N 94 22W
Nevada □ **72** 39 20N 117 0W
Nevada, Sierra, Spain **13** 37 3N 3 15W
Nevada, Sierra, U.S.A. **72** 39 0N 120 30W
Nevada City **72** 39 20N 121 0W
Nevada de Sta. Marta, Sa. **78** 10 55N 73 50W
Nevanka **25** 56 31N 98 55 E
Nevers **12** 47 0N 3 9 E
Nevertire **45** 31 50S 147 44 E
Neville **65** 49 58N 107 39W
Nevinnomyssk **23** 44 40N 42 0 E
Nevis **75** 17 0N 62 30W
Nevşehir **30** 38 33N 34 40 E
Nevyansk **22** 57 30N 60 13 E
New Albany, Ind., U.S.A. **68** 38 20N 85 50W
New Albany, Miss., U.S.A. **71** 34 30N 89 0W
New Amsterdam **78** 6 15N 57 36W
New Angledool **45** 29 5S 147 55 E
New Bedford **68** 41 40N 70 52W
New Bern **69** 35 8N 77 3W
New Boston **71** 33 27N 94 21W
New Braunfels **71** 29 43N 98 9W
New Brighton **43** 43 29S 172 43 E
New Britain, Papua N. G. **40** 5 50S 150 20 E
New Britain, U.S.A. **68** 41 41N 72 47W
New Brunswick **68** 40 30N 74 28W
New Brunswick □ **63** 46 50N 66 30W
New Bussa **53** 9 53N 4 31 E
New Caledonia **40** 21 0S 165 0 E
New Castile = Castilla La Nueva **13** 39 45N 3 20W
New Castle, Ind., U.S.A. **68** 39 55N 85 23W
New Castle, Pa., U.S.A. **68** 41 0N 80 20W
New Cristóbal **74** 9 22N 79 40W
New Delhi **32** 28 37N 77 13 E
New Denver **64** 50 0N 117 25W
New England **70** 46 36N 102 47W
New England Ra. **45** 30 20S 151 45 E
New Forest **7** 50 53N 1 40W
New Glasgow **63** 45 35N 62 36W
New Guinea **40** 4 0S 136 0 E
New Hampshire □ **68** 43 40N 71 40W
New Hampton **70** 43 2N 92 20W
New Hanover **57** 29 22S 30 31 E
New Haven **68** 41 20N 72 54W
New Hazelton **64** 55 20N 127 30W
New Hebrides = Vanuatu ■ **3** 15 0S 168 0 E
New Iberia **71** 30 2N 91 54W
New Ireland **40** 3 20S 151 50 E
New Jersey □ **68** 40 30N 74 10W
New Kensington **68** 40 36N 79 43W
New Lexington **68** 39 40N 82 15W
New Liskeard **62** 47 31N 79 41W
New London, Conn., U.S.A. **68** 41 23N 72 8W
New London, Minn., U.S.A. **70** 45 17N 94 55W
New London, Wis., U.S.A. **70** 44 23N 88 43W
New Madrid **71** 36 40N 89 30W
New Meadows **72** 45 0N 116 32W
New Mexico □ **66** 34 30N 106 0W
New Norcia **47** 30 57S 116 13 E
New Norfolk **44** 42 46S 147 2 E
New Orleans **71** 30 0N 90 5W
New Philadelphia **68** 40 29N 81 25W
New Plymouth, N.Z. **43** 39 4S 174 5 E
New Plymouth, U.S.A. **72** 43 58N 116 49W
New Providence **75** 25 25N 78 35W
New Radnor **7** 52 15N 3 10W
New Richmond **70** 45 6N 92 34W
New Roads **71** 30 43N 91 30W
New Rockford **70** 47 44N 99 7W
New Ross **9** 52 24N 6 58W
New Salem **70** 46 51N 101 25W
New Siberian Is. = Novosibirskiye Ostrava **25** 75 0N 142 0 E
New Smyrna Beach **69** 29 0N 80 50W
New South Wales □ **45** 33 0S 146 0 E
New Springs **47** 25 49S 120 1 E
New Town **70** 48 0N 102 30W
New Ulm **70** 44 15N 94 30W
New Waterford **63** 46 13N 60 4W
New Westminster **64** 49 13N 122 55W
New York □ **68** 42 40N 76 0W
New York City **68** 40 45N 74 0W
New Zealand ■ **43** 40 0S 176 0 E
Newala **54** 10 58S 39 18 E
Newark, Del., U.S.A. **68** 39 42N 75 45W
Newark, N.J., U.S.A. **68** 40 41N 74 12W
Newark, N.Y., U.S.A. **68** 43 2N 77 10W
Newark, Ohio, U.S.A. **68** 40 5N 82 24W
Newark-on-Trent **6** 53 6N 0 48W
Newaygo **68** 43 25N 85 48W
Newberg **72** 45 22N 123 0W
Newberry, Mich., U.S.A. **68** 46 20N 85 32W
Newberry, S.C., U.S.A. **69** 34 17N 81 37W
Newbrook **64** 54 24N 112 57W
Newburgh **68** 41 30N 74 1W
Newbury **7** 51 24N 1 19W
Newburyport **68** 42 48N 70 50W
Newcastle, Australia **45** 33 0S 151 46 E
Newcastle, Canada **63** 47 1N 65 38W
Newcastle, S. Africa **57** 27 45S 29 58 E
Newcastle, U.K. **9** 54 13N 5 54W

Novaya Ladoga

Newcastle, U.S.A. 70 43 50N 104 12W
Newcastle Emlyn 7 52 2N 4 29W
Newcastle Ra. 46 15 45S 130 15 E
Newcastle-under-Lyme 6 53 2N 2 15W
Newcastle-upon-Tyne 6 54 59N 1 37W
Newcastle Waters 44 17 30S 133 28 E
Newdegate 47 33 6S 119 0 E
Newe Etan 28 32 30N 35 32 E
Newe Sha'anan 28 32 47N 34 59 E
Newe Zohar 28 31 9N 35 21 E
Newell 70 44 48N 103 25W
Newenham, C. 60 58 40N 162 15W
Newfoundland □ 61 53 0N 58 0W
Newhalem 64 48 41N 121 16W
Newham 7 51 31N 0 2 E
Newhaven 7 50 47N 0 4 E
Newkirk 71 36 52N 97 3W
Newman 46 23 18S 119 45 E
Newmarket, Ireland 9 52 13N 9 0W
Newmarket, U.K. 7 52 15N 0 23 E
Newnan 69 33 22N 84 48W
Newport, Gwent, U.K. 7 51 35N 3 0W
Newport, I. of W., U.K. 7 50 42N 1 18W
Newport, Salop, U.K. 7 52 47N 2 22W
Newport, Ark., U.S.A. 71 35 38N 91 15W
Newport, Ky., U.S.A. 68 39 5N 84 23W
Newport, N.H., U.S.A. 68 43 23N 72 8W
Newport, Oreg., U.S.A. 72 44 41N 124 2W
Newport, R.I., U.S.A. 68 41 13N 71 19W
Newport, Tenn., U.S.A. 69 35 59N 83 12W
Newport, Vt., U.S.A. 68 44 57N 72 17W
Newport, Wash., U.S.A. 72 48 11N 117 2W
Newport Beach 73 33 40N 117 58W
Newport News 68 37 2N 76 30W
Newquay 7 50 24N 5 6W
Newry 9 54 10N 6 20W
Newry & Mourne □ 9 54 10N 6 15W
Newton, Iowa, U.S.A. 70 41 40N 93 3W
Newton, Mass., U.S.A. 68 42 21N 71 10W
Newton, Miss., U.S.A. 71 32 19N 89 10W
Newton, N.C., U.S.A. 69 35 42N 81 10W
Newton, N.J., U.S.A. 68 41 3N 74 46W
Newton, Tex., U.S.A. 71 30 54N 93 42W
Newton Abbot 7 50 32N 3 37W
Newton Boyd 45 29 45S 152 16 E
Newton Stewart 8 54 57N 4 30W
Newtonmore 8 57 4N 4 7W
Newtown 7 52 31N 3 19W
Newtownabbey 9 54 40N 5 55W
Newtownabbey □ 9 54 45N 6 0W
Newtownards 9 54 37N 5 40W
Neya 22 58 21N 43 49 E
Neyrīz 31 29 15N 54 19 E
Neyshābūr 31 36 10N 58 50 E
Nezhin 23 51 5N 31 55 E
Nezperce 72 46 13N 116 15W
Ngabang 34 0 23N 109 55 E
Ngabordamlu, Tanjung 35 6 56S 134 11 E
Ngami Depression 56 20 30S 22 46 E
Nganglong Kangri 33 33 0N 81 0 E
Nganjuk 35 7 32S 111 55 E
Ngaoundéré 54 7 15N 13 35 E
Ngapara 43 44 57S 170 46 E
Ngawi 35 7 24S 111 26 E
Ngoring Hu 37 34 55N 97 5 E
Ngorongoro 52 3 11S 35 32 E
Ngozi 52 2 54S 29 50 E
Ngudu 54 2 58S 33 25 E
Nguigmi 51 14 20N 13 20 E
Ngukurr 44 14 44S 134 44 E
Nguru 53 12 56N 10 29 E
Nha Trang 34 12 16N 109 10 E
Nhacoongo 57 24 18S 35 14 E
Nhangutazi, L. 57 24 0S 34 30 E
Nhill 45 36 18S 141 40 E
Nhulunbuy 44 12 10S 137 20 E
Niafounké 50 16 0N 4 5W
Niagara 68 45 45N 88 0W
Niagara Falls, Canada 62 43 7N 79 5W
Niagara Falls, U.S.A. 68 43 5N 79 0W
Niah 34 3 58N 113 46 E
Niamey 53 13 27N 2 6 E
Niangara 54 3 42N 27 50 E
Nianzishan 38 47 31N 122 53 E
Nias 34 1 0N 97 30 E
Nicaragua ■ 75 11 40N 85 30W
Nicaragua, L. de 75 12 0N 85 30W
Nicastro 18 39 0N 16 18 E
Nice 12 43 42N 7 14 E
Niceville 69 30 30N 86 30W
Nichinan 36 31 38N 131 23 E
Nicholás, Canal 75 23 30N 80 5W
Nicholasville 68 37 54N 84 31W
Nicholson 46 18 2S 128 54 E
Nicholson → 44 17 31S 139 36 E
Nicholson Ra. 47 27 15S 116 45 E
Nicobar Is. 3 9 0N 93 0 E
Nicola 64 50 12N 120 40W
Nicolet 62 46 17N 72 35W
Nicolls Town 75 25 8N 78 0W
Nicosia 30 35 10N 33 25 E
Nicoya, G. de 75 10 0N 85 0W
Nicoya, Pen. de 75 9 45N 85 40W
Nidd → 6 54 1N 1 32W
Niekerkshoop 56 29 19S 22 51 E
Nienburg 14 52 38N 9 15 E
Nieu Bethesda 56 31 51S 24 34 E
Nieuw Amsterdam 79 5 53N 55 5W
Nieuw Nickerie 79 6 0N 56 59W
Nieuwoudtville 56 31 23S 19 7 E
Nieuwpoort 11 51 8N 2 45 E
Nièvre □ 12 47 10N 3 40 E
Niğde 30 38 0N 34 40 E
Nigel 57 26 27S 28 25 E
Niger □ 53 10 0N 5 0 E
Niger ■ 50 17 30N 10 0 E
Niger → 53 5 33N 6 33 E
Nigeria ■ 53 8 30N 8 0 E
Nightcaps 43 45 57S 168 2 E
Nii-Jima 36 34 20N 139 15 E
Niigata 36 37 58N 139 0 E
Niigata □ 36 37 15N 138 45 E
Niihama 36 33 55N 133 16 E
Niihau 66 21 55N 160 10W
Nijkerk 11 52 13N 5 30 E
Nijmegen 11 51 50N 5 52 E
Nijverdal 11 52 22N 6 28 E
Nike 53 6 26N 7 29 E
Nikel 20 69 24N 30 12 E
Nikiniki 35 9 49S 124 30 E
Nikki 53 9 58N 3 12 E
Nikkō 36 36 45N 139 35 E
Nikolayev 23 46 58N 32 0 E
Nikolayevsk 23 50 0N 45 35 E
Nikolayevsk-na-Amur 25 53 8N 140 44 E
Nikolskoye 25 55 12N 166 0 E
Nikopol 23 47 35N 34 25 E
Nīkshahr 31 26 15N 60 10 E
Nîl, Nahr en → 51 30 10N 31 6 E
Nîl el Abyad → 51 15 38N 32 31 E
Nîl el Azraq → 51 15 38N 32 31 E
Niland 73 33 16N 115 30W
Nile = Nîl, Nahr en → 51 30 10N 31 6 E
Niles 68 41 8N 80 40W
Nimach 32 24 30N 74 56 E
Nîmes 12 43 50N 4 23 E
Nimmitabel 45 36 29S 149 15 E
Nimneryskiy 25 57 50N 125 10 E
Nīmrūz □ 31 30 0N 62 0 E
Nimule 54 3 32N 32 3 E
Nīnawá 30 36 25N 43 10 E
Nindigully 45 28 21S 148 50 E
Ninemile 64 56 0N 130 7W
Nineveh = Nīnawá 30 36 25N 43 10 E
Ningaloo 46 22 41S 113 41 E
Ning'an 38 44 22N 129 20 E
Ningbo 39 29 51N 121 28 E
Ningde 39 26 38N 119 23 E
Ningdu 39 26 25N 115 59 E
Ningjin 38 37 35N 114 57 E
Ningming 39 22 8N 107 4 E
Ningpo = Ningbo 39 29 51N 121 28 E
Ningqiang 39 32 47N 106 15 E
Ningshan 39 33 21N 108 21 E
Ningsia Hui A.R. = Ningxia Huizu Zizhiqu □ 38 38 0N 106 0 E
Ningwu 38 39 0N 112 18 E
Ningxia Huizu Zizhiqu □ 38 38 0N 106 0 E
Ningxiang 39 28 15N 112 30 E
Ningyuan 39 25 37N 111 57 E
Ninove 11 50 51N 4 2 E
Niobrara 70 42 48N 97 59W
Niobrara → 70 42 45N 98 0W
Nioro du Sahel 50 15 15N 9 30W
Niort 12 46 19N 0 29W
Nipawin 65 53 20N 104 0W
Nipawin Prov. Park 65 54 0N 104 37W
Nipigon 62 49 0N 88 17W
Nipigon, L. 62 49 50N 88 30W
Nipin → 65 55 46N 108 35W
Nipishish L. 63 54 12N 60 45W
Nipissing L. 62 46 20N 80 0W
Nipomo 73 35 4N 120 29W
Niquelândia 79 14 33S 48 23W
Nirmal 32 19 3N 78 20 E
Nirmali 33 26 20N 86 35 E
Niš 19 43 19N 21 58 E
Nişāb 29 14 25N 46 29 E
Nishinomiya 36 34 45N 135 20 E
Niskibi → 62 56 29N 88 9W
Nisutlin → 64 60 14N 132 34W
Niţā' 30 27 15N 48 35 E
Nitchequon 63 53 10N 70 58W
Niterói 79 22 52S 43 0W
Nith → 8 55 20N 3 5W
Nitra 15 48 19N 18 4 E
Nitra → 15 47 46N 18 10 E
Niuafo'ou 43 15 30S 175 58W
Niue I. 2 19 2S 169 54W
Niut 34 0 55N 110 6 E
Nivelles 11 50 35N 4 20 E
Nivernais 12 47 0N 3 40 E
Nixon 71 29 17N 97 45W
Nizamabad 32 18 45N 78 7 E
Nizamghat 33 28 20N 95 45 E
Nizhne Kolymsk 25 68 34N 160 55 E
Nizhneangarsk 25 55 47N 109 30 E
Nizhnekamsk 22 55 38N 51 49 E
Nizhneudinsk 25 54 54N 99 3 E
Nizhnevartovsk 24 60 56N 76 38 E
Nizhneyansk 25 71 26N 136 4 E
Nizhniy Novgorod = Gorkiy 22 56 20N 44 0 E
Nizhniy Tagil 22 57 55N 59 57 E
Nizhnyaya Tunguska → 25 64 20N 93 0 E
Nizip 30 37 5N 37 50 E
Nizké Tatry 15 48 55N 20 0 E
Njombe 54 9 20S 34 50 E
Nkambe 53 6 35N 10 40 E
Nkawkaw 53 6 36N 0 49W
Nkhata Bay 54 11 33S 34 16 E
Nkhota Kota 55 12 56S 34 15 E
Nkongsamba 54 4 55N 9 55 E
Nkurenkuru 56 17 42S 18 32 E
Nmai → 33 25 30N 97 25 E
Noakhali = Maijdi 33 22 48N 91 10 E
Noatak 60 67 32N 162 59W
Nobeoka 36 32 36N 131 41 E
Noblesville 68 40 1N 85 59W
Nocera Inferiore 18 40 45N 14 37 E
Nockatunga 45 27 42S 142 42 E
Nocona 71 33 48N 97 45W
Noel 71 36 36N 94 29W
Nogales, Mexico 74 31 20N 110 56W
Nogales, U.S.A. 73 31 33N 110 56W
Nōgata 36 33 48N 130 44 E
Noggerup 47 33 32S 116 5 E
Noginsk 25 64 30N 90 50 E
Nogoa → 44 23 40S 147 55 E
Noirmoutier, I. de 12 46 58N 2 10W
Nojane 56 23 15S 20 14 E
Nok Kundi 31 28 50N 62 45 E
Nokaneng 56 19 40S 22 17 E
Nokhtuysk 25 60 0N 117 45 E
Nokomis 65 51 35N 105 0W
Nokomis L. 65 57 0N 103 0W
Nola 54 3 35N 16 4 E
Noma Omuramba → 56 18 52S 20 53 E
Noman L. 65 62 15N 108 55W
Nome 60 64 30N 165 24W
Nonacho L. 65 61 42N 109 40W
Nonda 44 20 40S 142 28 E
Nong Khai 34 17 50N 102 46 E
Nong'an 38 44 25N 125 5 E
Nongoma 57 27 58S 31 35 E
Nonoava 74 27 28N 106 44W
Noonamah 46 12 40S 131 4 E
Noonan 70 48 51N 102 59W
Noondoo 45 28 35S 148 30 E
Noonkanbah 46 18 30S 124 50 E
Noord Brabant □ 11 51 40N 5 0 E
Noord Holland □ 11 52 30N 4 45 E
Noordbeveland 11 51 35N 3 50 E
Noordoostpolder 11 52 45N 5 45 E
Noordwijk aan Zee 11 52 14N 4 26 E
Nootka 64 49 38N 126 38W
Nootka I. 64 49 32N 126 42W
Noqui 54 5 55S 13 30 E
Noranda 62 48 20N 79 0W
Nord □ 12 50 15N 3 30 E
Nord-Ostsee Kanal 14 54 15N 9 40 E
Nord-Trøndelag fylke □ 20 64 20N 12 0 E
Nordegg 64 52 29N 116 5W
Nordhausen 14 51 29N 10 47 E
Nordkapp 20 71 10N 25 44 E
Nordkinn 4 71 8N 27 40 E
Nordland fylke □ 20 65 40N 13 0 E
Nordrhein-Westfalen □ 14 51 45N 7 30 E
Nordvik 25 74 2N 111 32 E
Nore → 9 52 40N 7 20W
Norembega 62 48 59N 80 43W
Norfolk, Nebr., U.S.A. 70 42 3N 97 25W
Norfolk, Va., U.S.A. 68 36 40N 76 15W
Norfolk □ 6 52 39N 1 0 E
Norfolk Broads 6 52 30N 1 15 E
Norfolk I. 3 28 58S 168 3 E
Norfork Res. 71 36 13N 92 15W
Norilsk 25 69 20N 88 6 E
Norley 45 27 45S 143 48 E
Norma, Mt. 44 20 55S 140 42 E
Normal 70 40 30N 89 0W
Norman 71 35 12N 97 30W
Norman → 44 17 28S 140 49 E
Norman Wells 60 65 17N 126 51W
Normanby → 44 14 23S 144 10 E
Normandie 12 48 45N 0 10 E
Normandin 62 48 49N 72 31W
Normandy = Normandie 12 48 45N 0 10 E
Normanhurst, Mt. 47 25 4S 122 30 E
Normanton 44 17 40S 141 10 E
Norquay 65 51 53N 102 5W
Norquinco 80 41 51S 70 55W
Norrbotten □ 20 66 30N 22 30 E
Norrby 20 64 55N 18 15 E
Nørresundby 21 57 5N 9 52 E
Norris 72 45 40N 111 40W
Norristown 68 40 9N 75 21W
Norrköping 21 58 37N 16 11 E
Norrland □ 20 66 50N 18 0 E
Norrtälje 21 59 46N 18 42 E
Norseman 47 32 8S 121 43 E
Norsk 25 52 30N 130 0 E
North Adams 68 42 42N 73 6W
North America 58 40 0N 100 0W
North Battleford 65 52 50N 108 17W
North Bay 62 46 20N 79 30W
North Belcher Is. 62 56 50N 79 50W
North Bend, Canada 64 49 50N 121 27W
North Bend, U.S.A. 72 43 28N 124 14W
North Berwick 8 56 4N 2 44W
North Canadian → 71 35 17N 95 31W
North C., Canada 63 47 2N 60 20W
North C., N.Z. 43 34 23S 173 4 E
North Caribou L. 62 52 50N 90 40W
North Carolina □ 69 35 30N 80 0W
North Channel, Br. Is. 8 55 0N 5 30W
North Channel, Canada 62 46 0N 83 0W
North Chicago 68 42 19N 87 50W
North Dakota □ 70 47 30N 100 0W
North Dandalup 47 32 30S 115 57 E
North Down □ 9 54 40N 5 45W
North Downs 7 51 17N 0 30 E
North East Frontier Agency = Arunachal Pradesh □ 33 28 0N 95 0 E
North East Providence Chan. 75 26 0N 76 0W
North Esk → 8 56 44N 2 25W
North European Plain 4 55 0N 20 0 E
North Foreland 7 51 22N 1 28 E
North Henik L. 65 61 45N 97 40W
North I. 43 38 0S 175 0 E
North Knife → 65 58 53N 94 45W
North Korea ■ 38 40 0N 127 0 E
North Lakhimpur 33 27 14N 94 7 E
North Las Vegas 73 36 15N 115 6W
North Loup → 70 41 17N 98 23W
North Minch 8 58 5N 5 55W
North Nahanni → 64 62 15N 123 20W
North Ossetian A.S.S.R. □ 23 43 30N 44 30 E
North Palisade 73 37 6N 118 32W
North Platte 70 41 10N 100 50W
North Platte → 70 41 15N 100 45W
North Pt. 63 47 5N 64 0W
North Portal 65 49 0N 102 33W
North Powder 72 45 2N 117 59W
North Ronaldsay 8 59 20N 2 30W
North Saskatchewan → 65 53 15N 105 5W
North Sea 4 56 0N 4 0 E
North Sporades = Voríai Sporádhes 19 39 15N 23 30 E
North Sydney 63 46 12N 60 15W
North Thompson → 64 50 40N 120 20W
North Tonawanda 68 43 5N 78 50W
North Truchas Pk. 73 36 0N 105 30W
North Twin I. 62 53 20N 80 0W
North Tyne → 6 54 59N 2 7W
North Uist 8 57 40N 7 15W
North Vancouver 64 49 25N 123 3W
North Vernon 68 39 0N 85 35W
North Wabasca L. 64 56 0N 113 55W
North Walsham 6 52 49N 1 22 E
North West C. 46 21 45S 114 9 E
North West Christmas I. Ridge 41 6 30N 165 0W
North West Frontier □ 32 34 0N 71 0 E
North West Highlands 8 57 35N 5 2W
North West Providence Channel 75 26 0N 78 0W
North West River 63 53 30N 60 10W
North West Territories □ 60 67 0N 110 0W
North York Moors 6 54 25N 0 50W
North Yorkshire □ 6 54 15N 1 25W
Northallerton 6 54 20N 1 26W
Northam 56 24 56S 27 18 E
Northampton, Australia 47 28 27S 114 33 E
Northampton, U.K. 7 52 14N 0 54W
Northampton, U.S.A. 68 42 22N 72 31W
Northampton □ 7 52 16N 0 55W
Northampton Downs 44 24 35S 145 48 E
Northcliffe 47 34 39S 116 7 E
Northern Circars 33 17 30N 82 30 E
Northern Group 43 10 0S 160 0W
Northern Indian L. 65 57 20N 97 20W
Northern Ireland □ 9 54 45N 7 0W
Northern Light, L. 62 48 15N 90 39W
Northern Marianas 40 17 0N 145 0 E
Northern Territory □ 46 16 0S 133 0 E
Northfield 70 44 30N 93 10W
Northland □ 43 35 30S 173 30 E
Northome 70 47 53N 94 15W
Northport, Ala., U.S.A. 69 33 15N 87 35W
Northport, Mich., U.S.A. 68 45 8N 85 39W
Northport, Wash., U.S.A. 72 48 55N 117 48W
Northumberland □ 6 55 12N 2 0W
Northumberland, C. 45 38 5S 140 40 E
Northumberland Is. 44 21 30S 149 50 E
Northumberland Str. 63 46 20N 64 0W
Northwich 6 53 16N 2 30W
Northwood, Iowa, U.S.A. 70 43 27N 93 0W
Northwood, N. Dak., U.S.A. 70 47 44N 97 30W
Norton 70 39 50N 99 53W
Norton Sd. 60 64 0N 164 0W
Norwalk, Conn., U.S.A. 68 41 9N 73 25W
Norwalk, Ohio, U.S.A. 68 41 13N 82 38W
Norway 68 45 46N 87 57W
Norway ■ 21 63 0N 11 0 E
Norway House 65 53 59N 97 50W
Norwegian Sea 21 66 0N 1 0 E
Norwich, U.K. 6 52 38N 1 17 E
Norwich, U.S.A. 68 42 32N 75 30W
Noshiro 36 40 12N 140 0 E
Nosok 24 70 10N 82 20 E
Noşratābād 31 29 55N 60 0 E
Noss Hd. 8 58 29N 3 4W
Nossob → 56 26 55S 20 45 E
Nosy Bé 55 13 25S 48 15 E
Nosy Boraha 57 16 50S 49 55 E
Nosy Mitsio 55 12 54S 48 36 E
Nosy Varika 57 20 35S 48 32 E
Notigi Dam 65 56 40N 99 10W
Notikewin → 64 57 2N 117 38W
Noto 18 36 52N 15 4 E
Noto-Hanto 36 37 0N 137 0 E
Notre-Dame 63 46 18N 64 46W
Notre Dame B. 63 49 45N 55 30W
Notre Dame de Koartac = Koartac 61 60 55N 69 40W
Notre Dame d'Ivugivic = Ivugivik 61 62 24N 77 55W
Nottaway → 62 51 22N 78 55W
Nottingham 6 52 57N 1 10W
Nottingham □ 6 53 10N 1 0W
Nottoway → 68 36 33N 76 55W
Notwane → 56 23 35S 26 58 E
Nouâdhibou 50 20 54N 17 0W
Nouâdhibou, Ras 50 20 50N 17 0W
Nouakchott 50 18 9N 15 58W
Nouméa 40 22 17S 166 30 E
Noupoort 56 31 10S 24 57 E
Nouveau Comptoir 62 53 0N 78 49W
Nouvelle Calédonie = New Caledonia 40 21 0S 165 0 E
Nova Casa Nova 79 9 25S 41 5W
Nova Cruz 79 6 28S 35 25W
Nova Friburgo 79 22 16S 42 30W
Nova Gaia 54 10 10S 17 35 E
Nova Iguaçu 79 22 45S 43 28W
Nova Iorque 79 7 0S 44 5W
Nova Lima 79 19 59S 43 51W
Nova Lisboa = Huambo 55 12 42S 15 54 E
Nova Mambone 57 21 0S 35 3 E
Nova Scotia □ 63 45 10N 63 0W
Nova Sofala 57 20 7S 34 42 E
Nova Venécia 79 18 45S 40 24W
Noval Iorque 79 6 48S 44 0W
Novara 18 45 27N 8 36 E
Novaya Ladoga 22 60 7N 32 16 E

Novaya Lyalya ... 24 59 10N 60 35 E
Novaya Sibir, Ostrov 25 75 10N 150 0 E
Novaya Zemlya .. 24 75 0N 56 0 E
Nové Zámky .. 15 48 2N 18 8 E
Novgorod .. 22 58 30N 31 25 E
Novgorod-Severskiy 22 52 2N 33 10 E
Novi Sad ... 19 45 18N 19 52 E
Novo Remanso .. 79 9 41S 42 4W
Novoaltaysk .. 24 53 30N 84 0 E
Novocherkassk .. 23 47 27N 40 5 E
Novokazalinsk .. 24 45 48N 62 6 E
Novokuybyshevsk . 22 53 7N 49 58 E
Novokuznetsk ... 24 53 45N 87 10 E
Novomoskovsk .. 22 54 5N 38 15 E
Novorossiysk .... 23 44 43N 37 46 E
Novorybnoye .... 25 72 50N 105 50 E
Novoshakhtinsk .. 23 47 46N 39 58 E
Novosibirsk .. 24 55 0N 83 5 E
Novosibirskiye
  Ostrava ... 25 75 0N 142 0 E
Novotroitsk .. 22 51 10N 58 15 E
Novouzensk .. 23 50 32N 48 17 E
Novska ... 18 45 19N 17 0 E
Novvy Port .... 24 67 40N 72 30 E
Now Shahr .. 31 36 40N 51 30 E
Nowgong .. 33 26 20N 92 50 E
Nowra .. 45 34 53S 150 35 E
Nowshera ... 32 34 0N 72 0 E
Nowy Sącz .. 15 49 40N 20 41 E
Nowy Tomyśl .. 14 52 19N 16 10 E
Noxon .. 72 48 0N 115 43W
Noyes I. .. 64 55 30N 133 40W
Nsanje ... 55 16 55S 35 12 E
Nsawam .. 53 5 50N 0 24W
Nsukka ... 53 6 51N 7 29 E
Nûbîya, Es Sahrâ En 51 21 30N 33 30 E
Nuboai .. 35 2 10S 136 30 E
Nueces → .. 71 27 50N 97 30W
Nueima → .. 28 31 54N 35 25 E
Nueltin L. .. 65 60 30N 99 30W
Nueva Gerona ... 75 21 53N 82 49W
Nueva Imperial .. 80 38 45S 72 58W
Nueva Rosita .. 74 28 0N 101 11W
Nueva San Salvador 75 13 40N 89 18W
Nuéve de Julio .. 80 35 30S 61 0W
Nuevitas .. 75 21 30N 77 20W
Nuevo, G. .. 80 43 0S 64 30W
Nuevo Laredo .. 74 27 30N 99 30W
Nuevo León □ .. 74 25 0N 100 0W
Nugget Pt. ... 43 46 27S 169 50 E
Nuhaka .. 43 39 3S 177 45 E
Nukey Bluff, Mt. .. 45 32 26S 135 29 E
Nukheila .. 51 19 1N 26 21 E
Nuku'alofa .. 43 21 10S 174 0W
Nukus .. 24 42 20N 59 7 E
Nulato .. 60 64 40N 158 10W
Nullagine → .. 46 21 20S 120 20 E
Nullarbor .. 47 31 28S 130 55 E
Nullarbor Plain .. 47 31 10S 129 0 E
Numalla, L. .. 45 28 43S 144 20 E
Numan .. 53 9 29N 12 3 E
Numata .. 36 36 45N 139 4 E
Numazu .. 36 35 7N 138 51 E
Numbulwar .. 44 14 15S 135 45 E
Numfoor .. 35 1 0S 134 50 E
Numurkah .. 45 36 5S 145 26 E
Nunaksaluk I. .. 63 55 49N 60 20W
Nuneaton .. 7 52 32N 1 29W
Nunivak .. 60 60 0N 166 0W
Nunkun .. 32 33 57N 76 2 E
Nunspeet .. 11 52 21N 5 45 E
Nuomin He → .. 38 46 45N 126 55 E
Nuremburg =
  Nürnberg .. 14 49 26N 11 5 E
Nurina .. 47 30 56S 126 33 E
Nuriootpa .. 45 34 27S 139 0 E
Nürnberg .. 14 49 26N 11 5 E
Nurran, L. =
  Terewah, L. .. 45 29 52S 147 35 E
Nurrari Lakes .. 47 29 1S 130 5 E
Nusa Barung .. 35 8 10S 113 30 E
Nusa Kambangan . 35 7 40S 108 10 E
Nusa Tenggara
  Barat □ .. 34 8 50S 117 30 E
Nusa Tenggara
  Timur □ .. 35 9 30S 122 0 E
Nusaybin .. 23 37 3N 41 10 E
Nushki .. 32 29 35N 66 0 E
Nutak .. 61 57 28N 61 59W
Nutwood Downs .. 44 15 49S 134 10 E
Nuwakot .. 33 28 10N 83 55 E
Nuweveldberge .. 56 32 10S 21 45 E
Nuyts, C. .. 47 32 2S 132 21 E
Nuyts Arch. .. 45 32 35S 133 20 E
Nxau-Nxau .. 56 18 57S 21 4 E
Nyah West .. 45 35 16S 143 21 E
Nyahanga .. 54 2 20S 33 37 E
Nyahururu .. 54 0 2N 36 27 E
Nyainqentanglha
  Shan .. 37 30 0N 90 0 E
Nyakanazi .. 52 3 2S 31 10 E
Nyakanyasi .. 52 1 10S 31 13 E
Nyâlâ .. 51 12 2N 24 58 E

Nyandoma ... 22 61 40N 40 12 E
Nyangana .. 56 18 0S 20 40 E
Nyanza .. 52 4 21S 29 36 E
Nyarling → .. 64 60 41N 113 23W
Nyasa, L. = Malawi,
  L. .. 55 12 30S 34 30 E
Nyazepetrovsk .. 22 56 3N 59 36 E
Nybro .. 21 56 44N 15 55 E
Nyda .. 24 66 40N 72 58 E
Nyeri .. 54 0 23S 36 56 E
Nyíregyháza .. 15 47 58N 21 47 E
Nykarleby .. 20 63 22N 22 31 E
Nykøbing .. 21 54 56N 11 52 E
Nyköping .. 21 58 45N 17 0 E
Nylstroom .. 57 24 42S 28 22 E
Nymagee .. 45 32 7S 146 20 E
Nynäshamn .. 21 58 54N 17 57 E
Nyngan .. 45 31 30S 147 8 E
Nysa .. 15 50 30N 17 22 E
Nysa → .. 14 52 4N 14 46 E
Nyssa .. 72 43 56N 117 2W
Nyurba .. 25 63 17N 118 28 E
Nzega .. 54 4 10S 33 12 E
N'Zérékoré .. 50 7 49N 8 48W
Nzeto .. 54 7 10S 12 52 E
Nzubuka .. 52 4 45S 32 50 E

O

Ō-Shima .. 36 34 44N 139 24 E
Oacoma .. 43 43 50N 99 26W
Oahe Dam .. 70 44 28N 100 25W
Oahe L. .. 70 45 30N 100 25W
Oahu .. 66 21 30N 158 0W
Oak Creek .. 72 40 15N 106 59W
Oak Harb. .. 72 48 20N 122 38W
Oak Hill .. 68 38 0N 81 7W
Oak Park .. 68 41 55N 87 45W
Oak Ridge .. 69 36 1N 84 12W
Oakbank .. 45 33 4S 140 33 E
Oakdale, Calif.,
  U.S.A. .. 73 37 45N 120 55W
Oakdale, La., U.S.A. 71 30 50N 92 38W
Oakengates .. 6 52 42N 2 29W
Oakes .. 70 46 14N 98 4W
Oakesdale .. 72 47 11N 117 15W
Oakey .. 45 27 25S 151 43 E
Oakham .. 6 52 40N 0 43W
Oakland, Calif.,
  U.S.A. .. 73 37 50N 122 18W
Oakland, Oreg.,
  U.S.A. .. 72 43 23N 123 18W
Oakland City .. 68 38 20N 87 20W
Oakley, Idaho,
  U.S.A. .. 72 42 14N 113 55W
Oakley, Kans.,
  U.S.A. .. 70 39 8N 100 51W
Oakover → .. 46 21 0S 120 40 E
Oakridge .. 72 43 47N 122 31W
Oamaru .. 43 45 5S 170 59 E
Oatman .. 73 35 1N 114 19W
Oaxaca .. 74 17 2N 96 40W
Oaxaca □ .. 74 17 0N 97 0W
Ob → .. 24 66 45N 69 30 E
Oba .. 62 49 4N 84 7W
Oban .. 8 56 25N 5 30W
Obbia .. 29 5 25N 48 30 E
Obed .. 64 53 30N 117 10W
Oberhausen .. 14 51 28N 6 50 E
Oberlin, Kans.,
  U.S.A. .. 70 39 52N 100 31W
Oberlin, La., U.S.A. 71 30 42N 92 42W
Oberon .. 45 33 45S 149 52 E
Obi, Kepulauan .. 35 1 23S 127 45 E
Óbidos .. 79 1 50S 55 30W
Obihiro .. 36 42 56N 143 12 E
Obilatu .. 35 1 25S 127 20 E
Obluchye .. 25 49 1N 131 4 E
Obo .. 54 5 20N 26 32 E
Observatory Inlet .. 64 55 10N 129 54W
Obshchi Syrt .. 4 52 0N 53 0 E
Obskaya Guba .. 24 69 0N 73 0 E
Obuasi .. 53 6 17N 1 40W
Ocala .. 69 29 11N 82 5W
Ocampo .. 74 28 9N 108 24W
Ocaña .. 13 39 55N 3 30W
Ocanomowoc .. 70 43 7N 88 30W
Ocate .. 71 36 12N 104 59W
Occidental,
  Cordillera .. 78 5 0N 76 0W
Ocean, I. = Banaba 40 0 45S 169 50 E
Ocean City .. 68 39 18N 74 34W
Ocean Park .. 72 46 30N 124 2W
Oceanside .. 73 33 13N 117 26W
Ochil Hills .. 8 56 14N 3 40W
Ochre River .. 65 51 4N 99 47W
Ocilla .. 69 31 35N 83 12W
Ocmulgee → .. 69 31 58N 82 32W
Oconee → .. 69 31 58N 82 32W
Oconto .. 68 44 52N 87 53W

Oconto Falls .. 68 44 52N 88 10W
Ocotal .. 75 13 41N 86 31W
Ocotlán .. 74 20 21N 102 42W
Octave .. 73 34 10N 112 43W
Ocumare del Tuy .. 78 10 7N 66 46W
Oda .. 53 5 50N 0 51W
Ódáðahraun .. 20 65 5N 17 0W
Odate .. 36 40 16N 140 34 E
Odawara .. 36 35 20N 139 6 E
Odda .. 21 60 3N 6 35 E
Oddur .. 29 4 11N 43 52 E
Odei → .. 65 56 6N 96 54W
Ödemiş .. 30 38 15N 28 0 E
Odendaalsrus .. 56 27 48S 26 45 E
Odense .. 21 55 22N 10 23 E
Oder → .. 14 53 33N 14 38 E
Odessa, Tex., U.S.A. 71 31 51N 102 23W
Odessa, Wash.,
  U.S.A. .. 72 47 19N 118 35W
Odessa, U.S.S.R. .. 23 46 30N 30 45 E
Odiakwe .. 56 20 12S 25 17 E
Odienné .. 50 9 30N 7 34W
O'Donnell .. 71 33 0N 101 48W
Odorheiu Secuiesc 15 46 21N 25 21 E
Odra → .. 14 53 33N 14 38 E
Odžak .. 19 45 3N 18 18 E
Odzi .. 57 19 0S 32 20 E
Oeiras .. 79 7 0S 42 8W
Oelrichs .. 70 43 11N 103 14W
Oelwein .. 70 42 41N 91 55W
Oenpelli .. 46 12 20S 133 4 E
Ofanto → .. 18 41 22N 16 13 E
Offa .. 53 8 13N 4 42 E
Offaly □ .. 9 53 15N 7 30W
Offenbach .. 14 50 6N 8 46 E
Ofotfjorden .. 20 68 27N 16 40 E
Oga-Hantō .. 36 39 58N 139 47 E
Ogahalla .. 62 50 6N 85 51W
Ōgaki .. 36 35 21N 136 37 E
Ogallala .. 70 41 12N 101 40W
Ogbomosho .. 53 8 1N 4 11 E
Ogden, Iowa, U.S.A. 70 42 3N 94 0W
Ogden, Utah, U.S.A. 72 41 13N 112 1W
Ogdensburg .. 68 44 40N 75 27W
Ogeechee → .. 69 31 51N 81 6W
Oglio → .. 18 45 2N 10 39 E
Ogmore .. 44 22 37S 149 35 E
Ogoja .. 53 6 38N 8 39 E
Ogoki → .. 62 51 38N 85 57W
Ogoki L. .. 62 50 50N 87 10W
Ogoki Res. .. 62 50 45N 88 15W
Ogooué → .. 54 1 0S 9 0 E
Ogowe =
  Ogooué → .. 54 1 0S 9 0 E
Oguta .. 53 5 44N 6 44 E
Ogwashi-Uku .. 53 6 15N 6 30 E
Ohai .. 43 44 55S 168 0 E
Ohakune .. 43 39 24S 175 24 E
Ohanet .. 50 28 44N 8 46 E
Ohau, L. .. 43 44 15S 169 53 E
Ohey .. 11 50 26N 5 8 E
Ohio □ .. 68 40 20N 84 10W
Ohio → .. 68 38 0N 86 0W
Ohre → .. 14 50 30N 14 10 E
Ohridsko, Jezero .. 19 41 8N 20 52 E
Ohrigstad .. 57 24 39S 30 36 E
Oil City .. 68 41 26N 79 40W
Oise □ .. 12 49 28N 2 30 E
Ōita .. 36 33 14N 131 36 E
Ōita □ .. 36 33 15N 131 30 E
Oiticica .. 79 5 3S 41 5W
Ojai .. 73 34 28N 119 16W
Ojinaga .. 74 29 34N 104 25W
Ojos del Salado,
  Cerro .. 80 27 0S 68 40W
Okaba .. 35 8 6S 139 42 E
Okahandja .. 56 22 0S 16 59 E
Okahukura .. 40 38 48S 175 14 E
Okanagan L. .. 64 50 0N 119 30W
Okandja .. 54 0 35S 13 45 E
Okanogan .. 72 48 6N 119 43W
Okanogan → .. 72 48 6N 119 43W
Okaputa .. 56 20 5S 17 0 E
Okara .. 32 30 50N 73 31 E
Okarito .. 43 43 15S 170 9 E
Okaukuejo .. 56 19 10S 16 0 E
Okavango Swamps 56 18 45S 22 45 E
Okaya .. 36 36 0N 138 10 E
Okayama .. 36 34 40N 133 54 E
Okayama □ .. 36 35 0N 133 50 E
Okazaki .. 36 34 57N 137 10 E
Oke-Iho .. 53 8 1N 3 18 E
Okeechobee .. 69 27 16N 80 46W
Okeechobee, L. .. 69 27 0N 80 50W
Okefenokee Swamp 69 30 50N 82 15W
Okehampton .. 7 50 44N 4 1W
Okene .. 53 7 32N 6 11 E
Okha .. 25 53 40N 143 0 E
Okhotsk .. 25 59 20N 143 10 E
Okhotsk, Sea of .. 25 55 0N 145 0 E
Okhotskiy Perevoz 25 61 52N 135 35 E

Okhotsko
  Kolymskoye .. 25 63 0N 157 0 E
Oki-Shotō .. 36 36 5N 133 15 E
Okiep .. 56 29 39S 17 53 E
Okigwi .. 53 5 52N 7 20 E
Okija .. 53 5 54N 6 55 E
Okitipupa .. 53 6 31N 4 50 E
Oklahoma □ .. 71 35 20N 97 30W
Oklahoma City .. 71 35 25N 97 30W
Okmulgee .. 71 35 38N 96 0W
Okolona .. 71 34 0N 88 45W
Okrika .. 53 4 40N 7 10 E
Oktabrsk .. 23 49 28N 57 25 E
Oktyabrskiy .. 22 54 28N 53 28 E
Oktyabrskoy
  Revolyutsii, Os. . 25 79 30N 97 0 E
Oktyabrskoye .. 24 62 28N 66 3 E
Okuru .. 43 43 55S 168 55 E
Okushiri-Tō .. 36 42 15N 139 30 E
Okuta .. 53 9 14N 3 12 E
Okwa → .. 56 22 30S 23 0 E
Ola .. 71 35 2N 93 10W
Ólafsfjörður .. 20 66 4N 18 39W
Ólafsvík .. 20 64 53N 23 43W
Olancha .. 73 36 15N 118 1W
Olanchito .. 75 15 30N 86 30W
Öland .. 21 56 45N 16 38 E
Olary .. 45 32 18S 140 19 E
Olathe .. 70 38 50N 94 50W
Olavarría .. 80 36 55S 60 20W
Ólbia .. 18 40 55N 9 30 E
Old Bahama Chan.
  = Bahama, Canal
  Viejo de .. 75 22 10N 77 30W
Old Castile =
  Castilla La Vieja . 13 41 55N 4 0W
Old Castle .. 9 53 46N 7 10W
Old Cork .. 44 22 57S 141 52 E
Old Crow .. 60 67 30N 140 5 E
Old Fort → .. 65 58 36N 110 24W
Old Town .. 63 45 0N 68 41W
Old Wives L. .. 65 50 5N 106 0W
Oldbury .. 7 51 38N 2 30W
Oldenburg .. 14 53 10N 8 10 E
Oldenzaal .. 11 52 19N 6 53 E
Oldham .. 6 53 33N 2 8W
Oldman → .. 64 49 57N 111 42W
Olds .. 64 51 50N 114 10W
Olean .. 68 42 8N 78 25W
Olekma → .. 25 60 22N 120 42 E
Olekminsk .. 25 60 25N 120 30 E
Olenegorsk .. 22 68 9N 33 18 E
Olenek .. 25 68 28N 112 18 E
Olenek → .. 25 73 0N 120 10 E
Oléron, I. d' .. 12 45 55N 1 15W
Oleśnica .. 15 51 13N 17 22 E
Olga .. 25 43 50N 135 14 E
Olga, L. .. 62 49 47N 77 15W
Olga, Mt. .. 47 25 20S 130 50 E
Olifants → .. 57 23 57S 31 58 E
Olifantshoek .. 56 27 57S 22 42 E
Ólimbos, Óros .. 19 40 6N 22 23 E
Olinda .. 79 8 1S 34 51W
Oliveira .. 79 20 39S 44 50W
Olivenza .. 13 38 41N 7 9W
Oliver .. 64 49 13N 119 37W
Oliver L. .. 65 56 56N 103 22W
Ollagüe .. 78 21 15S 68 10W
Olney, Ill., U.S.A. .. 68 38 40N 88 0W
Olney, Tex., U.S.A. 71 33 25N 98 45W
Olomane → .. 63 50 14N 60 37W
Olomouc .. 14 49 38N 17 12 E
Olonets .. 22 61 10N 33 0 E
Olongapo .. 35 14 50N 120 18 E
Olovo .. 19 44 8N 18 35 E
Olovyannaya .. 25 50 58N 115 35 E
Oloy → .. 25 66 29N 159 29 E
Olsztyn .. 15 53 48N 20 29 E
Olt → .. 15 43 43N 24 51 E
Olteniţa .. 15 44 7N 26 42 E
Olton .. 71 34 16N 102 7W
Oltu .. 30 40 35N 41 58 E
Olympia, Greece .. 19 37 39N 21 39 E
Olympia, U.S.A. .. 72 47 0N 122 58W
Olympic Mts. .. 72 47 50N 123 45W
Olympic Nat. Park . 72 47 48N 123 30W
Olympus, Mt. =
  Ólimbos, Óros .. 19 40 6N 22 23 E
Olympus, Mt. .. 72 47 52N 123 40W
Om → .. 24 54 59N 73 22 E
Ōmachi .. 36 36 30N 137 50 E
Omagh .. 9 54 36N 7 20W
Omagh □ .. 9 54 35N 7 15W
Omaha .. 70 41 15N 96 0W
Omak .. 72 48 24N 119 37W
Oman ■ .. 29 23 0N 58 0 E
Oman, G. of .. 31 24 30N 58 30 E
Omaruru .. 56 21 26S 16 0 E
Omaruru → .. 56 22 7S 14 15 E
Omate .. 78 16 45S 71 0W
Ombai, Selat .. 35 8 30S 124 50 E
Omboué .. 54 1 35S 9 15 E
Ombrone → .. 18 42 39N 11 0 E

Omdurmân .. 51 15 40N 32 28 E
Ometepe, I. de .. 75 11 32N 85 35W
Ometepec .. 74 16 39N 98 23W
Omez .. 28 32 22N 35 0 E
Omineca → .. 64 56 3N 124 16W
Omitara .. 56 22 16S 18 2 E
Ōmiya .. 36 35 54N 139 38 E
Ommen .. 11 52 31N 6 26 E
Omo → .. 51 6 25N 36 10 E
Omolon → .. 25 68 42N 158 36 E
Omono-Gawa → .. 36 39 46N 140 3 E
Omsk .. 24 55 0N 73 12 E
Omsukchan .. 25 62 32N 155 48 E
Omul, Vf. .. 15 45 27N 25 29 E
Ōmura .. 36 32 56N 130 0 E
Omuramba
  Omatako → .. 55 17 45S 20 25 E
Ōmuta .. 36 33 0N 130 26 E
Onaga .. 70 39 32N 96 12W
Onalaska .. 70 43 53N 91 14W
Onamia .. 70 46 4N 93 38W
Onancock .. 68 37 42N 75 49W
Onang .. 35 3 2S 118 49 E
Onaping L. .. 62 47 3N 81 30W
Onarhã .. 31 35 30N 71 0 E
Onavas .. 74 28 28N 109 30W
Onawa .. 70 42 2N 96 2W
Onaway .. 68 45 21N 84 11W
Oncócua .. 56 16 30S 13 25 E
Onda .. 13 39 55N 0 17W
Ondangua .. 56 17 57S 16 4 E
Ondjiva .. 56 16 48S 15 50 E
Ondo .. 53 7 4N 4 47 E
Ondo □ .. 53 7 0N 5 0 E
Öndörhaan .. 37 47 19N 110 39 E
Öndverðarnes .. 20 64 52N 24 0W
Onega .. 22 64 0N 38 10 E
Onega → .. 22 63 58N 37 55 E
Onega, G. of =
  Onezhskaya Guba 22 64 30N 37 0 E
Onega, L. =
  Onezhskoye
  Ozero .. 22 62 0N 35 30 E
Onehunga .. 43 36 55S 174 48 E
Oneida .. 68 43 5N 75 40W
Oneida L. .. 68 43 12N 76 0W
O'Neill .. 70 42 30N 98 38W
Onekotan, Ostrov . 25 49 25N 154 45 E
Oneonta, Ala.,
  U.S.A. .. 69 33 58N 86 29W
Oneonta, N.Y.,
  U.S.A. .. 68 42 26N 75 5W
Onezhskaya Guba . 22 64 30N 37 0 E
Onezhskoye Ozero 22 62 0N 35 30 E
Ongarue .. 43 38 42S 175 19 E
Ongerup .. 47 33 58S 118 28 E
Ongniud Qi .. 38 43 0N 118 38 E
Ongole .. 32 15 33N 80 2 E
Onguren .. 25 53 38N 107 36 E
Onida .. 70 44 42N 100 5W
Onilahy → .. 57 23 34S 43 45 E
Onitsha .. 53 6 6N 6 42 E
Onoda .. 36 34 2N 131 25 E
Onslow .. 46 21 40S 115 12 E
Onslow B. .. 69 34 20N 77 20W
Onstwedde .. 11 53 2N 7 4 E
Ontake-San .. 36 35 53N 137 29 E
Ontario, Calif.,
  U.S.A. .. 73 34 2N 117 40W
Ontario, Oreg.,
  U.S.A. .. 72 44 1N 117 1W
Ontario □ .. 62 52 0N 88 10W
Ontario, L. .. 62 43 40N 78 0W
Ontonagon .. 70 46 52N 89 19W
Oodnadatta .. 45 27 33S 135 30 E
Ooldea .. 47 30 27S 131 50 E
Oombulgurri .. 46 15 15S 127 45 E
Oona River .. 64 53 57N 130 16W
Oorindi .. 44 20 40S 141 1 E
Oost-Vlaanderen □ 11 51 5N 3 50 E
Oostende .. 11 51 15N 2 54 E
Oosterhout .. 11 51 39N 4 47 E
Oosterschelde .. 11 51 33N 4 0 E
Ootacamund .. 32 11 30N 76 44 E
Ootsa L. .. 64 53 50N 126 2W
Opala, U.S.S.R. .. 25 51 58N 156 30 E
Opala, Zaïre .. 54 0 40S 24 20 E
Opanake .. 32 6 35N 80 40 E
Opasatika .. 62 49 30N 82 50W
Opasquia .. 65 53 16N 93 34W
Opava .. 15 49 57N 17 58 E
Opelousas .. 71 30 35N 92 7W
Opémisca, L. .. 62 49 56N 74 52W
Opheim .. 72 48 52N 106 30W
Ophir .. 60 63 10N 156 40W
Ophthalmia Ra. .. 46 23 15S 119 30 E
Opi .. 53 6 36N 7 28 E
Opinaca → .. 62 52 15N 78 2W
Opinaca L. .. 62 52 39N 76 20W
Opiskotish, L. .. 63 53 10N 67 50W
Opobo .. 53 4 35N 7 34 E
Opole .. 15 50 42N 17 58 E
Oporto = Porto .. 13 41 8N 8 40W

Panama Canal

Opotiki 43 38 1S 177 19 E
Opp 69 31 19N 86 13W
Oppland fylke □ 21 61 15N 9 40 E
Opua 43 35 19S 174 9 E
Opunake 43 39 26S 173 52 E
Or Yehuda 28 32 2N 34 50 E
Ora 28 30 55N 35 1 E
Ora Banda 47 30 20S 121 0 E
Oracle 73 32 36N 110 46W
Oradea 17 47 2N 21 58 E
Öræfajökull 20 64 2N 16 39W
Orai 32 25 58N 79 30 E
Oran, Algeria 50 35 45N 0 39W
Oran, Argentina 80 23 10S 64 20W
Orange, Australia 45 33 15S 149 7 E
Orange, France 12 44 8N 4 47 E
Orange, Tex., U.S.A. 71 30 10N 93 50W
Orange, Va., U.S.A. 68 38 17N 78 5W
Orange → =
Oranje → 56 28 41S 16 28 E
Orange, C. 79 4 20N 51 30W
Orange Free State □ 56 28 30S 27 0 E
Orange Grove 71 27 57N 97 57W
Orange Walk 74 18 6N 88 33W
Orangeburg 69 33 35N 80 53W
Orangeville 62 43 55N 80 5W
Oranienburg 14 52 45N 13 15 E
Oranje → 56 28 41S 16 28 E
Oranje Vrystaat □ =
Orange Free
State □ 56 28 30S 27 0 E
Oranjemund 56 28 38S 16 29 E
Oranjerivier 56 29 40S 24 12 E
Or'Aquiva 28 32 30N 34 54 E
Oras 35 12 9N 125 28 E
Oraşul Stalin =
Braşov 15 45 38N 25 35 E
Orbetello 18 42 26N 11 11 E
Orbost 45 37 40S 148 29 E
Orchila, I. 78 11 48N 66 10W
Ord → 46 15 33S 138 15 E
Ord, Mt. 46 17 20S 125 34 E
Orderville 73 37 18N 112 43W
Ordos = Mu Us
Shamo 38 39 0N 109 0 E
Ordu 30 40 55N 37 53 E
Ordway 70 38 15N 103 42W
Ordzhonikidze 23 43 0N 44 35 E
Ore Mts. =
Erzgebirge 14 50 25N 13 0 E
Örebro 21 59 20N 15 18 E
Örebro län □ 21 59 27N 15 0 E
Oregon 70 42 1N 89 20W
Oregon □ 72 44 0N 121 0W
Oregon City 72 45 21N 122 35W
Orekhovo-Zuyevo 22 55 50N 38 55 E
Orel 22 52 57N 36 3 E
Orem 72 40 20N 111 45W
Orenburg 22 51 45N 55 6 E
Orense 13 42 19N 7 55W
Orepuki 43 46 19S 167 46 E
Orford Ness 7 52 6N 1 31 E
Orgūn 31 32 55N 69 12 E
Orhon Gol → 37 49 30N 106 0 E
Orient 45 28 7S 142 50 E
Oriental, Cordillera 78 6 0N 73 0W
Orihuela 13 38 7N 0 55W
Orinoco → 78 9 15N 61 30W
Orissa □ 33 20 0N 84 0 E
Oristano 18 39 54N 8 35 E
Oristano, G. di 18 39 50N 8 22 E
Orizaba 74 18 50N 97 10W
Orkanger 20 63 18N 9 52 E
Orkla → 20 63 18N 9 51 E
Orkney 56 26 58S 26 40 E
Orkney □ 8 59 0N 3 0W
Orkney Is. 8 59 0N 3 0W
Orland 72 39 46N 122 12W
Orlando 69 28 30N 81 25W
Orléanais 12 48 0N 2 0 E
Orléans 12 47 54N 1 52 E
Orléans, I. d' 63 46 54N 70 58W
Orlik 25 52 30N 99 55 E
Ormara 31 25 16N 64 33 E
Ormoc 35 11 0N 124 37 E
Ormond 43 38 33S 177 56 E
Ormond Beach 69 29 13N 81 5W
Orne □ 12 48 40N 0 5 E
Örnsköldsvik 20 63 17N 18 40 E
Oro → 74 25 35N 105 2W
Orocué 78 4 48N 71 20W
Orodo 53 5 34N 7 4 E
Orogrande 73 32 20N 106 4W
Oromocto 63 45 54N 66 29W
Oron 53 4 48N 8 14 E
Oroqen Zizhiqi 38 50 34N 123 43 E
Oroquieta 35 8 32N 123 44 E
Orós 79 6 15S 38 55W
Orotukan 25 62 16N 151 42 E
Oroville, Calif.,
U.S.A. 72 39 31N 121 30W
Oroville, Wash.,
U.S.A. 72 48 58N 119 30W
Orroroo 45 32 43S 138 38 E
Orsha 22 54 30N 30 25 E
Orsk 22 51 12N 58 34 E
Orşova 15 44 41N 22 25 E
Ortegal, C. 13 43 43N 7 52W
Orthez 12 43 29N 0 48W
Ortigueira 13 43 40N 7 50W
Ortles 18 46 31N 10 33 E
Ortón → 78 10 50S 67 0W
Ortona 18 42 21N 14 24 E
Orūmīyeh 30 37 40N 45 0 E
Orūmīyeh,
Daryācheh-ye 30 37 50N 45 30 E
Oruro 78 18 0S 67 9W
Orūzgān □ 31 33 30N 66 0 E
Orvieto 18 42 43N 12 8 E
Orwell → 7 52 2N 1 12 E
Oryakhovo 19 43 40N 23 57 E
Osa 22 57 17N 55 26 E
Osa, Pen. de 75 8 0N 84 0W
Osage, Iowa, U.S.A. 70 43 15N 92 50W
Osage, Wyo., U.S.A. 70 43 59N 104 25W
Osage → 70 38 35N 91 57W
Osage City 70 38 43N 95 51W
Ōsaka 36 34 40N 135 30 E
Ōsaka □ 36 34 30N 135 30 E
Osawatomie 70 38 30N 94 55W
Osborne 70 39 30N 98 45W
Osceola, Ark., U.S.A. 71 35 40N 90 0W
Osceola, Iowa,
U.S.A. 70 41 0N 93 20W
Oscoda 68 44 26N 83 20W
Ösel = Saaremaa 22 58 30N 22 30 E
Osh 24 40 37N 72 49 E
Oshawa 62 43 50N 78 50W
Oshkosh, Nebr.,
U.S.A. 70 41 27N 102 20W
Oshkosh, Wis.,
U.S.A. 70 44 3N 88 35W
Oshogbo 53 7 48N 4 37 E
Oshwe 54 3 25S 19 28 E
Osijek 19 45 34N 18 41 E
Osipenko =
Berdyansk 23 46 45N 36 50 E
Osizweni 57 27 49S 30 7 E
Oskaloosa 70 41 18N 92 40W
Oskarshamn 21 57 15N 16 27 E
Oskélanéo 62 48 5N 75 15W
Oslo 21 59 55N 10 45 E
Oslob 35 9 31N 123 26 E
Oslofjorden 21 59 20N 10 35 E
Osmanabad 32 18 5N 76 10 E
Osmaniye 30 37 5N 36 10 E
Osnabrück 14 52 16N 8 2 E
Osorio 80 29 53S 50 17W
Osorno 80 40 25S 73 0W
Osoyoos 64 49 0N 119 30W
Ospika → 64 56 20N 124 0W
Osprey Reef 44 13 52S 146 36 E
Oss 11 51 46N 5 32 E
Ossa, Mt. 44 41 52S 146 3 E
Óssa, Oros 19 39 47N 22 42 E
Ossabaw I. 69 31 45N 81 8W
Ossining 68 41 9N 73 50W
Ossokmanuan L. 63 53 25N 65 0W
Ossora 25 59 20N 163 13 E
Ostend = Oostende 11 51 15N 2 54 E
Österdalälven → 21 61 30N 13 45 E
Östergötlands län □ 21 58 35N 15 45 E
Östersund 20 63 10N 14 38 E
Østfold fylke □ 21 59 25N 11 25 E
Ostfriesische Inseln 14 53 45N 7 15 E
Ostrava 15 49 51N 18 18 E
Ostróda 15 53 42N 19 58 E
Ostrołęka 15 53 4N 21 32 E
Ostrów Mazowiecka 15 52 50N 21 51 E
Ostrów Wielkopolski 15 51 36N 17 44 E
Ostrowiec-
Świętokrzyski 15 50 55N 21 22 E
Ōsumi-Kaikyō 36 30 55N 131 0 E
Osuna 13 37 14N 5 8W
Oswego 68 43 29N 76 30W
Oswestry 6 52 52N 3 3W
Otago □ 43 44 44S 169 10 E
Otago Harb. 43 45 47S 170 42 E
Ōtake 36 34 12N 132 13 E
Otaki 43 40 45S 175 10 E
Otaru 36 43 10N 141 0 E
Otaru-Wan =
Ishikari-Wan 36 43 25N 141 1 E
Otavalo 78 0 13N 78 20W
Otavi 56 19 40S 17 24 E
Otchinjau 56 16 30S 13 56 E
Othello 72 46 53N 119 8W
Otira Gorge 43 42 53S 171 33 E
Otis 70 40 12N 102 58W
Otjiwarongo 56 20 30S 16 33 E
Otoineppu 36 44 44N 142 16 E
Otorohanga 43 38 12S 175 14 E
Otoskwin → 62 52 13N 88 6W
Otosquen 65 53 17N 102 1W
Otranto 19 40 9N 18 28 E
Otranto, C. d' 19 40 7N 18 30 E
Otranto, Str. of 19 40 15N 18 40 E
Otse 56 25 2S 25 45 E
Ōtsu 36 35 0N 135 50 E
Ottawa, Canada 62 45 27N 75 42W
Ottawa, Ill., U.S.A. 70 41 20N 88 55W
Ottawa, Kans.,
U.S.A. 70 38 40N 95 6W
Ottawa → =
Outaouais → 62 45 27N 74 8W
Ottawa Is. 61 59 35N 80 10W
Otter L. 65 55 35N 104 39W
Otter Rapids, Ont.,
Canada 62 50 11N 81 39W
Otter Rapids, Sask.,
Canada 65 55 38N 104 44W
Ottosdal 56 26 46S 25 59 E
Ottoshoop 56 25 45S 25 58 E
Ottumwa 70 41 0N 92 25W
Otukpa 53 7 9N 7 41 E
Oturkpo 53 7 16N 8 8 E
Otway, B. 80 53 30S 74 0W
Otway, C. 45 38 52S 143 30 E
Otwock 15 52 5N 21 20 E
Ou-Sammyaku 36 39 20N 140 35 E
Ouachita → 71 31 38N 91 49W
Ouachita, L. 71 34 40N 93 25W
Ouachita Mts. 71 34 50N 94 30W
Ouadâne 50 20 50N 11 40W
Ouadda 51 8 15N 22 20 E
Ouagadougou 53 12 25N 1 30W
Ouahran = Oran 50 35 45N 0 39W
Ouallene 50 24 41N 1 11 E
Ouanda Djallé 51 8 55N 22 53 E
Ouango 54 4 19N 22 30 E
Ouargla 50 31 59N 5 16 E
Ouarzazate 50 30 55N 6 50W
Oubangi → 54 0 30S 17 50 E
Ouddorp 11 51 50N 3 57 E
Oude Rijn → 11 52 12N 4 24 E
Oudenaarde 11 50 50N 3 37 E
Oudtshoorn 56 33 35S 22 14 E
Ouessant, I. d' 12 48 28N 5 6W
Ouesso 54 1 37N 16 5 E
Ouest, Pte. 63 49 52N 64 40W
Ouezzane 50 34 51N 5 35W
Ouidah 53 6 25N 2 0 E
Oujda 50 34 41N 1 55W
Oujeft 50 20 2N 13 0W
Ouled Djellal 50 34 28N 5 2 E
Oulu 20 65 1N 25 29 E
Oulu □ 20 65 10N 27 20 E
Oulujärvi 20 64 25N 27 15 E
Oulujoki → 20 65 1N 25 30 E
Oum Chalouba 51 15 48N 20 46 E
Ounguati 56 22 0S 15 46 E
Ounianga-Kébir 51 19 4N 20 29 E
Ounianga Sérir 51 18 54N 20 51 E
Our → 11 49 55N 6 5 E
Ouray 73 38 3N 107 40W
Ouricuri 79 7 53S 40 5W
Ouro Prêto 79 20 20S 43 30W
Ourthe → 11 50 29N 5 35 E
Ouse 44 42 38S 146 42 E
Ouse →,
E. Sussex, U.K. 7 50 43N 0 3 E
Ouse →, N. Yorks.,
U.K. 6 54 3N 0 7 E
Outaouais → 62 45 27N 74 8W
Outardes → 63 49 24N 69 30W
Outer Hebrides 8 57 30N 7 40W
Outer I. 63 51 10N 58 35W
Outjo 56 20 5S 16 7 E
Outlook, Canada 65 51 30N 107 0W
Outlook, U.S.A. 70 48 53N 104 46W
Ouyen 45 35 1S 142 22 E
Ovalau 43 17 40S 178 48 E
Ovalle 80 30 33S 71 18W
Ovar 13 40 51N 8 40W
Overflakkee 11 51 44N 4 10 E
Overijssel □ 11 52 25N 6 35 E
Overpelt 11 51 12N 5 20 E
Overton 73 36 32N 114 31W
Övertorneå 20 66 23N 23 38 E
Ovid 70 41 0N 102 17W
Oviedo 13 43 25N 5 50W
Owaka 43 46 27S 169 40 E
Owase 36 34 7N 136 12 E
Owatonna 70 44 3N 93 10W
Owbeh 31 34 28N 63 10 E
Owego 68 42 6N 76 17W
Owen Falls 52 0 30N 33 5 E
Owen Sound 62 44 35N 80 55W
Owendo 54 0 17N 9 30 E
Owens L. 73 36 20N 118 0W
Owensboro 68 37 40N 87 5W
Owensville 70 38 20N 91 30W
Owerri 53 5 29N 7 0 E
Owl → 65 57 51N 92 44W
Owo 53 7 10N 5 39 E
Owosso 68 43 0N 84 10W
Owyhee 72 42 0N 116 3W
Owyhee → 72 43 46N 117 2W
Owyhee, L. 72 43 40N 117 16W
Ox Mts. 9 54 6N 9 0W
Oxelösund 21 58 43N 17 15 E
Oxford, N.Z. 43 43 18S 172 11 E
Oxford, U.K. 7 51 45N 1 15W
Oxford, Miss., U.S.A. 71 34 22N 89 30W
Oxford, N.C., U.S.A. 69 36 19N 78 36W
Oxford, Ohio, U.S.A. 68 39 30N 84 40W
Oxford □ 7 51 45N 1 15W
Oxford L. 65 54 51N 95 37W
Oxley 45 34 11S 144 6 E
Oxnard 73 34 10N 119 14W
Oya 34 2 55N 111 55 E
Oyama 36 36 18N 139 48 E
Oyem 54 1 34N 11 31 E
Oyen 65 51 22N 110 28W
Oykel → 8 57 55N 4 26W
Oymyakon 25 63 25N 142 44 E
Oyo 53 7 46N 3 56 E
Oyo □ 53 8 0N 3 30 E
Ozamis 35 8 15N 123 50 E
Ozark, Ala., U.S.A. 69 31 29N 85 39W
Ozark, Ark., U.S.A. 71 35 30N 93 50W
Ozark, Mo., U.S.A. 71 37 0N 93 15W
Ozark Plateau 71 37 20N 91 40W
Ozarks, L. of the 70 38 10N 92 40W
Ozona 71 30 43N 101 11W
Ozuluama 74 21 40N 97 50W

P

P.K. le Roux Dam 56 30 4S 24 40 E
Pa-an 33 16 51N 97 40 E
Paarl 56 33 45S 18 56 E
Paatsi → 20 68 55N 29 0 E
Paauilo 66 20 3N 155 22W
Pab Hills 32 26 30N 66 45 E
Pabna 33 24 1N 89 18 E
Pacaja → 79 1 56S 50 50W
Pacaraima, Sierra 78 4 0N 62 30W
Pacasmayo 78 7 20S 79 35W
Pachpadra 32 25 58N 72 10 E
Pachuca 74 20 10N 98 40W
Pacific 64 54 48N 128 28W
Pacific-Antarctic
Basin 41 46 0S 95 0W
Pacific-Antarctic
Ridge 41 43 0S 115 0W
Pacific Grove 73 36 38N 121 58W
Pacific Ocean 2 10 0N 140 0W
Pacitan 35 8 12S 111 7 E
Padaido, Kepulauan 35 1 5S 138 0 E
Padang 34 1 0S 100 20 E
Padangpanjang 34 0 40S 100 20 E
Padangsidempuan 34 1 30N 99 15 E
Paddockwood 65 53 30N 105 30W
Paderborn 14 51 42N 8 44 E
Padloping Island 61 67 0N 62 50W
Pádova 18 45 24N 11 52 E
Padre I. 71 27 0N 97 20W
Padstow 6 50 33N 4 57W
Padua = Pádova 18 45 24N 11 52 E
Paducah, Ky., U.S.A. 68 37 0N 88 40W
Paducah, Tex.,
U.S.A. 71 34 3N 100 16W
Paeroa 43 37 23S 175 41 E
Pag 18 44 30N 14 50 E
Pagadian 35 7 55N 123 30 E
Pagai Selatan 34 3 0S 100 15W
Pagai Utara 34 2 35S 100 0 E
Pagalu = Annobón 48 1 25S 5 36 E
Pagastikós Kólpos 19 39 15N 23 0 E
Pagatan 34 3 33S 115 59 E
Page, Ariz., U.S.A. 73 36 57N 111 27W
Page, N. Dak.,
U.S.A. 70 47 11N 97 37W
Pago Pago 43 14 16S 170 43W
Pagosa Springs 73 37 16N 107 4W
Pagwa River 62 50 2N 85 14W
Pahala 66 19 12N 155 25W
Pahiatua 43 40 27S 175 50 E
Pahokee 69 26 50N 80 40W
Pahrump 73 36 15N 116 0W
Paia 66 20 54N 156 22W
Paignton 7 50 26N 3 33W
Päijänne, L. 21 61 30N 25 30 E
Painan 34 1 21S 100 34 E
Painesville 68 41 42N 81 18W
Paint Hills =
Nouveau Comptoir 62 53 0N 78 49W
Paint L. 65 55 28N 97 57W
Paint Rock 71 31 30N 99 56W
Painted Desert 73 36 0N 111 30W
Paintsville 68 37 50N 82 50W
Pais Vasco □ 13 43 0N 2 30W
Paisley, U.K. 8 55 51N 4 27W
Paisley, U.S.A. 72 42 43N 120 40W
Paita 78 5 11S 81 9W
Pakaraima Mts. 78 6 0N 60 0W
Pakistan ■ 31 30 0N 70 0 E
Pakistan, East =
Bangladesh ■ 33 24 0N 90 0 E
Pakokku 33 21 20N 95 0 E
Pakse 34 15 5N 105 52 E
Paktīā □ 31 33 0N 69 15 E
Pala 51 9 25N 15 5 E
Palacios 71 28 44N 96 12W
Palagruža 18 42 24N 16 15 E
Palam 32 19 0N 77 0 E
Palamós 13 41 50N 3 10 E
Palampur 32 32 10N 76 30 E
Palana, Australia 44 39 45S 147 55 E
Palana, U.S.S.R. 25 59 10N 159 59 E
Palanan 35 17 8N 122 29 E
Palanan Pt. 35 17 17N 122 30 E
Palangkaraya 34 2 16S 113 56 E
Palani Hills 32 10 14N 77 33 E
Palanpur 32 24 10N 72 25 E
Palapye 56 22 30S 27 7 E
Palatka, U.S.A. 69 29 40N 81 40W
Palatka, U.S.S.R. 25 60 6N 150 54 E
Palawan 34 9 30N 118 30 E
Palayankottai 32 8 45N 77 45 E
Paleleh 35 1 10N 121 50 E
Palembang 34 3 0S 104 50 E
Palencia 13 42 1N 4 34W
Palermo, Italy 18 38 8N 13 20 E
Palermo, U.S.A. 72 39 30N 121 37W
Palestine, Asia 28 32 0N 35 0 E
Palestine, U.S.A. 71 31 42N 95 35W
Paletwa 33 21 10N 92 50 E
Palghat 32 10 46N 76 42 E
Palgrave, Mt. 46 23 22S 115 58 E
Pali 32 25 50N 73 20 E
Palisade 70 40 21N 101 10W
Palitana 32 21 32N 71 49 E
Palizada 74 18 18N 92 8W
Palk Bay 32 9 30N 79 15 E
Palk Strait 32 10 0N 79 45 E
Palla Road =
Dinokwe 56 23 29S 26 37 E
Pallinup 47 34 0S 117 55 E
Palm Beach 69 26 46N 80 0W
Palm Is. 44 18 40S 146 35 E
Palm Springs 73 33 51N 116 35W
Palma 54 10 46S 40 29 E
Palma → 79 12 33S 47 52W
Palma, B. de 13 39 30N 2 39 E
Palma, La,
Canary Is. 50 28 40N 17 50W
Palma, La, Panama 75 8 15N 78 0W
Palma, La, Spain 13 37 21N 6 38W
Palma de Mallorca 13 39 35N 2 39 E
Palma Soriano 75 20 15N 76 0W
Palmahim 28 31 56N 34 44 E
Palmares 79 8 41S 35 28W
Palmas, C. 50 4 27N 7 46W
Pálmas, G. di 18 39 0N 8 30 E
Palmdale 73 34 36N 118 7W
Palmeira dos Índios 79 9 25S 36 37W
Palmeirinhas, Pta.
das 54 9 2S 12 57 E
Palmer 60 61 35N 149 10W
Palmer → 44 15 34S 142 26 E
Palmer Lake 70 39 10N 104 52W
Palmerston North 43 40 21S 175 39 E
Palmetto 69 27 33N 82 33W
Palmi 18 38 21N 15 51 E
Palmira 78 3 32N 76 16W
Palmyra = Tudmur 30 34 36N 38 15 E
Palmyra 70 39 45N 91 30W
Palmyra Is. 41 5 52N 162 5W
Palo Alto 73 37 25N 122 8W
Palopo 35 3 0S 120 16 E
Palos, C. de 13 37 38N 0 40W
Palouse 72 46 59N 117 5W
Palparara 44 24 47S 141 28 E
Palu, Indonesia 35 1 0S 119 52 E
Palu, Turkey 30 38 45N 40 0 E
Paluan 35 13 26N 120 29 E
Pama 53 11 19N 0 44 E
Pamanukan 35 6 16S 107 49 E
Pamekasan 35 7 10S 113 28 E
Pamirs 24 37 40N 73 0 E
Pamlico → 69 35 25N 76 30W
Pamlico Sd. 69 35 20N 76 0W
Pampa 71 35 35N 100 58W
Pampa de las
Salinas 80 32 1S 66 58W
Pampanua 35 4 16S 120 8 E
Pampas, Argentina 80 35 0S 63 0W
Pampas, Peru 78 12 20S 74 50W
Pamplona, Colombia 78 7 23N 72 39W
Pamplona, Spain 13 42 48N 1 38W
Pampoenpoort 56 31 3S 22 40 E
Pana 70 39 25N 89 10W
Panaca 73 37 51N 114 23W
Panaitan 35 6 36S 105 12 E
Panaji 32 15 25N 73 50 E
Panamá 75 9 0N 79 25W
Panama ■ 75 8 48N 79 55W
Panamá, G. de 75 8 4N 79 20W
Panama Canal 75 9 10N 79 37W

Panama City

Panama City **69** 30 10N 85 41W
Panamint Ra. **73** 36 30N 117 20W
Panão **78** 9 55S 75 55W
Panarukan **35** 7 42S 113 56 E
Panay **35** 11 10N 122 30 E
Panay, G. **35** 11 0N 122 30 E
Pancake Ra. **73** 38 30N 116 0W
Pančevo **19** 44 52N 20 41 E
Pancorbo, Paso **13** 42 32N 3 5W
Pandan **35** 11 45N 122 10 E
Pandegelang **35** 6 25S 106 0 E
Pandharpur **32** 17 41N 75 20 E
Pando **80** 34 44S 56 0W
Pando, L. = Hope, L. **45** 28 24S 139 18 E
Panevezys **22** 55 42N 24 25 E
Panfilov **24** 44 10N 80 0 E
Pang-Long **33** 23 11N 98 45 E
Pang-Yang **33** 22 7N 98 48 E
Pangalanes, Canal des **57** 22 48S 47 50 E
Pangani **54** 5 25S 38 58 E
Pangfou = Bengbu **39** 32 58N 117 20 E
Pangkah, Tanjung **35** 6 51S 112 33 E
Pangkajene **35** 4 46S 119 34 E
Pangkalanbrandan **34** 4 1N 98 20 E
Pangkalanbuun **34** 2 41S 111 37 E
Pangkalansusu **34** 4 2N 98 13 E
Pangkalpinang **34** 2 0S 106 0 E
Pangkoh **34** 3 5S 114 8 E
Pangnirtung **61** 66 8N 65 54W
Pangrango **35** 6 46S 107 1 E
Panguitch **73** 37 52N 112 30W
Pangutaran Group **35** 6 18N 120 34 E
Panhandle **71** 35 23N 101 23W
Panjgur **31** 27 0N 64 5 E
Panjim = Panaji **32** 15 25N 73 50 E
Panjinad Barrage **31** 29 22N 71 15 E
Panna **32** 24 40N 80 15 E
Panorama **80** 21 21S 51 51W
Panshan **38** 41 3N 122 2 E
Panshi **38** 42 58N 126 5 E
Pantar **35** 8 28S 124 10 E
Pantelleria **18** 36 52N 12 0 E
Pánuco **74** 22 0N 98 15W
Panyam **53** 9 27N 9 8 E
Panyu **39** 22 51N 113 20 E
Paola **70** 38 36N 94 50W
Paonia **73** 38 56N 107 37W
Paoting = Baoding **38** 38 50N 115 28 E
Paot'ou = Baotou **38** 40 32N 110 2 E
Paoua **51** 7 9N 16 20 E
Pápa **15** 47 22N 17 30 E
Papagayo → **74** 16 36N 99 43W
Papagayo, G. de **75** 10 30N 85 50W
Papakura **43** 37 4S 174 59 E
Papantla **74** 20 30N 97 30W
Papar **34** 5 45N 116 0 E
Paparoa **43** 36 6S 174 16 E
Papigochic → **74** 29 9N 109 40W
Paposo **80** 25 0S 70 30W
Papua New Guinea ■ **40** 8 0S 145 0 E
Papudo **80** 32 29S 71 27W
Papun **33** 18 0N 97 30 E
Pará = Belém **79** 1 20S 48 30W
Pará □ **79** 3 20S 52 0W
Paraburdoo **46** 23 14S 117 32 E
Paracatu **79** 17 10S 46 50W
Parachilna **45** 31 10S 138 21 E
Parachinar **32** 33 55N 70 5 E
Paradip **33** 20 15N 86 35 E
Paradise **72** 47 27N 114 17W
Paradise → **63** 53 27N 57 19W
Paradise Valley **72** 41 30N 117 28W
Parado **35** 8 42S 118 30 E
Paragould **71** 36 5N 90 30W
Paragua → **78** 6 55N 62 55W
Paragua, La **78** 6 50N 63 20W
Paraguaçu → **79** 12 45S 38 54W
Paraguaná, Pen. de **78** 12 0N 70 0W
Paraguarí **80** 25 36S 57 0W
Paraguay ■ **80** 23 0S 57 0W
Paraguay → **80** 27 18S 58 38W
Paraíba = João Pessoa **79** 7 10S 34 52W
Paraíba □ **79** 7 0S 36 0W
Paraíba do Sul → **79** 21 37S 41 3W
Parainen **21** 60 18N 22 18 E
Parakou **53** 9 25N 2 40 E
Paramaribo **79** 5 50N 55 10W
Paramushir, Ostrov **25** 50 24N 156 0 E
Paran → **28** 30 20N 35 10 E
Paraná, Argentina **80** 31 45S 60 30W
Paranã, Brazil **79** 12 30S 47 48W
Paraná □ **80** 24 30S 51 0W
Paraná → **80** 33 43S 59 15W
Paranaguá **80** 25 30S 48 30W
Paranaíba → **79** 20 6S 51 4W
Paranapanema → **80** 22 40S 53 9W
Paranapiacaba, Serra do **80** 24 31S 48 35W
Parang, Jolo, Phil. **35** 5 55N 120 54 E
Parang, Mindanao, Phil. **35** 7 23N 124 16 E
Paratinga **79** 12 40S 43 10W
Paratoo **45** 32 42S 139 40 E
Parattah **44** 42 22S 147 23 E
Parbhani **32** 19 8N 76 52 E
Parchim **14** 53 25N 11 50 E
Pardes Hanna **28** 32 28N 34 57 E
Pardo →, Bahia, Brazil **79** 15 40S 39 0W
Pardo →, Mato Grosso, Brazil **79** 21 46S 52 9W
Pardo →, São Paulo, Brazil **79** 20 10S 48 38W
Pardubice **14** 50 3N 15 45 E
Pare **35** 7 43S 112 12 E
Parecis, Serra dos **78** 13 0S 60 0W
Paren **25** 62 30N 163 15 E
Parent **62** 47 55N 74 35W
Parent, Lac **62** 48 31N 77 1W
Parepare **35** 4 0S 119 40 E
Parfuri **57** 22 28S 31 17 E
Parguba **22** 62 20N 34 27 E
Pariaguán **78** 8 51N 64 34W
Pariaman **34** 0 47S 100 11 E
Paricutín, Cerro **74** 19 28N 102 15W
Parigi, Java, Indonesia **35** 7 42S 108 29 E
Parigi, Sulawesi, Indonesia **35** 0 50S 120 5 E
Parika **78** 6 50N 58 20W
Parima, Serra **78** 2 30N 64 0W
Parinari **78** 4 35S 74 25W
Parîng **15** 45 20N 23 37 E
Parintins **79** 2 40S 56 50W
Pariparit Kyun **33** 14 55S 93 45 E
Paris, Canada **62** 43 12N 80 25W
Paris, France **12** 48 50N 2 20 E
Paris, Idaho, U.S.A. **72** 42 13N 111 30W
Paris, Ky., U.S.A. **68** 38 12N 84 12W
Paris, Tenn., U.S.A. **69** 36 20N 88 20W
Paris, Tex., U.S.A. **71** 33 40N 95 30W
Paris, Ville de □ **12** 48 50N 2 20 E
Pariti **35** 10 15S 123 45 E
Park City **72** 40 42N 111 35W
Park Falls **70** 45 58N 90 27W
Park Range **72** 40 0N 106 30W
Park Rapids **70** 46 56N 95 0W
Park River **70** 48 25N 97 43W
Park Rynie **57** 30 25S 30 45 E
Parker, Ariz., U.S.A. **73** 34 8N 114 16W
Parker, S. Dak., U.S.A. **70** 43 25N 97 7W
Parker Dam **73** 34 13N 114 5W
Parkersburg **68** 39 18N 81 31W
Parkerview **65** 51 21N 103 18W
Parkes **45** 33 9S 148 11 E
Parkside **65** 53 10N 106 33W
Parkston **70** 43 25N 98 0W
Parksville **64** 49 20N 124 21W
Parma, Italy **18** 44 50N 10 20 E
Parma, U.S.A. **72** 43 49N 116 59W
Parnaguá **79** 10 10S 44 38W
Parnaíba, Piauí, Brazil **79** 2 54S 41 47W
Parnaíba, São Paulo, Brazil **79** 19 34S 51 14W
Parnaíba → **79** 3 0S 41 50W
Parnassós **19** 38 35N 22 30 E
Pärnu **22** 58 28N 24 33 E
Paroo → **45** 31 28S 143 32 E
Páros **19** 37 5N 25 12 E
Parowan **73** 37 54N 112 56W
Parral **80** 36 10S 71 52W
Parramatta **45** 33 48S 151 1 E
Parras **74** 25 30N 102 20W
Parrett → **7** 51 7N 2 58W
Parris I. **69** 32 20N 80 30W
Parrsboro **63** 45 30N 64 25W
Parry Is. **58** 77 0N 110 0W
Parry Sound **62** 45 20N 80 0W
Parshall **70** 47 56N 102 11W
Parsnip → **64** 55 10N 123 2W
Parsons **71** 37 20N 95 17W
Parsons Ra. **44** 13 30S 135 15 E
Paru → **79** 1 33S 52 38W
Paruro **78** 13 45S 71 50W
Parvān □ **31** 35 0N 69 0 E
Parvatipuram **33** 18 50N 83 25 E
Parys **56** 26 52S 27 29 E
Pas-de-Calais □ **12** 50 30N 2 10 E
Pasadena, Calif., U.S.A. **73** 34 5N 118 9W
Pasadena, Tex., U.S.A. **71** 29 45N 95 14W
Pasaje **78** 3 23S 79 50W
Pascagoula **71** 30 21N 88 30W
Pascagoula → **71** 30 21N 88 35W
Pasco **72** 46 10N 119 0W
Pasco, Cerro de **78** 10 45S 76 10W
Pasfield L. **65** 58 24N 105 20W
Pashmakli = Smolyan **19** 41 36N 24 38 E
Pasirian **35** 8 13S 113 8 E
Pasley, C. **47** 33 52S 123 35 E
Pasni **31** 25 15N 63 27 E
Paso de Indios **80** 43 55S 69 0W
Paso Robles **73** 35 40N 120 45W
Paspébiac **63** 48 3N 65 17W
Passage West **9** 51 52N 8 20W
Passau **14** 48 34N 13 27 E
Passero, C. **18** 36 42N 15 8 E
Passo Fundo **80** 28 10S 52 20W
Passos **79** 20 45S 46 37W
Pastaza → **78** 4 50S 76 52W
Pasto **78** 1 13N 77 17W
Pasuruan **35** 7 40S 112 44 E
Patagonia, Argentina **80** 45 0S 69 0W
Patagonia, U.S.A. **73** 31 35N 110 45W
Patan, India **32** 23 54N 72 14 E
Patan, Nepal **33** 27 40N 85 20 E
Patani **35** 0 20N 128 50 E
Patchewollock **45** 35 22S 142 12 E
Patchogue **68** 40 46N 73 1W
Patea **43** 39 45S 174 30 E
Pategi **53** 8 50N 5 45 E
Patensie **56** 33 46S 24 49 E
Paternò **18** 37 34N 14 53 E
Pateros **72** 48 4N 119 58W
Paterson **68** 40 55N 74 10W
Paterson Ra. **46** 21 45S 122 10 E
Pathankot **32** 32 18N 75 45 E
Pathfinder Res. **72** 42 00N 107 0W
Pati **35** 6 45S 111 1 E
Patiala **32** 30 23N 76 26 E
Patkai Bum **33** 27 0N 95 30 E
Pátmos **19** 37 21N 26 36 E
Patna **33** 25 35N 85 12 E
Patos, L. dos **80** 31 20S 51 0W
Patos de Minas **79** 18 35S 46 32W
Patquía **80** 30 2S 66 55W
Pátrai **19** 38 14N 21 47 E
Pátraikós, Kólpos **19** 38 17N 21 30 E
Patrocínio **79** 18 57S 47 0W
Pattani **34** 6 48N 101 15 E
Patten **63** 45 59N 68 28W
Patterson, Calif., U.S.A. **73** 37 30N 121 9W
Patterson, La., U.S.A. **71** 29 44N 91 20W
Patti **18** 38 8N 14 57 E
Patuakhali **33** 22 20N 90 25 E
Patuca → **75** 15 50N 84 18W
Patuca, Punta **75** 15 49N 84 14W
Pátzcuaro **74** 19 30N 101 40W
Pau **12** 43 19N 0 25W
Pauillac **12** 45 11N 0 46W
Pauini → **78** 1 42S 62 50W
Pauk **33** 21 27N 94 30 E
Paul I. **63** 56 30N 61 20W
Paulis = Isiro **54** 2 53N 27 40 E
Paulistana **79** 8 9S 41 9W
Paullina **70** 42 55N 95 40W
Paulo Afonso **79** 9 21S 38 15W
Paulpietersburg **57** 27 23S 30 50 E
Pauls Valley **71** 34 40N 97 17W
Pavia **18** 45 10N 9 10 E
Pavlodar **24** 52 33N 77 0 E
Pavlograd **23** 48 30N 35 52 E
Pavlovo, Gorkiy, U.S.S.R. **22** 55 58N 43 5 E
Pavlovo, Yakut A.S.S.R., U.S.S.R. **25** 63 5N 115 25 E
Pavlovsk **23** 50 26N 40 5 E
Pawhuska **71** 36 40N 96 25W
Pawnee **71** 36 24N 96 50W
Pawnee City **70** 40 8N 96 10W
Pawtucket **68** 41 51N 71 22W
Paxton, Ill., U.S.A. **68** 40 25N 88 7W
Paxton, Nebr., U.S.A. **70** 41 12N 101 27W
Payakumbuh **34** 0 20S 100 35 E
Payette **72** 44 0N 117 0W
Payne Bay = Bellin **61** 60 0N 70 0W
Payne L. **61** 59 30N 74 30W
Paynes Find **47** 29 15S 117 42 E
Paynesville **70** 45 21N 94 44W
Paysandú **80** 32 19S 58 8W
Payson, Ariz., U.S.A. **73** 34 17N 111 15W
Payson, Utah, U.S.A. **72** 40 8N 111 41W
Paz → **75** 13 44N 90 10W
Paz, B. de la **74** 24 15N 110 25W
Paz, La, Entre Rios, Argentina **80** 30 50S 59 45W
Paz, La, San Luis, Argentina **80** 33 30S 67 20W
Paz, La, Bolivia **78** 16 20S 68 10W
Paz, La, Hond. **75** 14 20N 87 47W
Paz, La, Mexico **74** 24 10N 110 20W
Pazar **30** 41 10N 40 50 E
Pazardzhik **19** 42 12N 24 20 E
Pe Ell **72** 46 30N 123 18W
Peace → **64** 59 0N 111 25W
Peace Point **64** 59 7N 112 27W
Peace River **64** 56 15N 117 18W
Peach Springs **73** 35 36N 113 30W
Peak, The **6** 53 24N 1 53W
Peak Downs **44** 22 14S 148 0 E
Peak Downs Mine **44** 22 17S 148 11 E
Peak Hill, N.S.W., Australia **45** 32 47S 148 11 E
Peak Hill, W. Austral., Australia **47** 25 35S 118 43 E
Peak Range **44** 22 50S 148 20 E
Peake **45** 35 25S 140 0 E
Peake Cr. → **45** 28 2S 136 7 E
Peale Mt. **73** 38 25N 109 12W
Pearl → **71** 30 23N 89 45W
Pearl City **66** 21 24N 158 0W
Pearsall **71** 28 55N 99 8W
Pearse I. **64** 54 52N 130 14W
Pease → **71** 34 12N 99 7W
Pebane **55** 17 10S 38 8 E
Pebas **78** 3 10S 71 46W
Peč **19** 42 40N 20 17 E
Pechenga **22** 69 30N 31 25 E
Pechora → **22** 68 13N 54 15 E
Pechorskaya Guba **22** 68 40N 54 0 E
Pecos **71** 31 25N 103 35W
Pecos → **71** 29 42N 102 30W
Pécs **15** 46 5N 18 15 E
Pedder, L. **44** 42 55S 146 10 E
Peddie **57** 33 14S 27 7 E
Pedirka **45** 26 40S 135 14 E
Pedra Azul **79** 16 2S 41 17W
Pedreiras **79** 4 32S 44 40W
Pedrera, La **78** 1 18S 69 43W
Pedro Afonso **79** 9 0S 48 10W
Pedro Cays **75** 17 5N 77 48W
Pedro Juan Caballero **80** 22 30S 55 40W
Pedro Miguel Locks **74** 9 1N 79 36W
Peduyim **28** 31 20N 34 37 E
Peebinga **45** 34 52S 140 57 E
Peebles **8** 55 40N 3 12W
Peekskill **68** 41 18N 73 57W
Peel **6** 54 14N 4 40W
Peel →, Australia **45** 30 50S 150 29 E
Peel →, Canada **60** 67 0N 135 0W
Peera Peera Poolanna L. **45** 26 30S 138 0 E
Peers **64** 53 40N 116 0W
Pegasus Bay **43** 43 20S 173 10 E
Pegu **33** 17 20N 96 29 E
Pegu Yoma **33** 19 0N 96 0 E
Pehuajó **80** 35 45S 62 0W
Peip'ing = Beijing **38** 39 55N 116 20 E
Peixe **79** 12 0S 48 40W
Pekalongan **35** 6 53S 109 40 E
Pekanbaru **34** 0 30N 101 15 E
Pekin **70** 40 35N 89 40W
Peking = Beijing **38** 39 55N 116 20 E
Pelabuhan Kelang **34** 3 0N 101 23 E
Pelabuhan Ratu, Teluk **35** 7 5S 106 30 E
Pelabuhanratu **35** 7 0S 106 32 E
Pelaihari **34** 3 55S 114 45 E
Peleaga **15** 45 22N 22 55 E
Pelée, Mt. **75** 14 48N 61 0W
Pelee, Pt. **62** 41 54N 82 31W
Pelee I. **62** 41 47N 82 40W
Peleng **35** 1 20S 123 30 E
Pelham **69** 31 5N 84 6W
Pelican L. **65** 52 28N 100 20W
Pelican Narrows **65** 55 10N 102 56W
Pelican Rapids **65** 52 45N 100 42W
Pelkosenniemi **20** 67 6N 27 28 E
Pella, S. Africa **56** 29 1S 19 6 E
Pella, U.S.A. **70** 41 30N 93 0W
Pelly → **60** 62 47N 137 19W
Pelly Bay **61** 68 38N 89 50W
Pelly L. **60** 66 0N 102 0W
Peloponnese = Pelopónnisos □ **19** 37 10N 22 0 E
Pelopónnisos □ **19** 37 10N 22 0 E
Peloro, C. **18** 38 15N 15 40 E
Pelorus Sound **43** 40 59S 173 59 E
Pelotas **80** 31 42S 52 23W
Pelvoux, Massif de **12** 44 52N 6 20 E
Pemalang **35** 6 53S 109 23 E
Pematangsiantar **34** 2 57N 99 5 E
Pemba I. **54** 5 0S 39 45 E
Pemberton, Australia **47** 34 30S 116 0 E
Pemberton, Canada **64** 50 25N 122 50W
Pembina **65** 48 58N 97 15W
Pembina → **65** 49 0N 98 12W
Pembine **68** 45 38N 87 59W
Pembino **70** 48 58N 97 15W
Pembroke, Canada **62** 45 50N 77 7W
Pembroke, U.K. **7** 51 41N 4 57W
Pembroke, U.S.A. **69** 32 5N 81 32W
Pen-y-Ghent **6** 54 10N 2 15W
Peña de Francia, Sierra de **13** 40 32N 6 10W
Peñalara, Pico **13** 40 51N 3 57W
Penang = Pinang **34** 5 25N 100 15 E
Penápolis **80** 21 30S 50 0W
Peñarroya-Pueblonuevo **13** 38 19N 5 16W
Peñas, C. de **13** 43 42N 5 52W
Penas, G. de **80** 47 0S 75 0W
Pench'i = Benxi **38** 41 20N 123 48 E
Pend Oreille → **72** 49 4N 117 37W
Pend Oreille, L. **72** 48 0N 116 30W
Pendembu **50** 9 7N 12 14W
Pender B. **46** 16 45S 122 42 E
Pendleton **72** 45 35N 118 50W
Penedo **79** 10 15S 36 36W
Penetanguishene **62** 44 50N 79 55W
Pengalengan **35** 7 9S 107 30 E
Penglai **38** 37 48N 120 42 E
Pengshui **39** 29 17N 108 12 E
Penguin **44** 41 8S 146 6 E
Peniche **13** 39 19N 9 22W
Penicuik **8** 55 50N 3 14W
Penida **34** 8 45S 115 30 E
Peninsular Malaysia □ **34** 4 0N 102 0 E
Penmarch, Pte. de. **12** 47 48N 4 22W
Penn Yan **68** 42 39N 77 7W
Pennant **65** 50 32N 108 14W
Penner → **32** 14 35N 80 10 E
Pennines **6** 54 50N 2 20W
Pennsylvania □ **68** 40 50N 78 0W
Penny **64** 53 51N 121 20W
Penola **45** 37 25S 140 21 E
Penonome **75** 8 31N 80 21W
Penrhyn Is. **41** 9 0S 158 30W
Penrith, Australia **45** 33 43S 150 38 E
Penrith, U.K. **6** 54 40N 2 45W
Pensacola **69** 30 30N 87 10W
Pense **65** 50 25N 104 59W
Penshurst **45** 37 49S 142 20 E
Penticton **64** 49 30N 119 38W
Pentland **44** 20 32S 145 25 E
Pentland Firth **8** 58 43N 3 10W
Pentland Hills **8** 55 48N 3 25W
Penylan L. **65** 61 50N 106 20W
Penza **22** 53 15N 45 5 E
Penzance **7** 50 7N 5 32W
Penzhino **25** 63 30N 167 55 E
Penzhinskaya Guba **25** 61 30N 163 0 E
Peoria, Ariz., U.S.A. **73** 33 40N 112 15W
Peoria, Ill., U.S.A. **70** 40 40N 89 40W
Pera Hd. **44** 12 55S 141 37 E
Perabumilih **34** 3 27S 104 15 E
Percé **63** 48 31N 64 13W
Perche **12** 48 31N 1 1 E
Percival Lakes **46** 21 25S 125 0 E
Percy Is. **44** 21 39S 150 16 E
Perdido, Mte. **13** 42 40N 0 5 E
Perdu, Mt. = Perdido, Mte. **13** 42 40N 0 5 E
Pereira **78** 4 49N 75 43W
Perekerten **45** 34 55S 143 40 E
Perekop **23** 46 10N 33 42 E
Perenjori **47** 29 26S 116 16 E
Pereyaslav Khmelnitskiy **23** 50 3N 31 28 E
Pérez, I. **74** 22 24N 89 42W
Pergamino **80** 33 52S 60 30W
Perham **70** 46 36N 95 36W
Péribonca → **63** 48 45N 72 5W
Péribonca, L. **63** 50 1N 71 10W
Perico **80** 24 20S 65 5W
Pericos **74** 25 3N 107 42W
Périgord **12** 45 0N 0 40 E
Périgueux **12** 45 10N 0 42 E
Perijá, Sierra de **78** 9 30N 73 3W
Perlas, Arch. de las **75** 8 41N 79 7W
Perlas, Punta de **75** 12 30N 83 30W
Perm **22** 58 0N 57 10 E
Pernambuco = Recife **79** 8 0S 35 0W
Pernambuco □ **79** 8 0S 37 0W
Pernatty Lagoon **45** 31 30S 137 12 E
Peron, C. **47** 25 30S 113 30 E
Peron Is. **46** 13 9S 130 4 E
Peron Pen. **47** 26 0S 113 10 E
Perouse Str., La **40** 45 40N 142 0 E
Perow **64** 54 35N 126 10W
Perpendicular Pt. **45** 31 37S 152 52 E
Perpignan **12** 42 42N 2 53 E
Perry, Fla., U.S.A. **69** 30 9N 83 40W
Perry, Ga., U.S.A. **69** 32 25N 83 41W
Perry, Iowa, U.S.A. **70** 41 48N 94 5W
Perry, Maine, U.S.A. **69** 44 59N 67 20W
Perry, Okla., U.S.A. **71** 36 20N 97 20W
Perryton **71** 36 28N 100 48W
Perryville **71** 37 42N 89 50W
Persepolis **31** 29 55N 52 50 E
Persia = Iran ■ **31** 33 0N 53 0 E
Persian Gulf = Gulf, The **31** 27 0N 50 0 E
Perth, Australia **47** 31 57S 115 52 E
Perth, Canada **62** 44 55N 76 15W
Perth, U.K. **8** 56 24N 3 27W
Perth Amboy **68** 40 31N 74 16W

Port Alice

Peru, Ill., U.S.A. . . . 70 41 18N 89 12W
Peru, Ind., U.S.A. . . 68 40 42N 86 0W
Peru ■ 78 8 0S 75 0W
Peru-Chile Trench . 41 20 0S 72 0W
Perúgia . . . . 18 43 6N 12 24 E
Pervomaysk . . . . . . 23 48 10N 30 46 E
Pervouralsk . . . . . . 22 56 55N 60 0 E
Pésaro . . . . 18 43 55N 12 53 E
Pescara . . . . 18 42 28N 14 13 E
Peshawar . . . . 32 34 2N 71 37 E
Peshtigo 68 45 4N 87 46W
Pesqueira 79 8 20S 36 42W
Petah Tiqwa . . . . . . 28 32 6N 34 53 E
Petaluma 72 38 13N 122 39W
Petange . . . . 11 49 33N 5 55 E
Petatlán 74 17 31N 101 16W
Petauke . . . . 55 14 14S 31 20 E
Petawawa 62 45 54N 77 17W
Petén Itzá, L. 75 16 58N 89 50W
Peter Pond L. 65 55 55N 108 44W
Peterbell 62 48 36N 83 21W
Peterborough, Australia . . . . . . 45 32 58S 138 51 E
Peterborough, U.K. 7 52 35N 0 14W
Peterhead 8 57 30N 1 49W
Petersburg, Alaska, U.S.A. 60 56 50N 133 0W
Petersburg, Ind., U.S.A. 68 38 30N 87 15W
Petersburg, Va., U.S.A. 68 37 17N 77 26W
Petersburg, W. Va., U.S.A. 68 38 59N 79 10W
Petford . . . . 44 17 20S 144 58 E
Petit Bois I. 69 30 16N 88 25W
Petit-Cap 63 49 3N 64 30W
Petit Goâve 75 18 27N 72 51W
Petit Lac Manicouagan . . . 63 51 25N 67 40W
Petitcodiac 63 45 57N 65 11W
Petite Baleine ⟶ . 62 56 0N 76 45W
Petite Saguenay . . 63 48 15N 70 4W
Petitsikapau, L. . . . 63 54 37N 66 25W
Petlad . . . . 32 22 30N 72 45 E
Peto 74 20 10N 88 53W
Petone . . . . 43 41 13S 174 53 E
Petoskey 68 45 22N 84 57W
Petra . . . . 28 30 20N 35 22 E
Petrich . . . . 19 41 24N 23 13 E
Petrolândia 79 9 5S 38 20W
Petrolia 62 42 54N 82 9W
Petrolina 79 9 24S 40 30W
Petropavlovsk . . . . 24 54 53N 69 13 E
Petropavlovsk-Kamchatskiy . . . . 25 53 3N 158 43 E
Petrópolis 79 22 33S 43 9W
Petroşeni . . . . 15 45 28N 23 20 E
Petroskey 68 45 22N 84 57W
Petrovaradin . . . . . 19 45 16N 19 55 E
Petrovsk . . . . 22 52 22N 45 19 E
Petrovsk-Zabaykalskiy . . . 25 51 20N 108 55 E
Petrozavodsk . . . . . 22 61 41N 34 20 E
Petrus Steyn . . . . . 57 27 38S 28 8 E
Petrusburg . . . . 56 29 4S 25 26 E
Peureulak . . . . 34 4 48N 97 45 E
Pevek . . . . 25 69 41N 171 19 E
Pforzheim . . . . 14 48 53N 8 43 E
Phagwara . . . . 32 31 10N 75 40 E
Phala . . . . 56 23 45S 26 50 E
Phalodi . . . . 32 27 12N 72 24 E
Phan Rang . . . . 34 11 [illegible]N 10[illegible] 0 E
Phangan, Ko . . . . . 34 9 45N 100 0 E
Phangnga . . . . 34 8 28N 98 30 E
Phanh Bho Ho Chi Minh . . . . 34 10 58N 106 40 E
Phatthalung . . . . . . 34 7 39N 100 6 E
Phelps 70 46 2N 89 2W
Phelps L. 65 59 15N 103 15W
Phenix City 69 32 30N 85 0W
Phetchabun . . . . . . 34 16 25N 101 8 E
Philadelphia, Miss., U.S.A. 71 32 47N 89 5W
Philadelphia, Pa., U.S.A. 68 40 0N 75 10W
Philip 70 44 4N 101 42W
Philippeville . . . . . . 11 50 12N 4 33 E
Philippi L. . . . . 44 24 20S 138 55 E
Philippines ■ . . . . . 35 12 0N 123 0 E
Philippolis . . . . 56 30 15S 25 16 E
Philippopolis = Plovdiv . . . . 19 42 8N 24 44 E
Philipsburg 72 46 20N 113 21W
Philipstown . . . . 56 30 28S 24 30 E
Phillip, I. . . . . 45 38 30S 145 12 E
Phillips, Tex., U.S.A. 71 35 48N 101 17W
Phillips, Wis., U.S.A. 70 45 41N 90 22W
Phillipsburg 70 39 48N 99 20W
Phillott . . . . 45 27 53S 145 50 E
Philomath 72 44 28N 123 21W
Phitsanulok . . . . . . 34 16 50N 100 12 E
Phnom Dangrek . . . 34 14 20N 104 0 E
Phnom Penh . . . . . 34 11 33N 104 55 E
Phoenix 73 33 30N 112 10W
Phoenix Is. 40 3 30S 172 0W
Phra Nakhon Si Ayutthaya . . . . . . 34 14 25N 100 30 E
Phuket . . . . 34 7 52N 98 22 E
Piacenza . . . . 18 45 2N 9 42 E
Pialba . . . . 45 25 20S 152 45 E
Pian Cr. ⟶ . . . . . . 45 30 2S 148 12 E
Piapot 65 49 59N 109 8W
Piatra Neamţ . . . . . 15 46 56N 26 21 E
Piauí □ 79 7 0S 43 0W
Piave ⟶ . . . . 18 45 32N 12 44 E
Piazza Ármerina . . . 18 37 21N 14 20 E
Pibor Post . . . . 51 6 47N 33 3 E
Pica 78 20 35S 69 25W
Picardie . . . . 12 49 50N 3 0 E
Picardy = Picardie 12 49 50N 3 0 E
Picayune 71 30 31N 89 40W
Pichilemu 80 34 22S 72 0W
Pickerel L. 62 48 40N 91 25W
Pickle Lake 62 51 30N 90 12W
Pico Truncado 80 46 40S 68 0W
Picton, Australia . . 45 34 12S 150 34 E
Picton, Canada 62 44 1N 77 9W
Picton, N.Z. . . . . . . 43 41 18S 174 3 E
Pictou 63 45 41N 62 42W
Picture Butte 64 49 55N 112 45W
Picún Leufú 80 39 30S 69 5W
Pidurutalagala . . . . 32 7 10N 80 50 E
Piedad, La 74 20 20N 102 1W
Piedmont = Piemonte □ . . . . 18 45 0N 7 30 E
Piedmont 69 33 55N 85 39W
Piedmont Plateau . 69 34 0N 81 30W
Piedras, R. de las ⟶ 78 12 30S 69 15W
Piedras Negras . . . 74 28 35N 100 35W
Piemonte □ . . . . . . 18 45 0N 7 30 E
Pierce 72 46 29N 115 53W
Pierre 70 44 23N 100 20W
Piet Retief . . . . 57 27 1S 30 50 E
Pietarsaari = Jakobstad . . . . . . 20 63 40N 22 43 E
Pietermaritzburg . . 57 29 35S 30 25 E
Pietersburg . . . . . . 57 23 54S 29 25 E
Pietrosul . . . . 15 47 35N 24 43 E
Pigeon 68 43 50N 83 17W
Piggott 71 36 20N 90 10W
Pigüe 80 37 36S 62 25W
Pikes Peak 70 38 50N 105 10W
Piketberg . . . . 56 32 55S 18 40 E
Pikeville 68 37 30N 82 30W
Pikwitonei 65 55 35N 97 9W
Pilar, Brazil 79 9 36S 35 56W
Pilar, Paraguay . . . 80 26 50S 58 20W
Pilas Group . . . . . . 35 6 45N 121 35 E
Pilbara . . . . 46 21 15S 118 16 E
Pilcomayo ⟶ 80 25 21S 57 42W
Pilibhit . . . . 32 28 40N 79 50 E
Pilica ⟶ . . . . 15 51 52N 21 17 E
Pílos . . . . 19 36 55N 21 42 E
Pilot Mound 65 49 15N 98 54W
Pilot Point 71 33 26N 97 0W
Pilot Rock 72 45 30N 118 50W
Pilsen = Plzeň . . . . 14 49 45N 13 22 E
Pima 73 32 54N 109 50W
Pimba . . . . 45 31 18S 136 46 E
Pimenta Bueno . . . 78 11 35S 61 10W
Pimentel 78 6 45S 79 55W
Pinang . . . . 34 5 25N 100 15 E
Pinar del Río 75 22 26N 83 40W
Pincher Creek 64 49 30N 113 57W
Pinchi L. 64 54 38N 124 30W
Pinckneyville 70 38 5N 89 20W
Pińczów . . . . 15 50 32N 20 32 E
Pindar . . . . 47 28 30S 115 47 E
Pindiga . . . . 53 9 58N 10 53 E
Pindos Óros . . . . . . 19 40 0N 21 0 E
Pindus Mts. = Pindos Óros . . . . 19 40 0N 21 0 E
Pine 73 34 27N 111 30W
Pine ⟶ 65 58 50N 105 38W
Pine, C. 63 46 37N 53 32W
Pine, La 72 43 40N 121 30W
Pine Bluff 71 34 10N 92 0W
Pine City 70 45 46N 93 0W
Pine Falls 65 50 34N 96 11W
Pine Pass 64 55 25N 122 42W
Pine Point 64 60 50N 114 28W
Pine Ridge 70 43 0N 102 35W
Pine River, Canada 65 51 45N 100 30W
Pine River, U.S.A. . 70 46 43N 94 24W
Pinega ⟶ . . . . 22 64 8N 46 54 E
Pinehill . . . . 44 23 38S 146 57 E
Pinerolo . . . . 18 44 47N 7 21 E
Pinetop 73 34 10N 109 57W
Pinetown . . . . 57 29 48S 30 54 E
Pinetree 72 43 42N 105 52W
Pineville, Ky., U.S.A. 69 36 42N 83 42W
Pineville, La., U.S.A. 71 31 22N 92 30W
Ping ⟶ . . . . 34 15 42N 100 9 E
Pingaring . . . . 47 32 40S 118 32 E
Pingding . . . . 38 37 47N 113 38 E
Pingdingshan . . . . . 39 33 43N 113 27 E
Pingdong . . . . 39 22 39N 120 30 E
Pingdu . . . . 38 36 42N 119 59 E
Pingelly . . . . 47 32 32S 117 5 E
Pingguo . . . . 39 23 19N 107 36 E
Pinghe . . . . 39 24 17N 117 21 E
Pingjiang . . . . 39 28 45N 113 36 E
Pingle . . . . 39 24 40N 110 40 E
Pingliang . . . . 38 35 35N 106 31 E
Pingluo . . . . 38 38 52N 106 30 E
Pingnan . . . . 39 23 33N 110 22 E
Pingrup . . . . 47 33 32S 118 29 E
Pingtan Dao . . . . . . 39 25 29N 119 47 E
Pingwu . . . . 39 32 25N 104 30 E
Pingxiang, Guangxi Zhuangzu, China . . . . 39 22 6N 106 46 E
Pingxiang, Jiangxi, China . . . . 39 27 43N 113 48 E
Pingyao . . . . 38 37 12N 112 10 E
Pinhel 13 40 50N 7 1W
Pini . . . . 34 0 10N 98 40 E
Piniós ⟶ . . . . 19 39 55N 22 10 E
Pinjarra . . . . 47 32 37S 115 52 E
Pink ⟶ 65 56 50N 103 50W
Pinnacles . . . . 47 28 12S 120 26 E
Pinnaroo . . . . 45 35 17S 140 53 E
Pinos 74 22 20N 101 40W
Pinos Pt. 73 36 38N 121 57W
Pinrang . . . . 35 3 46S 119 41 E
Pinsk . . . . 22 52 10N 26 1 E
Pintados 78 20 35S 69 40W
Pintumba . . . . 47 31 30S 132 12 E
Pinyang . . . . 39 27 42N 120 31 E
Pinyug . . . . 22 60 5N 48 0 E
Pioche 73 38 0N 114 35W
Piombino . . . . 18 42 54N 10 30 E
Pioner, Os. . . . . 25 79 50N 92 0 E
Piorini, L. 78 3 15S 62 35W
Piotrków Trybunalski 15 51 23N 19 43 E
Pip . . . . 31 26 45N 60 10 E
Pipestone 70 44 0N 96 20W
Pipestone ⟶ 62 52 53N 89 23W
Pipestone Cr. ⟶ . . 65 49 38N 100 15W
Pipmuacan, Rés. . . 63 49 45N 70 30W
Pippingarra . . . . . . 46 20 27S 118 42 E
Piqua 68 40 10N 84 10W
Piquiri ⟶ 80 24 3S 54 14W
Piracicaba 80 22 45S 47 40W
Piracuruca 79 3 50S 41 50W
Piræus = Piraiévs . 19 37 57N 23 42 E
Piraiévs . . . . 19 37 57N 23 42 E
Pirané 80 25 42S 59 6W
Pirapora 79 17 20S 44 56W
Pírgos . . . . 19 37 40N 21 27 E
Pirin Planina . . . . . 19 41 40N 23 30 E
Pirineos . . . . 13 42 40N 1 0 E
Piripiri 79 4 15S 41 46W
Pirot . . . . 19 43 9N 22 39 E
Piru . . . . 35 3 4S 128 12 E
Pisa . . . . 18 43 43N 10 23 E
Pisagua 78 19 40S 70 15W
Pisco 78 13 50S 76 12W
Pisek . . . . 14 49 19N 14 10 E
Pishan . . . . 37 37 30N 78 33 E
Pising . . . . 35 5 8S 121 53 E
Pistóia . . . . 18 43 57N 10 53 E
Pistol B. 65 62 25N 92 37W
Pisuerga ⟶ 13 41 33N 4 52W
Pitarpunga, L. . . . . 45 34 24S 143 30 E
Pitcairn I. 2 25 5S 130 5W
Pite älv ⟶ . . . . . . 20 65 20N 21 2[illegible] E
Piteå . . . . 20 65 20N 21 25 E
Piteşti . . . . 15 44 52N 24 54 E
Pithapuram . . . . . . 33 17 10N 82 15 E
Pithara . . . . 47 30 20S 116 35 E
Pitlochry 8 56 43N 3 43W
Pitt I. 64 53 30N 129 50W
Pittsburg, Kans., U.S.A. 71 37 21N 94 43W
Pittsburg, Tex., U.S.A. 71 32 59N 94 58W
Pittsburgh 68 40 25N 79 55W
Pittsfield, Ill., U.S.A. 70 39 35N 90 46W
Pittsfield, Mass., U.S.A. 68 42 28N 73 17W
Pittston 68 41 19N 75 50W
Pittsworth . . . . 45 27 41S 151 37 E
Pituri ⟶ . . . . 44 22 35S 138 30 E
Piura 78 5 15S 80 38W
Pizzo . . . . 18 38 44N 16 10 E
Placentia 63 47 20N 54 0W
Placentia B. 63 47 0N 54 40W
Placerville 72 38 47N 120 51W
Placetas 75 22 15N 79 44W
Plain Dealing 71 32 56N 93 41W
Plainfield 68 40 37N 74 28W
Plains, Kans., U.S.A. 71 37 20N 100 35W
Plains, Mont., U.S.A. 72 47 27N 114 57W
Plains, Tex., U.S.A. 71 33 11N 102 50W
Plainview, Nebr., U.S.A. 70 42 25N 97 48W
Plainview, Tex., U.S.A. 71 34 10N 101 40W
Plainville 70 39 18N 99 19W
Plainwell 68 42 28N 85 40W
Plakhino . . . . 24 67 45N 86 5 E
Plankinton 70 43 45N 98 27W
Plano 71 33 0N 96 45W
Plant, La 70 45 11N 100 40W
Plant City 69 28 0N 82 8W
Plaquemine 71 30 20N 91 15W
Plasencia 13 40 3N 6 8W
Plaster Rock 63 46 53N 67 22W
Plata, La 80 35 0S 57 55W
Plata, Río de la . . . 80 34 45S 57 30W
Platani ⟶ . . . . 18 37 23N 13 16 E
Plateau □ . . . . 53 8 0N 8 30 E
Plateau du Coteau du Missouri 70 47 9N 101 5W
Platí, Ákra . . . . 19 40 27N 24 0 E
Plato 78 9 47N 74 47W
Platte 70 43 28N 98 50W
Platte ⟶ 70 39 16N 94 50W
Platteville 70 40 18N 104 47W
Plattsburg 68 44 41N 73 30W
Plattsmouth 70 41 0N 95 50W
Plauen . . . . 14 50 29N 12 9 E
Playgreen L. 65 54 0N 98 15W
Pleasant Bay 63 46 51N 60 48W
Pleasant Hill 70 38 48N 94 14W
Pleasanton 71 29 0N 98 30W
Pleasantville 68 39 25N 74 30W
Pleiku . . . . 34 13 57N 108 0 E
Plenty ⟶ . . . . 44 23 25S 136 31 E
Plenty, Bay of . . . . 43 37 45S 177 0 E
Plentywood 70 48 45N 104 35W
Plesetsk . . . . 22 62 40N 40 10 E
Plessisville 63 46 14N 71 47W
Pletipi L. 63 51 44N 70 6W
Pleven . . . . 19 43 26N 24 37 E
Plevlja . . . . 19 43 21N 19 21 E
Płock . . . . 15 52 32N 19 40 E
Ploieşti . . . . 15 44 57N 26 5 E
Plonge, Lac la 65 55 8N 107 20W
Plovdiv . . . . 19 42 8N 24 44 E
Plummer 72 47 21N 116 59W
Plumtree . . . . 55 20 27S 27 55 E
Plymouth, U.K. 7 50 23N 4 9W
Plymouth, Ind., U.S.A. 68 41 20N 86 19W
Plymouth, N.C., U.S.A. 69 35 54N 76 46W
Plymouth, Wis., U.S.A. 68 43 42N 87 58W
Plymouth Sd. 7 50 20N 4 10W
Plynlimon = Pumlumon Fawr . 7 52 29N 3 47W
Plzeň . . . . 14 49 45N 13 22 E
Po ⟶ . . . . 18 44 57N 12 4 E
Po Hai = Bo Hai . . 38 39 0N 120 0 E
Pobé . . . . 53 7 0N 2 56 E
Pobeda . . . . 25 65 12N 146 12 E
Pobedino . . . . 25 49 51N 142 49 E
Pobedy Pik . . . . . . 24 40 45N 79 58 E
Pocahontas, Ark., U.S.A. 71 36 18N 91 0W
Pocahontas, Iowa, U.S.A. 70 42 41N 94 42W
Pocatello 72 42 50N 112 25W
Pochutla 74 15 50N 96 31W
Pocomoke City . . . 68 38 4N 75 32W
Poços de Caldas . . 79 21 50S 46 33W
Podgorica = Titograd . . . . . . 19 42 30N 19 1[illegible] E
Podkamennaya Tunguska ⟶ . . 25 61 50N 90 13 E
Podolsk . . . . 22 55 25N 37 30 E
Podor 50 16 40N 15 2W
Podporozhy . . . . . . 22 60 55N 34 2 E
Pofadder . . . . 56 29 10S 19 22 E
Pogamasing 62 46 55N 81 50W
Poh . . . . 35 0 46S 122 51 E
Pohang . . . . 38 36 1N 129 23 E
Point Edward 62 43 0N 82 30W
Point Pedro . . . . . . 32 9 50N 80 15 E
Point Pleasant 68 38 50N 82 7W
Pointe-à-la Hache . 71 29 35N 89 55W
Pointe-à-Pitre 75 16 10N 61 30W
Pointe Noire . . . . . . 54 4 48S 11 53 E
Poisonbush Ra. . . . 46 22 30S 121 30 E
Poitiers . . . . 12 46 35N 0 20 E
Pojoaque Valley . . . 73 35 55N 106 0W
Pokaran . . . . 32 27 0N 71 50 E
Pokataroo . . . . 45 29 30S 148 36 E
Pokrovsk . . . . 25 61 29N 126 12 E
Polacca 73 35 52N 110 25W
Polan . . . . 31 25 30N 61 10 E
Poland ■ . . . . 15 52 0N 20 0 E
Polcura 80 37 17S 71 43W
Polden Hills 7 51 7N 2 50W
Polesye . . . . 22 52 0N 28 10 E
Polevskoy . . . . 22 56 26N 60 11 E
Polewali . . . . 35 3 21S 119 23 E
Poli . . . . 54 8 34N 13 15 E
Polillo Is. . . . . 35 14 56N 122 0 E
Políyiros . . . . 19 40 23N 23 25 E
Pollachi . . . . 32 10 35N 77 0 E
Pollock 70 45 58N 100 18W
Polnovat . . . . 24 63 50N 65 54 E
Polo 70 41 59N 89 38W
Polotsk . . . . 22 55 30N 28 50 E
Polson 72 47 45N 114 12W
Poltava . . . . 23 49 35N 34 35 E
Polunochnoye . . . . 22 60 52N 60 25 E
Polyarny . . . . 22 69 8N 33 20 E
Polynesia 41 10 0S 162 0W
Pombal, Brazil 79 6 45S 37 50W
Pombal, Portugal . . 13 39 55N 8 40W
Pomeroy, Ohio, U.S.A. 68 39 0N 82 0W
Pomeroy, Wash., U.S.A. 72 46 30N 117 33W
Pomona 73 34 2N 117 49W
Pompano Beach . . 69 26 12N 80 6W
Pompeys Pillar 72 46 0N 108 0W
Ponape . . . . 40 6 55N 158 10 E
Ponask, L. 62 54 0N 92 41W
Ponass L. 65 52 16N 103 58W
Ponca 70 42 38N 96 41W
Ponca City 71 36 40N 97 5W
Ponce 75 18 1N 66 37W
Ponchatoula 71 30 27N 90 25W
Poncheville, L. 62 50 10N 76 55W
Pond Inlet 61 72 40N 77 0W
Pondicherry . . . . . . 32 11 59N 79 50 E
Ponds, I. of 63 53 27N 55 52W
Ponferrada 13 42 32N 6 35W
Ponnani . . . . 32 10 45N 75 59 E
Ponnyadaung . . . . . 33 22 0N 94 10 E
Ponoi . . . . 22 67 0N 41 0 E
Ponoi ⟶ . . . . 22 66 59N 41 17 E
Ponoka 64 52 42N 113 40W
Ponorogo . . . . 35 7 52S 111 27 E
Ponta Grossa 80 25 7S 50 10W
Ponta Pora 80 22 20S 55 35W
Pontarlier . . . . 12 46 54N 6 20 E
Pontchartrain, L. . . 71 30 12N 90 0W
Ponte Macassar . . 35 9 30S 123 50 E
Ponte Nova 79 20 25S 42 54W
Pontedera . . . . 18 43 40N 10 37 E
Pontefract 6 53 42N 1 19W
Ponteix 65 49 46N 107 29W
Pontevedra 13 42 26N 8 40W
Pontiac, Ill., U.S.A. . 70 40 50N 88 40W
Pontiac, Mich., U.S.A. 68 42 40N 83 20W
Pontianak . . . . 34 0 3S 109 15 E
Pontine Is. = Ponziane, Isole . . 18 40 55N 13 0 E
Pontine Mts. = Kuzey Anadolu Dağlari . . . . 30 41 30N 35 0 E
Ponton ⟶ 64 58 27N 116 11W
Pontypool 7 51 42N 3 1W
Pontypridd 7 51 36N 3 21W
Ponziane, Isole . . . 18 40 55N 13 0 E
Poochera . . . . 45 32 43S 134 51 E
Poole 7 50 42N 1 58W
Pooley I. 64 52 45N 128 15W
Poona = Pune . . . . 32 18 29N 73 57 E
Pooncarie . . . . 45 33 22S 142 31 E
Poopelloe, L. . . . . . 45 31 40S 144 0 E
Poopó, L. de 78 18 30S 67 35W
Popanyinning . . . . . 47 32 40S 117 2 E
Popayán 78 2 27N 76 36W
Poperinge . . . . 11 50 51N 2 42 E
Popigay . . . . 25 72 1N 110 39 E
Popilta, L. . . . . 45 33 10S 141 42 E
Popio, L. . . . . 45 33 10S 141 52 E
Poplar 70 48 3N 105 9W
Poplar ⟶, Man., Canada 65 53 0N 97 19W
Poplar ⟶, N.W.T., Canada 64 61 22N 121 52W
Poplar Bluff 71 36 45N 90 22W
Poplarville 71 30 55N 89 30W
Popocatepetl 74 19 10N 98 40W
Popokabaka . . . . . . 54 5 41S 16 40 E
Porbandar . . . . 32 21 44N 69 43 E
Porcher I. 64 53 50N 130 30W
Porcupine ⟶, Canada 65 59 11N 104 46W
Porcupine ⟶, U.S.A. 60 66 35N 145 15W
Pori . . . . 21 61 29N 21 48 E
Porjus . . . . 20 66 57N 19 50 E
Porkkala . . . . 21 59 59N 24 26 E
Porlamar 78 10 57N 63 51W
Poronaysk . . . . 25 49 13N 143 0 E
Poroshiri-Dake . . . . 36 42 41N 142 52 E
Porretta, Passo di . 18 44 2N 10 56 E
Porsangen . . . . 20 70 40N 25 40 E
Port Adelaide . . . . . 45 34 46S 138 30 E
Port Alberni 64 49 15N 124 50W
Port Alfred, Canada 63 48 18N 70 53W
Port Alfred, S. Africa 56 33 36S 26 55 E
Port Alice 64 50 20N 127 25W

St. Lawrence, Gulf of

St. Lawrence, Gulf of 63 46 25N 62 0W
St. Lawrence I. 60 63 0N 170 0W
St. Leonard 63 47 12N 67 58W
St. Lewis ➤ 63 52 26N 56 11W
St.-Lô 12 49 7N 1 5W
St-Louis 50 16 8N 16 27W
St. Louis, Mich., U.S.A. 68 43 27N 84 38W
St. Louis, Mo., U.S.A. 70 38 40N 90 12W
St. Louis ➤ 70 47 15N 92 45W
St. Lucia ■ 75 14 0N 60 50W
St. Lucia, L. 57 28 5S 32 30 E
St. Lucia Channel 75 14 15N 61 0W
St. Lunaire-Griquet 63 51 31N 55 28W
St. Maarten 75 18 0N 63 5W
St.-Malo 12 48 39N 2 1W
St-Marc 75 19 10N 72 41W
St. Maries 72 47 17N 116 34W
St-Martin, I. 75 18 0N 63 0W
St. Martin L. 65 51 40N 98 30W
St. Martins 63 45 22N 65 34W
St. Martinsville 71 30 10N 91 50W
St. Mary Pk. 45 31 32S 138 34 E
St. Marys, Australia 44 41 35S 148 11 E
St. Mary's, U.K. 7 49 55N 6 17W
St. Marys, U.S.A. 68 41 27N 78 33W
St. Mary's, C. 63 46 50N 54 12W
St. Mary's B. 63 46 50N 53 50W
St. Marys Bay 63 44 25N 66 10W
St.-Mathieu, Pte. de 12 48 20N 4 45W
St. Matthews, I. = Zadetkyi Kyun 34 10 0N 98 25 E
St-Maurice ➤ 62 46 21N 72 31W
St. Michael's Mt. 7 50 7N 5 30W
St.-Nazaire 12 47 17N 2 12W
St. Neots 7 52 14N 0 16W
St.-Omer 12 50 45N 2 15 E
St-Pacome 63 47 24N 69 58W
St-Pamphile 63 46 58N 69 48W
St. Pascal 63 47 32N 69 48W
St. Paul, Canada 64 54 0N 111 17W
St. Paul, Ind. Oc. 3 38 55S 77 34 E
St. Paul, Minn., U.S.A. 70 44 54N 93 5W
St. Paul, Nebr., U.S.A. 70 41 15N 98 30W
St. Paul, I. 63 47 12N 60 9W
St. Peter 70 44 21N 93 57W
St. Peter Port 7 49 27N 2 31W
St. Peters, N.S., Canada 63 45 40N 60 53W
St. Peters, P.E.I., Canada 63 46 25N 62 35W
St. Petersburg 69 27 45N 82 40W
St. Pierre, Ind. Oc. 3 9 20S 46 0 E
St.-Pierre, St- P. & M. 63 46 46N 56 12W
St-Pierre, L. 62 46 12N 72 52W
St.-Pierre et Miquelon □ 63 46 55N 56 10W
St.-Quentin 12 49 50N 3 16 E
St. Regis 72 47 20N 115 3W
St. Sebastien, Tanjon' i 57 12 26S 48 44 E
St-Siméon 63 47 51N 69 54W
St. Stephen 63 45 16N 67 17W
St. Thomas, Canada 62 42 45N 81 10W
St. Thomas, W. Indies 75 18 21N 64 55W
St-Tite 62 46 45N 72 34W
St.-Tropez 12 43 17N 6 38 E
St. Troud = Sint Truiden 11 50 48N 5 10 E
St.-Valéry-sur-Somme 12 50 11N 1 38 E
St. Vincent 75 13 10N 61 10W
St. Vincent, G. 45 35 0S 138 0 E
St. Vincent and the Grenadines ■ 75 13 0N 61 10W
St. Vincent Passage 75 13 30N 61 0W
St-Vith 11 50 17N 6 9 E
Ste-Agathe-des-Monts 62 46 3N 74 17W
Ste Anne de Beaupré 63 47 2N 70 58W
Ste-Anne-des-Monts 63 49 8N 66 30W
Ste. Genevieve 70 37 59N 90 2W
Ste-Marguerite ➤ 63 50 9N 66 36W
Ste.-Marie 75 14 48N 61 1W
Ste-Marie de la Madeleine 63 46 26N 71 0W
Ste.-Rose 75 16 20N 61 45W
Ste. Rose du lac 65 51 4N 99 30W
Saintes 12 45 45N 0 37W
Saintes, I. des 75 15 50N 61 35W
Saintonge 12 45 40N 0 50W
Sairang 33 23 50N 92 45 E
Sairecábur, Cerro 80 22 43S 67 54W
Saitama □ 36 36 25N 139 30 E
Sajama 78 18 7S 69 0W
Sak ➤ 56 30 52S 20 25 E
Sakai 36 34 30N 135 30 E
Sakākah 30 30 0N 40 8 E
Sakakawea, L. 70 47 30N 102 0W
Sakami, L. 62 53 15N 77 0W
Sakarya ➤ 23 41 7N 30 39 E
Sakata 36 38 55N 139 50 E
Sakeny ➤ 57 20 0S 45 25 E
Sakété 53 6 40N 2 45 E
Sakhalin 25 51 0N 143 0 E
Sakhalinskiy Zaliv 25 54 0N 141 0 E
Sakhnīn 28 32 52N 35 12 E
Sakon Nakhon 34 17 10N 104 9 E
Sakrivier 56 30 54S 20 28 E
Sala 21 59 58N 16 35 E
Sala-y-Gómez 41 26 28S 105 28W
Salaberry-de-Valleyfield 62 45 15N 74 8W
Saladillo 80 35 40S 59 55W
Salado ➤, Buenos Aires, Argentina 80 35 44S 57 22W
Salado ➤, La Pampa, Argentina 80 37 30S 67 0W
Salado ➤, Santa Fe, Argentina 80 31 40S 60 41W
Salado ➤, Mexico 74 26 52N 99 19W
Salaga 53 8 31N 0 31W
Salālah 29 16 56N 53 59 E
Salamanca, Chile 80 31 46S 70 59W
Salamanca, Spain 13 40 58N 5 39W
Salamanca, U.S.A. 68 42 10N 78 42W
Salamis 19 37 56N 23 30 E
Salar de Atacama 80 23 30S 68 25W
Salar de Uyuni 78 20 30S 67 45W
Salatiga 35 7 19S 110 30 E
Salavat 22 53 21N 55 55 E
Salaverry 78 8 15S 79 0W
Salawati 35 1 7S 130 52 E
Salayar 35 6 7S 120 30 E
Salcombe 7 50 14N 3 47W
Saldaña 13 42 32N 4 48W
Saldanha 56 33 0S 17 58 E
Saldanha B. 56 33 6S 18 0 E
Sale, Australia 45 38 6S 147 6 E
Salé, Morocco 50 34 3N 6 48W
Sale, U.K. 6 53 26N 2 19W
Salekhard 22 66 30N 66 35 E
Salem, India 32 11 40N 78 11 E
Salem, Ind., U.S.A. 68 38 38N 86 6W
Salem, Mass., U.S.A. 68 42 29N 70 53W
Salem, Mo., U.S.A. 71 37 40N 91 30W
Salem, N.J., U.S.A. 68 39 34N 75 29W
Salem, Ohio, U.S.A. 68 40 52N 80 50W
Salem, Oreg., U.S.A. 72 45 0N 123 0W
Salem, S. Dak., U.S.A. 70 43 44N 97 23W
Salem, Va., U.S.A. 68 37 19N 80 8W
Salen 21 64 41N 11 27 E
Salerno 18 40 40N 14 44 E
Salfit 28 32 5N 35 11 E
Salford 6 53 30N 2 17W
Salima 55 13 47S 34 28 E
Salina, Italy 18 38 35N 14 50 E
Salina, U.S.A. 70 38 50N 97 40W
Salina Cruz 74 16 10N 95 10W
Salinas, Brazil 79 16 10S 42 10W
Salinas, Ecuador 78 2 10S 80 58W
Salinas, U.S.A. 73 36 40N 121 41W
Salinas ➤, Mexico 74 16 28N 90 31W
Salinas ➤, U.S.A. 73 36 45N 121 48W
Salinas, B. de 75 11 4N 85 45W
Salinas Ambargasta 80 29 0S 65 0W
Salinas de Hidalgo 74 22 30N 101 40W
Salinas Grandes 80 30 0S 65 0W
Saline ➤, Ark., U.S.A. 71 33 10N 92 8W
Saline ➤, Kans., U.S.A. 70 38 51N 97 30W
Salinópolis 79 0 40S 47 20W
Salisbury = Harare 55 17 43S 31 2 E
Salisbury, Australia 45 34 46S 138 40 E
Salisbury, U.K. 7 51 4N 1 48W
Salisbury, Md., U.S.A. 68 38 20N 75 38W
Salisbury, N.C., U.S.A. 69 35 20N 80 29W
Salisbury Plain 7 51 13N 1 50W
Salle, La 70 41 20N 89 6W
Sallisaw 71 35 26N 94 45W
Salmās 30 38 11N 44 47 E
Salmo 64 49 10N 117 20W
Salmon 72 45 12N 113 56W
Salmon ➤, Canada 64 54 3N 122 40W
Salmon ➤, U.S.A. 72 45 51N 116 46W
Salmon Arm 64 50 40N 119 15W
Salmon Falls 72 42 48N 114 59W
Salmon Gums 47 32 59S 121 38 E
Salmon Res. 63 48 5N 56 0W
Salmon River Mts. 72 45 0N 114 30W
Salo 21 60 22N 23 10 E
Salome 73 33 51N 113 37W
Salonica = Thessaloníki 19 40 38N 22 58 E
Salonta 15 46 49N 21 42 E
Salop = Shropshire □ 7 52 36N 2 45W
Salsk 23 46 28N 41 30 E
Salso ➤ 18 37 6N 13 55 E
Salt ➤, Canada 64 60 0N 112 25W
Salt ➤, U.S.A. 73 33 23N 112 18W
Salt Creek 45 36 8S 139 38 E
Salt Fork ➤ 71 36 37N 97 7W
Salt Lake City 72 40 45N 111 58W
Salta 80 24 57S 65 25W
Saltcoats 8 55 38N 4 47W
Saltee Is. 9 52 7N 6 37W
Saltfjorden 20 67 15N 14 10 E
Salthólmavík 20 65 24N 21 57W
Saltillo 74 25 30N 100 57W
Salto 80 31 27S 57 50W
Salton Sea 73 33 20N 115 50W
Saltpond 53 5 15N 1 3W
Saltville 68 36 53N 81 46W
Saluda ➤ 69 34 0N 81 4W
Salûm 51 31 31N 25 7 E
Salûm, Khâlig el 51 31 30N 25 9 E
Salur 33 18 27N 83 18 E
Saluzzo 18 44 39N 7 29 E
Salvador, Brazil 79 13 0S 38 30W
Salvador, Canada 65 52 10N 109 32W
Salvador, L. 71 29 46N 90 16W
Salwa 31 24 45N 50 55 E
Salween ➤ 33 16 31N 97 37 E
Salyany 23 39 10N 48 50 E
Salyersville 68 37 45N 83 4W
Salzburg 14 47 48N 13 2 E
Salzburg □ 14 47 15N 13 0 E
Salzgitter 14 52 13N 10 22 E
Sam Rayburn Res. 71 31 15N 94 20W
Sama 24 60 12N 60 22 E
Sama de Langreo 13 43 18N 5 40W
Samagaltai 25 50 36N 95 3 E
Samales Group 35 6 0N 122 0 E
Samangán □ 31 36 15N 68 3 E
Samani 36 42 7N 142 56 E
Samar 35 12 0N 125 0 E
Samaria = Shōmrōn 28 32 15N 35 13 E
Samarinda 34 0 30S 117 9 E
Samarkand 24 39 40N 66 55 E
Sāmarrā 30 34 12N 43 52 E
Sambalpur 33 21 28N 84 4 E
Sambar, Tanjung 34 2 59S 110 19 E
Sambas 34 1 20N 109 20 E
Sambava 57 14 16S 50 10 E
Sambhal 32 28 35N 78 37 E
Sambhar 32 26 52N 75 6 E
Sambre ➤ 11 50 27N 4 52 E
Samchŏk 38 37 30N 129 10 E
Same 54 4 2S 37 38 E
Sámos 19 37 45N 26 50 E
Samothráki 19 40 28N 25 28 E
Sampacho 80 33 20S 64 50W
Sampang 35 7 11S 113 13 E
Sampit 34 2 34S 113 0 E
Sampit, Teluk 34 3 5S 113 3 E
Samra 30 25 35N 41 0 E
Samsun 30 41 15N 36 22 E
Samui, Ko 34 9 30N 100 0 E
Samut Prakan 34 13 32N 100 40 E
Samut Songkhram ➤ 34 13 24N 100 1 E
San 50 13 15N 4 57W
San ➤ 15 50 45N 21 51 E
San Ambrosio 76 26 28S 79 53W
San Andreas 72 38 0N 120 39W
San Andrés, I. de 75 12 42N 81 46W
San Andres Mts. 73 33 0N 106 45W
San Andrés Tuxtla 74 18 30N 95 20W
San Angelo 71 31 30N 100 30W
San Antonio, Chile 80 33 40S 71 40W
San Antonio, N. Mex., U.S.A. 73 33 58N 106 57W
San Antonio, Tex., U.S.A. 71 29 30N 98 30W
San Antonio ➤ 71 28 30N 96 50W
San Antonio, C., Argentina 80 36 15S 56 40W
San Antonio, C., Cuba 75 21 50N 84 57W
San Antonio de los Baños 75 22 54N 82 31W
San Antonio Oeste 80 40 40S 65 0W
San Augustin, C. 35 6 20N 126 13 E
San Augustine 71 31 30N 94 7W
San Benito 71 26 5N 97 39W
San Bernardino 73 34 7N 117 18W
San Bernardino Str. 35 13 0N 125 0 E
San Bernardo 80 33 40S 70 50W
San Bernardo, I. de 78 9 45N 75 50W
San Blas 74 26 4N 108 46W
San Blas, Arch. de 75 9 50N 78 31W
San Blas, C. 69 29 40N 85 12W
San Borja 78 14 50S 66 52W
San Buenaventura 74 27 5N 101 32W
San Carlos, Argentina 80 33 50S 69 0W
San Carlos, Chile 80 36 10S 72 0W
San Carlos, Mexico 74 29 0N 100 54W
San Carlos, Nic. 75 11 12N 84 50W
San Carlos, Phil. 35 10 29N 123 25 E
San Carlos, U.S.A. 73 33 24N 110 27W
San Carlos, Amazonas, Venezuela 78 1 55N 67 4W
San Carlos, Cojedes, Venezuela 78 9 40N 68 36W
San Carlos de Bariloche 80 41 10S 71 25W
San Carlos del Zulia 78 9 1N 71 55W
San Carlos L. 73 33 15N 110 25W
San Clemente 73 33 29N 117 36W
San Clemente I. 73 32 53N 118 30W
San Cristóbal, Argentina 80 30 20S 61 10W
San Cristóbal, Dom. Rep. 75 18 25N 70 6W
San Cristóbal, Venezuela 78 7 46N 72 14W
San Cristóbal de las Casas 74 16 50N 92 33W
San Diego, Calif., U.S.A. 73 32 43N 117 10W
San Diego, Tex., U.S.A. 71 27 47N 98 15W
San Diego, C. 80 54 40S 65 10W
San Felipe, Chile 80 32 43S 70 42W
San Felipe, Mexico 74 31 0N 114 52W
San Felipe, Venezuela 78 10 20N 68 44W
San Felíu de Guíxols 13 41 45N 3 1 E
San Félix 41 26 23S 80 0W
San Fernando, Chile 80 34 30S 71 0W
San Fernando, Mexico 74 30 0N 115 10W
San Fernando, La Union, Phil. 35 16 40N 120 23 E
San Fernando, Pampanga, Phil. 35 15 5N 120 37 E
San Fernando, Spain 13 36 28N 6 17W
San Fernando, Trin. & Tob. 75 10 20N 61 30W
San Fernando, U.S.A. 73 34 15N 118 29W
San Fernando ➤ 74 24 55N 98 10W
San Fernando de Apure 78 7 54N 67 15W
San Fernando de Atabapo 78 4 3N 67 42W
San Francisco, Argentina 80 31 30S 62 5W
San Francisco, U.S.A. 73 37 47N 122 30W
San Francisco ➤ 73 32 59N 109 22W
San Francisco de Macorís 75 19 19N 70 15W
San Francisco del Monte de Oro 80 32 36S 66 8W
San Francisco del Oro 74 26 52N 105 50W
San Gil 78 6 33N 73 8W
San Gottardo, Paso del 14 46 33N 8 33 E
San Ignacio, Belize 74 17 10N 89 0W
San Ignacio, Bolivia 78 16 20S 60 55W
San Ignacio, Paraguay 80 26 52S 57 3W
San Ignacio, L. 74 26 50N 113 11W
San Ildefonso, C. 35 16 0N 122 1 E
San Javier, Argentina 80 30 40S 59 55W
San Javier, Bolivia 78 16 18S 62 30W
San Joaquin ➤ 73 38 4N 121 51W
San Jorge, B. de 74 31 20N 113 20W
San Jorge, G. 80 46 0S 66 0W
San Jorge, G. de 13 40 50N 0 55W
San José, Bolivia 78 17 53S 60 50W
San José, C. Rica 75 10 0N 84 2W
San José, Guat. 75 14 0N 90 50W
San José, Mexico 74 25 0N 110 50W
San Jose, Luzon, Phil. 35 15 45N 120 55 E
San Jose, Mindoro, Phil. 35 12 27N 121 4 E
San Jose, U.S.A. 73 37 20N 121 53W
San Jose ➤ 73 34 58N 106 7W
San José de Jáchal 80 30 15S 68 46W
San José de Mayo 80 34 27S 56 40W
San José de Ocune 78 4 15N 70 20W
San José del Cabo 74 23 0N 109 40W
San José del Guaviare 78 2 35N 72 38W
San Juan, Argentina 80 31 30S 68 30W
San Juan, Mexico 74 21 20N 102 50W
San Juan, Phil. 35 8 25N 126 20 E
San Juan, Puerto Rico 75 18 28N 66 8W
San Juan ➤, Nic. 75 10 56N 83 42W
San Juan ➤, U.S.A. 73 37 20N 110 20W
San Juan, C. 54 1 5N 9 20 E
San Juan Bautista 73 36 51N 121 32W
San Juan Capistrano 73 33 29N 117 40W
San Juan de los Morros 78 9 55N 67 21W
San Juan del Norte, B. de 75 11 0N 83 40W
San Juan del Rio 74 20 25N 100 0W
San Juan del Sur 75 11 20N 85 51W
San Juan Mts. 73 38 30N 108 30W
San Julián 80 49 15S 67 45W
San Justo 80 30 47S 60 30W
San Lázaro, C. 74 24 50N 112 18W
San Lázaro, Sa. 74 23 25N 110 0W
San Leandro 73 37 40N 122 6W
San Lorenzo 78 1 15N 78 50W
San Lorenzo ➤ 74 24 15N 107 24W
San Lorenzo, I., Mexico 74 28 35N 112 50W
San Lorenzo, I., Peru 78 12 7S 77 15W
San Lorenzo, Mt. 80 47 40S 72 20W
San Lucas, Bolivia 78 20 5S 65 7W
San Lucas, Mexico 74 27 10N 112 14W
San Lucas, C. 74 22 50N 110 0W
San Luis, Argentina 80 33 20S 66 20W
San Luis, U.S.A. 73 37 3N 105 26W
San Luis, I. 74 29 58N 114 26W
San Luis de la Paz 74 21 19N 100 32W
San Luis Obispo 73 35 21N 120 38W
San Luis Potosí 74 22 9N 100 59W
San Luis Potosí □ 74 22 10N 101 0W
San Luis Río Colorado 74 32 29N 114 58W
San Marcos, Guat. 75 14 59N 91 52W
San Marcos, Mexico 74 27 13N 112 6W
San Marcos, U.S.A. 71 29 53N 98 0W
San Marino ■ 18 43 56N 12 25 E
San Martín, L. 80 48 50S 72 50W
San Mateo 73 37 32N 122 19W
San Matías 78 16 25S 58 20W
San Matías, G. 80 41 30S 64 0W
San Miguel, El Salv. 75 13 30N 88 12W
San Miguel, U.S.A. 73 35 45N 120 42W
San Miguel ➤ 78 13 52S 63 56W
San Miguel de Tucumán 80 26 50S 65 20W
San Narciso 35 15 2N 120 3 E
San Nicolás de los Arroyas 80 33 25S 60 10W
San Nicolas I. 73 33 16N 119 30W
San-Pédro 50 4 50N 6 33W
San Pedro ➤, Chihuahua, Mexico 74 28 20N 106 10W
San Pedro ➤, Nayarit, Mexico 74 21 45N 105 30W
San Pedro ➤, U.S.A. 73 33 0N 110 50W
San Pedro de las Colonias 74 25 50N 102 59W
San Pedro de Lloc 78 7 15S 79 28W
San Pedro de Macorís 75 18 30N 69 18W
San Pedro del Paraná 80 26 43S 56 13W
San Pedro Mártir, Sierra 74 31 0N 115 30W
San Pedro Mixtepec 74 16 2N 97 7W
San Pedro Ocampo = Melchor Ocampo 74 24 52N 101 40W
San Pedro Sula 75 15 30N 88 0W
San Rafael, Argentina 80 34 40S 68 21W
San Rafael, Calif., U.S.A. 72 37 59N 122 32W
San Rafael, N. Mex., U.S.A. 73 35 6N 107 58W
San Ramón de la Nueva Orán 80 23 10S 64 20W
San Remo 18 43 48N 7 47 E
San Roque 80 28 25S 58 45W
San Rosendo 80 37 16S 72 43W
San Saba 71 31 12N 98 45W
San Salvador, Bahamas 75 24 0N 74 40W
San Salvador, El Salv. 75 13 40N 89 10W
San Salvador de Jujuy 80 24 10S 64 48W
San Salvador I. 75 24 0N 74 32W
San Sebastián, Argentina 80 53 10S 68 30W
San Sebastián, Spain 13 43 17N 1 58W
San Simon 73 32 14N 109 16W
San Valentin, Mte. 80 46 30S 73 30W
San Vicente de la Barquera 13 43 23N 4 29W

Valle Hermoso

Turabah 30 28 20N 43 15 E
Tūrān, Iran 31 35 39N 56 42 E
Turan, U.S.S.R. 25 51 55N 95 0 E
Turayf 30 31 41N 38 39 E
Turda 15 46 34N 23 47 E
Turek 15 52 3N 18 30 E
Turfan = Turpan 37 43 58N 89 10 E
Turfan Depression = Turpan Hami 37 42 40N 89 25 E
Turgutlu 30 38 30N 27 48 E
Turhal 30 40 24N 36 5 E
Turia → 13 39 27N 0 19W
Turiaçu 79 1 40S 45 19W
Turiaçu → 79 1 36S 45 19W
Turin = Torino 18 45 4N 7 40 E
Turin 64 49 58N 112 31W
Turkana, L. 54 3 30N 36 5 E
Turkestan 24 43 17N 68 16 E
Turkey ■ 30 39 0N 36 0 E
Turkey Creek 46 17 2S 128 12 E
Turkmen S.S.R. □ 24 39 0N 59 0 E
Turks Is. 75 21 20N 71 20W
Turks Island Passage 75 21 30N 71 30W
Turku 21 60 30N 22 19 E
Turlock 73 37 30N 120 55W
Turnagain → 64 59 12N 127 35W
Turnagain, C. 43 40 28S 176 38 E
Turneffe Is. 74 17 20N 87 50W
Turner, Australia 46 17 52S 128 16 E
Turner, U.S.A. 72 48 52N 108 25W
Turner Pt. 44 11 47S 133 32 E
Turner Valley 64 50 40N 114 17W
Turnhout 11 51 19N 4 57 E
Turnor L. 65 56 35N 108 35W
Tŭrnovo 19 43 5N 25 41 E
Turnu Măgurele 15 43 46N 24 56 E
Turnu Rosu Pasul 15 45 33N 24 17 E
Turnu-Severin 15 44 39N 22 41 E
Turon 71 37 48N 98 27W
Turpan 37 43 58N 89 10 E
Turpan Hami 37 42 40N 89 25 E
Turriff 8 57 32N 2 28W
Turtle Hd. I. 44 10 56S 142 37 E
Turtle L. 65 53 36N 108 38W
Turtle Lake, N. Dak., U.S.A. 70 47 30N 100 55W
Turtle Lake, Wis., U.S.A. 70 45 22N 92 10W
Turtleford 65 53 23N 108 57W
Turukhansk 25 65 21N 88 5 E
Turun ja Porin lääni □ 21 60 27N 22 15 E
Tuscaloosa 69 33 13N 87 31W
Tuscany = Toscana 18 43 30N 11 5 E
Tuscola, Ill., U.S.A. 68 39 48N 88 15W
Tuscola, Tex., U.S.A. 71 32 15N 99 48W
Tuscumbia 69 34 42N 87 42W
Tuskar Rock 9 52 12N 6 10W
Tuskegee 69 32 24N 85 39W
Tuticorin 32 8 50N 78 12 E
Tutóia 79 2 45S 42 20W
Tutong 34 4 47N 114 40 E
Tutrakan 19 44 2N 26 40 E
Tutshi L. 64 59 56N 134 30W
Tuttle 70 47 9N 100 0W
Tuttlingen 14 47 59N 8 50 E
Tutuala 35 8 25S 127 15 E
Tutuila 43 14 19S 170 50W
Tuva A.S.S.R. □ 25 51 30N 95 0 E
Tuvalu ■ 3 8 0S 178 0 E
Tuxpan 74 20 58N 97 23W
Tuxtla Gutiérrez 74 16 50N 93 10W
Tuy 13 42 3N 8 39W
Tuya L. 64 59 7N 130 35W
Tuz Gölü 30 38 45N 33 30 E
Ṭūz Khurmātū 30 34 56N 44 38 E
Tuzla 19 44 34N 18 41 E
Tweed → 8 55 42N 2 10W
Tweed Heads 45 28 10S 153 31 E
Tweedsmuir Prov. Park 64 53 0N 126 20W
Twentynine Palms 73 34 10N 116 4W
Twillingate 63 49 42N 54 45W
Twin Bridges 72 45 33N 112 23W
Twin Falls 72 42 30N 114 30W
Twin Valley 70 47 18N 96 15W
Twisp 72 48 21N 120 5W
Two Harbors 70 47 1N 91 40W
Two Hills 64 53 43N 111 52W
Two Rivers 68 44 10N 87 31W
Twofold B. 45 37 8S 149 59 E
Tychy 15 50 9N 18 59 E
Tyler, Minn., U.S.A. 70 44 18N 96 8W
Tyler, Tex., U.S.A. 71 32 18N 95 18W
Tynda 25 55 10N 124 43 E
Tyne → 6 54 58N 1 28W
Tyne & Wear □ 6 54 55N 1 35W
Tynemouth 6 55 1N 1 27W
Tyre = Sūr 28 33 19N 35 16 E
Tyrifjorden 21 60 2N 10 8 E
Tyrol = Tirol □ 14 47 3N 10 43 E
Tyrrell → 45 35 26S 142 51 E
Tyrrell, L. 45 35 20S 142 50 E
Tyrrell Arm 65 62 27N 97 30W
Tyrrell L. 65 63 7N 105 27W
Tyrrhenian Sea 16 40 0N 12 30 E
Tysfjorden 20 68 7N 16 25 E
Tyulgan 22 52 22N 56 12 E
Tyumen 24 57 11N 65 29 E
Tywi → 7 51 48N 4 20W
Tywyn 7 52 36N 4 5W
Tzaneen 57 23 47S 30 9 E
Tzukong = Zigong 39 29 15N 104 48 E

U

Uanda 44 21 37S 144 55 E
Uarsciek 29 2 28N 45 55 E
Uato-Udo 35 9 7S 125 36 E
Uatumã → 78 2 26S 57 37W
Uaupés 78 0 8S 67 5W
Uaupés → 78 0 2N 67 16W
Ubá 80 21 8S 43 0W
Ubaitaba 79 14 18S 39 20W
Ubangi = Oubangi → 54 0 30S 17 50 E
Ubauro 32 28 15N 69 45 E
Ube 36 33 56N 131 15 E
Ubeda 13 38 3N 3 23W
Uberaba 79 19 50S 47 55W
Uberlândia 79 19 0S 48 20W
Ubombo 57 27 31S 32 4 E
Ubon Ratchathani 34 15 15N 104 50 E
Ubundu 54 0 22S 25 30 E
Ucayali → 78 4 30S 73 30W
Uchi Lake 65 51 5N 92 35W
Uchiura-Wan 36 42 25N 140 40 E
Uchur → 25 58 48N 130 35 E
Ucluelet 64 48 57N 125 32W
Uda → 25 54 42N 135 14 E
Udaipur 32 24 36N 73 44 E
Udaipur Garhi 33 27 0N 86 35 E
Uddevalla 21 58 21N 11 55 E
Uddjaur 20 65 25N 21 15 E
Udgir 32 18 25N 77 5 E
Udhampur 32 33 0N 75 5 E
Udi 53 6 17N 7 21 E
Údine 18 46 5N 13 10 E
Udmurt A.S.S.R. □ 22 57 30N 52 30 E
Udon Thani 34 17 29N 102 46 E
Udupi 32 13 25N 74 42 E
Ueda 36 36 24N 138 16 E
Uele → 54 3 45N 24 45 E
Uelen 25 66 10N 170 0W
Uelzen 14 53 0N 10 33 E
Ufa 22 54 45N 55 55 E
Ufa → 22 54 40N 56 0 E
Ugab → 56 20 55S 13 30 E
Ugalla → 54 5 8S 30 42 E
Uganda ■ 54 2 0N 32 0 E
Ugie 57 31 10S 28 13 E
Uglegorsk 25 49 5N 142 2 E
Ugolyak 25 64 33N 120 30 E
Uhrichsville 68 40 23N 81 22W
Uíge 54 7 30S 14 40 E
Ŭiju 38 40 15N 124 35 E
Uinta Mts. 72 40 45N 110 30W
Uitenhage 56 33 40S 25 28 E
Uithuizen 11 53 24N 6 41 E
Ujjain 32 23 9N 75 43 E
Újpest 15 47 32N 19 6 E
Ujung Pandang 35 5 10S 119 20 E
Uka 25 57 50N 162 0 E
Ukerewe I. 54 2 0S 33 0 E
Ukhrul 33 25 10N 94 25 E
Ukhta 22 63 55N 54 0 E
Ukiah 72 39 10N 123 9W
Ukrainian S.S.R. □ 23 49 0N 32 0 E
Ukwi 56 23 29S 20 30 E
Ulaanbaatar 37 47 55N 106 53 E
Ulaangom 37 50 0N 92 10 E
Ulan Bator = Ulaanbaatar 37 47 55N 106 53 E
Ulan Ude 25 51 45N 107 40 E
Ulcinj 19 41 58N 19 10 E
Ulco 56 28 21S 24 15 E
Ulhasnagar 32 19 15N 73 10 E
Ulladulla 45 35 21S 150 29 E
Ullapool 8 57 54N 5 10W
Ullswater 6 54 35N 2 52W
Ullung-do 38 37 30N 130 30 E
Ulm 14 48 23N 10 0 E
Ulmarra 45 29 37S 153 4 E
Ulonguè 55 14 37S 34 19 E
Ulricehamn 21 57 46N 13 26 E
Ulster □ 9 54 35N 6 30W
Ulungur → 37 47 1N 87 24 E
Ulutau 24 48 39N 67 1 E
Ulverston 6 54 13N 3 7W
Ulverstone 44 41 11S 146 11 E
Ulya 25 59 10N 142 0 E
Ulyanovsk 22 54 20N 48 25 E
Ulyasutay 37 47 56N 97 28 E
Ulysses 71 37 39N 101 25W
Umala 78 17 25S 68 5W
Uman 23 48 40N 30 12 E
Umaria 33 23 35N 80 50 E
Umarkot 32 25 15N 69 40 E
Umatilla 72 45 58N 119 17W
Umba 22 66 50N 34 20 E
Umbrella Mts. 43 45 35S 169 5 E
Umbria □ 18 42 53N 12 30 E
Ume älv → 20 63 45N 20 20 E
Umeå 20 63 45N 20 20 E
Umera 35 0 12S 129 37 E
Umkomaas 57 30 13S 30 48 E
Umm al Qaywayn 31 25 30N 55 35 E
Umm Bel 51 13 35N 28 0 E
Umm el Fahm 28 32 31N 35 9 E
Umm Lajj 30 25 0N 37 23 E
Umm Qays 28 32 40N 35 41 E
Umm Ruwaba 51 12 50N 31 20 E
Umnak 60 53 20N 168 20W
Umniati → 55 16 49S 28 45 E
Umpqua → 72 43 42N 124 3W
Umtata 57 31 36S 28 49 E
Umuarama 79 23 45S 53 20W
Umzimvubu = Port St. Johns 57 31 38S 29 33 E
Umzinto 57 30 15S 30 45 E
Unac → 18 44 30N 16 9 E
Unalaska 60 53 40N 166 40W
Uncía 78 18 25S 66 40W
Uncompahgre Pk. 73 38 5N 107 32W
Underberg 57 29 50S 29 22 E
Underbool 45 35 10S 141 51 E
Ungarie 45 33 38S 146 56 E
Ungarra 45 34 12S 136 2 E
Ungava B. 61 59 30N 67 30W
Ungava Pen. 61 60 0N 74 0W
Unggi 38 42 16N 130 28 E
União da Vitória 80 26 13S 51 5W
Unimak 60 55 0N 164 0W
Unimak Pass. 60 53 30N 165 15W
Union, Miss., U.S.A. 71 32 34N 89 14W
Union, Mo., U.S.A. 70 38 25N 91 0W
Union, S.C., U.S.A. 69 34 43N 81 39W
Unión, La, Chile 80 40 10S 73 0W
Unión, La, El Salv. 75 13 20N 87 50W
Union, Mt. 73 34 34N 112 21W
Union City, Pa., U.S.A. 68 41 53N 79 50W
Union City, Tenn., U.S.A. 71 36 25N 89 0W
Union Gap 72 46 38N 120 29W
Union of Soviet Socialist Republics ■ 25 60 0N 100 0 E
Union Springs 69 32 9N 85 44W
Uniondale 56 33 39S 23 7 E
Uniontown 68 39 54N 79 45W
Unionville 70 40 29N 93 1W
United Arab Emirates ■ 31 23 50N 54 0 E
United Kingdom ■ 5 55 0N 3 0W
United States of America ■ 67 37 0N 96 0W
United States Trust Terr. of the Pacific Is. □ 40 10 0N 160 0 E
Unity 65 52 30N 109 5W
Unnao 33 26 35N 80 30 E
Unst 8 60 50N 0 55W
Unuk → 64 56 5N 131 3W
Ünye 30 41 5N 37 15 E
Upata 78 8 1N 62 24W
Upemba, L. 54 8 30S 26 20 E
Upington 56 28 25S 21 15 E
Upolu 43 13 58S 172 0W
Upper Alkali Lake 72 41 47N 120 8W
Upper Arrow L. 64 50 30N 117 50W
Upper Foster L. 65 56 47N 105 20W
Upper Hutt 43 41 8S 175 5 E
Upper Klamath L. 72 42 16N 121 55W
Upper L. Erne 9 54 14N 7 22W
Upper Lake 72 39 10N 122 55W
Upper Musquodoboit 63 45 10N 62 58W
Upper Red L. 70 48 0N 95 0W
Upper Sandusky 68 40 50N 83 17W
Upper Taimyr → 25 74 15N 99 48 E
Upper Volta = Burkina Faso ■ 50 12 0N 1 0W
Uppsala 21 59 53N 17 38 E
Uppsala län □ 21 60 0N 17 30 E
Upstart, C. 44 19 41S 147 45 E
Upton 70 44 8N 104 35W
Ur 30 30 55N 46 25 E
Uracara 78 2 20S 57 50W
Urad Qianqi 38 40 40N 108 30 E
Urakawa 36 42 9N 142 47 E
Ural → 23 47 0N 51 48 E
Ural, Mt. 45 33 21S 146 12 E
Ural Mts. = Uralskie Gory 22 60 0N 59 0 E
Ural Mts. 4 60 0N 59 0 E
Uralla 45 30 37S 151 29 E
Uralsk 22 51 20N 51 20 E
Uralskie Gory 22 60 0N 59 0 E
Urandangi 44 21 32S 138 14 E
Uranium City 65 59 34N 108 37W
Uranquinty 45 35 10S 147 12 E
Urawa 36 35 50N 139 40 E
Uray 24 60 5N 65 15 E
Urbana, Ill., U.S.A. 68 40 7N 88 12W
Urbana, Ohio, U.S.A. 68 40 9N 83 44W
Urbana, La 78 7 8N 66 56W
Urbino 18 43 43N 12 38 E
Urbión, Picos de 13 42 1N 2 52W
Urcos 78 13 40S 71 38W
Urda 23 48 52N 47 23 E
Urdzhar 24 47 5N 81 38 E
Ure → 6 54 20N 1 25W
Urengoy 24 65 58N 28 25 E
Ures 74 29 30N 110 30W
Urfa 30 37 12N 38 50 E
Urfahr 14 48 19N 14 17 E
Urgench 24 41 40N 60 41 E
Uribia 78 11 43N 72 16W
Urim 28 31 18N 34 32 E
Urique → 74 26 29N 107 58W
Urk 11 52 39N 5 36 E
Urla 30 38 20N 26 47 E
Urmia = Orūmīyeh 30 37 40N 45 0 E
Urmia, L. = Orūmīyeh, Daryācheh-ye 30 37 50N 45 30 E
Uruana 79 15 30S 49 41W
Uruapan 74 19 30N 102 0W
Urubamba 78 13 20S 72 10W
Urubamba → 78 10 43S 73 48W
Uruçuí 79 7 20S 44 28W
Uruguai → 80 26 0S 53 30W
Uruguaiana 80 29 50S 57 0W
Uruguay ■ 80 32 30S 56 30W
Uruguay → 80 34 12S 58 18W
Urumchi = Ürümqi 37 43 45N 87 45 E
Ürümqi 37 43 45N 87 45 E
Urup, Os. 25 46 0N 151 0 E
Uryung-Khaya 25 72 48N 113 23 E
Usa → 22 65 57N 56 55 E
Uşak 30 38 43N 29 28 E
Usakos 56 21 54S 15 31 E
Usedom 14 53 50N 13 55 E
Ush-Tobe 24 45 16N 78 0 E
Ushant = Ouessant, I. d' 12 48 28N 5 6W
Ushuaia 80 54 50S 68 23W
Ushumun 25 52 47N 126 32 E
Usk → 7 51 37N 2 56W
Üsküdar 30 41 0N 29 5 E
Usman 22 52 5N 39 48 E
Usoke 54 5 8S 32 24 E
Usolye Sibirskoye 25 52 48N 103 40 E
Usoro 53 5 33N 6 11 E
Uspallata, P. de 80 32 37S 69 22W
Uspenskiy 24 48 41N 72 43 E
Ussuriysk 25 43 48N 131 59 E
Ust-Aldan = Batamay 25 63 30N 129 15 E
Ust Amginskoye = Khandyga 25 62 42N 135 35 E
Ust-Bolsheretsk 25 52 50N 156 15 E
Ust chaun 25 68 47N 170 30 E
Ust'-Ilga 25 55 5N 104 55 E
Ust Ilimpeya = Yukti 25 63 26N 105 42 E
Ust-Ilimsk 25 58 3N 102 39 E
Ust Ishim 24 57 45N 71 10 E
Ust-Kamchatsk 25 56 10N 162 28 E
Ust-Kamenogorsk 24 50 0N 82 36 E
Ust-Karenga 25 54 25N 116 30 E
Ust Khayryuzova 25 57 15N 156 45 E
Ust-Kut 25 56 50N 105 42 E
Ust Kuyga 25 70 1N 135 43 E
Ust Maya 25 60 30N 134 28 E
Ust-Mil 25 59 40N 133 11 E
Ust-Nera 25 64 35N 143 15 E
Ust-Nyukzha 25 56 34N 121 37 E
Ust Olenek 25 73 0N 119 48 E
Ust-Omchug 25 61 9N 149 38 E
Ust Port 24 69 40N 84 26 E
Ust Tsilma 22 65 25N 52 0 E
Ust-Tungir 25 55 25N 120 36 E
Ust Urt = Ustyurt, Plato 24 44 0N 55 0 E
Ust Usa 22 66 0N 56 30 E
Ust Vorkuta 24 67 24N 64 0 E
Ústí nad Labem 14 50 41N 14 3 E
Ustica 18 38 42N 13 10 E
Ustinov 22 56 51N 53 14 E
Ustroń 15 49 43N 18 48 E
Ustye 25 57 46N 94 37 E
Ustyurt, Plato 24 44 0N 55 0 E
Usu 37 44 27N 84 40 E
Usuki 36 33 8N 131 49 E
Usulután 75 13 25N 88 28W
Usumacinta → 74 17 0N 91 0W
Usumbura = Bujumbura 54 3 16S 29 18 E
Uta 35 4 33S 136 0 E
Utah □ 72 39 30N 111 30W
Utah, L. 72 40 10N 111 58W
Ute Cr. → 71 35 21N 103 45W
Utete 54 8 0S 38 45 E
Utiariti 78 13 0S 58 10W
Utica 68 43 5N 75 18W
Utik L. 65 55 15N 96 0W
Utikuma L. 64 55 50N 115 30W
Utrecht, Neth. 11 52 5N 5 8 E
Utrecht, S. Africa 57 27 38S 30 20 E
Utrecht □ 11 52 6N 5 7 E
Utrera 13 37 12N 5 48W
Utsjoki 20 69 51N 26 59 E
Utsunomiya 36 36 30N 139 50 E
Uttar Pradesh □ 33 27 0N 80 0 E
Uttaradit 34 17 36N 100 5 E
Uttoxeter 6 52 53N 1 50W
Uudenmaan lääni □ 21 60 25N 25 0 E
Uusikaarlepyy 20 63 32N 22 31 E
Uusikaupunki 21 60 47N 21 25 E
Uva 22 56 59N 52 13 E
Uvalde 71 29 15N 99 48W
Uvat 24 59 5N 68 50 E
Uvinza 54 5 5S 30 24 E
Uvira 54 3 22S 29 3 E
Uvs Nuur 37 50 20N 92 30 E
Uwajima 36 33 10N 132 35 E
Uxin Qi 38 38 50N 109 5 E
Uxmal 74 20 22N 89 46W
Uyandi 25 69 19N 141 0 E
Uyo 53 5 1N 7 53 E
Uyuni 78 20 28S 66 47W
Uzbek S.S.R. □ 24 41 30N 65 0 E
Uzen 23 43 27N 53 10 E
Uzerche 12 45 25N 1 34 E
Uzhgorod 22 48 36N 22 18 E

V

Vaal → 56 29 4S 23 38 E
Vaal Dam 57 27 0S 28 14 E
Vaalwater 57 24 15S 28 8 E
Vaasa 20 63 6N 21 38 E
Vaasan lääni □ 20 63 2N 22 50 E
Vác 15 47 49N 19 10 E
Vacaville 72 38 21N 122 0W
Vach → 24 60 45N 76 45 E
Vache, I.-à- 75 18 2N 73 35W
Vadodara 32 22 20N 73 10 E
Vadsø 20 70 3N 29 50 E
Værøy 20 67 40N 12 40 E
Váh → 15 47 55N 18 0 E
Vaigach 24 70 10N 59 0 E
Val-de-Marne □ 12 48 45N 2 28 E
Val-d'Oise □ 12 49 5N 2 10 E
Val d'Or 62 48 7N 77 47W
Val Marie 65 49 15N 107 45W
Valahia 15 44 35N 25 0 E
Valcheta 80 40 40S 66 8W
Valdayskaya Vozvyshennost 22 57 0N 33 30 E
Valdepeñas 13 38 43N 3 25W
Valdés, Pen. 80 42 30S 63 45W
Valdez 60 61 14N 146 17W
Valdivia 80 39 50S 73 14W
Valdosta 69 30 50N 83 20W
Vale 72 44 0N 117 15W
Valença 79 13 20S 39 5W
Valença do Piauí 79 6 20S 41 45W
Valence 12 44 57N 4 54 E
Valencia, Spain 13 39 27N 0 23W
Valencia, Venezuela 78 10 11N 68 0W
Valencia □ 13 39 20N 0 40W
Valencia, Albufera de 13 39 20N 0 27W
Valencia, G. de 13 39 30N 0 20 E
Valencia de Alcántara 13 39 25N 7 14W
Valenciennes 12 50 20N 3 34 E
Valentia Harbour 9 51 56N 10 17W
Valentia I. 9 51 54N 10 22W
Valentim, Sa. do 79 6 0S 43 30W
Valentine, Nebr., U.S.A. 70 42 50N 100 35W
Valentine, Tex., U.S.A. 71 30 36N 104 28W
Valera 78 9 19N 70 37W
Valier 72 48 25N 112 9W
Valjevo 19 44 18N 19 53 E
Valkeakoski 21 61 16N 24 2 E
Valkenswaard 11 51 21N 5 29 E
Valladolid, Mexico 74 20 40N 88 11W
Valladolid, Spain 13 41 38N 4 43W
Valle d'Aosta □ 18 45 45N 7 22 E
Valle de la Pascua 78 9 13N 66 0W
Valle de Santiago 74 20 25N 101 15W
Valle Hermoso 74 25 35N 97 40W

Wendell

Vulcan, U.S.A. 68 45 46N 87 51W
Vulcano 18 38 25N 14 58 E
Vung Tau 34 10 21N 107 4 E
Vyatka → 22 56 30N 51 0 E
Vyatskiye Polyany 22 56 5N 51 0 E
Vyazemskiy 25 47 32N 134 45 E
Vyazma 22 55 10N 34 15 E
Vyborg 22 60 43N 28 47 E
Vychegda → 22 61 18N 46 36 E
Vychodné Beskydy 15 49 30N 22 0 E
Vyg-ozero 22 63 30N 34 0 E
Vyrnwy, L. 6 52 48N 3 30W
Vyshniy Volochek 22 57 30N 34 30 E
Vyshzha = imeni 26 Bakinskikh Komissarov 23 39 22N 54 10 E
Vytegra 22 61 0N 36 27 E

W

W.A.C. Bennett Dam 64 56 2N 122 6W
Wa 50 10 7N 2 25W
Waal → 11 51 59N 4 30 E
Wabakimi L. 62 50 38N 89 45W
Wabana 63 47 40N 53 0W
Wabasca 64 55 57N 113 56W
Wabash 68 40 48N 85 46W
Wabash → 68 37 46N 88 2W
Wabeno 68 45 25N 88 40W
Wabigoon L. 65 49 44N 92 44W
Wabowden 65 54 55N 98 38W
Wąbrzeźno 15 53 16N 18 57 E
Wabuk Pt. 62 55 20N 85 5W
Wabush 63 52 55N 66 52W
Wabuska 72 39 9N 119 13W
Waco 71 31 33N 97 5W
Waconichi, L. 62 50 8N 74 0W
Wad Banda 51 13 10N 27 56 E
Wad Hamid 51 16 30N 32 45 E
Wâd Medanî 51 14 28N 33 30 E
Waddeneilanden 11 53 25N 5 10 E
Waddenzee 11 53 6N 5 10 E
Wadderin Hill 47 32 0S 118 25 E
Waddington, Mt. 64 51 23N 125 15W
Waddy Pt. 45 24 58S 153 21 E
Wadena, Canada 65 51 57N 103 47W
Wadena, U.S.A. 70 46 25N 95 8W
Wadesboro 69 35 2N 80 2W
Wadhams 64 51 30N 127 30W
Wadi Halfa 51 21 53N 31 19 E
Wadsworth 72 39 38N 119 22W
Wafrah 30 28 33N 47 56 E
Wageningen 11 51 58N 5 40 E
Wager B. 61 65 26N 88 40W
Wager Bay 61 65 56N 90 49W
Wagga Wagga 45 35 7S 147 24 E
Waghete 35 4 10S 135 50 E
Wagin 47 33 17S 117 25 E
Wagon Mound 71 36 1N 104 44W
Wagoner 71 36 0N 95 20W
Wah 32 33 45N 72 40 E
Wahai 35 2 48S 129 35 E
Wahiawa 66 21 30N 158 2W
Wahoo 70 41 15N 96 35W
Wahpeton 70 46 20N 96 35W
Waiau → 43 42 47S 173 22 E
Waibeem 35 0 30S 132 59 E
Waigeo 35 0 20S 130 40 E
Waihi 43 37 23S 175 52 E
Waihou → 43 37 15S 175 40 E
Waikabubak 35 9 45S 119 25 E
Waikaremoana 43 38 42S 177 12 E
Waikari 43 42 58S 172 41 E
Waikato → 43 37 23S 174 43 E
Waikerie 45 34 9S 140 0 E
Waikokopu 43 39 3S 177 52 E
Waikouaiti 43 45 36S 170 41 E
Waimate 43 44 45S 171 3 E
Wainganga → 32 18 50N 79 55 E
Waingapu 35 9 35S 120 11 E
Wainwright, Canada 65 52 50N 110 50W
Wainwright, U.S.A. 60 70 39N 160 1W
Waiouru 43 39 28S 175 41 E
Waipara 43 43 3S 172 46 E
Waipawa 43 39 56S 176 38 E
Waipiro 43 38 2S 178 22 E
Waipu 43 35 59S 174 29 E
Waipukurau 43 40 1S 176 33 E
Wairakei 43 38 37S 176 6 E
Wairarapa, L. 43 41 14S 175 15 E
Wairoa 43 39 3S 177 25 E
Waitaki → 43 44 56S 171 7 E
Waitara 43 38 59S 174 15 E
Waitsburg 72 46 15N 118 0W
Waiuku 43 37 15S 174 45 E
Wajima 36 37 30N 137 0 E
Wajir 54 1 42N 40 5 E
Wakasa-Wan 36 35 40N 135 30 E
Wakatipu, L. 43 45 5S 168 33 E
Wakaw 65 52 39N 105 44W
Wakayama 36 34 15N 135 15 E
Wakayama-ken □ 36 33 50N 135 30 E
Wake Forest 69 35 58N 78 30W
Wake I. 3 19 18N 166 36 E
Wakefield, N.Z. 43 41 24S 173 5 E
Wakefield, U.K. 6 53 41N 1 31W
Wakefield, U.S.A. 70 46 28N 89 53W
Wakema 33 16 30N 95 11 E
Wakkanai 36 45 28N 141 35 E
Wakkerstroom 57 27 24S 30 10 E
Wakool 45 35 28S 144 23 E
Wakool → 45 35 5S 143 33 E
Wakre 35 0 19S 131 5 E
Wakuach L. 63 55 34N 67 32W
Wałbrzych 14 50 45N 16 18 E
Walbury Hill 7 51 22N 1 28W
Walcha 45 30 55S 151 31 E
Walcheren 11 51 30N 3 35 E
Walcott 72 41 50N 106 55W
Waldburg Ra. 47 24 40S 117 35 E
Walden 72 40 47N 106 20W
Waldport 72 44 30N 124 2W
Waldron 71 34 52N 94 4W
Wales □ 7 52 30N 3 30W
Walgett 45 30 0S 148 5 E
Walhalla, Australia 45 37 56S 146 29 E
Walhalla, U.S.A. 65 48 55N 97 55W
Walkaway 47 28 59S 114 48 E
Walker 70 47 4N 94 35W
Walker L., Man., Canada 65 54 42N 95 57W
Walker L., Qué., Canada 63 50 20N 67 11W
Walker L., U.S.A. 72 38 56N 118 46W
Walkerston 44 21 11S 149 8 E
Wall 70 44 0N 102 14W
Walla Walla 72 46 3N 118 25W
Wallabadah 44 17 57S 142 15 E
Wallace, Idaho, U.S.A. 72 47 30N 116 0W
Wallace, N.C., U.S.A. 69 34 44N 77 59W
Wallace, Nebr., U.S.A. 70 40 51N 101 12W
Wallaceburg 62 42 34N 82 23W
Wallachia = Valahia 15 44 35N 25 0 E
Wallal 45 26 32S 146 7 E
Wallal Downs 46 19 47S 120 40 E
Wallambin, L. 47 30 57S 117 35 E
Wallaroo 45 33 56S 137 39 E
Wallasey 6 53 26N 3 2W
Wallerawang 45 33 25S 150 4 E
Wallhallow 44 17 50S 135 50 E
Wallingford 6 51 40N 1 15W
Wallis & Futuna 40 13 18S 176 10W
Wallowa 72 45 40N 117 35W
Wallowa, Mts. 72 45 20N 117 30W
Wallsend, Australia 45 32 55S 151 40 E
Wallsend, U.K. 6 54 59N 1 30W
Wallula 72 46 3N 118 59W
Wallumbilla 45 26 33S 149 9 E
Walmsley, L. 65 63 25N 108 36W
Walney, Isle of 6 54 5N 3 15W
Walnut Ridge 71 36 7N 90 58W
Walsall 7 52 36N 1 59W
Walsenburg 71 37 42N 104 45W
Walsh 71 37 28N 102 15W
Walsh → 44 16 31S 143 42 E
Walsh P.O. 44 16 40S 144 0 E
Walterboro 69 32 53N 80 40W
Walters 71 34 25N 98 20W
Waltham Sta. 62 45 57N 76 57W
Waltman 72 43 8N 107 15W
Walvisbaai 56 23 0S 14 28 E
Wamba 54 2 10N 27 57 E
Wamego 70 39 14N 96 22W
Wamena 35 4 4S 138 57 E
Wamsasi 35 3 27S 126 7 E
Wana 32 32 20N 69 32 E
Wanaaring 45 29 38S 144 9 E
Wanaka L. 43 44 33S 169 7 E
Wan'an 39 26 26N 114 49 E
Wanapiri 35 4 30S 135 59 E
Wanapitei L. 62 46 45N 80 40W
Wanbi 45 34 46S 140 17 E
Wanda Shan 38 46 0N 132 0 E
Wandoan 45 26 5S 149 55 E
Wangal 35 6 8S 134 9 E
Wanganella 45 35 6S 144 49 E
Wanganui 43 39 56S 175 3 E
Wangaratta 45 36 21S 146 19 E
Wangdu 38 38 40N 115 7 E
Wangerooge 14 53 47N 7 52 E
Wangiwangi 35 5 22S 123 37 E
Wangjiang 39 30 10N 116 42 E
Wangqing 38 43 12N 129 42 E
Wanless 65 54 11N 101 21W
Wanning 39 18 48N 110 22 E
Wanquan 38 40 50N 114 40 E
Wanxian 39 30 42N 108 20 E
Wanyuan 39 32 4N 108 3 E
Wanzai 39 28 7N 114 30 E
Wapakoneta 68 40 35N 84 10W
Wapato 72 46 30N 120 25W
Wapawekka L. 65 54 55N 104 40W
Wapikopa L. 62 52 56N 87 53W
Wapsipinicon → 70 41 44N 90 19W
Warangal 32 17 58N 79 35 E
Waratah 44 41 30S 145 30 E
Waratah B. 45 38 54S 146 5 E
Warburton, Vic., Australia 45 37 47S 145 42 E
Warburton, W. Austral., Australia 47 26 8S 126 35 E
Warburton Ra. 47 25 55S 126 28 E
Ward 43 41 49S 174 11 E
Ward → 45 26 28S 146 6 E
Ward Cove 64 55 25N 132 43W
Warden 57 27 50S 29 0 E
Wardha 32 20 45N 78 39 E
Wardha → 32 19 57N 79 11 E
Wardlow 64 50 56N 111 31W
Ware 64 57 26N 125 41W
Warialda 45 29 29S 150 33 E
Wariap 35 1 30S 134 5 E
Warkopi 35 1 12S 134 9 E
Warley 7 52 30N 2 0W
Warm Springs 73 38 16N 116 32W
Warman 65 52 19N 106 30W
Warmbad, Namibia 56 28 25S 18 42 E
Warmbad, S. Africa 57 24 51S 28 19 E
Warnambool Downs 44 22 48S 142 52 E
Warnemünde 14 54 9N 12 5 E
Warner 64 49 17N 112 12W
Warner Mts. 72 41 30N 120 20W
Warner Robins 69 32 41N 83 36W
Waroona 47 32 50S 115 58 E
Warragul 45 38 10S 145 58 E
Warrawagine 46 20 51S 120 42 E
Warrego → 45 30 24S 145 21 E
Warrego Ra. 44 24 58S 146 0 E
Warren, Australia 45 31 42S 147 51 E
Warren, Ark., U.S.A. 71 33 35N 92 3W
Warren, Mich., U.S.A. 68 42 31N 83 2W
Warren, Minn., U.S.A. 70 48 12N 96 46W
Warren, Ohio, U.S.A. 68 41 18N 80 52W
Warren, Pa., U.S.A. 68 41 52N 79 10W
Warrenpoint 9 54 7N 6 15W
Warrensburg 70 38 45N 93 45W
Warrenton, S. Africa 56 28 9S 24 47 E
Warrenton, U.S.A. 72 46 11N 123 59W
Warrenville 45 25 48S 147 22 E
Warri 53 5 30N 5 41 E
Warrina 45 28 12S 135 50 E
Warrington, U.K. 6 53 25N 2 38W
Warrington, U.S.A. 69 30 22N 87 16W
Warrnambool 45 38 25S 142 30 E
Warroad 70 48 54N 95 19W
Warsa 35 0 47S 135 55 E
Warsaw = Warszawa 15 52 13N 21 0 E
Warsaw 68 41 14N 85 50W
Warszawa 15 52 13N 21 0 E
Warta → 14 52 35N 14 39 E
Warthe = Warta → 14 52 35N 14 39 E
Waru 35 3 30S 130 36 E
Warwick, Australia 45 28 10S 152 1 E
Warwick, U.K. 7 52 17N 1 36W
Warwick, U.S.A. 68 41 43N 71 25W
Warwick □ 7 52 20N 1 30W
Wasatch Ra. 72 40 30N 111 15W
Wasbank 57 28 15S 30 9 E
Wasco, Calif., U.S.A. 73 35 37N 119 16W
Wasco, Oreg., U.S.A. 72 45 36N 120 46W
Waseca 70 44 3N 93 31W
Wasekamio L. 65 56 45N 108 45W
Wash, The 6 52 58N 0 20 E
Washburn, N. Dak., U.S.A. 70 47 17N 101 0W
Washburn, Wis., U.S.A. 70 46 38N 90 55W
Washim 32 20 3N 77 0 E
Washington, D.C., U.S.A. 68 38 52N 77 0W
Washington, Ga., U.S.A. 69 33 45N 82 45W
Washington, Ind., U.S.A. 68 38 40N 87 8W
Washington, Iowa, U.S.A. 70 41 20N 91 45W
Washington, Mo., U.S.A. 70 38 35N 91 1W
Washington, N.C., U.S.A. 69 35 35N 77 1W
Washington, Pa., U.S.A. 68 40 10N 80 20W
Washington, Utah, U.S.A. 73 37 10N 113 30W
Washington □ 72 47 45N 120 30W
Washington, Mt. 68 44 15N 71 18W
Washington I. 68 45 24N 86 54W
Wasian 35 1 47S 133 19 E
Wasior 35 2 43S 134 30 E
Waskaiowaka, L. 65 56 33N 96 23W
Waskesiu Lake 65 53 55N 106 5W
Wassenaar 11 52 8N 4 24 E
Waswanipi 62 49 40N 76 29W
Waswanipi, L. 62 49 35N 76 40W
Watangpone 35 4 29S 120 25 E
Water Park Pt. 44 22 56S 150 47 E
Water Valley 71 34 9N 89 38W
Waterberge 57 24 10S 28 0 E
Waterbury 68 41 32N 73 0W
Waterbury L. 65 58 10N 104 22W
Waterford 9 52 16N 7 8W
Waterford □ 9 52 10N 7 40W
Waterford Harb. 9 52 10N 6 58W
Waterhen L., Man., Canada 65 52 10N 99 40W
Waterhen L., Sask., Canada 65 54 28N 108 25W
Waterloo, Belgium 11 50 43N 4 25 E
Waterloo, Canada 62 43 30N 80 32W
Waterloo, S. Leone 50 8 26N 13 8W
Waterloo, Ill., U.S.A. 70 38 22N 90 6W
Waterloo, Iowa, U.S.A. 70 42 27N 92 20W
Watersmeet 70 46 15N 89 12W
Waterton Glacier Int. Peace Park 72 48 35N 113 40W
Watertown, N.Y., U.S.A. 68 43 58N 75 57W
Watertown, S. Dak., U.S.A. 70 44 57N 97 5W
Watertown, Wis., U.S.A. 70 43 15N 88 45W
Waterval-Boven 57 25 40S 30 18 E
Waterville, Maine, U.S.A. 63 44 35N 69 40W
Waterville, Wash., U.S.A. 72 47 38N 120 1W
Watervliet 68 42 46N 73 43W
Wates 35 7 51S 110 10 E
Watford 7 51 38N 0 23W
Watford City 70 47 50N 103 23W
Wathaman → 65 57 16N 102 59W
Watheroo 47 30 15S 116 0W
Watkins Glen 68 42 25N 76 55W
Watling I. = San Salvador 75 24 0N 74 40W
Watonga 71 35 51N 98 24W
Watrous, Canada 65 51 40N 105 25W
Watrous, U.S.A. 71 35 50N 104 55W
Watsa 54 3 4N 29 30 E
Watseka 68 40 45N 87 45W
Watson, Australia 47 30 29S 131 31 E
Watson, Canada 65 52 10N 104 30W
Watson Lake 60 60 6N 128 49W
Watsonville 73 36 55N 121 49W
Wattiwarriganna Cr. → 45 28 57S 136 10 E
Watuata = Batuata 35 6 12S 122 42 E
Watubela, Kepulauan 35 4 28S 131 35 E
Waubay 70 45 22N 97 17W
Waubra 45 37 21S 143 39 E
Wauchope 45 31 28S 152 45 E
Wauchula 69 27 35N 81 50W
Waugh 65 49 40N 95 11W
Waukegan 68 42 22N 87 54W
Waukesha 68 43 0N 88 15W
Waukon 70 43 14N 91 33W
Wauneta 70 40 27N 101 25W
Waupaca 70 44 22N 89 8W
Waupun 70 43 38N 88 44W
Waurika 71 34 12N 98 0W
Wausau 70 44 57N 89 40W
Wautoma 70 44 3N 89 20W
Wauwatosa 68 43 6N 87 59W
Wave Hill 46 17 32S 131 0 E
Waveney → 7 52 24N 1 20 E
Waverley 43 39 46S 174 37 E
Waverly, Iowa, U.S.A. 70 42 40N 92 30W
Waverly, N.Y., U.S.A. 68 42 0N 76 33W
Wavre 11 50 43N 4 38 E
Wâw 51 7 45N 28 1 E
Wâw al Kabîr 51 25 20N 16 43 E
Wawa 62 47 59N 84 47W
Wawanesa 65 49 36N 99 40W
Waxahachie 71 32 22N 96 53W
Way, L. 47 26 45S 120 16 E
Wayabula Rau 35 2 29N 128 17 E
Wayatinah 44 42 19S 146 27 E
Waycross 69 31 12N 82 25W
Wayne, Nebr., U.S.A. 70 42 16N 97 0W
Wayne, W. Va., U.S.A. 68 38 15N 82 27W
Waynesboro, Ga., U.S.A. 69 33 6N 82 1W
Waynesboro, Miss., U.S.A. 69 31 40N 88 39W
Waynesboro, Pa., U.S.A. 68 39 46N 77 32W
Waynesboro, Va., U.S.A. 68 38 4N 78 57W
Waynesburg 68 39 54N 80 12W
Waynesville 69 35 31N 83 0W
Waynoka 71 36 38N 98 53W
Wazirabad 32 32 30N 74 8 E
We 34 5 51N 95 18 E
Weald, The 7 51 7N 0 9 E
Wear → 6 54 55N 1 22W
Weatherford, Okla., U.S.A. 71 35 30N 98 45W
Weatherford, Tex., U.S.A. 71 32 45N 97 48W
Weaverville 72 40 44N 122 56W
Webb City 71 37 9N 94 30W
Webster, S. Dak., U.S.A. 70 45 24N 97 33W
Webster, Wis., U.S.A. 70 45 53N 92 25W
Webster City 70 42 30N 93 50W
Webster Green 70 38 38N 90 20W
Webster Springs 68 38 30N 80 25W
Weda 35 0 21N 127 50 E
Weda, Teluk 35 0 30N 127 50 E
Weddell I. 80 51 50S 61 0W
Wedderburn 45 36 26S 143 33 E
Wedgeport 63 43 44N 65 59W
Wee Waa 45 30 11S 149 26 E
Weed 72 41 29N 122 22W
Weemelah 45 29 2S 149 15 E
Weenen 57 28 48S 30 7 E
Weert 11 51 15N 5 43 E
Wei He →, Hebei, China 38 36 10N 115 45 E
Wei He →, Shaanxi, China 39 34 38N 110 15 E
Weifang 38 36 44N 119 7 E
Weihai 38 37 30N 122 6 E
Weimar 14 51 0N 11 20 E
Weinan 39 34 31N 109 29 E
Weipa 44 12 40S 141 50 E
Weir →, Australia 45 28 20S 149 50 E
Weir →, Canada 65 56 54N 93 21W
Weir River 65 56 49N 94 6W
Weiser 72 44 10N 117 0W
Weishan 39 34 47N 117 5 E
Weiyuan 38 35 7N 104 10 E
Weizhou Dao 39 21 0N 109 5 E
Wejherowo 15 54 35N 18 12 E
Wekusko L. 65 54 40N 99 50W
Welbourn Hill 45 27 21S 134 6 E
Welch 68 37 29N 81 36W
Welkom 56 28 0S 26 46 E
Welland 62 43 0N 79 15W
Welland → 6 52 43N 0 10W
Wellesley Is. 44 16 42S 139 30 E
Wellin 11 50 5N 5 6 E
Wellingborough 7 52 18N 0 41W
Wellington, Australia 45 32 35S 148 59 E
Wellington, Canada 62 43 57N 77 20W
Wellington, N.Z. 43 41 19S 174 46 E
Wellington, S. Africa 56 33 38S 19 1 E
Wellington, Salop, U.K. 6 52 42N 2 31W
Wellington, Somerset, U.K. 7 50 58N 3 13W
Wellington, Colo., U.S.A. 70 40 43N 105 0W
Wellington, Kans., U.S.A. 71 37 15N 97 25W
Wellington, Nev., U.S.A. 72 38 47N 119 28W
Wellington, Tex., U.S.A. 71 34 55N 100 13W
Wellington □ 43 40 8S 175 36 E
Wellington, I. 80 49 30S 75 0W
Wellington, L. 45 38 6S 147 20 E
Wells, Norfolk, U.K. 6 52 57N 0 51 E
Wells, Somerset, U.K. 7 51 12N 2 39W
Wells, Minn., U.S.A. 70 43 44N 93 45W
Wells, Nev., U.S.A. 72 41 8N 115 0W
Wells Gray Prov. Park 64 52 30N 120 15W
Wells L. 47 26 44S 123 15 E
Wellsboro 68 41 45N 77 20W
Wellsville, Mo., U.S.A. 70 39 4N 91 30W
Wellsville, N.Y., U.S.A. 68 42 9N 77 53W
Wellsville, Ohio, U.S.A. 68 40 36N 80 40W
Wellsville, Utah, U.S.A. 72 41 35N 111 59W
Wellton 73 32 39N 114 6W
Wels 14 48 9N 14 1 E
Welshpool 7 52 40N 3 9W
Wem 6 52 52N 2 45W
Wen Xian 39 32 43N 104 36 E
Wenatchee 72 47 30N 120 17W
Wenchang 39 19 38N 110 42 E
Wenchi 50 7 46N 2 8W
Wenchow = Wenzhou 39 28 0N 120 38 E
Wendell 72 42 50N 114 42W